Understanding Modern Nige

MW00990596

The thrust of this book is in two sections: first, the diagnosis of the issues; second, policy prescriptions. Divided into six thematic parts, the first and second parts provide the introduction and a context to understand the country, locating it in its history, the choice of federalism as a political system, and religious and political pluralism that shape its institutions and practices. The third part speaks to the issues around ethnicity, democracy, and governance, focusing on the key features of each. The fourth part presents the outcome, manifested in hunger, violence, poverty, human rights violations, and constant threats of secession. Over the years, the country has become more and more corrupt; governance is messy, while power and resources are used to reproduce underdevelopment. In the fifth part, the book offers various ways of intervention to generate reforms or revolutions to change the country. The sixth concludes the study.

Toyin Falola is Professor of History, University Distinguished Teaching Professor, and the Jacob and Frances Sanger Mossiker Chair in the Humanities, at the University of Texas at Austin. He is an Honorary Professor at the University of Cape Town, and Extraordinary Professor of Human Rights at the University of the Free State. He has served as the General Secretary of the Historical Society of Nigeria, the President of the African Studies Association, Vice-President of UNESCO Slave Route Project, and the Kluge Chair of the Countries of the South, Library of Congress. He is a member of the Scholars' Council, Kluge Center, and the Library of Congress. He has received over thirty lifetime career awards and fourteen honorary doctorates. He has written extensively on Nigeria, including *A History of Nigeria*; *Nigerian Political Modernity*; *Violence in Nigeria;* and *Colonialism and Violence in Nigeria*.

Understanding Modern Nigeria

Ethnicity, Democracy, and Development

Toyin Falola

University of Texas at Austin

CAMBRIDGE
UNIVERSITY PRESS

CAMBRIDGE
UNIVERSITY PRESS

University Printing House, Cambridge CB2 8BS, United Kingdom

One Liberty Plaza, 20th Floor, New York, NY 10006, USA

477 Williamstown Road, Port Melbourne, VIC 3207, Australia

314–321, 3rd Floor, Plot 3, Splendor Forum, Jasola District Centre, New Delhi – 110025, India

79 Anson Road, #06–04/06, Singapore 079906

Cambridge University Press is part of the University of Cambridge.

It furthers the University's mission by disseminating knowledge in the pursuit of education, learning, and research at the highest international levels of excellence.

www.cambridge.org
Information on this title: www.cambridge.org/9781108837972
DOI: 10.1017/9781108936866

First published 2021

Printed in the United Kingdom by TJ Books Limited, Padstow Cornwall

A catalogue record for this publication is available from the British Library.

Library of Congress Cataloging-in-Publication Data
Names: Falola, Toyin, author.
Title: Understanding modern Nigeria : ethnicity, democracy and development / Toyin Falola, University of Texas, Austin.
Description: Cambridge, United Kingdom; New York, NY: Cambridge University Press, 2021. | Includes bibliographical references and index.
Identifiers: LCCN 2021009535 (print) | LCCN 2021009536 (ebook) | ISBN 9781108837972 (hardback) | ISBN 9781108936866 (ebook)
Subjects: LCSH: Nigeria – Politics and government. | Nigeria – Ethnic relations. | Social change – Nigeria. | BISAC: POLITICAL SCIENCE / American Government / General | POLITICAL SCIENCE / American Government / General
Classification: LCC DT515.59 .F35 2021 (print) | LCC DT515.59 (ebook) | DDC 966.905–dc23
LC record available at https://lccn.loc.gov/2021009535
LC ebook record available at https://lccn.loc.gov/2021009536

ISBN 978-1-108-83797-2 Hardback
ISBN 978-1-108-94763-3 Paperback

For Dr. Michael Oladejo Afolayan

Contents

Figures

Maps

Preface

Discussions on Nigeria have become routinized in all spaces, from small villages to the big cities, from the local to the global. Such discussions are filled with the familiar, the grandiose, and the bizarre. Both in private and public, no one is foolish or wise when discussing the country, as the wise can make silly statements and the foolish can proclaim great insights. There is love of country as pleasant talks in drinking places can celebrate the consumption of *ponmo* (cow skin) with that of "pepper soup" over cold bottles of beer. There is resentment of country as people give staggering figures of money stolen from the state, and there are politicians who keep the money in cemeteries, fridges, sewage tanks, and houses inhabited only by money. As theft becomes more staggering, missing money could have been swallowed by a cobra!

Familiar narratives speak to the following: discord, anomie, insecurity, hunger in the land, migration, individualism, and migrations. The religious people turn to God and prayer; the socialists speak to people who believe in violence; the modernists imagine Africa in terms of institutional efficiency; and the corrupt see opportunities in chaos. The blame is heaped on the colonial history and postcolonial leadership. Ethnicities complicate politics and, as of the time of writing this book, the conversation was about President Buhari and the "Fulanization" of Nigeria. Nigerian politics remains as complicated as ever and modernity remains elusive. There is no radicalism from the followers as the Left had hoped. In the concluding segment of this book, I provide multiple options for transformation.

The narratives on postcolonial Nigeria are full of ambiguities and contradictions – those that highlight its abundant positive assets and those that point to its failures. Some also express grave doubts about the capacity of the country to succeed, the ability of its leaders to ensure security and generate development. There are constant predictions of impending civil wars. The words and the analyses are painfully depressing. It is a corrupt country, called "fantastically corrupt" by a one-time

British prime minister. The objective of this book is to present the challenges of postcolonial Nigeria against the background of the expectations of its people.

The intellectual value of this book lies in two things: in the diagnosis of the issues and in policy prescriptions based on various alternative paths. Divided into four chapters, Part II of the book provides a context to understanding the country, locating it in its history, the choice of federalism that governed it, and political pluralism that shaped its institutions and practices. A huge country divided into thirty-six states and a Federal Capital Territory, Abuja, where the federal seat is located, the country is organized as a secular country with democratic institutions, but its coloration and management are shaped by ethnic and religious divisions. To reach its current state, the country has passed through a colonial phase where there was no democracy; a post–World War phase when nationalism became intense and fragmented into regionalism; a short-lived post-independence phase that prepared the grounds for a civil war (1967–70); the post-civil war phase with disjointed periods of military rule; and the so-called post-military corrupt civilian rule since 1999.

Part III of the book speaks to the issues around ethnicity, and democracy and governance, the three of which are united. The country comprises an agglomeration of hundreds of precolonial nations, called "tribes" by the British colonizers. Through their genius, the people created their cities, states, and kingdoms that the British organized into one country after 1885. A colonial state from 1914 to 1960, the people were governed in different administrative units without strong uniting forces. Strong ethnicities emerged, reinforced by a policy of Indirect Rule, which instigated the political option of federalism in the 1950s. Its independence in 1960 was immediately followed by serious political problems, with a civil war from 1967 to 1970. Different military regimes governed the unstable polity until 1999 when a so-called democratic regime began its complicated course. The democracy has produced a large bureaucracy, and a group of politicians who are interested in power for the money it can give them. Its statistics confirm its giant status – the seventh largest population in the world; the most populous in Africa; and, following China and India, the country with the third largest youth population.

Ethnicity, discussed in Chapter 7, remains a big issue, as identitarian politics generate instability. Violence is endemic; in the Niger Delta over the distribution of resources, and in the North-East by the insurgency of Boko Haram (Chapter 17). Politics in Nigeria is mainly about one thing: access to money. This access to money is connected to the manipulation of ethnicity to gain power and participate in corruption. Ethnicity also offers protection to crooked politicians who are clever in asserting their ethnic identities. As the masses get connected with politics via their manipulative leaders, ethnic identity becomes the basis to express grievances, articulate minority rights, and bring up issues of wrongs and genocide (as in the case of Biafra and the Igbo).

Part IV of the book presents the reality on the streets, the concrete consequences of democracy, and governance. Over the years, the country has become more and more corrupt. As the population grew, so did impunity. As oil revenues grew, so did poverty and theft. As politics became more centralized in a few hands, so did the units of administrative governance – from 3 regions to 36 states, from 24 provinces to 774 local governments – not to bring governance to the people, but for those in power to share money. Rather than progress, there are institutional declines. Power and resources have been used to reproduce underdevelopment. Rated as one of the leading economies in the world, the country has one of the largest numbers of poor people; overall, it is one of the poorest in the world. This poverty can best be seen in hunger, as well as in violence on the streets and in various communities, organized kidnappings, the marginalization of women, and long-lasting resistance to the state.

In Part VI, I offer various options for intervention to generate reforms or revolutions to change the country. Incentives for ethnic rivalries and rebellions must be channeled to the participation of youth in politics. Energies devoted to political parties and their dangerous schemes must be used for community mobilization and social movements for change. Violence in support of repression must give way to positive radical politics.

When Nigeria becomes successful, the indicators will be clear to see. People will be at the center of politics: rather than the masses serving the leadership, the leadership will work for the masses. The poorest members of society will be able to put food on their tables and meet their basic minimum needs. A system of economic justice will be in place. People's religions and places of birth will not set limits to their ambitions and goals. Opportunities for social and economic mobility will be everywhere, irrespective of regions, villages, and cities. Social justice will not be linked to ethnicity, religious beliefs, or places and accidents of birth. The well-educated citizens will use their education for the good of the country and will not represent a group of citizens who defend their primordial loyalties. They will be part of an engaged collective group of citizens that promote justice. The media will free itself from being captured by those in power and will not exist to represent the voices of those who control the state; instead, it will be watchful and critical.

For now, Nigeria is fragile; its reasons for existence lie in promises, not in major achievements. Not a single core element that defines a successful country exists here. Hopefully, new conversations, political activism, and a citizenry that can fight for its rights will produce the right sort of leadership and create the institutions to move the country forward.

Acknowledgments

A never-ending dialogue and debates since the mid twentieth century have provided the academic nourishment to compose this book on Nigeria. The sources of inspirations are many – from my students at the University of Texas at Austin to the intellectual community in the USA-Africa Dialogue, the Internet site that I created decades ago and manage on a daily basis, and the various universities that have invited me to give major lectures and convocation addresses. The conversations make room for revisions, fresh ideas that are expressed with conviction and energy in many pages of this book. The communities that sustained my interest in writing this book comprise university students, the nameless poor on the streets, and the face of poverty everywhere.

Too many friends had confidence in this project. I cannot but thank Professors Michael Afolayan, Bola Dauda, A. B. Assensoh, Samuel Oloruntoba, and Vik Bahl. These scholars and others offered both faith and passion – faith in strengthening intellectual commitments and passion in sustaining them. I remain truly grateful. To those who pushed me to rethink my ideas, I owe a debt of gratitude to Professor Olajumoke Yacob-Haliso, Dr. Ken Kalu, Dr. Samuel Oloruntoba, Devon Hsiao, Dr. Serges Kamga, Professor Bayo Oyebade, Adebukola Bassey, Dr. Uzoma Osuala, Dr. Ogechukwu Ezekwem, Chukwuemeka Agbo, Chima Korieh, Professor Bashir Salau, Dr. Samson Ijaola, Anna Lee Carothers, Adanna Ogbonna, Tolulope Oke, Farooq Kperogi, Damilare Bello, Nichole Griffin, Simi Hassan, Shannon Doyle, Abikal Borah, Dayo Adewole, Wale Gazhal, Damilare Osunlakin, and several anonymous readers. The success of some chapters, as that on food, would not have been possible without the difficult collection of data and statistics by my competent research assistant, Ms. Nicole Griffin of the University College, London. As these talented scholars and students read the final product of this book, I hope they do not lament my stubbornness in refusing to modify many of the ideas and statements they objected to. I also have to thank Nathan E. McCormack for co-doing the maps with me, and Michael Efionayi who assisted with the illustrations, all in mixed media, a combination of photo manipulation and digital oil paint.

In Biblical mythology on God and creation, Genesis 2:1–2 says the following:

Thus the heavens and the earth were completed, and all their hosts. By the seventh day God completed His work which He had done, and He rested on the seventh day from all His work which He had done.

Since the country called Nigeria was yet to be created by then, God's work remains to be fully done. God has rested enough – it is time to wake up and devote another six days to the making of Nigeria. Thereafter, He can take His final rest. My task of narrating the history and progress of Nigeria is also an incomplete project. When Nigeria, nicknamed "the giant of Africa," wakes up, I have to work on a new edition of this book. Meanwhile, the analyses and reflections in this book are based on what is current, real, observable, and messy. As Nigerians are fond to say when they read the preceding sentence, "It is well!"

Part I

Introduction

1   Narrating Postcolonial Nigeria

Introduction

This book's opening statements are formed by the perception and projection of postcolonial Nigeria's narratives. Nigeria, like most African states after their independence, has experienced subversions, extensions, and even new projections of narratives pertinent to its survival and development. Narratives are potent, flexible devices that endure the rigorous work of organizing experiences, fashioning collective identities, and projecting sociocultural realities. Here, the postcolonial is charged with multiple meanings, spiraling beyond the notion of temporality – indicating the postindependence period – to broadly include discourse related to and following colonialism.[1] Postcolonial thinking is evident in the political, economic, and sociocultural narratives of Nigeria that express ideologies for independence, self-awareness, and collective development.

Nigeria's narratives have undergone a pronounced shift from colonial experiences and criticism to postcolonial and neocolonial ones. This change is driven by the need to address the concerns of Nigeria's postcolonial and modern realities, including poverty, neocolonialism, illiteracy, democracy, and fraud. These concerns also include the tensions of modernity and development, mismanagement and corruption, political apathy, violence, and ethnic and religious rivalries. The shared concerns of these narratives search for Nigeria within the frame of global modernity, seeking to address the impact of modernity on the sustainability of Nigeria as an evolving nation-state. The perception of modernity has been imposed on all societies through Eurocentric constructs, but these postcolonial narratives navigate the intricacies of modernity as it is imposed, perceived, lived through, and adapted to, contrary to the idea of modernity as a static end result.

---

[1] An often-cited example is Chinua Achebe's *Things Fall Apart*, which was published two years before the independence of Nigeria in 1960. See Chinua Achebe, *Things Fall Apart* (London: Penguin Books, 1994).

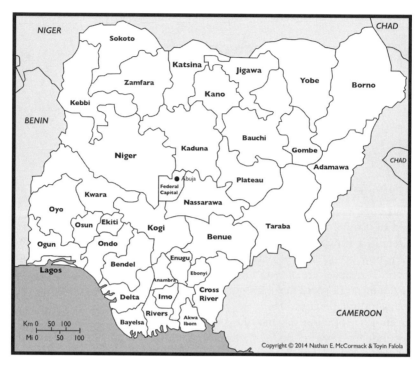

Map 1.1 Political map of Nigeria.

Postcolonial Nigerian narratives can be read as a microcosm of the "entire African postcolonial enterprise," in which Nigeria "continues to recommend itself as an important process of understanding,"[2] engaging, liberating, and developing Africa. There is a synchronic motion to the postcolonial temper: not only does it address immediate and emerging issues, it also reflects on colonial and precolonial issues that affect the present reality because "the postcolonial situation is about the present but a present which is not to be taken for a static moment or condition but as a dynamic reality that crosses borders of time, space, and aesthetics."[3] In grappling with its postcolonial and modern transition, "Nigeria has experimented with all sorts of political

---

[2] Wale Adebanwi and Ebenezer Obadare, "Introducing Nigeria at Fifty: The Nation in Narration," *Journal of Contemporary African Studies* 28, no. 4 (2010): 379.
[3] Klohinlwélé Koné, "Living and Narrating the Tensions of the Postcolonial Situation: Chinua Achebe Between Ambiguity and Ambivalence," *The International Journal of Social Sciences and Humanities* 3, no. 11 (2016): 2944.

systems, ideologies, economic policies and even cultural paradigms"[4] that have generated different narratives to sustain, redress, understand, and contribute to the development of the nation.

Postcolonial Nigerian aesthetics dominate the arts and humanities. Postcolonial ideology dominates the social sciences, expressed as cultural nationalism and nationalist historiography in history and political science, and postcolonial temperaments differ across regions and historical periods. Advocacy is prevalent for equality and other basic human rights in postcolonial Nigerian literary narratives. Jude Dibia, Chinelo Okparanta, Akwaeke Ameze, and others have increased the awareness of othering and criminalization imposed on lesbian, gays, bisexuals, and transgender individuals. In Nigeria, as in Africa and the rest of the world, these emerging concerns highlight the faults and intolerance of the present government, highlighting the shortcomings of democracy and the Eurocentric distortion of Africa's culture and history.

What Wole Soyinka, Chinua Achebe, and Buchi Emecheta are to Nigerian literature, J. F. Ade Ajayi, Yusuf Bala Usman, Kenneth Dike, Saburi Biobaku, Adiele Afigbo, and Toyin Falola are to Nigerian history; their reconstructionist work provides several narratives repurposing the image of Nigeria's culture and development into modernity. Simon Gikandi contends that Achebe's postcolonial aesthetic "is predicated on the belief that narrative can indeed propose an alternative world beyond the realities imprisoned in colonial and precolonial relations of power."[5] Nigeria's popular culture has recently been filled with vigor that gives hope while entertaining, or penetrating, the socioeconomic realities of Nigerian society to incite change.

The fluidity, relatability, and accessibility of various media allow popular culture to resonate with millions of Nigerians, making it a focal point of postcolonial Nigerian narratives. These narratives are charged with a nationalist duty to contribute to Nigeria's development. Beyond postcolonial nationalist narratives, pressing sociocultural issues have emerged and infiltrated the narrative of Nigeria. The recent history of violence, especially the Boko Haram insurgency, has generated diverse narratives in the social sciences to scrutinize new threats to the unity, peace, and development of the nation. Such discourse had been scarce before the year 2000.[6] Before the insurgency, there was the Niger Delta militancy in

---

[4] Adebanwi and Obadare, "Introducing Nigeria at Fifty," 383.
[5] Simon Gikandi, "Chinua Achebe and the Post-Colonial Esthetic: Writing, Identity, and National Formation," *Studies in 20th Century Literature* 15, no. 1 (1991): 31.
[6] See one of the most expansive studies on the subject till date: Marc-Antoine Perouse de Montclos, ed., *Boko Haram: Islamism, Politics, Security and the State in Nigeria* (Los Angeles: Tsehai Publishers, 2014).

the South-South region of the country. More recently, the herdsmen crises experienced throughout the nation generated narratives about the "Fulanization" and "Islamization" of Nigeria, reinforcing the narratives of Nigeria's possible fragmentation and its need for restructuring. New units, like Peace Studies, have been formed in government and tertiary institutions to address these emerging, fundamental narratives.

Digital media and social platforms are another significant dimension of Nigeria's postcolonial narrative. Digital media has been embraced in Nigeria as "sites of utilities for mobilization, sectarianism and for pursuits and practices that reflect offline tensions and grievances, but … also where alternative ways to redress them can be sought."[7] The psychological and emotional succor offered by these platforms contribute to the scope of nation building. Frustration, anger, and agitation can be channeled into constructive expressions and yield a positive outcome. Interventions through these channels have not been widely studied, but their effects have been noticeable for reducing and curbing social violence. Moral and cultural virtues, including love, solidarity, persistence, and patience are sustained through narratives of struggle and survival shared through digital media outlets.

The modernist approach of this book addresses the nation's most current challenges with updated resolutions by taking on the most dominant narrative preoccupations of postcolonial Nigeria: ethnicity, governance, democracy, and development. These interconnected frames explain the complications that shape the daily lives of Nigerians. These themes define how the country is organized by its government and evaluated by its citizens and outsiders; this book discusses the history and events that have shaped those themes and their far-reaching impact.

The common starting point is how the British laid modern Nigeria's foundations. Colonialism drove competition for resources and power, heightening tensions between the Hausa–Fulani, Yoruba, and Igbo ethnic groups forced together under the British rule. Preferential treatment fostered dissent and hatred – the British administration gave critical advantages to some groups, such as formal Western education, access to infrastructure, and the privileges of modernity.

Ethnic Politics

British manipulation of boundaries created an ethnic system, and the British ruled through the dissent it created. Tensions and inequalities

---

[7] Sokfa John, "Genocide, Oppression, Ambivalence: Online Narratives of Identity and Religion in Postcolonial Nigeria," *Open Library of Humanities* 4, no. 2 (2018): 2.

fueled the creation of political parties along ethnic lines in the 1940s, which persisted into the postindependence era that began in 1960. Each group served its ethnic constituents, and none fought for Nigeria's overall interests. With more than two hundred distinct ethnic groups in Nigeria, it is nearly impossible for each one to receive adequate representation. Despite the government's efforts to create a bill of rights, and political documents preserving minority representation, Nigeria still struggles with the complexities of ethnic identity and the effects of ethnic tension. Ethnic interests have distorted the allocation of state resources, and a primary source of contention is oil revenue – it is generated in the minority-occupied Niger Delta region, and there are constant concerns that it is not being allocated proportionately across the country.

Oil revenues, which allegedly lined the pockets of the same minority groups that had received preferential treatment from the British, became one of the reasons for the military coup in 1966. Prime Minister Tafawa Balewa was removed by military officers, assassinated, and replaced by Igbo General Johnson Ironsi. This sparked retaliatory violence against the Igbo people in Northern Nigeria. As the Igbo fled to southern Nigeria, the idea of Biafra was born; it was meant to be a conglomeration of southeastern states. Civil war raged for three years, from 1967 to 1970, as the Igbo endured prejudice and embargoes from the Nigerian government. Almost one million people were killed in the conflict, and as the concept of a fully free and legitimized Biafra seemed more appealing and attainable for millions of people, it further desta-bilized Nigerian nationalism.

Nigeria's long history of ethnic tensions and political unrest, com-bined with poor resource distribution, government corruption, and a relentless focus on oil production, has created systemic development issues that prevent the country from fully harnessing its natural resources. Prioritization of ethnic group identities over a united Nigerian identity has spawned mercurial government priorities; the stream of new arrivals constantly cycling through positions of power undermine long-term development efforts. As individual groups gain power, discrimination becomes institutionalized and access to educa-tion and other fundamental rights depend on the current government's attitude.

Nigeria's complex history with colonialism has deeply affected its politics, democratization, and development. It has led to years of instability, mutual distrust, conflict, and a civil war. The institution of colonialism and competition for power and resources pitted the largest ethnic groups against each other. The leaders of some groups supported the British crown and gained unparalleled access to the privileges of colonial power.[8] The preferential treatment they received led to disparities in access to education, infrastructure, and vital public services that included sanitation and access to electrical power grids.[9]

Some groups secured positions that allowed them to accumulate massive amounts of generational wealth and maintain dynastic advantages. The elites of dominant ethnic groups held government positions continuously through Nigeria's independence in 1960, which raised tensions to the point of civil conflict. The South's elites, who had received education in line with Western standards, believed that the Hausa–Fulani were given special dispensation within the structures maintained by Frederick Lugard, the British colonial administrator, to receive far more preferential treatment than other ethnicities.[10]

During Africa's decolonization, Nigerian political leaders conceptualized what it meant to be free, imagining a country without imperial control. It was a period of increased ethnic tension – as the institutional advantages of dominant groups became more apparent, so did the marginalization of other ethnic groups. The Nigerian National Democratic Party (NNDP), established by the well-known publisher and civil servant Herbert Macaulay, was the first formal political organization in Nigeria.[11] Under Macaulay, the NNDP focused on semi-autonomy and representation for Nigerians within the colonial government, working to dismantle practices of racial discrimination and subjugation under British rule.[12] For these reasons, Macaulay is often considered the father of Nigerian nationalism.[13] In 1941, the NNDP began to change as different factions promoted opposing viewpoints.[14] The Igbo-dominated NNDP became the National Council of Nigeria and the Cameroons, later becoming the National Council of Nigerian Citizens (NCNC) led by Nnamdi Azikiwe.

Other political parties were created on the basis of ethnic identities, focused on regional instead of national interests. The Action Group (AG)

[8] Belinda Archibong, "Historical Origins of Persistent Inequality in Nigeria," *Oxford Development Studies* 46, no. 3 (2018): 325–347.
[9] Ibid.
[10] Olufemi Taiwo, "Reading the Colonizer's Mind: Lord Lugard and the Philosophical Foundations of British Colonialism," in *Racism and Philosophy*, eds. Susan E. Babbitt and Sue Campbell (Ithaca: Cornell University Press, 1999).
[11] Bonny Ibhawoh, *Nations and Nationalism: A Global Historical Overview*, www.humanities.mcmaster.ca/~ibhawoh/documents/Nations%20&%20Nationalism.pdf.
[12] Ibid.
[13] "Herbert Macaulay," *ZODML*, September 19, 2014, zodml.org/discover-nigeria/people/herbert-macaulay#.XDbEzc9KhQJ.
[14] Ibid.

was established by Obafemi Awolowo,[15] a lawyer, in 1951. AG found its roots in the Yoruba cultural movement known as the Egbe Omo Oduduwa, or the Society of the Descendants of Oduduwa,[16] believed to be the common ancestor for all Yoruba people.[17] The organization was created to address fears of Igbo and Hausa–Fulani domination, providing leadership and representation for the Yoruba through prominent chiefs, professionals and intellectuals at the time.[18] The Northern People's Congress (NPC) was established in 1949 for the Hausa–Fulani Muslims of Northern Nigeria, who sought to establish regional autonomy and preserve traditional Islamic rule.[19]

The history of ethnic politics within Nigeria is central to the country's construction because it has been a pervasive force since independence. It has shaped political organization and socioeconomic endeavors. Before Nigeria's independence, early political parties cooperated for practicality and convenience. Afterwards, they seized postindependence opportunities to create a political atmosphere that reflected their own interests.

As Nigeria's independence became less about constructing a nation and more about advancing ethnic interests through regional political parties, many began to doubt the viability of a Nigerian state. The country has an estimated 350 to 400 ethnic groups, based on linguistic classifications,[20] making it nearly impossible to arrive at an agreement while maintaining adequate representation. Leaders such as Ahmadu Bello of the NPC and Obafemi Awolowo of the AG party openly questioned the Nigerian state's sustainability and implications.[21] Obafemi Awolowo's statement touches on such issues: "Nigeria is not a nation. It is a mere geographical expression. There are no 'Nigerians' in the sense as there are 'English,' 'Welsh,' or 'French.' The word 'Nigerian' is merely a distinctive appellation to distinguish those who live within the boundaries of Nigeria and those who do not."[22]

---

[15] John P. Mackintosh, "Politics in Nigeria: The Action Group Crisis of 1962," *Political Studies* 11, no. 2 (1963): 126–155, onlinelibrary.wiley.com/doi/pdf/10.1111/j.1467–92 48.1963.tb01055.x.

[16] Ibhawoh, "Nations and Nationalism: A Global Historical Overview."

[17] R. C. C. Law, "The Heritage of Oduduwa: Traditional History and Political Propaganda Among the Yoruba," *Journal of African History* 14, no. 2 (1973): 207–222.

[18] Mackintosh, "Politics in Nigeria: The Action Group Crisis of 1962."

[19] "Northern People's Congress (NPC)," in *The Oxford Dictionary of Islam*, ed. John L. Esposito (Oxford: Oxford University Press, 2004), www.oxfordislamicstudies.com/art icle/opr/t125/e1773.

[20] Felicia H. Ayatse and Isaac Iorhen Akuva, "The Origin and Development of Ethnic Politics and Its Impact on Post-Colonial Governance in Nigeria," *European Scientific Journal* 9, no. 17 (2013): 178–189, eujournal.org/index.php/esj/article/view/1165/1182.

[21] Ibhawoh, "Nations and Nationalism: A Global Historical Overview."

[22] Obafemi Awolowo, *Path to Nigerian Freedom* (London: Faber and Faber, 1947), 48.

The establishment of political parties only accommodated the three largest ethnic groups; it did not consider minority ethnic groups. The British colonial government attempted to address these concerns with a document known as the Willink Commission Report (1957), outlining the grievances and fears of minorities throughout the region.[23]

Many ethnic groups preferred to discard the idea of a "Nigerian" nation in favor of creating separate states, but the Willink Commission proposed creating a bill of rights to guarantee the protection of rights for minorities; the commission was wary of political power concentrating solely in one political party, ethnicity, or region. When Nigeria gained independence in 1960, Abubakar Tafawa Balewa, of the NPC, became the prime minister. Awolowo was appointed as leader of parliament's opposition party, and Azikiwe, of the NCNC, became governor general[24] to cultivate a sense of unification and inclusion.

Beneath the budding nationalism and symbolic acts of unity, Nigeria still struggles with the complexities of ethnic identity and the associated tensions. Efficient and fair resource allocation is vital to the stability of any country, especially one with multiple ethnic divisions, but ethnic concerns continued to subvert the allocation of state resources.

Significant amounts of oil are present in Niger River Delta land that has historically belonged to the Ijo and other groups. In the 1960s, Igbo leaders believed that discrimination was preventing them from receiving meaningful amounts of the oil revenue that originated in their territory.[25] Oil, which accounts for a substantial amount of the Nigerian economy, is the backbone of the nation. It affects foreign exchange earnings, export production, and the nation's overall revenue. However, the Ijo region receives the least benefit from the proceeds, which is reflected in the nation's revenue sharing formula, the lack of development in the region, and the devastating destruction of the region's environment. From 1960 through 1966, the Northern Region received a larger portion of federal funds than the Western or Eastern Regions. This could have been due to several reasons, but Balewa, a Muslim from the North, was Prime Minister at the time. Resource distribution evokes the memories of the alleged preferential treatment received by those in the North and strengthens the deep-seated distrust among ethnic groups.

---

[23] Secretary of State for the Colonies by Command of Her Majesty, *The Willink Commission Report: Report of the Commission Appointed to Enquire into the Fears of Minorities and the Means of Allaying Them* (Adaka Boro Centre, 1958), https://ijawnation.org/wp-content/uploads/2019/01/The-Willink-Commission-Report_conc_recom_lt.pdf.

[24] Molefi Kete Asante, *The History of Africa: The Quest for Eternal Harmony* (New York: Routledge, 2019).

[25] Herbert Ekwe-Ekwe, "Biafra 1966–1970," *Combat Genocide Association*, n.d., combat-genocide.org /?page_id=90.

In 1966, Prime Minister Balewa was ousted in a military coup, which was organized primarily by Igbo soldiers. Balewa was assassinated along with Ahmadu Bello, and Igbo General Johnson Aguiyi Ironsi claimed power.[26] The sudden, violent shift of power shook the country and magnified preexisting weaknesses in national cohesion. In retaliation for the coup, many of the Igbo in northern Nigeria were killed. As thousands of Igbo fled the predominantly Hausa–Fulani north, the idea of Biafra was born.

In 1967, Lieutenant Colonel C.O. Ojukwu declared a conglomeration of southeastern states in southern Nigeria to be sovereign and autonomous, naming it Biafra. This new Igbo nation sought to defend itself from violence, injustice, and discrimination at the hands of the Nigerian government.[27] The Biafra movement ended after three years of embargo-induced famine[28] and other acts of war carried out against the group in Eastern Nigeria.[29] As a movement, Biafra represented more than an Igbo desire for succession; it inspired others with their own dreams of autonomy and independence from the Nigerian government. In this role, Biafra was the biggest threat to Nigerian nationalism since the country's conception.[30]

Governance and Democracy

The words "good governance" and "Nigeria" are often used as antonyms. Widespread corruption, involving money laundering, misallocated funds, political nepotism, and paternalism, have made it almost impossible to identify a time when Nigeria was a truly functional democracy. These conditions did not develop overnight, and they do not need to remain chronic issues within the state.

Before Nigeria's independence in 1960, the British exerted total control over the colony without seeking input from its subjects. Their indirect rule system used existing ethnic structures to exert power without requiring a physical presence on the ground,[31] and this set the tone for Nigeria's

---

[26] Ibhawoh, "Nations and Nationalism: A Global Historical Overview."

[27] American Historical Association, "Biafran Declaration of Independence," American Historical Association, n.d., www.historians.org/teaching-and-learning/teaching-resour ces-for-historians/teaching-and-learning-in-the-digital-age/through-the-lens-of-history-biafra-nigeria-the-west-and-the-world/the-republic-of-biafra/biafran-declaration-of-independence.

[28] World Peace Foundation, "Nigeria: Civil War." *Tufts Mass Atrocity Endings*, August 7, 2015, sites.tufts.edu/atrocityendings/2015/08/07/nigeria-civil-war/.

[29] Ibid.   [30] Ibhawoh, "Nations and Nationalism."

[31] American Historical Association, "England's Indirect Rule in Its African Colonies," American Historical Association, n.d., www.historians.org/teaching-and-learning/teach ing-resources-for-historians/teaching-and-learning-in-the-digital-age/through-the-lens-

struggle to achieve democracy. Nigeria gained independence without a blueprint for how a democratic country should operate; it had been ruled arbitrarily by the British Crown. National borders did not follow established ethno-linguistic lines, and the political system was foreign to the region's indigenous groups, which are two reasons why British colonialism increased the new state's instability and vulnerability. Colonial decisions had completely uprooted and replaced centuries-old practices and traditions. Postcolonial Nigeria barely moved beyond the legacies of colonial enterprise, failing to harness its potential and develop into modernity. It currently maintains an inherited system of governance and administration that perpetuates frustration and failure.

Colonialism is not the sole cause of Nigeria's struggle with political corruption, but it is a starting point. The country's tumultuous relationship with ethnic politics has encouraged different ethnic groups to engage in violent struggles to gain and maintain political power. The prioritization of regional interests over national ones has created a culture of nepotism and paternalism to mirror the British administration. There is no democracy when power is shared among family members or closely held within a single ethnic group. Nigeria's political elites have been counterproductive for democracy. These elites are often the products of colonial education and the privilege that comes from working closely with the British government,[32] distinguishing themselves by their proximity to political power. It is unsustainable to have a privileged few represent almost 200 million citizens, especially when the needs and grievances of the citizens are seemingly incomprehensible to the elites. Such inequality, which is woven into the fabric of Nigeria, is not healthy for democracy.

The military has also interfered with Nigeria's efforts to build a functional democracy. The country's political trajectory has been altered by military intervention since independence.[33] It has generated feelings of disillusionment within Nigerian society, encouraging an increasingly militarized political system. The military evolved into an institution of its own, viewing itself as its own class within society[34] and attempting to exert control over Nigeria's political and economic affairs. Initially, the military served as a force that could hold political actors accountable for their actions and policies, but it ultimately weakened public faith in the democratic process and amplified instabilities.

of-history-biafra-nigeria-the-west-and-the-world/the-colonial-and-pre-colonial-eras-in-nigeria/englands-indirect-rule-in-its-african-colonies.

[32] Cyril I. Obi, *Nigeria: Democracy on Trial* (Uppsala: The Nordic Africa Institute, 2004), nai.uu.se/research/publications/electronic_publ/obi_nigeria.pdf.
[33] Ibid.   [34] Ibid.

Another factor hindering Nigeria's democratization is its existence as a "petro-state," with weak institutions and an anemic public sector, allowing the revenue from oil production to be concentrated in the hands of a few individuals.[35] The Nigerian government holds a monopoly on oil income, but transnational corporations have control over oil extraction, which allows other countries to exert influence over Nigerian policies. It is nearly impossible for the state to regulate these multinational companies when they control the flow of oil and money, and that has extreme effects on the oil-producing Niger River Delta region. It is difficult to maintain a robust democracy when the country is so heavily invested in a single economic sector, and Nigeria's political arena is dominated by petroleum interests.

Sustainable Development

Nigeria's tumultuous political history has stifled economic growth. Nigeria possesses both natural and human resources for rapid development, but fundamental, systemic issues have impaired national progress. Inequitable access to resources and services, an extreme emphasis on oil production, and government corruption have been persistent problems. Ethnic identity and the issues that stem from it have also played a role in state development. Ethnic groups in Nigeria are obsessed with securing and maintaining power, whether political or economic, at the expense of national development and unity. The struggle over the country's oil reserves is a struggle for power where ethnic ties are exploited for personal gain.[36] The fragmentation of ethnicities discourages development and erects systemic barriers that prevent many people from advancing. Certain positions are inaccessible for specific ethnic identities, regardless of a candidate's professional and academic merits. Alienation and erasure are not compatible with a single, unified goal of Nigerian development.

Many people prefer to identify with specific ethnic identities instead of Nigerian citizenship. Disproportionate access to education and job opportunities has affected livelihoods and diminished interest in democratic or economic endeavors; their corrosive effects have made national stability almost unattainable. The political instability brought on by ethnic rivalries has led to inconsistent development, and different administrations pursue development projects that reflect conflicting goals and

---

[35] Ibsen Martinez, "The Curse of the Petro-State: The Example of Venezuela," *Library of Economics and Liberty*, September 5, 2005, www.econlib.org/library/Columns/y2005/Martinezpetro.html.

[36] Richard Ilorah, "Ethnic Bias, Favouritism and Development in Africa," *Development Southern Africa* 26, no. 5 (2009): 695–707.

interests. When government changes as frequently and as drastically as it does in Nigeria, it is difficult for these projects to be completed, which sets the country back further.

What can be done to dismantle the institutional discrimination, economic and political nepotism, and ethnic power consolidation within Nigeria? Drafting and implementing a comprehensive human rights accord is one way to address ethnic discrimination. However, if these rights are to be guaranteed, there must be serious consequences for breaking the law. For thirty-eight years, human rights issues have been handled by the African Commission on Human and Peoples' Rights; it is a quasi-judicial body. Organizations such as the African Court on Human Rights deal with human rights issues, but there are limits to their jurisdiction. These institutions typically deal with inter-state conflicts, rarely addressing grievances brought forth by individuals or nongovernmental groups. The African Court must also obtain state permission before conducting any investigation or inquiry.[37]

Without the autonomy to conduct independent investigations, the entire purpose of human rights organizations is called into question. What real change can be implemented when the African Court does not have the authority to address human rights violations grounded in ethnic discrimination? The ability to enforce a human rights accord is necessary for Nigeria to remedy years of ethnic tensions, avoid another civil war, and work toward more sustainable, rapid development.

Violence

Nigeria has become a violent state. The Nigerian Civil War of the 1960s is an example of the violence, communal crises between neighbors, and religious divisions induced by ethnic politics. Development has spurred many forms of violence, including those that occur on a daily basis in the struggle for resources. Democracy in Nigeria is undermined by violence in pursuit of power. Elections are marred by chaos and destruction. Examining this violence within the nation-state's development reveals foreign and domestic factors at work. External forces exert pressure to influence economic decisions. Political sovereignty is altered in ways that affect the power dynamics between a government and its people and between one nation and another, fostering conditions that lead to further inequality, irreconcilable disagreements, and eruptions of violence.

Internal challenges include shifting dynamics between the government and its citizens, citizens and domestic groups, and citizens and their

---

[37] Ibid.

environment. The undeniable impact of external and internal influences presents multiple opportunities for conflicts to be resolved through violence. These factors, along with technology's advancement and the evolution of interpersonal ideologies connected to social and political practices, have created unmanageable conflicts in the attitudes and governance of many countries.

Within the state, evolving social and political forces can encourage change, adapting policy and practice to support the ideologies and needs of the people. Policy decisions exercised within a single state's boundaries are often beneficial, allowing local government to adopt effective principles, such as that of an overarching bureaucracy, for organizing people and resources. However, it is no longer possible to isolate individual nation-states in the interconnected presence of globalization and neocolonialism: international relationships and communications – at diplomatic and informal levels – have created fast-paced social cultures whose ideologies challenge established conventions. The state must recognize that shifting values and contexts have altered the structure of many systems. Without growth and evolving values, the developing needs within a state create vast dissent and disagreement leading to the disruption of order and outright chaos. This exposes the fragility of power structures, and force is a common outcome, regardless of the instability's cause.

The position and role of the state, either by causing or resolving an issue, consolidates the authority of a nation's governing body. The actions and structures executed and implemented by overarching systems are the state's power in relation to its citizens and society. Max Weber's theory, regarding the government monopoly on force, emphasizes the necessity of the state's success in this task – it distinguishes the modern state from alternate forms of organization.[38] The state not only holds power to intervene in the lives of the governed, but it also serves as the only correct source of justice. The second half of Weber's understanding of the state's legitimate use of force[39] further establishes the state's validity as a governing body equipped to protect itself and its people. Legitimizing this power creates a collective understanding amongst the citizens and those in power: citizens must recognize the state's power and accept its role as the sole enforcer of regulations, laws, and conditions necessary to live within a country.

The static perspective of the state, controlling the lives of its citizens domestically and internationally through the establishment of police and

---

[38] Markus Jachtenfuchs, "The Monopoly of Legitimate Force: Denationalization, or Business as Usual," *European Review* 13, no. S1 (2005): 37–52.
[39] Ibid.

military forces, has transcended the boundaries of political organization. In the modern age, national government cannot be defined in a single, specific formation – the creation, maintenance, and dispersal of force has become a necessary requirement for all modern nation-states. Weber's recognition of the state's monopoly of force has developed into a key survival characteristic for many nations. However, Weber's ideologies have been challenged by advances in the practices of globalization, foreign policy positions, cultural awareness, and global human rights understandings.

These developments support the assertions of Bruce Kapferer and Bjørn Enge Bertelsen regarding the government's position as a continually changing and progressing body.[40] In their view, the government continually adjusts to the body that constitutes its power. The state must constantly adjust in order to survive, and many states have adapted through the implementation of new military policies. Kapferer and Bertelsen suggest that the government's power is continuously challenged, because the forces[41] driving its change can never be completely controlled. This leads to the inevitable necessity of power institutions advancing in the face of the future.

Relatively new states face danger and threats of violence more frequently than those with preestablished structures and positions. The historical use of violence, to conquer territories, create new civilizations, or take command of citizens, suggests that severe action is needed to destroy old systems. Revolutions for independence, such as those that created countries in the Americas and granted independence to the former colonies of Western nations, often involve violence. Innovative countries formed after these events have experienced their own rebellions against ineffective postcolonial governments, and they have experienced social unrest that stems from the inadequate distribution of resources.

Embedded systems and ideologies have generated persistent issues within the African continent. The country of Nigeria has experienced surges of violence from multiple sources during its postcolonial existence. Large-scale conflicts within the nation have seen force exercised through coups, military regimes, and civil war. It has experienced centralized violence, carried out by monopolized sources of force, in response to the shifting values and priorities of the nation's people.

Centralized force, embodied in the forms of the police and the military, has embraced its essential function as a manifestation of state violence in

---

[40] Bruce Kapferer and Bjørn Enge Bertelsen, "Introduction: The Crisis of Power and Reformations of the State in Globalizing Realities," in *Crisis of the State: War and Social Upheaval*, eds. Kapferer Bruce and Bertelsen Bjørn Enge (New York: Berghahn Books, 2009), 1–26.

[41] Ibid.

domestic and international settings; this force is not foreign in any capacity or form. Nigeria's military coups demonstrate a public belief in the
efficacy of using force to change institutions. This understanding of
military organization and its role in securing government, combined
with ongoing sociopolitical conflicts, has led various militant ethnic campaigns to overthrow existing power structures and institute new ones.

The military coups of 1966 were attempts at political cleansing.
Groups sought to eradicate corruption in the civilian system.[42] Ethnic
conflicts,[43] fueled by underrepresentation and the divides created by
previous government authorities, led to attacks and counter-attacks
from military forces that redistributed political power. The attacks that
occurred during the Nigeria's early postcolonial history established that
the military was the primary influence over the country's political and
social structures.

In 1966–79 and 1983–99, Nigeria was ruled by multiple military
regimes that sought to secure a stable future for the country. They
continued the tradition of separating ethnic groups through ethnicity-
driven politics that affected the composition of the military groups
themselves.[44] Specific ethnic groups maintained majority power within
the country through the allocation of positions and resources within
military systems. The ability to use force against civilian entities, including the civilian government, forwarded the political agenda of dominat-
ing groups. New heads of state steered development and appointed
positions within departments to reduce the separation between public
and private sectors. Governments projected their needs and values into
the private sphere, declaring their intent to purge corruption from
existing structures.

The Nigerian Civil War demonstrates the expansion of government
power and the marginalization of minority ethnic groups. The state's
ability to distribute oil revenues was established through violent means,
resulting in the deaths of millions and highlighting the absence of mediated diplomacy under military rule.[45] Beyond the civil war, repeated
incidents of militancy and insurgency in the Niger Delta region have
violently protested the discrimination and neglect that have crippled the
area's socioeconomic development.

---

[42] A. R. Luckham, "Institutional Transfer and Breakdown in a New Nation: The Nigerian
Military," *Administrative Science Quarterly* 16, no. 4 (1971): 387–406.
[43] Ibid.   [44] Ibid.
[45] J. O. Ahazuem, "Nigeria: Gowon Regime, 1966–1975," in *Encyclopedia of African
History*, ed. Kevin Shillington (London: Routledge, 2004), http://ezproxy.lib.utexas.ed
u/login?url=https://search.credoreference.com/content/entry/routafricanhistory/nigeria_
gowon_regime_1966_1975/0?institutionId=4864.

The Biafra war challenged the validity of Major-General Gowon's military structure, separating the state of Biafra from ineffective rulers who had failed to protect the interests of the Biafran people and their territory. It challenged the prevalent view of the military as a central force for power and the construct of Biafran territory as a state within the nation of Nigeria. The Nigerian Civil War also intensified the complex relationship between the country's political and social spheres. The inescapable intersection of multiethnic citizens – and their desire for the redistribution of power and wealth – made the military a focal point for involvement in ethnic conflicts and attempts to maintain control over the entire nation.

At the base of Nigeria's independence, the weak foundation of an inconsistent government created a struggle for power; the military assumed command through its monopoly on violence and its sociopolitical elevation before and after Nigeria's colonization. Despite several attempts to establish an effective government and root out the remaining corruption and self-serving interests in Nigeria, the country has experienced continual challenges from internal conflict that led to economic and political disintegration.

Electoral democracy was instituted after these regimes ended in 1999, and Nigeria's military pursued policies that were less directly interventionist. Decreased military involvement and factors such as citizen investment, open debates, an emphasis on accountability, and the rising importance of input from civil society institutions have generated alternative methods for conflict resolution and stronger foundational support for institutions within the current developing nation. The evolving government structure has not completely alleviated the country's socioeconomic or political tensions, but changing approaches to governance, foreign policy, and growth under this period of democracy have made a noticeable change in the nation's future trajectory.

Moving Forward

Years have been spent brainstorming possible solutions for Nigeria's ethnic politics, underdevelopment, and political instability, but they remain elusive. Political corruption and gross economic mismanagement have allowed these issues to latch onto the country like parasites. Freedom from institutionalized discrimination and ethnic power dynamics has two requirements: establishing serious, enforceable human rights protections and diversifying the economy away from oil production. Discarding the petro-state economic model would encourage more egalitarian job creation and shield the government from ethnic allegiances and favoritism, allowing Nigeria to improve crucial infrastructure and redistribute wealth more equitably.

There must be a clean break with the political practices of the past, including nepotism and favoritism along ethnic and religious lines. Efforts to protect the interests of different ethnic identities have been detrimental for national development and state security. There must be an inclusive push toward grassroots activism that avoids othering and involves citizens outside of the group considered to be Nigeria's "elite." Nigeria's path to democracy depends on accessibility and transparent political processes where everyone can participate actively and proudly. The country's debilitating dependence on its petroleum sector weakens its democratic process: diversifying away from this dependence could result in more transparent policymaking and a more democratic government that is free from foreign influence.

There are no easy solutions; a plethora of approaches must be carefully examined if Nigeria is to transition successfully into democracy. Nigeria's story is like that of a woven blanket: aspects of colonialism, independence, and ethnic identity are some of the fibers threaded together to shape Nigeria's relationship with ethnic relations, development, and democracy. No problems can be addressed without considering and finding tangible solutions for the issues outlined in this chapter. Fortunately, Nigeria is still a nation in the making that possesses the potential for growth and development unlike anything the continent has seen before.

Political instability and government militarization are enduring sources of conflict within Nigeria. Socioeconomic divisions are propagated by societal values and reinforced by state action in pursuit of national interests. Divisions created by ideologies and unequal resource distribution cause conflict. Internal disputes, stemming from differentiations of status and ideology, create their own conflicts among citizen groups and magnify existing issues of corruption in public and private sectors. Arguably, corruption has been established and embraced both as a ritual and a norm, and discourses have been drawn away from eliminating corruption but are rather subjected to the degree of corruption; hence, by failing to address corrupt practices, and by failing to hold individuals accountable, the state cannot foster effective development on either macro or micro levels. Political and economic leaders pursue interests dictated by individuals and dominant majorities, deliberately marginalizing subsets of the population. Domestic confrontations between segregated ethnic, religious, and regional groups strain a society that expects violence to resolve issues and deliver stability. These conflicts compromise the quality of life for individual Nigerians, and state violence against citizens remains a common occurrence for many.

National disputes involve preestablished social ideas, behaviors, and attitudes that are enabled by a larger social infrastructure that generates inequality and marginalizes specific groups. These disputes often involve settlement patterns or the distribution of people across a territory, depending on regional history. Some communities determine their physical boundaries through geographic features and the resources necessary to survive. In Nigeria's case, the historical boundaries, relationships, and rights to natural resources were disrupted by external forces. British colonial rule had a devastating impact, affecting the country's preservation of ethnic identities, communities, and traditions. Intentional divisions, and the deliberate placement of specific people in strategic locations, altered the dynamics between geographic regions.

Nigeria is currently divided into six geopolitical zones[46] reflecting diverse compositions of citizens, ideas, beliefs, identities, and interests.[47] National violence can be observed in the interactions between the country's Northern and Southern regions, which differ most prominently in the composition of their citizenry. Ethnic and religious tensions among regional populations, and their impact on the overall struggle between North and South, cannot be overstated. Both regions have diverging amounts of infrastructure investment and resource allocation, resulting in different comparative rates of development. Northern states experience greater poverty rates; the average household size is also larger.[48]

Western education levels within the Southern zones are greater than those in the Northern zones, due to educational initiatives that included exposure to Western education and the development of private universities.[49] Education remains largely underdeveloped and overlooked as a root cause of the numerous setbacks Nigeria is entangled in. Much of ethno-political and religious violence, poverty, unemployment, and health crises have inadequate education as a remote cause. The reluctance to make the necessary investments in education is not without serious consequences: lack of proper education or miseducation of the masses helps to advance divisiveness while ensuring that political power remains within the grip of the elites.

Cultural attitudes of individuals in the Northern zone emphasize religious and traditional teaching styles along with a commitment to the

---

[46] Tolu Ogunlesi, "Nigeria's Internal Struggles," *The New York Times*, December 21, 2017, www.nytimes.com/2015/03/24/opinion/nigerias-internal-struggles.html.
[47] Ibid.   [48] Ibid.
[49] Zuhumnan Dapel, "Poverty in Nigeria: Understanding and Bridging the Divide between North and South," *Center for Global Development*, April 6, 2018, www.cgdev.org/blog/poverty-nigeria-understanding-and-bridging-divide-between-North-and-South.

growth of families,[50] and these attitudes have combined with resource allocation decisions and economic policies to widen the gap between the two regions. The pressures positioning North and South as competitors inhibit the ability to form a unifying Nigerian identity. Attitudes of hostility and inferiority are cultivated for political gain, preventing constructive relationships from developing between North and South. Ongoing disputes are encouraged by religious beliefs and ethnic groups, and external influences include separationist movements and international terrorism that could have catastrophic effects. Each region's uncoordinated attempts to address these problems could result in large-scale, cross-regional violence.

Regional perspectives have been shaped by geographic differences, individual settlement patterns, established communities, and religious identities. Like ethnicity, religion is a source of identity creation. Religious identity influences decision-making and affects political agenda. The political elites have appropriated the significance and functionality of religion and religious identities to further accrue political power for themselves and exploit the willing and unwilling masses. The ability of the elites to maximally profit from religion and religious identities is tied to the use of the country's resources in favor of specific ethnic and religious groups.

The relationship between religious identity and politics is transactional; politicians using religion as a mobilizing force for legitimacy and self-aggrandizement. The geopolitical and religious foundation of the country remains a core source of instability and differences. Islamic politics have introduced many important questions regarding the integration of religion and new-found political interests – especially regarding the role of Islamic practices and Sharia law within a framework for self-rule.[51] In the North, the status of Sharia law as a focal point for governance within the new nation emphasized the presence of Islam in the North and created a consistent system of laws.[52]

Taxation, trade policies, and business administration in the North, along with political organization, criminal justice policies, and the distribution of resources, steered the region's development under Muslim rule. These policies were integrated into the postcolonial state because Muslim leaders held positions of power. However, their advancement was met with opposition that called for restrictions within the region and the rest of

---

[50] Ibid.
[51] Olufemi Vaughan, *Religion and the Making of Nigeria* (Durham: Duke University Press, 2016), www.doabooks.org/doab?func=search&query=rid:20703.
[52] Ibid.

the nation. The Muslim government's values did not match the priorities held by everyone under its jurisdiction.

The widespread proliferation of Christianity was sanctioned by British interests during the 19th and 20th centuries. Under this influence, native Nigerians adopted Christian values and were exposed to Western ideologies. Colonial administrators and religious leaders also introduced the Christian school system, building missions in the Southern territories and parts of the Northern region. Education initiatives led to opportunities for civic engagement that were accessed by those in power and those educated under their administration.[53] While Christianity was advanced by the missionary and the colonialists, the North has been fundamentally homogenized by the ideals of Islam prior to the colonial period. The strength of religion to homogenize disparate ethnic groups across the geopolitical regions of Nigeria was accentuated by colonialism and remains to date as a dominant dynamics of power control as they resist one another.

The intersection of Christian faith and indigenous traditions shifted social practices and the symbolism of tradition.[54] Concepts such as marriage gained alternate meanings,[55] reflecting a new understanding of the union and the benefits of being bound in matrimony. Economic strategies also changed through the Christian emphasis on moral practices, the abolition of slave trade and slave labor,[56] and the involvement of native and colonial Christian networks. The rise of Pentecostalism, influenced by Christian structures and African culture, also changed Nigeria's social and political climate. By promoting social change and modernization through new media technology and popular culture,[57] faith has allowed larger, more socially expressive autonomy. These adaptive forces have increased the prominence of faith through active participation and placement within government systems and structures; globalization efforts approached from this perspective have encouraged greater economic advancement and increased social mobility.[58]

The conflicting agendas of the major religions, and their desire to assert political dominance, have led to numerous violent conflicts. The role of religion in national politics is an ongoing source of conflict – the right to apply Sharia law across the nation remains a contested issue. This conflict, which grew intense in 1986 and again in 1999, is an active concern in the political arena.[59] Small-scale conflicts between individuals persist into the

[53] Ibid.   [54] Ibid.   [55] Ibid.   [56] Ibid.   [57] Ibid.   [58] Ibid.
[59] Bede E. Inekwere, "A History of Religious Violence in Nigeria: Grounds for a Mutual Co-existence between Christians and Muslims," Order No. 3711053, University of the West, 2015, http://ezproxy.lib.utexas.edu/login?url=https://search.proquest.com/docview/1703030998?accountid=7118.

present day, but large-scale conflicts are embedded in the history of relationships between Christians and Muslims. Violence across college campuses in the North and the South served as outlets for students expressing anxiety and prejudice against different religious groups.[60] In the 1980s and 1990s, schools endured multiple attacks on Christian students, initiated by Muslims who felt that their religious freedom was threatened.

The 1987 attack in Kaduna State,[61] the 1992 Zango-Kataf confrontation,[62] and the 1994 incident at Goron Dutse prison[63] showed that military regimes had not eradicated the presence of Islam and its followers. Each of these events was sparked by tensions between Muslim sects and their surrounding non-Muslim communities, erupting into conflict that claimed lives. In 1999, the democratic process allowed Northern states to adopt Sharia law selectively. This allowed Islamic justice to be implemented, but it resulted in harsher punishments for those who broke the law and non-Muslims expressed their disapproval.[64] Although religious confrontations continued, the imposition of Sharia law took a back seat to other ethnic and political conflicts.

Religious conflicts have claimed lives and destroyed property, and they have eroded tolerance for the different approaches to modernization and social influence that different faiths can foster. The Boko Haram terrorist group continues to plague Nigeria, providing an extreme example of a community that resists the ideologies of others. The group, which was born from political conditions in postindependence Nigeria, has disrupted the development of the people and their nation. They claim to proliferate "true" Islamic ideology through heinous acts of bombing, killing, and kidnapping, although they target other Muslims along with the Christian community. This subset of Islamic followers has repeatedly required large-scale military interventions.[65] The dedicated efforts of government and civil society organizations have prevented these conflicts from destroying the entire nation.

Intra-Islamic relationships affect Boko Haram's ability to spread its influence. Differences between Shi'ite and Sunni adherents within the Islamic religion spawn conflict and violence to determine political and religious autonomy.[66] Civil society institutions with religious affiliations, such as the Christian Association of Nigeria[67] and Islamic civil society groups, have helped decouple the Boko Haram attacks from the general conflict between Muslims and Christians, but Northern and Southern

[60] Ibid.   [61] Ibid.   [62] Ibid.   [63] Ibid.   [64] Ibid.
[65] W. Ehwarieme and N. Umukoro, "Civil Society and Terrorism in Nigeria: A Study of the Boko Haram Crisis," *International Journal on World Peace* 32, no. 3 (2015): 25–48.
[66] Inekwere, "A History of Religious Violence in Nigeria."
[67] Ehwarieme and Umukoro, "Civil Society and Terrorism in Nigeria."

regions handle the attacks differently. Politicians antagonize their opposition for personal gain, and continued intolerance remains capable of generating catastrophic violence.

Bridging the ethnic divisions between Hausa–Fulani, Igbo, and Yoruba must be integral to political organization that addresses violence in Nigeria. In the postcolonial era, violent clashes between these groups have continued the struggle for power within the fragmented government left behind by the colonial regime. The strategies of these three major groups, combined with the political strategies developed under indirect rule, enable regional and ethnic conflicts.[68] These groups, their leadership strategies, and their involvement in the larger scope of government ensured a struggle for majority control after the British powers had left.

Ethnic conflict led to the decline of Nigeria's First and Second Republics, followed by the rise of ethno-military powers imposing new heads of state. The three groups struggled to maintain a balance of power; the Hausa–Fulani group repeatedly declared their supremacy but ultimately acquiesced to democracy in 1999. Despite the eventual success at maintaining a singular form of political organization, ethnic struggles have continued. The Nigerian Civil War was a struggle for recognition mounted by the Biafran people under the control of the Igbo state; it established a precedent for the continued use of force between groups that oppose each other.

The exploitation of public resources for private gain has also fueled these conflicts. Government officials allocate resources to benefit their own ethnic groups.[69] Government-controlled oil operations have driven conflict between regions and groups, pitting minority and majority groups against each other to determine the distribution of land.[70] The stunted mindsets of fractional, factional interests have stalled internal development, preventing wider cooperation, and challenging the expression and validation of ethnic group identities.

Inter-ethnic conflict is a serious issue that threatens the safety of individuals and the orderly distribution of power, while intra-ethnic conflict has become an issue within regions. The consolidation of smaller ethnic groups recreated the forced unity of former ethnic groups, clans, and kinships that were imposed by colonial rule. Under colonialism, the involuntary fusion of alterative ideologies, traditions, and relations caused problems for individuals trying to identify with those around them. The homogenization of language, symbolism, and customs devalued the smaller groups that were merged into larger identities.

[68] April A. Gordon, *Nigeria's Diverse Peoples: A Reference Sourcebook (Ethnic Diversity Within Nations Series)* (Santa Barbara: ABC-CLIO, 2003).
[69] Ibid.   [70] Ibid.

Without British support behind the centralized government, smaller ethnic groups and identities expressed themselves freely and created their own distinct communities. The nation's federal system allowed these smaller entities to practice their traditions within their own state boundaries.[71] The creation of additional states for specific ethnic groups encouraged continuous defections of individuals from these minority groups, believing that their interests were not represented in a larger system.[72] This is seen in the conflict between Kogi State and the Ebira Tao people protesting limited political and economic mobility. [73] Discrepancies in political representation and unequal opportunities for generating wealth have driven people to violently assert their power.[74] The destruction of lives and property, along with the reduction of opportunities, show that the interests of smaller groups must be recognized, and leadership's attitude must change regarding intervention in intra-ethnic conflicts.[75]

Individuals within Nigeria's established regional and ethnic boundaries have chosen occupations based on their surroundings. Some groups, such as the Yoruba, favor farming initiatives while other groups, such as the Hausa–Fulani, engage in herding activities. Clashes between herders and farmers are common among all three major ethnic groups, regularly involving disputes over land usage. For example, Fulani cattle grazing on established farmland have led to violence that destroys crops and possessions.[76]

Continued ethnic disputes over land use have led to the deaths of thousands and the displacement of hundreds of thousands of individuals.[77] Farmers in Benue and Enugu states have experienced direct and indirect aggression from militant Fulani groups.[78] These disagreements have spread violence across the country, involving multiple states and wasting political and economic resources by disrupting agricultural agreements and social relationships between groups. Cattle and arable land are destroyed, denying either farmers or herders an opportunity for economic gain.[79] Ineffective government intervention has held no party accountable for the damages or losses inflicted.[80] Political instability and the lack of meaningful support have resulted in the violation of rules that govern agricultural

[71] Ifeanyi Onwuzuruigbo, "Researching Ethnic Conflicts in Nigeria: The Missing Link," *Ethnic and Racial Studies* 33, no. 10 (2010): 1797–1813.
[72] Ibid.
[73] Marietu S. Tenuche, "Intra-Ethnic Conflict and Violence in Ebiraland," *Afrigov* 27, no. 2 (2002), http://works.bepress.com/marietu_tenuche/7/.
[74] Ibid.   [75] Ibid.
[76] Aluko Opeyemi, "Urban Violence Dimension in Nigeria: Farmers and Herders Onslaught," *Agathos: An International Review of the Humanities and Social Sciences* 8, no. 1 (2017): 187–206.
[77] Ibid.   [78] Ibid.   [79] Ibid.   [80] Ibid.

operations.[81] The livelihoods of farmers, herders, and their families have been diminished, limiting their capacity for development and degrading their quality of life.

Violence within Nigeria has become commonplace for too many of its citizens. The country faces these issues in the age of modernization and globalization, and its critical infrastructure has failed to develop ways to address the domestic threats imposed by historical divisions. The military was a successful tool for developing an independent colonial state, but Nigeria's government has failed to maintain its monopoly on violence. Specific, segregated populations are victimized by violent subgroups, and the corruption at institutional and national levels has prevented the nation from addressing it. Efforts to increase tolerance and develop collective agreements have been ineffective at establishing meaningful political and economic structures.

The pursuit of self-interest in domestic and foreign policy decisions has led to neocolonialist policies undermining political and economic stability within the nation. Violence between religious, ethnic, and socioeconomic groups will continue until consistent principles of accountability and justice have been firmly established to improve the quality of life for all people.

Oil is a major component of Nigeria's economy. Originally discovered in the southern state of Bayelsa in 1956, it now accounts for 95 percent of Nigeria's exports and 80 percent of its revenue.[82] These extremes indicate an over-emphasis on the petroleum sector to the detriment of others, such as agriculture and textiles. Economists have identified a pattern called the "resource curse," where countries with abundant natural resources develop at much slower rates than those where resources are scarce.[83] The majority of Nigeria's oil is produced in the area surrounding the Niger River Delta, but corruption denies the inhabitants of that region the ability to benefit from the oil revenue – many of them live on less than US $1 per day.[84] Some villages in the Delta cannot consistently access clean drinking water, adequate medical care, or functional schools. Only

---

[81] Mabel Ukamaka Dimelu, Edward Danjuma Salifu, and Edwin M. Igbokwe, "Resource Use Conflict in Agrarian Communities, Management and Challenges: A Case of Farmer-Herdsmen Conflict in Kogi State, Nigeria," *Journal of Rural Studies* 46 (2016): 147–154.

[82] Organization of the Petroleum Exporting Countries, "Nigeria Facts and Figures," Organization of the Petroleum Exporting Countries, n.d. www.opec.org/opec_web/en/about_us/167.htm.

[83] Jeffrey D. Sachs and Andrew M. Warner, "The Curse of Natural Resources," *European Economic Review* 45, no. 4–6 (2001): 827–838.

[84] Amnesty International, "Oil, Poverty, and Violence," Amnesty International, August 1, 2006, web.archive.org/web/20070819155442/www.web.amnesty.org/library/Index/EN GAFR440172006?open&of=ENG-NGA.

about 27 percent of people in the region have access to clean water, only 30 percent of households have access to electricity, and although 30–40 percent of children attend primary school, the government and various corporations divvy up 100 percent of the earnings amongst themselves.[85]

The rapid deterioration of infrastructure in one of Nigeria's most oil-rich regions is almost paradoxical, but the situation in the Delta is directly tied to corruption in the region. Oil is the government's most profitable activity, and much of its development and investment is linked to petroleum production. The needs of other sectors, especially agriculture, have been ignored. Rural actors, such as farmers, are frequently excluded from Nigeria's development discussions. Neglected sectors of the economy could bolster productivity and develop ways to reduce Nigeria's reliance on petroleum if these rural communities were able to create their own development projects.

Oil not only causes massive income inequality in Nigeria, it also harms the environment. Oil spills, occurring due to negligence and failing equipment, substantially alter the surrounding area. The Niger Delta was previously one of the most biodiverse places in the world, and now it has lost entire species because of recurring oil spills; entire ecosystems have succumbed to this fate.[86] Oil has marked Nigeria so indelibly that there seems to be no way to slow its production or to break the country's dependency. Investing all of Nigeria's resources into the development of a single sector has done incredible damage.

Science, technology, engineering, and math (STEM) disciplines have overcome these obstacles to become a booming source of growth for Nigeria. Engineers, mathematicians, doctors, and computer scientists are vital to Nigeria's modernization and development. As the country becomes more established, and domestic and foreign companies expand their operations, they need people who can work in STEM positions. If Nigeria is willing to cut back on oil production to develop other sectors – especially those involving increased STEM education efforts – it could develop research that supports safer, more efficient petroleum production practices. The country could employ thousands of people while simultaneously reducing the environmental impact of oil in the Niger Delta.

Investment in other sectors could also reduce the number of highly trained professionals who emigrate from Nigeria. This phenomenon,

---

[85] Daniel Egiegba Agbiboa and Benjamin Maiangwa, "Corruption in the Underdevelopment of the Niger Delta in Nigeria," *Journal of Pan African Studies* 5, no. 8 (2012): 108–132, www.researchgate.net/publication/254259040_Corruption_in_the_Underdevelopmento f_the_Niger_Delta_in_Nigeria.
[86] Ruth Krause, "Oil Spills Keep Devastating Niger Delta," *DW*, March 20, 2015, www .dw.com/en/oil-spills-keep-devastating-niger-delta/a-18327732.

known as "human capital flight" or "brain drain," happens when people look elsewhere for stable work, higher salaries, and more advanced technology.[87] Improving a broad range of economic sectors would diversify the available job opportunities and encourage these professionals to stay and work in their home country. Nigeria's loss of human capital hinders its development because the country is unable to advance its research, institutions, or intellectual potential. The country is caught in a self-reinforcing spiral that damages the economy.[88]

Development is more than economic endeavors, and it is more than oil. It can be measured in terms of infrastructure projects such as roads, railways, and power grids. Infrastructure keeps a country afloat, acting as a tool to transport natural resources for production and human capital for labor. It is the manifestation of a country's inner workings: like a machine, the entire process depends on its components remaining well maintained and running smoothly. Nigeria's infrastructure shortfalls are related to the government's misuse of funds and inefficient spending, which impairs economic growth and development.[89] Repairing infrastructure is not a simple task, and it requires years of careful planning and execution. However, it is vital for putting development and growth at the forefront of Nigeria's agenda.

[87] Sunita Dodani and Ronald E. LaPorte, "Brain Drain from Developing Countries: How Can Brain Drain Be Converted into Wisdom Gain?" *Journal of the Royal Society of Medicine* 98, no. 11 (2005): 487–491.

[88] E. E. Emeghara, "Brain Drain as a Clog in the Wheel of Nigeria's Development," *International Journal of Development and Management Review* 8, no. 1 (2013): 110–121.

[89] Dhruv Gandhi, "Figure of the Week: Gaps in Nigeria's Public Infrastructure," *Brookings*, March 14, 2018, www.brookings.edu/blog/africa-in-focus/2018/03/14/figure-of-the-week-gaps-in-nigerias-public-infrastructure/.

2   In Search of Modernity

Within the Nigerian state – which is a colonial construct and a modern project – modernity is an illusion. The colonialism that created Nigeria as a political and socioeconomic unit is a product of European modernity along with Europe's global push to spread its version of modernity. This modernity saw the rise of the welfare state, individual subjectivity, the decline of religion and kingship authorities, a rise in industrialization, increased reliance on science and logic, increasingly democratic governance, notions of liberty, and capitalism. All of these developments are tied to the Enlightenment that preceded them, and the drive to impose Europe's concept of modernity on other nations galvanized the scramble to colonize Africa. It was anchored in pretentious ideas of "civilizing" the Black race and saving it from its own cultures, despite European modernity's status as a summary of Europe's cultural orientation. Their lofty aspirations and global imposition turned European ideals into benchmarks for many societies that were encouraged to see them as standards for modernization.

Nigeria was created from European aspirations of modernity fusing a group of independent and sovereign nations together. Although the country exhibits many elements of European modernity, some assert that it belongs to the category of the not-yet-modern.[1] This argument is supported by pervasive levels of underdevelopment that ravage many African nations, affecting some of the fundamental features associated with modernity, but the European brand of modernity is obsolete. Nigeria, and much of the globalized world along with it, has evolved. Modernity is now expressed in other dominant Western nations, such as the United States, and through localization in other countries, such as the countries of the global South. China, Japan, and Singapore are current sites of modernity, expanding the definition of modernity

---

[1] Ulrich Beck, Wolfgang Boss, and Christopher Lau, "The Theory of Reflexive Modernization: Problematic, Hypotheses and Research Programme," *Theory, Culture and Society* 20, no. 1 (2003): 1–34.

Figure 2.1 An aerial view of Ibadan city, combining the past and contemporary landscape.

through manufacturing strength, market influence, and effects on the global economy.[2]

Enwezor has argued that Asian countries are sites of modernity's revitalization, designating European countries as "morticians of modernity" that have infrastructures, societal practices, and policies that preserve modernity's earliest ideals.[3] European countries can be viewed as relics of modernity, and some Asian countries are redefining what it means to be modern, along with the processes of modernization. This does not dismiss the questions regarding Nigeria's achievements, but it challenges the idea of modernity as something that encompasses or underscores fixed indices. If one feature consistently marks modernity as a condition of affairs or a state of civilization, it is continuity: modernization, which results in the state of being modern, is a process. Modernity itself is an ongoing process.

Apart from the obvious implication of the "not-yet-modern" label, which flattens modernity's expansive definition as a continually self-regenerative and self-reflexive state of culture, its use affirms European–colonialist ideals

[2] Okwui Enwezor, "Modernity and Postcolonial Ambivalence," *South Atlantic Quarterly* 109, no. 3 (2010): 595–620.
[3] Ibid., 598.

of European modernity required for any nation deemed modern. European forms of cultural renewal, which distinguished the region as a site of wide-ranging renaissance across facets of society, are expected as essentialist features of a modern state. These expectations developed because European modernity, espoused and introduced globally through colonialism and adopted by many colonized nations, set the stage for versions of modernity that presently exist. Okwui Enwezor calls these versions "petit" in contrast to a "grand" type of European modernity. Petit modernity, according to Enwezor, "represents the export kind, ... [designated as] a mimic modernity through its various European references."[4] Wittock Bjom supports this idea with his take on the European origins of modernity as a global state and the multiple modernities arising from this condition of global domestication.[5]

The structures, paradigms, and ideals of European modernity retain their influence in countries that are said to achieve global modernity, a status common for countries around the world but originating from and administered by the West. This is partly because cultural structures of the West, especially those of the United States, are indebted to European cultural formations exported through colonialism and other encounters with non-European societies. Special priority was given to cultural systems associated with the renaissance that stemmed from the Enlightenment. If "global" modernity is essentially Western dominance over countries that adopt, adapt, and domesticate these sociocultural systems, it is merely European modernity by another name. The ideas and cultural shifts that entrenched European modernity in global consciousness persist in the political and social formations of Western nations.

Others have argued that the West's brand of global modernity pays tribute to the European version. Chakrabarty's take on the hetero-temporal history of modernity accentuates this idea, stating that modernity undergoes habituations as multiple locales provincialize modernity in their struggle toward modernization, resulting in the creation of several modernities.[6] Chakrabarty's position implies that grand and petit modernities exist. The former is European in its fundamentals, structure, and progress, and the latter is exported. Enwezor has described it as a "quotation," continually referencing Europe, regardless of the particularities imbued in it by each locale. If the centers of modernity are in the

---

[4] Ibid., 596.
[5] See Bjorn Wittrock, "Modernity: One, None or Many? European Origins and Modernity as a Global Condition," in *Multiple Modernities*, ed. Shmuel Eisenstadt (New Brunswick: Transaction Publications, 2002).
[6] See Dipesh Chakrabarty, *Provincializing Europe: Postcolonial Thought and Historical Difference*, 2nd ed. (Princeton: Princeton University Press, 2008).

West, and nations of the global South depend on the localization or habituation of this brand of modernity to realize their own versions, then the nations dependent on the West's cultural directions are localizing a Eurocentric grand modernity. In a sense, Euro-North America is a descendant of "Western" Europe[7] – America was one of the first sites of European victory during the campaign for global dominance.[8]

Two strands of arguments concerning modernity and nation-states are pre-eminent and vital: modernity is uniquely European, and it can be locally domesticated. This accedes to modernity's European origin, but it also accentuates modernity's universal character, highlighting its domestication and translatability into several cultures. If these were the case, if modernity could be domesticated despite its European foundations, it would be a rash judgment to declare that Nigeria is not-yet-modern. This is also the case if modernity is regenerative and the logical process of modernization is continuous. Modernity is always self-reflexive, at risk of being redefined and expanded by localizing contexts.

Although some features can distinguish a modern state from the not-yet-modern, these features are not set in stone – they are continually acted upon by the conditions they engender. Identifying these features requires an understanding of the contexts in which they have been localized. It also requires comprehension of the progress toward modernization that has been made by and in such locales. Judging a given setting's state of modernization demands an investigation into the locale's search for modernity. One must consider the social practices and governmental activities, policies, ratifications, and agencies created, as well as the political formations, structures put in place, and cleavages promoted to demonstrate a conscious movement toward modernization. Because modernization is a process, and modernity is an ongoing state, a nation can continually be in search of modernity while remaining modern, redefining its modern status and localizing global features. By globalizing its contributions, modernity can self-inflect, be reflexive, and also thrive in continuity.

By employing this approach to modernity, one avoids generic conclusions that gloss over a state's unique conditions and the specific circumstances of that state's modernization efforts. It is an approach that eliminates fixed expectations of what modernity looks like in a nation; even Third World countries contribute to the cultural formations and social streams that feed into and constitute global modernity. The default

---

[7] Anibal Quijano, "Coloniality and Modernity/Rationality," *Cultural Studies* 21, no. 2 (2010): 168–178.
[8] Ibid.

approach to modernization views the condition as an end of civilization or a given period's social history.

Nigeria's experience of modernity might be incomplete or unsatisfactory, but that cannot justify claims that the nation is not-yet-modern. What is modern when modernity is continuous and open to remediating properties from other cultural centers? If this is one of the fundamental features of modernity, especially as demonstrated by nations that lay the foundations for and chart the course of modernity, then it is not missing from Nigeria. Modernity is continually reinvented and open to remediation, meaning that anything short of complete hostility to civilization on Nigeria's part should be seen as efforts and initiatives, either failed or successful, to achieve modernity.

Like other nation-states, Nigeria has experienced failures and successes at modernization, even if its failures occur to an appalling extent. Nigeria's efforts to exhibit modernity may be dismal, but its failures as a modern state are insights into its ongoing struggles and attempts at modernization. Nigeria's history as a state, from precolonial, colonial, and postcolonial eras, is that of a country in search of modernity. Many transformations that occurred during colonialism, including segregationist policies, cultural destruction, social control, and the forced adoption of cultural items, are all "skewed" attempts to rapidly modernize Nigeria.

The imposition of European values, the prioritization of European civilization and knowledge production, and the denial of African visibility were attempts to transition Nigeria from its existing state to one that was modern and civilized. These motives also drove the denial of core African epistemologies and knowledge patterns and the limitations imposed on African expressions. The forced adoptions of European lifestyles and the normalization of European coloniality, along with the policies that led to and maintained the amalgamation of the northern and southern protectorates, were more modernization efforts executed in bad faith. They are an example of indigenous epistemic practices treated as substandard modes of cultural expression that are inadequate to engage the developing world.

These attitudes are visible in treatment of indigenous sites of knowledge. They have been relegated to mere sites of data, or spaces of inspiration for European creativity and civilization that are not sites of knowledge production in their own right. The exoticization and objectification of Africa were the results of European policies governing non-European indigenous spaces. They created an increasingly modernized nation with a fragmented spirit and fractured foundation. European dismissal of native culture caused fractures that affect Nigeria's exhibition of modernity: modernization was not a natural progression in the country's cultural history, and it created tensions between existing aspects of culture and the modern features introduced by Europe. An antagonistic relationship developed between Nigerian indigenous cultures and the features of modernity, which, ironically, set up Nigeria's native cultural expressions and systems as antipodes of modern structures. In some instances, rather than localize European modernity, Nigeria merely translocated it and proceeded from there.

The objectionable colonial administration created structures and patterns of expression that encouraged Nigeria's move toward being modern. Some narratives point out the benefits of European colonialization, encouraging a view of Africa's colonization as a drive toward civilization that supports the idea of a "white man's burden," or a compulsion to civilize other nations and shield their cultures from self-induced decay. Although these views minimize the colonizers' brutal exploitation of Africa, benefits can be found in any type of inter-cultural encounter. Independent Nigeria maintained some colonial structures in its administration: representative governance, ideas regarding liberty, legal jurisprudence, constitutional amendments, accountable governance, the separation of religion and state, the creation of a Federal Civil Service, formal education, and even infrastructure has been seen as either directly influenced by or deliberately based on European patterns of civilization.

Continued European dominance in former colonies, even after the defeat of colonialism, suggests that Nigeria is a nation struggling toward being modern. The coloniality of being, a phrase used to describe this dominance, is sustained by postcolonial practices that have been endorsed or created by the state. International inequalities have retained the modes of exploitation and hegemony that enabled European colonialism in Africa, where European superiority steered all development.

Many precolonial African cultures already had distinct civilizations that would have naturally progressed into the modern era on their own terms without colonial interruption. Modern Nigeria is a narrative of transitions from ancient social and cultural habits to new patterns of behavior. The primary features of modernity – "permanence of change and innovations" and "universality of social development"[9] – emphasize the self-reflexive, fluid, and continually regenerative nature of modernity along with its global character. Nigeria's experience of modernity must also reveal constant change, and this perpetual change must keep pace with the modernity that shapes global developments. This has multiple implications; Nigeria's

---

[9] Yuriy Savelyev, "Essential Features of Modern Society in Sociological Discourse," *Journal of Humanities and Social Sciences* 6, no. 11 (2013): 1673–1691.

ability to localize modernity is unquestionable, but its capacity to keep pace with global modernity is less certain.

Some claim that Nigeria is not a modern state due to its inability to evolve an expression of modernity that keeps pace with the global version. Because modernity is defined by continuity, and because these terms are defined by the West, it is difficult for Africa's localizing nation-states to remain current. Western countries have the infrastructure in place to identify and adapt to the changes imposed by modernity, and African nations do not. African nations require both the adaptability and the ability to sustain the tempo necessary for change – it is one thing to adapt a system to reflect modern changes, and it is another to maintain those systems to facilitate the continual changes demanded by modernization. This challenge is a defining characteristic of modernity and the countries that pursue it. Eisenstadt puts the matter in sharp relief, describing the primary challenge for nations pursuing modernity as the failure to adapt their systems for the continually evolving demands of modernization. When these evolutions are difficult to absorb from a policy-making standpoint, Eisenstadt says that it spells problems for the state's capacity to match the tide of ever-altering demands that shape modernization.[10]

How does Nigeria continue its pursuit of modernity, and how does it deal with the tide of change that characterizes modernity? Nigeria's struggle to adopt the Western version of modernity and create a unique brand, localizing the sociocultural structures of global modernity, provides a narrative of Nigeria's struggle. This narrative describes the country's successes and failures with modernization. Nigeria's narrative as an independent state is that of a country navigating its way toward modernity.

Nigeria's political history and reality provides insight into the nation's ongoing struggle. The Nigerian political space has a history of changes, radical renewals of political structures, and constitutional amendments attempting to remedy or advance the nation's status as a sovereign entity with defined goals, protecting the rights and liberties of its citizens. The struggle to achieve the political requirements of a modern nation is visible in the structures that make up Nigeria's political reality. Sovereignty is a crucial aspect of the modern Nigerian state; it allows each state the capacity to derive methods of habituating modernity and to keep up with its changing features. It also facilitates the creation of policies to support a unique configuration that considers each state as autonomous. Nigeria has over 250 ethnic groups, numbering up to 400. The country has six

[10] Shmuel N. Eisenstadt, "Social Change and Modernization in African Societies South of the Sahara," *Cahiers D'études Africaines* 5, no. 19 (1965): 453–471.

geopolitical zones, with several ethnic cleavages and formations. The nation's political system and its component states must accommodate these considerations.

Shortly after independence, Nigeria maintained a divide-and-rule system of democratic government patterned after the European admin-istration of Nigeria. Although there were attempts at regional auton-omy, power was concentrated in the Northern part of country, and other regions were subordinate. The military governments that seized power suspended all forms of democracy, creating a unitary system of government. The military's entrance into Nigerian politics has been rationalized in some quarters as a necessary intervention designed to halt the corruption, ethnic favoritism, nepotism, and other bad govern-ance that ailed the political structure under civilian rule. The reality of Nigeria's military administration revealed that little had changed, fur-ther degrading the nation and suspending any hope of modernization: democracy was stopped in its tracks and the country was plunged into despotism.

After independence, Nigeria's parliamentary system of governance mirrored the European strategy of the time, allowing for structural imbal-ances that favored a lopsided power distribution, skewed representation, and unequal access to the country's resources despite the intent to develop a federalist system. This was an insurmountable obstacle in the race toward modernization; the newly created country could not accom-modate its inherent schisms and mutual distrust. Although its structure favored a weak center and more powerful regions, the larger population of the North (according to a contested census) meant greater representation in the central government. The system failed to adequately address the imbalances in demographic and geographic strength between the North and the less populated Southern and Western regions.

Regional governments felt overshadowed by the North, which was viewed as socially in the minority due to its low levels of education. However, the North was not a political minority; it was underrepresented in the federal civil service because of its aversion to Western education. Reforms to the 1951 and 1957 constitutions failed to address the conse-quence of substantive representation reinforcing the power of an already powerful region. Tyrannies drove the nation farther back in its struggle toward modernity – Elaigwu described them as "tyranny of population and tyranny of skills,"[11] since the embrace of Western education led the South and the West to dominate the civil service.

---

[11] Isawa J. Elaigwu, "Federalism in Nigeria's New Democratic Polity," *Publius: The Journal of Federalism* 32, no. 2 (2002): 73–95.

The resultant schism was revealed in 1966; the first coup was allegedly a reaction to the country's unequal distribution of power. The North's acquisition of power, with its demographic strength leading to representative and political power, fostered ethnic schisms and distrust that invited military takeover. Power swung temporarily to the East and then back to the North, and it has remained there.

After overthrowing the parliamentary government, the unitary government lasted for decades. Nigeria's military government was hostile to several components of modern states, including political representation, the protection of rights, freedom, liberty, democracy, and equality. Restrictions on freedom of expression and freedom of the press were the actions of a state that disavowed liberty, which is a core component of the modernization process. The military government removed the federal structure that had been giving considerable autonomy to the regions and imposing restrictions on a weak central government. A powerful center was intended to promote unity, unlike the regional individuality and autonomy promoted by a federal structure that divided the country. This centralization handicapped the regions and the states carved from them in the long run, fertilizing spaces where a do-or-die type of state politics would germinate, and it increased the corruption and ethnic favoritism that the military had sworn to eradicate.

The military government would be removed by 1999, but some of its programs would remain in effect, laying the foundations for the democratic government's federalism. Federalism supports aspirations of modernization not only by promoting democratic policies but also by safeguarding the rights of groups and individuals. The core features of federalism, such as units of government that share power, exercise jurisdictional autonomy, and coordinate authority,[12] are also the means of modernizing a state; they ensure that democracy thrives and achieves its potential. Nigeria adopted a formal federalist structure and embraced democratic governance as part of the wave of modernity that swept the globe. However, Nigeria's federal structure is different due to its efforts at localizing an important component: its power is concentrated at the top and distributed downward as a vestige of the military government.

The regional autonomy and power of Nigeria's early parliamentary system was absent from its later federal structure. The creation of thirty-six states from four regions – Northern, Western, Eastern, and Midwestern – was intended to aid substantive representation and allocate resources to minority groups that were overshadowed by larger groups. The creation of states and hierarchical governments within those states,

---

[12] See Kenneth C. Wheare, *Federal Government* (London: Oxford University Press, 1946).

for state and local governments were consociational means of distributing power and allocating resources between the several ethnic groups, meant to ensure stability and unity in the country.

Even consociational interventions can fail. Despite Nigeria's inclusion of veto power, segmental autonomy, and proportionality, a considerable amount of power remained concentrated in the central government. The federal government could intervene in matters that violated regional autonomy, permitting regions and the ethnicities bound within them to grow without undue restrictions. But Nigeria's political system is a system of ethnic cleavages, and federal power is often abused by the ethnic group at the center. This allows ethnic favoritism and unintended consequences to halt the progress of the nation.

Concurrent, executive, and residual legislative lists were created to address these issues, allowing the constitution to create scenarios where all tiers of government could exercise powers without infringing on each other. Yet previous Nigerian constitutions, such as the 1960 and 1963 constitutions, permitted the central government to decide regional matters. The 1999 constitution still empowers the central government at the expense of state governments, regardless of the quota system or constitutional provisions made to address federal infringement of state authority. Constitutional amendments are ongoing efforts to transition the government to a modernized state. The federal character principle contained in the 1979 and 1999 constitutions attempted to ensure substantive representation of ethnic groups in federal structures. The idea was to establish equality and the protection of individual rights by ensuring representation in government entities that ranged from the civil service to educational institutions. But the strong ethnic cleavages in Nigeria transcend barriers to continue practicing ethnic favoritism. Some measures, like the principle of proportionality, only functioned as a type of affirmative action that perpetuated hegemony: Northerners continue to occupy government seats based on a quota system that tries to increase the representation of social minorities, because the system is influenced by the low levels of education in the North.

Transitions from democratic government to military rule and back are the struggles of a country not only searching for a means of adapting modern ways of governance, but also fashioning ways to contribute to the currents of modernity that shape the world.

The protection of human rights is a basic feature of modern states. Several African countries, including Nigeria, have ratified human rights instruments to protect their citizens. Nigeria has also drafted policies to protect the interests of several groups within the country. Freedom, fundamentally defined as the right to exist in ways that do not harm others, is a primary component of the modern state, and it is often a feature of democratic governance. Nigeria's claim to being democratic is linked with its ability to secure and safeguard the interests and rights of its citizens.

Nigeria's history as an independent nation has been one of contradictions. Attempts to safeguard the rights and interests of specific groups have either been temporary fixes that cause long-term damage, or actions that empower the perpetrators of hegemonic polities, or moves that eventually append minorities to their oppressors. Legislation was passed in 1962, during the first republic, to create a new region: Mid-west. A major reason for the change was to allow better representation and greater autonomy for non-Yoruba ethnicities living in the Yoruba-occupied Mid-west Region. Theoretically, the bill would empower each ethnic group and guarantee substantive representation – this was necessary in a newly created country where Yoruba, Igbo, and Hausa ethnic groups outnumbered every other group in their respective regions. These groupings were inadequate to provide considerable autonomy, and the problems became more pronounced as the creation of additional states followed.

The four regions were divided into thirty-six states, allowing more ethnicities to exercise relative autonomy and control of their resources. Ethnic groups could also implement practices that promoted cultural sensibilities, ideals, and heritages, and these changes allowed for greater representation. The right to political participation is vital for a country with a pluralist political system; pluralism is pivotal for democracy.

A multiethnic political system should create an atmosphere for political pluralism that provides space for ethnic groups and their representatives to exercise their rights to political participation, good governance, and enfranchisement. According to Ejobowah, such a political structure "takes into account regional, ethnic, and group-specific matters,"[13] enabling the growth, progress, and harmony that drives democracy. It also protects cultural differences and allows cultures to thrive without being overshadowed, subsumed, or collapsed into others. The right to cultural participation also promotes the right to political participation, since nations like Nigeria have political parties that formed around cultural identities.

When these rights are protected, and political participation is encouraged, representative members can draft policies that benefit members of every ethnic group. The quota system and consociational policies implemented by Nigeria are methods of addressing inequality for greater access

---

[13] See John C. Ejobowah, "Political Recognition of Ethnic Pluralism: Lessons from Nigeria," *Nationalism and Ethnic Politics* 6, no. 3 (2000): 1–18.

and maintenance of rights, but they are often done at the expense of merit. In the educational system, quotas have been implemented that target students from Northern Nigeria – this protects the right to education for Northern Nigerians. Nigeria has ratified rights instruments like the Universal Declaration of Human Rights (UDHR), expressly advocating for the right to education. (Implementing and ensuring compliance with these instruments is a separate matter.) Such actions improve the short-comings of the quota system by addressing the root of the problem: limited educational opportunities.

Although Nigeria has ratified human rights instruments, including the UDHR and the African Charter, to protect fundamental human rights, their implementation has been problematic. The rights of the girl-child are protected, as an African child, by the national constitution. Girls have an equal right to education, but the consti-tution makes allowances for Islamic law declaring that the marriage-able age for a girl is puberty or around age 13. Not only does this have adverse economic and health implications, it also impacts edu-cation. Early marriage often interferes with access to education, and girls are disadvantaged on several fronts.

The African Charter recognizes the right to development and self-determination, and it recognizes the rights and protects the welfare of children, women, and persons with disabilities. It emphasizes the role of the family and other collective social units, protecting civil, political, economic, social, and cultural rights. In Nigeria, women are the social minority, and their rights are barely protected. Women have not been fielded as representatives for either the People's Democratic Party or the All Progressives Congress, the nation's two major political parties. No woman has been elected as a Nigerian president or as a deputy.

In a bid to increase the pace and tempo of modernization, Nigeria ratifies many human rights instruments, adopting and adapting inter-national agreements to fit the country's structures, vowing to support the rights of its citizens in the process. These are often empty gestures. Several ethnicities continue to agitate for greater representation and more favorable quota systems, claiming to be disadvantaged without commen-surate allocations from the Federation Account based on the resources they provide. Less productive states continue to receive greater support from the center, determined by a lopsided sharing formula that favors the North.[14] This denies regional rights for development and self-realization,

---

[14] For more explanation on this, see Adeleke Salami, "Taxation, Revenue Allocation, and Fiscal Federalism in Nigeria: Issues, Challenges, and Policy Options," *Economic Options* 56, no. 189 (2011): 27–49.

an important feature of the African Charter, but it is also a subtle indictment of ethnic cleavages. It essentially denies rights to federation resources based on affinities with specific ethnic groups. The Federal Character Principle also hints that Nigeria has mismanaged opportunities to protect citizens' rights – it is a struggle for power between elites and an ethnic-centered quota system that favors specific groups at the expense of those in the minority. Dibua accurately describes the situation by calling it a power-sharing exercise.[15]

Ethnicity and religion are inseparable in Nigeria, and this relationship shows how the rights of religious affiliation and participation can be indirectly repressed. Ethnic interests become state interests in the context of Nigerian politics, and the religious sentiment of the dominant ethnic group seeps into political decisions, indirectly demonstrating that ethnic connections can be used to access state resources. The practice, interpretation, and state support for religious affiliation in Nigeria has had an awful consequence of standardizing some interests as the norm, or as national interests that sideline others, to the point where ethnic roots often determine the level of access to state power.

Nigeria's inability to facilitate the participation of adults in representative government is an indictment of its efforts to protect the right to political participation. Nigeria's Age Reduction Bill was intended to increase the age of participation for Nigerian youths. The minimum age required to run for office was lowered: down to twenty-five from thirty for the Houses, to thirty from thirty-five for governorship positions, and to thirty from forty for the office of the president. The bill reveals decades of bias repressing the political ambition of a specific cohort across elected positions – it has been a systematic repression of political rights. The bill is a step in the right direction, although diehard conservatives insist that age is tantamount to experience. Their cultural view has maintained this barrier in the 1999 constitution.

The Age Bill signifies a country struggling toward modernization, but the Social Media Bill proposed by the Senate threatens the freedom of expression. Although it has been camouflaged as a way to reduce hate speech or protect against internet falsehoods, it follows previous bills that attacked internet freedom, such as the Hate Speech Bill that was read by the Senate and the National House of Representatives (the Hate Speech Prohibition Bill 2019 and the National Commission for the Prohibition of Hate Speeches Bill 2019, respectively). The Social

---

[15] J. I. Dibua, "Ethnic Citizenship, Federal Character, and Inter-Group Relations in Postcolonial Nigeria," *Journal of the Historical Society of Nigeria* 20 (2011): 1–25.

Media Bill is related to a Digital Rights Bill that was rejected by the president for being vague and needlessly extensive, despite claims that it was meant to protect the rights, well-being, and safety of internet users.

The Social Media Bill, known as the "Protection from Internet Falsehoods and Manipulations and Other Related Matters," targets the freedom of expression associated with the Internet. The bill threatens the rights of individuals expressing opinions; it deems contradictory opinions as potential threats to state security. Nigeria ranks 120th on the world Press Freedom Index, which is an appalling development, and the country should not favor policies that threaten freedom of expression. Vague, poorly conceived, and contrived bills with blanket repercussions threaten the rights of its citizens.

Social media and its hash-tag revolution continue to provide platforms for change agents and youth participating in the country's governance, largely owing to its democratic spaces. Enacting bills that limit this activity, whether intentionally or otherwise, not only stems the creation of political spaces outside normative political structures, it also perpetuates the repression of important voices that sustain the nation's modernity. A modern nation gives voice to its grassroots activists, offering opportunities to participate and encouraging political activism on all fronts and across all levels. These actions are ways to ensure and preserve a place for democracy.

Nigeria's economy is another area showing weak attempts at modernization. After independence, the three regions that were relatively autonomous had almost total control over their economies, but the current national economy depends on imports and tethers itself to the fluctuations of the international market. In the past, a competitive spirit allowed each region to support the country by creating infrastructure that increased productivity: the West produced cocoa, the North had groundnuts, and the East had palm oil. Nigeria competed favorably in the international marketplace until the discovery of oil and the centralization of political power that allowed ethnic politics to erode the nation's economy. These developments reinforced a federal structure where the center held all the power while the regions, later turned into states, became subordinate. An exclusive focus on oil as the major export eventually crippled Nigeria's economy. Nigeria's problems, especially in relation to its modernization, have an economic base.

The centralization of power allowed ethnic interests to steer national interests, especially for the ethnicities that occupied the ruling center. Revenue from oil production was centrally controlled and distributed downward, which enticed other states and ethnicities to focus on oil production and aim to occupy central government positions, neglecting other sources of income and development. Revenue-sharing formulas favored groups allied with those at the center, controlling the allocation of resources and the Federation Account. Taxes are mostly controlled by the central government, from Value Added Tax to the income tax and custom and excise duties. The lack of constitutional restrictions on federal spending has increased the fiscal supremacy of the center at the expense of the states.

Nigeria's revenue-sharing formula, which allocates 52.68 percent, 26.72 percent, and 20.60 percent of revenue to federal, state, and local governments, respectively, contributes to the country's economic malaise.[16] In the first republic, 60 percent of revenue went to the regions, before petroleum revenues captured the government's attention, becoming the major export while other resources and sources of federal revenue were neglected.[17] Nigeria's derivation principle, which allowed regions producing resources to receive special consideration in revenue-sharing decisions, affects its economic strength. The derivation was 50 percent before independence. By the fourth republic, it had dropped to 13 percent, showing why the Niger Delta region continually suffers despite generating most of Nigeria's revenue. It is a dismal performance of fiscal policy, and it serves as a reminder that states can receive allocation benefits without doing anything.

When population size and the equality of states are given greater weight than derivation principles of the past, states can sit back and do nothing.[18] This is detrimental to nation building. Nigerian fiscal policy encourages indolence, ethnic favoritism, and nepotistic governance, showing neither foresight nor planning on the part of the government. States in the North region receive the greatest sums from the Federal Allocation Account while generating almost nothing compared to states in the West.

In 2018, Nigeria overtook India as the world's poverty capital, with about 87 million people living in extreme poverty. Although this reality contradicts claims of progressive modernization, it is not surprising from a country riddled by ethnic politics at every point, including its democracy, protection of human rights, and fiscal policies. A country that depends on imports – which practices hegemonic fiscal policies that offer no incentives for state growth – will only regress away from modernization.

---

[16] Salami, "Taxation, Revenue Allocation, and Fiscal Federalism in Nigeria."   [17] Ibid.
[18] See ibid. for the formulas.

Nigeria continues to pursue several policies and strategies in its drive toward being modern, but it faces self-imposed challenges and external obstacles. One cannot claim that Nigeria is not modern, and like many other nations, Nigeria continues to search for modernity through policies, ratified instruments, and the creation of new structures. Some of these approaches fail, and others assist in this quest.

Part II

Context and History

3   Colonial Modernity

Colonial discourse will continue eliciting interest in scholarship for a long time to come, with a view to understanding contemporary African states and the predicaments facing their inherited identities.[1] Understanding the colonial epoch as part of society's evolution in Africa has become the focal point of debates: through colonialism, this nomenclature invokes the tripartite evil of poverty, ignorance, and disease,[2] invoked as the primary explanation for all that is deficient in modern African states.

In such discourse, colonialism takes the form of a mysterious leviathan casting a powerful spell; its impact was total and absolute, with the colonized people having no agency in the course of history that led to the domination and maintenance of its structure. One can fall into the trap of parochial analyses that frame the colonial history of these states in the realm of morality – good and evil – rather than what it really represented for their history. It was an integral stage of evolution that required negotiation and compromise, having seismic impacts on sociopolitical and economic configurations.[3]

The moralist view of colonization supports a myth that poverty persists because innocents have been conditioned to remain poor due to external, evil forces. Within these confines, colonialism becomes synonymous with society's retrogression; it served no constructive purpose to advance

---

[1] See Tunde Decker, *Matrix of Inherited Identity: A Historical Exploration of the Underdog Phenomenon in Nigeria's Relationship Strategies, 1960–2011* (Ibadan: University Press, 2016), on the challenges of this identity and the state's reputation in the international community.

[2] Some discussions, which have been classified as Afro-pessimism, approach these challenges from a perspective of hopelessness and despair. Abubakar Momoh, "Does Pan-Africanism Have a Future in Africa? In Search of the Ideational Basis of Afro-Pessimism," *African Journal of Political Science* 8, no. 1 (2003).

[3] As such, Ajayi cautioned that, "The partition of Africa at the end of the nineteenth century should be seen as the result, not the cause of the incorporation of Africa into the world-economy." J. F. Ade Ajayi, ed., *General History of Africa VI: Africa in the Nineteenth Century Until the 1880s*, abridged edition (Paris: UNESCO Publishing, 1998), 10.

society. Under this line of thinking, colonialism contaminated the unique attributes of Africans and their steady journey toward peace and glory – a kind of El Dorado, vilifying colonialism as the sole source of modern societal ills.

On the other side of the discussion, colonialism is viewed as a transitional period in the history of Africa's cultures and people. Its unprecedented effects followed the usual laws of historical evolution: gain and loss. Colonialism can be seen as a double-edged sword, often accompanying the cultural shift of societies from one extreme to another. The modern state in Africa is the product of imperial machinations and the period's centripetal and centrifugal forces. The colonial period, which officially spanned about six decades for the various cultural groups inhabiting the area currently known as Nigeria, was a period of exploitation and manipulation to claim the colony as an appendage of Britain and the West. These influences, especially in pursuit of profit, shaped the sociopolitical and economic morphology that would be inherited by the independent state of Nigeria.

The true implications of colonialism were not lost on the emerging, Western-educated class that would lead nationalist agitations and occupy

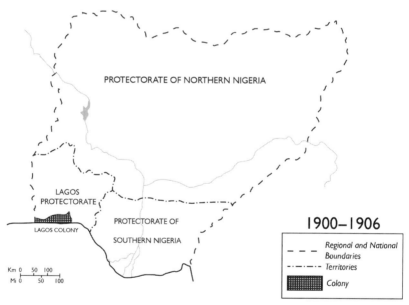

Map 3.1 Nigeria, colonial regions, 1900–6.

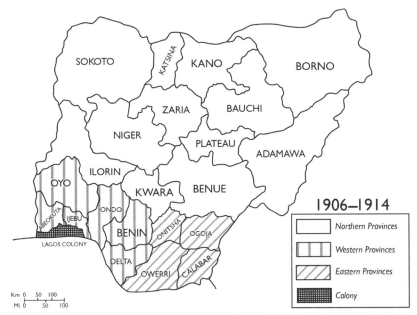

SOKOTO KATSINA KANO BORNO

ZARIA BAUCHI

NIGER PLATEAU

ADAMAWA

ILORIN
OYO KWARA BENUE

ABEOKUTA IJEBU ONDO
BENIN ONITSHA OGOJA
LAGOS COLONY
DELTA CALABAR
OWERRI

1906–1914

	Northern Provinces
	Western Provinces
	Eastern Provinces
	Colony

Km 0 50 100
Mi 0 50 100

Copyright © 2016 Nathan E. McCormack & Toyin Falola

Map 3.2 Nigeria, colonial regions, 1906–14.

important bureaucratic and political positions in the emergent state.[4] They knew that colonial boundaries and divisions were not established to reflect aspects of the people within and outside these boundaries – none of those people were consulted in the process – but rather due to imperial calculation and personal ambition. Indirect rule, the larger policy under which these structures were created, encouraged people to consent to their societies' exploitation based on loyalty to their traditional rulers.[5]

Indirect rule reduced the number of British officers necessary to administer the colonial enterprise, and it was the cheapest, safest, and shrewdest approach for political and economic penetration into the heart of the

---

[4] This consciousness is seen in the presidential address delivered by Honorable Chief Obafemi Awolowo, Federal President of the Action Group and Premier of Western Region of Nigeria, at the Fourth Congress of the Action Group, held at Calabar on Monday, April 8, 1958. Chief Obafemi Awolowo, "Presidential Address" (address, Fourth Congress of the Action Group, Calabar, Nigeria, April 8, 1958).

[5] This suggests how the precolonial sociopolitical culture of colonial territories in Africa would be used to benefit the new elite, and this trend continued in the hands of the postindependence political elites. For more on this, see Keith Somerville, *Africa's Long Road Since Independence: The Many Histories of a Continent* (London: Penguin Random House, 2017), 1–48.

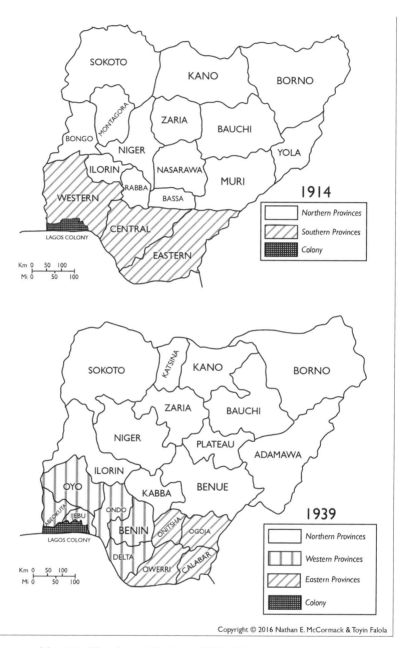

Map 3.3 Nigeria, subdivisions, 1914–39.

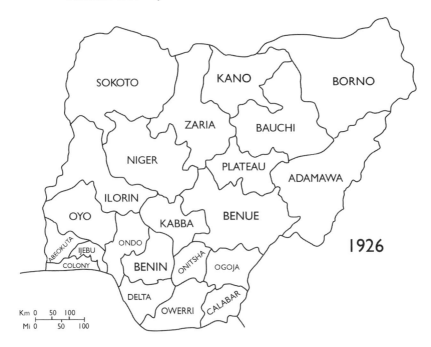

Map 3.4 Nigeria, 1926.

colony. The arrangement bred discontent among several cultural groups
that were placed under the authority of traditional institutions that had
previously been considered separate. The arbitrary nature of colonial
boundaries became more problematic toward the colony's independence,
when the question of minority representation became one of the leading
issues. The truth about colonial boundaries, and the formation of modern
African states, is that societies rarely emerge from homogeneity, and the
relative homogeneity of a nation does not automatically guarantee peace,
progress, and development.[6]

None of the imperial powers that gathered in Berlin to design modern
African states had such an advantage of homogeneity; they were states

[6] Apart from recent examples, consider Somalia, where a homogenous group still experiences conflict. To cite another example, the colonization of Yoruba territory took its form
from the incessant instability and quest for dominance by one group over another. See
Toyin Falola and G. O. Oguntomisin, *Yoruba Warlords of the Nineteenth Century* (Trenton:
Africa World Press, 2001).

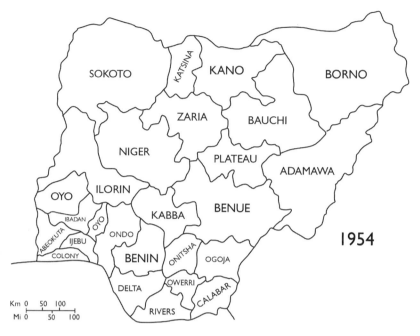

Map 3.5 Nigeria, 1954.

with concentrations of people from multiple cultural backgrounds. Having emerged through wars of conquest and diplomacy, they faced the inevitable task of consciously maintaining their differences despite the seamless identity they developed over the years.[7] This was the obstacle that the United States had to overcome following its independence – the epigraph on Washington's tomb reads: "Let prejudices and local interest yield to reason. Let us look to our National character and to things beyond the present period."[8]

The popular expression describing Nigeria as a "mere geographical expression" was originally applied to Italy during its formative years.

[7] In a *London Times* report from December 13, 1957, the British Prime Minister had to contend with the fact that, regardless of the position of the English people, the interests of the Welsh were best served and protected in a union with Britain: "Wales has not only her own language but her distinctive needs and culture, and any system of Government must be based on a full recognition of those facts." The *London Times*, quoted in "Presidential Address," delivered by Honorable Chief Obafemi Awolowo.

[8] The George Washington Masonic National Memorial, Washington, DC.

Examples of independent, precolonial states, which are often cited to challenge colonial boundaries, were described by Ikime as the "fusion of many strands of migrants"[9] who jealously retained their primordial identities. These changed as they adapted to the evolving reality and as competing interests required them to take on identities for leverage.[10] The fusions took place at various times in the lives of these cultural groups for a reason that is missing from the postcolonial state project: faith, either rational or otherwise, in the state's ability to protect their interests.[11] Colonization contributed to this mindset, but it can also be seen as a continuation of precolonial contests for domination and the mutual suspicion that they encouraged.

The challenge of Nigerian unity and the nation building project is complicated by fundamental ideological differences between the North and the South; colonial powers exploited these differences to maintain dominance over the entire region with a divide-and-rule mechanism.[12] The colonial administration deliberately restrained missionary activities in the North to maintain the sociopolitical and economic structures that already existed due to the spread of Islam. These structures became the dominant pedestal upon which the societal superstructure was developed. History books have studied how this morphology maintained the subjugation and domination of people of this region, developing under the imperial colonial bureaucracy along the same lines as it had developed during the imperial religious indoctrination of the Sokoto Caliphate.[13]

[9] Obaro Ikime, *Can Anything Good Come out of History?* (Ibadan: Bookcraft, 2018), 97.

[10] Cf. Fredrik Barth, ed. , *Ethnic Groups and Boundaries* (London: George Allen and Unwin, 1969).

[11] Years ago, it would have been unthinkable for Scottish people to demand independence from Great Britain, and the people of Northern Ireland have been patriotic British nationals to a large degree. Fractures in these relationships, strained by Brexit proceedings, have led them to question whether their interests are being well represented. For the first time in the centuries-old relationship, Scotland is considering a break from the union, and the people of Northern Ireland are contemplating their choices against the backdrop of Brexit negotiations with the EU. In both cases, the English-dominated union must consider the interests of these two regions to maintain the United Kingdom. Similar issues of faith and interest have arisen in the recent demands of the Catalans in Spain and other examples.

[12] Colonial rule emerged from the unending rivalry among several cultural groups in the precolonial state. The role of the Sokoto Caliphate and the Oyo Empire, both of which rose to prominence during this rivalry, has been documented in several historical writings. For more on this transition, see, among others, Toyin Falola and Matthew M. Heaton, *A History of Nigeria* (New York: Cambridge University Press, 2008).

[13] See Saidu H. Adamu and Yahaya A. Abdullahi, "Rural Economy and Society in Nigeria Since 1900," in *Seminar on Nigerian Economy and Society Since the Berlin Conference*, vol. 2, eds. Musa Adamu Mamman et al. (Zaria: Ahmadu Bello University Press Ltd., 2005), 137; Mohammed Ahmed Modibbo, *European Trade, Imperialism and Under-Development in Northern Nigeria 19th and 20th Centuries* (Zaria: Ahmadu Bello University Press Limited, 2016).

This model was later applied to the whole colony of Nigeria, after colonial administrators realized that additional sources of revenue were needed to support the ailing Northern economy that could not meet colonial needs. The event is known as the amalgamation of the Northern and Southern protectorates of 1914.[14]

The integration of political structures in these areas, making decisions as a single entity that affects the entire country, increased mutual suspicion and tensions among the people. Colonial policies ensured that the Nigerian state was birthed on an imbalanced slope, and every member demanded relevance despite those imbalances. One such imbalance was due to the spread of Western education, which was intended to prepare people for modern governance and responsibilities. Its influence began creating problems even before independence.

Nigeria's independence was delayed for years, based on the concerns of Northern delegates who feared domination by the Southern part of the colony. Levels of education in the northern region were very low, due to many factors. Anti-Western sentiment had been cultivated internally, by people who saw it as antithetical to their Islamic doctrines, as taught by the ulamas,[15] and applied by colonial administrators who wanted to avoid changing the ideological landscape of the region, which was a ready-made tool for control to aid the colonial enterprise. The end result was the creation of two states within one geographical entity, along with the continued, cynical manipulation of the masses to benefit the elites.

After independence, this disparity led to the official relinquishment of meritocracy, reinforcing all sorts of favoritism. Through the quota system, the educationally disadvantaged region of the North was evaluated according to lower standards. A Southern candidate with competent skills and a rich educational background, considered for admission into university or a job appointment, would face more scrutiny than a Northern candidate with fewer qualifications. This was initially meant to encourage educationally disadvantaged people from the North and to strike a balance in public appointments within the federation, but such magnanimity and privilege was later claimed as a right for Northerners – particularly for the elites, as in the case of Oranmiyan and his brothers in the Yoruba traditions.

---

[14] For more discussion on the amalgamation of Nigeria, see Richard A. Olaniyan, ed., *The Amalgamation and Its Enemies: An Interpretive History of Modern Nigeria* (Ile-Ife: Obafemi Awolowo University Press, 2003).

[15] See Aliyu S. Alabi, "Voices after the Maxim Gun: Intellectual and Literary Opposition to Colonial Rule in Northern Nigeria," in *Resurgent Nigeria: Issues in Nigerian Intellectual History: A Festschrift in Honour of Dahiru Yahya*, eds. Sa'idu Babura Ahmad and Ibrahim Khaleel Abdussalam (Ibadan: University Press, 2011), 124–146.

This encouraged people to view themselves as superior in the nascent state, which they saw as the continuation of the 1804 conquests and expansion; it gave birth to the idea of one "born to rule." It did not end there. Other regions saw the preferential treatment received by the North. The deliberate composition of a larger Northern region, over and above the Western and Eastern regions combined, meant a larger number of Northern representatives in parliament, affecting the quality of debate and decision-making abilities within the House. The result was more regional parochial politics and less nation building. It reinforced the cynical proclivity of political actors within these regions, turning the soon-to-be-independent state into an estate of contested interests.

Minority groups became the most disadvantaged in the process of state formation, regardless of their levels of education or competence. They were occluded from expressing themselves or wielding state power at various levels. The diversity of cultures and peoples in the state meant that changing the system of government from parliamentary to presidential, creating states, local governments, and more local government areas, could not placate the anxiety of these minorities. Society had never been governed based on equality, and justice was only relative, but the colonial antecedent of the Nigerian state had entrenched the feeling of marginalization and injustice among many. There was little room for various people to be sure that their interests would be protected in the state's new composition.[16]

The underlying challenge of the postcolonial Nigerian state is the absence of a common national goal – the ideal state enacts policies that address all senses of marginalization, suspicion, and tension. The sense of entitlement, held by political elites on behalf of their people, has created a society that cannot be said to have been built on equality, justice, and fraternity. Members of a fraternity do not necessarily share the same ideology, but they all share equally fundamental ideologies that support their survival in society. They concentrate on this area of convergence, while managing their differences in the best way possible, to avoid disintegration. Members of a nation share the same history and fear the same fear; they share the same interests. To members, this is more important than anything else.[17] In the postcolonial Nigerian state, these shared interests boil down to concerns for their economic well-being and

---

[16] Cf. Terhemba Wuam, Chris S. Orngu, and Elijah Terdoo Ikpanor, eds., *Ethnic Minority Agitations and Political Development in Nigeria*, vol. 2 (Abuja: Donafrique Publishers, 2015).

[17] The previous examples of the imperial powers remain instructive.

survival. However, a fraternity has not formed around these interests, fears, and history in Nigeria because the inherent differences have been manipulated and amplified by political actors.

Some have asked why the ethno-religious affiliation of leaders should be a concern, as long as those leaders provide basic amenities for the people and create a society built on justice and equality. Concerns over primordial identity often arise when the basic principles are missing to develop a nation and its people.[18] The irony is that people only understand their problem after their kinsmen are given political power: the problem lies not with their primordial identity and its marginalization by others, but with the elites who control their resources. For some complex reason, possibly connected to the bio-power of the elites exercised through various means, these people are content to see their kinsmen at the center of state power, even if it means that they do not experience material gain of their own.

What the British achieved for their imperial gain in 1914 has been described as "territorial amalgamation." It had nothing to do with the integration of the people, although colonial dictate held that the duty of the postindependence state was to promote historical consciousness that could be used to evolve a central philosophy. Ikime, considering this issue, opined that the root cause of Nigeria's problem is "sin," describing it as the inability of the people to know and understand one another. Therefore, "repentance has to be based on knowledge of ourselves; and history holds the key to that knowledge, though Nigeria may not acknowledge this truth."[19]

The main consideration, when forming societal superstructures, is the formation of identities for different elements that compose the geographic entity. Before the colonial enterprise recalibrated this setting, societies that failed to manage these structures collapsed through the machinations of groups contending to assert themselves.[20] It is taken from Barth, and other scholars of identity, that ethnic boundaries are perceived identity formations used to secure primordial rights for economic, social, and

---

[18] This is how illusive ethnic identity can be. Jenkins concluded that, "A boundary is a cumulative social construction that occurs when people who are identified as say, Lupitan interact with others who are identified differently in any context or setting in which being Lupitan matters. In the process the relevant criteria of membership of Lupitan – Lupitan Identity – are rehearsed, presented and developed, as are the consequences of being Lupitan. These are political processes: negotiating, transaction, mobilization, imposition and resistance." Richard Jenkins, *Social Identity*, 4th ed. (London & New York: Routledge, 2014), 160.

[19] Ikime, *Can Anything Good Come out of History?* 265.

[20] See J. A. Atanda, *The New Oyo Empire: Indirect Rule and Change in Western Nigeria 1894–1934* (London: Longman Group Limited, 1973), 56–57.

political relevance.[21] Once these interests are protected, there is less emphasis on these boundaries.

Colonization's greatest impact on Nigeria may not be the structures it created for maximum imperial gain, but the ideology it implanted. This ideology took on a life of its own, enduring into the present. Political elites, educated elites, and middle-class workers – some representing the modern government structure of the state – can recognize the problem identified by Awolowo, but they are overwhelmed by the ideological base upon which the government was premised. Nigeria and Nigerians had moved beyond colonial boundaries even before they were created, as can be seen in the level of economic, social, and political integration of precolonial societies. However, they revert back to these boundaries in the face of prevalent inequality and injustice. The essential problem lies in the institutionalization of the idea of making it out of the system, to join the trend of modernization, rather than driving that modernization them-selves. To appreciate the complexity of the past's influence on the modern Nigerian state, one must appreciate the fact that:

Nigeria is in a hurry towards its destined goal of full nationhood. It is inevitably pressed for time in finding effective solution for those of its problems which must be solved and solved rightly if the emergence of a Nigerian nation in 1960 is to mean freedom and happiness for, and harmony among, all its citizens.[22]

The urgency goes farther than the race to "full nationhood"; it fuels a need to become accepted as "human" in modern society. The colonial mentality ensured that subjects lost sight of their own ingenuous capacity for productivity outside the dictates of the West. The cocoa prosperity that created another wealthy class in the colonial state had maintained patterns of economic participation that were established by managers of the colony in service to the imperial government. Structures created during the colonial period were part of a shrewd quest for domination – imperial powers knew that any structure created to support the ruling class must involve an appealing myth that could reinforce the realities created by their manifestation and the continued recycling of the myth. The deliberately schemed policies and actions of colonial agents have less of an impact on the independent state, unlike the domino effects of these activities that had been reflected in the authentication and entrenchment of their human proclivity for power and hegemonic consolidation through instruments of force and intimidation.

---

[21] Perceived because of its highly mutable susceptibility; see among others Barth, *Ethnic Groups and Boundaries*.
[22] "Presidential Address," delivered by Honorable Chief Obafemi Awolowo.

Through these mechanisms, political elites became less accountable, institutions became less responsive, and society became entangled in the quest to survive on the colonial economy's crumbs. Educated elites of the colonial period busily tried to make names for themselves as those closest to imperial culture in the evolving milieu, and their contemporaries faced the same race to relevance with a limited amount of time to prove themselves. Trying to outsmart the system became the preferred means for addressing the time constraints, which is what anthropologists, led by the likes of Guyer, have consistently interrogated in the concept of *kos'ona miran* (no other way). They have extensively captured it in the idea of "the Political Economy of Everyday Life," this time in Africa.

These forces explain "how people attempt to impose some measure of order and stability on their lives, even in the context of acute precarity, poverty and various forms of fiscal, social or political instability," which in turn has created a "continent with a huge informal sector that is 'recalcitrant to regulation and taxation.'"[23] Although this shows the resilience and innovation of Africans, it also shows the preoccupation of every person for themselves, even when in government. No person and no institution is left consciously building the nation, although its foundations had been built, even before the colonial experience, with a collective guiding philosophy.

This reality allows agents of the status quo to persistently manipulate the state. The untidy race to modernization has made everyone so busy for survival in the hemorrhagic state that there is little room for national consciousness or civic responsibilities. Thinking less of this reality – one that makes the West's supposedly accurate mechanisms for collecting data irrelevant in most cases – is to think less of the innate African capacity for "rational adaptation to environment." This happens even when such adaptation would seem irrational within the Western ontological truth, acting in ways that demonstrate "passive resistance to a predatory state – and the relativity of their 'faithfulness to cultural principles or ancestral dictates.'"[24]

In other words, Nigeria cannot be on the path to nation building by all indices because the colonial mentality demands that its subjects survive in an environment designed to exploit them. A cursory look at this epoch shows that the colonial state, much like the contemporary independent state, ensured the production of forceful policies to pursue its parochial, exploitative agenda. It largely neglected the development of human

---

[23] Wale Adebanwi, ed., *The Political Economy of Everyday Life in Africa: Beyond the Margins* (London: James Currey, 2017), 2.
[24] Jane Guyer, quoted in Adebanwi, *The Political Economy of Everyday Life*, 8.

capacity to ensure a society built on common interests and purpose. This cacophonic structure came to define status in the modern state, and it reformed the definitions of status and hierarchy that formed the basis of social relations in precolonial times.

Changing symbols of social status within society predated the colonial experience, occurring in the period of trading contact between Africans and European merchants. Some foreign items became distinguished as items of nobility.[25] Traditionally, nobles and ruling classes exerted their authority through distinctive features on display outside of their residences. This was introduced during the colonial period as the government would,

> ... not only seize the whole colonial space as one of the most critical indices of hegemonic (European) power, but, also, and this is crucial, organized the colonial space as a reflection of the racial hierarchies that they had constructed and as the material evidence of domination and difference. Therefore, forbidden or prohibited spaces emerged in the African city as a marker of this difference between the white/colonizers and the native/colonized.[26]

This would later come to authenticate and incentivize the human proclivity for conspicuous relevance in the natives, leading to further social stratification as they inherited this special hierarchy. As Obadare and Adebanwi have observed, "Unlike in the colonial era, postcolonial cities are sharp reflections of the incompetence, ineffectiveness, and corruption of the postcolonial ruling elite."[27] In these cocoons, they became unconcerned with the reality of their society.

Many nationalist leaders became involved in the struggle for independence after becoming direct victims of the colonial system; the solutions they proffered were largely to protect their primordial interests. This explains the concept of elitism, which is a formidable force in societal formation. Cohen brought a detailed representation of this social category to the fore when he opined that, given the inevitability of public sentiment and support for an agenda to wield influence in society, "an elite can be located on a continuum from the most particularistic, least universalistic, at one end, to the most universalistic, least, particularistic, at the other."[28]

---

[25] The intensity of trading activities, and fierce competition for limited resources, led African states to shed their much-acclaimed communalism. People began competing for foreign goods to reinforce their status in the society; the contest has continued into the present.

[26] Wale Adebanwi and Ebenezer Obadare, "Introduction: Excess and Abjection in the Study of the African State," in *Encountering the Nigerian State*, eds. Wale Adebanwi and Ebenezer Obadare (New York: Palgrave Macmillan, 2010), 15.

[27] Ibid.

[28] Abner Cohen, *The Politics of Elite Culture: Explorations in the Dramaturgy of Power in a Modern African Society* (Berkeley: University of California Press, 1981).

Beyond the question of colonial impact on modern Nigeria, it is important to examine the inherited elite culture that the colonial structure adapted and expanded through its institutions. These became the legacy of the contemporary state. Somerville provides us with an anecdotal piece of this trajectory, embedded in the tale of the dependent economy managed by the contemporary state:

The history of African is not one of discrete chapters or momentous ruptures .... Slavery became an early example of what Jean-François Bayart calls the extraversion economy, in which African rulers "live chiefly off the income they derive from their position as intermediaries vis-à-vis the international system." An early example of the gatekeeper function of African rulers developed in which they were the source of slaves, gold and ivory for export and gained power through the trade and the weapons, manufactures and wealth it brought in. The combination of pre-colonial and colonial gatekeeping and extraversion had a profound effect on the development of the economies and trading relations of independent states. The slave trade helped make Africa a subordinate and subject part of the international economic system. This happened through the development of dependency on exports of primary commodities and labour, and reliance on imported manufacturers in exchange, reduced the potential for the development of diversified economies, even before the distorting effects of colonial occupation and exploitation of export commodities.[29]

Although the colonial government used force and intimidation to compel order, logic and reason cannot explain the same actions undertaken by the contemporary state. No precedent could warrant this, apart from the abstract nature of freedom that often transforms the proletariat of today into the bourgeois class of tomorrow, or the activist of today into a tyrant-in-waiting.

The independent Nigerian state became a "military state" not because of the colonial government's intolerance of antiestablishment sentiments in the colony, but because the elite project needed to be protected by asserting governmental authority. Applying such force could deter dissenting voices, as it had in the colonial days. Such assertions can also maintain the status quo that maintains their power, wealth, and influence. Cohen offers further insight:

An elite is a collectivity of persons who occupy commanding positions in some important sphere of social life, and who share a variety of interests arising from similarities of training, experience, public duties, and way of life. To promote these interests, they seek to cooperate and coordinate their actions by means of a corporate organization.[30]

[29] Somerville, *Africa's Long Road Since Independence*, 1 and 4–5.
[30] Abner Cohen, *The Politics of Elite Culture, Explorations in The Dramatology of Power in a Modern African Society* (Berkeley: University of California Press, 1981), xvi.

Depending on the magnitude of their demands and where they fall in the sociopolitical composition of the state, several tactics are used to achieve these "interests." As in the colonial state, political gimmicks are often employed. On the defensive front, this could include a mixture of force and diplomacy.

These mechanisms, applied as a carrot-and-stick approach, do not correct the state's underlying issues. The state, along with those who make demands, are all represented by elites who resort to quick-fix agreements that are premised on deceit from both groups. Addressing the fundamental issues of the state would harm the political elites, the educated elites, and the middle-class workers who are privy to the rot in the system, sacrificing their life of Western-induced privileges to achieve national cohesion.

How do you know whether someone is important in postcolonial Nigeria? As in colonial times, they enjoy medical treatment in other parts of the world, receive education at foreign institutions, own properties in foreign countries, maintain foreign accounts and a generous amount of currency, and possess the latest automobiles, gadgets, and clothing. Western ideals are generally embraced in the pursuit of these goals. The quantity of these extravagances signifies the relevance and influence of the person who possesses them. Of course, none of the elite status symbols are produced domestically, setting a tone of consumer culture. Religious bodies organize special prayers for visas and divine foreign partnerships. Prayers for travel abroad are matched by prayers for salvation in the afterlife. Society emphasizes the exploitation of resources, including humans, to fuel the improvement of other cultures, and this mindset has been entrenched and institutionalized through the colonial mentality.

In lieu of enhancing health and educational services provided in the independent state, the colonial mentality encourages elites to distance themselves from the rest of the society; they consider themselves to be "privileged recipients" of these modern amenities abroad. In a society longing for change and progress, it is considered an act of prestige to flaunt one's wealth and go abroad for medical treatment, rather than developing such capacity inside the country. By creating special facilities and access for a particular class of people, the colonial government established the pattern that the elites follow to massage their egos in the emergent state. In most cases, the opportunities later enjoyed by the indigenous educated elites, the middle class, and the political elites reinforced the status of these classes – they mostly consisted of Britons, over and above the colonial subjects. As in the colonial state, they were consciously and unconsciously indoctrinated to become the new agents of neocolonialism.

A stark difference between the colonial state's economy and that of the postindependent state can be seen in the areas where biopolitics were deployed to sustain an extractive imperial economy and develop the colonial headquarters in Britain. Biopolitical structures, such as railways, roads, health facilities, and other infrastructure, began deteriorating – they were no longer central to the purpose of the state that had emerged. Nigeria's government has become a rentier state, managed through a form of petro-capitalism controlled by expatriates, foreign investors, and the petite-bourgeoisie class of a society that consists of political opportunists. Biopolitics became irrelevant under this set of priorities.

Who cares if taxation dwindles because fewer people are meaningfully engaged in the economy? Who cares about the mortality rate, even though reductions could boost the labor force and the state's productivity? Who cares about a porous educational system, although it is essential to reverse the decay and aid the state's industrialization drive? Who cares about the condition of the railways and roads needed to transport raw materials from the farms to the villages and cities? Who cares about the anemic power grid that is essential for the industrialization and technological advancement of the state? Who cares about the environmental degradation of Niger Delta areas – it has left the people unproductive, although their oil has continued to flow – or that investors sign off on their participation through which the state is reliant, and which is managed by the virtue of their remittances?[31]

These points support Somerville's argument that "the tragedy of slavery for those enslaved was paralleled by the increased wealth and power it conferred on those in Africa engaged in the trade."[32] Effective biopolitical structures are a marked difference between colonial and postcolonial governments, but the two administrations show close affinity in other areas, maintaining an exploitative state through any means possible, including force and diplomacy. Both were deployed to enable a carefully planned, predatory economic order. There was no state during the colonial period, but rather a people within a colonized boundary meant to be exploited for the benefit of the colonial powers.

In the postindependence period, starting with the flag raised on October 1, 1960, the Nigerian "state" emerged. It was allegedly created by the so-called nationalist leaders to ensure a systemic nation building process that equalized the different ethnic nationalities in the nascent

---

[31] The oil economy, or rather the extractive economy on which the state is built, has pushed administration into autopilot, where the state is run by chance and individuals receive benefits based on luck. In this form of extractive economy, there is no planning and the only planning that exists is to continue the survival of the "self."

[32] Somerville, *Africa's Long Road Since Independence*, 5.

state. This was not the case in reality; the state became a perpetual object of exploitation. Frivolous policies and transactions were enacted to serve the material and immaterial lusts of political elites seeking visibility through their access to state institutions, agencies, and general government apparatuses.

People who had been powerless under colonial domination still survived the odds through flexibility, resilience, innovation, negotiability, and entrepreneurship. Colonial control has been broken, but people are continuing to apply their strengths and find paths outside the state's sphere of influence. In this reality, the government takes advantage of the people's struggle to survive and their limited opportunities and methods for survival. It retains a certain form of bio-power over the people, exerting control over their private lives and thought processes.[33]

The complexity of relations between the state and the populace have made scholars ask fundamental questions in different ways: "Is the state real for those who encounter it and its agencies, or is it a mere fetish, a fantasy, or even a pathology? ... are there really 'citizens' in Nigeria, even though there are those who are formally called citizens of Nigeria ... ?"[34] These questions are assisted by insights from Larry Diamond – either the idea of a state is an illusory configuration of man for the pursuit of allied interest(s), or not:

The oldest and most enduring story of human political life is this: the strong exploit and abuse the weak. Those who wield political power use it to extract wealth from the powerless ... Historically, force was typically the means by which the wielders of power acquired it and held it. And force remains the ultimate guarantor of power ... Political development can be viewed as a quest to solve three basic problems in the organization and exercise of power. First, how can violence be subdued and contained so that power is acquired and exercised by (largely) peaceful means? Second, how can the abuse of power the exploitation of the powerless by the powerful be restrained? And, third, how can the powerless be empowered, so that all members of the collectivity benefit to some fair if not exactly equal degree from the exercise of power, and hence the holders of power are held accountable to the people?[35]

---

[33] Civil servants consider their salary to be a grand favor from the government, and the general public takes the same view of government services, such as the construction of a road – regardless of the inefficiencies and waste involved in the award and execution of the project. Through the bio-power mechanism of political elites, people are conditioned to accept a state where they have no rights, they only receive favors from the government.

[34] Adebanwi and Obadare, "Introduction: Excess and Abjection," 3 and 10.

[35] Larry Diamond quoted in Adigun Agbaje, "Kos'ona Miran? Patronage, Prebendalism & Democratic Life in Contemporary Nigeria," in Adebanwi, *The Political Economy of Everyday Life*, 318.

Nigeria's current predicament is not solely due to the colonial government's failure to start down the path of economic prosperity – that was never its intention. The problems do not persist because of a political composition with little regard for the precolonial formation of society. Instead, these problems exist because of the colonial ideology that was successfully implanted in people through various means, centered around foreign consumption and reinforced by religion, education, material goods, and the general worldview.

After development became a topic of discussion, particularly in the Global South in the 1960s, several models were touted; many made careers out of promoting development models in a relationship similar to that of a doctor with patients. However, the rise of Asian countries in the second half of the twentieth century – bringing a voodoo term into the Western political–economic lexicon, describing it as the "Asian miracle," for want of a logical explanation – has brought a renewed focus on the place of culture in the development of states.

The unconscious erosion of culture through the colonial mentality has consistently shaped the postindependence state. The modernization process that was brought to the society could not be internalized and domesticated. People were told, by the state's various agents of modernization, that their traditions were enmeshed in paganism. Traditions were dismissed as primitive and antithetical to progress and transformation; these assertions were put forward by the missionaries and repeated by instructors within the colonial educational system. People were told that redemption could only come from the West, the sole source of "salvation."

The government served as the legal background through which a policy of indigenous cultural eclipse was pursued. Christianity became synonymous with Westernization, and education became tantamount to integration with Western culture. Western ideals were considered supreme, to the detriment of indigenous cultures relegated to the background. Indigenous knowledge production became less relevant for schoolchildren and the general public. The ontological and epistemological design of education reinforced Western ideals – and limitations – as the standard of what could be achieved and how it could be accomplished.

It took a separate fight for history departments in African colleges to start offering African history courses; the students had been conditioned to value the study of European art, history, and civilization as the admiration of a race "born to conquer." In the 1980s, the government of Nigeria prohibited the study of history as a stand-alone subject for elementary and junior secondary schools. It remains to be seen how a people who know nothing about their past, or how they arrived at their present situation, could proffer a meaningful diagnosis of their challenges and hopes. Society only progresses when there is a common cultural bond between the people and the process of development.[36]

The domino effect of this curriculum was a nation increasingly ridden with primordial prejudices and stereotypes; people lacked a historical consciousness that could heal their ignorance of primordial compositions. Although the study of history was banned only at elementary and junior secondary levels, the policy gradually led to the pitiable state of historical study at all other levels. The postindependence government, like its colonial counterpart, saw no value in integrating the subject into its plans for nation building; it never intended to embark on cultural revitalization of the state. As discussed previously, such an effort would be tantamount to the state digging its own grave.

This attitude maintained the colonial educational structure, keeping the government in power and oiling its wheels. The educational system in northern Nigeria has remained unchanged, and the region continues to be regarded as an educationally disadvantaged area after more than half a century since independence. Public sentiment in other regions drew attention to the difficulties of bearing many children – as they would say in the Western Region: *omo bere, osi bere/* multiple children, enormous poverty – but elites had indoctrinated the people of the North to remain focused on the opposite message: more children, greater blessings from Allah. This was not because Allah would bless these ignorant folks who had more children than they could support, but because colonial powers had shown these elites that a larger population would dominate the political space of the emergent state.

It is not enough to maintain a large population; political elites keep them in perpetual ignorance and servitude to fleece them for political gains. Policies of the colonial state were continued, systematically withdrawing Western education and creating a vast network of *almajiri* – a thieving and destitute population. The entire country maintained an educational structure that divides "the town and the gown," linking the acquisition of education with the colonial economy that produced lawyers, journalists, teachers, clerks, and secretaries who consume luxuries that society does not produce domestically.

In the postcolonial North, where Western education was restricted with the aid of the colonial state, and other parts of the region, where the

[36] See Qian Yingyi, quoted in Chukwuma C. Soludo, "Can Nigeria Be the China of Africa?" (Lecture, University of Benin, Benin City, Nigeria, November 23, 2006), 15–16.

educational system was meant to produce a subservient population, educational conditions have remained unchanged. During the colonial period, the school curriculum was designed to ensure that "vibrant" minds could think along the lines of European taxonomic modernity, within the colonial/Western ontological and epistemological world. It remains to be seen how this curriculum, which has been maintained by the postindependence state, could yield a fundamental change from colonial conditioning.

The postindependence government's approach to education is not an anomaly. Colonial agents had vigorously resisted the concept of African traditions and history prior to European contact. This was due to the culture of those who preserved indigenous history, traditions, and civilization, primarily in oral forms. Ironically, these same colonial agents collected traditions from different cultural groups for documentation, intending to use them for policy making and to enhance the colonial enterprise. For this reason, Smith has argued that "from the vantage point of the colonized, a position from which I write, and choose to privilege, the term 'research' is inextricably linked to European imperialism and colonialism."[37]

These findings, along with other government documents of the era that could teach future generations about their past, were documented and later housed in a facility called the Archives. Three such facilities were established in the country, one in Enugu and the other two in Kaduna and Ibadan, for historical preservation and ostensibly to see the emergent state engage this trove of data as part of a conscious nation building process. Less than three decades after independence, the management of this structure became one of the country's greatest challenges to historical research.

A letter written by the Historical Society of Nigeria to the government, delivered to the Minister for Education, stated that "the national committee on the Archives has not met for over ten years. As of the time of this Memorandum there still exists no effective policy-making body for our National Archives outside whatever ministry it is located."[38] This is a sharp contrast with the colonial government that sought to understand the people it governed (for its own imperial gains). The application of

---

[37] Because of its enduring effect on the colonized, even in the postcolonial period where the trend of collecting data from indigenous peoples has persisted – albeit for individual aggrandizement, intellectual visibility, and promotion – she continued that, "The word itself, 'research,' is probably one of the dirtiest words in the Indigenous world's vocabulary." Linda Tuhiwai Smith, *Decolonizing Methodologies: Research and Indigenous Peoples*, 2nd ed. (London: Zed Books, 2012), 1.

[38] Historical Society of Nigeria, memorandum presented to the Hon. Minister of Education of the Federal Republic of Nigeria, September 10, 1984.

historical knowledge to craft policy considerations has been a key component of governance in the imperial states and in other progressive societies. The colonial state applied this knowledge for effective exploitation, and it has been used over the years for effective biopolitics in their imperial headquarters.

While the Historical Society of Nigeria begged the government for an audience, hoping to deliver a sermon on the relevance of history to the nation building process "without any impact on my nation,"[39] the British Education Secretary asked the Historical Association of Great Britain for assistance justifying a plan to teach history to everyone up to the age of sixteen. At that point, youths are expected to reach a certain level of education and exposure to the composition of the state and the world around them.[40]

If historical study and the country's archives were neglected under colonial rule, one could assume that it was meant to hide the skeletons in their cupboard. However, what explains this neglect in the current context? The poor planning and porous documentation culture of the postindependence state is in sync with the colonial mentality, entrenching a feeling of state ownership by the elites. This feeling, which was already inherent from the precolonial practices of the people,[41] implies that those in power can do anything and get away with it. They are only concerned with the exploitation of the state, and keeping records seems to be of limited use in this endeavor. Safeguarding the history of the state's people has became an irrelevant effort to their parochial task; this explains the rotten traditional heritage of the various cultures and peoples of Nigeria in the postindependence state.

Colonial agents can be forgiven for their part in this process – one can only garner effort to transform another to suit one's taste when given the opportunity. They were unconcerned with traditions and practices of people that they did not care to understand beyond the imperial purpose they were meant to serve. But what justifies the sustenance at best, or debasement of this endeavor at worst, by the postindependence

---

[39] This was an expression of regret from a leading African historian who spent more than three decades of his career making a case for the relevance of history and historical study to the progress of the Nigerian state. Ikime, *Can Anything Good Come out of History?* 265.

[40] The Historical Society of Nigeria, "The Place of History in Nigeria's School System and the Nation" (official memorandum, 1987).

[41] Aside from the submissions of Somerville represented previously, see further the discussions of Ranger and Vaughan, particularly on the precolonial Zulu Kingdom in South Africa and the Buganda, both of which are reflective of the traditional power relations in the precolonial African states. Terence Ranger and Olufemi Vaughan, eds., *Legitimacy and the State in Twentieth Century Africa: Essays in Honour of A. H. M. Kirk-Greene* (Oxford: Palgrave Macmillan, 1993), 3–15.

government of Nigeria? Is there any explanation other than the colonial mentality that enables their thieving proclivity? They see the state as the colonialists saw it; it is a mechanism of exploitation.

Colonialists were in charge of this estate in the past. Postindependence governments, claiming indigenous ownership, took up the role of an estate agent – which Somerville would prefer to call a gatekeeper role – as they ridiculously manage affairs of the state with foreign aid, loans, and grants often paid to them by managers they supposedly pursued, using funds recovered from the same source.[42] This mental flexibility, which has ensured a dependent economy, further illustrates what Awolowo described as the "street beggar economy."[43]

Postindependence governments have no intention of nation building beyond the extent of protecting their cynical interests, to the detriment of the masses.[44] When they do attempt to reform the system, the widespread colonial mentality among the populace, and the perception of a limited amount of time for action, leads them to short-term, shoddy policies. Many scholars have asserted that sustainable development cannot be cultivated in a society before consistent attention is paid to "intangible cultural heritage that will provide the 'bank of cultural images' as our guide for acceptable behaviour ... These qualities cannot be bought with money. They can be taught, acquired and internalized through a system of cultural socialization."[45] In this view, tangible developments such as railways, roads, hospitals, and schools would be useless without paying attention to the intangible developments among the people. Without support from an appropriate culture, physical developments cannot be sustained.

Colonial powers concentrated energy on the systematic creation of a "bank of cultural images," institutionalizing a mindset of production and consumption. Its predecessor had been unconsciously created

---

[42] Cf. Tunde Decker and Damilola Osunlakin, "Rodney, Development and Africa in the Twenty First Century," in Benjamin U. Anaemene and Olusegun J. Bolarinwa, eds., *Agenda 2030 and Africa's Development in the 21st Century* (Kuala Lumpur: United Nations University International Institute for Global Health, 2017), 13–30.

[43] Here, complaint was made of the "complete lack of imagination and initiative on the part of the Federal Government in exploiting the many sources of revenue available to it. It has always pursued what I once described as a 'street beggar economy' in its public finance, and has not yet been able to get out of the rut." "Presidential Address," delivered by Honorable Chief Obafemi Awolowo.

[44] Cf. Leena Koni Hoffman and Raj Navanit Patel, *Collective Action on Corruption in Nigeria: Social Norms Approach to Connecting Society and Institutions* (London: Royal Institute of International Affairs, May 17, 2017), www.chathamhouse.org/sites/default/files/events/Latest_ACS_LaunchSlides_ED.pdf.

[45] Akinwumni Isola, "Making Culture Memorable: The Literary Contributions of Isaac Oluwole Delano" (Isaac Oluwole Delano Inaugural Memorial Lecture, Muson Centre, Lagos, Nigeria, December 20, 2004).

through precolonial economic relations with different parts of Africa. At the time, the Westernization of society was soothing. It was a succor for many that had been disadvantaged in the precolonial setting. Its relevance is evident in the roles it played during other cultural evolutions, such as in Japan during the Meiji Restoration. Only the ignorant and the hypocrite could think that European taxonomic modernity, without its apparent gains and advancement over some traditional practices, could displace age-old conventional practices in less than a century of colonization. It brought a decisive end to shenanigans and wars of conquest that intensified in the nineteenth century, allowing the elites of several cultural groups to achieve that which had been elusive. The emergence of a nation-state in this society followed the European model, designed by wars of conquest that had been present since before colonization, bringing about what Fukuyama once referred to as the "End of History."[46]

The model of larger state formation, with different populations of cultural groups controlled by a central authority within a modern complex structure, appears to be the ultimate end of world politics, intrigues, and permutations before the twentieth century.[47] European civilization became the explicit model that generations pursued when building their civilizations, either by imposition or adoption to achieve Western ideals with varying degrees of success. This was achieved through imposition in Nigeria and other African countries; for example, the victory of a Sokoto Caliphate in the Niger area would not have formed a nation-state drawn with a boundary and cultural composition of current-day Nigeria. The gains and advancements of that civilization, which would have been inevitable for realizing a progressive society in recent times, have not been successfully utilized to develop the unique culture and reality of Nigeria. Relentless effort was necessary to fit a square peg, upon which its civilization had been built, into the round hole gouged out by the colonizers. It is a stark contrast to the development of great civilizations.

---

[46] Francis Fukuyama, "The End of History?" *The National Interest* 16 (1989): 3–18.

[47] The argument for "the End of History" is the premise that, following the French revolution of 1789, all demands by the masses from every corner of the world remained within the precinct of the demands of that year. Demands can only be relatively met by states, and although the level of compliance varies by state, the basic demands have always been about freedom, justice, and equality. With the recalibration of other cultures and society, in the light of state composition in Europe through colonization, these demands became globalized. This brought to the fore, for the very first time, global demands and agitation from states. Cf. Tim Gee, *Counterpower: Making Change Happen* (Oxford: New International Publications Ltd., 2011), 14.

To be clear, great civilizations consist of ideas adopted and developed by a group of people, with close affinity, working to build a unique culture. These great civilizations influence other civilizations and their cultures in turn. Because they are developed through conscious cultivation, and not through the use of magic wands, no great civilization has a complete and total remedy for the needs of another. Great civilizations select ideas from others and domesticate them to fit their own requirements. Greek civilization became great by learning from Egypt, the Romans learned from the Greeks, the West learned from the Romans, and East Asian countries learned from the West. In all of these places, borrowed ideas were refined to suit a wide variety of cultural visions and peculiarities. This process, from borrowing to cultivating, was heavily influenced by events of the time.

Nigeria, like other African states, had little say in the civilization that was imposed on it. It took shape under a colonial structure operated by those looking to reinforce their own culture. There was no opportunity to cultivate a civilization that could suit the specific nature of the society, allowing people shape their civilization, not the other way around. Decades after power has been transferred to indigenous "rulers," it is incumbent on them to take charge; it is pitiable that society has remained stuck in a colonial quagmire without any meaningful effort to address its cultural deficit.

Colonial impact on modern Nigeria goes beyond the structures it created or the actions of its agents – an examination of union politics in Nigeria is instructive. In the professional unions and the so-called youth movements, the replication of the state's political ambience is palpable. The colonial administration did not create these bodies, but it entrenched a mindset that embraces a crude proclivity for power and hegemonic consolidation, through the instruments of force, intimidation, and other forms of maneuvering for cynical and parochial gains. The news of the Nigeria Bar Association's (NBA) elections, National Union of Road Transport Workers' (NURTW) politics, and the operation of the Student Union Governments (SUG), among many others, are examples of the rot that goes far beyond the colonial structure.

This mentality was not built on an innocent soul. The nobles and elites in African societies before this period were lords who could trample on the rights of commoners without fear of repercussion; the extent of their accountability was their cabinet chiefs' ability to challenge them. This is similar to the colonial administration, which was only accountable to the Queen of England. Postindependence governments painstakingly supervised failed institutions, dancing to their macabre rhythm to renew their influence through the machinery of state power. A society's elite culture is the incubator of its behavioral model, and the general rot in the Nigerian state, along with other parts of Africa, should not be surprising.

Conclusion

It has been noted that "market and politics are two important social mechanisms for the generation and distribution of wellbeing."[48] The question is to what extent modern African states – especially Nigeria – are willing to go to reconstitute these two essential areas, nurturing a culture of production and ingenuity in their people. Ultimately, success will be seen as a deep synergy between the town and the gown, as well as enhanced relations between the state and the informal sector that accounts for more than half of indigenous production.

Apart from a few areas, there is hardly any social conditioning introduced by the colonial state that had not existed in various forms during precolonial times. As we talk about the impact of colonial rule on the postindependence state, it may be best to examine the inherent features of the precolonial state that enabled the colonial state and continue to haunt the postcolony. For "what is significant in Indigenous discourses is that solutions are posed from a combination of the time before, *colonized* time, and the time before that, precolonized time. Decolonization encapsulates both sets of ideas,"[49] owing to the fact that the colonial experience of indigenous peoples was informed by *precolonial* experiences and practices that were manipulated – either entrenched or replaced – for effective imperial enterprise in a colonized entity.

Beginning from the position that knowledge and culture are harbingers of societal structures and the conduct of its people, commanding a greater force than military strength, it can be understood that the decolonization process in the Nigerian state is a war against colonial ideology, described as the institutionalization of precolonial order and the introduction of others to achieve the imperial goals of the West. One problem with this idea – foremost of all, because it is the means through which political power is attained and political leadership is selected – lies in the democratic practices of the emergent state. It has led scholars from the first generation of the state's modern intellectual community, like

---

[48] Adebanwi, *The Political Economy of Everyday Life in Africa*, 7.
[49] Smith, *Decolonizing Methodologies*, 25.

Delano, to doubt whether people were mentally prepared for this form of government.[50]

The modern form of democracy works better in a society that evolves through the realization of its people, demanding a complete reformation of the political order. Its imposition on the emergent state, through the prodding of European taxonomic modernity,[51] has reduced the society to its precolonial state. Only the privileged few, the elites and the nobles in the "proper clique," have rights and are infallible.[52]

Regardless of the manner in which this system was adopted and incorporated into society, there is nothing in the DNA of Nigerians to suggest that this could not be nurtured into a rational state. In this planetary age, which is equivalent to the idea of the End of History, consistent demands are made for more inclusive democratic practices. In the context of the colonized people, this is tantamount to the much-needed decolonization process for a progressive society to evolve. It entails the deconstruction of exploitative, dysfunctional structures that have restricted the wealth of the state to the hands of those few who constitute the elite class. Instructively;

There are always lessons to be learned in the process of decolonizing: it is not enough to hope or desire change. Systemic change requires capacity, leadership, support, time, courage, reflexity, determination and compassion. It is hard work and the outcome often seems a distant vision. Paulo Freire referred to this as praxis; theory, action and reflection; Graham Smith has called it indigenous transforming praxis.[53]

---

[50] A lot of sharp practices have gone into this process even before independence, raising the moral question of the fairness upon which the society was established in the first place. Be that as it may, the political climate as we have it today in the state is a replica of this early period of modern political transitioning. See Toyin Falola, *Cultural Modernity in a Colonized World: The Writings of Chief Isaac Oluwole Delano* (Austin: Pan-African University Press, 2020).

[51] Ulrich Beck, Wolfgang Boss, and Christopher Lau, "The Theory of Reflexive Modernization: Problematic, Hypothesis, and Research Programme," *Theory, Culture and Society* 20, no. 1 (2003): 1–34.

[52] It is general knowledge that the Nigerian president wields an absolute monarch's power; the extent of the position's accountability is the cabinet chiefs' ability to challenge him. The illusion of modern democracy gives the impression of popular acceptance, and precedence has given the role a blank cheque for choosing his cabinet members. The head of state has grown to become second only to the gods and worshipped by all. The absolute power concentrated in this office corrupts the nation; the presidency has become an arena of irresponsibility and validation of porous political sagacity, rather than a bastion of responsibility and service to the state. At all levels of political leadership in the state, you have what Adebanwi and Obadare called the "Baba-rization of power." These features are specific to the adoption of this system in Nigeria and other African states. Adebanwi and Obadare, *Encountering the Nigerian State*, 4; see also Jesusegun Alagbe, "No World Leader Is as Irresponsible as a Nigerian President–Kukah," *Punch News*, October 6, 2018, https://punchng.com/no-world-leader-as-irresponsible-as-a-nig erian-president-kukah/.

[53] Smith, *Decolonizing Methodologies*, Xiii.

Unless this is enforced in Nigeria by a coalition of stakeholders, the existence of the country will remain as an estate on the precipice, where rent is to be collected by agents from occupants and those who do business in it.[54] In this situation, it may never get the chance to transform into a "state"[55] before its collapse.

---

[54] For the efficacy of this, see Gee, *Counterpower,* 17.

[55] A state, in this context, is a sovereign geographical entity where people make conscious efforts to build a society with a unifying philosophy. They share a common image for projecting themselves to the world, and they work towards this in daily government policies and actions, as well as in the people's reactions.

4   Political Pluralism

Introduction

Political pluralism is the idea that in a true liberal democracy, power should never rest with any individual or group of elites. Power should be evenly distributed across all groups that have a variety of economic interests and ideological beliefs. Under this philosophy, distribution or diversification of power is not a hindrance to society – these things benefit society. Diversity and mutual respect should be embraced and enjoyed by all political groups, religious groups, economic groups, and ethnic groups.[1] To be a pluralist means to "accept disagreement because they take dissensus to be an inevitable feature of the imperfect world in which we live."[2] Pluralists strive to make disagreements acceptable, not expendable. This contrasts with consensualists who believe that disagreement should be avoided at all costs.[3]

English authors such as Richard H. Tawney, Frederic Maitland, Harold Laski, Samuel G. Hobson, Howard Cole, and George Douglas advocated fiercely for pluralism in the early part of the last century. These men advocated for political pluralism because capitalism was creating damaging individual alienation in societies. They argued that, in lieu of capitalism, societies should aim to integrate as much as possible, much like in a medieval guild sense. They believed that modern industrial society does not benefit the modern person, because he or she lacks any feeling of community or commonality. They proposed that the modern person would be much happier and more fulfilled if societies become pluralistic, allowing integration, and enforcing the decentralization of the economy and administrative groups.[4]

---

[1] *Encyclopedia Britannica*, "Pluralism: Politics," *Encyclopedia Britannica*, n.d., www.britannica.com/topic/pluralism-politics.

[2] Ibid.

[3] Michele Marsonet, "Pragmatism and Political Pluralism: Consensus and Pluralism," *International Scientific Journal* 25, no. 12 (2015): 47.

[4] *Encyclopedia Britannica*, "Pluralism."

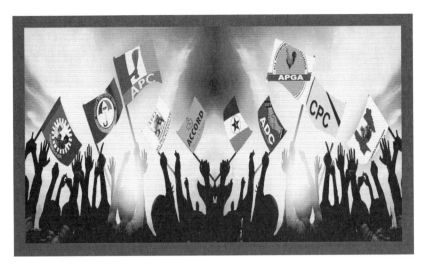

Figure 4.1 Symbols of Nigerian political parties.

In the more "classical" sense, pluralism is considered a fundamental part of a truly democratic system or society. It must rely on people having diverse political interests and values, instead of belonging to a single party or group. In such a way, barriers to peace and productivity can be avoided.[5] According to Truman, "no tolerably normal person is totally absorbed in any group in which he participates."[6] For this to occur, a pluralistic society must provide people with the necessary organizations, allowing them to establish communications between society and the state. Pluralism bolsters democracy, because it involves the intersections of various interest groups and a "flexibility of interest association across time."[7] These two conditions allow pluralism to function in its traditional, theoretical sense.[8] However, as developed countries in the West have learned, the best way to ensure the validity of this system is by having a robust multiparty system – which is exactly what Africa struggles with, as we shall see later.[9]

Although pluralism is usually conceptualized in a more traditional, classical standpoint, it has evolved in other parts of the world. In the Arab world, pluralism has taken its own distinctive forms. Marwan Muasher, Vice President of the Carnegie Endowment and previously Jordan's deputy prime minister, foreign minister, and ambassador of

[5] Carrie Manning, "Assessing African Party Systems After the Third Wave," *Party Politics* 11, no. 6 (2005): 712.
[6] Ibid., 713.   [7] Ibid., 712.   [8] Ibid., 713.   [9] Ibid., 708.

Jordan to the United States, has explained that public uprisings that occurred in Libya, Egypt, and Yemen in 2011 point toward a growing movement for political pluralism and democracy. This is the subject of Muasher's book, *The Second Arab Awakening and the Battle for Pluralism*.

Although pluralism and democracy seem to be desired by the people, Muasher is cautiously optimistic; the change to pluralism and democracy cannot happen overnight. Even if a despot is overthrown, it cannot be claimed as an immediate victory for democracy and pluralism. For this reason, Muasher believes that the title applied to the 2011 "Arab Spring" movement is a misnomer. It was not the instant growth of a new life, but it was not followed by "Arab winter" either. It is a constant act in progress that will take decades to complete. The ideal political pluralism that Muasher envisions, and that which much of the Arab world strives toward, involves a "peaceful rotation of power" and "the right of all political parties to exist and organize at all times." And it must involve women's rights. Without women's rights, Muasher argues, the Arab world – which contains Tunisia and Egypt – cannot achieve the sort of political pluralism it desires. Political pluralism must include gender pluralism. Political pluralism requires the government and the people to recognize and respect all ethnic, religious, and political ideologies.[10]

The 2011 uprisings are what Muasher calls the "second awakening," but the "first awakening" he references is the period from the mid-nineteenth century to the early-twentieth century, when various Arab countries, such as Lebanon, Syria, and Egypt, broke free first from the Ottoman Empire and then from colonial rule. This awakening was certainly a great achievement, but these countries did not establish societies based on democracy and pluralism. According to Muasher, these countries did not create the institutions needed to develop democratic, pluralistic societies because their primary concern was independence. Even after independence was established, pluralism and democracy were less of a priority than the Arab-Israeli conflict and the push to free Palestine. Even after the Palestine issue, any thought of Pan-Arabism or Arab nationalism died alongside thoughts of democracy or pluralism.

This was a time when the slogan "Islam is the solution" became popularized. Those in power – the Islamists – seemed to be the only remaining hope. This sort of dysfunctionality was also a symptom of the Sykes-Picot agreement in 1916, when communities were merged without any sense of cohesion or national unity, and "borders were artificially created."[11]

---

[10] Marwan Muasher, "The Second Arab Awakening," interview by Diane Rehm, *National Public Radio* (February 20, 2014).

[11] Ibid.

Happily, Muasher believes that the Second Arab Awakening was the realization that the government does not have to be ideological, particularly in regard to religious values; the government must only deliver a stable economy. This is a sign of progress in the Arab world, even if it takes decades to establish true pluralism and democracy. This economic focus was seen in 2013, when Egypt overthrew the Islamists in power because they could not deliver a strong economy. In 2014, about 90 percent of Egyptians said that they were religious and conservative, but only 2 percent said that they wanted an ideological government. Meanwhile, 70 percent of Egyptians wanted a government focused primarily on strengthening the economy. The downside is that the scars left by the Sykes-Picot Agreement and previous ideologues in power mean that Arab countries must continue suffering through wars in the meantime.[12]

Even though it will take time for pluralism and democracy to become reality across the Arab world, it is important to remember that Tunisia adopted a constitution in 2014 – the "best constitution in the Arab world," in Muasher's opinion – that values inclusivism in all forms. It establishes equality between men and women, religious freedom, and the expectation that all transitions of power should be done peacefully.[13] Tunisia's current government can be described as "unitary semi-presidential democratic." It is a striking contrast to the previous government, which was essentially a dictatorship under President Zine El Abidine Ben Ali. He was overthrown during the Jasmine revolution in 2011, and a new constitution was solidified by 2014. It declared that Tunisia would exist under a decentralized government, with executive power divided between a president and prime minister.[14] Although Islam is considered the state religion,[15] the constitution does not require Sharia law to be the law of the land. The rest of the Arab world could learn from this document. No single power can completely resolve the problems infesting the Arab world today; only pluralism can address them, at least in the eyes of Muasher.[16]

Ultimately, Muasher believes that the Arab world must adapt to pluralism and democracy to survive. These efforts do not have to be linked to any specific religion; a country can have a majority-Muslim or majority-Christian population and still have a democratic society. Unfortunately, the Arab world does not have a key figure leading a movement toward

[12] Ibid.   [13] Ibid.
[14] Joyce Chepkemoi, "What Type of Government Does Tunisia Have?" *World Atlas*, August 1, 2017, www.worldatlas.com/articles/what-type-of-government-does-tunisia-have.html.
[15] Ibid.   [16] Muasher, "The Second Arab Awakening."

democracy and pluralism, meaning that the fight will last for decades and require cooperation between citizens and those in power. It can certainly be done – as long as those in power do not use pluralism and democracy to manipulate others.[17]

Let us now consider the rest of the African continent apart from Tunisia and Egypt. How has the continent adapted to or responded to pluralism, and what does pluralism look like across Africa? Religion and pluralism appear to be intertwined in much of Africa. The resurgence of Sharia law in Nigeria coincided with the democratization of Nigeria in 1999 and new assertiveness for religious pluralism. Ahmed Sani, the governor of Zamfara State, was the first to adopt a more rigid Sharia law. Eleven other states followed his example, including Kebbi and Kaduna – both of which are poignant examples of how demographics and history affect the implementation of Sharia law and the aftereffects of a pluralized, democratized society.

Even though a clause in the 1999 Nigerian constitution stipulated how a state assembly could use a Sharia Court of Appeal, state interpretation and implementation of Sharia law was not uniform by any means.[18] The introduction of Sharia sparked panic among Christians, and scholars began to predict the end of Nigeria. Paul Marshall, in a 2002 report, explicitly stated that Sharia law unquestionably violated human rights, particularly those of non-Muslims. Marshall concluded Sharia's allegedly disgraceful nature could make Nigeria into a "new Afghanistan"[19] under an oppressive force like the Taliban.[20] Nigeria's diversity prevented this from happening, as can be seen in Kebbi and Kaduna states.

The demographical similarities and differences of Kebbi and Kaduna make them good case studies for adapting Sharia law to suit a region. The differences in implementation are important, because they have implications for how pluralism and democracy have responded. Both states have a majority-Muslim population, and both states have ethnically diverse non-Muslim people. Both states are also in northwestern Nigeria, the geographical location of a former Islamic state that existed under the Sokoto Caliphate before the colonial period.[21] However, the similarities between Kebbi and Kaduna stop here.

---

[17] Ibid.
[18] Eyene Okpanachi, "Between Conflict and Compromise: Lessons on Sharia and Pluralism from Nigeria's Kaduna and Kebbi States," *Emory International Law Review* 25, no. 2 (2011): 897.
[19] Quotation marks mine.
[20] Paul Marshall, *The Talibanisation of Nigeria: Sharia Law and Religious Freedom* (Washington: Freedom House, 2002), 8 and 62–66.
[21] Okpanachi, "Between Conflict and Compromise," 899.

The Muslim percentage of the population is quite different in the two states. In Kebbi, Muslims make up 84 percent of the population. In Kaduna, Muslims hold a slight majority at 56 percent of the population. Kebbi is also a much newer state. It was created in 1991, fifteen years after the 1976 creation of Kaduna.[22] These differences make Kaduna much more "heterogeneous and cosmopolitan"[23] than Kebbi. This heterogeneity and growth may be the reason why Kaduna is more susceptible to ethno-religious violence. A newer, more homogeneous state like Kebbi has offered less stimulus for conflict.[24]

Sharia rule began in Kaduna on December 14, 1999, when an eleven-person, all-Muslim committee known as the Kaduna State Assembly was created to express a Muslim desire for a Sharia legal system in the state.[25] This assembly was not created quietly. It was met with great resistance from the House of Assembly's Christian members. Christians in the House accused Muslims of subterfuge, because they appeared to have a hidden agenda and because the motion had not been properly approved. The Muslims in the House accused the Christians of panicking over something that did not concern them and rejected the nomination of two Christians put forward to participate in their committee.

Animosity festered in the general public. Christians and Muslims instigated rallies and talks about their differing points of view on Sharia law and the consequences of its implementation. The government established two more committees, composed of Muslims and Christians in equal parts, to address the growing tensions.[26] Soon afterward, the Kaduna State branch of the Christian Association of Nigeria organized a public protest in February of 2000 – the protest soon became violent. A similar outbreak of violence occurred in May of the same year. Only armed intervention could restore balance to the state.[27]

The then-governor of Kebbi State, Alhaji Muhammed Adamu Aliero, encountered less resistance when he established the Committee on the Implementation of Sharia Law in October of 1999. The committee's main purpose was to advise the government on effectively merging Sharia with current state laws. In December of 2000, the government officially established the legal code of Sharia. At its launch, announced in

[22] Ibid., 900.   [23] Ibid.   [24] Ibid.
[25] Abdu Hussaini and Lydia Umar, "Ethnic and Religious Crisis in Kaduna," in *Hope Betrayed: A Report on Impunity and State-Sponsored Violence in Nigeria*, eds. I. Bawa and V. I. Nwogwu (Lagos: World Organization against Torture and Center for Law Enforcement Education, 2002), 83 and 88.
[26] Hussaini and Umar, "Ethnic and Religious Crisis in Kaduna," 89.
[27] Okpanachi, "Between Conflict and Compromise," 901–902.

Haliru Abdu stadium, Aliero said that Sharia law was democratically legitimate.[28] New law created Sharia and Upper Sharia Courts to apply Sharia to civil law and criminal law.[29] The government also established a Sharia Court in every state district and an Upper Sharia Court in all government headquarters.[30] Other legislation was passed that targeted behavior contradicting Muslim customs. For example, boxing, prostitution, gambling, and interactions between unrelated men and women were prohibited.[31]

Clearly, Kaduna and Kebbi experienced different reactions to the implementation of Sharia. But there were some intrinsic similarities in the more pervasive aftermath and in responses from people and governments. The implementation of Sharia in Kaduna and Kebbi allowed for changes in ethnic and religious identity in both communities, because it evoked democratic questions about relations between the majority and minority, especially regarding "representation, fair distribution, and religious freedom."[32] Kebbi's Sharia implementation was smoother, but non-Muslims still experienced increasing fear, just like in Kaduna. Non-Muslims in both states feared that the rights promised by pluralism and democracy would be stripped away. These fears galvanized non-Muslims in both states to create change.[33]

Minorities encouraged both governments to create pluralistic systems through "Sharia-free zones" that focused more on the social justice aspects of Sharia, seeking adjustment within a "constitutional democratic system."[34] Religion in both states was a massively influential force in pluralistic policies and politics.[35] In both Kaduna and Kebbi, the government had to respond to concerns of diminishing rights. The Kaduna government used more pluralistic means, establishing organizations that adhered to a more "pluralist version of Sharia law."[36] Some of the new organizations in Kaduna included the Kaduna Peace Forum, which included Christian and Muslim members, and the Bureau of Religious Affairs, which settled Christian and Muslim religious matters.[37] Kebbi's homogeneous demography did not require this type of strategy.

Kaduna and Kebbi's methods of restoring peace were quite different due to their differences in demographics and history. Because Kaduna's demographics were much more heterogeneous, the non-Muslim citizens

---

[28] Ibid., 902.
[29] *White Paper on the Report of the Committee on the Implementation of Sharia in Kebbi State*, in Sharia Implementation in Northern Nigeria, note 2, 177.
[30] *White Paper*, 178–189.
[31] Okpanachi, "Between Conflict and Compromise," 902–903.   [32] Ibid., 902.
[33] Ibid., 903.   [34] Ibid., 905.   [35] Ibid.   [36] Ibid., 912.   [37] Ibid.

arguably had to fight harder and demand more from their government before peace was restored. One example was the Interfaith Mediation Center (IMC), an organization formed by an imam named Muhammad Ashafa and a pastor named James Wuye. IMC advocates for open discussion of peace in schools and the community at large.[38] One of its major accomplishments occurred in 2002, when twenty-two leaders from Muslim and Christian communities signed a declaration of peace, known today as the Kaduna Peace Declaration. The declaration would "create a platform of collaboration between religious stakeholders and government to foster greater understanding between religious adherents and the State."[39] Through the declaration, leaders vowed to work together peacefully to enable future generations of Muslims and Christians to coexist peacefully. The leaders also established the Kaduna Peace Committee to carry out recommendations found in the declaration.[40] The Kaduna strategies are evidence for the democratization of the state because issues have become decentralized. Conflicts play out more on the local level and not on the national level.[41]

One cannot make the mistake of thinking that Kaduna has remained peaceful with its more pluralistic rules. It has often been the opposite. Democracy in Kaduna has allowed for more protests and an increased focus on the differences between Muslims and Christians. Violence was rampant in Kaduna after the 2011 presidential election. It was sparked by Goodluck Jonathan, a Christian vice president, becoming president after the death of his Muslim predecessor, Umaru Yar'Adua. The situation allowed Patrick Yakowa, a Christian who was also part of the People's Democratic Party (PDP), to be considered for the role of deputy governor. Yakowa was the first Christian ever considered for the position, and his candidacy assuaged Christian fears that Muslims were deliberately restricting access to the position.

However, some Muslims felt it was best to vote for Muhammadu Buhari, a Muslim who was part of the Congress for Progressive Change (CPC). Some people mistakenly believed that the PDP was a Christian party and that the CPC was a Muslim party.[42] When Jonathan, a PDP candidate, was projected to win the position, CPC supporters engaged in violent protests. They declared that the election was fraudulent, and CPC protesters burned the campaign offices of the PDP. They also burned the

---

[38] Ibid.
[39] Muhammad Ashafa and James Wuye, "Warriors and Brothers," in *Peacemakers in Action: Profiles of Religion in Conflict Resolution,* ed. David Little (Cambridge: Cambridge University Press, 2007), 247 and 272.
[40] Okpanachi, "Between Conflict and Compromise," 913.   [41] Ibid., 915.
[42] Ibid., 915–916.

businesses and homes of nearby PDP supporters – ironically, most of the victims were Muslim.[43] This was followed by Christian attacks on mosques in Christian-majority southern Kaduna. It is estimated that 680 people died in this chaos, and about 26,000 people were displaced[44] and moved to 100 centers across Kaduna.[45] This led to concerns that Muslims and Christians would become even more divided and antagonistic toward one another.[46] Pluralism came at a deadly price for Kaduna, even with its benefits.[47]

Kaduna and Kebbi responded differently to the introduction of Sharia law. The heterogeneous demographics of Kaduna required pluralism to restore peace. However, its peace has not been maintained consistently, meaning that pluralism is no guarantee of prosperity. Even with Kebbi's homogeneous demographics and peaceful transition to Sharia influence, non-Muslim individuals still felt threatened with insignificance and had to question how democratic issues would be handled. This case study demonstrates how "pluralism" is not a system that can be understood or implemented in a single way. Instead, it may work ideally in some conditions and less ideally in others; it must adapt to the demographics and societal structure at hand.

Let us assess how pluralism in Africa compares to its Western counterparts. In more traditional theory, pluralism involves the intersection of various political interest groups and a "flexibility of interest association across time."[48] According to Carrie Manning, this traditional structure is not readily applicable across the African continent. Africa's emerging democratic societies, which are only a few decades old, may not have many interest groups available, and individuals might not belong to more than one interest group.[49] Instead of hosting multiple organizations that people can join, developing countries in Africa have party systems that "define [their] members' identity completely."[50] In many African countries, one party effectively rules the government and the people's social life, meaning that the multiparty system in place is not nearly as strong or efficient as it could be.[51]

States can also serve as the center of political and socioeconomic development because it was a means of survival during the postcolonial

---

[43] Ibid., 916.

[44] Ikechukwu Amaechi, "In Defence of Muhammadu Buhari (1)," *Iyke*, May 24, 2011, http://ikechukwu.wordpress.com/2011/07/16/in-defence-of-muhammadu-buhari-1.

[45] Scott Stearns, "Nigerian Human Rights Group: At Least 500 Killed in Post-Election Violence," *VOICE AM*, April 24, 2011, http://voanews.com/english/news/africa/Nigeria-Human-Rights-Group-At-Least-500-Killed-in-Post-Election-Violence-120579459.html.

[46] Okpanachi, "Between Conflict and Compromise," 917.   [47] Ibid., 919.

[48] Manning, "Assessing African Party Systems," 712.   [49] Ibid., 713.   [50] Ibid., 714.

[51] Ibid.

era in Africa.[52] And according to Emmanuel Gyimah-Boadi, African countries without political or economic stability cannot establish professional associations for the middle class, which are the "strongest of civil society organizations." As a result, African people do not have the means to join multiple organizations that are vital to the pluralistic philosophy.[53]

Manning argues that even if African people have the opportunity or money to belong to various organizations, those organizations do not contribute to political identities – according to classical pluralism, multiple political identities are essential for people to give to society and for society to give back to people. When citizens are part of multiple interest groups, either tacitly or explicitly, and those groups have political motivations, the values of the interest groups will overlap. If the values of one organization are violated, for whatever reason, then the values of another organization are violated, incentivizing more people to act.[54] According to Manning, "overlapping memberships and shared belief in the fundamentals are what make a pluralistic political system possible – they are the brakes on both unrestrained diversity and enforced homogeneity."[55] Even though African states tout the virtues of pluralism, they cannot feasibly rely on classical versions of pluralism. African states do not have the infrastructure for it.[56]

Even though Africa does not normally see great turnover or exchange of power among parties,[57] Africa still maintains multiple parties. This corroborates the evidence from Kaduna and Kebbi; pluralism's classical form is not necessary for some form of functional democracy, although the degree to which that democracy functions is another factor worth scrutinizing. Immediately after African countries achieved independence, they formulated single-party systems. However, African countries shifted to multiparty systems after 1990. By the year 1995, almost all countries in sub-Saharan Africa had at least one multiparty election.[58] According to the African Development Bank, these parties have allowed African countries to regularly engage in legitimate democratic elections. However, information cited from the Economist Intelligence Unit found that only Mauritius was ranked as having full democracy. Ten other African countries were ranked as having some form of flawed democracy. African countries were ranked as undemocratic in nature because they were classified as "hybrid regimes" or "authoritarian regimes." The Economist Intelligence Unit based these

---

[52] Ibid., 715.
[53] Emmanuel Gyimah-Boadi, "Civil Society in Africa," in *Consolidating the Third Wave Democracies*, eds. Larry Diamond et al. (Baltimore: Johns Hopkins University Press, 1997), 278–294.
[54] Manning, "Assessing African Party Systems," 713.   [55] Ibid., 714.   [56] Ibid.
[57] Ibid.   [58] Ibid., 709.

rankings on a matter of opinion, although the rankings show how Africa's multiple parties are far from stable, fully fleshed democracies.[59]

African countries tend to select incumbents from majority parties in power. Among twenty-five of forty-six African countries, majority parties win more than two-thirds of the vote in elections.[60] This could be influenced by the fact that several African countries "[provide] the incumbent party with both easy access to public resources and enormous capacity to intimidate the private sector, preventing it from financing the opposition."[61] It may also be due to state control of social life[62] and economics.[63]

According to Manning, this system of democracy has allowed African parties to develop these characteristics:

1. The parties' connections to pluralism are feeble. They are generally associated with "kinship-based networks," but not with organizations that have pluralistic interests.
2. A multitude of small, feeble parties may have central figures, but these figures often lack support from within their regions. Furthermore, these parties do not have an extension of organizational structure.
3. A predominant single party tends to be either the previous incumbent's party or the party that was victorious in the first "transitional elections."
4. The parties do not easily fall along a spectrum from conservative to liberal. Instead, they have similar economic and political agendas. Generally, the parties are also restrained by the need for aid and "structural adjustment."[64]

The structure of these parties does not correspond to the parties seen in the West, partly because parties in Africa emerged from totally different circumstances. Political parties in the West arose from socioeconomic changes, such as the Industrial Revolution. Western parties are also connected to a social base that was relevant for the period. On the other hand, African parties arose from political changes, such as a noticeably young democracy. This means that they are often searching for

---

[59] African Development Bank Group, "Democratic Elections in Africa – Opportunities and Risks," *African Development Bank Group*, April 24, 2012, www.afdb.org/en/blogs/afdb-championing-inclusive-growth-across-africa/post/democratic-elections-in-africa-opportunities-and-risks-9117/.

[60] Dieter Nohlen, Michael Krennerich, and Bernhard Thibaut, "Elections and Electoral Systems in Africa," in *Elections in Africa: A Data Handbook*, eds. Dieter Nohlen, Michael Krennerich, and Bernhard Thibaut (Oxford: Oxford University Press, 1999).

[61] Jennifer Widner, "Political Parties and Civil Societies in Sub-Saharan Africa," in *Democracy in Africa: The Hard Road Ahead*, ed. Marrina Ottaway (Boulder: Lynne Rienner, 1997), 79.

[62] Manning, "Assessing African Party Systems," 714.   [63] Ibid., 716.   [64] Ibid.

supporters, even when their preferred policies do not have clear long-term results.[65] Western parties also allow a "bottom-to-top" strategy, where people with diverse opinions affect politicians who must find ways to reconcile those opinions. In contrast, African parties are controlled by elites, meaning that they do not represent a diverse set of opinions, and they do not try to strike a balance. Instead, African parties are inherently biased and willing to manipulate the people's diverse opinions in a "top-to-bottom" strategy.[66]

What can we conclude from this evidence? Ultimately, Manning asserts that it is two things:

1. The social structure of Africa, and the multiparty structure of Africa, cannot support the classical form of pluralism considered to bolster democracy.[67]
2. Africa's example shows that we cannot assume that party politics rely on pluralism.[68] Party politics, as damaged as they may be, have emerged in Africa without a solid pluralistic system.

Why Is Political Pluralism Important?

In Nigeria, a multicultural and multiethnic space, political pluralism is essential for key reasons. Pluralism is a pivotal aspect of democracy, which "takes into account regional, ethnic, and group-specific matters"[69] and which allows cultural identities to survive without being collapsed into a monolithic whole. This is not fully implemented in the culturally pluralist atmosphere of Nigeria. It is a country where there is a claim to democracy, but there is a dearth of democratic practices or people belonging to multiple groups and parties. The absence of overlapping relationships and interests between existing groups equates to the absence of a full democracy; it can culminate in nepotism or elite interests taking precedence over those marginalized. Full democracy in Nigeria would be an indication of successful pluralism.

Possessing a multigroup identity is a consequence of belonging to and having multiple group interests. It is one of pluralism's crucial advantages, especially in relation to national democracy that requires collective effort from various segments of society – political, religious, ethnic, cultural, and gender-based. For these segments to participate and contribute substantially to national development, there is the need for pluralism, which will allow them to be recognized and rewarded in substantive

---

[65] Ibid., 718.   [66] Ibid., 718–719.   [67] Ibid., 717.   [68] Ibid., 723.
[69] See John C. Ejobowah, "Political Recognition of Ethnic Pluralism: Lessons from Nigeria," *Nationalism and Ethnic Politics* 6, no. 3 (2000): 1.

measures, resulting in equality and representation. It is done by "design-ing political arrangements around groups,"[70] a position favored by con-sociationalists where democracy is fostered; then mistrust and ill will arising from nepotism and bias can be easily nipped in the bud. Cross-membership relationships between existing groups would ensure that such arrangements are geared toward nation building instead of the interests of an elite few.

Nigeria as a nation is a "social order," with functional and integrated parts. This is why sociologists consider a nation like Nigeria as an "inte-grated system of social structures and functions."[71] Each part that con-tributes to the whole has its own purpose. To emphasize that Nigeria is a social order – with functional and integrated rational systems, thought systems, institutions, and human and non-human resources – is to restate one of sociology's main principles: in the modern world, "even nonhu-man objects are increasingly seen as key actors in networks."[72] This is even true in primordial societies where the principle of reciprocity between society and the individual, which is a principle now characteriz-ing the modern world, underpins most joint associations. For each com-ponent of reciprocal relationships to attain relevance in a modern construct like Nigeria, some level of pluralism is required where society and individuals are constantly interacting. Agentive groups with political significance must be active so that equality through representation can be achieved.

In a pluralist state, individuals must have interests that transcend the group divide, and their groups must have visibility and representation in crucial political positions. (It is strongly advised that such agency has political relevance, contributing to the formation of political identities.) By fostering representation across society's different interests, pluralism deals with inequality, under-representation, and "incomplete liberaliza-tion, lack of inclusiveness and deficient application of rule of law."[73] The presence of all these in a modern society like Nigeria is why Ritzer posits that "[a]lthough it appears that the . . . world has undergone a process of liberalization, in fact it has grown increasingly oppressive."[74]

Nigeria supports Ritzer's argument. The absence of true pluralism is visible in many places, including hegemony and the continued ruling of an elite executive. There is a group of political elites defined by a single party affiliation, even though the country boasts a multiparty system – this situation

---

[70] Ibid., 1.   [71] George Ritzer, *Sociological Theory* (New York: McGraw-Hill, 2010), 2.
[72] Ibid., 1.
[73] Henry Kifordu, "Political Elite Composition and Democracy in Nigeria," *The Open Area Studies Journal* 4 (2011): 29.
[74] Ritzer, *Sociological Theory*, 2.

feeds the illusion identified by Ritzer. There are more than 100 political parties in Nigeria, but the representation of women and minority ethnicities is minimal in the upper tiers of Nigeria's political structure, exposing the lack of substantive equality in the region. In the 2019 presidential election, only a handful of women are among the seventy-three candidates under consideration. In parties steered by tribal interests, especially those with Northern origins or affiliations, a woman's candidacy would be abhorrent.

Women are legitimate members of the social order. The presidential contest is always fought between two super-parties, PDP and APC, and their current presidential candidates are from the Northern Region. It reveals the state of things: Nigeria has a multiethnic, pluralist setting that does not support a pluralist philosophy or a pluralist government. The party system of Nigeria claims to be inclusive, but it is bound by ties of kinship and ethnicity.

Citizenship differentiated by particularized cultural identities in a multiethnic construct can enable elite political regimes, the continuity of those regimes, and the exclusion of outsiders, which contradicts pluralism's claims of providing equal rights and opportunities. Tensions exist between equal treatment and recognizing aspects of individualism, but to deny the expression of multiple forms of identity is to engender a greater tension. By recognizing pluralism's role in circumventing or neutralizing unintended consequences, Ejobowah asserts that the way forward is to find and establish structures that preserve unity while concurrently supporting expressions of such groups.[75]

Pluralism's risk of allowing political elites to seize executive positions explains the hybridized and half-formed democracy practiced in Nigeria. Kifordu argues that this "situation is at odds with the democratic spirit of liberal pluralist assumptions, which reflect equality of participation."[76] The nature of the governing elite and the nature of the democratic structure that enables them is representative of the political climate. The glaring disparity in the representation of ethnicities across political groups is a symptom of false integration, indicating a system of government that has "failed to move away significantly from an oligarchic past since independence."[77] Political pluralism, the type that recognizes and safeguards the interests of the minority, must be implemented.

Political pluralism is essential for maintaining social order, which requires integration, inclusiveness, and unity through diversity. In other words, heterogeneity should be superimposed on homogeneity. Precolonial Nigeria functioned well as a region with independent cultural

[75] Ejobowah, "Political Recognition of Ethnic Pluralism," 3.
[76] Kifordu, "Political Elite Composition and Democracy," 29.   [77] Ibid.

units; each unit was differentiated from others sharing the boundaries now designating Nigeria. The increasing influence of modernization, industrialization, and globalism – all attendant features of colonialism – gave an advantage to integration and heterogeneity over homogeneity. Notions like homogeneity, which served as an antidote to the ethnic violence occurring well into the twentieth century,[78] lost relevance as viable solutions.

In the present century, integration that does not blur the individuality of previously independent cultural groups and ethnicities has become the way forward. Mutual respect and substantive equality are pivotal for achieving this level of inclusivity. Differences can be tolerated through mutual respect. Tolerance of differences would ease the integration of several groups, leading to a sense of national belonging and national identity. This is possible because national identity is a function of shared identities among groups, which is the case in Nigeria. As noted by Edewor et al., any social order is reliant on the degree to which a shared identity exists among members of the society.[79] The presence of a shared identity among culturally diverse groups is a symptom of mutual trust, shared membership, and equal treatment of such groups, especially through political representation. These are all manifestations of effectively implemented, pluralist policies and pluralism.

Unity in diversity, as a result of pluralism, leads to social cohesion. It increases national consciousness and improves nation building because all parties are involved, which is a requirement for groups in any social order. A national identity, premised on shared fundamentals, can unite disparate groups, especially in a country like Nigeria with its large number of ethnic groups. It is possible for national identity and cultural identity to coexist, without hindering each other. This is why multiple groups involving themselves in the political state of the nation is germane to the functioning of pluralism – it engenders cross-sectional interests and avoids the hegemony of one group over another.

To Edewor et al., cultural identity signifies freedom of involvement, with agencies and ideologies that can extend beyond nationalized boundaries.[80] These identities are and can be complementary, such as ethnic, social, gender, religious, or work identities. This level of complementarity can harness the strengths of each group toward progressive nation building. Under the ideology of nationalism, natural resources have been harnessed in Nigeria's Niger Delta region and the proceeds

---

[78] Patrick Edewor A, Yetunde Aluko A., and Sheriff Folarin, "Managing Ethnic and Cultural Diversity for National Integration in Nigeria," *Developing Country Studies* 4, no. 6 (2014): 70.
[79] Ibid.   [80] Ibid.

have been distributed nationwide. This interrelation of diverse, group-derived identities is an example of the benefits that come from integrating previously exclusive parts of a society.

Human and natural resources are opportunities for each region to contribute to nation building. According to Edewor et al., "success stories of peaceful societies world-wide highlight the positive results of this coexistence." Acceptance of cultural identity within a national identity prevents stifling of social relationships and promotes dynamic inter-actions, creativity, critical thinking, and acceptance of history as a shared legacy and the future as shared aspirations."[81]

In places where cultural identity is suppressed, there are cases of exclusion from elite political groups and continued inequality and inequity in representation. Conflict and war can even develop – the first Civil War in Nigeria is an example. Although this is dangerous, it is equally dangerous to have proportional-but-not-substantive representa-tion of cultural identities in institutional contexts. Such representation only allows for the insertion of cultural identities into a national frame-work, especially under biased and preconceived parameters. It does not necessarily allow for integration, which is the more pressing benefit of pluralism.

Back in 2017, Nigeria's president was able to claim that he had given about four substantive ministry positions to the Southeast in response to criticism that his appointments had a uniformly Northern character. The response was offered as though he gave special consideration to the Southeast group. Similar incidents show that the existence of multiple ethnicities and other multicultural signifiers in a nation-state ostensibly practicing democracy, especially the kind practiced in a country like Nigeria, is not a guarantee of successful pluralism. As Edewor et al. put it, they "may increase tensions, rather than resolve them"[82] – it is one of the consequences of non-integrative pluralism in Nigeria.

The equal footing that a pluralist state affords its various ethnicities and groups would automatically promote and support the growth of cultural values and systems, enhancing their inclusion in the national structure. One such instance is the creation of customary courts as part of a country's constitutionally recognized legal systems, and the creation of Sharia law courts and Islamic Law. The political ramifications of establishing judicial systems catering to grassroots issues alongside sys-tems that are more national in outlook enables the proliferation of legal systems that maintain the normative values of traditional or primordial societies and keep them alive. Cases like these lead to legal pluralism and,

---

[81] Ibid., 71.   [82] Ibid.

according to Gwaza, Nigeria "has manifested first of all in the ethnic, cultural and religious multifaceted nature of the country."[83] Political power in a country like Nigeria rests on ethnic character, while legal pluralism is "the coexistence of two or more autonomous or semi-autonomous legal orders in the same time–space context."[84]

The perpetuation of traditional values through customary legal systems owes a lot to globalization, especially the "process of norm formation"[85] that increases their chances of being recognized in the same light as state laws. As Paul Berman has argued, legislation is predicated on community definition and acceptance.[86] It is easy for various ethnicities to politically contribute to nation building through legal pluralism in places where customary and more traditional legal systems have been instituted. When legislative power is not the sole preserve of the state, and it can be claimed by different types of communities,[87] it allows non-state groups to move from unrecognized legislative sidelines to the domain of legitimate law.

In fact, such primordial laws can become useful or adopted by other communities or the State. This is possible when the original communities can fulfill the condition of "jurispersuasion," which Berman describes as successfully convincing others of one's legitimate legislative power. The degree to which such legal orders are applied depends on the constitutional provisions deciding the extent of their applications. In the words of Gwaza, "where any legal order fails to comply with the provision of the Nigerian constitution, it becomes null, void and inapplicable.[88]"

Any nation that accommodates and recognizes pluralism, in any form, contributes to the survival and continuity of its primordial heritage and values. This pluralism can be ethnic, or a legal pluralism built on the ethnic and religious structure of the community, or political pluralism, which is also immensely affected by the previous two – assuming that it does not contradict the provisions made for it in the appropriate constitution. As seen in the case of Nigeria, this is often not the reality on the ground. Through pluralism, any nation-state can admit the legislative power of its communities.

In a proper pluralist state, democracy would be in full practice; a totalitarian elite class, or an elite structure renewed by members of

---

[83] Paul Gwaza, "Romanticising Legal Pluralism through Religious Revival in Democratic Nigeria: Crusaders, Criminals, and Casualties" (paper presentation, the International Conference on Ethnicity, Religion and Peace Building, University of Jos, Jos, Nigeria, February 18–20, 2013), 8, https://ssrn.com/abstract=2544836.

[84] Ibid., 7.   [85] Ibid.

[86] See Paul S. Berman, "From International Law to Law and Globalization," *Journal of Transnational Law* 43 (2005): 485.

[87] Gwaza, "Romanticizing Legal Pluralism."   [88] Ibid., 8.

a particular group, would not exist. In such a state, pluralism would be fully observed as equal and substantive representation of all groups. There would be elite renewal, and not the continuity that incites hegemony. In the case of Nigeria, the Hausa–Fulani dominance that has persisted since independence would have been checked.

Pluralism would also enhance the freedom of association and encourage multiple group memberships. This would not only advance progressive and national interests, but also lead to political legitimacy – pluralism would require the creation of political agencies that allow citizens from different cultural backgrounds to interact and contribute to a mutually beneficial project, such as nation building. Multiple group memberships, and the subsequent integration of disparate groups, would ensure the creation of common ground and progressive dialogues from and through which democracy can sprout and operate freely. Democracy is a confluence of equality and participation, integration and dialogue, and representation and allied interests, all of which are possible outcomes of pluralism.

There are many forms of pluralism associated with political pluralism, all of which are products of the cultural structure of a nation-state. To understand how pluralism functions in a country like Nigeria, it is not enough to examine political pluralism and ignore the associated realities in which it operates. Pluralism, as it exists in Nigeria, is a far cry from its ideal form, which is obvious from the lacuna between the state of the country and the benefits of pluralism discussed here.

The State of Things: The Nigerian Experience of Pluralism

To understand pluralism in Nigeria, one must begin with the premise that Nigeria is a modern state built on a (now-fragmented) cultural frame. The modern world is trans-cultural, and pluralism is a central part of this trans-cultural framework. It is responsible for much of the cosmopolitan and multicultural structure of the twenty-first century world.

The twenty-first century world is a mix of cultures. These cultures are socially meaningful patterns of behavior, traditions, and man-made material goods with social implications,[89] and they are also the manifested implication of the nature or forms of human occupancy of a space through which diversity or distinctions of patterns of civilization might be established and examined.[90] These traditions, cultures, and forms of occupancy

---

[89] John Zadrozny, *Dictionary of Social Science* (Washington, DC: Pacific Affairs Press, 1959).
[90] See Richard Tuthill, "Geographic Aspects of Cultural Pluralism in Nigeria," *The High School Journal* 56, no. 1 (1972): 26–44.

overlap severally, characterizing the world as a global space, which is often the reason why it is considered a melting pot of diverse cultures.[91]

In the twentieth and, more increasingly, twenty-first centuries, borders and boundaries are continually being removed; geographies are collapsed, and new regions created. These fusions can lead to cultural conditions such as hybridism, syncretism, and heterogeneity. In Nigeria alone, thirty-six states were created at different periods toward the end of the twentieth century, and the region itself had its Southern and Northern Protectorates annexed in 1914. These have been monumental periods in the country's history. In Africa, colonialism brought about the fusion of various ethnic groups, chiefdoms, kingdoms, and empires that had shared close geographic connections while remaining independent and sovereign. The history of many African countries is a narrative of such fusions. This is how a country like Nigeria can include over 400 ethnicities. These unions explain the continent's multicultural nature.

Interconnectedness is perceptible in every facet of the modern world, including politics, religion, and education. Pluralism, a consequence of heterogeneity or diversity and that which Tuthill considers an "acceptable project,"[92] is the backbone of civilization. The idea of a melting pot is often invoked as a fitting metaphor for a multicultural and hybridized reality – or a Third Space,[93] to use a more technical term. Pluralism and its philosophies are fastening agents that hem together an increasingly heterogeneous world. This pluralism begins with culture before manifesting in other forms, such as ethnic plurality, political plurality, religious plurality, liberal plurality, and legal plurality. To understand how pluralism operates in Nigeria, one must engage in an explorative view of cultural pluralism.

Cultural pluralism can be explained in many ways, but the dominant idea is the coexistence of several cultural groups in a single national or social framework. This principle underscores several notions on cultural pluralism, which may be narrow or broad.[94] Tuthill, attempting to broaden cultural pluralism, describes it "as a state in which each ethnic

---

[91] See works like Timothy Cresswell, *Place: A Short Introduction* (Oxford: Oxford University Press, 2004); see also John Urry, *Sociology beyond Societies: Mobilities for the Twenty-First Century* (London: Routledge, 2000); and Peter Barry, *Beginning Theory* (New Delhi: Viva Books Pvt. Ltd, 2010), especially the chapter on postcolonialism, for how the modern world can be a meeting point of diverse cultures.

[92] Tuthill, "Geographic Aspects of Cultural Pluralism," 26.

[93] A third space – in cultural, postcolonial, sociological, and migration studies – is the neutral meeting point of diverse cultures, where contact and clashes occur, leading to cultural pluralism. Third Space is a place of multiculturalism. Works of multiculturalist and postcolonial scholars, such as Homi Bhabha, Henri Lefebvre, Chinweizu, Spivak, and Edward Said, all comment critically on this.

[94] Tuthill, "Geographic Aspects of Cultural Pluralism," p. 27, criticizes Zadrozny's definition of cultural pluralism – "which he defines as co-existence of diverse cultural groups

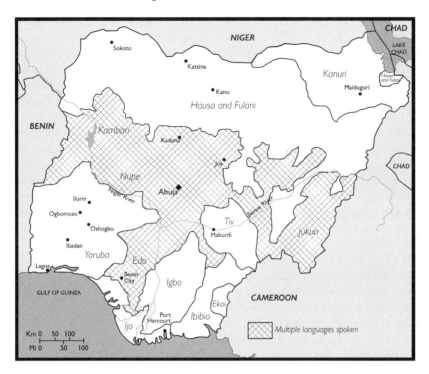

Map 4.1 Nigeria, ethno-linguistic groups.

group maintains in large measure, a separate way of life, with its own customs, its own supplementary schools, its special organizations and periodicals, and perhaps its favored secondary languages."[95] The conception of Edewor et al. finds ideological balance between the unspecific and the broad as criticized by Tuthill: Edewor considers cultural pluralism to be "the variety of human societies and culture in a specific region or in the world as a whole."[96] Three things are pertinent here: coexistentiality; uniqueness, in terms of identity and custom/way of life; and variety. These are discovered in any conceptual attempt to capture the essence of cultural plurality.

To reemphasize cultural pluralism's role as the bedrock of any pluralist reality in the modern world, and in Nigeria by extension, we must

within a multi-national state" (see Zadrozny, "Dictionary of Social Science," 78) as an all-embracing position whose delineation is not enough.

[95] Tuthill, "Geographic Aspects of Cultural Pluralism," 27.

[96] Edewor et. al., "Managing Ethnic and Cultural Diversity."

reexamine the idea of culture. It is usually delineated in two senses, according to Edewor et al.: one focuses on cultural products and expressions, such as aspects of folklore that include dance, songs, sculpture, painting, and other arts, or architecture and other physical cultural institutions; the other, which is more universal and popular, presents culture as a way of life.[97] The conceptions are considered narrow and broad, respectively.

When carefully examined, Edewor et al. provides a second sense of culture that is more expansive and inclusive, making recourse to the two definitions that Meyer and Strietelmier and Zadrozny stated earlier. Culture encompasses everything that defines a human, both physical and immaterial, traditional and modern, and philosophical and political, as well as the customary, the natural, and the man-made. It is in the wisdom passed down through the ages, the patterns of survival, and the practices and edicts separating and uniting people. If culture is all these, incontestably carrying the learned, socially meaningful conduct that is practiced in a given context, and it reflects the ways in which humans have occupied the time–space construct and expressed themselves in it, then cultural pluralism is the motherboard upon which a pluralistic state draws expression and functions. Cultural pluralism – a term that was introduced into scholarly usage by M. H. Kallen in a seminal work,[98] even though it existed long before Kallen employed it – accommodates other forms of pluralism.

Countries like Nigeria claim to practice pluralism through their level of multiculturalism. The Yoruba, Igbo, and Hausa – three of Nigeria's major ethnicities – existed as kingdoms, regions, and empires, exercising sovereignty over independent territories. The 1914 annexation, by Lord Frederick Lugard and his colonial administration, made Nigeria a colonial project. It is the reason why Nigeria has over 250 independent ethnic groups within its national framework.[99] Several scholars put the number at over 200. Paul Andrew Gwaza[100] puts the number above 400, and Alubo rounds it off to about 370.[101] According to Kifordu, the Hausa–Fulani constitute about 29 percent of the entire Nigerian population, and the Yoruba and Igbo ethnicities comprise 21 percent and 18 percent, respectively.[102] Kifordu identifies other minority groups,

[97] Ibid., 71.
[98] See his *Cultural Pluralism and the American Idea* (Philadelphia: University of Philadelphia Press, 1956).
[99] Kifordu, "Political Elite Composition and Democracy."
[100] Gwaza, "Romanticising Legal Pluralism through Religious Revival in Democratic Nigeria."
[101] O. Alubo, *Nigeria: Ethnic Conflicts and Citizenship Crises in the Central Region* (Ibadan: PEFS, 2006).
[102] Kifordu, "Political Elite Composition and Democracy," 17.

such as the Ijo, making up 10 percent; the Kanuri, 4 percent; the Ibibio, 3.5 percent; the Tiv, 2.5 percent; and the Edo, 2 percent. There are also several others, like Nupe, Urhobo, Idoma, and Jukun.

Each culture is complete on its own, with language and dialectal varieties, ethos, thought and knowledge systems, landmarks, spatial territories, and institutions. These cultures are maintained within the national framework constructed by the colonialists and maintained by the earliest Nigerian political ideologues, including Nnamdi Azikiwe and Obafemi Awolowo, who fought for independence. The successful unification of ethnic groups – in execution and not implication, because Nigeria's history of cultural diversity is not without its ironies – is symptomatic of the pluralist tag's appropriateness for Nigeria. Ogbole Friday Abu's position on pluralism, as the consequence of social transformations causing the union of people of different beliefs, values, and customs in a social relationship, reveals the tag's suitability for the Nigeria situation.[103] But it would be reductive and untrue to claim that ethnicity is the only reason for Nigeria's pluralistic nature.

Nigeria also accommodates religious pluralism. "Roughly half of all Nigerians are recorded as Muslims, residing mostly in the North but with certain southwestern converts [and] 40 per cent are Christians, the large majority of whom live in the South,"[104] Kifordu states. He notes that the remaining 10 percent maintain traditional religions. Nigeria is a religiously pluralist nation because it perpetually manifests conditions where different religious persuasions exist within a given institutional frame.[105] This is a consequence of the nation's cultural dynamics. There is a strong bond between religion and culture. For example, Nigerian northerners experience their religion of Islam not only as a spiritual affair, but it also encompasses other aspects of their lives, including political orientation, legal orders, and education.

The many religions in Nigeria establish conditions of difference that suggest, at the very least, duality. Nigeria is religiously pluralist because it is multireligious. Different religions and sub-religious groups exist, nurturing different doctrines, philosophies, interpretations, and ideals. The region now considered Nigeria was already pluralistic in religion before the coming of the Europeans. Each group had its own traditional religion, with different sets of religious laws, edicts, legislatures, myths, and spiritual and cosmological views along with different pantheons and

---

[103] Friday A. Ogbole and Adewale O. Akinrinade, "Nigerian Pluralistic Society and the Relevance of Religious Dialogue as an Instrument of Peace," *Journal of Educational and Social Research 3*, no. 3 (2013): 343–350.

[104] Kifordu, "Political Elite Composition and Democracy," 17.

[105] Ogbole and Akinrinade, "Nigerian Pluralistic Society," 344.

celestial beings or deities that they worshipped. As Ogbole and Akinrinade have posited, precolonial societies were ideologically regulated from within because of relatively minimal contact with foreign ways and cultures. This led to cultural homogeneity and societies that were internally regulated and isolated,[106] conditions that Kifordu asserts have been the preference of preliterate societies well into the twentieth century.[107] Colonialism, Westernization, migration, and globalization have intruded on such internal modes of regulation, resulting in desertion. Societies have become multicultural, multireligious, and politically pluralistic.

Africans are highly religious people, and their religions inform their philosophies and laws, serving as templates for legislative jurisprudence, political reforms, and judicial laws. It is no surprise that judicial agencies promoting traditional consciousness are accorded legitimacy. In Nigeria, some of these are the customary courts and Sharia laws running concurrently with more secular, national legal orders. In Nigeria, these kinds of arrangements are popular and constitutional. The idea is that the heterogeneous reality of a pluralist nation can be governed by an impartial government guaranteeing equality under law to different religions, whether the religions have a handful of adherents or millions.[108] Such a government would guarantee and protect the rights and freedoms of those choosing to either join or abstain from joining any religion. In a country like Nigeria, with pluralist religious and legal settings, each legal event determines which law or legal order is applicable in that instance, supported by the dictates of the constitution. Section 101 of the Nigerian constitution declares that it is a secular state, and "the Government of the Federation or of a State shall not adopt any religion as State religion."[109] However, this is hardly the case.

Constitutional affordances were initially the guiding principles during the adoption and implementation of Sharia law under the Zamfara State Government in 1999. Governor Kure of Niger State, adopted Sharia and said it would

submit to the supremacy of the nation's constitution ... assuring that were the system [to run] contrary to the provisions of the constitution, Shari'a would bow to give the constitution the right of way. ... He said that having vowed to preserve and protect the nation's constitution during his swearing in, his administration would do nothing to flout the provisions under any guise.[110]

---

[106] Ibid., 343.   [107] Edewor et al., "Managing Ethnic and Cultural Diversity," 70.
[108] Ogbole and Akinrinade, "Nigerian Pluralistic Society," 344.
[109] See Nigerian Constitution.   [110] Gwaza, "Romanticising Legal Pluralism," 8.

A similar statement is associated with Governor Sani, who was instrumental to the establishment of Sharia in the North: "[w]hatever I am doing must be . . . within the agreement signed by the people of Nigeria to live together which is referred to as the Constitution."[111] The same statement was referenced when he was accused of violating Child Rights laws by marrying a minor, and he claimed that "I do not work with such law that runs counter to my religion."[112] This is one of many examples, prevalent in the northern region, where Sharia law and Islamic religion override the Nigerian Constitution. It is a consequence of religious pluralism in a defective democracy, where the rule of law is not applied and where pluralist policies and the federalism that should aid them are often relegated to the sidelines.

Freedom to choose or abstain from choosing a religion extends to all religions existing within the dictates of the law, even if "an individual religion accepts that other religions are legitimate or [not]."[113] This edict allows Nigeria to exhibit symptoms of pluralism and safeguard the rights of non-religious persons. But allowing many religions to exist in a national frame is not enough to sustain pluralism on its own. Inter-religiosity can lead to chaos, as seen in the Abuja riot of 2000 and the Jos riot of 2001, both of which were results of Muslim–Christian tensions. Acceptance of Sharia law in eleven states is not without uproar and bedlam. The Boko Haram menace presently ravaging the northern part of the country is a consequence of an extreme religious group's intolerance against Christians, Westernization, and the national government.

The Boko Haram insurgency started in 2009. It probably has ties to Al-Qaeda, and it is responsible for the deaths of hundreds of thousands, as well as millions of internally displaced persons. Abduction, kidnapping, bombing, raiding, and killing – the insurgency has developed beyond a form of religious intolerance to become a terrorist group and a gradual attempt to disintegrate the nation. This terrorist movement has agriculturally crippled northern states, such as Yobe, Adamawa, and Bornu, which were popular for producing cowpeas, onions, corn, sorghum, millet, and tomatoes.

According to the UN High Commissioner for Refugees, "more than 1.5 million people, mostly farmers have been forced to flee their homes."[114] Amaru argues that if these insurgent attacks continue, the country might be plunged into long-term, chronic food insufficiency; the North is known to be the agricultural foundation of the country. The

---

[111] Ibid.   [112] Ibid., 9.   [113] Ibid., 344.
[114] Nneka S. Amalu, "Impact of Boko Haram Insurgency on Human Security in Nigeria," *Global Journal of Social Sciences* 14 (2015): 38.

same terrorist group is responsible for the breakdown of healthcare facilities in the states they have attacked, reducing their capacity to around 37 percent as medical workers are hindered and healthcare centers are destroyed.[115] In Adamawa, the US Agency for International Development discovered that free medical prescription stocks were either inadequate or unavailable.[116]

To avoid these situations, mutual respect must exist between religions. Obviously, religion and religious groups are linked with and contribute to political formation and identities. The North's political structure is linked to its religiosity. The BBC has reported that the Emirs, who are the religious and traditional rulers and custodians, continue to wield political power even in a democratic government. Recognized by the constituency and also acting as religious heads, they determine who gets which political appointments, even if the moves are covert.[117] Parties often approach these heads to acquire political goodwill, and their functions include reinforcing the importance of civic duties and adherence to Northern heritage, advising Local Government Council leaders, and providing guidance on the choice of political candidates. This is also true of other regions; traditional rulers are religious leaders.

Religion is second only to ethnicity in determining candidacy and political strategizing, especially in relation to upper-level political positions, although these maneuvers are now less overt than they had been in the past. To sell their presidential candidates, political parties often push forward a coalition of Christian and Muslim candidates, as the APC did in Nigeria's 2015 Presidential Election. The strategy was adopted by the PDP opposition party in Nigeria's 2019 election. It is an improvement from the regionally and ethnically dominated political parties created immediately after colonialism. By respecting each other's religions, "[d]ifferent religions must then acknowledge the fact that they need each other and that is why dialogue is very crucial in a religiously pluralistic society."[118] For growth to flourish, and for religious plurality to deliver the heterogeneity, diversity, and progress required to function properly, mutual respect of religions and their values must be cultivated, which can only be done through conscious dialogue.

It is no wonder that a religiously pluralist country like Nigeria is legally pluralist, which leads to political pluralism. This cyclical causation is manifested in the Nigeria federation's legal structure. As Gwaza argues, "choice of normative system or legal order enacted by the legislature or

---

[115] Ibid.   [116] Ibid.
[117] Dan Isaacs, "Nigeria's Emirs: Power Behind the Throne," *BBC*, February 18, 2019, www.bbc.com/news/world-africa-11418542.
[118] Ibid., 345.

developed by the judiciary ... seek to define the criteria by which a decision is reached as to which of the contending systems of law is applicable in a way that appears reasonable."[119] This means that the legal order in Nigeria, applied in an instance requiring judicial intervention, is a function of the order that is considered most appropriate. Family, land, and ethnic disputes, for example, can be settled by customary courts. Northern States, such as Zamfara and Bornu, allow for the practice of Sharia and Islamic Law. In 1999, Governor Alhaji Ahmed Sani advocated for religious reforms by strategically moving apparatuses for motion reforms – his efforts, along with those of the Zamfara state government, enacted Sharia Law to be practiced as a legitimate legal order.[120] About eleven other Northern states followed suit, eventually accommodating Islamic and Sharia Law alongside the existing, democratic, and nationally recognized legal order.

As Gwaza noted, it is often difficult to determine which legal order is applicable to a particular event or transaction because of the compound character of Nigerian reality's sociolegal environment. This is a testament to the existence of legal plurality in the Nigerian nation. Legal pluralism would be "the coexistence of two or more autonomous or semi-autonomous legal orders in the same time–space context." Nigeria is a good subject of pluralist legality, or inter-legality, a termed coined by Boaventura de Sousa Santos and explained as "the impact of legal plurality on the legal experiences, perception and consciousness of the individuals and social groups living under conditions of legal plurality, [whose] everyday life crosses or is interpenetrated by different and often contrasting legal orders and legal cultures."[121]

There is a multiplicity of laws and centers of law. The legal structure of a country is affected by the intersection or collision of these multiple legal orders, which Gwaza itemizes as including "symbiosis, subsumption, imitation convergence, adaptation, partial integration, and avoidance as well as subordination, repression, or destruction."[122]

The impact of legal plurality on Nigeria has been manifold, and it does not necessarily follow the designs that birthed it. In the example with Governor Sani, minors would have expected their interests to be defended by the constitution, and their rights were limited under Sharia law. It is also clear that the logicality or reasonableness that Gwaza describes is absent in Nigerian legal plurality; there is no rationality in marrying minors or girls under the age of eighteen. The United Nations

---

[119] Gwaza, "Romanticising Legal Pluralism," 7.   [120] Ibid., 6.
[121] See Boaventura de Sousa Santos, "Law: A Map of Misreading, Towards a Postmodern Conception of Law," *Journal of Law and Society* 14, no. 3 (1987): 279–302.
[122] Gwaza, "Romanticising Legal Pluralism," 7–8.

Children's Fund expressly states that "marriage before the age of 18 is a fundamental violation of human rights,"[123] declaring that interrupted education, early pregnancy, career disruption, social isolation, and truncated vocation are the consequences of such violations. Consequences of early pregnancy can include "vaginal fistula, anemia, high blood pressure, premature birth, malnutrition, sexually transmitted diseases, suicide, and postpartum depression."[124]

Cases like these are rampant in Northern Nigeria, where the constitution is repressed or subordinated, if not destroyed outright, in favor of Islamic/Sharia Law to accommodate these acts. In 2013 alone, the United Nations Population Fund (UNFPA) found that 47 percent of married women between the ages 20 and 24 had been wed before they reached the age of eighteen. In 2017, UNICEF reported that 17 percent of girls had been wedded before the age of fifteen, and 43 percent married before the age of eighteen. Article 21 of the Child Rights Act reestablished that eighteen was the legal age for marriage, yet the Nigeria Demographic and Heath Survey found that only twenty-three out of thirty-six states had enacted this law by 2016.[125] In 2014, 276 girls were kidnapped from a government school in Chibok by Boko Haram, and most were under the age of eighteen. In Yobe, about 110 girls were also kidnapped in 2018.

These circumstances reveal that ethnicity and religion have political connections and repercussions in Nigeria. They are consequences of society's pluralist nature on cultural, ethnic, and religious levels. Each ethnic group is complete in itself, having normative systems and legal orders that are unique and different from those of other groups. On a religious level, Islam has been accepted into Nigerian public space through Islamic Law. Gwaza explains that this is due to "Islamic person status, Sharia Courts of Appeal in the constitution, accreditation of Sharia law by the National Universities Commission, and other education regulatory bodies in Nigeria."[126] Public institutions and government agencies, such as hospitals, schools, and secretariats, now have civil servants wearing religious garb like the hijab alongside or on top of recommended official clothing.

[123] See UNICEF, "Monitoring the Situation of Children and Women," UNICEF, April 2020, http://data.unicef.org/topic/child-protection/child-marriage/.
[124] This link leads to a different article, and I can't find Raja's article. Debolina Raja, "9 Health Risks and Realities of Teenage Pregnancy," www.momjunction.com/articles/health-risks-of-teenage-pregnancy_00377831/#gref. Accessed February 17, 2019.
[125] Mohammed Ibrahim, "Child Marriage in Northern Nigeria," Nigerian Reporter, August 20, 2016, http://nigerianreporter.com/2016/08/20/child-marriage-in-northern-nigeria-nigerian-newspaper/.
[126] Ibid., 8.

A recent case that caused much uproar was when Amasa Firdaus, a law school student, insisted on wearing her hijab during her call-to-bar ceremony. The school originally refused to allow her to participate in the ceremony while wearing the hijab, and the Muslim Students' Society of Nigeria claimed that denying her access would deny her rights. A similar incident led to the closure of Ibadan International School, a government-owned institution, when Muslim parents campaigned to allow their children to use the hijab. In Nigeria, the religious cannot be separated from the political. The country's institutions should be as secular as its constitution.

The political climate of Nigeria itself is pluralistic. The nation is a social project, established through socialization processes anchored on culture and its expressive frames.[127] The political domain of a nation, which is an expression of its political institution, is affected by its level of cultural diversity. As the socialization processes governing social order become more polycentric, diverse, and competing interests are created at an increasing rate. These interests are drawn along cultural, ethnic, and religious lines, and they compete for representation, power, and other social benefits that can only be acquired through political agency. This creates the condition of pluralism, the existence of varied and contending interests. These and their actualizations are signifiers of "democratic equilibrium"[128] and true democracy – not electoral democracy alone.

Political elites in Nigeria, those who are responsible for regime change and the renewal of the elite executive class, develop social order and form alliances that are underscored by ethnic ties, interests, and cultural affinities. Political groups, such as the parties providing candidates that populate core political offices, are guided by cultural and ethnic sentiments when making appointments to positions that Kifordu defines as "the echelon of the national political power structure where major policy decisions are taken and where control lies over the treasury."[129] For example, the North and the Hausa–Fulani politicians have enjoyed the largest number of political executive offices since the 1950s.[130] From the 1999 transition to a democratic government up until 2019, there have been one western, two northern, and a southern representative occupying the presidency through about five democratic elections. Kifordu's work shows a decline in Hausa–Fulani presence from 37 percent to 30.5 percent, and an incremental increase in the Yoruba presence from 17 percent

[127] Colombo Maddalena, "Introduction: Pluralism in Education and Implications for Analysis," *Italian Journal of Sociology of Education* 5, no. 2 (2013): 1–16. See also, Di P. Maggio, "Culture and Cognition," *Annual Review of Sociology* 23 (1997): 263–287.
[128] Maddalena, "Pluralism in Education," 2.
[129] Kifordu, "Political Elite Composition and Democracy," 17.   [130] Ibid.

to 29 percent.[131] APC, the incumbent party, and their most powerful opposition, PDP, still fielded two Northerners as presidential candidates, showing that Northerners still hold an advantage.

This is a testament to the state's political ambience and the character of the executive elite, who rest largely on political patronage. Patronage ensures continuity, and continuity demands that the "recruitment of the political elite from ethnic groups is ultimately dependent on the institutional power and resources of the chief executive, which stems from both formal and informal sources."[132] As Kifordu rightly asserts, the Hausa–Fulani have dominated the elite executive throughout Nigeria's political history, beginning at independence in 1960.

The Northern ethnic group's influence has been continuous for many reasons, but one of them is the patronage system embedded in the executive system of democracy. Institutionalized forms of patronage bestow advantages to individuals from one's own ethnic group, a kind of retrogressive politics at play in Nigeria's political terrain; institutions are maintained through biased party systems: Kifordu states that the political parties formed since independence have been predicated on ethnic leadership support. After the election of Muhammadu Buhari, there was public criticism asserting that his appointments favored the North. As of 2016, Northerners headed fourteen of the seventeen security agencies, and most of them were appointed by President Buhari. The presidency claims that substantive ministerial positions have been given to individuals from the South-east region, but a quick glance at the current cabinet shows better representation for Northerners than for other regional or ethnic groups. This is inevitable since the Constitution demands that there must be a cabinet representative from each state and the North has nineteen of the thirty-six states!

Another fitting example is the character of early Nigeria's political nature after colonialism, or since decolonization (1951–60): "The National Party of Nigeria and Cameroon (NCNC-East), the National People's Congress (NPC-North) and the Action Group (AG-West), all of which are the earliest political groups, emerged and grew from the three major ethnic groups (Igbo, Hausa-Fulani and Yoruba)."[133] Now there are close to ninety-one registered political parties. As of October 2018, Punch Newspaper reported on information given by the INEC National Chairman, head of the body responsible for regulating electoral practices in the nation. Professor Mahmood Yakubu, INEC head, reported that about seventy-three political parties are fielding presidential candidates for the 2019 presidential elections – a glaring difference from the initial

---

[131] Ibid., 24.   [132] Ibid., 25.   [133] Ibid.

three political parties that sprung up in the '60s. As of December, the number dwindled to thirty-five.[134]

Although the earliest practice of democracy after colonialism included principal continuity criteria and a patronage system that favored an ethnic-centered pattern – a pattern where executive elite continuity was maintained through strong ethnic ties and party-sustaining affiliations were drawn along cultural lines – there have been significant changes allowing for more inclusiveness in the representation of ethnic groups in political parties. In the nation's current political climate, the two top political parties (APC and PDP) both fielded Northerners (Mohammadu Buhari and Atiku Abubakar, respectively) as presidential candidates. However, Yemi Osinbajo (a Western Yoruba) and Peter Obi (an Eastern Igbo) are their running mates, creating an image of equal and substantive representation and inclusiveness in the political elite structure. The presidency of Olusegun Obasanjo, 1999–2007, had Yoruba and Hausa–Fulani representation; his vice president was a northerner.

The Buhari administration pointed to a shift in political orientation toward the kind of pluralism that is effective and pivotal to the nation's democracy. These parties are mostly representative of the major ethnic group, and they still perpetuate the hegemony of one group over others, but inter-ethnic affiliations and compromises have been made. A federal structure, however faulty, has been adopted and maintained to afford equal, substantive equality for the various cultures and facilitate the true purpose of pluralism or liberal pluralism, which emphasizes equality in participation. This present state agrees with Kifordu's conception of liberal pluralism, observing that "transformation in the elite power structure depends on periodic renewals, i.e. the entrance of new persons and ideas as regimes and resources change."[135] In Nigeria, the renewal recycles the same people using newer platforms. Interest, not ideology, has become the binding force in place of more glaring ethnic ties.

True pluralism should culminate in a federal structure, but Nigeria practices a type of federalism that is a far cry from this. Federal attempts to encourage integration and unity in diversity are only applied in theory. Boko Haram terrorists are given amnesty, but Indigenous People of Biafra (IPOB) are labeled as terrorists by the present administration; it is an indication of ethnic favoritism in defiance of the law. The menace of Northern herdsmen, who are responsible for a series of killings across the

---

[134] Samson Toromade, "List of Presidential Candidates Contesting in Next Year's Election," last modified, December 29, 2018, www.pulse.ng/news/politics/2019-preseidentila-elections-list-of-presidential-candidates-contesting-in-next-years'/3w287 c1//.
[135] Kifordu, "Political Elite Composition and Democracy," 16.

country, is treated with apparent levity – beginning with the present administration's refusal to identify them as terrorizing forces within the nation, and the political gimmicks of denial and blame games.

The present administration attempts to splinter the country further through insensitive laws and bills. Although the country should be a federation, the National Grazing Reserves Bill attempts to serve a specific ethnic group through injustice, ethnic meddling, inequality, and territorial infringement. The bill, sponsored by APC Senator Rabiu Musa Kwankwaso, Kano-central, has the potential to dispossess people of their land and cede it to the Hausa–Fulani, the group known for cattle herding. The assumption is that this bill, coming at a time when herders are killing farmers, ought to be the solution to violence between the Hausa–Fulani herdsmen and farmers in the country. However, it has all the markings of a political attempt to give preference to one ethnic group over others.

The National Grazing Reserves Bill provides occasions to map out grazing routes all over the country, and a commission would be created to implement it. The commission's work would deny many ethnic groups the use of their lands, invalidating the character of a true federation where regions are equally protected by a governing center that allows some measure of autonomy. Ultimately, the resources of other regions and ethnicities would be harnessed to serve a specific group of elites in power. It contradicts the constitution, which assigns power to each state to hold land. The bill is rejected on multiple fronts as anti-people, but the fact that this bill has surfaced is another testament to the ill state of pluralism in the country. It challenges the state–federal principle that holds a federation together.

Incidents like these are manifestations of ethnic distrust and hegemonic tendencies in the country. They also reveal the ties between religious biases and political conflicts. Such conflicts can spread beyond their ethnic and religious origins to become full-scale political conflicts. Parties tout superficial integration, cloaking their ethnic sentiments with a veneer of legitimacy, meaning that tensions can erupt, and political conflicts can break out on any possible occasion. The crises plaguing the 2019 Nigerian elections are examples of how true political pluralism is absent.

The Independent National Electoral Commission (INEC) postponement of the presidential elections, announced on the eve of the event, was a result of political violence that led up to election day. Attacks in some Nigerian states, just a few days before the election, destroyed important materials that included permanent voter cards, voting cubicles, card readers, and ballot boxes. In Plateau State, INEC offices were burned to the ground alongside materials for presidential and national assembly elections. Similar incidents occurred in Anambra and Abia States, constituting major setbacks that culminated in postponement of the election. In Benue, the vehicle conveying INEC materials was attacked.

These incidents display the political instability present in an unhealthy political system where democracy is lost and ethnicity, nepotism, and distrust run rampant. In Nigeria, political parties are a means of committing national sabotage and renewing elite interests at the expense of the populace. Pluralist initiatives like multiparty systems are agenda-driven instruments of discord instead of vital supports for democracy. They have resulted in violent clashes of opposition parties at rallies in Yola, Lagos, Bayelsa, Kano, Akwa Ibom, Adamawa, and all over the country. Careful scrutiny always implicates the two main parties, APC and PDP, along with their loyalists.

The dialogue and diplomacy that are associated with democracy, and required for its practice, are absent in the Nigerian political sphere, especially during the public campaigns and rallies when they are needed the most. Conferences that build dialogues, and pledges to avoid exploiting divisions for personal gain, along with the legal redress of grievances in ways that do not resort to inflammatory rhetoric, especially in areas prone to conflict – all these are absent. Security Report identified 181 election-related deaths that occurred between October 2018 and February 2019, stemming from recurring violence fueled by party politics. The Southwest had 17.5 percent of the general crises, Northwest 3.5 percent, Southeast, 3.5 percent, South, 35.7 percent, Northcentral, 31.6 percent, and Northeast had 8.2 percent of the election deaths counted.[136]

Although Nigeria is a pluralist country in terms of culture, religion, and ethnicity, it does not have pluralist policies that encourage democracy, the policies that are most needed, because of the political divide caused by religious and ethnic sentiments. Politics in Nigeria involve pluralist agencies, but they do not rely on the theories of pluralism. Nigeria experiences incomplete pluralism.

Way Forward: How Pluralism Can Work in Nigeria

Moving pluralism from theory to practice, especially in an unstable poly-cultural atmosphere like Nigeria, would encounter significant difficulties. However, it can be accomplished through genuine democratic governance. One way to address the problems arising from multiple cultures

---

[136] I can't find a link for this. *Gatefield*, "Security Report: Election Related Death Toll Rises to 181 in Nigeria," *Gatefield*, 2009.

interacting in a broader nationalist framework is to work with Ejobowah's prescription of "designing political arrangements around groups."[137] Political agendas and their execution should be framed around existing groups – cultural, religious, ethnic, political, and even gender groups – to foster an environment of mutual trust, respect, and shared heritage where all parties are actively involved in the political process. This would ensure the cross-sectional involvement of multiple groups, and it would lead to legitimacy and transparency of process. It could even entrench a dialogic spirit, akin to democracy, that gets projects executed efficiently. The feeling of inclusiveness engendered by such strategies would enshrine the practice of accountability; each group would be held responsible for the role they play in democracy. Transparency is enthroned, and sabotage, propaganda, inflammatory rhetoric, ulterior motives, and political scheming are discouraged.

Normative consensus is birthed in and through such processes of collectivity. Normative consensus, owing to its collective impulse, enhances the deployment of those democratic practices that are pivotal to the pluralistic network needed in Nigeria. The cultivation of a supportive public culture – another avenue toward true pluralism – can elevate shared values and conventionalize them as norms in a way of establishing normative consensus. Seeking normative consensus will have direct consequences for several organs of society that react positively to it.

Education is a sure means for engineering pluralist philosophies and integrative policies that can be instilled and injected into society and members of the body polity. Education can secure a pluralist system. Integrated diversity, or unity in diversity, could be pursued at early stages; this collapses "the differentiation between institutions [that] originates from specific sub-cultures, each showing its own specificity, interpretational code, and mode of functioning."[138] Out of many things, the school is a reflection of the society, or what Maddalena calls the "main prototype of an organization, one that is based on culture, made of culture and generates culture."[139] Hostility and intolerance, and other forms of cultural distrust and disrespect between ethnicities, can be handled in pluralist and instructive spaces, such as educational institutions. Qualities and ideas of nationalism, integration, ethnic coexistence, and tolerance of differences, as well as heterogeneity, can be encouraged to create an inclusive system of governance. Nationalist sentiments, loyalty, unity in diversity, and ethnic tolerance and a spirit of accommodation are some of the principles that can be instilled in younger members of society.

---

[137] Ejobowah, "Political Recognition of Ethnic Pluralism," 1.
[138] Maddalena, "Pluralism in Education," 1.   [139] Ibid., 3.

Programs of national consciousness and integration, like the needed National Youth Service Corps program, should be consciously encouraged, implemented, and judiciously funded and managed. They are a means toward a nationalistic, political end. Other programs that foster inter-ethnic interaction and awareness should be at the forefront of the Nigerian budget.

Having citizens of the body polity belong to multiple political groups or different organizations with political significance would dissuade selfish interests. By belonging to religious and political groups, and by having other sociocultural affiliations, those holding sensitive positions in the highest national hierarchies would dissolve the one-sided affiliation or hydra-headed ethnicity problems wrecking the nation's democracy. A display of balanced interests affects whatever bills or policies are advanced and implemented.

Providing capital, infrastructure, and other assets that allow members of society to become members of such organizations is a process guaranteed to facilitate this strategy. But it can only be done by providing members of society with enough capital and opportunities to pursue multiple group membership, which requires economic policies targeted to alleviate the burden of meeting Nigeria's cost of living. Fiscal policies, financial plans, and reform strategies and sensitization plans developed on a national scale and aimed at the grassroots and the middle class can provide the infrastructure needed to foster multiple group membership. The absolute identities of the party system – the principal sources of political agency that are immobilized by religious and ethnic chokeholds – would be tempered. It would weaken the ethnic or kinship influences that covertly direct parties to serve elite interests.

Regionalism and true federalism are effective ways for practicing pluralism beyond existence of many ethnic groups. A regional government, where power is de-centralized and shared between regions, is a way to assure ethnicities and states of their relevance and autonomy, especially in a national construct where power seems to be directed by a small number of elites. Regionalism has not fulfilled its purpose in the region, as can be seen in the Niger Delta crisis and the menace of the Fulani herdsmen.

The Niger Delta region claims to be sidelined when its oil resources are allocated; the activity that creates profits from oil is also responsible for environmental degradation that wrecks the region through oil spillage, gas flares, and water pollution. Taking a region's mineral resources while denying that region the benefit of the proceeds – especially when those proceeds are shared with other regions at the expense of the host community – is no different from an incursion and a disregard for democracy.

Claims of inequality originating from those who live in the Niger Delta region are not spurious; the neglect of an oil-producing region during revenue allocation is a product of a faulty constitution and fake federalism. In the words of Edewor et al., "[t]he undemocratic 1999 federal constitution lacks the support of the citizens. The constitution was drafted by military dictators and handed over to the people. It has not gone far enough to resolve the problems of ethnicity that the country has faced since independence."[140] A huge part of the problem stems from a lack of proper implementation, shortsighted political visions, and bad governance.

Shortsighted political vision is a consequence of politicians harboring do-or-die outlooks, seeing elections as opportunities to remove opponents and entrench grand ethnic schemes. Nigeria's political parties require a shift in ideologies and principles; organizing philosophies should have more cosmopolitan outlooks. Debate, campaigns, and dialogues should stem from real economic and political strategies, not from empty hate or inflammatory talk with agendas that have no real effect on the nation. It means that points of convergence and divergences between political parties should not be anchored on elite interests, ethnicity, religion, or kinship ties. The masquerade of fake alliances should be replaced by practical policies and democratic philosophies, along with implementable fiscal plans and other signifiers of a conservative or liberal political economy. Fickle alliances are the reasons why party members jump ship and parties are splintered into many cells.

More importantly, unity should be encouraged. Heterogeneity should be promoted over homogeneity; this can be done through a feasible federal character. The classical form of pluralism cannot work in Nigeria, but a form can be implemented that accounts for its strengths and weaknesses, the converging points and shared interests of cultures. It can work if it is coupled with regionalism, where each region is allowed to develop measures of autonomy in a democratic setting, and a federal structure that distributes power between the regions and a center, held together by a binding constitution that is appropriate.

---

[140] Edewor, "Managing Ethnic and Cultural Diversity," 74.

5   Religious Identities

Introduction

One of the basic characteristics of religion resides in its persuasive capacity to structure a common identity among people who recognize themselves as belonging to the same faith. People often accept their religion as a means of identification to the extent that other indices of separation or difference are blurred or considered as unimportant in their interrelationships. Naturally, therefore, people who find themselves in different religious identities do consciously or otherwise understand that something that they identify with and rely on makes them unique from others who belong to another identity or hold different values. For these people, it is morally binding on them to follow the directions and instructions laid out from their religious institutions, as this remains the only proof that they are committed to the course of their religion. Meanwhile, there is a long history of struggles among different religious sects to recruit and retain members so as to extend their influence. Consequently, various religious persuasions have become extremely strong in the country with sometimes overbearing attitude. In Nigeria, religion continues to dictate several actions and activities.

Quite a number of anti-state involvements, which deserve national dissuasion, if not complete abhorrence, have escaped necessary harsh reactions because of the religious coloration that they are embroiled in. Thus, religious identities in Nigeria have become an integral part of the country's national political culture that is difficult to separate from the general condition of the country. The deep-seated assumption that religion is usually controlling or sometimes meddling with political issues finds its validity in Nigeria, as religious differences have become the most fearful indicator of national unrest. Although religious differences are only an ill wind that does no one any good, religious differences have not come without their comforting benefits irrespective of their capacity to trigger contradictions. Despite the minimal advantage that religious identities have ensured in national growth, however, they have remained one of the nastiest impediments to the collective advancement of the country. The rate at which growing religious identities continue to influence the socioeconomic and sociopolitical landscape remains very alarming. This is principally because many conflicts ordinarily spring up and are given religious coloration even when they are triggered by or for nonreligious reasons. As a result, efforts at national development are impaired by incessant religious conflicts in a way that threaten not only the political condition of the country, but also its economic power.

Historical Formation of Religious Identities

There is a growing literature on religious identities and the corresponding political and social impacts they make in the Nigerian environment, and this suggests that religion and its identity formation process has become a worthy national debate.[1] While the majority of these research engagements have indicated that the plural religious identities are potentially indicted by their involvement in bubbling altercations that are capable of crushing the collective peace, quite a number of them do not provide the historical overview of the religious identities in the country. Subsequent upon this, this segment of the chapter is dedicated to a short historical review of the spread of religion and its consequences. Obviously, the current religious pluralities in the country date back to the beginning of Euro-Arabic expansionism and influence where people accepted the world religions. Subsequently, their spread became ubiquitous, and Nigeria became one of the countries where both religions spread remarkably well. Since the underlying reason for their expansion was the extension of their sociocultural and sociopolitical influence, the two dominant religions, Christianity and Islam, became competitors in shaping religious identities.

In what would be explored subsequently, religious identities in Nigeria have ethnic persuasions, making it a complex web of social and political phenomena using the platform of religion to pursue hegemonic agendas.[2] Islam has been used to construct the idea of a homogenous North. The North, for example, is also divided along class lines: the aristocratic elite and the economically deprived lower structure, the poor, known as the *Talakawa*. Given the closeness of Northern geography to countries

---

[1] See the long-standing book by Toyin Falola and Hassan Mathew Kukah, *Religious Militancy and Self-Assertion: Islam and Politics in Nigeria* (London: Avebury, 1996); and Pat Williams and Toyin Falola, *Religious Impact on the Nation State: The Nigerian Predicament* (London: Avebury, 1995).
[2] Ibid.

already influenced by Islam, the extension of commercial transactions and other networks of relationships led to the spread of Islam.[3] Islamic influence spread over several centuries, ultimately creating a religious identity that serves as a unifying force and reinforces the class structures already in existence.

The existing indigenous religion in the North put forward strong resistance that threatened the adaptive strategy already embraced by the elite class. Resistance was inevitable for a community that was principally divided along class lines where the occupiers of the lower rung were exploding in huge numbers. However, the commitment of the ruling class was irrevocable as it seemed to be prepared with unprecedented determination that was bent on incorporating the new religion into the social structure of the Northern society. For Islam to therefore gain additional attention and power, it was necessary for Muslims to take over important positions in the political system of the extraction so that the institutions of Islam would sweep contenders and win doubters to its side in the end. For more than three centuries, the elite schemed potential frameworks and strategies to assist in making Islam an incontestable religion grafted to the political establishment. As a result, Muslim administrations and their institutions got additional recognition through the *ulama*, the clerics, ultimately involved in spreading the religion to different government departments and their leadership. At various times, different clerics of the religion campaigned for the absolute embrace of Islam, therefore influencing the people to abandon their indigenous religions. At the end, the incorporation of Islam into the region comes with the advantage of creating a political-cum-religious identity.

Conversely, the time when Islam was spreading with amazing speed in the North coincided with the time when the influence of Christianity was being planted in the Southern region of the country that covers many groups. These groups include the Edo, Ijo, Yoruba, and Igbo ethnic extractions. Apparently, Western evangelical and theocratic departments had set out on a mission to expand their geographical space to extend their ecumenical influence. West Africa seemed to become the cynosure of interests that sought to explore the opportunities available in the continent's region with a view to establishing the Christian faith. The assurance of success, therefore, became the driving force of the evangelists and they became emboldened to pursue their religious agenda. In what would seem like a joint effort between the notable Europeans who were averse to slavery and its destructive

---

[3] Olufemi Vaughan, *Religion and the Making of Nigeria* (Durham: Duke University Press, 2016).

influence, the evangelical assignment of the missionaries was corroborated by figures who were doubling as European merchants with specific interests in economic exploration, or exploitations, of the continent. Their synergy therefore produced inaugural results measured in the establishment of a missionary group called the Church Missionary Society (CMS). The combined interests of these two groups proved particularly important to the establishment of the Christian identity in Nigeria.

With moderate influence by the Sierra Leone Christian missionaries who extended it to Nigeria, it became obvious that the geographical concession of Western Nigeria to Christianity would mean that the country which would later be merged by Lord Lugard would be defined by various religious identities. Samuel Ajayi Crowther, who was a liberated slave from Sierra Leone, alongside a German missionary, Reverend Jacob Friederichs Schon, established a strong bond that enhanced the continuation of the Christian gospel in Nigeria. Fortunately, their religious campaigns were accepted by the colonialists, who consolidated their quest for spreading the gospel by creating the enabling environment. Samuel Ajayi Crowther – with appreciable understanding of the people's culture because of his cultural identity – became a reckoning voice in the propagation of the Christian faith in Southern Nigeria. As such, the agency of Usman Dan Fodio – with his overwhelming influence in the establishment of Islamic institutions in the North – and that of the figures from the South, a combination of Ajayi Crowther and his English accessories, was notably apparent in the formulation of religious identities in Nigeria.

On the flip side, however, the indigenous religious institutions were available, with heterogeneous identity, before the ascension of the external propagation of the alien religions of Christianity and Islam. It is important to reiterate the argument that indigenous religious identities are themselves plural, and this fact was tied to the religious tolerance of the precolonial African world, whose beliefs about the "cosmic intelligence" do not entertain hegemonic evaluation of others or their inferiorization. Therefore, every group making up the country had its different religious views and philosophies it practiced in its own environment for ages based on in-group convictions. This presupposes the idea that the provision of nominal identity on the African belief systems, known today under the aegis of African Traditional Religion (ATR), was relatively recent, and it was created because of the sociopolitical necessity to prevent unnecessary controversy usually sparked by religious fundamentalists. Despite the statistical evidence that the country is religiously demarcated along the Christian and Muslim lines, there is growing evidence that corroborates the idea that African Traditional Religion still enjoys patronage and expansion.

Figure 5.1 Christians at a ceremony in Northern Nigeria.

Clusters of Religious Identities

The construction of identity predominantly in Nigerian recent history has added religion to the available indices of representation.[4] In other words, belongingness in the country has taken the dimension of religion around the typology of Islam, Christianity, and African Traditional Religion. Notably, these identities are necessitated by diverse sociocultural and sociopolitical influences attached to each group. Except for ATR, the other two expressions of religion have experienced massive political mobilization in their colonial and postcolonial conditions, and the tendency to attract several advantages has continued to dictate the need for belonging to a particular religious group, even if one does not show any membership commitments. For a country that is as diverse and culturally heterogeneous as Nigeria, bearing any mark of religious identity comes with sufficient benefits. By identifying with a religious group, people become qualified to enjoy some sociopolitical benefits that are attached to the group. In fact, it is based on this understanding that various denominations begin to expand, and new ones are formed for similar

---

[4] Toyin Falola and Chukwuemeka Agbo, "Nigeria," in *The Routledge Handbook to Religion and Political Parties*, ed. Jeffrey Haynes (London and New York: Routledge, 2020), 298–310.

purposes. It would be exposed soon as how different expressions, even of the same religion, become a modern divisive tool for political purposes.

Islam

Islam is a religious identity with group members across the country with their conviction in the identity and a commitment to remain steadfast to the philosophies of the religion. The adherents of this faith are generally guided by the ecumenical regulations identified by Islamic laws, the Sharia. Islam, especially with the ways it is being practiced by a few groups, seems to be opposed to many modifications as the general understanding is that Islam is inherently perfect, immune to evolution, and with an unnegotiated absolutism. Because of this, therefore, among those people (sometimes labeled in the media as "extremists"), Islam is now synonymous with immobility as it resists every effort for updating it. The attending tensions arising from this absolutism usually manifest in the constant contestations among adherents of different faiths which always result in infractions and eventually create fragmented relationships. Islam is practiced predominantly in Northern Nigeria because of the region's historical antecedents and experience. Their relationship spanned centuries and their proximity to countries that are grounded in Islamic theocracy foregrounds their reason for massively taking a side or identifying the religion as their domestic source of identity.

Christianity

Another religious identity that Nigerians intimately connect with is Christianity. Usually, there are more Southern adherents of this religion than there are Northern, and this is not unconnected to the South's historical past that brought missionary relationships that saw to the establishment of Christian institutions and philosophies in the South. Just like the Islamic religion, Christianity has developed into different sub-identities, although with a common creed. The mutation into various subgroups, which had occurred for centuries, was connected to the political behavior of the country that seems to encourage multiple identities. The struggle for converts in the country remains intense because there are possibilities for getting social and political acknowledgment depending on the population control of each religion. However, the Christian South appears to be less forceful in their campaign for religious adherents compared to what obtains among the Muslims in the North. Other than the fact that the Pentecostal extremism of Nigerian Christianity takes a supremacist approach to ensure the maximum control of members and an instrument of sensitization for the yet-to-be-impressed fencists, Christianity presents itself as a better organized religious identity in the country. The commanding influence of Christianity in the region is built on the contemporary realities of the then-Southern environment that was shaped by wars and conflicts, such as the Biafran war of 1967 to 1970. Both the Muslim and Christian missionaries continue to compete.

African Traditional Religion (ATR)

Logically, this religious identity remains the oldest, even though the officialization of its identity coincided with the time that external religions came to contend for its space. The religion is different in style and approach. Unlike others, ATR does not demonstrate any possibility to evangelize millions of people. Its development over time has been borne out of personal interest of the adherents, rather than their being influenced by any evangelical movement. Given the fact that ATR was considered an inherited identity, it did not, and does not, struggle to attract worshippers as the Muslims and Christians do. Even though there are swelling numbers of Christians and Muslims in the country, there are a majority of these two who secretly parade the ATR because of a consensus that it is their origin that cannot be entirely separated from them.[5] Over this assumption, there are very many Nigerians who seek urgent assistance from the religion in cases of emergencies and do not consider that as inhibitive of their Christian or Muslim identity. Because of the pressure to become a recognized and organized identity in the postcolonial environment, ATR has elected to adopt this popular identity.

What remains undeniable is the understanding that the cluster of these religious structures or identities is informed by the rise of missionary evangelism and Islamic jihad that made conversions into them a competitive exercise. Ever since the two missionary religions surfaced in the continent, there has risen the necessity to fashion out an identity with religious persuasions and permutations. Consequently, the politics and commerce of the Nigerian people have been dictated continuously by the various religious identities. With the installation of Muslim clerics in Northern Nigeria and the collaboration of British imperialism aiding the expansionist missionaries in their religious agenda, the Nigerian sociopolitical environment was set for

---

[5] Luis Lugo, "Tolerance and Tension Islamic and Christianity in Sub-Saharan African," *Pew Research Center*, April 15, 2020, www.pewforum.org/2010/04/15/executive-summary-islam-and-christianity-in-sub-saharan-africa/.

the enthronement of competition in religious politics and other aspects of their national existence. Except for the recent reincarnation of ATR in diplomatically competing for its rightful position and having understood the privileges and sympathy accorded to the other religions, ATR was secluded exclusively from taking part in national affairs. This means that the privileges enjoyed by both Christianity and Islam became the rallying reason behind ATR's challenge for relevance.

Religious Associations in Nigeria

Soon, the societal growth of the available religions in the country would be determined by their structural power since the primary focus of these external religions was to achieve unimaginably high popularity and patronage. Sequel to this, therefore, the stage for competition rouses religious permutations from different religious groups in the country, as the basic precondition to achieving their aims was to develop a structure useful for the enhancement of their ascension to sociopolitical power. As Nigeria was moving forward after independence, various religious identities were seeking to consolidate power by way of the perversion of mutual distrust from others. Different denominations of these religions therefore forged a formidable bond to establish a foundation that would guide their activities generally and protect their interests in situations where they are exposed to some threatening circumstances. Hence, there are religious associations like the Christian Association of Nigeria (CAN), Muslim Rights Concern (MURIC), Pentecostal Fellowship of Nigeria (PFN), the Shiites, the Sunnis, Nigerian Supreme Council for Islamic Affairs (NSCIA), Muslim Students' Society (MSS) of Nigeria, Jama'atu Nasril Islam or Society for the Support of Islam, Ahmadiyya Muslim Community, Ansar-ud-Deen Society Nigeria, and Nasrul-lahi-li Fathi Society of Nigeria (NASFAT). Amidst the popular religious groups are the ones identified previously in Nigeria.

The Christian Association of Nigeria (CAN)   At the inception of this religious group in Nigeria, there were thirteen denominations representing two major Christian blocs: the Catholics and the Protestants.[6] The formation of this religious group, CAN, was benchmarked on an assumption of ecumenical purity where the merger of politics with religious activities would enhance their theological and social growth. Creating a union as such was considered an official registration of their

[6] Iheanyi M. Enwerem, *A Dangerous Awakening: The Politicization of Religion in Nigeria* (Ibadan: Institut français de recherche en Afrique, 1995).

presence, and this would facilitate consolidation of their religious existence with political decisions. The membership of CAN was restrictive
because the ideological focus of the group was resistant to churches which
are too liberal or too materialistic in their outlook. Thus, CAN experienced some contradictions at the incubation stage of its identity formation. The group was even challenged by various Christian organizations
whose demands for membership were not granted. As the controversy for
membership of CAN became heightened, the religious identity therefore
reconsidered reviewing its membership policies to accommodate other
Christian denominations, despite their doctrinal variances. Perhaps for
reasons that are political, very many other Christian identities, irrespective of their ideological or theological reservations, considered joining
CAN for underlying sociopolitical benefits.[7]

Pentecostal Fellowship of Nigeria (PFN)   PFN is another Christian
religious identity that shares a similar theocratic philosophy with CAN,
but seeks to pursue its evangelical agenda using different approaches and
means. Against the group's denial into CAN membership, PFN developed as an alternative organization seeking to establish its values and
agenda through mature coordination and organization. Without making
these efforts, it was becoming prohibitively challenging for a group that
professes the same religion as another group to decide to shut them out of
possible collaboration. Instructively, these religious identities were by
then getting some ethnic coloration because of the heterogeneity of the
country that creeps into every activity that has a national persuasion. PFN
charges itself as the body that coordinates the activities of Pentecostal,
Evangelical, and Charismatic ministries to enhance internal unity and
sustain the pursuance of interest under a common religious creed and
identity.

Shiism/Sunni   Shiism and Sunni are the two predominant subdivisions that arose from the core Islamic culture. While the former
precisely believes in the supremacy of the Prophet Muhammad and
fundamentally supports the religious injunctions of the prophet about
his pronouncement of succession on Ali ibn Abi Talib, the latter group
shares a different perspective. Otherwise known as Shia Islam, anyone
who is bound by the creed of this group is referred to as a Shiite. Their
theocratic ideology is characterized by the belief in the Prophet and the

---

[7] Toyin Falola, "Christian Radicalism and Nigerian Politics," in *Dilemmas of Democracy in Nigeria*, eds. Paul A. Beckett and Crawford Young (Rochester: University of Rochester Press, 1997), 265–282.

successor he bequeathed the Islamic leadership prior to his demise, who is believed to be Ali ibn Abi Talib. The foundation of controversy that led to the formulation of the two basic identities identified above came from the differences in the understanding of this particular injunction. It seems, however, that the demarcation between the members of these two groups is political when closely considered. The leadership of Islam was designated to be Ali and his followers, called Shiites, who profoundly supported his mandate, irrespective of the ensuing contradictions that it brought. On the other hand, however, the Sunni are another Islamic identity in Nigeria that shares the universal ideologies of Sunnism. Principally, the Muslims under this canopy refuse to share the conviction of Shiites about any designation of Islamic leadership to Ali after Prophet Muhammad's death. They reject generally the idea that Ali was a legitimate successor of their Prophet. Without swerving from the attention on their prophet, this group accepts and internalizes all actions and engagements of the Prophet Muhammad.

Muslim Rights Concern (MURIC)   MURIC is a human rights organization that seeks to promote, protect, and defend the rights and interests of Muslims in Nigeria against suppression and instances of intimidation. The foundation of this organization is linked to the general understanding that religious affairs deserve to be given increased organization through the formulation of appropriate institutions that could be directed to the promotion of their national interests in both a political and social sense. Unlike Sunnism and Shiism, which were created from the conviction of variegated ideologies, MURIC seeks to speak for all Muslims in Nigeria if they are within the umbrella of Islam. However, there are indications that MURIC seeks to gain equal political recognition as other religious groups in the country because of its sometimes-extreme measures in speaking about issues that concern the Nigerian religious setting. For the group, pursuing the Islamic agenda was primary and important because the identity of Islam appears to take precedence over every other issue of national or public emergency. MURIC seems to be rid of ethnic concerns, as their mandate has shown their preference for anything Islamic uncolored by sentiment surrounding ethnic or political affiliation. Generally, however, MURIC is an expression of religious philosophies seeking to be recognized in Nigeria as equally important.

Jama'atu Nasril Islam or Society for the Support of Islam (JNI)
Founded after the Premier, Alhaji (Sir) Ahmadu Bello (Sardauna of Sokoto), an erstwhile leader of the Northern region, returned from a pilgrimage to Mecca, JNI was created to undertake Islamic crusade

through the proper organization of the affairs of Muslims and their social engagements. The spread of Islamic teachings was the basic reason for founding the group, and its beginning was necessary to aid the expansion of Islamic culture. As the founder was from the Northern part of the country, its headquarters were situated in Kaduna, where they began the process of sociocultural integration of the religion. Just like other groups of religious making, JNI sought to represent the Muslims within the country's sociopolitical space so that their interests would be catered for and managed accordingly.

Other Muslim groups that are popular in the country are the Ahmadiyya Muslim Community, Muslim Students' Society (MSS) of Nigeria, Ansar-ud-Deen Society of Nigeria, and Nasrul-lahi-li Fathi Society of Nigeria (NASFAT), all of which represent Muslims and their religious inclinations.

Religious Identities with Intercultural Persuasions

If we are to entertain the propensity of religious groups to be susceptible to infractions, we would begin to problematize religion and its divisive capacity in Nigeria and how it stands to increase contradictions and intensify controversies. By doing this, we would therefore be pitching our tent with scholars who assert that there are intricate connections between identity development and the escalations of tensions in every human society. Obviously, tendency for the clash of interest is palpitatingly high in an environment where struggles dictate the distribution of power and influence. In a multicultural and heterogeneous country like Nigeria, the complexities of identities usually reflect in their national politics, which usually experience a level of division that promotes violence and tensions. Nigeria, therefore, remains a laboratory where varying interests are pushed in competition for national recognition and resource control. The predominant reason for the creation of religious identities in Nigeria is to establish a creed with common interest that will be valuable in pursuing a collective agenda in political, social, and economic development. This becomes obvious from the commitment of group members to their creed even in situations when national interests should take precedence.

More importantly, religious identity in Nigeria seeks to create an intercultural awareness where members are deliberately blind to all other indices of separation. Trading on the shared values and bonded beliefs, religion becomes an instrument for geopolitical mobilization, legitimacy, and a weapon for the promotion of group (oftentimes antithetical to ethnic and national) interests and the allocation or sharing of the commonwealth. In other words, a Yoruba Muslim can sometimes demonstrate a level of loyalty to a Hausa–Fulani Muslim even in issues bordering on the wellness or the well-being of his ethnic members who are not Muslims. The Muslim identity and creed have become an instrument for carving out a different identity that can be insensitive to people's cultural and political persuasions as long as they belong to the same religion. For many reasons, those who identify with the same religion preferably consider internal theocratic rules and philosophies that bind them together with other members as opposed to using their background differences to delineate themselves. As such, creed loyalty can be spotted in members, perhaps in their silence, especially when there arises the need to condemn individuals who have violated some social codes. In some other instances, members of the same religion always stand in defense of other members because they accept their religious identity as another indicator of a different society, and their belongingness is protected by showing solidarity to the members who are confronted with existential challenges.

One fundamental reason behind the creation of identity generally is to enhance control, especially of those with whom we share the identity tag. Apart from cultural identity, which predominantly is determined by accident of birth, there is hardly any identity that does not have its aims and motives. It is within this context that the religious identities in Nigeria would be treated. What is clearly apparent about the identity is their aim to spread their influence across cultures and economic divides so that the members in different categories can be persuaded to support the ideas and values as identified by the group. Therefore, when one sees a Christian or Muslim in Nigeria, one tends to defend or rationalize the activities of members not on the grounds that they have been involved in morally commendable engagements, but because they belong to a common creed; such an action depicts the essence of religious identities. This means that religious groups are fledged out to enhance in-group protection and identification. Hence, the construction of an identity that is founded on religious conviction entails the embracing of diverse groups with which one would be bound to defend and identify even in uncomfortable situations.

Beyond the intercultural persuasion of religious identities in Nigeria is the understanding that any group that is formed to attract members regardless of their cultural and political creed would always stand a higher chance of attaining increased popularity. It is commonly known that members of the same religion usually identify with one another, as would be seen in the modern creation of groups in every situation that involves people of different cultural backgrounds. For example, among Nigerian students, there are Muslim Students Society of Nigeria (MSSN), Campus Christian Fellowships (CCN), Muslim Corpers' Association of Nigeria (MCAN), and Nigeria Christian Corpers' Fellowship (NCCF). The reality, however, that this would become another avenue to expand in membership across the country using the transcultural influence of the formulated group to win converts cannot be overstated. Having realized that the student's demographics, for example, would always expend their energy to expand the control of their religious goals and objectives, identities that are based on religion are used to achieve specific primary objectives.

The growing influence that both Christianity and Islam have gathered in recent history remains an indicator of the usefulness of forming religious identity. They have both consolidated the goodwill enjoyed in the Nigerian sociopolitical space to expand their territorial space and influence. The fact that the spark of any controversy usually attracts interests from different political groups confirms the assumption that Nigeria's claim to secularity can, in some cases, be bogus and unfounded. Very many affairs of national interest have escaped from public access because they are dressed in the toga of religious identities. Equally, there are some other issues of national or sectional politics that however have ignited controversy because different groups decided to introduce religion to politics in order to win the sympathy of their members. Perhaps, when discussing how the power ascribed to religious identities in Nigeria has forced lopsided development, we would examine the underlying dangers inherent in the appropriation of power to different religious groups against national interest. While Christianity and Islam enjoy these privileges, ATR is compelled to take a back seat.

Power Ascription to Religious Identities

One of the most alluring ways to understand the gravity of the power ascribed to religion in Nigeria is to begin by considering the massive amount of money dedicated annually to pilgrimage in the budget of the country. This is perhaps because taking such routes would reveal the sympathy directed toward the religious identities in the country. The dedication of a country's commonwealth to theological support reveals the definition of a "secular" society. In ways that may not be easily explained, the commitment of the national treasury to the pursuance of religious tourism signals everything but indifference to secular politics. According to Gabriel Omoh, the country committed an amount approximating N34.63 billion to pilgrimage in 2008 with pilgrimage to Mecca taking the lion's share while journeys to Israel accounted for the rest.[8] Such statistics, apart from showing that Nigeria excessively treats the Abrahamic religions with some preference, also reveals a disturbing reality about how Nigeria unconsciously supports the creation of additional religious identities and the controversy they birth. Basically, the two popular religions, Christianity and Islam, despite the outward perception of the country as a secular entity, get sufficient financial backings from the national purse to run their affairs, amidst other things. Against this background, therefore, there are increasing conflicts in the country.

Following the recognition of these two religions even in the allocation of national budget, the leaders of these various religious groups tend to dive into politics under the camouflage of religion. They seek to control resources of the state using their population strength. Since 1999, Nigeria's presidency, which primarily includes the president and the vice president, has been decided using religious identities. As such, from 1999–2007, General Olusegun Obasanjo and Atiku Abubakar were the occupants of those positions as the president and the vice president respectively. While the president was from the Christian South, the vice president was a Muslim from the North. Succeeding these two political representatives were Alhaji Umar Yar'adua, deputized by Dr. Goodluck Ebele Jonathan, also with the former as a Muslim from the North and the latter a Christian from the South. And at the death of President Yar'adua, Jonathan, on succeeding him, chose a Muslim from the North as his vice president. This religious permutation seemed to generate less uproar, and also did not attract people's interests until a third force sought to wrestle power from the ruling People's Democratic Party (PDP) in the year 2015. The All Progressives Congress (APC) with the mandate to dislodge the ruling party from the seat of power, was confronted with the problem of choice as they elected to make a Northern Muslim their flag bearer in the 2015 elections. However, they faced the challenge of choosing someone who would deputize him.

Because of the inherent contradictions manifesting in the people's sentiment around religion, it was becoming prohibitively challenging to choose among the available options, especially among those qualified candidates who were Muslims. Importantly, making a wrong choice could jeopardize the collective dream of overtaking power, as voters were essentially sensitive because of the mutual distrust and suspicion around a Muslim–Muslim ticket, or a Christian–Christian choice for the

---

[8] Gabriel Omoh, "Nigeria: Citizens Spend N35 Billion on Pilgrimages," *All Africa*, January 5, 2009, https://allafrica.com/stories/200901051100.html.

positions. Apparently, the choice of Professor Yemi Osinbajo as the vice president, even without any political concession coming from any political party, was informed by the probable sociocultural influence his candidacy would command. In fact, his religious identity became one of the strongest reasons behind his selection, having understood how it would persuade people of different ethnic groups and cultures to give their votes to the two candidates. For those who were unconvinced by the mouthed and touted transformation of the presidential candidate from being a military officer to a democrat, the APC, to convince their Southern electorates, invented a catchy expression to curate their support and sympathy in the imminent elections: "think Osinbajo, vote Buhari." The results of the election revealed that the permutations worked successfully and again validated the assumption that political power is ascribed to religious identities in Nigeria. At different occasions, religion has demonstrated its ability to influence decisions of Nigerians as people are compelled to identify with their religious groups even in areas where it defeats moral reasoning.

Considering the seemingly unending power unconstitutionally accredited to religious identities in Nigeria, it is easily observed from the contrived influence of these societies that Nigeria truly has accepted religious beliefs as another important marker of division. Against this background, there are countless conflicts that have erupted because of clashes of interest in religious and related issues. It is instructive to recognize the influence of British imperialists who handled the political system that allows such a process to be identified generally. The Northern extraction has for centuries been under the control of Islamic culture, and this arrangement remained so even under British leadership, as these colonialists identified that their concession to the religion had a better opportunity for them to control the populace by proxy. This culture became the legacy during the postcolonial Nigeria, which saw to the fortification of the religious identity even beyond the pre-independence era. In fact, the understanding brought from the suspicion that the unchecked allowance of Northern citizens to dominate the political spectrum would come with a costly consequence made Southern Nigerians dive more into the politics of division by creating additional religious groups to compete with the Islamic ones in national politics.

Therefore, the mobilization of religious movements as a negotiating factor for policies and other important national engagements was founded on the belief that religious groups are given a significant recognition and regard even in the constitution. Based on this condition, different responsibilities, which originally should be shouldered by various religious groups, were imposed on the Nigerian government. Consequently, the government is responsible for building mosques and churches that are considered as national interests. Despite laying claims to secularity, the country already undertakes religious responsibilities in a manner that reveals their bias and intent. In fact, the country is engrossed in such religious politics that it becomes exceedingly difficult for many individuals to occupy national political positions without any affiliation to the two major religions. This ideology, however, has perforated into other aspects of Nigerian culture. Jobs, positions, and appointments are allocated based on the religious convictions of Nigerians. Although it is not within this chapter to consider how it is already affecting the progress of the country generally, the gravity of the challenges confronting the country continues to reflect ubiquitous religious permutations. Given these underlying conditions, Nigerians are especially creating additional identities along religious lines because of the propensity for mobilization during national events that, in the end, would bring about the desired outcomes that will change their lives.

Religious Identities and Self-Protection

Arising from the existence of multiple identities are increased tendencies of tension, struggles, and conflicting interests, as well as the need to defend these anomalies when they surface. Struggles are inevitable when there are different interest groups, irrespective of their moral structures that may or may not be averse to belligerent dispositions. Accordingly, the primary instinctual response of humans to competition, or any situation that warrants it, is that of protection of identity, brand, interest group, or integrity. This is usually because the lack of it is an indirect invitation to being marginalized or driven into marginality. Apparently, the situation of religious groups and different identities in Nigeria is one that is descriptive of this simple analogy. In fact, the protective ability residuc in large identity remains one of the strongest reasons for the conviction of members to identify within the same group. Once there are assurances of in-group protection of interests, people tend to flock into an identity camp for various personal reasons, a majority of which are the protection of their interests and the provision of their core demands of life. This undoubtedly coincides with Nigeria's reality within the context of various human identities that can be observed – ethnic, religious, political, and even class.

Depending on the identity group one finds oneself in, the requirement to win support is to show loyalty to them and adhere to their basic principles, even if this is satisfied only in public. One thing is undebatable about group identity, and that is the reality of self-protection. In all groups, regardless of their size and coverage, it is a common provision that reverberates through every form of human identity. In our own case, it is how religion and its protruding identities in Nigeria continue to offer protection to members for self-preservation. It is important that we establish the socioeconomic dimension of Nigeria's susceptibility to the formation of various identities, and how this constitutes the predominant reason for the justification of creating different or additional groups to the existing one. It is alluded previously that the creation of CAN, for example (and its sustenance experienced), encompassed contradictions and controversies because the pioneer founders of the group restricted membership to some sects of the religion due to many factors that they considered important and indispensable to their mission. This led to the sudden resurgence of various other groups even while demanding membership from CAN. Apparently, without the sociopolitical, socioeconomic, or sociocultural values attached to groups like CAN, having an influx of members would be improbable.

What therefore becomes important when discussing religion and its identities is the existence of in-group defenses that members enjoy in political, economic, and cultural affairs. In fact, the protection of individuals belonging to similar religious groups manifests in different dimensions. In the political form, for example, access to positions or the qualification to run for public offices are many times determined by religious membership, such as the one found in the unconstitutional but tacit declaration of a Muslim-Christian candidacy for the office of president. Beyond this level, therefore, this is corroborated by the provision of economic opportunities reserved for members of a particular group. Even when the constitution of the country recognizes a quota formula, for example, the choice of the candidate picked could trigger controversy if the selection process is insensitive to the Christian–Muslim dichotomy that thrives in the country. With the availability of mobs of deliberately underprivileged citizens waiting to be used and mobilized for the agenda of the political elites, Nigeria is always disposed to tension and its needless intensification when political positions are shared without recourse to the different religious identities available in the country. This therefore confirms the assumption that social or political protection of members of a religious group remains one of the incontestable benefits offered to members by these religious groups. Hence, the rationalization behind the competition for new members.

Interestingly, religious groups do not particularly withdraw their support for members on national issues. Even when members are confronted with debilitating anguish manifesting in pervasive hunger, social insecurity like unemployment, and are clinically abandoned, the politicians are still able to frame the conversation in ways that are advantageous to them. Strictly therefore, this signals that the interest of these groups is for mere political relevance or domination, as their aloofness to the challenges of individual members does not create problems for them. For example, it is common knowledge that Nigeria maintains an enviable position in the poverty index, notwithstanding the reality that most of its citizens are overly religious. It therefore betrays the sense of identity stretchable across the different religious groups, as these interest groups are unable to channel their religious powers as vehicles to improve the conditions of their members, at least economically. In fact, by the time we add the rising insecurities in Northern Nigeria in relation to the numbers of Muslim representatives they have in political offices, it is not out of line to talk about religious or identity protection as a mere nomenclature.

The masses, whether during political or sociocultural problems, are always mobilized with a view to protecting their members, especially when they are under prohibitive emergencies. When controversial issues involving different religious groups arise, chiefly Christian–Muslim conflicts, these people are always recruited for the protection of their faith. In very recent history, there was an uproar among some Muslim sects protesting the arrest and the detention of their member, Ibrahim El-Zakzaky. This individual, a leader of the Shiite Muslims, was arrested by the federal government on an allegation of being an accessory to violence in the country and was detained. In reaction to that, a religious group affiliated to Shiism, the Islamic Movement of Nigeria (IMN), condemned the action of the federal government over the continuous detention of its leader, which it considered unlawful and in violation of his citizenship rights.[9] Despite the court injunction given in exoneration of the Islamic leader, it was obvious that the government was unwilling to obey the court's ruling. Given the position of the arrested leader, the face of the faith in Nigeria, the followers decided to take resistant actions as they were convinced that this was the only actionable plan to restore their leader's freedom.

In all, members of the same religious groups in Nigeria are evidently protective. Religious groups are concerned about the safety of their members in national affairs because of the sensitivity to that environment of politics. When instances of religious controversies arise at any time and have national coloration, religious identities usually project the interests of members against what they see as a predation that must be met with

---

[9] Halimah Yahaya, "IMN Replies Presidency, Says Buhari Cannot Be Separated from Continued Detention of El-Zakzaky," *Premium Times Nigeria*, July 21, 2019, www.premiumtimesng.com/news/top-news/342143-imn-replies-presidency-says-buhari-cannot-be-separated-from-continued-detention-of-el-zakzaky.html.

equal or stronger resistance. Muslims easily identify with their members and protect them; likewise, the Christian groups and factions. They are mainly putting their support behind members who are perceived as endangered.

Conclusion

Each region of the country is dominated by citizens who are divided by religion. The North is predominantly Muslim while the South is dominated by Christians. For this basic reason, therefore, there are religious identities that arise with the mandate to safeguard their groups in matters of national interest first, and other arising challenges as secondary. In fact, this mindset is conveniently and sufficiently reflected in the ways Nigerians go about their religious practices and institutions.

It is indisputable that contemporary religious associations in Nigeria have intercultural persuasion where members primarily align with their religious philosophies in protecting identity, even if it means denying other markers of identity such as ethnic belonging or their political creed. Therefore, religion could be said to have been another important marker of identity to determine memberships that are not bounded by either blood or geography but are nonetheless immutable. For this reason, Nigerians have religious members who are committed to identity defense in their quest to sustain their names and improve their collective yearnings. Therefore, identities in Nigeria, especially those bordering on religious convictions, have had their negative and positive sides and continue to forge relevance through their growing display of interest in group activities. This is usually reinforced because an appreciable level of power is ascribed to religion and this, therefore, explains why the creation of different religious groups continues to enjoy the goodwill of the people generally. The trend of identity formation around religion appears to be continuous because minority religions would most predictably join the wagon as that would, at a point, become their reason for survival.

6   Federalism and Its Fault-Lines

Introduction

Federalism, as a concept, can be understood as a system of government that divides political authority between a nation-state and subnational polities, so that both the national and subnational units govern individuals within their jurisdiction.[1] In other words, federalism occurs when the central or federal government and regional governments (provincial, state, territorial, or other subunits) share the governing power. There are numerous different models of federalism and various examples of how individual units of governance share power and form a union. Certain governments, like that in the United States, have a "bottom-up" model, where the provincial units or states are virtually sovereign but cede certain powers in order to form a union. The reverse of this are "top-down" models, like that of India and Nigeria, which have a stronger central government with less powerful federated units underneath it.[2] Additionally, federalism is not limited to a single state or country and can refer to a federation, such as the European Union.

This chapter will uncover the various definitions of federalism and explore how the different federal models work by observing some of the countries that follow it. Furthermore, I will take a closer look at Nigeria's practice of federalism, the history behind it, and what it lacks today in comparison to other countries. I will answer questions such as: Is federalism as a model of governance the best option for Nigeria? How are people being affected by Nigeria's current model of federalism? In what ways can the system be improved or transformed to better serve the people of Nigeria? And finally, what components of federalist structures in other countries should Nigeria grasp onto?

---

[1] P. H. Schuck, "Federalism," *Case Western Reserve Journal of International Law* 38, no. 1 (2006): 5–12, http://ezproxy.lib.utexas.edu/login?url=https://search-proquest-com.ezproxy.lib.utexas.edu/docview/211122202?accountid=7118.
[2] A. Singhvi, "Federalism," *Indian Journal of Public Administration* 53, no. 4 (2007): 742–758.

Figure 6.1 Three men, representing the ethnic groups of the majority, firmly holding the Nigerian national flag as a symbol of unity, peace, and strength.

Models of Federalism

The United States The United States has perhaps the most famous example of federalism at work, and it is one of the most fundamental concepts contained in the US Constitution, despite the word "federalism" never once appearing in it. As the individual states existed long before the United States gained independence, the creation of a new national government focused heavily on maintaining the sovereignty of each of the states. Thus, the US Constitution designated which powers and prerogatives should go to the federal and state governments in order to establish a federal union, rather than a unitary democracy.[3] The different powers of the federal and state governments have changed and evolved since the Constitution was first written, with the states gradually losing aspects of their

---

[3] William T. Pound, "The State of Federalism Today," *National Conference of State Legislatures*, July 24, 2017, www.ncsl.org/bookstore/state-legislatures-magazine/the-state-of-federalism-today636359051.aspx.

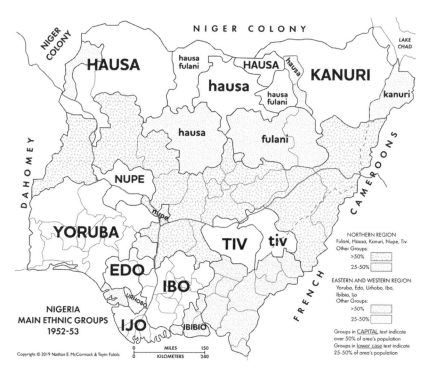

Map 6.1 Nigeria, main ethnic groups, 1952–3.

sovereignty in exchange for a stronger national government in times of
need, such as during the aftermath of the Civil War, World Wars I and
II, and the Great Depression.

Over the course of US history, two major models of federalism have
dominated politics and political theory. The first of these is dual federalism, meaning that the federal and state governments are equals, and
each other's powers are limited to what is explicitly stated in the
Constitution. The second is cooperative federalism, inferring that governments at the national, state, and local levels interact collectively and
work together, but the national government holds power over the
states.[4] As stated previously, following the American Revolution, the
United States concentrated on protecting the sovereignty of the states,
therefore granting them numerous powers of their own, but this did not
remain the case.

[4] *US Legal*, "Federalism," *US Legal*, n.d., https://system.uslegal.com/federalism/.

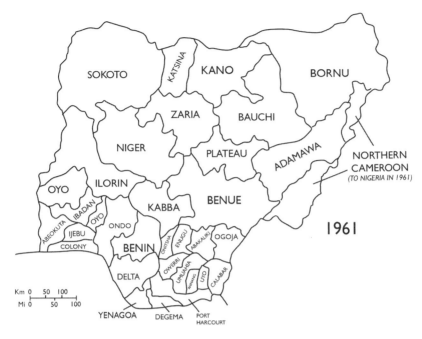

Map 6.2 Nigeria, 1961.

Regardless, federalism in the United States divides powers between different units of government, some of which are specific to one unit or another while others are shared. The delegated powers, those specifically given to the federal government, include the regulation of trade, currency, war, armed forces, treaties, and the postal system. Meanwhile, the reserved powers are those designated for the states to enforce, such as education and the police force. Powers shared between the state and federal governments are called concurrent powers, and they include infrastructure and the power to tax and maintain courts.[5] The Constitution also specifies what the federal and state governments do not have the power to do, therefore preventing one unit of government from gaining too much power over the other. For example, the national government cannot change state boundaries, and the states cannot print money.

There are numerous levels of governance in the United States, all with multiple branches and balances of power. Each of the fifty states is made

[5] Ibid.

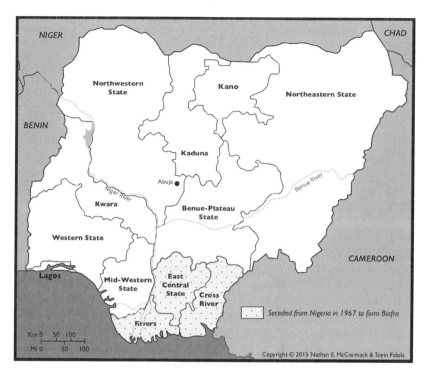

Map 6.3 Nigerian regions, 12 states.

up of counties with elected representatives. The federal government is made up of three branches, two of which are elected positions – the legislative and the executive. As for just how the federal and state governments have powers divided between them, the federal branches each have their own designated roles as well as checks placed on them, so no branch has significantly more power than the others.

The Top-Down: Indian Federalism   While the United States' concept of federalism grew out of largely independent colonies wanting a union of states, federalism in India was not a product of states coming together, but rather the conversion of a unitary system into a federal system.[6] While the states or "units" in India have some degree of autonomy and independence, the central government is far more powerful and

---

[6] Raj Kumar et al., "Indian Federalism – 15 Issues That Challenge the Federal Structure of India – Clear IAS," *ClearIAS.com*, May 12, 2017, www.clearias.com/indian-federalism-issues-challenges/.

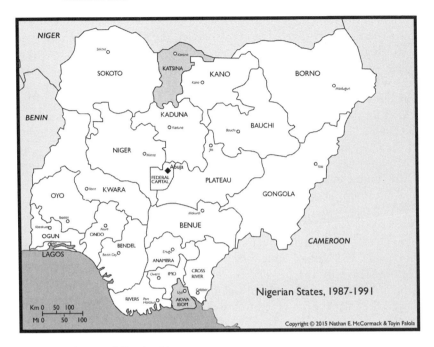

Map 6.4 Nigeria, 21 states.

has control over the individual states. The only check on the central government is the Indian Constitution itself, which lawfully cannot be nullified by either of the governing bodies.[7]

India has what is known as a "top-down" model of federalism. Protected by the Indian Constitution, the individual units have certain powers that cannot be stripped away. The same goes for the central government of India, but more power is granted to it than to the states.[8] On the other hand, like that of the United States, the central government of India is divided amongst the executive, legislative, and judiciary bodies. The federal courts are in place to put checks on those who make and enforce laws, as well as prevent violations of the Indian Constitution. The Constitution is in itself a federal one, as it divides powers among multiple branches of government instead of giving a single group or individual all of the power.[9]

[7] Ibid.
[8] Arnav Raj Chakravorty III, "Federalism in India," *Legal Service India.com*, n.d., www .legalservicesindia.com/article/686/Federalism-in-India.html.
[9] Ibid.

Indian federalism stands out by the fact that even amongst the constituent units, there are variations of power dynamics. Jammu and Kashmir, a state in northern India, has a higher degree of autonomy than the other states under Article 370 of the Indian Constitution.[10] Jammu and Kashmir, otherwise known as J&K, is the only state in India to have a separate constitution and therefore enjoys a greater sense of independence. The reason for this dates back to 1947, when India gained independence from the United Kingdom and Pakistan was created during the partition of India. At the time, J&K had not officially aligned with either country as they were a Muslim-majority, princely state ruled by a Maharaja.[11] Because of this, when Jammu and Kashmir eventually became part of India, they were given special circumstances and allowed to keep their own constitution.

Not Quite Federal: The United Kingdom   The path to being a truly federal state has been a long and arduous one for the UK. According to the *Herald*, the United Kingdom is a single state which, over time, has been modified by varying degrees of devolution.[12] The parliaments in Scotland, Wales, and Northern Ireland all have different distributions of power; they all have limited power to make laws, but anything they decide on can be removed by the Westminster Parliament in London. For centuries, Ireland battled over the issue of having practically no power, and in recent years, it has been Scotland which has been especially vocal about federalism and even held a vote for independence from the UK in 2014.[13]

It wasn't until 1999, a short time after the accession of the Labour government in 1997, that the UK took a step toward becoming more federal.[14] Scotland regained a parliament in Edinburgh after three centuries of not having one, and the Welsh gained their own elected assembly for the first time. Despite centuries of increasingly centralized rule, each of the individual countries within the UK maintained their own sense of national identity and distinctness.[15] For the longest time, the Welsh, Northern Irish, and Scottish had no real government of their own and yet never considered themselves to be English.

---

[10] Riyaz Punjabi, "Autonomy in Jammu and Kashmir," *Strategic Analysis* 35, no. 2 (2011): 308–311.

[11] Ibid.

[12] *Herald Scotland*, "The Big Read: Can Federalism Ever Work in the UK?" *Herald Scotland*, April 22, 2018, www.heraldscotland.com/news/16175777.the-big-read-can-federalism-ever-work-in-the-uk/.

[13] Ibid.

[14] Martin Laffin and Alys Thomas, "The United Kingdom: Federalism in Denial?" *Publius* 29, no. 3 (1999): 89–107.

[15] Ibid.

However, what they have nowadays is still very devolved from the parliament in the UK capital, and questions about autonomy and devolution of power have risen again in the wake of the Brexit vote.[16] Now, it seems as though the UK's imbalanced federalist system is threatening to break itself apart, as Scotland's 62 percent vote to remain in the EU has been largely ignored by the Westminster Parliament.[17] Despite the vote happening almost three years ago, Parliament has been struggling to find a solution and a plan moving forward to compensate for all four countries in the UK. For Scots, it either means following the rest of the UK in leaving the European Union, despite not voting in favor of it, or leaving the UK to be an independent nation, forced to become self-reliant.[18]

From Confederation to Federation: The European Union   Speaking of which, the European Union as it exists today falls somewhere between a confederation of sovereign states and a federation of interconnected, dependent states. It moves far beyond being an international organization, but there is still quite a degree of autonomy within each of the states involved.[19] The question is, and has been since its formation, whether the EU is moving toward becoming more like a federation. What unites the members of the EU are almost entirely economical, rather than political reasons. Every country maintains their own leaders and election processes, while their economies are largely regulated by the EU.

The Single European Act (1987) enforced the free movements of capital, goods, labor, and people all across the EU, and the European Central Bank created the Euro as the common currency throughout all EU states except the UK. Apart from economic integration, the EU still lacks much of what it means to be a federal state. The EU does not regulate national welfare systems in each of the states, nor does it have any kind of united defense or military powers, let alone a central governing body.[20] Nonetheless, the EU presents a unique model of federalism, one that unites historically divided nations, ones with different languages, government structures, and borders.

---

[16] *Herald Scotland*, "The Big Read."

[17] Martin Kettle, "Now Brexit Really Is Threatening to Tear the UK Apart | Martin Kettle," *The Guardian*, October 10, 2018, www.theguardian.com/commentisfree/2018/oct/10/brexit-threat-theresa-may-uk-scotland-northern-ireland-union.

[18] Ibid.

[19] Henna Bagga, "The Future of Europe: Is Europe Really Moving Forward to Federalism?" *Jurist*, October 31, 2017, www.jurist.org/commentary/2017/10/sedeftopal-future-of-europe/.

[20] Ibid.

Federalism in Nigeria

Federalism, as it functions in Nigeria, has struggled since 1960. For almost sixty years, the country has battled to find a real sense of identity because of ethnic rivalries, tension between different regions, and religious conflict. As Nigeria is composed of a diverse population with many different interests, values, and power dynamics, rivalries between different groups of people can corrupt or prevent the federal system from functioning peacefully and productively.[21] It often happens that rival groups from different political regions are more focused on gaining power and promoting their own interests than working toward harmony and equality for all Nigerians.[22]

Nigeria's elected government contains three levels – federal (or central) government, state government, and local government. At the legal level, Nigeria lists three subjects of jurisdiction – a long list of powers held exclusively by the federal government, a shorter list designated to the state governments, and powers that the two cooperate on called coordinate jurisdiction.[23] The interaction and supposed cooperation between the federal and state governments comes in the form of liaison officers, representatives from each of the thirty-six states who live in the capital and communicate with federal ministries. In reality, much of their time is spent tracking payments that the Federal Ministry of Finance owes their individual states. As the system is so inefficient, the amounts due to the states may not be paid if the Ministry of Finance is not reminded in person.[24]

Historically, the major ethnic groups in Nigeria – the Hausa, the Yoruba, and the Igbo – have all dominated each of their regions, holding the most power and shutting out the voices of minority ethnic groups. Because of this, minorities in the North, West, and East have expressed desire for their own regions to avoid suppression and to have their own people represented in government.[25] The question is, would that be the right solution? In terms of the ongoing struggle to create a sense of Nigerian national identity, it seems counterproductive to separate every ethnic group into their own political region. However, it is understandable that minority ethnic groups want to participate in the national government and not be forced to go along with decisions made by the three major ethnic groups.

---

[21] Diana Ibori, "The Concept of Federalism and Its Features in Nigeria," *Legit Nigeria*, November 28, 2018, www.legit.ng/1136924-major-features-federalism-nigeria.html.
[22] Ibid.
[23] M. Dent, "Nigeria: Federalism and Ethnic Rivalry," *Parliamentary Affairs* 53, no. 1 (2000): 157–168.
[24] Ibid.   [25] Ibid.

The Quest for True Federalism Despite being a "Federal Republic" on paper, authority in Nigeria is largely top-down. The central government has almost all control over natural resources, infrastructure, education, and health throughout the state. Indeed, since the 1974 Udoji Civil Service Review, the federal government has imposed a unified salary structure for all the tiers of government and all the agencies of government. Due to continuous bad governance, underdevelopment, and unemployment, many Nigerians have called for greater federalization in Nigeria, where more power is allocated to the local levels of government, giving minority groups and those whose interests are neglected by elected officials greater control and representation.[26] Many individuals, particularly those in the South and South-East of Nigeria, feel that they do not benefit from the current system and claim that they, as citizens, can hold their local politicians more closely accountable if more powers were devolved to the state and local levels.

In July 2017, the push for restructuring federal powers culminated in a bill presented at the Nigerian National Assembly. The proposed bill sought to transfer a number of powers from the central to state governments, including railways, education, agriculture, and healthcare.[27] However, the bill was heavily defeated, despite the fact that the All Progressives Congress (APC) party, which supports the devolution of federal powers, had control of both houses of parliament.

The phrase "true federalism" is a somewhat newfound term in Nigeria, and it means different things to different people. Since the democratic transition in 1999, Nigerians have expressed increasing desire and agitation for a working federal system due to the many defects in the current system.[28] Some Nigerians don't even see their government as federal but instead as unitary, as those at the center practically have all control and power. As we have seen from the examples of other countries and confederations, there is no one model of federalism, but there are some factors that distinguish a good example from a bad one. Most important is that the constituent units or governments within a federal system have a certain degree of authority over that region and function independently of each other.[29] If the constituent governments are practically meaningless, corrupt, or ineffective, then the system is not truly federal. One body

---

[26] Festus Iyorah, "True Federalism Beckons for Nigeria," *African Arguments*, September 12, 2017, https://africanarguments.org/2017/09/12/true-federalism-beckons-for-nigeria/.

[27] Ibid.

[28] Dele Babalola, "Nigeria: A Federation in Search of Federalism," *50 Shades of Federalism*, September 4, 2018, http://50shadesoffederalism.com/case-studies/nigeria-federation-search-federalism/.

[29] Ibid.

of government cannot have sole authority over the other – there must be checks and balances.

True Federalism: Federalism in Theory, Federalism in Practice

As explained previously, "true federalism," especially in the context of the Nigerian political space, is something of a newfound term, and even if its significance is immediately denotative, its application requires some measure of caution. This is because the placement of "true" in relation to federalism to examine a specific nation's political arrangement and the extent to which political and economic power are separated between a central government and subnational forms of government suggests that the premise of evaluation is expressly universalist.

The aforementioned position is true because while there are varied general definitions of federalism, like that of Joseph Ebegbulum that captures federalism as a system of government "where the component units of a political organization participate in sharing powers and functions in a cooperative manner,"[30] or that of Inegbedion and Omoregie that presents it as a system "where powers are shared between two levels of government ... and [e]ach has exclusivity in certain areas while exercising concurrent powers in other areas,"[31] one feature is always invariable: power and the devolution of it. This kind of power (political and economic) is an elusive concept.[32] Thus, to comprehend it to a significant extent requires, equally, a robust understanding or familiarity with the political, economic, and social processes of the specific region in which it is being deployed. The same applies to the utility and devolution of said power. In that case then, to understand how "true federalism" works or what it could signify in plural spaces like Nigeria demands a judicious understanding of the sociopolitical dynamics and economic power plays in Nigeria as a specific political frame.

In light of this level of relativity in the application of true federalism, it comes as no surprise that the Nigerian federal system has oftentimes been tagged the dynamic type that changes with time, just like any other federal

---

[30] C. Joseph Ebegbulum, "Federalism and the Politics of Resource Control in Nigeria: A Critical Analysis of the Niger Delta Crisis," *International Journal of Humanities and Social Science* 1, no. 12 (2011): 218–229.

[31] N. A. Inegbedion and Egite Omoregie, "Federalism in Nigeria: A Re-Appraisal," *Journal of Commonwealth Law and Legal Education* 4, no. 1 (2006): 70.

[32] Egite Oyovbaire, *Federalism in Nigeria: A Study in the Development of Nigeria States* (New York: St. Martin's Press, 1984).

system.[33] This is because governments and regimes vary on a contextual basis. The political history in sub-Saharan Africa is unlike that of the countries of the Global South. To put it more emphatically, the political climate in countries of West Africa differs from those of the East, with whom it shares borders. Just as has been briefly explained previously, the type of federalism practiced in India differs from that of the United States or Canada, even though all are said to be federal states. Indeed, in the case of Nigeria, the federal structure in place in the First Republic, which had a weaker central government, contrasts sharply with that of the second, third, and fourth, which at present has a stronger and dominant central government.

Might we then argue that the desire for true federalism translates to an absence of it, or, to put it more appropriately, the presence of a defective type? The response to this query lies in the subsequent analysis to follow. Some[34] have even argued through essays on Nigerian political history that during the military regimes that sacked Nigerian democracy to the sidelines and instituted a unitary system of government, there was some measure of federalism in place. A principal indication of this was the state creation exercise that transformed the country from a three–four largely autonomous regional structure – although heavily imbalanced, with the Northern Region towering over others through its demography and geography, and, hence, politically – into a thirty-six-state federal structure.

This move, in Inamete's view, helped in neutralizing the dominance of one region over the others, and afforded marginalized groups some degree of local autonomy, political agency, and representative power. This, one can say, is a feature of federalism – the interdependency, representation, and autonomy of subnationalities. However, others like Elaigwu, expressly contend this view, positing that instances that seemed like expressions of federalism during military regimes were pretentious.[35] Such pretensions manifested in self-tagged nomenclatures such as "The Federal Military Government," and administrations that were neither pyramidal in federal structure nor tolerant of power devolution.[36] Truly, its system of governance was hierarchical and unitary, and power was centralized in the federal government at the expense of the autonomy of the created states; also, the power that existed was mostly delegated, not divided or decentralized.

---

[33] Ufot B. Inamete, "Federalism in Nigeria: The Crucial Dynamics," *The Round Table: The Commonwealth Journal of International Affairs* 80, no. 318 (1991): 191–207.

[34] See Inamete, "Federalism in Nigeria."

[35] See Isawa J. Elaigwu, "Federalism in Nigeria's New Democratic Polity," *Plubius: The Journal of Federalism* 32, no. 2 (2002): 73–95.

[36] Ibid., 75.

While these positions are valid and are vital, depending on contexts, to accurately evaluate the extent of federalism in Nigeria in order to fully recognize its lack of the true type, especially when compared with more progressive types, we must first examine the structures that separate the Nigerian experience of federalism from those of other federal states. These experiences are contained and bound up in what Inamete describes as "[t]he profile of the relative powers of the national and the state (before 1967, regional) governments, and the nature of the stability of the polity."[37] This means the body polity and its experiences, and the political processes of Nigeria, determine the extent of its federalism. Putting it succinctly, federalism should itself be determined by its structure and process. Only through this way is the abstract quality of a term like "true federalism" made apparent. When made apparent and then applied to the Nigerian space, the relatively erroneous belief that often follows from this – that Nigeria is not at all federal owing to the fundamental changes in its political climate and the incursive military campaign that altered it – is revealed.

This position cannot be more insular; after all, it is only when it is federal that its federalism can be faulty, and only when it is faulty can it be truly not-federal. Another argument is that changes in political history are part of the particular dynamics that separate a nation-state's federal system from others with which it shares space on a broad spectrum of federal systems. The import is that the differences that characterize the Nigerian political frame from others do not make it more or less a federal system; it is how these changes are expressed within that spectral precinct of permissions that does. Just as it is often championed by theorists of federalism, all forms on the "spectrum of federal systems are still federal systems (their being in the left, middle, or right of the federalism spectrum does not make them any more or less federal)."[38] Accordingly, then, practicing federalism as a national strategy and political system does not call for all federal systems or nations to have exactitude of features or comprise similarities to the same degree and extent.

Inegbedion and Omorogie's view lend credence to this argument by acknowledging that although certain minimum indices must be found in any federal structure, it is impracticable to have a model ideal federalism.[39] The political history and experience of the specific nation-state or country would determine how federalism obtains in that context. To quote Ayua,

---

[37] Inamete, "Federalism in Nigeria," 191.

[38] Adele L. Jinadu, "A Note on the Theory of Federalism," in *Readings on Federalism*, eds. A. B. Akinyemi, P. D. Cole, and Walter Ofonagoro (Lagos: Nigerian Institute of International Affairs, 1980), 19.

[39] Inegbedion and Omoregie, "Federalism in Nigeria."

"there is nothing like true federalism or a true federal system. A federal constitution may have the tendency of centralization or decentralization depending on the strength of centripetal or centrifugal forces existing in the country."[40] In that case, a nation-state either practices a faulty federalism – that is, its practice of it is faulty – or does not.

Aspects of federalism as propounded by Wheare, and popularly cited as identifiers of federalism, include the sharing of power between a central and subnational governments, jurisdictional autonomy, and coordinational collaboration or coordinate control – where each tier of government is willing to let go and retain limited powers in accordance to respective functions – like each government being "limited to its own sphere of action and each being within that sphere independent of the others."[41] These have been criticized as out of place as absolute features, since in many modern federal nations the central governments have waded into or shared in the jurisdictions of regional governments. As is evident today, many regional governments of federal countries have their activities dependent on financial aids from a central government. That this is a common feature that provokes one to hold the opinion that absolute takes of such characters as "true federalism," or how a federal system should operate, are manifestations of the exemplification of the United States' type of federal structure as the standard.

To Egbebelum, who shares similar sentiments, the popular definition of Wheare that is often cited as an apt take is borne of his fascination with the United States' form of federalism, which in Egbebelum's opinion incited Wheare to have described some constitutions as being quasi-federal because such constitutions tie or subordinate, to some extent, regional or state governments to the central government.[42] In reality, were this to be the case, many federal nations would be culprits. Although, in the case of Nigeria, a good example would be the pre-1966 Nigeria Constitution that Wheare deems quasi-federal because a section of it, Section 66, permits the Federal Government to declare a state of emergency in any region and to assume the role of running that region's government for a specific period.[43]

It is not enough to impress a standard federalism on a sovereign country to determine its federalism or to what extent it manifests true federalism, especially if the federalism of a nation-state is defined by the

---

[40] I. A. Ayua, "The Nigerian Constitutional Scheme on the Sharing of Its Resources and Its Implementation: An Assessment," in *Major Issues in the 1999 Constitution*, eds. I. A. Ayua, D. A. Guobadia, and A. O. Adekunle (Lagos: NIALS, 2000), 130.

[41] John P. Mackintosh, "Federalism in Nigeria," *Political Studies* 10, no. 3 (1962): 223.

[42] Egbebulum, "Federalism and the Politics of Resource Control in Nigeria," 210.

[43] Ibid.

provisions of its constitution and is both a structure and a process. Although, such nations like Nigeria can borrow a leaf from the pages of more successfully federal nations were its federalism, that is, its structures and process, faulty. Two equally apt positions on federalism cited by Egbebulem that emphasize structure and process in relation to the proper functioning of federalism are Kolawole's, which centers on the notion that federalism must be moored on a consentient relationship between available tiers of government;[44] then Eleazar's, which stipulates that federalism can only manifest where there is instituted a significant level of open-mindedness toward diversity and the desire to implement political action through conciliation, even when the power to act unilaterally is available.[45]

These positions underscore one thing: federalism must necessarily be a confluence of a meaningful structure where the process of implementing political action toward governance is constitutional, as well as reflective of federalist principles and a public culture where the body polity has a stake in governance through appropriately autonomous and integrated mechanisms according to jurisdictional functions that must be in operation. As a result, it is mandatory that for federalism to function, the state and local governments and the central government must dissolve powers in constitutionally acceptable ways.

To add to this matter of true federalism, we must return to Ayua's position, which aside from reemphasizing the tenuous implication of the term "true federalism," also underscores the value of power in determining the quality of a federal system. The dynamics of power play is so sacrosanct to federalism that its distribution as both political and financial instruments should enable each tier of government – just as is expected of and in each federal system – to remain relevant, competent, and functional according to constitutionally assigned roles. The place of power has been emphasized by foremost scholars of federalism like Wheare, who envisaged power and its constitutional backing as instigators of federalism in such ways that each tier of government can be competent, independent, and coordinate. Wheare saw federalism as a constitutional arrangement dividing powers and functions between tiers of government.[46] This makes a constitution a prime code of federalism.

For that reason, it is vital to bear in mind that in identifying federalism in a performed space, the basic features of federalism must be found, even if in varying degrees. These basic features can be summed as the political

---

[44] Ibid.   [45] Ibid.
[46] See Kenneth C. Wheare, *Federal Government*, 4th ed. (London: Oxford University Press, 1946).

and economic autonomy of integrated structures within a legislative space as provided by a governing constitution. If these, alongside the division of power, are the basic ingredients with which a federated system of government can be identified as federal, the notion of true federalism would be, by and large, a fluid concept, considering its leanings toward being ideal. More so, the extent of political and economic autonomy always differs from nation-state to nation-state.[47] In addition, the governing constitution that makes provisions that serve as measures through which division of power and political as well as economic autonomy can be achieved and maintained are region based; so, specific country and constitutional provisions are necessary agents to consider in instituting true federalism, not some ideal principle of what federalism should be. It is the gross absence of these features in structure and process that warrants the charge that Nigeria does not practice true federalism.

A careful consideration of the points raised so far makes clear two claims. First, Nigeria, regardless of its history of political turbulence, is a federation, even if only on paper (which is predominantly the case). Second, the features or factors that constitute Nigeria's federalism, that is, that enable its claim to being a federal state, are the same features that encroach on its federalism, rendering it inactive – a bad case of an unpleasant irony. Thus, while Nigeria cannot be said to practice true federalism in any sense, its federalism is visibly impeded by the features that ought to promote it reveals that the type of federalism it claims to practice is non-functional or a bad and poor one. It also reveals that while on paper there is a structure and process that should effectively enhance the implementation of federalist policies, the usual culprit of poor transition of theory to practice is at play.

Nigeria practices a bad type of federalism; this is evidenced by the far cry between what has been theorized and what is being effectuated. Features like religion, state creation and statism, ethnicity, federal character principles, affirmative action types, federal fiscal policy, revenue allocation, local government systems, constitution and legislative lists, and government regimes and their effects on the body polity are instances that map out points of breakdown between federalism in theory and federalism in practice in Nigeria. While these factors are not mutually exclusive, and as such cannot be totally examined in isolation from one another, examining these factors would afford us two things. First, an understanding of the nature and trajectory of Nigerian federalism since the First Republic. The second would be the nature of the faults dividing

---

[47] Inegbedion and Omoregie, "Federalism in Nigeria."

the lines, that is, the postures imposing negatively to the point of total breakdown of the type of federalism Nigeria claims to practice.

Nigerian Federalism: The Faults

The framework of Nigeria's federalism is increasingly reliant on a power structure with an economy background, which, as rightly argued by Toyin Falola,[48] is a foundation for many of the political issues affronting Nigeria's brand of federalism. Underlying all these are power tussles that manifest in fiscal and economic patterns. In recognition of this, I begin by tracing the faults in Nigeria's federalism from Nigeria's unification to the civil war, and the nature of Nigeria's federal fiscal policy.

The Indelible Military Footprints: Civil War and Federal Fiscal Policy

In a country where federalism ought to be the prevalent political philosophy, subnational governments should be autonomous enough to have the capacity to be economically viable, generate public revenue, and determine expenditures without having to wait on or rely totally on the central government, which sadly is the case with Nigeria. There are many reasons why the central government sits at the apex of the Nigerian political and economic pyramid, wielding fiscal power and controlling resources and revenue allocations, so much so that it dictates the extent to which the local and state governments are self-sufficient, if they are at all. The incursion of the military into the Nigerian democratic space to suspend democracy triggered a power alteration and structure change.

The First Republic comprised three regions: Southern, Northern, and Western, with the Mid-west Region as the fourth created later in 1962 when a federal legislature, supported by the required two-thirds majority in the two houses of government, passed.[49] The original three regions were integrated after the Richards Constitution in 1946, and this structure was maintained right till after independence, with various reforms to the constitution in 1951 and 1957.[50] The distrust that manifested at the level of governance required that each region grow itself into a formidable stature that could compete at the national level. The corollary of this is the autonomous self-sufficiency that the regions manifested right into

---

[48] Toyin Falola, *Nigerian Political Modernity and Postcolonial Predicament* (Austin: Pan-African University Press, 2016).

[49] Adele L. Jinadu, "Federalism, the Consociational State, and Ethnic Conflict in Nigeria," *Plubius: Federalism and Consociationalism: A Symposium* 15, no. 2 (1985): 71–100.

[50] Elaigwu, "Federalism in Nigeria's New Democratic Polity."

independence, even though as far back as 1956, both Eastern and Western Regions had gained political self-sustaining status, with the Northern Region gaining it later in 1959 in a mostly deliberate fashion. This fissure in political foresight itself suggested the presence of strains that would later press gravely on the newly independent state.

While the first Nigerian constitution provided a federalist structure that operated in the context of a parliamentary democracy, the tensions that would eventually invite the military forces had increased exponentially. One of the manifestations of this was the structural imbalance of the body polity. Owing to the divide-and-rule strategy of the colonial administration that left power with the North – which had the numbers, geographic power, representation, and hence political power – ethnic distrust and political maneuvering of ethnic bents were palpable. The Northern Region, by virtue of its demographic and geographic strength, towered over both the Western and Eastern Regions, and as such monopolized political power. A census taken in 1963 put the percentage of the Northern, Southern, Eastern, and Mid-west Regions at 53.5, 22.3, 18.4, and 4.6, respectively.[51] In terms of the country's total area, the Northern Region took 79 percent, with the three others sharing the remaining 21 percent.[52]

The fear of the Northern Region's representative and hence political power, in lieu of the democratic process that supported substantive representation, and the South's dominance of the civil service and economic sectors by virtue of their impressive embrace of education, culminated in a condition of mutual distrust; a kind of subtle rivalry or, as Elaigwu puts it, "tyranny of population and tyranny of skills."[53] The tyranny of population in a federal context that afforded autonomy to regional governments meant that the North had the political power, while the tyranny of skills meant the South wielded the economic power. This was a relatively balanced system of power separation that supported the federal structure of the First Republic, however warped it seems now.

The military coup of 1966 counteracted this rather brittle balance by concentrating political power in the hands of the Southern political leaders, as it is often argued that the key actors of that coup were of Southern extraction, and the main victims Northern. As Elaigwu rightly argues, "Political power had been the North's safeguard against the South's economic and educational advantages. The South's advantage in the bureaucracy, which, if anything, was strengthened by the coup, was greatly augmented. The North reacted violently as it saw its last card – the

[51] Ibid.   [52] Ibid.   [53] Ibid., 74.

political card – suddenly [taken away]."[54] The counter-coup by the North and the pogrom that followed consolidated military rule and Northern dominance. Three different military regimes culminated in the military ruling from January 15, 1966, to October 1979, from December 31, 1983, to August 1993, and from November 1993 to May 29, 1999. In all these regimes, the country was run as a unitary government, especially after General Aguiyi Ironsi's Decree No. 34 in 1966, with power centralized at the center and the regions made subordinate to it. Although the Ironsi-led government was not able to implement the unitary structure he had decreed, continuing with the federal structure he inherited, successive military regimes starting with General Yakubu Gowon's did. The argument in support of this was that a weak central government and powerful regional governments were remote causes that bred the ethnic bias and distrust that led to the catastrophe of 1966. Furthermore, unifying the nation would foster nationalist character and transfer allegiance from the regions, which had ethnic moorings, to the center. This was the first great misstep in the history of Nigeria's federalism.

Implementing a unitarist philosophy and creating a unitary state meant the regions lost their economic autonomy, fiscal strength, authority over their resources, and hence revenue power. With a more powerful central government and a top-down approach of government, the regions became dependent constitutionally, politically, and economically. The discovery of oil and the constitutions that have presided over revenue allocation and its sharing formula have all the more concentrated power at the center, affecting the supposed federalism that had fostered some level of progressive integration in the country. The discovery of oil and the transition to complete reliance on petroleum revenue as the major source of the nation's GDP catapulted and sustained federal revenue power.

To further consolidate federal fiscal power, the four regions, which were larger and economically viable, were broken up into several states – all during the military regime. The four-region federal structure of the First Republic is now the thirty-six-state federal structure of the Fourth Republic. This state-creation exercise transferred economic and political power to the center, as the states were smaller in size compared to the regions from where they were carved out. This caused an incapacity that made efforts by the states to gain power at the expense of the federal government cumbersome;[55] it fueled their continued dependence on the military center. By the time democratic governance was reinstituted in 1999, the center had become so powerful that the federal structure that was created was woven around it. This owed to, among many other

---

[54] Ibid., 75.   [55] Inamete, "Federalism in Nigeria."

factors, increased revenues from oil production that were secured by the central government, leaving the state governments to raise revenues to fulfill the constitutionally allocated roles, and in most cases depend on the center for allocations and grants. This dependency took away the economic powers of the states and local governments and made them some sort of appendages to the central government. Presently, many states like Kebbi, Borno, and Katsina, only get by through the allocations made to them by the central government.

In maintaining the fiscal hold at the center, provisions were made – constitutionally, of course – to generate formulas that would consolidate fiscal power at the hands of the national government by controlling the allocation of resources. This made the state governments dependent. A Federation Account was also managed by the center. This means resources that were once region-bound were now vested in the hands of the national government, which then redistributed them back to the states and local governments. Through constitutional backing, the tyranny of the federal head was instituted. The lack of strong constitutional limitations on federal spending further increased the fiscal hegemony of the federal government at the expense of the states, laying bare the pretensions of federalist practices in the nation. Even on tax basis, the central government is supreme, having a near-total control over VAT, company income tax, custom and excise duties, education, and petroleum product taxes.

Consequently, the Civil War, military rule, petroleum revenue, and reduction of the regions into mini-states, reinforced power in the hands of the central government of each successive regime, from the military down to the civilian, so much so that presently even the constitution that ought to be the prime determinant of a federal structure consolidates the hegemony of and the concentration of power at the center.

A Strange Case of Irony: Constitutional Provisions, Consociationalism, and Affirmative Actions

It should follow logically that in the face of a blatant misapplication of federalist principles and practice of defective federalism, the Nigerian constitution, in its preceding and current form(s), would be a certified approach at righting the defects and instituting a more practical and progressive federalism. But, ironically, the constitutional provisions, the manner of their implementation, the philosophies of the policies and bills, as well as the affirmative actions that have been provided as solutions to Nigeria's political problem (which betrays ethnic distrust), have generated unintended consequences of perpetuating the continued dominance of the center and the elite class that populate it. This means federalism in Nigeria is beset with a strange case of irony; it is being choked by the remedies that ought to cure its defects.

The constitution has concentrated power in the hands of the center government based on the logic that constitutions are attempts by the political class to manage ethnic-based conflicts and tensions by separating authority constitutionally derived between tiers of governments. But, as visible and as opined by Jinadu, this separation of constitutional power (should be) consociational in nature.[56] Nigeria has had several constitutions whose legislative lists favored the center government at the expense of both state and local governments. The legislative list, as it should be in any federated economy, consists of powers that, according to capacity and allocated functions, are separated between the different tiers in categories of federal, concurrent, and residual lists.

Case in point: the 1960 Independence Constitution and 1963 Republican Constitution facilitated federal preeminence that undermined regional autonomy.[57] Emergency provisions were made that encouraged or vindicated grounds wherein the federal government could intervene in regional matters. In May 1962, after a series of in-house squabbles, the center exercised this power by declaring a state of emergency in the Western Region and appointed a federal administrator to perform executive and legislative functions in the region, suspending the regional government. This type of provision challenges the viability of regional governments and their claims toward a measure of self-sustenance. It also imposed upon and made useless the consociational element of segmental autonomy that, among others like veto powers, grand coalitions, and proportionality, was derived to manage the ethnic problem of Nigeria. Segmental autonomy, which necessarily does not translate to absolute autonomy, would afford the regions made of related ethnicities the space they needed to grow at their own pace and legislate on matters within their jurisdiction.

Segmental autonomy was deemed an affirmative-type of action that would eliminate or lessen the ethnically engineered conflicts and bias affecting the federation. The logic was to make the center less attractive and the regions more attractive, so as to stem the do-or-die affair that characterized government politics at the center. It was also to protect the center government from being dominated by one ethnic group or a region, or the bias of a group playing out politically to the expense of

---

[56] Jinadu, "Federalism, the Consociational State, and Ethnic Conflict in Nigeria."
[57] Ibid.

the autonomy of the others, which was what played out in the creation of the Mid-west Region back in the 1960s. The constitution provided that a new region or boundary could be made if two out of the three regions supported by the federal government pushed a bill in that regard. In March 1962, the federal legislature passed such bill and submitted same for approval. While the Western Regional Legislature rejected the bill, the Northern and Eastern passed it, and thus the Mid-west Region was created. The Yoruba translated this as an ethnic coalition against the West, saying that the Northern Region consisted mainly of the Hausa–Fulani and the East, the Igbo, and other minorities.

This is an instance that demonstrated the desire to empower each ethnic group by granting autonomous power that made them viable and less dependent on the center, fostering interdependency and consensual coordination, unless in specific instances which were provided for. But the challenges that derived from this are manifold. One, there is no clear-cut way to determine when such situations were legit and demanded federal interventions, and when they were manifestations of attempts by the dominant ethnic group at the center to undermine the political powers of the others. Two, the regions are not absolute structures in terms of their ethnic configurations. Each region, aside from being populated by a major ethnic group, also consists of minorities. As a result, the segmental autonomy granted to the regions only favored the main ethnic groups – the Yoruba, Hausa–Fulani, and Igbo – who were, in population and cultural presence, more dominant than the rest. Although it should be said that while minority groups could not be granted segmental autonomy through the creation of states, several benefits were prepared for them such as the Special Area Scholarship Awards created for those from the Niger Delta.[58] Yet, by the mere fact that many states were eventually created just to appease some of the marginalized identities and stem ethnic distrust and structural imbalance, they consolidated power at the center and eventually still created instances where certain minorities were marginalized.

Furthermore, another constitutional provision that rivaled autonomy of the states was the monopoly of fiscal revenue. The central government had in its legislative list control over defense, export, import, trade, currency, revenue allocation, foreign affairs, tax, and interstate commerce, which rendered the states dependent. Not only is the executive list overloaded, which is a cause for concern, the federal government, especially benefiting from the 1979 and 1999 Constitutions, has been imbued totally with powers that are fundamental to a nation's running. This means that without them, the nation cannot function properly. The

[58] Ibid.

state governments are then only afforded cosmetic powers. The irony of the situation is that the meddlesomeness of the federal government in state matters is as evident today as it was back then. There are cases of the federal government being involved in the election of officials into local government offices.[59] Furthermore, while in the 1999 Constitution the concurrent and executive lists do not reveal provisions made for the federal government to partially or fully control agriculture and health,[60] an assessment of the political terrain and federal cabinet since 1999 would reveal that there have been ministries of health and agriculture whose heads were appointed by the federal government. More so, these ministers who head these ministries are aided by junior ministers.

So, while the Constitution should, naturally, make provisions for the federal government to be in charge of matters whose implications and importance transcend state boundaries, and the state governments should be in charge of those with geopolitical boundaries like education, public health, agriculture, and cultural issues, the 1999 Constitution presently used by Nigeria clearly flouts this principle. The interference or complete takeover of issues relating to labor evidences this. The federal government is afforded legislative jurisdiction over labor, including adjudicating over matters of trade unions and industrial disputes, and prescribing a national minimum wage for the nation or any part of it. This severally contradicts the principle of residual and concurrent lists, and it was why, when the former President Olusegun Obasanjo declared a new national minimum wage of 5,500 naira for state governments and 7,500 for federal government, it was perceived by the governors as a rude oversight of due process. The insistence was on the continued perpetuation of an overt centralization of power started by the military that made the civilian government that immediately succeeded it to impose such measures without due consultation. The end result led to incessant industrial actions, as some states could not meet up. This same scenario also played out in 2018, when President Buhari declared the new minimum wage as 30,000 naira and the governors rejected it, stating the same grounds as those of Obasanjo's tenure; these are clear impositions by the overtly powerful center on the state and local governments.

To add to how constitutional provisions further strain federalism in Nigeria is to cite the matter of revenue allocation. Revenue allocation is contained in the concurrent list; yet, it is listed and managed in such a manner that sidelines the state governments, making it, in practicality, an exclusively central government matter.[61] As argued by Inegbedion and

---

[59] Inegbedion and Omoregie, "Federalism in Nigeria: A Critical Appraisal."   [60] Ibid.
[61] Ibid.

Omoregie, the entire "concurrent list of the 1999 Constitution is structured in such a way as to substantially confine the extent of State powers in respect thereof to the level of near insignificance."[62] This, as further contended, is a poor implementation of the idea of covering the field, which suggests that in any federal structure, the state governments are barred from legislating on matters in conflict with the central government.[63]

Resource allocation and its sharing formula do not properly reflect the principles of segmental autonomy. Allocation of resources in Nigeria covers all distribution of scarce but distributable resources such as enrollment or recruitments into political offices and public services. Chief among these is also the distribution of petroleum revenue. To ensure that resources are equitably distributed among the states and ethnicities represented, especially with regard to appointment into the Federal Public Service, strategies or affirmative action types such as federal character and quota systems were developed. The Federal Character Commission, created by the federal government, was responsible for monitoring the patterns of appointment employed by agencies into federal, state, and local governments work sectors.[64] This was to ensure and promote a nationalist identity and sense of belonging, especially considering the claims of marginalization by minorities. In a real sense, the unity that was produced as a result of this affirmative action type engineered to foster national integration and development, resulted in elite dominance.

This national integration context provided justification for the appearance of federal character in the 1979 and 1999 Constitutions, where it was interpreted as a means of preventing the domination of the federal government and, hence, national resources, by a particular ethnic group. And because, as stated previously, state boundaries are not denominated by ethnic margins, which was not the case with the regions, it was easier for this affirmative action-type strategy to be included in the Constitution as a provision that catered for the substantive representation of all ethnic groups. It was underneath this context that it appeared in all three Constitutions, and would be reflected as implemented in the appointments of "Federal Ministers, Nigeria's permanent representatives overseas, chairmanship and membership of the boards of parastatals and public bodies set up under the constitution, judicial offices, commissioned and non-commissioned personnel of the armed forces, federal permanent secretaries and Presidential advisers."[65]

---

[62] Ibid., 74.   [63] Ibid.   [64] Elaigwu, "Federalism in Nigeria's New Democratic Policy."
[65] See B. J. Dudley, *An Introduction to Nigerian Government and Politics* (Bloomington: Indiana University Press, 1982), 162.

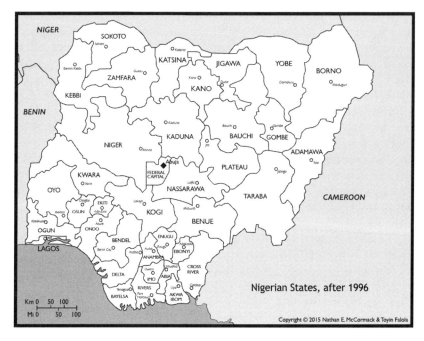

Map 6.5 Nigeria, 36 states.

This may seem to be a progressive contribution to the ethnic problem in Nigeria, aside from bad leadership, which is also another gargantuan foe of Nigerian federalism. In reality though, it equates, as hinted previously, upper/elite class interest unification with national unity. Like Dibua argues, it was, in practice, "[f]irst and foremost, more of a power sharing exercise and an ethnic-based quota system."[66] This is apparent in the proposition of the Federal Character Principle as a compromise in the demands by the Southern delegates to the Constituent Assembly in 1978 for rotational presidency, in order to sidestep or put an end to the perceived dominance of the Northern Region; it was also manifested in the opposition to the same rotational presidency by the Northern delegates.[67] More so, because the states themselves are representative of the dominance of three big ethnicities – Igbo, Yoruba, Hausa–Fulani – over other minorities, the emphasis on the state as basis for appointments

[66] J. I. Dibua, "Ethnic Citizenship, Federal Character, and Inter-Group Relations in Nigeria," *Journal of the Historical Society of Nigeria* 20 (2011): 1–25.
[67] Ibid.

still perpetuates ethnicity as a key component in the implementation of the principle.

The foregoing means that emphasis on indigeneity to a state, which the federal character and quota system require, only rehashes the use of ethnicity as criterion to ascend into offices. In the words of Dibua, "The principle in effect produced the antithesis of national unity in that it fostered ethnically salient candidates whose primary loyalty were to their respective ethnic groups."[68] This way, the minority ethnic groups are discriminated against; and even the elites of the minority groups are also discriminated against, which means power is only shared between the elites of the dominant ethnic group, leading to a lopsidedness in the inter-elite integration and accommodation structure that ought to benefit from this. That is why the federal character principle is often declaimed as a power-sharing avenue between the dominant ethnic groups. So, while ethnic citizenship was granted eminent status in the context of federalism, where citizens could hold rights to identities that fed into the broader national identity, it was often weaponized in various pseudo-progressive forms to defraud the provisions of federalism.

Unlike in the United States and the United Kingdom in which historical gender and racial inequalities were being redressed with "positive affirmative action" without compromising meritocracy, the Nigerian quota system as an affirmative action type that should enable the substantive representation of ethnic groups and states, as a way of furthering the federalist principle of resources allocation and sharing, became counterproductive as it not only pitched ethnic representation over competency or afforded dominant ethnic groups and those constituted in the political elite class to control resources for their ethnic group; it also further incentivized ethnicity as a bargaining or access card to national resources. This is why in the Nigerian context of federalism, consociational items like proportionality and grand coalition are themselves masquerading vehicles concealing attempts to advance the interests of dominant ethnic groups through emphasis on ethnic membership and ethnicity. Proportionality, which is a measure that allows the inclusion of or gives accessibility to institutions and resources to minority members that would otherwise have been subjected to competitive selection procedures, followed a quota nature that, in consequence, led to the appointment of less-than-credible persons into the federal, state, and local administrative levels. In the case of the North, Northerners who were trailing behind in educational qualifications were beneficiaries, as the principle afforded them to be represented in the different levels of the national/federal

---

[68] Ibid., 11.

administration. This, of course, has led to the influx of Northerners into competitive cadres; it has also led to accusations that the country was being run by less educated people when viable and qualified candidates were left out.

Another instance would be the reduction in entry qualifications for Northerners into the Nigerian army by Alhaji Ribadu, the Minister of Defense, in 1961.[69] Quota systems were also employed in institutions of learning, and were in favor of Northerners in many instances, especially in the federal civil service. Although, according to Jinadu, this did not translate into the haphazard and overt inclusion of unqualified Northerners into the civil service pool, in instances of promotions, strict requirements like seniority and merit were bypassed, much to the chagrin of other ethnicities. That these actions existed at all contradict to some extent the 1959/1960 and 1963 Constitutions that sought to protect citizens from discriminations, which is what conferring on a group certain privileges not conferred on others is. More so, conferring such on a group not of the minority seems to make useless the provisions for the protection of the fundamental rights of minorities in the 1960 Constitution, or the constitutional arrangements that sought to ensure the equitable representation of minorities in the civil service. This is most especially seen in the 1960 Constitution, where provisions were made to protect the minorities from discriminatory acts produced by the application of any law by the federal or regional government to which other groups are not made subject. Although it could be argued, as Jinadu did, that the Northerners were socially of the minority – evidenced by their poor presence in the administrative cadres – they are still of the majority, a fact continually reinforced by their numerical and geographic strength, even after the Northern Region was divided into several smaller states.

Also, while the argument that the 1960 and 1963 Constitutions did not expressly make provisions for proportionality in the context of appointments and promotions in the civil service and agencies of the nation, a lot of federal executive decisions were made that rest on or betrayed consociational principles and affirmative action such as the quota or proportionality rule.[70] To date, considering the kind of leadership Nigeria has and the choke hold ethnicism has on the nation, it is no surprise that overtly and covertly, certain kinds of quota systems are still being used in running the country, as was done in 1977, to maintain some semblance of compositional balance in the Federal Executive Council, the Supreme Military Council, and the National Council of States.[71] During this time, strategies like those were also pursued in the education sector through

---

[69] Jinadu, "Federalism, the Consociational State, and Ethnic Conflict in Nigeria."
[70] Ibid.   [71] Ibid.

appointments of principal staffs and admission of students.[72] In the 1981/2 session, a federal government mandate compelled universities to use a quota system in admission procedures. The gradual reliance on such consociational methods made it so that the 1979 Constitution pronouncedly accommodated and expressed consociational principles. The presence of the grand coalition, proportionality, segmental autonomy, and mutual veto in the 1979 Constitution were framed by the requirement of section 14(3) of the Constitution that demanded that federal government appointments should reflect "the federal character" of the country. The 1999 Constitution only followed suit, making it possible for the president to follow the principle of substantive equality and appoint ministers from several states in the country. The sustenance of these principles that continually feed Northern domination is born out of the idea, in certain quarters, that it helps to increase the representation of the socially minority Northerners and reduce the entrance of Southerners (from both the West and East) into the administrative and institutional structures. The result of employing this principle of proportionality to reverse hegemonic tendencies, especially in the current administration, has resulted in the political cabinet being filled with Northerners.

Let us now return to the matter of revenue allocation, which also greatly affects any pretense Nigeria has to practicing federalism. Over the years, several criteria have been generated to determine which strategies are best in deriving a workable formula for sharing the nation's wealth resources among its constituent parts. According to Salami, there have been about nine fiscal commissions, six military decrees and one act of parliament to ensure appropriate revenue allocation, chief among which are "the Hicks-Phillipson Commission (1951), Chick's Commission (1953), Raisman Commission of 1958, Binns Commission (1964), Dina Commission (1968), Aboyade Technical Committee (1972), Okigbo Commission (1980), and Danjuma Commission 1988 (Salami, 2007). The recommendations of all the commissions were all based on the need to have equitable and balanced horizontal and vertical allocation structure for the country."[73]

Yet, despite the many attempts, the results have always negated the provisions of federalism with regard to political and economic power divisions. Just like many other factors that affect Nigeria's brand of

---

[72] See Jinadu for more on how proportionality as reversed discrimination action or quota was employed in tertiary institutions, public projects, and secondary and primary schools.

[73] Adeleke Salami, "Taxation, Revenue Allocation, and Fiscal Federalism in Nigeria: Issues, Challenges, and Policy Options," *Economic Options* 56, no. 189 (2011): 27–49. See also Egbebulem, "Federalism and the Policy of Resource Control in Nigeria."

federalism, the major hiccup started with the military imposition on Nigerian politics. The Phillipson-Adebo Commission marked the first significant attempt at engineering a workable formula for revenue allocation in 1946.[74] Again, ethnicity prevailed and allocating factors – which themselves were heavily underscored by private, sectional, and ethnic bias – trumped other more important aspects. These factors could be largely separated into population and derivation. The South pushed for the derivation principle, based on being in possession of significant resources; the Northerners, having demographical and geographical strength, pushed for population. The Hicks-Phillipson Commission of 1951 eventually settled the dispute by providing parameters such as derivation, national interests, population, needs, and development as some of the criteria to be used in allocating resources.[75] The regions, based on their considerable fiscal, economic, and political autonomy and the nature of Nigeria's federalism in the First Republic that made Regions more powerful than the center, enjoyed and had considerable amount of control over the revenues from their resources. The 1960 Constitution made provisions that 50 percent of returns from mineral extraction and mining should be returned to the regions based on the derivation principle. This further consolidated the political relevance of the regions. With the appearance of the military and the overt centralization of powers, revenues became increasingly concentrated in the hands of the center government, diminishing the powers of the regions. More so, the discovery and subsequent misguided heavy reliance on petroleum as the mainstay of the country's exports required that the center government regard petroleum and lands as property of the national government. This way, the regions and the minority groups were disempowered. On another note, it paved the way for more ethnic schism as the majority ethnic groups in power had more access to control this resource without regional intervention, since the political power required to do so was already centralized, and the revenue generated from it would be allocated nationwide. Here again, ethnicism and ethnic citizenship were at play.

In a horizontal revenue allocation format, by 1969 revenue allocation, following General Yakubu Gowon's (the then-military leader) Decree No.30 that revenue allocation should follow a formula of 55 percent of royalty and rents from crude oil for the federal government and 45 percent for producing states,[76] favored the center. By 1970 and 1980, the center government had gained increased control. Another decree by Gowon conferred the rights of the states in the minerals of their continental

---

[74] Dibua, "Ethnic Citizenship, Federal Character, and Inter-Group Relations in Nigeria."
[75] Ibid.   [76] Ibid.

shelves, ownership and title of territorial waters, and royalties and rents derived or related to exploration- and petroleum-related services on the federal government.[77]

With regard to the general allocation of the resources sharing formula, the derivation principle was granted the greatest weight pre-1960, 50 percent, which allowed the corresponding regions to benefit from their contributions to the body polity and be equally invested in nation building. From 1964 to 1976, the principle of derivation was discarded in favor of the principle of equality of population and state in a 50 percent formula.[78] By 1975, the percentage for sharing based on derivation was reduced to 20 percent, and by 1979 it was stopped. The years between 1977 and 1981 saw the use of principles such as equal access to development opportunities, which carried a 25 percentage, and national minimum standard, absorptive capacity, independent revenue efforts, and fiscal efficiency, which carried 22, 20, 18, and 15 percent, respectively,[79] to allocate resources. By 1982 to 1998, equality of states, population, independent revenue efforts, land mass and terrain, and social development had 40, 30, 10, 10, 10 percent, respectively.[80] Post-1999, equality of states gained the biggest percentile, having 40 percent, while population had 30 percent, and the other 30 percent had to be shared by other factors.[81] The major increment in the horizontal revenue allocation was the derivation, which saw a 13 percent increase, from its previously low positions in past years. Shehu Shagari in 1982 had raised this percentage of royalties based on derivation to 1.6 percent; Babangida and his government, in 1992, raised it back to 3 percent, establishing a commission that would utilize the amount allocated to enhance development in the oil-producing region of the Niger Delta. Corruption of the commission, bad leadership, elite interests, and the careful omission of proceeds from offshore oil exploration in the derivation percentage led to the neglect of the oil-producing regions, which led to ethnic resentment, political unrest, terrorism, vandalism, and clamor for resource control. These also promoted ethnic citizenship, negating the philosophy of national integration, interest and unity, under whose guise resources were controlled by the federal government.

The return of civilian government improved things for the states. In vertical allocation, because the federal government reserves part of the federally collected revenues as part of its independent revenues, the states occupy the lower position, which was a far cry from the pre-independence allocation structure where the sharing formula was 40:60; this was in favor of the regional governments now separated. In 1992, according to

[77] Ibid.   [78] Salami, "Taxation, Revenue Allocation, and Fiscal Federalism in Nigeria."
[79] Ibid.   [80] Ibid.   [81] Ibid.

Salami, vertical allocation – which mapped out allocation between the center, state, and local governments – increased to 48.5, 24, and 20 percent, respectively.[82] From 2002, it followed the percentage of 52.68, 26.72, and 20.60, respectively. Presently, since the Obasanjo regime, the derivation formula has been 13 percent.

A close scrutiny of revenue sharing in Nigeria, especially that of the horizontal revenue allocation as aided by the Constitution, reveals that the state and local governments, or non-centralized forces, are at the mercy of the center, a case which makes an absolute mockery of federalism and its emphasis on fiscal autonomy. This is because the Federation Account is solely in the care of the federal government, and even the allocation formula is presided upon by the federal government and the National House of Assembly, without the State House of Assembly having a reasonable say in the matter. This is a tremendous assault on the division of powers and interdependency, because clearly only one party is dependent: the subnational government. In addition, and as consequence, the principles of separateness and independence of each government are violated. If this were not the case, then there would not be a clamor for resource control by the Niger Delta. The issue of equality of states is also a nonissue because the formula only enriches some states at the expense of others who are being impoverished, like in the Niger Delta region. The constitution is clearly faulty and old, and the techniques for dividing powers are ethnocentric; they favor a national frame where power is highly concentrated at the center and can be a means to control other ethnic groups and their resources. Obviously, the verdict is that Nigerian federalism has been ridiculed by forces that ought to improve it.

This revenue-sharing pattern that places more emphasis on population than independent revenue effort is a call to applaud indolence on the part of the state governments, who must wait on the federal government for allocations without worthwhile efforts at generating revenue, especially if they have the numbers. This case is rampant among many states in the country. More so, the near oversight of the derivation principle betrays the odious presence of ethnicism, lack of foresight, and political domination of elite interests, considering the irony between Nigeria's heavy reliance on petroleum and the continuous neglect of the region that produces the oil.

Owing to the heavy reliance of the subnational governments on the center, there have often been skirmishes and tensions between the state government and the local governments as a result of infringements on division of powers and on state authority by the center.

[82] Ibid.

State of the States and Vertical Bypassing: The Center, State, and Local Governments

The presence of the military on the Nigeria political scene not only led to the implementation of the unitary system of government that concentrated power in the hands of the national government at the expense of regions; it further led to the creation of states out of the regions, for the reasons of granting segmental autonomy to ethnic groups, especially the major ones, protecting ethnic interests, and reducing the power of the regions, as opposed to the idea of bringing the government closer to the people. The states created eventually culminated in the top-down model of federalism currently practiced in the country.

The interdependency of the states and the central government would transform into the dependence of former on the latter. This nullifies the impression of economic viability of the states as a criterion for their creation. Aside from many of the states surviving on allocations from the center, the rationale that led to their creation was ethnically and politically driven. Inamete's view that the creation of new states enables marginalized ethnic groups to gain a prominent voice in national and state affairs shows that representation is given precedence over economic viability, which undoes federalism's emphasis on economic and political viability and power diffusion. [83] Although sources like Nwabueze[84] champion the idea that federalism thrives on a multiplicity of group interests reacting upon one another to generate parity and balance, and that this can be achieved by the existence of multiple states, the current pattern of government in which the states are allocated yields from resources drawn from the purse of the federal government, which itself is enriched by the resources sourced from specific states, means some states benefit more from this kind of interrelationship at the expense of others. The current derivation principle and its effect on oil-producing regions is a good example of this. Furthermore, economically weaker states with high population numbers benefit more compared to those who contribute more to nation building through Internally Generated Revenues (IGRs). This is why, as of 2017, many states were deemed impossible to survive without the federation allocation as a result of dismally low internally generated revenues. Borno State, according to the 2017 Annual States Viability Index published by the Economic Confidential, produced an embarrassing 2.6 billion naira, a far cry from the 73.8 billion naira in allocations it received from the Federation

---

[83] Inamete, "Federalism in Nigeria."
[84] B. O. Nwabueze, *The Presidential Constitution of Nigeria* (Enugu: Nwamife Publishers, 1982).

Account (FAA).[85] Other states are Ebonyi, producing 2.3 billion naira compared to the 46.6 billion it received from the FAA; Kebbi, with 3.1 to 60.88 billion naira; Jigawa with 3.5 to 68.52 billion naira; Yobe with 3.24 to 53.93 billion naira; Gombe with 2.94 to 46 billion naira; Ekiti with 2.99 to 47.56 billion naira; Katsina with 5.54 to 83 billion naira; and Sokoto with 4.54 to 65.97 billion naira it received from the FAA.[86] More so, these revenues are obtained mainly from direct assessment, pay-as-you-earn tax, road taxes, and revenues from various Ministries, Departments, and Agencies (MDAs).[87] Upon further analysis, it is glaring that most of the insolvent states are Northern states. This of course reinforces the theory of some states benefiting from the sweat of others, because the same report has it that Lagos state, with 302 billion naira, has the IGR of thirty states combined, except Ogun, Kwara, Rivers, Edo, and Delta states, whose IGRs are more than 30 percent of their federal allocation. More so, these insolvent states further buttress the problem of the centralization policy and the delegation – not division – of economic power with which Nigeria's current federalism operates; these states are having their laziness buoyed and indirectly encouraged by the lifelines offered by the national government. As of 2016, only two states, Lagos and Ogun, generated additional revenues other than their allocations from the FAA.[88] In 2017, the National Bureau of Statistics reported that the low-performing states performed even lower, like Anambra, Bauchi, Osun, and Taraba,[89] while Lagos, Ogun, and Rivers states increased their IGRs, raising (with a few others) the total IGR across country by 100.04 billion naira – a 12.03 percent increase from 2016.

While this is a disturbing improvement occasioned by Nigeria's interpretation of federalism, which reveals that its defects are interlinked on multiple levels, it would not be enough to argue for the benefits of state creation alone as the viable solution to the problem of ethnicity and its adverse effects on the polity. This is because state creation only leads to more ethnic problems that have immense economic and political blowbacks, such as the clamor for resource control, which would further divide the country – especially if the resource of one state is used to power others. Were states to be given a measure of economic and political control over their resources, without incursive or officious intrusion by the central

---

[85] Oladeinde Olawoyin, "14 Nigerian States Insolvent Have Ridiculously Low Internal Revenue – Report," *Premium Times Nigeria*, May 30, 2017, www.premiumtimesng.co m/business/business-news/232507–14-nigerian-states-insolvent-%E2%808have-ridicu lously-low-internal-revenue-report.html.

[86] Ibid.   [87] Ibid.   [88] Ibid.

[89] *Sahara Reporters*, "NBS Data Reveals How Much Nigeria States Generated Internally in 2017," *Sahara Reporters*, March 24, 2018, https://saharareporters.com/2018/03/24/nbs-data-reveals-how-much-nigerian-states-generated-internally-2017.

government, and the states were empowered and not made subordinate to the center, with interdependency allowed to fully run its course, the resultant economic buoyancy through healthy competition and consensus on policies would improve the state of the nation.

Rather than allow for the smooth effectuation of policies, even within the vertical structure, the federal government still gives reasons for the state governments to accuse it of bypassing its legislative jurisdiction and infringing on its constitutional rights. One of such ways is the maintenance of law and order and the issue of local governments. The state governments, through constitutional provisions, have had the power to institute or create police forces stripped from them. The federal government controls the police forces that protect the states. In the 1999 Constitution, Section 214(1), which is the same as Section 198(1) of the 1979 Constitution, provides that the establishment of the Nigerian Police Force must be for the federation, while none other must be created for it or any of its parts.[90] Furthermore, evidently, the 1999 Constitution omitted provisions that backed any state that wished to form its own police force.[91] Consequently, the entire nation, backed by the Constitution, is policed by a federal-controlled police force, the Nigerian Police Service. This itself has led to a flouting of the rule of division of political power, because the result is the inability of a state Governor, as the Chief Security Officer, to command the Commissioner of Police in charge of the state arm of the force. This is because under the current structure as provided by the Constitution, the Commissioner of Police answers only to the authority constituted in the federal government. The reasons given for this, as tended by Inegbedion and Omorogie, are that underneath the control of state governments, the police force could be put to self-serving uses; yet, this accusation also implicates the federal government. Moreover, the fact that the local police authorities of the old regime and previous republics were put to use that threatened to divide the nation, or were used as instruments of oppression, does not absolve the present police force. That a federally controlled police force would prevent political repression is an overstretch judging by the state of the nation and the oppressive practices of the dominant elite groups and elite executives. It is not entirely wise that a region or subnational entity that claims to have political and economic autonomy and jurisdiction to a certain reasonable extent, under a constitution, would not have to an equally reasonable extent some degree of control over the police authority manning its territory. It would seem that this has been rectified, as posited

---

[90] Inegbedion and Omoregie, "Federalism in Nigeria: A Re-appraisal."   [91] Ibid.

by Inegbedion and Omorogie, but to the extent to which it has been implemented in the Constitution is a different matter altogether.

In continuation of my point of governmental interference and vertical power usurpation, not only are the state governments bypassed in terms of authority in their jurisdictions, they are also bypassed in matters relating to local governments. The local governments see the state governments as overbearing; the latter are often accused of not recognizing the local governments' constitutional powers by removing local government chairmen at will, and withholding allocations from the federal government reserved for them. The summary of the state governments' approach to the local governments is reminiscent of that of the federal to the state. The states accuse the local governments of desiring sovereignty and not relative autonomy when they do no generate revenue, as if all states generate significant revenues. They are accused of not having executive capacity and are as such useless.[92] Consequently, in some states, the tenure of local governments has been truncated from three to two years, while others maintain the usual three. More so, the State Houses further generate functions for the local government officials as deemed fit under the constitution. The fluctuation in tenure caused uproar at some point, and the Senate set up a committee to make recommendations to the National Assembly on the matter. This was perceived as a slight and a flouting of the constitutional provision Section 7, that guaranteed the legislative rights of the States to establish, structure, finance, and share functions to such councils.[93]

Constitutionally, the creation of local governments must be approved by the federal government. States that created local governments without approval received no allocations for those local governments. Lagos State is a good example of this: Governor Tinubu created additional local governments and President Olusegun Obasanjo refused to acknowledge the existence of those local governments. Bayelsa State tried the same approach, and it was considered a null attempt by the Senate who quoted Section 8(3) of the Constitution, where provisions are made for the creation of local governments. Quoting Elaigwu, "unless the list of local governments as contained in the first schedule, Section 3, Part 1, is duly amended, no new local government is legal."[94]

There have been cases of further undue processes between the state and the local governments, such as that in Sokoto, where the state government was taken to court by fifteen local governments for deducting 3 percent from its statutory allocation for funding the Sokoto Emirate Council.[95]

---

[92] Elaigwu, "Federalism in Nigeria's New Democratic Polity."   [93] Ibid.   [94] Ibid., 82.
[95] Ibid.

There have also been underhanded practices like state governors colluding with State Houses to shorten the tenures of local government (elected) officials in order to install their supporters, especially if the incumbent political party at the state level differs from that of the elected chairmen.

It is evident that, clearly, there is a misuse and misallocation of power in Nigeria across all levels and tiers of governance that affects its federal structure. Even its constitution is faulty and its application poor.

Conclusion: The Way Forward

This chapter would not be conclusive if certain questions are not answered. Is federalism the best course of political strategy in Nigeria? Considering the nation's military history and pluralist foundations, the answer is an affirmative yes. Regionalism, which would afford each region the chance to develop politically and economically and control its own resources before contributing to the national purse, manifests the principles of federalism. More so, if each state is granted relative autonomy, with due consultation processes instituted between its Houses and that of the national body, feelings of intrusion and hegemony would be drastically done away with. In the current system, everybody wants to have a seat at the table, owing to the concentrated authority at the center. Concentrated efforts in reviving state power and decentralizing the maximum power of the center would reduce the powers associated with the center that warrant the negative competitive spirit displayed by ethnic groups and political parties contesting for political seats at the center. This way, even ethnic conflicts and hegemonic tendencies would be reduced.

Federalism is the best way to establish and maintain vested interests in nation building. Through appropriately defined and applied principles of power devolution, separation of powers, legislative lists, regional character of political parties, segmental autonomy, mutual veto, and other consociational methods, and a constitution that expressly makes provision for intergovernmental consultation and development, federalism would reveal itself as the most viable option for Nigeria. Autonomy would improve standards of living and the lives of citizens, as each state and local government would be directly connected to its people and be responsible for their economic welfare and security.

By being in control of agriculture, labor, security, education, tax, health, revenue, and resources, the states would adequately provide for the development of related institutions that would react positively on the economy of that region. In particular, more healthy competition that would impact the nation positively would have been engendered. This is because without the heavy reliance on federal allocation, states that are less productive would increase efforts to be on par with the rest in terms of resource and human capital. This would also lessen the hold the center has, as well as the elite executive and the occupying ethnic group, on others in the society. It would also do away with the embarrassment that is the current sharing formula and derivation principles, affording the nation the chance to tap into its varied resources, and subvert the reliance on petroleum as well as the federal government's fiscal power. Clear devolution of power would mean that local governments should be also autonomous to some extent. This also means revenue allocated to them should not be directed to or redistributed by the State Joint Allocation Committee.

Properly instituted federalism that is practiced with a properly crafted constitution that effectively spells out ways and manners of performing democracy are ways through which human life can be enhanced in Nigeria. But, as it is glaringly obvious that Nigeria practices a strange case of federalism, it is important, as previously suggested, that we look up to countries where federalism is practiced in a progressive way as a system of governance. Nigeria could borrow from the dual federalism the United States uses; this would clearly divide powers between the national and subnational governments, without unnecessarily subordinating one under the other. Even though Nigeria's political history is at variance with that of the United States, wherein previously independent states merged to surrender some of their autonomy to a center government, Nigeria could take a cue from the legislative list structuring. The federal government can only be in control of international trade, currency, war, armed forces, treaties, and the postal system, while the individual states would be in control of aspects such as education, health, mainland security, and the police force. The powers to control infrastructure, tax, and maintain courts can be shared. Most importantly, there should be a system of check and balances.

Part III

Democracy and Governance

7   Ethnicities and Political Identities

Introduction: Ethnicity and Politics

The relationship between ethnicity and political identity raises several questions. What is their relationship, and what does it mean to examine ethnicity against a backdrop of politics? What does it mean to locate identity, as a construct, within the purview of ethno-politics? Historical dynamics are invoked when ethnicity and politics are bound together, especially in a pluralist space like Nigeria. These questions are inseparable from discussions of the character of modern politics – they reflect the multicultural, multiracial, and multiethnic texture of global society, where identity is a universal currency.

Spatial connections, such as territoriality, ancestral roots, and boundaries and borders are applied as invariable indices of political validation. At the very least, they operate as undercurrents. They reveal that traditional notions of kinship and relational ties are mechanisms to explore tides of belonging and nonbelonging, even in the modern world. In many political environments, kinship bonds are often wielded as tools of sociopolitical negotiation alongside ties anchored on spatial or nonphysical notions of boundary and permissibility.

The logic behind this kind of transference, carrying features of ethnic grouping from the cultural front to the political, is built on the notion that the characteristics of an ethnic unit should be used to define a political unit – its permissions and the reach of its ideology.[1] In Africa, the political structure is undergirded by definitions of sociocultural units. An ethnic group is one founded on shared ideologies, defined binding ties, modes of rationality, systems of communication, and performative procedures. Over time, these come to be seen as cultural or as a group-specific way of existing. Shared ancestry, ideology, defined systems of executing tasks, and even language are some of the transferred features.

---

[1] Here, "cultural" refers to some sort of organic or structured unit.

Figure 7.1 A group of Northern Nigerian men dressed in flowing gowns and turbans.

These features define ethnic groups and political groups in varying degrees. In a country like Nigeria, the political parties that first sprang up in the wake of increased nationalism were ethnically oriented: AG, Action Group in the Southwest; NCNC, National Council of Nigeria and the Cameroons; and NPC, Northern People's Congress, in the North are examples.[2] They were headed by indigenous members of cultures: Nnamdi Azikiwe championed the cause of the NCNC, Ahmadu Bello led the NPC, and Obafemi Awolowo was the dominant figure within the AG. Over time, these parties transitioned through shrinkage and expansion, internal crises that led to bifurcations, and de facto military decrees that led to unlawful disbandment. Additional dictates of time and space, such as the Civil War and the horrifying reign of General Sani Abacha, changed these party types further and provided the impetus for contemporary political parties. Partisan politics and political parties today carry on the legacy of these earlier groups.

[2] See Richard Sklar, *Nigerian Political Parties* (Princeton: Princeton University Press, 1963).

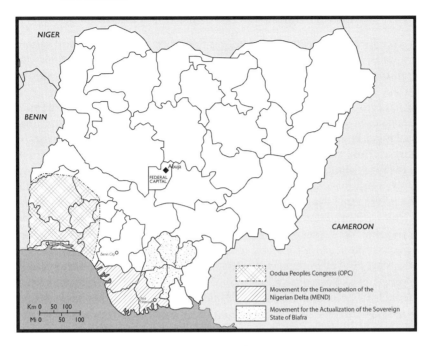

Map 7.1 Nigerian southern-separatist groups.

   The political groups were once national groups, owing to their nationalistic temper and ideology. At their core, they were ethnically oriented,
which is striking for two reasons: first, the definition of ethnicity, or what
an ethnic group can be, is expansive; the definition depends on how the
features defining ethnicity are harnessed and expressed. The other observation is that ethnic groups are not simply "tribes," which is a term that
carries its own significant derogatory symbolism. The term is routinely
used in discussions of "Third World" countries and excluded from discussions of comparable European sociocultural units. Arguments have
been made against Eurocentric apologists or scholars designating ethnic
groups as tribes.[3]

---

[3] For further arguments on ethnic groups as national groups that should not be seen as
"tribes," especially since Western cultural groups do not receive the same treatment,
see Chukwuemeka Onwubu, "Ethnic Identity, Political Integration, and National
Development: The Igbo Diaspora in Nigeria," *The Journal of Modern African
Studies* 13, no. 3 (1975): 399–413; and Adebayo O. Olukoshi and Liisa Laakso,
Challenges to the Nation-State in Africa (Uppsala: Scandinavian Institute of African
Studies, 1995).

Framing Ethnicity in the Context of Politics

It is challenging to establish working definitions of ethnicity and ethnic groups; excessively specific definitions or undue overgeneralizations can limit their usefulness. The definition of ethnicity has recently seen various inputs that expand its meaning, accommodating other identity-based formations like religion for their legitimacy informing primordial identity cleavages around a religious base.[4] It provides organic and institutional backing, allowing the use of group identity to negotiate, compete for, or prey on public resources and democratic power – or to engage in these activities while simultaneously pursuing self-advancing interests. A straightforward definition comes from Osaghe, who defines it as the "employment [of]identity and difference to gain advantage in situations of competition, conflict or cooperation."[5]

Osaghe's definition has its advantages: it identifies ethnicity as a construct by conscious social actors, and it does not exclude ethnicity's potential for positivity. However, this general definition only accounts for two possible approaches to conceptual categories of definition: constructivist and instrumentalist. Deriving a working definition for ethnicity is not that simple, especially when it can be viewed from other conceptual lenses, such as the primordialist, or essentialist (emphasizing ethnicity as inscribed or natural identity), or institutionalist (identifying formal policies and political institutions as factors to consider in defining ethnic groups). And ethnicity's connection to religion is continually presented as a basis for its definition.

The basic conception of ethnicity does not overtly centralize external categorization or identification. Ethnicity is ascribed identity as much as it is inscribed identity; it is underscored by shared characteristics that differentiate its members from others. Current applications of ethnicity, as a term, often involve the use of multiple conceptual framing points[6] – one does not necessarily exclude the other. There is a general agreement on constitutive elements of ethnicity, even if they vary from group to group, but there is often divergence regarding the formation of ethnicities or ethnic identity, or to which purposes they are put. Conceptual frameworks often identify specific factors in the formation of ethnicity, and if there are significant disparities in the perception of how ethnicity is formed, it might be simplistic to slap

---

[4] See Onwubu, "Ethnic Identity, Political Integration, and National Development"; and Abubakar Dauda, "Ethnic Identity, Democratization, and the Future of the African State," *African Issues* 29, no. 1/2 (2001): 31–36.

[5] E. Eghosa Osaghae, *Structural Adjustment and Ethnicity in Nigeria* (Uppsala: Nordic African Institute, 1995).

[6] Claude Ake, *The Feasibility of Democracy in Africa* (Dakar: CODESRIA Books, 2000).

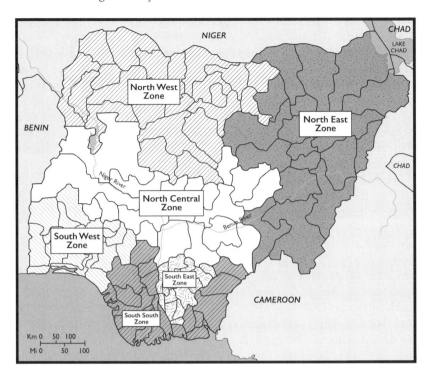

Map 7.2 Nigeria, political zones.

a definition on it. There is also the matter of religion being seen along the lines of ethnicity.

Northern Nigeria organizes its political identity around the religion of Islam, and eleven northern states are governed under the permissions of Sharia Law.[7] The 1999 National Constitution is still in place, which institutes a kind of plural legal order. Religion is politicized in the same way as ethnicity,[8] and Nigeria's political history testifies to this. Shortly after independence, when Nigeria was well federated and divided into Northern, Western, and Eastern Regions, political parties controlled each region. The NPC, AG, and NCNC shaped politics in their regions to benefit the dominant ethnicities and privilege their preferred religious leanings.

---

[7] Paul Gwaza, "Romanticising Legal Pluralism through Religious Revival in Democratic Nigeria: Crusaders, Criminals, and Casualties" (paper, International Conference on Ethnicity, Religion, and Peacebuilding, University of Jos, Jos, Nigeria, February 18–20, 2013), https://ssrn.com/abstract=2544836.

[8] Dauda, "Ethnic Identity, Democratization."

The NCNC sought to strengthen its relations with the Vatican. Christianity, especially when spread by missionaries, flowered in the East, as is evidenced by the number of Easterners that belong to any of the orthodox denominations. The NPC furthered its region's relations with other Muslim countries, campaigning to integrate Islam and the state. Both ethnicity and religion are socially constructed, wedded to the realities of the social fabric that produces them. This means that identities rooted in either ethnicity or religion are vulnerable to emotional manipulation. Ultimately, they bear a political burden, and their instrumentality as assets or liabilities cannot be ignored.[9]

Another nuance contributing to the intricacy of defining ethnicity is the issue of political correctness. An ethnic group is said to be bound by a defined language with a primordial quality and a unique native culture. It is a term used in relation to African countries that are considered heterogeneous because they are populated with diverse, organic cultural groups. European countries like Scotland are regarded as homogenous nations – 98 percent of the population are white, and Scottish whites make up 88 percent. South Asians, Chinese, mixed-race peoples, and Blacks make up 1.09, 0.32, 0.25, and 0.16 percent of Scotland's population, respectively.[10] Scots are referred to as a national group, with the sense of a nation-state, instead of an ethnic group. The designation of "nation" is also used by the indigenous peoples of America, who refer to each indigenous group as a Nation (Navajo Nation, for example). In the case of indigenous Americans, the backing of international recognition is absent.

Nigeria is composed of multiple ethnicities, and the Scotland–Nigeria example points to a lopsided usage of ethnicity. Arguments may be made about differences in demographics and percentages, but it does not explain why one is considered heterogeneous, using the term "ethnicity," and the other is considered homogenous, using the term "nation." Both countries comprise dominant and minority ethnic groups. Ethnicity itself is considered a modern phenomenon, constructed by the colonial machinery.

Nnoli[11] has done extensive work to emphasize colonial imprints in the architecture of ethnicity and, together with Mbah and Mwangu,[12] identifies the development of ethnicity as a politically activated tag; it is an

[9] Adebayo O. Olukoshi and Liisa Laakso, *Challenges to the Nation-State in Africa* (Uppsala: Scandinavian Institute of African Studies, 1995).

[10] *World Population Review*, "Scotland Population 2019," *World Population Review*, 2019, http://worldpopulationreview.com/countries/scotland-population/.

[11] Okwudiba Nnoli, *Ethnic Politics in Nigeria* (Enugu: Fourth Dimension, 1978).

[12] Peter Mbah and Chikodiri Nwangwu, "Sub-ethnic Identity and Conflict in Nigeria: The Policy Option for the Resolution of the Conflict Between Ezza and Ezillo in Ebonyi State," *Mediterranean Journal of Social Sciences* 5, no. 2 (2014): 681–688.

encompassing construct arising in urban centers as a result of colonialism's influence shaping the development of the nation's civilization and ushering in modernity. They viewed the identity-based cleavages currently informing ethnicity as a mode of organically organizing in response to urban factors that included perceived outsiders, intruders, or competitors. This organization allows groups to address social exclusion, competition for scarce resources, growing poverty, contestation of boundaries, and the drive for state power. If ethnicity carries a modern heritage, then how were these groups recognized prior to colonialism, especially if colonialism hemmed together separate, indigenously sovereign, and organically different communities?

Nigeria nationalist and premier of the then–Eastern Region, Nnamdi Azikiwe, recognized the grey areas involved in defining ethnic groups and national bodies, referring to the Igbo ethnic group as the Igbo nation on several occasions.[13] Obafemi Awolowo, another nationalist who possessed a brilliant understanding of Yoruba political history, only used the term in reference to the various Yoruba ethnicities (Egba, Awori, Ijebu, and Oyo) as they existed prior to colonialism. These ethnicities were independent of each other before being merged into a group labeled with the term Yoruba. The concept of a "Yoruba nation" as a single and unified entity is a modern construct.

Ethnicity, used as an umbrella term or political signifier, is fluid in its definition. It also carries political undertones, betrayed by an appropriateness that is largely underscored by the specific context and the degree of shared characteristics among members of the group being referenced. These characteristics are judged based on how they can or have been forged into a solid framework to create an identity that can compete and control.

Ethnic groups implicate political formation in more ways than one, and the implications are complex, manifold, and intricate. Nigeria exemplifies an effect that occurs in many African (and even Western) countries: ethnicity can rub off on the definition of political identity. Overt ethnocultural groups have been birthed through strong nationalist ideology, as seen in Awolowo's AG, which became a political group. The AG was a political party with a strong Yoruba base that grew out of the Egbe Omo Oduduwa (The Group of the Descendants of Oduduwa) group created in 1945,[14] focused on harnessing Yoruba heritage in an inclusive way to allow various Yoruba sub-ethnicities, as they presently exist, to compete

---

[13] See Nnamdi Azikiwe, *My Odyssey: An Autobiography* (London: C. Hurst, 1970).

[14] John Ayoade, "Party and Ideology in Nigeria: A Case Study of the Action Group," *Journal of Black Studies* 16, no. 2 (1985): 169–188.

on a national level with other ethnic groups. The group provided the impetus, ideology, and machineries that introduced a Yoruba-focused political party to Nigeria's political scene.

Considering the frequency and extent to which ethnic groups provide templates for advancing political identities in Nigeria's political climate, it is logical that ethnicity continues to entrench itself as a major determinant of political identity and legitimacy. Glazer and Moynihan argue that ethnicity has been instrumentalized, especially in Africa and the Third World, to become integral to a country's political structure. Politically conscious groups, social groups, support groups, ethnic groups, and even racial groups now organize politically to advocate for their ideas and pursue their interests.[15]This sums up ethnicity's function in a political system. Countries in Africa provide prime examples, but the advanced West also sees this kind of formation, suggesting that ethnicity is both pervasive and invasive in political formation.

Cultural identity – defined by spatial, ancestral, and paternal ties, or simply indigeneity – finds abundant resonance within politics. For example, during the 2008 US presidential campaign of Barack Obama, continuous references were made to his Kenyan (Luo) roots, regardless of how poorly founded the arguments were. This sort of identity politics, playing out on such an advanced stage, is a strong signal that announces how (post)modern philosophies of "being," largely characterized by fluid and liberal notions like migration, multiculturalism, hybridism, syncretism, and other "-isms" of globality, still accommodate orthodox indices of identity.

The global definitions for some types of belonging, like citizenship, are based on some of the parameters used to construct primordial identities. As Mbah and Nwangwu argue, a basic condition for this type of belonging is anchored on one's attachment to the community and, through it, to the ancestors.[16] Primordial definitions emphasize attachment by ancestry – birth or blood. In Obama's case, modern definitions did not cancel these parameters; they added the conditions of migration and a substantial period of exile in constructing his identity. And in constructing an identity, primordial indices are appropriated. All notions of belonging are exclusionary; Obama's identity as an American, and more importantly, as an American president, rests on the extent of his divorce or attachment to his Luo ethnicity in Kenya.

Regardless of which side of the debate is being championed, or the degree to which recourse is made to Obama's Kenyan roots, or how much

---

[15] Nathan Glazer and Daniel P. Moynihan, *Ethnicity: Theory and Experience* (Cambridge: Harvard University Press, 1975).

[16] Mba and Nwangwu, "Sub-ethnic Identity and Conflict in Nigeria."

generational migration is sufficient to validate his American identity, connections to his Luo roots situate ethnicity as an essential aspect of his political identity. It is linked to the condition of indigeneity through ancestry and land, and both are primordial templates. Any claim to an African root rests on how much Obama embraces his Luo ethnicity. Such complexities exemplify the extent to which aspects of ethnic definitions have permeated or now exist as criteria for reinforcing political identity.

Ethnic definitions include spatialized ancestral ties, or indigeneity defined by connections to a lineage through land. Spatial politics, or the politics of space along ancestral lines, has always been present in the invocation of ethnic affiliations, especially toward politically oriented goals. It has also been a principal feature of ethnic conflict management,[17] especially in countries with warring or conflicting institutionalized identities. Obama's case unveils the connectivity of the aforementioned approaches for understanding ethnicity in relation to politics:

1. Constructivist approaches that engineer identities into being rely on institutionalist methods, because migration and citizenship themselves are defined by formal political policies. Notions of belonging, borders, and boundaries are all defined by political bills and institutionalized procedures for absorption. The construction of identity follows set patterns defined by political, organized, and formal procedures.
2. Primordialist approaches are implicated in instrumentalist constructs of identity, especially in mixed-ethnicity cases where an identity can be beneficial for a specific cause. Africa is a great example of this.
3. All four approaches to understanding the construction of ethnicity and its implication in politics are intricately woven together; they should be approached as such.[18]

Ethnic identity can be fluid and expansive, reinforcing the logic of the constructivist school holding that ethnic-affiliated identity can be constructed. However, it can also be inherited, which is a major point of primordialists who hold identity as partly biological and fixed. In the modern–traditional dyad, both schools have their logics and fall neatly into either category. For example, Obama's identity as an American is constructed and fluid due to the effects of hybridity, migration, and multiple consciousness. These are evoked by the condition of shift in notions of home, globality, and modernity. However, Obama's identity as an African, a Kenyan with Luo ancestry, is defined by primordial

[17] Henrik Angerbrandt, "Struggles over Identity and Territory: Regional Identities in Ethnoreligious Conflict in Northern Nigeria," *Nationalism and Ethnic Politics* 22, no. 2 (2016): 172–192.
[18] Ibid.

conditions of indigeneity and blood ties, which evoke notions of being fixed and inscribed. Ethnic-based identity can be both fixed and fluid.

The logic is simple: the cultural route toward self-definition intersects with the modern as obtainable in politics. In Obama's case, references to his Kenyan root imply a relationship, however subtle and indirect, between descent-related ties and territoriality that are an index of identity and mainstays of primordial definitions. Although more modern indices can be spatial related – citizenship is hinged on several modes and duration of inhabitation – they do not particularize ancestral ties.

Ethnicity and political identity are constantly in a state of flux, with the one trying to influence the other in an unstable combination of ancient and modern notions of being. In Africa, this struggle takes on additional layers of importance. There may be implicit reference to ethnicity through ancestral ties and space elsewhere, occurring as a significant aspect of the process of political identity building, but ethnicity is institutionalized as a political category in Africa, especially in Nigeria. The mobilization of ethnic affiliations for political gains is pervasive, and political consciousness is organized along ethnic lines as a foundational part of the political process.

Regardless of differences in degree or expression, one vital conclusion is to be made: in either Africa or the West, political history continues to emphasize the pervading potency of ethnicity as a mode of identification in politics. Alongside this, ethnicity can function as a mode of social organization and a conduit for framing political claims.[19] If this is so, then what is the point?

1. Political identity and ethnic identity are forever locked in an embrace. Any individual or group identity bears echoes of ethnic definition because ethnicity is imbued in most expressions or formations of identity, regardless of geographic specificity.
2. Regardless of civilization, advancement, and the transition of political processes through time, the essentialism of ethnicity is sustained.
3. When points 1 and 2 are fused to generate a coherent argument, it is clear that the criteria maintaining the essentialism of ethnicity in antediluvian times remains the same.
4. Ethnicity and politics are tangled in a process that can be best presented as the ethnicization of politics and the politicization of ethnicity.[20]

The argument is that ethnicity, as a defining feature, has been completely transported from its primal expression into a modern context and its

---

[19] Rogers Brubaker, "Religion and Nationalism: Four Approaches," *Nations and Nationalism* 18, no. 1 (2012): 2–20.
[20] Ibid.

attendant connotations. The principal differences between now and then are the textures and manifestations of these connotations; they are merely particulars that adjust to the specifics of a time and space. But how have these connotations been expressed in modern context, and to what extent?

To answer this question, one must understand the implication of ethnic connections and kinship ties. This understanding is achieved by holding a historical lens against several African countries, and perhaps countries in other continents. The enduring presence of ethnicity in global politics and culture cannot be missed; it is either ominous or it is forged into a tool that advances group ideology. Ethnicity has been wielded as a separatist instrument, or a tool of "othering," to borrow the post-colonial term. It has been used in countless examples as markings for extermination. It has led to genocides: in Rwanda, it served as a product of socially and culturally engineered hate in 1994, leading to the death of thousands of Tutsis by members of the Hutu militia and political elite. One ethnic group was animated to extremes of incivility by perceived notions of superiority over another.

A calamitous experiment in ethnic performance also played out in Romania as the Nazis marked Gypsies for extermination in the early twentieth century. The Polish were subjected to this atrocity during Nazi Germany's invasion of Poland in World War II. Burundi and the Democratic Republic of Congo also saw Tutsi–Hutu rivalries play out to extremes.[21] Further back in time, the Wu Hu genocide in Northern China is another poignant historical example: Ran Min's extermination order against the Jie and the Wu Hu, issued after they challenged his legitimacy, led to a contemptible genocide. The same goes for Pol Pot's Cambodian genocide in 1975. These are a minuscule fraction of the instances where ethnicity has been used as basis for crimes against humanity.

The 2017 case of the Muslim Rohingya in Southeast Asia is a more recent example, and the Igbo of Nigeria is another example close to home. Each was the result of one identity's calculated, organized killing of another – the Myanmar government and the Hausa, respectively. The California genocide is another example of ethnic cleansing, perpetuated by a body of people now considered to inhabit the last bastion of freedom and progress; the genocide decimated the indigenous population of California and much of the territory now identified as the United States of America. The Jews may be the greatest victims of such hostile use of ethnicity or kinship ties: they have been repeatedly massacred throughout

---

[21] Dauda, "Ethnic Identity, Democratization, and the Future of the African State."

history by several governments, including the Russians and the Soviet Union, the Nazis, the Romans, and Islamic countries.

The use of ethnicity is most visibly used as an instrument of selfish interest, hate, and massive destruction in the World Wars. Groups of people sharing cultural traits, heritages, values, and mythology – amongst other systems of knowledge and group-distinctive traits or forms of ethnic affiliation – perceive themselves to be naturally born to dominate the world and determined to do so by any means. Examples of ethnicity-induced violence are too many to contain in a single volume, were such a work to be commissioned. Patterns of ethnically induced violence are too apparent to be missed, leading one to theorize on the instrumentality of ethnicity. Ethnicity and political identity are never mutually exclusive, even when ethnicity is not defined in more primal senses.

Ethnicity's possibilities are boundless, not only as a tool of affiliation but also in its applications and what it can achieve. It depends on the orientation of those who invoke it, which further embeds the essentialism of ethnicity within politics. To identify with an ethnic composition is to present the self as loyal to it. It can be either a product of destruction or a weapon of progress – even if human conceptions of progress and how to actualize it lie in grey areas. Empires, such as those of Rome, Mali, and Macedonia, have thrived on their ability to forge ethnic affiliation for productive purposes.

Ethnicity can be used as a universal currency. But if ethnicity can instigate political action by humans toward and against others on a global scale, then how then does it operate in a specific setting, especially a pluralist one like Nigeria? These are the major ideas I will be exploring:
1. The ways in which political identity – and politics generally, in a manner that highlights consequences – and ethnicity are fused together;
2. How ethnicity is ensconced in the Nigerian political framework; and
3. How the four approaches to understanding ethnicity are intricately implicated in one another and, in the case of Nigerian political reality, cannot be cleanly separated.

Ethnicity and Diversity

As noted in an earlier chapter, Nigeria is home to over 200 clearly defined ethnic groups. It accommodates, and even promotes, ethnicity as a form of identification, enough for it to become a mainstay in Nigerian politics.[22] To appreciate diversity, we must understand its relevance to

---

[22] For figures and sizes of ethnic groups, see Chapter 4.

the Nigerian situation. Diversity thrives through variety, and variety – in its purest, non-agenda-driven form – is a source of strength. The reliance on variety informs civilization in several ways, and it informs many African countries. Before Nigeria's reliance on oil, it allowed the country to thrive economically. The Southwest Region produced cocoa, which contributed significantly to the country's foreign as well as domestic earnings. The Southern Region provided palm oil and later crude oil. The Northerners, especially the Fulani, are largely herders, and they produce groundnuts; both of their activities aided the national economy.

Diversity was present in more than commerce. Easterners and Westerners, who privileged Western education as pivotal to identity and nation building, populated administrative cadres at federal and state levels of the civil service. The civil service, judiciary, and House of Representatives were regionalized; it promoted diversity and allowed each region to grow at its own pace. They harnessed home-grown means of advancing political and economic power, competed favorably with others, and avoided becoming federal appendages or being forced to assume subservient status. Attention was focused inward, spreading the benefits of regional success to positively affect the country in the long run. At the time, Nigeria's political structure was a far cry from that of the present day.

In arts and music, diversity enhanced and sustained Nigeria's stature. The Eastern Region contributed to the growth of Highlife music in Nigeria through maestros such as Dennis Osadebe, Bright Chimezie, Lexy Mella, Victor Uwaifo, Rex Lawson, and Nelly Uchendu. They reenergized the performance arts in Africa and cast a spotlight on its countries. In the West, music such as Juju, Afrobeats, Apala, Afrojuju, Fuji, and even Highlife by Victor Olaiya influenced the melodies of the age, generally affecting the ambience of the period. It made positive contributions to domestic earning and economic progress through sponsored shows, festivities, and organized events. People like Ebenezer Obey, Fela Kuti, and Sunny Ade performed outside the country, earning nominations for prestigious awards like the Grammys.

Nigeria's arts and cultural space saw a proliferation of cultural programs, like FESTAC in the late 1970s, along with the growth of distinctive blends of traditional and modern art. There were cross-cultural influences, borrowing, collaborations, and multicultural programs. The National Youth Service Corps program grew out of the need to harmonize the nation and increase the benefits of diversity. Region-specific traits, such as cuisine, ceremonial wear and attire, and the traditions undergirding them, were adopted by others. Each region, and the ethnic groups within them, revived and improved Nigeria's cultural atmosphere. The nation harnessed the strength of its rich demographic diversity and hinged its progress on it. It was the opposite of diversity being used as a tool for political division, which is what happened in Nigeria's Civil War.

The instrumentality of diversity is determined through use, or through the desires of those wielding it for personal purposes. It becomes a source of discord in the presence of irreconcilable differences, and the Nigerian situation is no different. The 400+ ethnic groups in the region testify to a richness of diversity, but the problems of representation in politics, government, and civil service signal the presence of disunity. With diversity comes territoriality, especially in urban centers or in the wake of increasing civilization. Mobilization around shared cultural traits becomes the means to an end, rather than an end itself, because diversity suggests the possibility of competition. Ethnic and religious conflict can stem from such competition, frequently defined by state resources, land, and other forms of capital. In these conflicts, indigeneity becomes the first tool of defence; groups plot to manufacture forms of cleavage that are organic enough to compete and arrogate resources. Spatial politics are a recurrent outcome, often approached as a knee-jerk remedy to identity-based conflicts, whether religious or ethnic.[23]

The creation of additional states was a key indication that ethnic diversity had created an arena for the growth of discord and unhealthy spatial politics. Constitutional efforts to carve out territories that satiated the hunger of ethnic groups were formal attempts to curb the violence, but they only ended up increasing ethnic rivalry and distrust. The Mid-western Region was created in 1963; it followed a bill that had been passed, approved, and backed by a constitution providing grounds for a new region to be created when two of the three existing regions supported it. The Mid-western Region was carved out of the Western Region because the Northern Region and the Eastern Region supported the Bill. The coalition provided four lessons:

1. Spatial politics often require odd capitulations and coalitions. The Eastern Region, dominated by the Ibos, and the Northern Region, populated with a Hausa–Fulani majority that also held power at the center, were not fond of each other.
2. Diversity breeds contempt in Nigeria's case. This plays out in the way constitutional provisions are structured, exploited, and molded to suit specific desires. Political decisions are textured by heavy ethnic leanings, and the Constitution is vulnerable to undue influence from ethnic groups.

[23] Angerbrandt, "Struggles over Identity and Territory."

3. Approaches to settling ethnic disputes, or appeals to divisive expressions of differences, have implicated politics. Although they can be glaringly prejudicial, they often carry formal and constitutional appeal.
4. Institutional approaches to resolving ethnic problems can create new ways for affected groups to form identities along ethnic lines. The Mid-western Region's example reveals that formal policies can lead to the construction of new, ethnic-based formations.[24]

The creation of states in Nigeria follows the same pattern. Regional boundaries are not coterminous with ethnic boundaries, and regions with clear boundaries can accommodate more than one ethnic group, as is the case with the Eastern and Northern Regions. Creating a new, Mid-western Region did not douse the tensions of the period; the country was already in an "ethnic trap," a situation where ethno-regional and religious identities shaped the character and patterns of political activities.[25] The Civil War, whose immediate cause was Northerners exterminating Igbos in the north, is an example. Diversity can lead to integration, inter-ethnic relationships, and cross-border migration. Territoriality, regionalist politics, and ethnic intolerance treated the Igbos as outsiders in the north, where they had made their home.

Affirmative action measures, such as segmental autonomy, failed to stem ethnic rivalry and unhealthy contests, largely because of the diversity within the regions themselves. The philosophy behind affirmative action can be reduced to two points: (1) bring government closer to the people[26]; and (2) provide ethnic groups the space to grow without being overshadowed by others within a region. The action failed because minority groups did not feel that the regional government considered their interests. The political maneuvering, intended to provide regions with a substantial degree of autonomy, recreated the ethnic dominance and centralization of power that occurred at the federal level. Minority ethnic groups complained that they were regularly being excluded from regional dialogues conducted by the dominant ethnic groups that were the face of the region, at all levels of representation.

A governmental transformation was initiated to fight this new inequality and the domination of elites, catering to the minorities who clamored for representation and the dethronement of the Big Three in each region. A four-region federal government became a thirty-six-state federal structure. Yakubu Gowon's government created twelve states from the four regions: North-western State, Kaduna State, Kano State, North-eastern

---

[24] Ibid.
[25] Dauda, "Ethnic Identity, Democratization, and the Future of the African State."
[26] Ibid.

State, Kwara State, Benue-Plateau State, Western State, East-central State, Lagos State, Bendel State, Cross River State, and Rivers State. Seven more states were created in 1976, bringing the number of states to nineteen. From 1987 to 1991, twenty-one states existed along with a Federal Capital Territory. By 1996, thirty-six states had been created.[27]

The hope was that dividing the nation into states would provide ethnic groups with the agency necessary to contribute to national development, keeping them from being stifled by the domineering Big Three. The political action that endured four consecutive military governments was shaped by ethnic considerations. The pressure to restructure the nation's federal organization and satisfy the groups clamoring for constituent units has led Nigerian political formation to be described as sobering, and the territorial arrangement of the nation's federal system has been called unstable.[28]

These approaches were intended to prevent outbreaks of ethnic-based crises, but a solution could not be engineered successfully. States often witnessed large-scale, intra-ethnic battles. Crises – like the one in Kafanchan in 1987, and in Zangon Kataf in 1992, or Ife-Modakeke in the West in 1997, and Ezza–Ezillo occurring in the East in 2008 and 2009 – are examples of intra-ethnic wars where groups, distinguished either by religion or ethnic affiliation, sought each other out with murderous intent. Other examples were the Tiv–Jukun, Tiv–Hausa, Andoni–Ogoni, and Umuleri–Aguleri conflicts.[29] The Kafanchan crises stemmed from religious intolerance in the Northern region, specifically Kaduna state.[30]

Many attempts have been made to stem ethnic conflicts: federalism to ensure the decentralization of power, creation of a third arm of government, state creation, quota systems, consociational paradigms, revenue allocation formulas, the cancellation of ethnic-based political parties and the creation of broad-spectrum ones, federal character, adoption of a presidential system of governance, and modifications to the Constitution. These political strategies to address the negative corollaries of the diversity problem have only widened the divide.

The federal character and quota system, designed for an effective process and equitable distribution of resources and substantive representation

---

[27] Abdul-Majeed Alkali, "Federalism and the Creation of Sub-national States in Nigeria: Appraising the State-Creation Exercise Under Babangida Administration," *Journal of Humanities and Social Sciences* 22, no. 1 (2017): 1–8.

[28] Ibid.

[29] See Patrick A. Edewor, Yetunde A. Aluko, and Sheriff F. Folarin, "Managing Ethnic and Cultural Diversity for National Integration in Nigeria," *Developing Country Studies* 4, no. 6 (2014): 70–76.

[30] For details of these crises, see Dauda, "Ethnic Identity, Democratization, and the Future of the African State," *Journal of Humanities and Social Sciences* 22, no. 1 (2017): 1–8.

among multiple ethnic groups, were adopted by the government to harness strength in diversity and to foster nation building and national development. These affirmative-action mechanisms were defined in the 1989 and 1999 Constitutions to prevent ethnic domination or monopolization of resources. They were introduced into the civil service and reflected in the appointments of ministers, ambassadors, military personnel, and federal permanent secretaries.[31]

These policies perpetuated ethnic dominance and monopolization, enacted by dominant ethnic groups at state levels, leading to the advancement and concentration of power for specific ethnic-elite groups. They also renewed the age-old problem of unwitting reliance on ethnicity as a conduit for political organization, effectuating national objectives, and nation building. The consequences remain the same: ethnic affiliation is used as a pass card, leading to othering and discrimination against members of minority groups. In more overtly critical spaces, the federal character principle is designated as a power-sharing exercise.[32] The federal character principle even multiplies divisions at the grassroots level, promoting instances of local rivalry over who or what constitutes indigeneity. Scholarships, federal appointments, and federal resources are shared vertically, based on the idea of regional nativity.[33]

Ethnic belonging, ancestral ties, and roots to ancestral lines have become required access cards for individuals trying to benefit from federally allocated resources. Corrective measures have unintentionally created divisive lines within inter- and intra-ethnic relationships. Ukoha Ukiwo captures the position perfectly when he states: "while these initiatives have solved some old problems, they have generated many unintended consequences that have exacerbated ethnicity. What is more, they have been destabilizing for the Nigerian state system."[34]

State creation, alongside consociational and affirmative-action strategies, could have expanded room for diversity to flourish. However, it did not stem the problems arising from diversity or prevent diversity from being perverted for political gain by politically motivated, ethnic stalwarts.

The Colonial Project

Ethnicity is often described as a recent construct. The constructivist view – and the individualist view, to some extent – lend essential truth

[31] See J. I. Dibua, "Ethnic Citizenship, Federal Character, and Inter-Group Relations in Postcolonial Nigeria," *Journal of Historical Society of Nigeria* 20 (2011): 1–25.
[32] Ibid.   [33] Angerbrandt, "Struggles over Identity and Territory."
[34] Ukoha Ukiwo, "On the Study of Ethnicity in Nigeria," *CRISE: Centre for Research on Inequality, Human Security and Ethnicity* 12 (2005): 14.

to this stance, and the Nigerian case emphasizes it. Ethnicity as a modern construct implicates key players who engineered it. A construct owes its existence to a group of creators who must have been incentivized by ideology or means. If we are to take the constructivist stance seriously, constructivist thought traces the identity formation of ethnic groups along invented paths created by the activities of external and internal factors,[35] such as colonial authorities, missionaries, and emergent nationalists. The contributions of colonial forces in creating ethnic sentiments and ethnicity must take center stage, alongside the way that ethnicity has been crafted to implicate political authority.

On the other hand, Nigeria's example, especially in the case of the Yoruba, is fitting because it exists as a colonial project. Lord Frederick Lugard's amalgamation of the Northern and Southern protectorates in 1914 suggests that the regions were separate. In reality, they were; the Southern protectorate housed what would become the Eastern and Western Regions that were divided further, becoming states populated by various ethnic formations. The merger suggests that Nigeria existed prior to colonialist unification as independent entities. Prior to the unification, there also existed those which can now be called sub-ethnicities of ethnicities: a Yoruba person identified as either Ijebu, Ekiti, Ijesa, Oyo, or Egba, among many other possibilities, based on territorial and ancestral ties. Northerners identified as Kanuri, Kafta, Tiv, Idoma, Hausa, or Fulani, and other indices of identification existed within these subsets.

Ethnic peculiarities abounded before colonialism, but the organic nature and umbrella image that ethnic groups adopted in contemporary times, and the ways that they are currently addressed, owe a great deal to the actions and managerial impulses of colonialists and the agendas of ethno-nationalists/activists. For example, the Yoruba had several independent kingdoms that maintained contact through commerce and trade without forfeiting sovereignty – as defined in present times – except through cases of war. Through wars, political boundaries were blurred, thrones were usurped, citizens were carted away as prisoners of war, and communities were made into protectorates of larger kingdoms.

The various Yoruba sub-ethnicities were in a constant state of war: examples include the Owu and the Ijaye wars. The Owu war reveals the shift that often follows conquest; it impacted the political formation of the pre-colonial Yoruba region by eclipsing two former dominant city-states, Oyo and Owu. The conflict provided space for the emergence of new centers of power, such as Abeokuta, Ilorin, Ibadan, and Ijaye. The documented effects of this war included the spread of Islam and the

---

[35] Ibid.

introduction and expansion of Christianity through freed slaves. It also led to the dismantling of existing political structures, where authority was conferred on the basis of hereditary or ancestral ties within specific descent groups.[36] It impacted the region's political ambience and shaped the architecture of its future politics.

Some Yoruba subgroups existed independently of others: Igbomina, Ijumu, Ikale, Ekiti, Ijesa, Ondo, Owe, Owo, and Akoko in eastern Yorubaland; Ana, Anago, Egbado, Ketu, Awori, and Sabe in western Yorubaland; and Awori, Egba, Ife, Ijebu, Oyo, and Owu in the center.[37] Each group had subunits: Oyo comprised the metropolitan of the city of Oyo, as well as Ibolo, Ibarapa, and Epo districts; Ekiti had sixteen chiefdoms; Egba had Ake, Gbagura, and Okeona divisions; and Ilaje was carved into Ikale, Mahin and Ugbo chiefdoms.[38] These ethnicities were largely independent groups before they were fused together into what is now the Yoruba race.

In the precolonial Yoruba region, each city-state's sovereignty was complete without any recourse to a pan-Yoruba framework. Systems of belief, institutions, political structures, and codes of social conduct did not rely on a generally accepted frame between Yoruba groups, the way it does now. Each city-state had its own political head in the form of the Oba: the Ijebu had the Awujale, the Ife had the Ooni, and Oyo had the Alaafin. None was superior to the other – each king was a sovereign ruler, installed by and through local, context-specific rules and procedures.

Local governments had some similarities in structure. The Oba had institutionally recognized court officials that formed a political elite class and assisted him in ruling. The political structure of each state had three branches (executive, legislative, and judiciary) with checks and balances. This was due to the universal nature of a political configuration's fundamental aspects, regardless of its level of centralization or its method of expression. None of the city-states had their political structure managed or influenced by Pan-Yoruba political ideologies.

Yoruba city-states were geographically separated, organically autonomous, and able to stand on their own. The *orisa*, the religio-spiritual governing forces that are now about 401 in number, were originally

---

[36] For more on the cause and effects of this war, see J. F. Ade Ajayi and Robert Smith, *Yoruba Warfare in the Nineteenth Century* (London: Cambridge University Press, 1971); and Akinlawon L. Mabogunje and John Omer-Cooper, *Owu in Yoruba History* (Ibadan: University of Ibadan Press, 1971). See also, R. C. C. Law, "The Owu War in Yoruba History," *Journal of the Historical Society of Nigeria* 7, no. 1 (1973): 141–147.

[37] For further clarification on the distribution of the Yoruba, see Olatunji Ojo, "Heepa' (Hail) Òrìṣà: The Òrìṣà Factor in the Birth of Yoruba Identity," *Journal of Religion in Africa* 39, no. 1 (2009): 30–59.

[38] Ibid.

provincial. Deities and orisa were never contained in a single pantheon, as they are now. Sango was as important to the Oyo as Agemo was to the Ijebu.

Relationships were formed around trade; each city-state had products it could export. The Oyo traded in Ofi, a type of fabric, and Iseyin, a town north-west of Ibadan in present-day Oyo State, was more of an industrial base. The Egba were known for Adire, a type of cloth predominantly manufactured in Abeokuta. Ilesa and Osogbo were known for pottery or aro. These towns received visitors from other city-states, like Ijebu, who journeyed down to Eko (Lagos) for trade because of its access to the coast. Even at the dawn of modernity, clear-cut social–cultural demarcations existed. Focusing on textiles alone, the independence of each city-state is evident in the way that each had its own commercially successful market for Adire, regardless of its origin: Itoku (in Abeokuta), Akerele (in Lagos), Gbagi and Oje (in Ibadan), Oja-Oba (in Ilorin), Powerline (in Osogbo), and Erekesan (in Akure).[39]

Ibadan, capital city of Oyo State and once the largest city in West Africa, was a military base for the Oyo Empire. It housed the empire's Military Commander-in-chief, the Aare Ona Kankanfo. Ibadan existed separate from present-day Osun, home to Ilesa, Ife, and Owo, and each had its own deity, cultural affinities, ways, and systems of subsisting. Despite these differences, Osun State was carved from Oyo, largely Ibadan, during state creation. How is this not evidence of haphazard merging? Just as the Berlin Conference carved Africa into manageable bits, Yorubaland was carved into a manageable size for proper administrative functioning and ease.

Linguistic parameters and ancestral ties were used as distinguishing criteria for administrative districts. The benefit of using a linguistic index for constructing a blueprint to carve out separate Yoruba states was that it allowed culturally close groups to be squeezed together under a single banner. City-states were fused together for this purpose.

The colonial input that anchored national politics – and political identity by extension – by using ethnicity can be seen in the contradictions of its administrative strategy and process. The colonial project separated the nation into ethno-conscious divisions in a bid to achieve a unified identity. The various administrative and political units of a modern state were colored by ethnic considerations from inception, considering that the rationale behind them followed an ethnic path. In the words of Okolie,

---

[39] Adeyemi B. Oyeniyi, "Dress and Identity in Yorubaland, 1880–1980," *Leiden University Repository*, 2012, http://hdl.handle.net/1887/20143.

they were kept socially, culturally, and politically separate.[40] The separation fostered a systematic procedure that conducted national affairs in a pattern reflecting the earliest divisions along ethnic considerations. It stirred unhealthy competition that birthed a distrust capable of leading to war, rancor, and other forms of state disturbance that hindered unity, peace, and growth.

The other contradiction, tied to the first, was a consequence that rebirths itself and aggravates the initial cause: the ethnically defined divisions of the colonialists unwittingly suppressed nonethnic or nonreligious identities that could have moderated the concentrated ethnic character of the sociopolitical atmosphere. In trying to build a modern nation, the colonial administration's efforts attracted an influx of diverse people to urban centers, such as Lagos, Kano, Kaduna, and Enugu. This diversity led to competition for resources, capital, space, and power. The people drawn to the cities were already divided along ethnic lines; they had grown accustomed to forming associations and cleavages based on ethnic or religious ties, which only increased the divide. Ethnicity became a tool for organizing against competitors, viewed as a viable method of group survival.

The colonial administration's act of grouping the nation into three regions did not foster integration. Instead, it kept the regions isolated. The move was even more counterproductive because the regions did not contain individual ethnic groups; the grouping was for administrative efficiency, which took its toll on the unity of the nation. By demarcating boundaries with geographical lines cutting across economic, political, and cultural groups, the colonial regime sowed and nurtured the seed for ethnic intolerance. Regions had very little in common, even though they inhabited the same political space.

The regions did not grow at the same pace: The North did not have an experience with Western education similar to that of the other two regions. The Northern region did not permit Western culture to flower for an extended period, and it did not allow much transfer of Western influence from the South, which had undergone significant cultural transformations. Prior to the 1914 amalgamation, the North had fastidiously retained its ways, religion, and traditionally centralized political structure. Unlike the South, the North had the colonial government's permission to continue its primordial ways within tolerable limits. Not until 1946, well after the 1914 amalgamation, did the two regions cease

---

[40] Andrew C. Okolie, "The Appropriation of Difference: State and the Construction of Ethnic Identities in Nigeria," *Identity* 3, no. 1: (2003): 67–92.

their distinct political identities and administration characterized by degrees of cultural fidelity to primordial ways of life.[41] Without sufficient contact, each region remained ignorant of the other, wrapped in individual cocoons. This arrangement divided the nation to the point where ethnic misunderstandings, especially involving cross-cultural elements, quickly escalated into conflicts. The Jos riots are an example; many Igbo were killed by Northern Hausa.

Colonial influences were central factors in the ethnic cleavages affecting Nigerian politics. The colonial governor limited the movement and influx of Southern traders, missionaries, and educated and professional men and women entering the North. There were concerns that migrants from the educated South would undermine the authority of the Northern political heads that were more easily influenced by the colonial government. The North's Indirect Rule System was effective because the colonial government ruled through the Emirs; to protect this structuring, they blocked any form of oppositional influence, especially influence from the South. It was an attempt to perform surgery on a nonexistent injury. One such policy was the Land and Native Rights Ordinance of 1910, which transferred many Northern lands to the colonial governor so that the Southerners' activities could be limited.[42]

The colonial government's inability to capitalize on the diversity of the nation, beyond a random merging that did nothing to integrate its various units, guaranteed division along regional lines. The divisions were ethnic and promoted at the economic level. Each region's major export – groundnuts in the North, palm oil in the East, and cocoa in the West – was developed for trade with the international market; there was no support for interregional markets that could foster national development. This isolationist arrangement was unofficially adopted by the subsequent regions after independence.

Consciously or otherwise, another adopted policy was the use of propagandist literature to caricature or criticize ethnic groups as impatient, uncivilized, overambitious, uncooperative and distrustful rivals, competitors, conspirators, and saboteurs. These attacks perpetuated stereotypes created by the colonial authorities, trivializing groups with unflattering descriptions and applying parochial ideas to condition ethnic interaction. Communities that were slowly adapting to the benefits of education and gradually gaining awareness of others would read about their neighbors and fellow citizens in distorted accounts that sowed ethnic distrust and groomed them for rivalries that escalated into killings and bloodshed.

---

[41] Ibid.   [42] See Nnoli, "Ethnic Politics in Nigeria."

Misleading information would create false impressions of others and reinforced harmful predispositions, shaping interactions between groups across generations. Claims of Igbo superiority, articulated over time and reinforced by Nnamdi Azikiwe in the political arena, have at least been influenced by such colonial legacies. Terms like "conquer," "lead," "responsibility," and "bondage," used in the speeches of party leaders like Nnamdi Azikiwe and Obafemi Awolowo, are part of a political rhetoric that validates a long-standing perception of superiority. Awolowo explicitly referred to the Hausa and Fulani as conservative and significantly opposed to Western civilization; he claimed that the Igbo had a low cultural background when explaining how Igbos could achieve self-government before Hausas.[43] Awolowo employed colonial methods of classifying natives based on their embrace of Western education, listing Efik, Ijo, Ibibio, and Igbos as most likely to achieve self-government, in that order, if the race went to the swift.[44]

Each ethnic group's political relevancy and agency was determined by the colonial administration's ideologies, following the groupings created by its anthropologists and ethnologists. Ethnicities were agreeable or non-agreeable, liberal or radical, moderate or extremist, and civilized to varying degrees based on Western standards. These unofficial criteria would be the basis for the distribution of political power. In many instances, political power was transferred from moderate groups to elites.[45]

The political power that the North received after independence supports this idea. The region's size and population are the basis of its political strength, and the importance of these factors was established by colonial administrative machinery. Colonial administrators carved out a Northern Region that was not ethnically homogenous, so ethnicity alone could not justify the boundaries of the region. By making the Northern Region bigger than the other two regions combined, the colonial administration ensured that the North would establish political dominance. In a nation like Nigeria, where territoriality, ancestral ties, geographic proximity, and kinship ties determine political power, size and population would always determine who has a seat at the table.

Eventually, the North created a formidable political identity based on cleavages provided by the colonial administration. Rather than remain ethnically heterogeneous, the nationalist and elite class clamored for Northerners to rally around a political identity. The collective identity pursued by the Northern Region would compete with and outdo its competitors. The NPC's creation, and its successful division from the

---

[43] See Obafemi Awolowo, *Path to Nigerian Freedom* (London: Faber and Faber, 1947).
[44] Ibid.   [45] Okolie, "The Appropriation of Difference."

South on all possible fronts, supported this plan. The NPC, which took over governance from the colonialists, adopted a motto that speaks to this agenda: "One North, One People, under One God." The ideology supports a collective Northern identity that Hausa and non-Hausas, such as the Kanuri, Bachama, and Mambilla, along with Muslims and non-Muslims, such as the Idoma, Tiv, and Birom, could organize. As Okolie argued, the success of this agenda is evident in the way that every Northerner is assumed to be Hausa – even when the assumption is clearly erroneous.[46] The colonial vestiges of this formation are apparent in the identity's anti-Igbo, anti-South, anti-Christian, and pan-Islamic sentiments, however subtle.[47]

Nigeria's current political orientation regarding ethnic divisions and ethnic frameworks owes a great deal to the colonial government's blurring of clear-cut boundaries between interdependent communities; they were fused into three unevenly divided and mutually exclusive regions. The administration of these regions followed a "divide and conquer" route, paving the way for the instrumentalization of ethnicity and the organization of political structures that would maintain the legacies of colonialism. These legacies would manifest in various forms: not only material forms, but also nonmaterial forms such as notions and ideas of belonging, whose implications would be felt visibly and physically. One example of this legacy is captured by what I call "ethnic ghettos" and how they combine with colonially instigated notions of "home" to reinforce the divide.

Home and the Ethnic Ghetto

In Africa, the notion of home and how it shapes identity generally encompasses how land defines a person and the extent of that person's inclusion in group activities. It is a precolonial concept, and the colonial empire's policies and activities did nothing to temper these sharp distinctions when it merged previously disparate regions. By crafting policies and performing functions that further regionalized national activities, if not ethnicizing them outright, the colonialists oiled machinery that would sustain ethnic divisions and their input in the construction of political identity. One example is their use of geography.

Colonialists failed to appreciate how Africa's environment – where ancestral ties can take precedence over place of birth to define "home" – would

---

[46] Ibid.

[47] Antagonistic sentiments were revealed by calls for the creation of a Middle Belt identity; the region's inhabitants are largely Christians. Claims that minority and non-Muslim or non-Hausa–Fulani would be marginalized showed that the "One North" agenda is more political than cultural.

shape future consequences when carving out separate places for non-indigenes. They did not consider how it would impact integration. Sabo, for example, is generally considered "home away from home" for Northerners in the West and South. Colonialists concentrated non-indigenes in separate enclaves within regions, which reinforced the idea of migration's temporality. This sort of concept does not foster inter-ethnic cooperation; how can a Hausa man feel safe, or see a Yoruba as his brother, when he does not see the West as his home?

Colonial strategy eliminated any feeling of belonging, entrenching distrust and identifying foreigners as a specific group to be ostracized and blamed for communal setbacks. This perception encourages inter-ethnic clashes within regions or states that almost always spread elsewhere. Colonialist stereotyping of ethnic groups fueled these structural divisions, ensuring that geographic partitions were maintained from both sides. Easterners preferred to maintain close ties with kin, instead of exploring possible relations with the Northerners that were portrayed as conservative and remote. Northerners preferred to stay away from Easterners who had been demonized as infidels and usurpers. Awolowo's remark reveals how such conditioning can characterize political ideology and state action:

[A] deep religious gulf runs between the Northern [Hausa–Fulani] and Southern [Igbo and Yoruba] portions of the country. The peoples in the Western [Yoruba] and Eastern [Igbo] Regions of the south, approach religion with remarkable moderation and nonchalance: Christians, Mohammedans, and so-called Pagans mix in society without restraint. The people in the North, however, are extremely fanatical about Islamism. They have an open contempt for those who do not share their religious belief.[48]

The creation of Sabon-Gari, which translates as "stranger's quarters,"[49] implicates the colonialists. These systematic divisions kept northern-dwelling Southerners in specific areas for observation. Other places, such as Tudun Wada, housed migrants from other parts of the north[50] and replicated this separation in various ways after independence. For the African, whose notion of home is characterized by ancestral ties and spatial dynamics, the separation impairs the necessary and natural understanding that follows cultural contact after migration, especially on such a large scale. Competition for resources is heightened in such environments, and temporary "homes" like Sabo and Sabon-Gari become methods for scapegoating migrants and vilifying them during inter-ethnic rivalries.

---

[48] Awolowo, "Path to Nigerian Freedom," 49.
[49] See Okolie, "The Appropriation of Difference."   [50] Ibid.

The Nigerian Civil War is another example. One of the factors leading to the declaration of Biafra was the massive killing of Igbo in the North. The low level of integration was unable to encourage dialogue, and allegiances with original ethnic roots were strengthened at the expense of regional or national bonds. Igbo were discouraged from seeing themselves as Nigerians, an identity that could be shared with Yoruba and Hausa. Instead, their loyalties to their original Igbo identities and homes were invoked against groups trying to confine them within specific regions.

These enduring realities have manifested in contemporary politics, despite increasing levels of intranational migration and cross-cultural contact. The feeling of being an outsider, or of seeing outsiders as saboteurs, remains present. It shapes political orientations. In the 2019 elections, Igbos in Lagos were identified as "backstabbers" and "saboteurs" for allegedly refusing to support the dominant party's candidate for governor. The millennial culture that reduces movements and counter-movements to shorthand rhetoric became embroiled in "#otoge," a hashtag applied to a Yoruba word meaning "it is enough." The bickering and mini conflict characterizing the Lagos Governorship Elections involved these positions:

1. That the Igbos in Lagos were saving the Yoruba from political tyranny. This claim replicated the pomposity of the earliest nationalists, who ethnicized political rhetoric with claims that the Igbos would be the messiahs for the African race. ·

2. That "#otoge" was a manifestation of hypocrisy and covetousness. Many parts of the East, where the Igbos hail from, experience similar political tyranny. Critics asserted that Igbo claims of moral superiority were exhibiting shortsightedness and greed, frequently invoking the biblical proverb of a man with a beam in his eye who thinks he can remove the mote from another's.

3. That Igbos are not indigenous to Lagos, whose original inhabitants are the Aworis. These arguments claimed that Igbos had no political standing for determining who to oust, who to follow, and who to enthrone, especially when opposing the original inhabitants.

4. That ancestral ties and roots do not matter when exercising rights to franchise. Some argued that Igbo land ownership and their capital-building investments were enough to make them indigenes.

5. That metropolitan cities, like Lagos, are a neutral ground. Their increase in multiculturalism, due to migration, has allowed them to accommodate and benefit from contributions made by various non-indigenes.

6. That these divisions, trying to decide who belongs and who does not, are products of elite machinations that seek to benefit from the conflict.

7. That Nigerians, like most Africans, do not think beyond ethnic lines. Calls to replace the dominant party's candidate were belittled as attempts to strengthen an Igbo-backed, and therefore Igbo-controlled, opposition candidate.

These arguments surround a context-specific situation, but the ideologies are common to Nigeria's political climate. Approaching the Lagos matter as an ethnicized issue shows how the seven points above can play out at national levels. The 2019 presidential election also saw its own share of ethno-politics. Arguments were made that:

1. A particular presidential candidate, especially one of the Northerners put forward by the two dominant parties in the country, meant opportunities for other ethnic groups in the next election.
2. A victory for the incumbent president, a Hausa–Fulani candidate, would automatically mean a shift in political power in the next election, from the center toward the Southwest.
3. The dominant opposition party's candidates, an Easterner and a Northerner as running mates, were a slap in the face to Igbos, who had not held the presidency since 1999.
4. A political alliance with the North, due to its size and population, would create more chances for the other two groups. The People's Democratic Party had a Northerner as the presidential candidate and an Easterner as the running mate, while the incumbent All Progressive Congress had a Northerner as its presidential candidate and a Southwesterner as the running mate. Party politics appeared to be an ethnic game.

The fourth scenario has played out frequently in Nigeria's political history; candidates have made ethnic calculations and forged unusual alliances. Former president Olusegun Obasanjo's victory over opposition Chief Olu Falae was often framed as the result of dominant Northern support for a Southwesterner.

The reasons for this assumption are speculative and diverse. It could be argued that Northerners – who wielded greater political authority in the region through a Northern-dominated military government and damage done to the body politic – chose to support a Yoruba over an Easterner because the candidate would reliably protect Northern interests. On the other hand, Obasanjo astutely presented himself as a national brand, defying the boundaries of ethnic specificity to cut a national-oriented figure; it was similar to the way President Buhari presented himself as belonging to no one and everyone. Popular opinion held that Obasanjo's military tenure did not completely accommodate Yoruba interests, and that he refrained from fully supporting Abiola in the 1990s and opposed Awolowo in the 70s, because he was a shrewd operator capable of making tactical alliances. Most Yoruba support during the 1999 elections went to Obasanjo's opponent, Olu Falae, but Obasanjo had the North and the remainder of the Yoruba behind him. Obasanjo's political maneuvering has led Yoruba to alternately deny and accept him many times over.

This same ethnic game played out after Obasanjo's tenure; various Yoruba bigwigs have endorsed Northern candidates over time and sold them to the West. Obasanjo endorsed Umaru Yar'Adua, a Northerner, in 2007; Goodluck Ebele Jonathan, a South-southerner, in 2011; and President Muhammadu Buhari, a Northerner, in 2015. Each one was largely supported by the Yoruba. Subsequent fallouts between Obasanjo and each candidate – except for Yar'Adua, who died in office – revealed the brittle nature of each alliance, which were more interest oriented than in service to the body politic. Obasanjo's endorsed candidate for the last election was another Northerner, Atiku Abubakar, who served as vice president during Obasanjo's 1999–2007 presidential tenure. The two later had a public and political falling-out.

If Obasanjo's example reflects the fragile, ethnocentric scaffold supporting Nigerian politics, then even the body politic is exercising its franchise in ethnocentric ways. It can also be seen in the shifting alliances between ethnic group elites, who are responsible only to themselves. The Lagos example played out in the 2015 elections, when the state was said to be a no man's land by the Igbo. In some ways, the examples may be specific to historical timelines. However, it is a manifestation of the tendency to follow a constructivist approach, which easily allows for a redefinition of political identity that organizes around ethnic lines for political gains.

These examples show how the ideals defining ethnicity can be manipulated over time for political profit, exploited by political stalwarts, party members, and the elite class. By revealing how ethnic identity can be both binding and fluid, and how ethnicity's only constant is that it can be deployed as an instrument and reconstructed, these instances map out colonialist efforts to "unite" the nation that merely divided it in their favor, laying foundations for the centralization of ethnicity in Nigeria's politics.

Executive Class and the Pursuit of Power

If colonialists provided blueprints to form political cleavages around ethnicity, the elite class further institutionalized and instrumentalized ethnicity for political gains. The formation of the NPC, and other such regional political parties, is a pattern following the fissures left by the colonial empire along ethnic lines. Nationalists moved into the interior of rural settlements, mobilizing ethnic sentiment for nationalistic gains.

Ethnic unions and social groups with political orientation, such as the Egbẹ Ọmọ Oduduwa, were formed to advance ethnic group interests. The group spearheaded by Awolowo was created primarily to foster a pan-Yoruba identity that could challenge other groups at the national level. These unions embarked on community development initiatives highlighting allegiance to primordial ethnic identities, and they became useful tool in the hands of emergent political parties;[51] they also gave impetus to the formation of political parties.

The Egbẹ Ọmọ Oduduwa example is instructive: the name means "the group of the descendants of Oduduwa," and it created ideologies in 1945 favoring the Yoruba.[52] Its philosophies were woven around the flowering and sustained unity and cooperation among Yoruba groups – they had been unified under the ancestry of Oduduwa during colonialism and later saw themselves as descended from the same patriarchal lines. The group promoted educational and cultural programs, encouraging the maintenance of traditional political institutions that would be relevant to the nation's political structure. The group's members included educated and traditional elites, and one of its objectives was to consolidate Yoruba unity. Its pan-Yoruba focus would eventually be felt throughout the nation; not only did it compete with groups such as the Igbo State Union and The Association of Peoples of the North, it also denied a substantial Yoruba following to the leaders of those groups.[53]

By the time the Macpherson constitution allowed for democratic elections, the Egbẹ had a strong presence in the Southwestern Region as a cultural organization. Action Group was formed in 1950 and declared itself to be a political party the following year. The Egbe served as the political party's springboard; Chiefs who were stakeholders in the Egbẹ were invited to support the party.[54] The aim and objectives of both groups overlapped, which led to support from the members of the cultural group. By endearing and popularizing itself among the Yoruba through the Egbẹ, the party created room for cross-membership. The group eventually became the core of the party and faded into the background.

The growth or evolution from cultural groups to political parties was not unique to the Southwest. The Northern People's Congress (NPC) started as a cultural group for Northerners, and the National Congress of Nigeria and the Cameroons, a Southeastern formation of Igbo ethnic

[51] Ukiwo, "On the Study of Ethnicity in Nigeria."
[52] John Ayoade, "Party and Ideology in Nigeria: A Case Study of the Action Group," *Journal of Black Studies* 16, no. 2 (1985): 169–188.
[53] Ibid.   [54] Ibid.

unionists, became National Council of Nigerian Citizens (NCNC).[55] Other, less identified groups or unions that became nationally focused parties include the Northern Elements People's Union (NEPU) and the United Middle Belt Congress (UMBC).[56]

The creation of ethnically focused parties, especially by ethnic-oriented groups looking to influence national elections, speaks to the dominant orientation of educated elites at the time. It resembles the ethnically structured political blueprints that the colonial administration had left behind. The desire to arrogate political power to the regions, and the distrust of other ethnic groups, did not allow for broad-spectrum, inter-ethnic political organizations.

These groups were led by ideologues, like Awolowo and Azikiwe, who already saw other ethnic groups as competitors. Coalitions and schemes were quickly devised to outdo each other. Between 1960 and 1966, the NCNC and the NPC formed coalitions that sidelined the AG, although this would be short-lived. The Civil War took on an ethnic character, pitting Igbos and Hausas against each other, and the political class began to manipulate ethnicity for political power. Cleavages were strengthened around ethnic ties for political support. The push for state creation, zoning, and a rotational presidency were all supported by ethnic interests. Each ethnic group's elite class used demographic and geographic justifications to reposition themselves as beneficiaries of federally controlled resources and redistributions.

The ethnic considerations determining which requests are granted at the federal levels have led to political strategizing along ethnic lines. Because of features such as size and population that determine revenue allocation, the Constitution sports phrases such as religious group, ethnic group, places of origin, and indigenous groups.[57] These words indicate the essentialism of ethnicity in Nigerian politics. The politicization of identity is instituted to acquire state power, and numbers are politicized as a criterion. This is visible in the North, whose population and geographical size exceed those of the other regions; they are used to canvas for more revenue allocation. Many Northern states receive larger distributions from the Federal Allocation Account than they contribute into it.[58] And yet the revenue allocation formula favors the North over other states

---

[55] Edewor et al., "Managing Ethnic and Cultural Diversity."   [56] Ibid.

[57] Angerbrandt, "Struggles over Identity and Territory."

[58] For an idea of Northern representation among the Nigerian states that would fail miserably without govern mental locations, see Oladeinde Olawoyin, "14 Nigerian States Insolvent, Have Ridiculously Low Internal Revenue – Report," *Premium Times Nigeria*, May 30, 2017, www.premiumtimesng.com/business/business-news/232507-14-niger ian-states-insolvent-%E2%808have-ridiculously-low-internal-revenue-report.html.

that generate more revenue.[59] The "One North" principle is being applied by the Northern political elites, even if it is not true in practice. The case of Kaduna, where political and economic tensions exist between Muslim and non-Muslim groups, is a fitting example. Various claims of marginalization are contested by opposing factions.

In local areas of Southern Kaduna, Hausa–Fulani Muslims are considered non-indigenes and politically marginalized through unequal substantive representation;[60] this contradicts the political dominance of the Hausa–Fulani in the North, which includes Kaduna. The "One North" claim reveals the instrumentalization of ethnicity – extensive political structuring was applied in the North to span nineteen states, including the Middle Belt region and, by extension, non-Muslim groups. However, if a religious yardstick were to be used to measure ethnic representation, the number of Northern states would be twelve.

Depending on circumstances, the goals at hand, and the classes making the claims, defining boundaries have been shifted and enlarged. The Northern-based Arewa Consultative Forum (ACF), for example, favors a region-influenced definition for political units, de-emphasizing the aspects of indigeneity and religion. This structuring follows colonial-based regionalization to define political units. Geographic-oriented political mobilization extends the construction of Northern political identity across state-based ethnic and religious lines. This reconstruction explains the North's size.

The ACF motto of "One North" was adopted from the NPC to engender a united political front based on numbers and regional unity. Political backing for the ACF came from powerful elites and traditional rulers in the North, and from what is often called the "Kaduna Mafia."[61] In a series of counter-claims, the Middle Belt rejected the dominance of the Hausa–Fulani in the North to favor political representation for the non-Muslim southern part of the region above "One North" aspirations. This separated the interests of non-Muslim ethnic groups, mainly Christians, from those of areas dominated by the Hausa–Fulani. The movement peaked with the rise of the United Middle Belt Congress in the 1950s.

Arguments against rejecting the "One North" motto point to divisive actions. It is also the case with the proponents of the "Core North" claim, which is often described as "used to designate areas associated with the traditional power personalities."[62] The "Core North" claim has also been rejected by the Northern elite class as unnecessarily divisive.

---

[59] For more on how Northern states continue to dominate the FAA, despite producing dismally low turnout, see Olawoyin, "14 Nigerian States Insolvent," for a clear breakdown of the revenue allocation and generation of each Nigerian state.

[60] Angerbrandt, "Struggles over Identity and Territory."   [61] Ibid.   [62] Ibid., 184.

In 1957, the colonial administration suggested, prior to independence, that the Northern Region should be divided into smaller regions to accommodate the interests of minorities. The premier of the Region, Ahmadu Bello, claimed that the agitation was promoted by alien ideologies imported from outside the region.[63] Just as in the cases of the "Core North" and "One North" movements, the picture was painted of a unified North, although the dominance of the Hausa–Fulani was apparent. The creation of a new region, which would be the Middle Belt, could thwart the united regional front project that sustained the North's dominance at the center, both politically and economically, where it enjoyed increased access to resources. Ethnicity's local constructions or variations within a region's political structure can be accommodated or disregarded, depending on the political goals of the elite class. In other words, political elites often manipulate territorial boundaries. Territoriality is implicated in the construction of ethnic identity, and geographic boundaries are implicated in the political process, meaning that shifts in territorial boundaries also determine ethnic character.

To this end, elites manipulate ethnic identities to access resources, which often leads to the politicization of ethnicity. The size of an ethnic group often becomes the means to an end in political processes, such as a census, because state resources can easily be diverted to a region that appears to have the strength of numbers. What else could be the case when the revenue allocation formula allots 30 percent to the population factor? Various Nigerian Constitutions have assigned significant portions of the revenue allocation based on population.[64] By defining and redefining political boundaries based on ethnic, religious, and regional affiliations, the political class not only reveal their inheritance from the colonial government, but also expose themselves as constantly trying to monopolize state power. It is exploited for resource accumulation and to oppress those who stand their way. This is tantamount to what Abubakar calls "regarding the state as the instrument of its will."[65] The resultant effect, as seen in the case of the Middle Belt, is that people find solace by mobilizing around new ethnic cleavages or primordial ones.

Conclusion: Asset or Liability?

Is ethnicity an asset or a liability for the Nigerian political process, since they are symbiotically related? Ethnicity can be a positive force for

[63] Ibid.
[64] See Adeleke Salami, "Taxation, Revenue Allocation, and Fiscal Federalism in Nigeria: Issues, Challenges, and Policy Options," *Economic Options* 56 (2011) 189: 27–49.
[65] Abubakar, "Ethnic Identity," 31.

diversity when it is harnessed by actors with a broader, nationalistic political scope. Ethnic groups can benefit from a structured political process. And ethnicity can enhance capacity building and boost a nation's profile as long as the body politic and the elite classes of several ethnicities can align based on ideology, without resorting to ethnic divisions that divert state resources.

A progressive ideology, held by individuals of diverse cultural backgrounds, automatically creates room to accommodate significant inputs from several sources, which leads to a vibrant and dynamic political reality. Ethnic diversity can lead to healthy competition between groups that impact on the nation on economic and political fronts. But this is often not the case with Nigeria, where ethnicity is perverted from inception and instrumentalized for personal gains by political actors. In Nigeria, the manifestations of ethnicity in relation to political identity tilt toward the negative, implicating the colonialists, the masses, and the elites.

An understanding of ethnic influences, in relation to political identity, requires an intersectional approach conducted from four angles. Examining the Nigerian political reality in relation to ethnicity shows that subtracting the institutionalist view from the constructivist, or the primordialist from the instrumentalist, or any one view from the others is to sidestep a significant aspect of Nigerian political reality.

8 Religion and Geopolitics

Introduction

Nothing more can elaborate the sociopolitical influence of religion in Nigeria than the almost unending display of politicians' pictures showcasing their enrollment in various religious activities either in churches or mosques when elections are approaching. For every political office chaser, getting the media attention to capture their involvements in religious engagement during electioneering is primarily for the endorsement of their candidature from the unassuming and sometimes unsuspecting public. The manipulative politician wants to claim membership in a religious identity and to promise that those of the same faith will see the privileges of power. The identity of religion takes precedence in the lives of those who feel powerfully connected to political candidates because they belong to the same religion. The slow journey into this contemporary thinking was perhaps midwifed by the assumption that sharing religious identities with political figures may approximate to belonging to the same social class as them. This assumption is justified over the entrenched social codes infused into the two popular religions, Christianity and Islam, through their scriptures, where leaders are interpreted as cosmically ordained representatives doing the earthly assignment of God for the "benefit" of the people. Without giving exemption, the un-elitist interpretation of portions of the scriptures like this has misinformed many believers. This is even more prevalent when people are neither grounded in religion nor in political machinations.

It should be recalled that the Nigerian President, General Muhammadu Buhari, a diehard Muslim with rigid reverence to Islamic ideologies and injunctions, was seen enrolling in a Redeemed Christian Church of God's (RCCG) religious program in the prelude to the 2015 election, when his political campaign was ongoing. Even if it contradicted his personal religious beliefs, the time was inevitably ripe for making a courageous compromise for the assurance of success and the remodeling of his political image that many people believed was too rigid to mend. If doing it because of his political ambition was uncalled for, the demands of his reputation managers to follow this process would be too intimidating to waive for him for obvious reasons. One, not appearing in religious gatherings different from his (Islam), particularly when his chosen deputy comes from an opposite and fervent religious group, the Redeemed Christian Church of God (RCCG), would help his detractors to do an easy character assassination on him as they would spread a narrative that would de-market the man from the coming elections.

Again, that would most predictably influence the election turnout of Nigerians of varying ethnic extractions who naturally would have accepted his coming to the church as a tacit declaration of support from their spiritual head. Complementing this case are the flocks of Nigerian politicians who move from one end to the other seeking the religious validation of their political ambition to which members of the same religious gatherings would automatically key in for their support. It is a common reality in the Nigerian environment, therefore, to come across situations where the political office chasers scout for different prominent religious groups for endorsement prior to the election periods. They usually leverage on the opportunity provided by the Internet to spread their religious engagements across different media outlets so that the campaign exercise would be completed for the flood of Nigerians married to social media. Hence, finding optics with religion remains one of the most electorally profitable strategies in which Nigerian politicians are always engaged during election time, and this behavior has a beginning in Nigerian politics.

Beginning of Religion and Politics

The reference to Nigerian democracy invokes multiple reactions, as the country's political journey is saturated by varying political ideologies alternating between democracy and dictatorship. The inherited democracy during the youthful age of Nigerian identity was truncated in 1966 following the fragmentation of representation considered as unhealthy for the development of the country by some interest groups. Subsequent efforts around 1979–83 met a similar fate and contradictions that again aborted the dream of democratic independence and rule. Riding on the rough pebbles of administrative leadership that took a straightforward but unceremonious trajectory, democracy became relatively stable in 1999 at the ascension of General Olusegun Obasanjo into office as the President of Nigeria for eight consecutive years. Incidentally, religion, alongside its popular index of division, ethnicity, began to dictate the political behavior of the country generally where candidates to be elected into different offices must satisfy these two unconstitutional, however fundamental, factors before their endorsements both by their party and the masses become guaranteed. Unintentionally, Nigeria introduced a version of democracy whose descriptions and characteristics can be adjudged "Nigerian" because of the dimensions of the system in the country. Nigeria won itself the notorious status of being one of the few countries with a "religious democracy," or a democracy that is religious.

Following the succession of Nigerian democratic struggles from the time stretching back to the eve of Nigerian independence through the contemporary time, the intervention of religion in Nigerian politics dated disparagingly to these periods and has mutated into the full-blown result that is generally observed today. Since the British saw a confounding relationship between distancing themselves from the internal political structures in Northern Nigeria and a successful proxy control through their leaders, they became bland and indifferent to likely results which would erupt by merging a region that depended on Islam as the major source of law with the liberal South that delineated religion from politics. This, therefore, would not come without major consequences. The constitutional conferences haphazardly organized by the colonialists to provide the avenue for the different ethnic extractions to engage in national dialogue in preparation for postcolonial leadership and its eventual results revealed extensively how the impending Nigerian future would be marred by ideological contradictions as the two geopolitical poles, the North and the South, were not only guided by irreconcilable ideologies but also by a certainty that they had different perceptions about the separation of religion and the state. To the Northern bloc, Islam was enough to be accepted as the sources of law. To the South, the focus was different.

All these religious reservations were placed during the series of deliberations that preluded the country's independence, and the finality of the conferences showed that the religious minority in Northern Nigeria and the Northeast, who have been under age-long domination of the Islamic Hausa–Fulani, were in for an extended rollercoaster journey in the political junction of the regional North.[1] These people therefore were confronted with despair as their minority status, religion-wise, would limit their democratic freedom and put their religious survival in jeopardy. Apparently, the Hausa–Fulani administrators during the period established a nexus between the expansion of Christianity and the allowance of Western education, and their aversion to the former forced them to reject

---

[1] Toyin Falola, *Violence in Nigeria: The Crisis of Religious Politics and Secular Ideologies* (Rochester: University of Rochester Press, 1998).

the latter with unusual energy. For the Northern Nigerians therefore, political and economic opportunities are to be laced with religious permutations so that their interests would be adequately catered for. Having its humble beginning at the pre-independence era, the intrusion of religion in the determination of political leaders and offices, which initially began in the North, became a countrywide appeal in the later stages of their democracy, and remained unshaken. It continues to remain a primary determinant of various sociopolitical projections as the networks of religious alliance have always been invoked for power contest. The spillover of this permutation would later smuggle its way into the other part of the country, given the increased interest of the people to use religious identities to consolidate political gains.

Religious infiltration into Nigerian politics is animated by the ethno-political party formed by the Northern leaders, the Northern People's Congress (NPC), underscored by internal structures that were predominantly colored by religious beliefs. The party was considered useful for the consolidation of the national political positions that were expected to be won by Northern members because of their population strength. However, the minorities within the region would not allow the religion to be used as the yardstick for determining or distributing political dividends as that would further destabilize their relationship with the dominant Hausa–Fulani, who generally were Muslims. Against this background, therefore, various political parties were formed within the region with the mandate to checkmate the NPC's dominance. The Tiv Progressive Union (TPU), Middle Zone League (MZL), Middle-Belt People's Party (MBPP), United Middle-Belt Congress (UMBC), Northern Nigeria Non-Muslim League, and Birom Progressive Union (BPU), among other parties, were formed within striking influence of the minority Christian groups from the Middle Belt and the Northeast.[2] Although these political theatrics would demonstrate the existential resistance against the hegemonic structures of the Northern oligarchs even within the region, they did not succeed in bringing them down.

From the South, however, religion also has recently been given prominence in the delineations of interest and allocation of opportunities to the people. However, it is not as deep-seated there as are instances in the Northern hemisphere. The reason for this is not alien. The Southern Nigerians are naturally inclined to be tolerant of opposing religious views and would rarely allow it to determine their political or social relationships. However, since the language of religion has been deeply etched into the

---

[2] Hakeem Onapajo, "Politics for God: Religion, Politics and Conflict in Democratic Nigeria," *The Journal of Pan African Studies* 4, no. 9 (2012): 42–66.

political system of the Northern Nigerians, there are clear indications that the contemporary South is tilting toward that trajectory. In essence, the beginning of the religious intermingling into Nigeria's politics is associated with their precolonial internal politics which was deliberately fractured by the colonialists' arrangement because of the understanding that such a method would aid their control of the country generally. The allowance of Sharia, for example, strengthened the confidence of the North and allowed consideration of religious affiliations and identities before the continuation of any national relationship. Therefore, the modern concession to forces of religion in the determination of candidates vying for political offices can be interpreted as a coping mechanism or survivalist strategy for the other Nigerians who do not intend to get caught in the web of Northern domination or presumed Northernization agenda.

Religion and Ethnic Politics

Since the NPC was fundamentally synonymous with regional politics, even if it was dressed under the toga of religion, the South therefore reacted in promoting a political system that supported an ethnic configuration. The expiration of Northern religio-ethnic identity domination of Nigeria and its political space was a dream that was nursed by conflicted Southerners who were appalled by extensive recalcitrance from the side that seemed condescending and prohibitively controlling. Apparently, the dissolution of the democratic process of the country as early as 1966 was representative of the resentment of the South against the dominant NPC in the political spectrum. The unsuccessful attempts to control power, which by implication meant resource control, contributed significantly to the expression of secessionist interest by the East which analytically appeared antagonistic of the Northern control-them-all strategy, at least, as seen by the minority groups in the Middle Belt who were predominantly Christians. Although the secessionist dream was stillborn, the resulting outcome manifested in different dimensions across the different ethnic extractions making up the country. For one thing, it signaled to the Northern oligarchs that the other parts of the country would not be repressively restrained from protesting against instances of domination.

As an extension of this, the Southern part of the country that includes both Western Nigeria and its Eastern bloc, became unprecedentedly alert to the reality of ethnic politics. Even if they had already shown a disposition to this in the past, the reaction of Northern Nigeria toward anything with the emblem of Nigeria's leadership reinforced their suspicion and, therefore, forced them to develop a sense of preservation of their type in national politics. Therefore, the creation and the sustenance of ethnic politics reflective in party formation or agenda pushing immediately became ubiquitous, and each region began to mobilize ethnic support for political engagements. Subsequently, when General Ibrahim Badamasi Babangida was challenged from office as a military head, the underlying reason for the invalidation of his leadership status was related to his religious convictions, as the Orka Coup of 1990 protested in their take-over speech. The military competence of Babangida was primarily not faulted; instead, the fact that the Northern Muslims had annexed the political system of the country under their control cumulated in contestations of various ethnic groups, chief of which were the Southern Nigerians who insisted that the symbolism of Northern Muslims with Nigerian leadership was to be delegitimized. Even though Orka's coup was counterintuitive, it did not go without registering its disaffection.

This incidence, however, ruffled some feathers in the Nigerian sociopolitical landscape. Shortly after the successful countercoup, finger-pointing became a popular culture among the people at the political front. For the Northern bloc, who saw the Major Gideon Gwaza Orkar coup as an act of insubordination and a vote of no confidence on the Northern leadership in the country, the Christian faith became the target of attacks as the candidate that brought the revolutionary idea against General Ibrahim Babangida was a practicing Christian. As a result, the action of a military officer who considered changing the power structures of the country's highest echelon became an indictment on religion and was therefore employed as a tool to further the existential acrimony that had overtaken the country on religious grounds. The resultant consequence of all these experiments cannot but have political and socioeconomic permutations and configurations. The infusion of religion into the political system of the country remains the very reason for the escalation of tensions, struggles, and conflicts that characterized the country's political spectrum eventually. Even when the affront of the Muslim Hausa–Fulani bloc was ideologically unbearable for the reticent South, they were not reluctant to recoil for improved strategy on ways to wrestle their political opponents using the religious agenda. Therefore, as the country was already fragmented along ethnic lines, the fragmentation was foregrounded by the inclusion of another index of division: religion. From then on, the country traveled along religiously divisive lines, and this has continued to influence many policies made in the country. Earnestly speaking, even within the minority groups which had hitherto accepted their minority status and decided to play national politics, there arose extensive interest in ethno-religious politics.

In retrospect, the assaulted minority Middle Belt that found protracted difficulty, metaphorically speaking, breathing comfortably while being tightly kept under the kneading influence of the Hausa–Fulani Muslims, had differently aired their grievances about the totalitarian rule of the Northern oligarchs in the region generally. They had complained that the majority Hausa–Fulani were using their authority to intimidate members from participating in the democratic process of the country and repressing their voices where they mattered. However, the deliberate oppression of this group was an indirect demonstration of arrogance attached to power. Many Hausa–Fulani political interest groups were convinced of their absolute right to control and dominate those they perceived as minorities. The victims, however, could only show their protest in political aspects and the only avenue through which they could fulfill that agenda was to create a political party with religious signs and colorations. The reason for the fixation of interest on the evolution of politics in Northern Nigeria is because there is no other ethnic extraction that exclusively linked religion with politics as demonstrated by the Northerners even today. Perhaps this is caused by the fact that other regions have a moderate percentage of the two popular religions, Christianity and Islam.

Because religion is a binding and bonding leveler that has the propensity to gather members who share common scriptural opinions into the same identity group, whether political or economic, Northern leaders therefore sought to consolidate the popularity of the NPC by appealing to the religious sense of members from other regions. However, the South would not allow the religious politics of the North to tear down their fabric of national unity, and neither would they allow their ethnic differences to degenerate so much that they became observers in the political progression and scheming of the North. The only realizable goal to truncate such a dream of continuous domination by the Northern Region was to collaborate and consolidate their political gains through synergy. Therefore, the coalition that led to the unveiling of a political party under the umbrella of the Unity Party of Nigeria was an amalgam of Western and other Nigerians whose intent was to unseat the North from their excessive domination of power and the intransigent introduction of religious beliefs to the political system of the country. Meanwhile, there was the political party formed in the East seeking a similar mandate. This, therefore, led to the coloration of Nigerian elections along religious and ethnic lines. Subtly but steadily, religious identities began to dominate Nigerian politics and influence the choices of leaders and their deeds.

Participation of Clerics in Vote Mobilization

The mobilization of political power through the encouragement of clerics and many members' support and their influence began honorably in Northern Nigeria following the introduction of Sharia principles by the then-governor of Zamfara State, Ahmed Sani Yerima, in the period after the return to the democratic process. Taking such a political decision was a sequel to the electioneering campaigns of the governor before his ascension to power. Apparently, he had pledged to introduce Sharia law to the state during the campaign period, and the realization that the predominant religious philosophy in the North, Islam, prepared the ground for its popularity made this possible. This unavoidably led to the subjugation of displeased oppositions or defenseless minorities. Taking this bold step was democratically condemnable but it was politically useful for the advancement of the man's political ambition in the state. Further, the support gathered for the endorsement of Yerima as a reliable solution to the myriad of political challenges facing the region was unprecedented. The masses, to whom the mandate of Islam has been understood as a divine movement against which their welfare and wellness takes a secondary view, became religiously committed to Yerima and would not be discouraged to provide their support for him as long as he declared an interest in pursuing a political agenda.

Under the flagship of the All People's Party (APP), Zamfara State became actively synonymous with Islamic identity and this influenced its social acceptability by the neighboring states and international admirers, among those who shared the same religico-political leanings. Apparently, to them, the Islamization of the Northern Region was becoming more realistic than a mere fantasy, with the actualization of such a political move in the environment.[3] Although the Northern Nigerians were attached to this update, it had an opposite effect on the observing Southerners who immediately understood the masked intention of the Northern politicians. For one thing, they were shaken to their roots and confronted with harsh realities that would influence them to make immediate changes in their political approaches, particularly when it came to national emergencies. It was difficult to understand the motivation of the Zamfara governor who pulled such a mind-blowing stunt and political effrontery. Maybe he was only using that to curate the persuasion and support of his people from whom he would demand unwavering loyalty if he decided to run for national political office in the future. Or he was seriously pursuing a religious agenda under a federation that was constitutionally considered secular. Whatever was the background motivation, the Southern elites were left in the dark.

Subsequently, the unimaginable support that such an action gave to the candidacy of Yerima within the state and beyond was even enough to

---

[3] Hakeem Onapajo, "Politics and the Pulpit: The Rise and Decline of Religion in Nigeria's 2015 Presidential Elections," *Journal of African Elections* 15, no. 2 (2016): 112–135.

convince him to focus on that trajectory and provide his initial motivation for the step taken for mere political cosmetics. Predominantly, emotions overrode humanistic decency and thereby escalated the tendency of similar actions to rise to the exponential peak following the adoption of the same method by a neighboring governor, Ibrahim Shekarau of Kano.[4] Convinced that the class of political elites in the region was now waking up to their religious assignments as entrenched in their religious values, the Islamic clerics, both in Kano and Zamfara, began to capitalize on their theocratic influence to mobilize support for these political leaders in those two states particularly. The message was simple and the strategy to achieve it succinct; by taking such gradual steps, they would someday conquer the minorities in the region, a dream that began during the Usman dan Fodio's jihad expedition. The strategy therefore was to create an intimidating atmosphere for the minorities, as that might force them to embrace the Islamic religion. Gabriel Ntaniu et al., provided a beautiful image of the social dialectics of the era in words:

Chanting of Allahu Akbar (God is Great) was most popular at major political rallies in the state. All this successfully gave an Islamic coloration to the regime, because this had taken the political order of the day. The case was not different in Kano state as Shekarau under the same political platform (APP) adopted the same strategy; again the Muslim clerics vigorously campaigned for him during the elections because of his agenda for Sharia and also headed major state agencies such as the Shura Committee, Zakat and Husbi Commission and the Hisbah board established in the spirit of Sharia after his emergence as the governor of the state between 2003 and 2011.[5]

In Nigeria, the pluralities of identity naturally presuppose struggles as the survivalist instinct is always activated by jungle residents against predatory species. With the available political arrangement and the unmasked intentions by Northern politicians, the Southern people were forcibly instigated to come up with coping strategies in the political atmosphere of a country that they saw as quickly becoming inhabitable. Even if it meant swallowing their internal grudges, the Christian blocs in the region began to mobilize very strong moral support for the leadership of General Olusegun Obasanjo who doubled as a Southerner and a Christian while piloting the affairs of the country in 2003.[6] Underneath, the Christian South organized a series of sensitization programs to coordinate

---

[4] Ibid.

[5] G. U. Ntamu et al., "Religion in Nigerian Political Space: Implication for Sustainable National Development," *International Journal of Academic Research in Business and Social Sciences* 4 (2014), http://dx.doi.org/10.6007/IJARBSS/v4-i9/1159.

[6] Oluwaseun O. Afolabi, "The Role of Religion in Nigerian Politics and Its Sustainability for Political Development," *Journal of Social Sciences* 3, no. 2 (2015): 42–49.

themselves with regard to the ensuing contradictions that had emerged nationally over the ambition of Northern politicians to consolidate political power using Islam. With religious identities that border on Christian and Muslim indexes becoming emboldened, the reincarnation of religious conflicts became inevitable and was complicated by the sociopolitical, socioeconomic, and sociocultural conditions.

It has been noted that the formation of political parties in Nigeria has tended toward the accentuation of a mutual understanding that religion and ethnicity are important indices of identity formation and the consolidation of power. Thus, the constant mutations of political parties into different nominal identifications – for example, from the NPC to the People's Democratic Party; from the Alliance for Democracy to the Action Congress; from the Action Congress for Democracy to the Action Congress of Nigeria – all still have the religious undertones.[7] One interesting orientation of the Northern politicians is that they see their distance from the political control of the country as a negative omen for the actualization of their imperialist agenda. To prevent this, they are always committed to mobilizing the Northern demographics for electoral involvement, banking on their numerical strength. This is sometimes pursued at the expense of the common Northerner who has been used as cannon fodder for the achievements of their political goals. Since the politicians have created an impression that their political dominance is the fulfilment of a religious philosophy, the people are easily manipulated in the political process.

Religious Activism

Whether displayed outright or masked under a bigger movement, religious activism is as old as politics itself in Nigeria, especially from the time when the British colonialists provided opportunities for Nigerians to participate in governance. For deeply rooted emotional reasons, religion has always convinced its followers over the assumption that in-group safety should take precedence over other things, as the survival of a group presupposes the survival of the individuals under the identity of such a group. Now that religion is considered inseparable from politics, it is therefore understandable why religious believers are susceptible to being mobilized by their religious leaders to carry out civil responsibility, predominant of which is political activism. Based on this understanding, it is natural that religious leaders endorse political candidates who belong to the same religious identity. The reason for this is usually the survival of

---

[7] Falola, *Violence in Nigeria*.

self-interest. Thus, the content of the character of the individuals or their administrative skills to run for offices are secondary. Any attempt to pitch one's intent to someone with opposite religious ideologies is an exposure to an imminent danger of predatory groups which could deploy their influence to inflict maximum pain or threat on a powerless group. By powerless, I mean an identity group without the political authority to exert an influence or enforce a significant national opinion.

The manifestations of religious activism appear in different but compelling forms. For example, CAN has always expressed interest in national affairs that involve Muslim–Christian differences because of an understanding that not to do so will hurt the interest of Christians. Given that the two dominant religions in Nigeria, Christianity and Islam, are exceedingly popular in their different blocs, each of them allows their own strong religious convictions to influence policy, education, and the allocation of major offices and contracts. Different literatures have emphasized how influential the Christian religion is in ensuring that the recruitment of employees is dependent on their relationship with the religion. Even in schools, admission and the subjects taught can be influenced by religion.[8]

The same forces shape the competition for power and elected offices.[9] The manifestation of this activism, especially to the Christians, has been overt and covert. On the other side of the coin, the Muslims have always banked on the religious philosophy across the country to vociferously influence the educational system and sociopolitical engagement in different ways.

Indeed, there have been different cases of activism of different religious groups in Nigeria, even in their immediate social activities. The hallmark of every activism is the registration of influence on issues that are wider spread and keep members' interest. For example, many institutions associated with CAN are created on the platform of protest and activism, against the general practice. As such, inauguration of the Christian Health Association of Nigeria Pharmacy Project (CHAN-PHARM),[10] for example, was geared toward the imposition of the Christian presence in delivery of good healthcare services as a supportive strategy to the government and the establishment of their presence. In another

---

[8] Y. Sodiq, "Can Muslims and Christians Live Together Peacefully in Nigeria?" *The Muslim World* 99 (2009): 646–688.

[9] M. Joseph and I. Benjamin, "Jonathan Gave CAN N7bn not N6bn, Pastor Dikwa Alleges," *Leadership*, 2015, http://leadership.ng/news/412848/jonathan-gave-can-n7bn-not-n6bn-pastor-dikwa-alleges.

[10] Iheanyi Enwerem, *A Dangerous Awakening: The Politicization of Religion in Nigeria* (Ibadan: IFRA-Nigeria, 1995).

realization, there have been obvious protests from Christian groups, especially CAN, against the religio-centric selection of political appointments by any government that has a soft spot for Islam. On a few occasions, the Buhari-led administration has been accused of such sentiment by people who believe that his selection of Muslims to positions is a demonstration of uncanny bias. Equally, MURIC has collectively complained about administrators who do not consider Muslims in their selection or choice of appointments. In 2020, the governor of Oyo State, Seyi Makinde, was accused by MURIC of promoting a Christianization agenda. These are some of the methods used to negotiate political offices and power in Nigeria.

Anti-political Christians

Despite the fact that Nigeria is filled with politically inclined religious people who comfortably blur the dichotomy between religion and politics, realistically there are also people who do not share any interest in partaking in Nigerian politics or endorsing members for political offices. Their apolitical disposition is not descriptive of any indifference to community, leaders, or representation in any administration. Rather, it is reflective of their fundamental interpretation of scriptural opinions on governance generally. While some sects of Christianity are open to welcoming the prospect of political participation, these religious sects are antagonistic or indifferent to issues that border on politics or leadership, as such embarkation contradicts the tenets of their religious philosophy. Unfortunately, the sect of Christianity that rejects the involvement of members in a political system is often confronted with harsh realities that push them to evolve and accommodate the changes that come with advancement. Regardless of this development, there remain some groups that are ideologically tied to the traditional philosophy of the Christian religion that forbids its members from participating in elections and political offices. Some of these groups would attract our attention here, and the scriptural backings always used for the justification of their positions would be appraised.

To enable this understanding, it is important to invoke some instances that bear a mark of resemblance on the current issue. The United States of America's values and political philosophies, for example, are rooted in Christian culture from its beginning as a country. Nothing more crystalizes their religious sentiment than their popular slogan inscribed in their collective psychology, boldly printed on their currencies (paper and coins): "In God we trust." This expression summarizes important information about America in relation to their reliance on God, and their pursuance of that agenda. America's involvement in the grand political affairs of the world generally provides an overview about their determination to employ all means to remain politically relevant across the world. In fact, it was its political inclinations and practices that made it occupy the enviable position it maintains even today. To many American citizens, there should be no separation between the theocratic Christian philosophy and an engagement in deep political affairs, as one continues to remain the instrument to achieve the other. So, when the Christian scripture stipulates that its members should go and dominate the world, there are Americans who implicitly interpret that to mean conquest using political strategies. Some missions, such as the American Southern Baptists, advocated a separation of Church and State. However, there are Nigerian Christians who share a contradictory view of this philosophical opinion about politics. Politics, especially in the Nigerian environment, involves dirty processes that would challenge one's morality and force socially identified people of God into taking some questionable decisions.

Against this understanding, there are Nigerian Christian denominations that consider it appalling and religiously abhorrent to venture into politics. One must be incredibly careful in passing unreflective judgment on these groups of people. Political history and experience in the country have enriched the knowledge of Nigerians enough to make some decisions and conclusions that could be wrongly interpreted. The country has recorded instances of deliberate deception and political calculations that confound the average individual repeatedly. As such, Nigerian politics is thereby interpreted by groups that are antagonistic to participation in political engagements as the biblical allusion to worldly affairs capable of distracting individuals who should be working in the way of God. These groups tenaciously maintain that the domain of politics is the domain of secularity that involves distractive engagement through the provision of ephemeral materialism that can sway people to the side of the devil. Two churches, for example, take this apolitical disposition to the extreme, projecting the aversion to materialism in various religious injunctions. The Deeper Christian Life Ministry and the Mountain of Fire and Miracle Ministry (MFM) are two popular denominations that offer sermons and teachings that actively target and castigate religious believers who partake in politics. Obviously, these denominations understand politics as something to be taken away from religion because of its capacity to destroy human morality.

Meanwhile, the anti-political Christians who employ scriptural injunctions to justify their political aloofness also consider the idea of being essentially materialistic as a contradiction to God's moral and ideological positions: life, to them, is generally observed chiefly from the binary angle of good and bad, godliness and the opposite, and religious and secular. These groups dissociate themselves from possessions that reveal they are engrossed or entangled with life's luxuries. Therefore, their aversion to political issues can be understood within the context of their observation of spiritual and theological affairs. When one understands that the group that shuns political engagements in Nigeria is quite indifferent to countries that engage in politics – especially the United States and some European countries – it would prepare an understanding that there is something curious about Nigerian politics that scares them away. The political terrain of the country is slippery and sloppy, and being entangled in it requires sufficient tact and a measure of carefulness. From the postindependence era to the present time, Nigerian politics is an assortment of violence, greed, and excessive sentiment. The elections are characterized by bloodshed and struggles, both of which push these religious denominations to extend their distance from the political practice that would come with a negative influence on them and their social engagements.

The Christians who share dissimilar ideologies and views about Nigerian politics have been given the chance to function at different levels of politics.

Figure 8.1 Aftermath of religious violence.

As an instance, different political figures who are considered as clerics in their various religious sects have occupied the highest political offices and served in many capacities. It has been observed that some pastors, especially from the Southern divide, have recorded some laudable endorsements from their ethnic and religious extractions, including from their Christian members who have decided to distance themselves from active political engagements. Some Pentecostal leaders, like Pastor Tunde Bakare, Chris Okotie, and Yemi Osinbajo, are Christians who had once vied for political offices or occupied them. Because of this, many of the apolitical Christians are retracing their steps and modifying their opinions about politics generally as they are becoming less critical of the participants of it. Generally, there is a shift from their common perception about materialism, and this has equally affected their relationship with politics. The force of technological revolution, which is making it difficult for anyone to hold tenaciously to ideas and perceptions that do not conform with modern life, has changed the perception of these adherents about materialism. Therefore, the idea that politics is linked to excessive materialism does not take the important position it used to, and this has changed the people's view.

Religious Fundamentalism, Violence, and Its Politicization

Religious fundamentalism is globally understood as a committed impediment to progress. Any country where religion is placed above secular philosophy is bound to be confronted with any of the following challenges. One, they are under the risk of disintegration provided members of the religion are tolerant of other religious expressions which rarely happens. In fact, religious tolerance is usually impossible in an area where the adherents of a particular religious group are fundamentalists, for they would seek the perfectly dogmatic pursuance of their religious philosophies which would, in most, if not in all, cases infringe on the rights of others. Following this, a country of fundamentalist religious adherents basically would be faced with the challenge of stagnation, as ideas to which they are religiously tied are not practical in the contemporary environment. This is usually because most of the injunctions given by religious groups are time-tied. They came up because of the prevailing circumstances of the era and may not conform to the modern dictate. Therefore, fundamentalists would always believe that these laws and codes are absolute, and any attempt to modify them is interpreted as an attack on the religion itself. Again, in a place where religious fundamentalism is popular, the society is usually prone to violence and unending contradictions. It is commonplace among fundamentalists to be embroiled in violence because of the struggles for supremacy.

At the introduction of Sharia law in the North during the country's fourth republic, the environment where it was introduced equally enforced laws that would ensure that the Islamic ethos was imbibed by the commoners, the failure of which would attract punitive reactions. Then, the Hisbah police, the religious law enforcers, were simultaneously inaugurated by politicians and empowered to carry out legal action against those who did not conform to the Islamic injunctions. The atmosphere became very hostile to those who naturally express different opinions on religion generally, and even less conducive for those who professed religions other than Islam, especially in Kano or Zamfara. In this reality, every measure of freedom was thrashed, and there was no inkling of democracy achievable in such an environment where religion takes strong precedence in the administration of social justice. More than expected, the minority (people of different religious expressions) are bound to live in despair and become traumatized to force themselves to conform to the dictates of the society in which they find themselves. The reality that the country is a secular one which advocates legitimacy for migrations of Nigerians who are neither Muslims nor from northern Nigeria reveals that the culture of fundamentalism is unhealthy for the progress of the country.

In July 2016, a Deaconess, Eunice Elisha, of the Redeemed Christian Church of God at a parish in Abuja, was killed by a group of religious fundamentalists over the allegation that she was projecting her faith in consternation of the Muslims within the environment.[11] Eunice Elisha, the victim, was outside doing her daily religious routine before being attacked and murdered by unidentified dissidents who obviously were not from the Christian community. The killing sparked outrage as the death of the woman attracted protests from people, especially Christians, registering their displeasure for the inhumane attitudes of the Northern Muslims to anyone with opposing religious views. Condemnation came from different quarters, each consolidating arguments that the Northern Muslims on the wrong side of religion would become the undoing of the group. This action, however, was preceded by an equally confusing expedition. In 2015, a Northern man by the name of Mubarak Bala was arrested, detained, and molested on the account of committing apostasy.[12] Born to a Muslim family, the renunciation of the Islamic

---

[11] Immanuel Jannah, "How RCCG Evangelist Was Murdered while Preaching," *Vanguard Nigeria*, 2016, www.vanguardngr.com/2016/07/abuja-evangelist-murdered-preaching/.
[12] Ibid.

religion earned Bala public outrage from the Muslim majority who concluded that he had lost his mind. Added to the occasional arraignment of individuals alleged to be homosexuals, Northern Nigerians are deeply into religious fundamentalism, and they seem to go unscathed usually because they are either supported by the leaders' silence, or even sponsored by them. Ordinarily, the governor that imposed Sharia law tacitly already accepts the possibility of contentions because of the fact and possibility that people would always believe differently.

The reality is that the North suspects the South has been a silent reinforcement for fundamentalist behavior and dispositions. It is inconsequential that the South, a region that espouses attitudes and attributes of an opposing religion, is trusted and given the serene atmosphere to thrive. This sentiment reverberates through the thinking of the Northern Muslims who have been supported by acts of silence from their political representatives and have therefore continued in their forceful relationship with politicians from the South. This, unfortunately, has shattered trust and confidence. At the inception of internal struggles and conflicts that led to the formulation of a terrorist organization like Boko Haram, for example, it is popularly announced that the group is against Western culture and the philosophy entrenched in the educational system introduced by the colonialists. For them to repel this system, they considered it instrumental to take the route of force to exert violence and hostility on the whole country. Therefore, this graduated to the normalization of violence and terrorism, where different religions are constitutionally recognized and accepted. Therefore, it has become a politicized issue and it is becoming more difficult to proffer solutions to the myriad of challenges and threats brought by religious fundamentalism.

Conclusion

From all indications, religion has infiltrated politics in Nigeria and this combination has brought some results that are worthy of national reflections because most of them are wreaking havoc. Nigeria's democracy has experienced political instability because it has, at different times, been punctured by military overtaking and dictatorial actions that challenge the country's growth. Politics in Nigeria has been affected by ethnic sentiments and has produced questionable results for the people and the country compared to their contemporaries around the world. Even when the politics of ethnicity appeared unseparated from a heterogeneous country like Nigeria, the fact that the religious dimension is a consideration at all is a bad omen as far as the country's development is concerned. It is so because these religious fundamentalists are either dragging the country backward by politicizing religions or using politics as a tool to achieve a parochial agenda. For example, religion has been used at different times to mobilize support for candidates, therefore creating a mindset of otherness where the people who share the same religion consider those in another religion to be an existential threat and enemies against whom to fight for political control. This mindset has affected the country's collective progress. It has at least seen to the enforcement of candidates with fewer intellectual qualifications or less capacity to pilot the affairs of the country, or other political offices. These lesser candidates then ascend political offices, reducing the possibility of driving the country forward. There are unending scheme-making Nigerian elections that are difficult to adjudge as free and fair, as people are conditioned to follow candidates based on different factors like ethnicity and religion. Apart from political parties, which are necessary platforms for following the ideologies of candidates, religion has been a major factor.

To the extent that members raise their grievances when members are found in threatening situations, religion has always been used as a platform to challenge authority, especially when their members have been unlawfully treated. Accordingly, religious activism has become commonplace among Nigerians. When the horrible incidence of the murder of Eunice – the earlier-referenced RCCG member – surfaced, CAN and other notable religious bodies, condemned the action and encouraged the Nigerian government to embark on a fact-finding mission to unveil those who perpetrated the evil. No matter how deafening the protests of national emergencies that are bordered around religion are, they are either rationalized or explained away, using illogical arguments that are responsible for birthing them in the first instance. Perhaps, it is because of this reality that some denominations of Christians distance themselves from political engagement in Nigeria. Thus, their appropriation of scriptural injunctions to justify their apolitical disposition is commonsensical. Sadly though, the paradoxical reality is that those who sermonize against participation in politics are always encumbered by a lack of knowledge concerning the political processes which they consider to be evil. What remains constant, therefore, is that religion and politics in Nigeria are intertwined and have become difficult to separate. The fact that religion continues to be a useful instrument for elites to pursue their agenda animates its importance.

9   Democracy and Its Limits

Introduction

In this chapter, the problems of government and governance in Nigeria, one of the most populous, yet least popular conglomerates of democracy (with additional reference to other parts of Africa) will be examined. For obvious reasons, Nigeria is proof that democracy is not necessarily the total solution to a nation's problems because, as favorable as it is, there are other factors needed for a country's development, the absence of which expose the limitations of democracy.

There are clear expectations of what the country wants, which have been defined dating back to the 1970s. The country's objectives were listed in Nigeria's Second National Development Plan. This list has been repeated and is now part of the daily conversation and media narrative:

a. A united, strong and self-reliant nation.
b. A huge and powerful economy.
c. A fair and egalitarian society.
d. A land full of bright and adequate opportunities for all citizens.
e. A free and democratic society.[1]

When African countries became independent of European powers in the second half of the twentieth century, many welcomed the so-called democratic governments, but they were short-lived. Political parties were formed and there was contest for power; however, election rigging, electoral frauds, and violence defined the contests. Power was sought by all means because the dividends of power were too attractive. The results of the contests could not be left to the electoral process, since a party could not predict what the other would do. With the police and judiciary compromised, the army struck, and the country began what was to be a long stretch of military rule. Also, in other parts of Africa where there were no coups or military rule, a one-party state was the norm, such as in

---

[1] *Second National Development Plan 1970–8* (Lagos: Federal Ministry of Information, 1970), preamble.

218

Kenya, Cote d'Ivoire, Tanzania, and so on. The leadership and institutional crises of the postindependence era were very troublesome: State institutions exercised punitive and coercive powers without much care for human rights. The judiciary was subordinated to dictatorship, and rarely allocated justice with equity and fairness. Paradoxically, misgovernance and a slow rate of development incited the demand for democracy everywhere; it was a long process, lasting almost four decades in some countries.

Although the desire for democracy and the struggle to attain it have a long history, worthy of note is the fact that its contemporary history is not yet thirty years old. What scholars such as Samuel Huntington refer to as the "third wave of democratization" is as recent as the mid-1990s.[2] The wave coincided with worldwide political changes with the disintegration of the Soviet Union, the collapse of communism, the fall of the Berlin Wall, and the end of the Cold War. Democracy entered its triumphant moment, and was described as the best political system, which, along with capitalism, was said to signal "the end of history."[3] In this "third wave of democratization," there are important developments, which some refer to as achievements: the number of countries under military dictatorship has greatly reduced; apartheid ended in South Africa and there have been four successful elections thereafter. While there were four electoral democracies in 1985, it increased to ten in 1993, eighteen in 1995, and twenty-four in 2006; between 2000 and 2002, forty-two countries in sub-Saharan Africa conducted multiparty elections; and in that same period, the ruling parties in Ghana, Mauritius, Mali, and Senegal conceded defeat and handed power over to opposition parties in their countries. By 2003, only 39 percent of African countries were seen as unfree, and Nigeria's various republics, including the Fourth Republic was in its twentieth year by 2019, which is a huge feat in comparison to the First Republic which lasted less than six years, the second for four years, and the third was actually aborted. A number of African countries are presently members of the Community of Democracies, an international, intergovernmental coalition of states committed to the promotion of democratic values.[4]

Nigeria returned to civilian democracy in 1999, but it was an elite exercise and the governance has been disappointing. There has been much violence, religious and ethnic conflicts, rising poverty, and blatant

---

[2] Samuel Huntington, *The Third Wave: Democratization the Late Twentieth Century* (Norman: University of Oklahoma Press, 1991).
[3] Francis Fukuyama, *The End of History and the Last Man* (Washington, DC: Free Press, 1992).
[4] On this organization, see www.community-democracies.org/.

looting of public funds by the same people entrusted with the funds meant for the development of the nation. In this chapter, the change in the state is taken as hidden context, while the critique of governance is regarded as similar to that of democracy. Despite the propaganda about its advantages and the near-global consensus about its values, democracy is riddled with a lot of contradictions that limit its functional value to most of the citizenry. It is expected that political modernity would cause an evolution of political culture and lead to the appearance of viable, resilient institutions that would produce stable politics.

Former Nigerian president, Goodluck Jonathan, who is a beneficiary of anti-military conflict, defines democracy as "a system to comprise interdependent and mutually enforcing rights, systems, norms, and institutions aggregated into what can be referred to as an essential element of democracy."[5] He went further to list out the essential elements:

1. Respect for human rights – which includes freedom of expression, freedom of the press, freedom of religion and conscience.
2. The rule of law and due process.
3. Holding periodically, clearly defined, free and fair elections based on secret balloting and universal suffrage, and monitored by independent election observers.
4. Freedom of association which includes the right to form independent political parties.
5. Impartial and transparent administration of elections by an independent body.
6. Separation of powers, with an independent judiciary.
7. Constitutional subordination of all state institutions, including the military, to the legally constituted civilian authority.[6]

It seems that he is very aware of the complexities that plague democracy, in terms of electoral democracy that put him in power versus liberal democracy which his people desire. The rule of law is essential to a liberal democracy – that is, assuming that the law enforcement agencies and judiciary are not corrupt.

Freedom of speech is also ensured. Citing Goodluck Jonathan here is deliberate, since he was a practitioner at the highest level of governance, rather than using the words of a scholar or someone who could be regarded as a non-African voice and be dismissed as spreading a Western idea. His definition and list of elements however, leave out issues relating to development and governance, which are the main

---

[5] Goodluck Jonathan, "Consolidating Our Democratic System," in *Strengthening Democratic Traditions and Institutions in Nigeria*, eds. Martin Uhomoibhi and Ehiedu Iweriebor (Abuja: Ministry of Foreign Affairs, 2014), xviii.
[6] Ibid.

sources of the problems in Africa. There is also no connection between the theoretical definitions and practical reality, as his administration made abundantly clear.

Disturbing Trends and Dangerous Signals

Africa is currently witnessing the problems of governance in a democratic framework. The problems are too many, hopes are constrained, and expectations are high. The problems seem to be similar in Nigeria, Tunisia, and Kenya, and they include violence, election malpractices, fraud, corruption, judicial manipulation, ethnic rivalries, immense theft of public funds, and many others.[7] Sometimes, these problems become obstacles, which are converted to negative ideas, some of which will be later discussed.

What are the problems? The legacies of European control in the first half of the twentieth century had a lasting effect on institutions and governance. Major issues include those around identities that were merged with ethnicities whose members constantly fight for power. Some are minority ethnicities and as such can be excluded from power, while religious identities are stronger and they continually create serious pressures from their side. Sudan had to be divided into two countries with the Muslims in North Sudan, and the Christians and other religions in South Sudan, where not long after independence in 2011, they succumbed to power rivalries and a civil war.

In liberal theory, it is assumed that democracy is the solution to political dissolution, but on the contrary, democratic political communities are divided as well. Regional, ethnic, and religious rifts shape the emanation and orientation of political parties. The electoral process is marked by bloc voting, which shows regions and ethnicities. Arguments based on ethnicity compromise those of merit and thus emphasize choosing leaders based on where they come from and not about building inclusive institutions to give everyone a sense of belonging to exercise their rights and brilliance and contribute to nation building. As stated in the following, the democratic process is tied to violence and there have been cases of bloodshed.

Postcolonial economic problems have overwhelmed the democratic processes and institutions. In the 1980s and 1990s, many countries were destabilized by economic conflicts. Africa had the highest number

---

[7] For instance, see Olufemi O. Ajayi, *Crises of Democracy* (Lagos: Self-Published, 2012); and Saliba Sarsar and Julius O. Adekunle, eds., *Democracy in Africa: Political Changes and Challenges* (Durham: Carolina Academic Press, 2012).

of poor countries in the world, and this led to conditions of violence. Economic growth is evident in a few places, while poverty is still endemic in many countries. In poor countries, democracy and governance cannot be detached from poverty. While to the poor, the ballot box is a tool of positive change in their lives, the rich and the powerful believe it grants them access to higher levels of accumulation, influence, and power.

The problems become a vicious cycle and electoral malpractice is widespread. Campaigns are filled with promises and not challenges concerning corruption, insecurity, unemployment, energy, health, education, and so on. Programs are promised without consideration for the cost, and when cost is considered, it is already inflated. The tolerance for corruption and an ugly environment (ugly buildings and landscapes) is connected to declining civic culture and deterioration of traditional ethos. An observer of Nigerian politics, writing in pain and disappointment, states the problem of corruption:

> There is no other time in the political history of Nigeria that corruption has thrived so amazingly and alarmingly than since 1999 when the current democratic structure became operational. The extent, nature, trend and content of corruption in Nigeria have altogether assumed sophisticated dimensions. Is it among governors, law-makers, public office holders, or within government establishments? Corruption is pervasive. Apparently, democracy seems to have become the guise under which corruption thrives in the public sector. Those who are officially responsible for operating government machinery in Nigeria use the opportunity to exploit the state thereby using the democratic structure to their personal advantage.[8]

He reiterates the voices of many others, as the most common topic in the Nigerian media is about public corruption, missing funds, and abuse of power. This action is not limited to politicians, but extends to the judges, police, civil servants, and the army. This is to show that office holders have no regard for accountability. Therefore, the cost of democracy is too high, and its dividends too small to the populace.

Poor leadership is a common narrative and the crises of institutions are visible all around, with that of the leadership always conspicuous for all to see. Fixing institutional problems and promoting the rule of law could persuade leaders to behave, but leaders need to create the necessary institutions. Corruption is an obstacle to producing great leaders, so the civil society needs to work hard, and first, transform the mindset of the citizens to promote values of respect and honesty, to seek the collective good to work for. It is quite common to see citizens asking God for good

---

[8] Zimako O. Zimako, *Face of a Nation: Democracy in Nigeria, Foreign Relations and National Image* (Lagos: Modern Approach, 2009).

and 'godly' leaders, probably because politics is instilled with faith or as a reflection of the people's frustration.

The Mo Ibrahim Prize offers the largest prize in the world ($5 million over ten years, and $200,000 each year for a lifetime) for a democratically elected African leader who governed well, reduced poverty, and generated sustainable development.[9] You might regard the Mo Ibrahim Prize as either pragmatic or silly, but it is aimed at encouraging the emergence of good leadership, and so far, only the former presidents of Mozambique (Joaquim Alberto Chissano, 2007), Botswana (Festus Gontebanye Mogae, 2008), Cape Verde (Pedro de Verona Rodrigues Pires, 2011), and Namibia (Hifikepunye Pohamba, 2015) have won it. Not only is it difficult to get winners, but presidents of rich countries like Nigeria would not care about amounts that represent peanuts in comparison to what they amass through their wanton greed and insatiable appetite for stealing from their nation's treasuries. It is indeed the proverbial drop of water in a mighty sea!

Problems and Limits in Context

Democracy is still unsettled in Africa, both theoretically and practically. Theoretically, its definitions are yet to be clarified in many countries, and in some cases, it is less understood in different applications. While some insist that democracy is universally applicable – meaning it should ignore race, ethnicity, religion, nationality, and culture – on the other hand, there is a wide range of theories and arguments that there is a need to make it fit for different cultural communities and adapt it to different cultures. However, the leaders alter this meaning in practice, so as to serve their personal interests.

Thus far, the stress has been on electoral democracy, meaning the country is democratic because of elections held and ballots counted. However, voting is not the same as counting of ballots. In many cases, numbers are just declared, sometimes more than the number of registered voters. Elections are rarely free and fair, and only the winners agree with the results. The cheated losers and their supporters therefore, have no respect for those in power. Ultimately, election periods show the fragility of the state, and fear of the collapse of the entire nation is evident. Whoever is in power sees power as a game, and the voters, the so-called electorate, relate democracy to an avalanche of problems. Due to the backdrop of failures of authoritarian military regimes that lasted for many

---

[9] *Mo Ibrahim Foundation*, "Ibrahim Prize for Achievement in African Leadership," *Mo Ibrahim Foundation*, n.d., www.moibrahimfoundation.org/prize/.

years, the expectation is that democracy will put an end to ethnic problems and bring about development; in fact, many see democracy as the solution to human rights problems, environmental degradation, unemployment, and many other relentless issues.

Corruption and neo-patrimonialism destroy democratic institutions and prevent the emergence of credible leadership. From various sources such as Transparency International (a global watchdog against corruption), Nigeria is one of the most corrupt nations in the world, a place where the purpose of political participation for most of the leaders is to have access to state money and not public service. Politics is very lucrative, therefore, the differences between a democratic and nondemocratic government is negligible as regards to the use of power for personal interest. The salaries and benefits of Nigerian politicians are among the highest worldwide, with the total package of a senator being N354 million per annum, the equivalent of over $2 million, while members of the house of representatives earn slightly less. On the Local Government Council, which hardly generates any significant revenue but is dependent on the federal allocation, the chairman earns N1 million (about $5,000) monthly, N5 million as security vote, 100 percent of annual salary for accommodation, 400 percent of annual salary for car loan, 300 percent of annual salary for furniture, 30 percent of annual salary for utility bills, and 75 percent of annual salary for domestic staff. Also, after the stipulated terms of politicians and civil servants are over, they continue to collect significant pensions.

The political class in Nigeria has developed a depraved sense of entitlement and the system in general rewards those in public service not to do any analytical work or contribute to nation building, but rather rewards personal ambition. There are structures of accumulation in place that have no regard for the poor nor the aspiration of the majority of the country's population. The political philosophy suggests that members of the political class want to convert the majority of the citizens into beggars in order to have total control, using democracy as a ruse. Democracy in Nigeria works for a few, expending 85 percent of its resources to sustain a minute percentage of the population. An ex-governor of the Central Bank of Nigeria once purported that it cost Nigeria more than 25 percent of the government's recurrent expenditure to maintain the National Assembly!

A Series of Contradictions

Liberal democracy must be evaluated based on governance, institutions of governance, policies, leadership, and their outcomes. Some analysts advance the evaluative yardstick to include civil and political rights, economic freedom, and also cultural freedom to give room to women's rights and the right to same-sex marriage, so that people are allowed to live the way they want and also express their grievances and desires.[10]

In Nigeria's case, the most critical matrices are those of economic development and political stability. Is there overall security? With respect to the economy, what is the GDP growth rate? Are prices stable to check inflation? What about the unemployment and poverty rates? The conditions for democracy and governance to function are in the creation process. In 1979, the presidential system of the United States was copied without considering the cost or the cultural and historical context that shaped its development. So-called democratic freedom translates to the combination of religious and ethnic lines instead of creating cross-cutting national institutions and citizenship. Political aspirants divide the society and are quick to suggest the use of violence in a bid to win elections. Western liberal democracy does not have its intellectual origins in Africa, and the intellectualization of the political process by the likes of Aristotle, Plato, and so on were rooted in the experiences of their own societies and cultures. Therefore, there will be some transition problems when Africa tries to adapt such. Democracy in Africa is thus treated as an imported idea, and it is sometimes separated from the cultures and philosophy of the West that pitched the idea to or forced it on Africa. The West is richer economically with the ability to sustain its form of liberal democracy, but Nigeria drains its resources and elections hardly lead to major changes; victory to a new leadership merely increases the number of those eligible to steal.

The fact that a country is democratic does not mean it is not repressive. Democratic and repressive regimes go together; a nation can be a threat to itself by repressing its citizenry, tearing their rights to shreds, and torturing and detaining its citizens unlawfully. Democracy does not translate to the emergence of democratic institutions to manage the lives of the people; thus, presidents and governors could be elected but they may not govern democratically. That is, state agencies, universities, etc., may not run as democratic institutions, but the leaders of such institutions act like emperors, and democracy is a mere disguise.

Democracy does not always promote meritocracy, which is the search for the most qualified to govern; but democracy could become a tool to advance prebendalism. It privileges the mediocre in power, who are appointed because of loyalty to the party and party leaders, and not for

---

[10] An expansive definition is offered in Shireen Hassim, "Democratization: A View from Africa," *Signs: Journal of Women in Culture and Society* 31, no. 4 (2006): 928–932.

any other qualification. Democracy in Nigeria does not mean that the rights of the marginalized are protected. For instance, the way the minorities are treated is a way of undermining the rights of citizens.

Constitutionalism ignores the boundaries of democracy. A constitution reveals the shortcomings of human nature and its interpretations and practices may reflect elite interests that, in some cases, may nullify the interests of most of the population. The wealthy make up the minority that control power, and as members of the political class, they rotate themselves in power, replicating one another by adding their children, wives, and close friends to the network. There is a lust for power in order to profit from the state. This minority is the "constituent power," to use a term of Hardt and Negri, who govern the majority – the "constitutive masses."[11]

In order to make the constitution work, political parties might devise systems that disenfranchise. For example, the zoning of political offices in order to balance the interest of political identities may deprive the nation of qualified people. As demonstrated during the President Olusegun Obasanjo–led administration, while the constitution was in place and the system democratic, activities showed personal whims and caprices, ambition, and political intrigues. According to those who served during this administration, there were inconsistencies in the balance of rights and obligations. Even Obasanjo schemed hard to adjust the constitution to have a third term in office. El-Rufai who was an insider to the Obasanjo led government confessed in his long memoir:

[B]ut we all remain disappointed at the blemish our administration got by the pursuit of the tenure extension, and the consequences of what has turned out to be poor outcomes resulting from his personal choice of successors. The very notion of thinking that no third term means the end of Nigeria seems to suggest that he considered himself more important than Nigeria. It was a breath-taking realization: all his decisions and actions since that fateful evening [that is, May 16, 2006 when the Senate voted to reject a constitutional amendment to elongate the presidential term] indicated to me that he believed that Nigeria was a creation of nature for him to use at will, that wherever and whenever the narrow interest of Obasanjo and the broad interests of Nigeria conflicted, Obasanjo's preferences must trump Nigeria's interest. One still does not know how he arrived at that conclusion, but it was quite clear to me that this was what he had come to believe, and perhaps what he still thinks.[12]

To be clear, it is good to note that the above statement was not in reference to a military general in an autocratic regime, but to a civilian in

[11] Michael Hardt and Antonio Negri, *Multitude: War and Democracy in the Age of Empire* (New York: Penguin, 2004).
[12] Nasir Ahmad El-Rufai, *The Accidental Public Servant* (Ibadan: Safari Books, 2013), lvii–lviii.

a so-called democratic era. Many narrations in the book revealed that the people counted for less in various calculations and schemes. Obasanjo handpicked his successor, Umaru Yar'Adua, who had complicated health problems and who, after an unfair election, spent more time in the hospital than his office. Obasanjo being able to handpick his successor is a pointer to one of the weaknesses and limitations of democracy. While political parties claim to be agents of democracy, this does not mean that politicians run a democratic government. According to Robert Michels' remark in the examples of political parties in Europe, their internal workings may not be just or egalitarian.[13] Diverse testimonies and narrations of those who have served under civilian democratic regimes are consistent about the excesses and abuse of power, and the blatant disregard for the citizens and their rights. The institutions do not give expression to the majority of the population. The politicians are not committed to programs that will benefit the people, but to pacts among themselves to distribute largesse. The pacts work because they have created institutional, social, and political barriers to develop a credible system. Politicians create chaos and profit from it as underdeveloped infrastructures disenfranchise the populace from participating in pursuits that will emancipate them.

Obasanjo was the first to deny that his actions were authoritarian and out of place in a democratic system, and this must be identified as yet another contradiction and limitation: democracy is not the absence of patriarchy. African theorists have their work cut out for them in this regard, because from homes to the highest level of power, patriarchy is the norm of governance. For many centuries, the kings, chiefs, and men have created substantial authority systems that marginalize women and disempower youths. Authority has a base in patriarchal power, even at the simple household level, where the man is the head. It is either that patriarchy as a cultural model of authority is totally destroyed or it is accepted as one of the cultural parameters of the African domestication of democracy. One question – and a serious consideration in which theorists have to come up with new ideas or at least, a new kind of explanation – is: Can patriarchy be aligned with liberal democracy? The fact that Nigerians called Obasanjo "Baba" (Father) in place of President shows how even the vernacular of communication captures the reality of patriarchy and the language of authority!

There are definitely places worse than Nigeria, such as the Gambia, under the mercurial figure Yahya Jammeh, who referred to citizens of his

---

[13] Robert Michels, *Political Parties: A Sociological Study of the Oligarchical Tendencies of Modern Democracy* (Kitchener: Batoche Books, 2001).

nation as witches and sorcerers, and claimed to cure HIV/AIDS, Ebola, and other diseases. Thus, while the Gambia was seen as being under liberal democracy, Jammeh's governing institutions were not. Commonplace in many so-called democratic governments in Africa is that the person in power manipulates the constitution to stay in power. (For instance, Paul Biya of Cameroon and Robert Mugabe in Zimbabwe devised means not to leave power.) Elections can be annulled if they don't favor those who want to be in control of the nation, the executive can ignore the legislative and judicial arms, extra-judicial actions can be taken against the opposition, for instance, the assassination of M. K. O. Abiola, etc. Democracy becomes a way to hold on to power, which someone like Jammeh did for twenty years. Gerard Roland tried to advance this argument:

> A democracy and an autocracy also often differ in a number of other critical aspects related to economic development. In autocratic countries, a small group of elites usually controls a large part of the country's wealth and productive assets. The elite will tend to use the political regime to perpetuate its economic control and privileges by discouraging both the entry of new firms into the economy and market competition, favoring instead to erect barriers to market entry via laws and regulations. In contrast, in a democracy, while special interests and political lobbies generally favor established firms, there are also countervailing tendencies as consumers favor market competition and low prices, and small medium enter- prises favor low costs of entry into the economy.[14]

For example, Jammeh controlled the economy and Gambia's resources were used to maintain his loyalists. The rule of law operated under the pleasure of a single person, whose official title was His Excellency Sheikh Alhaji Dr. Professor Jammeh, who had the monopoly of power and violence. He had the power to invade anybody's house, confiscate his or her assets, and extort or take over lucrative businesses of citizens. Some so-called democratic leaders in countries such as Equatorial Guinea also behaved in this manner. Teodoro Obiang Nguema Mbasogo has been in power since 1979, with his son as vice president. Zimbabwe's former president Robert Gabriel Mugabe, the oldest head of state in Africa, ruled between 1980 and 2017. In Angola, President Jose Eduardo Dos Santos was also in power from 1979 to 2017, and Paul Biya has ruled Cameroon for over thirty years.

Democracy is not the solution to inequality in income. Where majority of the people are poor, there is limited participation. Some theorists believe that liberal democracy does not thrive in poor societies because the poor have no advantage over the rich who are able to exploit the

---

[14] Gerard Ronald, *Development Economics* (Boston: Pearson Publishers, 2014), 241.

system in their favor and control electoral politics.[15] Party politics can be extended, and the result will be such that the poor have limited benefits.

Critical Challenges

Islam Islam's relationships with democracy are many and sometimes contradictory. First is the argument that predominantly Islamic populations, like those in the Middle East, are undemocratic. Some are much older civilizations, such as the case of Egypt, but they have always been confronted with the tensions between authoritarianism and democracy. Second, some people see the religion and the culture it promotes as undemocratic. Third, some argue that Islam is being misinterpreted and that while it is true that democracy and other issues (such as the West's past, present, individualism, and freedom of thought) are feared, Fatema Mernissi argues that some of these issues misappropriate the blame. As regards democracy and Islam, she opines:

Arabs do not so much have a fear of democracy as suffer from a lack of access to the most important advances of recent centuries, especially tolerance as principle and practice. By this I mean the secular humanism that has allowed the flowering of civil society in the West. Humanistic ideas – freedom of thought, the sovereignty of the individual, the right to freedom of action, tolerance – were propagated in the West through secular schools. With a few rare exceptions (notably Turkey), the modern Muslim state has never called itself secular, and has never committed to teaching individual initiative. On the contrary, individualism always held a rather ambiguous place among the "reformers" of the nineteenth-century nationalist movement. This movement, focused on the struggle against colonization and therefore viscerally anti-Western, was obliged to root itself more deeply than ever in Islam. Facing the militaristic, imperialistic West, Muslim nationalists were forced to take shelter in their past and erect it as a rampart – cultural hudud to exorcise colonial violence. The Muslim past they reactivated did not anchor modern identity in the rationalist tradition. In fact, the nationalists were prisoners of a historical situation that inevitably made modernity a no-win choice. Either they might construct modernity by claiming the humanistic heritage of the Western colonizer at the risk of losing unity (for when we speak about the rationalist tradition, we are talking about ra'y, "individual opinion," and 'aql', "reason," and therefore about the possibility of divergence of opinion); or they could carefully safeguard a sense of unity in the face of the colonizer by clinging to the past, favoring the tradition of ta'a, "obedience," and foreclosing all Western innovation.[16]

---

[15] See, for instance, Del Dickson, *The People's Government: An Introduction to Democracy* (New York: Cambridge University Press, 2014), chapter 11.

[16] Fatema Mernissi, *Islam and Democracy: Fear of the Modern World*, 2nd ed., trans. Mary Jo Lakeland (New York: Basic Books, 1992), 42–43.

According to Mernissi, Arab leaders made the choice that would ensure the unity of their people with consequences on freedom of thought and the freedom to differ.

Fourth, as in the case of Nigeria, violence connected with Islamic radicalism has been seen to constitute a danger to democracy. This is particularly true in the case of the Boko Haram (BH), which has created serious chaos since 2009. The inability of the state to curtail the BH crisis has impacted negatively on democracy and undermined the credibility of those in power.

Boko Haram has shown that the Nigerian Army and federal police forces are incompetent. It has therefore, destroyed villages and towns, captured some places easily, and engaged in ruthless killing and extortion as terrorists. So-called caliphate flags have been raised to proclaim them as territories that are independent of Nigeria. There have been massacres and bombings in Abuja, Kano, Kaduna, and Borno, among others. As of 2018, 112 of the abducted 276 girls from Chibok were still missing, while on February 19, another 110 girls were kidnapped in Dapchi. All these crimes were perpetuated by Boko Haram.

Violence   Sometimes, the route to power is violence in various forms. Power can be seized by violence through military coups. Existing power structures may collapse and be usurped by an alternative leadership as in the overthrow of Muammar Gaddafi in Libya, Ben Ali in Tunisia, Blaise Compaore in Burkina Faso, and some other instances. Violence can also be employed to retain power, in addition to fraudulent adjustments to constitutions, as in Paul Biya's case in Cameroon and the late Robert Mugabe's in Zimbabwe, where both Presidents refused to leave power. Political crises may lead to civil war, which is always long lasting and difficult to resolve as in Liberia, Sierra Leone, and Sudan.

The most severe is in relation to transfer of power when a new leader has to emerge, or an incumbent retained through an electoral process. Elections are supposed to be the means by which choice, succession, and legitimacy are determined. The rules and regulations that guide the conduct of elections and electoral laws are theoretically simple and can be replicated from other countries. However, in the real world, they are very difficult to practice, and their failure can lead to political instability and violence which impact on the political process and the society at large. A country can move from conducting an election to civil war, as happened in Nigeria following the June 12, 1993, election that produced the victory of late Chief M. K. O. Abiola, but the results were annulled by the military government of retired General Ibrahim Babangida. All the major elections in Nigeria (1964, 1979, 1983, 1993, 1999, 2003, 2007, 2011) produced violence. The process was a disappointment because it was expected that the country would transition from being governed by a single party to a more open and competitive electoral system.

The desire for power creates a breeding ground for violence. As the power seekers manipulate religion and ethnicity, political narratives become verbally violent and physically create ethno-religious militias. Thugs are hired, vigilante groups created, and rival gangs extort money from people. These thugs take to kidnapping and demand huge ransoms. The Boko Haram terrorists are not the only people with access to dangerous weapons and guns; all kinds of firearms are everywhere, purchased by criminals, party thugs, and even leading politicians. In villages, rival political parties fight with knives, machetes, spears, clubs, and bows and arrows, as seen many times in Jos. But where there are higher rewards of power, thugs use AK-47s, assault rifles, bazookas, submachine guns, double-barreled shotguns, and Beretta pistols.

Violence has become an important part of the democratic culture. A former Inspector General of Police, the head of the country's police force, Mike Okiro gives three reasons:

Whenever there is political competition, there is always an element of electoral violence.
    Violence has been used by groups holding power and by groups in the process of losing power.
    Violence has been pursued in the defiance of order, by the privileged; in the name of justice, by the oppressed; and in fear of displacement, by the threatened.[17]

The connections between politics and violence are very strong, and Okiro's cogent points can be cited again:
  i. Democratic governance in Nigeria is yet to institute sufficient policies and programs to alter the structures of imbalance and inequity rooted by colonialism and prolonged autocratic military rule.
  ii. Because of the multiethnic nature of the country and the inability of the nationalistic project to produce a true nation and a corresponding national identity; ethnic, religious and primordial points of reference became more important in democratic processes.
  iii. The desperation for political power, and by extension unrestricted access to state resources, amplifies the feeling of insecurity in the people. Hence, the premium on power is exceptionally high, and because the system lacks the institutional arrangements to moderate

[17] Mike Mbama Okiro, "Law Enforcement, the Electoral Process and Democracy in Nigeria," in *Strengthening Democratic Traditions and Institutions in Nigeria*, eds. Martin Uhomoibhi and Ehiedu Iweriebor, 97.

political competitions, political campaigns in Nigeria tend to assume the nature of warfare.

iv. The closeness between the militants who were political foot soldiers to politicians makes efforts to curb insurgency or directives against them difficult to effect. This is because the politicians know that the militants could be needed during future elections against their opposition in their respective states.[18]

Paul Collier describes political violence as a curse and an obstacle: "It is a curse because the process of violent struggle is highly destructive. It is an obstacle because where power rests on violence; it invites an arrogant assumption that government is there to rule rather than to serve."[19] He devoted his book, *Wars, Guns, and Votes*, to explaining why political violence is indigenous, fostered by the three things in the book's title, which he characterized as the "technologies" of violence. He argued that the three "have destroyed societies that were confidently expected to develop."[20] He views democracy as universal but plagued by the promotion of its wrong features, by which he means electoral politics, instead of its infrastructure. The façade is not capable of promoting democratic accountability: "[W]hen political power is won through violence, the results are usually awful. The political strongman in a divided society is seldom a visionary leader; he is more likely to be self-serving, or in thrall to the interests of a narrow support group."[21] When violence is endemic, it means democracy is dangerous or destructive, and its outcome is not genuine. If democracy is not capable of reducing or minimizing violence, then fundamentals are flawed.

Globalization   The forces that created African countries as an imperialist project continue to manifest themselves in new dimensions of globalization with implications for democracy. The West preaches democracy, but the global structures of power are not based on democracy. The international system is structured on political and economic inequalities. International power and global financial institutions are exploitative.

Failed states have awful effects globally. A failed state can destabilize an entire region and consequently produce internally displaced refugees, instigate migration within and outside the region, and encourage the emergence of terrorist cells. While Nigeria is not a failed state, it is clearly dysfunctional. Maybe democracy will prevent the fall down the political slope, but this is only possible if good governance produces development.

---

[18] Ibid.

[19] Paul Collier, *Wars, Guns, and Votes: Democracy in Dangerous Places* (New York: Harper Perennial, 2009), 2.

[20] Ibid., 8.   [21] Ibid., 9.

Globalization has different effects on various countries and their economies. While some impacts are direct, such as those affecting immigration, the environment, and nationalism; some may be indirect, such as those on citizenship, education, religion, and health. In a recent book, *Africanizing Democracies*, the authors listed as challenges issues around health and healing, women, gender, and sexuality, as part of the problems of democracy.[22] The thinking on these issues became part of the conversation on modernity and democracy in Africa. According to Claude Ake, democracy is imperiled by globalization: global financial institutions, he argues, can disempower national financial institutions.[23] To Benjamin Barber however, globalization has destructive impact on local cultures and can sabotage how states control the use and consumption of their own cultures.[24]

A silver lining is for Africans to connect with people from other parts of the world in order to create a larger social movement for justice, to form the empowered "multitude" that Michael Hardt and Antonio Negri optimistically think can rise to redress the imbalances in global power.[25]

Antidemocratic Impulses   The need for democracy has been questioned by the people in places where leadership is corrupt and the pace of development has been slow. Many voices have asked for the relevance of civilian governments, and some have even called for the return of military regimes. The connection between democracy and development has been questioned, as many call attention to how an authoritarian government in Japan, after the Meiji Restoration, brought about changes and how the same model changed development in Singapore, South Korea, Taiwan, and China under authoritarian regimes. To develop good governance and effective institutions many not necessarily require democracy, and there is an argument that authoritarian regimes may even govern better. The shock from the remunerations and salaries of politicians has made citizens wonder if the cost of democracy is actually worth it. How can a country that boasts of liberal democracy have a government that cannot supply electricity and drinking water? Why is the quality of education degraded? Why is human capital poorly developed? And why do most people make less than $2 a day?

[22] Alicia C. Decker and Andrea L. Arrington, *Africanizing Democracies, 1980–Present* (New York: Oxford University Press, 2015).

[23] Claude Ake, "Dangerous Liaisons: The Interface of Globalization and Democracy," in *Democracy's Victory and Crisis*, ed. Alex Hadenius (Cambridge: Cambridge University Press, 1997), 282–296.

[24] Benjamin Barber, *Strong Democracy: Participatory Politics for a New Age* (Berkeley: University of California Press, 1984).

[25] Michael Hardt and Antonio Negri, *Multitude: War and Democracy in the Age of Empire* (New York: Penguin, 2004).

Correctives and Future Possibilities

A very common phrase in African politics is the "roadmap to democracy," as one analyst after another offers ideas on how to make democracy a possibility. Larry Diamond declared that it is a "spirit," which is global in outreach.[26] It is also complimentary to talk about a roadmap to authoritarianism, as democracy doesn't work all the time, hence the efficacy of the system is being questioned. The number of electoral democracies declined from twenty-four in 2008 to nineteen in 2012, and the number of countries referred to as "unfree" by the Freedom House increased from 35 percent in 2003 to 41 percent in 2013.[27] Some countries have experienced political turmoil and reversals: Burkina Faso, Central African Republic, Cote d' Ivoire, Guinea, Guinea-Bissau, Lesotho, Mali, Madagascar, Mauritania, and Togo.

Democracy has not enhanced accountability thus far; neither has it brought a higher standard of living to the poor. Many analysts admit that it is a process and can be long. Former President Jonathan of Nigeria spoke the mind of leaders and scholars:

The establishment of a functional democratic system in any society is a long and complex process with ups and downs because it requires full understanding of the cultural, and social and political environment in which this democratization process is taking place. But since political systems are also cultural systems, the makers and actors of the democratic order have to deliberately undertake a creative application of the political, social and cultural heritage with the formal tenets of democracy for it to take root and become truly national.[28]

President Goodluck Jonathan was right about seeing democratization as a "process," and he recognized the need to think about its "creative application." General Muhammadu Buhari, a former dictator who is now a democracy convert and Nigeria's president, worried about the quality of elections and warned that "mere elections do not democracy make."[29] Democracy should be treated "not as an event, but a journey . . . to attain democratic consolidation."

---

[26] Larry Diamond, *The Spirit of Democracy: The Struggle to Build Free Societies throughout the World* (New York: Henry Holt and Company, 2008).

[27] Reports on "free" and "unfree" can be found in annual reviews by the Freedom House based in New York. https://freedomhouse.org.

[28] Goodluck Jonathan, "Consolidating Our Democratic System," in *Strengthening Democratic Traditions and Institutions in Nigeria*, eds. Martin Uhomoibhi and Ehiedu Iweriebor (Abuja: Ministry of Foreign Affairs, 2014), xviii.

[29] General Muhammadu Buhari, "Prospects for Democratic Consolidation in Africa: Nigeria's Transition" (lecture, Chatham House, London, England, February 26, 2014), www.vanguardngr.com/2015/02/chatham-house-buharis-speech-on-nigerias-transition/.

With this important destination in mind, it is clear that though many African countries now hold regular elections, very few of them have consolidated the practice of democracy. It is important to also state at this point that just as with elections, a consolidated democracy cannot be an end by itself. I will argue that it is not enough to hold a series of elections or even to peacefully alternate power among parties. It is much more important that the promise of democracy goes beyond just allowing people to freely choose their leaders. It is much more important that democracy should deliver on the promise of choice, of freedoms, of security of lives and property, of transparency and accountability, of rule of law, of good governance and of shared prosperity.[30]

Africa needs to question its current practices of democracy: as they are not serving the people, it can be described as failure and it is definitely a drawback to collective progress.

The search is not for a perfect democratic system or a governance model devoid of problems. Rather, it is to rethink the borrowed ideas and see how democracy and governance can deliver its promises to the populace, ensure accountability, produce credible leadership, and secure legitimacy to political leadership. Even in the West, where liberal democracy is rooted and whose constitutions shaped those of Africa, democracy underwent different phases emerging from criticism, modification of practices, and responses by people to misgovernance, wars, power of religious institutions, and secularization.

All these adjustments and rethinking are responsible for the long list of thinkers on the subject, which notably include Niccolo Machiavelli, author of *The Prince* and the idea of realism and force; Thomas Hobbes, whose "Leviathan State" called for a strong government that must ensure peace so that life will not become "solitary, poor, nasty, brutish, and short"; and Edmund Burke, an advocate of the place of tradition in stabilizing institutions. John Stuart Mill observed democracy in the nineteenth century and regarded it as a way of protecting the private interest of few, while the majority voted just to have a sense of belonging in the system. Max Weber argued that liberal democracy could give legitimacy, but this does not mean that it is ethical. Similarly, there have been debates about the role of government; the use of funds in the electoral process, which allows the rich and powerful to control power; and the manipulation of democracy to use public resources for private purposes.[31] It is not unusual to witness the fact that citizens no longer bother to vote and that

---

[30] Ibid.

[31] See, for instance, extensive writings on public choice theory, for example, Dennis C. Mueller, *Public Choice III* (Cambridge: Cambridge University Press, 2003). See also the argument that democracy can undermine public interest, by Michael J. Crozier, Samuel P. Huntington, and Joii Watanuki, *Democracy: Report on the Governability of Democracies to the Trilateral Commission* (New York: New York University Press, 1975).

Figure 9.1 A young Nigerian man gracefully shouldering the Nigerian flag against the background of children playing outside a family compound in a rural setting.

understanding the intricacies of democracy may be time consuming, and fighting for one's rights may be too costly. The result of apathy has led to the formation of a theory of "rational ignorance," which means that people choose not to know.[32]

Politics is central to the solution of the country's problems. The country needs to produce first-rate theoreticians of democracy; the citizens have to merge to create powerful pressure groups, using the civil society to reform governance. Political demands must be combative and aggressive, to remove corrupt people from power, to institutionalize accountability, and to be less afraid of state violence. Citizens must see politics as the agency that will enable them to function, that is, politics must defend their freedom of association and freedom to participate in the marketplace. Professor Samuel Zalanga, a critical voice in the search for an alternative to the present system, has been extremely disturbed that he has lost

---

[32] Olson Mancur, *The Logic of Collective Action: Public Goods and the Theory of Groups* (Cambridge: Harvard University Press, 1971); Olson Mancur, *The Rise and Decline of Nations: Economic Growth, Stagflation and Social Rigidities* (New Haven: Yale University Press, 1984).

respect for Nigeria's type of democracy: "there are non-liberal democratic societies today that are run by authoritarian regimes but are functioning very well, and the countries are well-governed." He believes that meeting the demands by the people as one of the key solutions to what he perceives as a crisis of the failure of democracy:

> I will argue without hesitation that the Nigerian elites and the political system have not only prevented but have made it a major concern of theirs to not allow the ordinary Nigerian [to] develop the capability to function to the point he or she can hold his leaders accountable and live as a human being with dignity. It is not enough for the Nigerian government to adopt a presidential system of government or write a new constitution without sincerely asking: what are the conditions that will truly ensure the true functioning of the political system, in order to uplift the lives of the least advantage[d] people. We should measure our development not by the number of expensive cars driven by rich Nigerians, the skyscrapers or the money people have to buy the conscience of others. Rather it is the human development and the capability to function of the least advantage[d] people that matters. We should be able to achieve that while allowing others who have great talents to excel [and] function as well. This requires working hard to balance equality and liberty. But this is not a simple question of getting a constitution written or even having a process adopted.[33]

Zalanga is in search of another political system that delivers development as in Singapore and China. He is definitely not alone in the critical interrogation of the failure of democracy and its weak linkage to good governance. In other words, he and some others tend to suggest that democracy is not the only route to good governance. When he endorsed the nondemocratic model of Asia, he invoked the statement by Deng Xiaoping of China that "it does not matter whether a cat is black or white, as long as it catches mice."[34] Private and media accounts believe that the differences between military and democratic regimes are limited, and liberal democracy is not suited to places that have critical needs to build infrastructures and create jobs.

No matter how bad democratic practices may be, return to military rule is not an option. A military regime appoints a dictator who is difficult to remove. It can also unleash violence on the people. Even in its mildest form, past experiences have shown that military rule will take away civil liberties, rights, and rule of law. It curtails the freedom of the press and free speech generally. While the cost of running the government is truly cheaper, the motivation of power "for profit" remains. Overall, records show that the military tenures did not bring about impressive economic

---

[33] https://groups.google.com/forum/#!searchin/usaafricadialogue/$20Zalanga$20on$20de mocracy/usaafricadialogue/uOtAPnx6ugY/dixNz0k-tkoJ.
[34] Ibid.

development and progress. Nigeria has been under military regimes in the past, and the record of the dictator, General Sani Abacha is enough to frighten everyone from proposing the return of the military. A regime of tyranny, his government lacked respect for freedom of speech and human rights, and also lacked the vision of nation building. Even though democracy is not a guarantee of instant development, it offers the most effective way of resolving political conflicts in a country as plural as Nigeria.

It is better to engage in dialogue and struggles to reform democracy than to opt for a benevolent military dictator. It has become necessary to have a conversation in order to seek ways for democracy to serve the people, be less expensive, and be grafted into local cultures. Democracy is not an abstract subject to be taught in schools but, rather, it must be created from applied governance experienced on street corners. The serious questions begging for answers include: Can the cost of running democratic governments be reduced so as to have enough funds for developmental purposes? Are there elements in past cultures which are better suited to our present conditions and can be worked into modern practices? Are there new positive democratic cultures which can be used to redefine current practices? How can the obligations between the leaders and the citizenry be respected?

Truly, constitutional panels were formed, and a National conference convened that has produced significant documents; however, many of the constitutions have been imposed both by the departing British colonial government and by the military. The political class members interested in power sharing and revenue allocations tinkered with these constitutions. It is commonplace to hear people talk about "grassroots democracy" to suggest a non-elitist adaptation, but there has been no suggestion on how to organize dialogue around it. Can there be an African democracy? The "contents" of such democracy must deal less with borrowed political models and more with what bothers Africans: mismanagement, corruption, accountability, human development, conflicts, peace, hunger, etc.

The contextual importance must be well defined. The factual reality must link governance with the ability of the people to pursue their aspirations and liberate themselves from poverty. Borrowed liberal democracy needs to be scrutinized. The oft-quoted statement by John Dewey, "The foundation of democracy is faith in the capacities of human nature; faith in human intelligence and in the power of pooled and cooperative experience,"[35] must be questioned if there is no faith in leadership, or the agencies of governance are not governed by logic of rationality, and if

---

[35] John Dewey, "Democracy and Educational Administration," *School and Society* 45 (1937): 457–467.

communities are in a state of conflict. In fairness to Dewey, he sees democracy as "[m]uch broader than a special political form, a method of conducting government, of making laws, and carrying on governmental administration by means of popular suffrage and elected officers."[36] He continues:

> Universal suffrage, recurring elections, responsibility of those who are in political power to the voters, and the other factors of democratic government are means that have been found expedient for realizing democracy as the truly human way of living. They are not a final end and a final value. They are to be judged on the basis of their contributions to an end.[37]

Minimally, democracy must ensure a peaceful and developed future. Democracy is yet to produce a land without serious ethnic politics, social and political conflicts, and fragmented citizenship. Democracy has not eliminated our fears: the fear of neighbors, of communities, and of people of other faiths. Democracy has not solved the problems of intolerance either. It has, rather, produced a type of authoritarian leadership. There are cases of dictatorship, as seen in some of the leadership styles of President Olusegun Obasanjo. All these are indeed proof that democracy does have its limits.

Pluralism is a common fate of the country. Democracy must, however, enhance the capacity to dialogue, and to respect diversity and differences. The ultimate goal is development; therefore, democracy must deliver development. Both are connected and they cannot be separated, either intellectually or in practice. Sadly, leadership is yet to figure out how to deliver development. The state itself is not an efficient agent of development. There are pressures to reconstitute the space, which are even sometimes extreme suggestions of secession and creation of smaller and manageable states.

In order to reform democracy, attention can be shifted to the means of developing a much stronger civil society. People know what they want, and they have developed the language to express resistance. However, the values that reject and oppose corruption are still weak as many continue to think in terms of aristocratic values and it is commonplace to see wealthy citizens, including corrupt politicians, as role models. In this regard, the culture of discourse must be decisively hostile to corruption. The citizens, too, are willing collaborators and participants to say nothing of nursing the desire to acquire power in order to participate in looting and stealing.

---

[36] Ibid., 457.   [37] Ibid.

Conclusion

A democratic culture and system will emerge over time. There will definitely be moments when some will call for benevolent dictatorship, but
forces in support of democracy will continually be strong. The transfer of
power will always be a problem and will always be predisposed to political
violence. As long as corruption is tied to power, the competition for power
and the ambition for lucrative positions will remain a driving force. The
ruling class, through the democratic system, grapple with different styles
and methods of campaign, and, in some cases, recognize that they may lose
power. As those in power realize that incumbency does not guarantee
victory, this may reduce the recourse to violence to settle their differences.

Disappointments with those in governance will instigate pressures to
reform practices, and also demand for radical democracy, or the use of the
revolutionary possibilities that democracy offers. A silver lining is that
a number of politicians in power now talk about change and
a "transformation agenda," thus, demonstrating an awareness that the
exercise of power should not be linked always to their pockets, but to the
delivery of public goods. Indeed, in the expressions of political leaders,
they now use the language of democracy of governance, pointing to what
it means. To return to the example of President Jonathan, he said there is
a "collective conviction and commitment toward:

1. Ensuring the sustainability of democratic government in Nigeria
2. Regional and international assistance in restoring and sustaining
   democratic systems in our sub-regions and beyond
3. Timely delivery of democratic dividends to our people in these critical
   and sensitive areas:
   Rule of Law, respect for human rights, and due process
   Electoral reforms, and free and fair elections
   Women's empowerment and equality in all spheres of Nigerian life
   Freedom of information
   Job creation and poverty reduction
   Education
   Infrastructural development and upgrade
   War against terrorism."[38]

His list shows that governance is key, and change is necessary. It is
instructive that he leaves out corruption. The overall quality of debate
around governance must be enhanced.

Good leadership is critical, but not enough. Reconstruction and recon-
stitution of institutions of governance and democracy are needed. While

---

[38] Goodluck, "Consolidating Our Democratic System," xxi.

leadership on its own may lack the ability to produce good institutions and promote the rule of law, strong and effective institutions are more likely to produce good leadership. Beyond the institutions are, however, the issues of values and ethics. Owing to the commodification of life being fostered by the global forces of neoliberalism; values of integrity, diligence, hard work, and delayed gratification have been sacrificed on the altar of immediacy, and instant self-gratification. Due to the lack of commitment to punishing corruption, this cankerworm has become endemic at both micro and macro levels. Therefore, in order for democracy to deliver development, there is need for value reorientation by both the leaders and the citizens. Particularly, integrity and delayed gratification should be promoted through the agents of socialization such as religious institutions such as mosques, churches, and shrines. Elementary and high schools need to revamp civic studies that emphasize the importance of enduring values to development.

To be clear, democracy, in its recent manifestations, is a Western-derived idea, copied as a label and practice. Since it is assumed that it is the government of the people, its theoretical premise is derived from whether "the people" are seeking freedom or security or both. There are normative and cultural issues that must be included in the definition and understanding of the behavior of politicians or the application of democratic principles.

Social engineering is needed to deal with the issues of religious differences, ethnic identity, Islamic radicalism, and violence. Because there are no jobs or social services, it is easier to build an alliance of the oppressed to destabilize the polity. For instance, the case of the notorious Boko Haram, demonstrates how an insurgency by misguided citizens can destroy the progress of others and attack the fundamental rights of the majority of the population to freedom of religion and opinion, even to carry out their day-to-day activities. Boko Haram claims the right to special privileges and political exclusivism that is impossible in a democracy.

Constitutions need to be reexamined to restore confidence in political pluralism, provide active ways to live in peace, destroy all dictatorial tendencies, create conditions for reform and development, and condemn corrupt practices. In order to strengthen democratic institutions, a number of things are necessary: the creation of an independent judiciary, an electoral commission that can conduct free and fair elections, respect for all citizens, free and independent media, enlightened and educated citizenry, a committed civil society, promotion of human rights, the rights of citizens to choose their leaders, equality before the law and respect for the rule of law, honest political communication between the leaders and the citizens, and decentralization of authority and political power.

The next fight, which is urgent, must be over accountability. The account books for all levels of government must be open, budget discussions must be made public, leakages must be prevented, and corruption must be severely checked. There must be an overall increase in the efficiency per naira or dollar spent. Unless the battle over accountability is won, the dividends of democracy will continue to be disappointing and its limitations will grow.

In order to achieve accountability, and for a genuine people-oriented constitution to materialize, that is, for social engineering to work, the civil society and media have to be stronger and fortified with the capacity to tap into their freedom to circulate information, criticize the government, and organize protests. The mission of the civil society is to monitor the activities of politicians, curb their excesses, prevent abuses, and insist on economic management that focuses on job creation.

Creating a coalition of Nigerians in place of a coalition of politicians or a coalition of ethnic identities will be a better way to manage an emergent democracy. This coalition will wage war against corruption, and lead the country toward genuine development. It will have organizations in place to intervene in policies and will not yield space to the myrmidons of politics who could not care less about people's lives and welfare as long as they have protected comforts and secure bunkers. The civil society has to create the knowledge and skills to create production systems such that the majority of people can be mobilized to minimize poverty. People who want to defend their jobs and employments, their health and education, can be politically organized and work for social welfare programs.

In order for democracy to work in Nigeria, it is best to place less hope in politicians who have a vested interest in wealth accumulation rather than in public service, less hope in leadership that has shown itself as selfish and uncaring, and less hope in the military that is arrogant, self-serving, and corrupt; but more hope in institutions of nation building that can endure and function, and far more hope and commitment in institutional strategies that will uplift the poor. The common interests by the majority of the population can be organized around democracy, economic development, and the creation of a unified identity that will transcend ethnic and religious divides and sustain the existence of a viable nation state.

10   Governance, Citizenship, and the State

Introduction

The term "governance" has been used in many related contexts. Academic, corporate, government, and informal conversations have tried to fathom its essence and its ideal role in human society. Philosophers, political scientists, sociologists, anthropologists, ethnographers, economists, historians, and others have contributed to its usage, understanding, and evolution in the humanities and social sciences. These disciplines have something in common: they are preoccupied with the task of understanding governance of the human society. The different approaches of these disciplines have given us a more complete picture of what constitutes humanity, society, and public or private governance. The term has gained more currency in the public space due to its ability to assess the quality of life and everyday living conditions of individuals, families, groups, and entire societies when used in relation to a state.

Discussions of inclusivity, marginalization, discrimination, poverty, development, growth, war, tranquility, politics, inflation, deflation, debt, death rates, birth rates, environmental conditions, security, human development capacity, fundamental human rights, and other issues revolve around the efficiency and effectiveness of governance. When citizens in Nigeria, India, Congo, France, Britain, Hong Kong, America, Venezuela, and elsewhere stage a protest, they are protesting how a particular aspect of their lives is governed by the state.[1]

A major concept for discussion is the means of assessing the pros and the cons in any society's system of government, as well as the extent to which ideas of governance have been collectively domesticated by the state and its people. Human society has evolved through several mechanisms of governance, from monarchy to other forms. Despite society's evolution from predominately religious governments – still found in the Middle East and

---

[1] Secessionist agitations in Nigeria and the yellow-vest protests in France are some of the movements protesting the effect of governance through state policies and politics.

the Vatican today – to embrace secular bureaucracies, the rules governing behavior remain largely drawn from religious tenets. At the core of any inquiry into governance is the question of morality vis-à-vis the promotion of common humanity and justice. By considering what governance portends and its implications over time, one can begin to understand the roots of modern governance and the Nigerian experience.

Historicizing Governance in the Modern State

The practice and theory of governance has been with humanity since the origin of civilization. Even in a space inhabited by two people, norms and rules are required to guide their behavior and establish boundaries. Four students sharing a hostel room must have rules, and so must a family be guided by expectations and restrictions. As the number of people increases to form villages, cities, states, and nations, rules and regulations expand to define rights and responsibilities, create sanctions, provide incentives, promote order, ensure prosperity, and prevent chaos and violence. Even ancient societies and nationalities created rules to govern families, villages, towns, markets, and every other human interaction that the modern world is built upon.[2]

In Africa's precolonial state formations, power and governance were arranged in networks of relationships and control. The king was usually at the apex, especially in centralized settings.[3] Elaborate institutions and laws were formulated in all states with norms, attitudes, and words. Political processes were derived from conventions, established practices, the division of power, and sometimes even at the whims of kings, princes, and their allies. The king enforced laws and market regulations, monitored trade routes, and upheld principles of crime and punishment.[4] This capacity – the ability to believe in a common story and organize around a shared goal – separates humans from other animals.[5] Over the ages, human societies have been faced with questions and challenges to leadership that result in reforms and changes.[6] Regardless of the culture or

---

[2] Cf. John Burrow, *A History of Histories: Epics, Chronicles, Romances and Inquiries from Herodotus and Thucydides to the Twentieth Century* (London: Penguin Books, 2009).

[3] M. P. K. Sorrenson, *Land Reform in the Kikuyu Country: A Study in Government Policy* (Nairobi: Oxford University Press, 1967), 4.

[4] See Toyin Falola, ed., *The Collected Works of J. A. Atanda* (Austin: Pan-African University Press 2017), 97–100.

[5] Yuval Noah Harari, *Sapiens: A Brief History of Humankind* (New York: Harper Collins, 2014).

[6] Cheikh Anta Diop, *The African Origin of Civilization: Myth or Reality*, ed. M. Cook (New York: Lawrence Hill Books, 1974); Timothy Ubelejit Nte, *African Traditional Institutions: An Illustrative Perspective* (Port Harcourt: Shupea Publishers, 2017); Tesemchi Makar, *The*

system of government in place, the idiosyncrasies of a leader can determine and shape the path of the society, and this has remained with humanity to the present day. The preponderance of organization and governance in human affairs goes beyond the subject of politics, or any other secular discourse.

Religious scripts, notes, and texts all discuss the governance of humanity. Ideas that are considered religious today laid the foundation for secular governance; they are rules, laws, and regulations guiding human behavior. Without this guidance, humans recede to the state that Thomas Hobbes described as nasty, brutish, and short.[7] Religious ideas, passed through various phases of governance and philosophy over the centuries, were repeated as dogma that was later refined and coded into nonreligious regulations and stated in national constitutions in the present day.[8] This explains religion's influence from past to present.

Even when religion and state are separated, religion and religious leaders still wield substantial influence over state affairs. Modern China, with its extreme secularity, may be an exception. However, the Chinese experience shows that a rigid, conscious structure must be in place to defend state politics from religious influence, similar to the way that a lack of constraints in Africa has shown the danger that such influence can pose. Despite this, religious codes can still be seen in the laws governing the affairs of the modern Chinese state.[9]

From the time that religion and state were separated, until the likes of Braithwaite drew our attention to the root of modern-day laws and governance, many scholars tend to forget democracy's intellectual lineage. Modern-day states continually try to reinterpret constitutions that are deeply based in religious ethos to conform with modern secularist terms.

The rule of law and its need to be a state's supreme guiding principle has been at the fore of many texts and philosophical enquiries.[10] Most of these rules were drawn from various religious doctrines and texts before the modern era, but the rules of modern states were polished and

---

History of Political Change Among the Tiv in the 19th and 20th Centuries (Enugu: Fourth Dimension Publishers, 1994).

[7] David Boucher, "Inter-Community and International Relations in the Political Philosophy of Hobbes," *Polity* 23, no. 2 (1990): 207–232.

[8] See, for instance, Tunji Braithwaite, *The Jurisprudence of the Living Oracles* (Bloomington: Trafford Publishing, 2011) for a succinct interrogation of this dynamic.

[9] Even in China, laws prohibiting murder and demanding obedience to recognized authorities have been in existence for centuries.

[10] Cf. John of Salisbury, *The Statesman's Book*, trans. John Dickinson (New York: Alfred A. Knopf, 1927), 3, 33–34, 243–244, and 258; Thomas Aquinas, *Governance of Rulers*, trans. G. B. Phelan (Toronto: Medieval Studies of Toronto, Inc., 1949).

incorporated into what would be known as a state constitution.[11] The success or failure of a leader is judged by their compliance with these rules and the extent to which laws are upheld during that leader's time in office. In times of war and peace, a government's success depends on a leader's ability to administer the state in accordance with the rule of law.

It is important to note the evolution of these laws. Society is never static, and neither are the laws governing its population. New circumstances introduced new laws, establishing a fundamental convention for future responses to similar circumstances. By the eighteenth century, which has been styled the Age of the Enlightenment, the likes of Adam Smith, Giambattista Vico, Voltaire, Jean Jacques Rousseau, and other great philosophers in Europe emerged to scientifically assess the state's role outside of religion. Their efforts were similar to that of Galileo, who had sought to understand the world and the natural environment outside of religious influence. Because society is continually progressing, the societal scrutiny performed by these great intellectuals could only build on previous ideas.

These inquiries became important to what is known as governance today, concerning the state and the relationship between leadership and followership. If previous ages had contributed to the understanding of these phenomena, the Age of Enlightenment is the intermediary between those ages and contemporary times. Like the priests and ulamas who were their theological predecessors, these philosophers and intellectuals taught lessons that were ontologically coherent, although there were slight differences in the way that they saw society. For example, Jean Jacques Rousseau wrote the "social contract and the general will,"[12] attacking the individualism advanced by John Locke and generating a new set of philosophical ideas that contributed to the foundation of democracy, partly instigating the French Revolution.

Both Locke and Rousseau were scientifically interpreting old practices, governed by religious interpretations of violence and legitimacy, for an ideal modern state. Premodern states commonly expanded their territory through invasions, legitimizing their rule over other cultures through violent repression linked with religious and spiritual sanction, and Locke provided a philosophical justification for this paradigm's power mechanism. In contrast, Rousseau questioned the use of violence to obtain consent – his idea of state power was that which is drawn from the will of the people, in what he described as a social contract.

---

[11] Braithwaite, *The Jurisprudence.*
[12] Jean Jacques Rousseau, *The Social Contract and Discourses*, trans. G. D. H. Cole. (New York: E. P. Dutton & Co., 1950).

Rousseau's ideal society is one where individuals consciously participate in the process of governance. The premise is that people are born free, or with the freedom of choice, and the social conditions inherent in a person's environment place them under many restrictions, most of which are beyond their control. Rousseau believed that anyone thinking of themselves as superior to others, seeking to rule over others without their consent, is enslaved to a greater extent than those they would dominate. The servitude of one who would be master is not the same as those who water or cultivate the ground; there are greater constraints on the means by which a person rules and hopes to retain power without their subjects' consent. This person is a greater slave to mundane constraints as he robs the people of their freedom of choice.

Rousseau undertook an extensive interrogation of what he called the social contract to suggest better ways for the state to acquire power and wield it legitimately while keeping the natural rights of humanity intact. Key highlights of this contract have become the thinkables in today's liberal democracy in which the collective will of the people forms and defines the state. Democratic movements, largely shaped by Rousseau's ideas, emerged in many places across Europe.

The rethinking of politics, power, governance, and institutions has been endless and continues to this day.[13] In the search for a fitting model of governance that promotes human dignity and collectivity, the nineteenth century saw Engels and Marx introduce ideas with far-reaching implications for the relationship between classes. By the twentieth century, communism and fascism were thrown into the contest, redefining the boundaries of the relationship between the state and its people. Vladimir Lenin, arguing that revolutionary theory must form the basis of a revolutionary movement, shunned democracy formulated by other philosophers and demanded a dictatorship of the proletariat to displace the "bourgeois state." Lenin's view of governance gives another meaning to violence and repression in relation to the will of the people: he saw violence, repression, and alienation as justified in state governance if it is perpetuated by a class of people, which he termed the proletariat, against the other class, called the bourgeoisie. The proletariat dictatorship that Lenin envisioned sought to empower common people in defense against exploitation from the powerful. In reality, such system replaces one set of elites with another, but this time they are fewer in number. The attainment of elite status allows so-called representatives of the people to wield greater influence.

---

[13] Tim Gee, *Counterpower: Making Change Happen* (Oxford: New International Publications Ltd., 2011).

Ultimately, only a few of the proletariat become elites who are empowered to anchor the "people's dictatorship" and think for the whole state. This model sought to restrict democracy to what Lenin defined as "democracy for the poor, democracy for the people, and not democracy for the rich folk."[14] In a way, this is a reversion to the premodern justification of violence and coercion, which Locke supported in the acquisition and perpetuation of power – the rule of the powerful – and which was opposed by Rousseau, who favored the rule of the people. By Lenin's time, the ideas of governance had been established in the West from philosophical ideas that dated back to Plato. Plato's interpretation of governance as "steering" may be the most dominant usage of the term today. In England, people had been discussing governance of the realm since the fifteenth century. When Charles Plummer published *The Governance of England* in 1885, it was based on a translation of a fifteenth century document. By the nineteenth century, constitutional history had emerged to discuss various aspects of governance. Ideals and practices of democracy continued to be debated and refined.

There were many resources available for people to examine Lenin's ideas of governance and ideal statehood. Despite a resounding victory in Russia during the Bolshevik revolution of 1917, which created the Union of the Soviet States, Lenin's ideal state encountered problems during the Cold War less than a century later. Liberal democracy and the actualization of its tenets increasingly became the force driving social movements and making up the central demands of activist groups across the world.[15] In the 1930s and 40s, an alteration of Lenin's ideal state emerged with the rise of fascism in Italy and Germany, which led to further conversations on the role of the state and legitimization of democratic governance. In "The Doctrine of Fascism," written in 1932, Mussolini dismissed both democracy and socialism, transferring almost all power to the state. According to its logic, the free will of the individual resides with the state, and the only recognizable entity in the state is the government. To understand what the government connotes, Mussolini's logic explains, "the man of Fascism is an individual who is nation and fatherland."[16]

When the British created their colony called Nigeria, ideas and practices of governance had been with its people for many centuries. These societies were still governed by religious laws and principles, and the state and

[14] Vladimir Lenin, *State and Revolution* (New York: International Publishers, 1932), 73.
[15] Gee, *Counterpower*, 14.
[16] Benito Mussolini, "The Doctrine of Fascism," in *Italian Encyclopedia* (1932).

religion remained largely intertwined. The British took their established ideas of governance – tainted by objectives of conquest, domination, and exploitation – and imposed them on their subjects.

The 1914 amalgamation of the territory later known as Nigeria would be marked by two practices that characterized the British administration. One was autocracy, in which power was taken from the people and given to a select few who were only accountable to their masters in London. The other was exploitation, in which the government transferred resources from Nigeria to Europe. These would later characterize governance in the postindependent state, modified to suit the postcolonial "conquistadors." Not only was the governance of indigenous societies modified to suit the Western model, but the social setting of these societies was also adjusted to fit the political modifications. The acquisition of Western education gained new importance, and a new class of elites emerged in society: the educated elites.[17]

Figure 10.1 A group of stranded travelers scampering for a ride on a truck transporting farm produce.

[17] See E. A. Ayandele, *The Educated Elite in the Nigerian Society* (Ibadan: Ibadan University Press, 1974), for the intricacies of this new class in the modern society.

The initial successes of Lenin's ideal state in the Soviet Union, China, and Cuba allowed new educated Africans to draw ideas from democracy, capitalism, and socialism, introducing Nigeria to different sources of governance that had been developed in Europe. The idea of fascism – destroyed in theory and in practice by Allied forces during World War II – was not officially considered by pioneering political elites in Nigeria, because it had been discredited for its totalitarian and brutish tendencies. Unofficially, its elements would later support military dictatorships and civilian regimes to some extent.[18] In theory and in practice, governance has always been about securing a mandate from the people through their free choice, coercion, or elements of both. The goal is to deliver security, meet human needs, and enhance the progression of the culture's civilization. In the contemporary state, the last point is understood as the modernization project.[19]

Governance and Politics: Two Sides of the Same Coin?

The World Bank and the International Monetary Fund began using the term "governance" in the 1990s, and it quickly became entrenched vocabulary in the policy and social sciences world. The topic is divided into subfields that cover public, nonprofit, private, and other organizations, and those fields are further fragmented into issues that include regulations, project management, security, and infrastructure. In each of these discussions, governance has a different meaning. However, it all boils down to the management of available human and nonhuman resources. Corporate governance is concerned with balance sheets and the generation of profit. In its original usage, "governance" is used by the World Bank and international agencies to discuss the management of resources, the policing of debtor nations, and the reconciliation of governmental activities and resource allocation in political systems that were struggling to become democratic.[20] Today, widespread use of the Internet has led companies and nations to create the field of Internet and Technology governance.[21]

---

[18] Cf. Masoud Msellem, "Democracy and Dictatorship Are Two Sides of the Same Coin," *The Khilafah*, July 20, 2016, www.khilafah.com/democracy-and-dictatoship-are-two-sides-of-the-same-coin.

[19] For a succinct view of what this entails, see Shmuel N. Eisenstadt, "Modernity and Modernization," *Sociopedia* 25, no. 1 (2010): 1–15.

[20] For more on this, see K. Sarwar Lateef, *Evolution of the World Bank's Thinking on Governance: Background Paper for 2017 World Development Report* (Washington, DC: World Bank, 2017), https://openknowledge.worldbank.org/bitstream/handle/10986/26 197/112916-WP-PUBLICDR17BPEvolutionofWBThinkingonGovernance.pdf? sequence=1&isAllowed=y.

[21] Jesse Hirsh, "Technology Governance in 2018," *Platform Governance, Internet Governance*, December 24, 2018. www.cigionline.org/articles/technology-governance-2018.

Any major aspect of existence can have a governance framework created around it, as with products and supply chains. There are so many branches that academic departments can award governance degrees at all levels. Governance and politics cannot be separated into two distinctive concepts, as some analysts have attempted. In this work, "governance" is used in relation to the state, conjoining with politics, authority, and accountability. This raises the issue of normativity: can there be justice, or can governance be fair? A developing country like Nigeria cannot avoid evaluation through the lens of "good governance." And the notion of good governance cannot be detached from that of sustainable development and the overall welfare of citizens.[22]

The separation of politics and governance should be seen as a theoretical fallacy and an error of judgment. In Nigeria and else-where, governance and politics are tied to the way power is obtained and used to allocate resources. Governance cannot be separated from the methods through which those in power create policies or make decisions that are enforced by different branches of their government. An evaluation of politics cannot be divorced from the evaluation of governance.

In addressing this link holistically, the distinction between politicians and the bureaucratic class should not be exaggerated; the bureaucratic class does not necessarily operate independently of the political. Bureaucrats are constrained by rules, and only some of those rules are defined in legal documents. They are all subject to the political culture of the state, which makes bureaucrats a part of state politics because they are prone to follow the rules of the state politics.[23]

It is ill conceived to think of management without considering the politics of management. Cultural affiliations are a dangerous feature, putting obstacles in the path of democracy and sustainable develop-ment anywhere in the world, but they drive both politics and govern-ance, especially in a plural society.[24] In different contemporary states, the politics of consociationalism can leave room for incompetence and

---

[22] Arch Paddington and Tyler Roylance, "Anxious Dictators, Wavering Democracies: Global Freedom under Pressure," *Freedom House*, 2016, https://freedomhouse.org/repo rt/freedom-world/2016/anxious-dictators-wavering-democracies-global-freedom-unde r-pressure.

[23] Yushau A. Shuaib, "Most Corrupt: Between Politicians and Civil Servants in Nigeria," *YaShuaib*, 2011. https://yashuaib.com/2010/12/most-corrupt-between-politicians-and-civil-servants-in-nigeria-by-yushau-a-shuaib/.

[24] As shown in the landmark anthropological findings of Barth, this is made manifest at any level of societal organization. F. Barth, ed., *Ethnic Groups and Boundaries* (London: George Allen and Unwin, 1969).

252 Governance, Citizenship, and the State

undermine merit in state governance when such politics are not well managed.[25] In Nigeria, oil politics cannot be divorced from the governance of the state. Because oil revenues are over-deterministic in the country's management, the governance of the oil sector and national politics cannot be discussed in isolation of each other.[26] Needless to say, the bureaucratic management of the oil sector is shaped by the wielders of state power (i.e., the custodians of the state politics).

As many Nigerianist scholars have observed, everything in the country revolves around the state. The survival of the state relies on crude oil and its management, which means that the survival of every other sector, including private enterprises and the everyday political economy of the state, depends largely on the distribution and redistribution of this wealth. In Nigeria, the private sector is considered more efficient than the public sector, but the "language" that governs both is similar; they can be influenced by religion and ethnicity because they evolved within the same environment and culture. In the private and public sectors, elite behavior is born from the same mother: as much money as possible must be made as quickly as possible to support their aristocratic lifestyles. Whoever is harmed by this behavior is none of their concern – they are held accountable for neither their actions nor their inaction.

The payment of workers in the Niger Delta offers an example of poor governance. The private sector does not pay a living wage, expecting workers to exist on a bare minimum that leaves most of them vulnerable to harsh conditions. The government has failed to address this problem, and government responsibilities are distributed across many different Ministry Departments and Agencies (MDAs) – allegedly, for effective governance – with the ministries at the top of the hierarchy led by commissioners at the state level and ministers at the federal level. Unintended circumstances and conscious political calculations have led these government ministries, along with various departments, agencies, and parastatals, to increase, shrink, and restructure over time. Sometimes these changes were made in the name of continuity, and at other times they were to break from previous practice.[27] They are all governed by

[25] Cf. Crawford Young, *The Politics of Cultural Pluralism* (Madison: The University of Wisconsin Press, 1993).

[26] See, for instance, James Fennell, "Nigeria: Unity or Democracy? A Conflict Analysis," 2006; Kenneth M. Amaeshi et al., "Corporate Social Responsibility in Nigeria: Western Mimicry or Indigenous Influences?" *The Journal of Corporate Citizenship*, no. 24 (2006): 83–99.

[27] Cf. *Punch News*, "Buhari Unbundles Ministries, Merges, Creates Others," *Punch News*, August 21, 2019. www.google.com/amp/s/punchng.com/breaking-buhari-unbundles-m inistries-merges-creates-others/amp/.

similar norms, regardless of the new forms that they take, and they always link public activity with private financial gain. Their operations convert regulations into opportunities for personal enrichment, and the positive effects of these MDAs and government parastatals are very difficult to evaluate.

These attitudes begin with the political leadership and are shared by the bureaucrats. Over time, it has become hard to identify which group influences the other; the relationship between politicians and bureaucrats has become a chicken-or-egg chain of cause and effect. Citizens do not believe that their leaders are committed to the country; leaders hold power but they do not practice genuine service, humility, or sincerity. The face of power in Nigeria, like elsewhere in Africa, is the face of arrogance. Leadership upholds norms that support tyranny, encourage greed, foster covert and overt corruption, and discourage a sense of selflessness, dedication, or humanitarianism. There is neither a sense of nationhood nor patriotism from either the leaders or the led. Many so-called activists and NGOs lack credibility because some bad actors exploit activism and NGOs for personal enrichment opportunities. Genuine activists are ridiculed and accused of not being in it for change, but to "chop." The political culture of the state has influenced more than governance, contaminating corporate behavior and other forms of organization within its boundaries.

Families and individuals are also affected by the leaders' attitudes. People who are indoctrinated by this culture of impunity begin to engage society with this mindset, replicating state–society relations[28] and victimizing each other in order to survive. These values have even influenced religion – religious bodies do not champion the cause of the poor or practice liberation theologies: the work of Bishop Hassan Kukah is one of a small number of exceptions.

It is not clear whether religious figures hear the voice of God, or their own voices, or even satanic voices. They politicize whichever voice they choose to hear, and the governance of their organizations is on par with state politics. They feed the fear of their congregation for personal gain, deceiving and exploiting their followers in ways that create platforms for political elites to manipulate the masses on a greater scale. There are various reasons why religious leaders support political goals; they may seek access to those in power for obtaining resources or other privileges

---

[28] Cf. Sola Akinrinade, "A Society Under Pressure: Thoughts on Leadership, Followership and The Re-Invention of the Nigerian State," *Journal of the Historical Society of Nigeria* 15 (2016): 1–17.

like tax exemptions, oil considerations, and other sorts of patronage mechanisms.

In traditional institutions across Africa, kings and chiefs look after their own self-interests. Maintaining their palaces and their prestige calls for clever mechanisms to tap into the wealth of others and extract resources from state and local governments. Some kings feel shortchanged when they see politicians living in grandeur; if racing to dismantle the bonds of humanity and statehood can offer them similar benefits, then why should they sit on the sidelines?

The governance of traditional institutions now depends on the state, and their custodians have become contributors to state politics and societal rot. Nigeria and her counterparts in the sub-Saharan region officially operate democratic governments based on popular participation, choosing representatives for the people through elections. Unfortunately, nothing in this process reflects the will of the people.[29] Individuals acquire power through this process not to advance the public good, but to increase their own fortunes, leading to a disconnect between governance and the common good of society. The state is not viewed as an instrument of development for the people. In a democracy, the assumption is that politics will deliver public goods. In Nigeria, experience has taught people not to be deceived by the promises of politicians – those promises are expected to be broken. Voters have avoided complete loss by learning to "improvise," selling their votes and voices.[30]

Democratic governance promotes the rule of law, delegitimizing the rule of men. This ensures the sanity of the state and prevents it from sliding into anarchy. However, in military and civilian governments in any part of Africa, the rule of law is not always the force that governs the state; it is often the rule of those with political power and their cronies living in affluence. Powerful individuals can twist the laws or bribe judges to receive their preferred outcomes.

These states, part of an international system since its colonial foundation, represent a subaltern power in global governance. There are many external influences on their activity, especially those activities that generate revenue linked to external markets. In the international arena, the voices of these states may be drowned out by the countries of the Global North exercising dominance. The politics of the state is the administration of state affairs at different levels, with similar manifestations. In

---

[29] Akin Mabogunje, "Issues and Challenges of Governance in Nigeria" (speech, Olabisi Onabanjo University, Ago Iwoye, Nigeria, March 10, 2016), www.transparency.org/news/feature/cpi_2019_sub_saharan_africa.

[30] Cf. Wale Adebanwi and Ebenezer Obadare, eds., *Democracy and Prebendalism in Nigeria: Critical Interpretations* (New York: Palgrave Macmillan, 2013).

Nigeria's case, the corrupt norms of governance have been consistent since the country's independence in 1960; reforms on paper have been consistently subverted in practice.

Government of the People ... ? A Survey of Governance since 1960

Nigeria was established as an entity ruled by rent-seekers who used access to state power for personal gain. Governance in the postindependence state has remained unchanged, but Nigeria finally received a report card in 2018 that reflects years of graft and corruption. According to the World Poverty Clock survey, Nigeria's estimated 86.9 million people living in poverty – out of a total population of about 180 million people – has surpassed India's estimated 71.5 million people living in poverty, making Nigeria the world poverty capital.[31]

The extreme wealth inequality between leaders and ordinary citizens has been pronounced and persistent. After General Sani Abacha, the former Nigerian Head of State, died in 1998, the United States Senate reported that his wife was found at a Lagos airport with thirty-eight suitcases filled with money. One of their sons was found with $100 million in cash.[32] Their family was so notorious for siphoning public funds that some Nigerians joke about US currency appearing in mysterious places, saying that it must be the remains of the Abachas' stolen loot.[33] This is just one of many disturbing examples of corruption in Nigeria. Destructive, corrupt practices have eroded the core cultural values of society for decades, and poverty in Nigeria has increased since 1980. Records from the National Bureau of Statistics classified 6.2 percent of the Nigerian population as "extremely poor" in 1980, increasing to 12.1 percent in 1985, 13.9 percent in 1992, 29.3 percent in 1996, 22.0 percent in 2004, and 38.7 percent in 2010.[34] While poverty in

---

[31] Yomi Kazeem, "Nigeria Has Become the Poverty Capital of the World," *Quartz Africa*, June 25, 2018. https://qz.com/africa/1313380/nigerias-has-the-highest-rate-of-extreme-poverty-globally/.

[32] Financial Action Task Force, *Laundering the Proceeds of Corruption* (Paris: Financial Action Task Force, July 2011), 25, www.fatf-gafi.org/media/fatf/documents/reports/Laundering%20the%20Proceeds%20of%20Corruption.pdf, cited in Anna Markovska and Nya Adams, "Political Corruption and Money Laundering: Lessons from Nigeria," *Journal of Money Laundering Control* 18, no. 2 (2015): 170.

[33] Markovska and Adams, "Political Corruption and Money Laundering," 171.

[34] National Bureau of Statistics, *The Nigerian Poverty Profile 2010 Report* (Abuja: National Bureau of Statistics, 2012), 12–14, cited in ActionAid, *Corruption and Poverty in Nigeria: A Report* (Garki: ActionAid Nigeria, 2015), 15, www.actionaid.org/sites/files/actionaid/pc_report_content.pdf.

Nigeria varies by demography and region, it is more likely to affect Nigerian mothers, youths, and children.

Despite these statistics, Nigeria is considered one of the top ten fastest-growing economies in the world.[35] Between 2003 and 2013, Nigeria's economy grew between 6 and 7 percent,[36] and Nigeria was recognized as the largest economy in Africa in 2013: the country was ranked the twenty-sixth largest economy in the world, with a gross domestic product of US $509 billion.[37] These impressive numbers mask an unstable political environment shaken by religious extremism, terrorism, inequality, poor infrastructure, illiteracy, poverty, ignorance, poor health, and poor education.[38] The current administration has touted an anticorruption stance, but the words have not been matched with effective action. Although larger numbers of anticorruption convictions have been reported, removing corrupt officials is not as effective as reforming the system that breeds them. The current strategy, which is not a new one, only changes the identity of the cabal looting public funds and abusing state power.

The whole "fight" against corruption is a political ruse, leaving massive cases of fraud – which have substantial effects on the country's annual budget – unreported and unsolved. The minor gains supposedly made against corruption leave the state's financial strength unchanged, because they neither assuage the thirst for loans nor demand accountability from current public officials. Government communication with the public is remarkably opaque. Transparency International's Corruption Perception Index (CPI) 2019 report noted that Nigerian citizens' perception of the government has become extremely negative.[39] Other numbers from the survey show how shallow and ineffective the government's anticorruption stance has been.[40] Governance cannot be understood without considering the welfare of the citizens, and Nigeria has failed its duty of governance because it has chosen personal gain over public good. Nigeria's people have been left ignorant and suffering, without true aid.

---

[35] ActionAid, 15.
[36] U. David Enweremadu, "Nigeria as an Emerging Economy? Making Sense of Expectations," *South African Journal of International Affairs* 20, no. 1 (2013): 56–77, cited in ActionAid, *Corruption and Poverty in Nigeria*, 16.
[37] Enweremadu, "Nigeria as an Emerging Economy?" 56–77, cited in ActionAid, *Corruption and Poverty in Nigeria*, 1.
[38] Markovska and Adams, "Political Corruption and Money Laundering," 171.
[39] *Transparency*, "Corruption Perceptions Index," *Transparency*, 2019, www.transparecy.org /cpi2019.
[40] Ibid.

Not all of Nigeria's corruption takes place outside the law. Goods are exchanged illegally and public resources are criminally mismanaged, but a separate strain of corruption is accepted as a normal way of conducting business. This "corruption inside the law" serves and increases state bureaucracies to offer new avenues of patronage and prebendalism, "at the expense of the public through increasing the inefficiency of state bureaucracy."[41] Excessive government programs impose additional expenses on the common taxpayer while delivering ineffective results.[42] Formal and informal governmental processes have increased Nigeria's corruption and social deterioration.

The discovery of oil in the Niger Delta area laid the foundation for activities that would later define corruption in Nigeria. The country's entire economy and agricultural foundations changed over a decade; everything became focused on oil. Countries such as Germany found strength through productive engagements with multiple economic opportunities, while Nigeria suffered weakness through rent collection that flowed mainly from oil. The country's weakness became the strength of its political elites, and Nigerians became desperate to obtain those riches. Those who were successful joined the 1 percent of Nigerians who seized about 80 percent of oil revenues.[43]

Public officials, entrusted with substantial national revenue, do not hold one another accountable for illegal or immoral deeds, despite laws in place to control such misbehavior. Lawmaking is only the first step to contain corruption; politicians must follow up with the political will to transform law into action. Institutional capacity is important to ensure that those who hold office are subject to the laws of the land, not the other way around. Government institutions must be able to carry out their work without political interference.

Today, Nigeria's government is run like a dubious cartel. Members justify their mass appropriation of public funds through false assurances and ambiguity: consider the monthly payments of "security votes" to state governments, which neither secure the states nor provide any accountability to the people they are meant to secure.[44] The breakdown of monthly handouts to state governments from the

---

[41] William Ewharieme and Jude Cocodia, "Corruption and Environmental Degradation in Nigeria and Its Niger Delta," *Journal of Alternative Perspectives in the Social Sciences* 3, no. 3 (2011): 448–449.

[42] Ibid.

[43] Daniel Egiegba Agbiboa, "Serving the Few, Starving the Many: How Corruption Underdevelops Nigeria and How There Is an Alternative Perspective to Corruption Cleanups," *Africa Today* 58, no. 4, (2012): 111–132.

[44] Obiamaka Egbo et al., "Security Votes in Nigeria: Disguising Stealing from the Public Purse," *African Affairs* 111, no. 445 (2012): 597–599.

federal government are public knowledge in most cases,[45] but never the security votes.[46]

The reality is that Nigeria's oil revenue is given to a select few – government elites – who will do anything to retain power, and the security vote is part of this deal. To maintain their structure of exploitation, the state's balance sheet is opaque and shrouded in secrecy.[47] These elites also create an atmosphere of uncertainty that threatens the security of the state to enable their looting. Oil politics breeds violence and rebellions that include incidents of stolen pipelines, the kidnapping and ransom of oil workers, and bombings. Many stakeholders try to accrue power by creating or supporting various militant groups.[48] This explains the undeclared security votes, billions of naira allocated to the same items in the annual budget, and an intermittent scramble for additional funds during the year to address security challenges despite the absence of obvious threats. Nigerians must use their senses to recognize that governance issues are pervasive in their country, but somehow they are always hopeful that improvements are near.

Beyond the misappropriation of funds through security ruses, public officials embark on infrastructure development projects that support their own interests. They manipulate the process of awarding contracts, inflate prices, and sometimes leave projects in perpetual planning stages, if actual projects exist in the first place.[49] Even when the projects are executed, corners are cut to generate additional profits.

Ewharieme and Cocodia have found that the situation is aligned with the World Bank's 1997 definition of corruption: "the illegal diversion of

[45] Cf. Bassey Udo, "Federal, States, LGAs Share N769.523 Billion for July," *Premium Times*, August 22, 2019, www.premiumtimesng.com/news//more-news/34098-federal-states-lgas-share-n769-523-billion-for-july.html; Bamidele Samuel Adesoji, "FAAC Disburses N190 Billion to 36 States in August as Allocation Drops [Full List]," *Naira Metrics*, September 26, 2019, https://nairametrics.com/2019/09/26/faac-disburses-n19-billion-to-36-states-in-august-as-allocation-drops-full-list/&hl=ig-NG.
[46] Cf. Matthew T. Page, "Camouflaged Cash: How 'Security Votes' Fuel Corruption in Nigeria," *Transparency International*, May 1, 2018, https://carnegieendowment.org/2018/05/01/camouflaged-cash-how-security-votes-fuel-corruption-in-nigeria-pub-77297.
[47] Michael Herb, "No Representation without Taxation? Rents, Development, and Democracy," *Comparative Politics* 37, no. 3 (1985): 298, cited in Egbo, et al., "Security Votes in Nigeria," 598.
[48] Elias Courson, *Movement for the Emancipation of the Niger Delta (MEND) Political Marginalization, Repression and Petro-Insurgency in the Niger Delta* (Uppsala: Nordiska Afrika Institute, 2009).
[49] In many cases, these are phantom projects. When they do exist, they are normally abandoned after public funds are squandered on them. For more on these dynamics, see Tunde Decker and Damilola Osunlakin, "Rodney, Development and Africa in the Twenty First Century," in *Agenda 2030 and Africa's Development in the 21st Century*, eds. Benjamin U. Anaemene and Olusegun J. Bolarinwa (Kuala Lumpur: United Nations University International Institute for Global Health, 2017), 13–30.

state revenues as well as patronage or nepotism by government officials or theft of state assets."[50] Public corruption exists where those entrusted with public projects consider their own personal gains to be more important than those of the public they represent. It remains to be seen what political office holders in Nigeria would do without putting their personal interests ahead of the public they are meant to serve.[51] This form of corruption is unlikely to end any time soon, because the more they engage in these sharp-elbowed practices, the more visible and "respected" they become in society.

In the words of former Nigerian president Goodluck Jonathan, "It would be difficult to form a viable citizenry that could call government to account for its stewardship if the economy depends solely on oil revenue."[52] The division of the country along ethno-religious lines has also made it difficult to mobilize the people against corrupt government practices.[53] One would have thought the transition to democracy in 1999 would have heralded some changes, but it did not. Instead, Nigeria's multiparty system has encouraged practices such as the abuse of security votes because there is no central authority to stop them. Neither the military nor civilian systems seem to work for Nigeria. The illegal exchange of goods and the mismanagement of public resources for self-advancement often goes hand-in-glove with the proliferation of the bureaucratic processes to expand the scope of prebendal engagement.

In 2017, the United Nations Office on Drugs and Crime released a report on a survey administered by Nigeria's National Bureau of Statistics that involved 33,000 Nigerian households.[54] The survey asked individuals whether they had been asked to pay a bribe and whether they had complied between June 2015 and May 2016. About one third of Nigerian adults who had been in contact with public officials during this period reported instances where they were either asked to pay a bribe or where they agreed to pay a bribe. The survey also found that Nigerian

---

[50] The World Bank, *Helping Countries Combat Corruption: The Role of the World Bank* (Washington, DC: The World Bank, 1997), 8, quoted in Ewharieme and Cocodia, "Corruption and Environmental Degradation," 447.

[51] Cf. Maira Martini, *Nigeria: Evidence of Corruption and the Influence of Social Norms* (Berlin: Transparency International, September 26, 2014), www.u4.no/publications/nigeria-evidence-of-corruption-and-the-influence-of-social-norms.pdf; Decker and Osunlakin, "Rodney, Development."

[52] James Emejo, "Jonathan: Pay Taxes, Hold Govt Accountable," *This Day (AllAfrica)*, October 11, 2010, https://allafrica.com/stories/201010120384.html.

[53] Toyin Falola, *Colonialism and Violence in* Nigeria (Bloomington: Indiana University Press, 2009).

[54] United Nations Office on Drugs and Crime, *Corruption in Nigeria: Bribery: Public Experience and Response* (Vienna: United Nations Office on Drugs and Crime, 2017), https://drive.google.com/file/d/0B6jj-ulM0cLrOXFpMDh1Q1l1bm8/view.

adults, on average, pay a bribe every other month, or six times a year. It amounts to about $4.6 million per year solicited by public officials in a country where almost half of the citizens are in poverty.

Most adults, a little over 46 percent, paid bribes to police officers. Others paid the following officials, sometimes in addition to police officers: prosecutors (33.0 percent), judges (31.5 percent), tax officers (27.3 percent), customs officers (26.5 percent), and public utilities officers (22.4 percent). The survey reported that money obtained by public officials was mostly used for activities such as getting land ownership licenses, getting a driver's license, paying for water and electricity, and paying fines for traffic violations. Only 3.7 percent of the adults who paid bribes reported the incidents to the authorities – not because of ignorance, but due to a lack of trust. Adults in the survey felt that authorities would not take action if the cases were reported.[55] The report also concluded that these forms of corruption will persist within the state because of the structure and culture that backs them.

Nigeria's culture of corruption breeds a cycle of poverty that harms the people and the environment. The Niger Delta region, pumping the petrodollars that the state relies on, is a case in point.[56] Instead of developing a supportive environment for people in the Niger Delta region and compensating them for the livelihoods that have been denied to them, the government's web of corruption, within and outside the law, increases their precarious state.[57]

The execution of policies in Nigeria is closely linked to personal interest, meaning that negligence and indifference to the plight of the people precede any corrupt act. This explains why the Niger Delta region has seen some of the worst environmental disasters. In 1987, the Koko disaster was caused by 18,000 barrels of chemicals containing PCB, dioxin, and asbestos fiber discarded by devilish Italian businessmen and their Nigerian collaborators. Other catastrophes have included pipeline

---

[55] Yomi Kazeem, "Nigeria's First Ever Corruption Survey Is as Bad as Most People Imagined," *Quartz Africa*, August 21, 2017, https://qz.com/africa/1058356/how-bad-is-corruption-in-nigeria/.

[56] Sam Oyovbaire, "Political Stability and the African Union," in *The Ministry of Cooperation and Integration in Africa (the Presidency), The African Union and the Challenges of Cooperation and Integration: Proceedings of the National Seminar* (Ibadan: Spectrum Books, 2002), 37.

[57] Cf. Chukwunonye Ezeah and Clive L. Roberts, "Waste Governance Agenda in Nigerian Cities: A Comparative Analysis," *Habitat International* 41 (2014): 121; *Sahara Reporters*, "Six Years of Waste: How Niger Delta Ministry Blew N800b between 2009 and 2015," *Sahara Reporters*, August 23, 2016, https://saharareporters.com/2016/08/23/six-years-waste-how-niger-delta-ministry-blew-n800b-between-2009-and-2015; *AllAfrica*, "Nigeria: Save Niger Delta Ministry from Corruption," *AllAfrica*, September 2, 2016, http://allafrica.com/stories/201609020657.html.

leakages, oil spills, gas flaring, and other hazardous practices in the region. These disasters have harmed the essence of the culture, traditions, economy, and spirituality of the region's people. If public officials cannot line their pockets by enforcing laws and regulations, then they are not interested in upholding them.[58]

A 1995 World Bank study found that most of Nigeria's pollution came from local businesses, such as restaurants, hotels, and workshops. Dangerous fumes are also released by generators that citizens use to generate electricity,[59] despite official records showing that billions of dollars have been – and continue to be – spent generating a better power supply for the people.[60] The government has left the people to govern themselves in matters that cannot be exploited for profit.

As people generate their own power, they also provide water for themselves[61] and secure their own neighborhoods. This leaves those who cannot afford it without water, electricity, or security. Deforestation and flooding have become rampant in the country as businesses strain the environment for short-term gain and individuals struggle to ensure their own survival. As the multinational oil companies and other businesses maximize their profits, people are left to struggle on their own and the environment suffers damage from both groups.[62] The government's over-centralized structure has made local governments irrelevant to developmental policy considerations, despite constitutional acknowledgment of their importance.[63] Landfills and facilities for sanitation are absent from many localities, leaving the people to burn waste or dispose of it in ways that harm the environment.

---

[58] Cf. Fennell, "Nigeria: Unity or Democracy?"

[59] Cf. Egwu Ben Obasi, "Deaths and Electricity Generator Fumes," *Guardian*, September 25, 2018, https://m.guardian.ng/opinion/deaths-and-electricity-generator-fumes/&hl=ig-NG.

[60] Government corruption and self-dealing in the electricity sector explains the absence of improvements. See, among others, Uzochukwu Amakom and Uche Collins Nwogwugwu, "Financing Energy Development in Nigeria: Analysis of Impact on the Electricity Sector," *Australian Journal of Business and Management Research* 2, no. 3 (2012): 54–61.

[61] In the twenty-first century, communities with means dig their own wells and construct infrastructure for pipe-borne water, while many communities use stream water.

[62] For instance, bush burning and the use of logs for preparing food became rampant in modern Nigeria following the economic crisis of the 1980s caused by the Structural Adjustment Program. S. O. Tomori and O. W. Tomori, "Revisiting the African Alternative Framework to Structural Adjustment Programmes for Socio-economic Recovery and Transformation (AAF-SAP) in Contemporary Nigeria," in *African Development and Governance Strategies in the 21st Century: Looking Back to Move Forward (Essays in Honour of Adebayo Adedeji)*, eds. Bade Onimode et al. (London and New York: Zed Books, 2004), 37–47.

[63] Emmanuel Ibiam Amah, "Federalism, Nigerian Federal Constitution and the Practice of Federalism: An Appraisal," *Beijing Law Review* 8, no. 3 (2017): 141–158.

The culture of corruption does not rest solely within the circle of corrupt public officials. It has become part of the societal culture, created by the political ambience of the state. People hardly have any place of refuge. Consider the practices of nongovernmental organizations (NGOs) and so-called activists in Nigeria, whose numbers increased rapidly due to the socioeconomic conditions of the 1980's and the outbreak of AIDS. Hundreds of millions of US dollars were contributed to several NGOs – supposedly campaigning against AIDS in Nigeria – between 2002 and 2011; the US President's Emergency Plan for AIDS Relief (PEPFAR) and the Global Fund for AIDS, Tuberculosis, and Malaria gave $2.25 million to a number of NGOs in Nigeria.[64] An accurate count of the money received by NGOs is nearly impossible, but they received hundreds of millions of dollars over the years.

Although these NGOs can be sources of help for those in need, Nigerians know that these organizations can easily become corrupted through their ongoing contact with government officials. The fraudulent acts of some NGOs are often seen as contributing to greater inequality in the country. The reality is that these bodies not only produce inequality, they are products of inequality themselves. Studies have shown that although Nigerians are aware of the sharp practices among these NGOs, in some circumstances they tolerate this behavior and indirectly encourage it.[65] If an individual distributes misappropriated money to help others within their social circle, the act is viewed as acceptable, though an individual hoarding misappropriated money for selfish gain is viewed as unacceptable.[66] Collective corruption can ultimately be viewed as legitimate; some practical instances have been cited by Smith.

An individual identified as Okadigbo, who worked for an NGO helping public health efforts in Abia State, was named head of the Umuahia office of the United against AIDS (UAA). He began misusing money meant to run the organization, purchasing only the very best for himself: the latest and most expensive office facilities, the finest clothing, and the most lavish furniture. After accruing much wealth and prestige, he adopted an unapologetic air of overt braggadocio. He was characterized by his colleagues as arrogant, often demanding special privileges that he did not deserve, and he would publicly ridicule staff members that he deemed inferior. His remarkable sense of self-importance was a characteristic of "naira chiefs" (a term that Nigerians use for those who feel they can buy honors, respect, and titles), according to his colleagues.[67] He was referred

---

[64] Daniel Jordan Smith, "AIDS NGOs and Corruption in Nigeria," *Health & Place* 18 (2012): 475.
[65] Ibid.   [66] Ibid.   [67] Ibid.

to as a poser – someone who tries to appear more important than they actually are. Because of his behavior, he was terminated from his position.

Okadigbo's staff exposed his wrongdoings, but not because of his misappropriation of NGO funds. His staff had been bothered by the way he treated others and how he spent money so ostentatiously. If he had spent his misappropriated money on others, his staff would have accepted the corruption without seeking his termination.[68]

Another individual, named Alozie, started her own NGO that developed into an active organization and collected substantial amounts of donations. It is difficult to say whether Alozie took money from her own projects, but she was able to expand her house and purchase a car, appearing to have funds apart from her salary. Unlike Okadigbo, she used the money to help others and remained moderate in her spending and appearance. Alozie treated her staff with dignity while using extra funds to build a new home for her mother and to care for her four children as a single mother.[69] This behavior meant fewer complaints against her. According to Smith, even though corruption should not be supported, in a sense, Alozie's case was overlooked.

These narratives are a microcosm of Nigeria's larger polity, and indeed, the whole of Africa. Although sub-Saharan African states have received more aid than any other region in the world over the last fifty years, these interventions have not changed the lives of people in the region. If anything, they have created a "culture of dependency."[70] Nigeria, like other countries in the region, has received monetary assistance from several sources – especially the United States.[71] Considering foreign aid's adverse effects on Africa, many were relieved when the Trump administration's "America First" policy cut foreign spending, especially in the form of aid. One of these optimists, Angelle Kwemo, the chair and founder of "Believe in Africa," stated that "this reduction [should] be seen as an opportunity for the continent to rise and for the relationship between the US and Africa to evolve."[72] If foreign aid cannot help Nigeria get to the core of its poverty problem, then Nigeria must reorganize itself from within. Instead of fighting for foreign aid, Nigeria must fight the corruption crippling its democracy and its economy.

---

[68] Ibid., 478.   [69] Ibid.
[70] Luminous Jannamike, "Poverty: Foreign Aid Doing Nigeria More Harm than Good – Kalu," *Vanguard*, August 9, 2018, www.vanguardngr.com/2018/08/poverty-foreign-aid-doing-nigeria-more-harm-than-good-kalu-2/.
[71] Angelle B. Kwemo, "Making Africa Great Again: Reducing Aid Dependency," *Brookings*, April 20, 2017, www.brookings.edu/blog/africa-in-focus/2017/04/20/making-africa-great-again-reducing-aid-dependency/.
[72] Ibid.

Conclusion

The essence of governance is the well-being of the people, which is undoubtedly linked to the generation, distribution, and redistribution of public wealth: it all boils down to the challenges of sustainable development in Africa. This discussion has considered the trajectory of modern governance, why governance and politics are inseparable, and the dynamics of governance patterns that have impacted Nigeria. It may seem simplistic, but corruption led to the purgatory in which Nigeria now resides. The phenomenon and practices called corruption cannot be completely erased from state governance,[73] but curbing these activities to the barest minimum through responsive and efficient state institutions, transparency, and accountability will provide public benefits. Kukutschka and his team described this as the path to political integrity:

> Political integrity means exercising political power consistently in the public interest. However, defining exactly what constitutes the public interest is both difficult and contestable. At minimum, the public interest implies that decisions are taken independently of private interests and are not intended to simply sustain power holders' own wealth or position.[74]

Ensuring political integrity is not only political power applied in the public interest, it is also a refinement of the political process to prevent political power from being used against the public interest. This starts with the electioneering process and continues through the selection and appointment of public officials and state contractors. Governance in a democratic state cannot become "government of the contractors, by the contractors and for the contractors,"[75] and undue influence must be removed from the formation and execution of state policies. These reforms will ensure that there is a level playing field for all qualified members of society to aspire to and attain on merit.

These considerations, when handled as abysmally as they have been to create the current reality in Africa, deplete state resources and benefit a small minority who gain prominence by mortgaging their society.[76] Maira describes this current situation as a "'hybrid' state" where "[the]

---

[73] No state, not even among the OECD countries, was free from the perception of corruption in either the latest (2019) TI reports or in the previous years.

[74] Roberto Martinez B. Kukutschka et al., "Building Political Integrity to Stamp Out Corruption: Three Steps to Cleaner Politics," *Transparency International*, January 23, 2020, www.transparency.org/news/feature/cpi_2019_political_integrity.

[75] General Ishola Williams, Chairman of AFSTRAG, quoted in Fennell, *Nigeria*, 10.

[76] Cf. Kenneth Kalu and Toyin Falola, "Introduction: Exploitation, Colonialism, and Postcolonial Misrule in Africa," in *Exploitation and Misrule in Colonial and Postcolonial Africa*, eds. Kenneth Kalu and Toyin Falola (Switzerland: Palgrave Macmillan, 2019), 1–24.

distinction between the public and private spheres exists at least formally, but in practice real decision-making happens outside the formal institutions. Instead, decisions about policies and resources are made by powerful politicians and their cronies who are linked by informal, personal and clientelist networks that co-exist with the formal state structure."[77]

Maira, quoting Erdman and Engel, identified four different harbingers of corruption in Nigeria: presidentialism, defined as the systemic concentration of power within an individual; legitimization of political power through the personalization of state resources; a rent-seeking culture perpetuated by a tiny group of political elites; and clientelism practiced in the awarding of contracts and appointments.[78] It is a general consensus among Africanist scholars that the situation has brought penury into the space.[79] The misappropriation of Africa's abundance in these states has played a role in breeding the evil tripartite of poverty, ignorance, and disease.

Kukutschka and his colleagues have noted the daunting task of eradicating elements of corruption in a state: their 2013 Global Corruption Barometer (GCB) found that 55 percent of citizens around the world shared the view that their governments were run by few big interests out to serve themselves. Additionally, "overwhelming majorities in 17 out of 28 OECD countries were amongst them. In 2017 the GCB Europe also revealed that 65 percent of citizens in the region shared the opinion."[80] In Africa, the effect of these practices is abysmal; the proceeds of corruption in these countries develops and strengthens the economies of OECD countries.[81]

---

[77] Maira Martini, "Nigeria," 2.   [78] Ibid.
[79] Cf. Joseph C. Ebegbulem, "Corruption and Leadership Crisis in Africa: Nigeria in Focus," *International Journal of Business and Social Science* 3, no. 11 (2012), 221–227.
[80] Kukutschka et al., "Building Political Integrity."
[81] Cf. Leena Koni Hoffman and Raj Navanit Patel, *Chatham House Report: Collective Action on Corruption in Nigeria, a Social Norms Approach to Connecting Societies and Institutions* (United Kingdom: Royal Institute of International Affairs, May 2017).

Part IV

Development Crises

11   Corruption

Introduction

Historically, Nigeria has always been among the most corrupt countries in the world. In fact, Nigeria led this "league" in 1996 when the Transparency International Corruption Perception Index (CPI) report of that year found it to be the most corrupt of the fifty-four countries surveyed.[1] Compared to previous years, the report indicated that nothing changed over the years in this respect.[2] While all these years of corruption took place under military rule, in 1999, the country transited into a democratic dispensation ushering in the Fourth Republic. This was led by Chief Olusegun Obasanjo, himself a retired military General and former military Head of State. Following internal and external pressures – particularly the designation of Nigeria as one of the noncooperative states by the Financial Action Task Force (FATF) in 2001 and the post-9/11 crisis in the United States, which led the American government and the United Nations (UN) to pressure UN member states to strengthen, or put in place where none existed, measures to combat financing of terrorism – the Nigerian government "adopted its multipronged anticorruption campaign with the creation of the EFCC (Economic and Financial Crimes Commission), the Due Process Office in the Presidency and the ICPC (Independent Corrupt Practices and Other Related Offences Commission)."[3] Subsequently, other measures were taken to strengthen the fight against corruption in the country.

---

[1] Johann Graf Lambsdorff, "TI Corruption Perception Index 1996," *Transparency International and Göttingen University* (1996), https://images.transparencycdn.org/image s/1996_CPI_EN.pdf.
[2] Ibid.
[3] Emilia Onyema et al., "The Economic and Financial Crimes Commission and the Politics of (In)effective Implementation of Nigeria's Anti-Corruption Policy," *SOAS Consortium*, Anti-corruption Evidence: Making Anti-Corruption Real, Working Paper 007, November 2018, 12.

Therefore, in addition to the aforementioned offices, other bodies put in place and equipped at varying degrees for preventing, tracking, and prosecuting financial crimes include the Code of Conduct Bureau (CCB) and the Code of Conduct Tribunal (CCT), Nigerian Financial Intelligence Unit (NFIU), Public Complaints Commission (PCC), Bureau of Public Procurement (BPP), Nigerian Extractive Industry Transparency Initiative (NEITI), and Special Control Unit Against Money Laundering (SCUML). Treasury Single Accounts (TSA), Bank Verification Numbers (BVN), and Integrated Personnel and Payroll Information Systems (IPPIS) have also been introduced and implemented at different times since the current democratic dispensation in 1999.

Regardless, in its latest survey on the perceived level of corruption in the public sector of 180 countries in the world, the 2019 Transparency International report marks the country abysmally low at 26 on a scale of 100, and ranks it among the countries thought to be highly corrupt, putting it at number 146 out of the total number of the countries surveyed.[4] Again, when this is put in comparison with the previous years' records, including that of 1996, the report indicates that the prevalence of corruption in the country has seen little or no change over the years, in spite of system reforms. Most of these cases are found within the government, but there are a lot more going on in the private sector and at different levels of the state as well.[5] Instructively, the yearly Transparency International CPI cannot be said by any measure to be comprehensive and absolutely deterministic of the prevalence of corruption in any country; however, it certainly reflects the trend and spread of corruption in these entities. In all of these, corruption has been related to or defined strictly in monetary terms. The act, however, goes further than this, as it reflects the moral decadence of the society. In what follows, the intricacies of corruption in Nigeria are examined using the simple definition of the willingness to gain, or the act of gaining, what one is reasonably not in the position to earn or has not earned.

The Culture of Corruption

All practices become known as the culture of a society the moment they are ubiquitous in the everyday living experience of the people.[6] But

---

[4] "Corruption Perceptions Index 2019."

[5] See, for detail taxonomy of corruption in Nigeria: Mathew T. Page, *A New Taxonomy for Corruption in Nigeria* (Washington DC: Carnegie Endowment for International Peace, 2018), https://carnegieendowment.org/files/CP_338_Page_Nigeria_Brief_FINAL.pdf.

[6] See Greg Urban, *Metaculture: How Culture Moves Through the World* (Minneapolis: University of Minneapolis Press, 2001).

practices do not just gain this ground in vacuum. They are like a plant: they survive on a set of structures that enhances their fertility and growth.[7] Therefore, through human evolution, cultures are built in response to the environment, including the sociopolitical formation and economic structure of the place.[8] Barring the periods Nigeria was ruled by military dictatorships, the country has been a democratic state since independence in 1960, at least officially. In practical terms, the democratic credentials of the state read something like "the government of the contractor, for the contractor and by the contractor," as succinctly described by General Ishola Williams.[9] Between the period of independence and the present, the country has embarked on a process of cosmetic restructuring of the state. Fundamentally, the state in this evolution has moved from regional to state formation and from operating a parliamentary to a presidential system of government, all within which its pervasive democratic practices have been conspicuously optimized, operationalized, and measured.[10] The General's description of the Nigerian state captures the whole of the pervasive manifestation of democracy and dictatorship alike, in the country since independence.

Beyond the General's interpretation, the contractors in this case include the voters; political thugs; public officers; government institutions; organized groups, including the civil society organizations (CSOs) and nongovernmental organizations (NGOs); those in the private sector, both the formal and informal; media; students; and every other conceivable human entity in the state. Either as a group or as individuals, these entities position themselves as potential contractors, not citizens, to the state. The differences that exist between contractors and citizens are wide. For one, the demeanor of contractors is to take advantage of situations, be competitive, lobby, bargain, maximize profit, and, in all, execute cynical interest(s), making them susceptible to corruption. On the other hand, citizenship offers the propensity for collective commitment, tendering of a viable culture, and above all, patriotism. Meanwhile, the tenets of democracy only speak to the zeal and morality of citizenship.[11] Contractors seldom

---

[7] See, Karen Barber, *The Anthropology of Texts, Persons and Publics: Oral and Written Culture in Africa and Beyond* (Cambridge: Cambridge University Press, 2007), 23, in particular.

[8] See, Toyin Falola, *The Power of African Culture* (Rochester: University of Rochester Press, 2003).

[9] General Ishola Williams, Chairman of AFSTRAG, quoted in James Fennell, "Nigeria: Unity or Democracy? A Conflict Analysis" (2006): 10, www.academia.edu/4457697/Nigeria_Unity_or_Democracy.

[10] See, for example, Richard Joseph, "Political Parties and Ideology in Nigeria," *Review of African Political Economy* 13 (1978): 78–90.

[11] Guillermo O'Donnell, J. V. Cullell, and O. M. Iazzetta, eds., *The Quality of Democracy* (Notre Dame: University of Notre Dame Press, 2003).

work in synergy unless it's a profit-making venture in which strict business rules are evoked. Cloaked in its cynical self, a contractor would go to any length to get a contract deal; and taking what one cannot reasonably earn or had not earned is always a game changer because it's more profitable. This succinctly explains the social relations that are often described as corruption in Nigeria.[12]

At any rate, from despotism to nepotism, cronyism to prebendalism, and patronage to rent seeking, democracy as practiced in Nigeria has never been anything close to what was envisaged by its modern interpreters.[13] If anything, democracy liberalizes malfeasance and expands the reach of corrupt practices, as it creates an elastic space for the "contractors" to seek rent from the Nigerian state. On the one hand, it provides the political elites in Nigeria with the pretense with which they gain legitimacy for power acquisition, while despotism and manipulation have been the tools for sustaining the acquired power. This makes the Nigerian democracy what could be called autodemocracy, which is a combination of autocracy and democracy; a practice which denies any form of accountability or transparency. On the other hand, it provides the people with the opportunity to forfeit their right to the dividends of democracy through the electioneering process during which they exchange their votes for instant material gains.[14] This democracy does not serve the collective interest of the society, and it is not structured to nurture a viable nation-building process. Instead, it represents the cynical interests of the few in power and the short-term gains of the people when they are negotiating the forfeiture of their right to the real dividends of the democratic exercise of voting.[15]

Historically, this culminated in the first military coup in 1966, which terminated the First Republic, and the fourth coup which ended the Second Republic in 1983.[16] Virtually all major events that shaped the postindependence Nigerian state are heavily dotted with the footprints of democratic failures that do not need a forensic expert to detect. In addition to the coups, the schema to use this pervasive democratic tool in favor of a powerful cabal in the polity, which also led to the stillborn status of the 1993 general elections and the hope of earlier democratic transition before

[12] Page, "A New Taxonomy for Corruption."

[13] Ebenezer Obadare, "Democratic Transition and Political Violence in Nigeria," *Africa Development* 24, no. 1 (1999).

[14] Onome Osifo-Whiskey, "Triumph of Money," *Tell* (1993): 3.

[15] Meanwhile, "this year's Corruption Perception Index (CPI) shows corruption is more pervasive in countries where big money can flow freely into electoral campaigns and where government listen only to the voices of the wealthy or well-connected individuals." "Corruption Perceptions Index 2019," 6.

[16] See Adewale Ademoyega, *Why We Struck: The Story of the First Nigerian Coup* (Ibadan: Evans Brothers, 1981).

1999. The Biafra war also struck because of the abysmal functioning of democracy in the First Republic and the loss of hope in the military for its revival.[17] Whether democracy has done more harm than good to the Nigerian state is certainly a matter of perspective. What is telling, however, is that democracy as practiced in Nigeria has contributed immensely to the nurturing of malfeasance and corrupt practices in the country. There is so much corruption that it is hard to argue against Richard Joseph's position: "Democratic politics and prebendal politics are two sides of the same coin in Nigeria."[18] And indeed, nothing can be worse for a country than the systemic nurturing of corruption on a prebendal scale.[19]

The evidence of this in Nigeria has its history dating back to the days of the so-called nationalist leaders at the height of the independence movement in the country.[20] The first taste of democracy by the people of Nigeria was encountered during this period as they were made to vote for representatives into the Legislative House in Lagos. What was supposed to be a representation and service to the people became widely known as an avenue to make quick money and live above the rest of the society they were supposedly representing. Rather than preparing for public service, elected officials were usually perceived to be preparing for looting and the subversion of public interests. Rather than protesting, the people, like contractors, reacted by positioning themselves to benefit from this.[21] Hence, the modern genesis of patron–client politics in Nigeria. The colonial government played a vital role in nurturing this evolution through the precedent that set a certain standard of living for senior public officials, usually whites, which could only be attained by this class of people in the society, due to the socioeconomic structure of the colony. Their cohorts were those who had benefitted from the "benevolence" of the state (i.e., the colonial administration). This way, we see the colonial administration, which is a contractual government anyway, laying the foundation of a contractual state populated by contractors and not citizens.[22] The government became

---

[17] Karl Maier, *This House Has Fallen: Nigeria in Crisis* (Colorado: Westview Press, 2000).

[18] Wale Adebanwi and Ebenezer Obadare, "Democracy and Prebendalism: Emphases, Provocations, and Elongations," in *Democracy and Prebendalism in Nigeria: Critical Interpretations*, eds. Wale Adebanwi and Ebenezer Obadare (New York: Palgrave Macmillan, 2013), 1.

[19] Larry Diamond, "Foreword," in Adebanwi and Obadare, *Democracy and Prebendalism in Nigeria*, xi.

[20] See Bola Ige, *People, Politics and Politicians of Nigeria (1940–1979)* (Ibadan: Heinemann Educational Books, 1995), 27–47, in particular.

[21] For more on this, including an empirical detail example of how this took shape, see Toyin Falola, *Cultural Modernity in a Colonized World: The Writings of Chief Isaac Oluwole Delano* (Austin: Pan-African University Press, 2020), 231–236.

[22] Atul Kohli, *State-Directed Development: Political Power and Industrialization in the Global Periphery* (New York: Cambridge University Press, 2004), 291–367.

the only means through which tangible social mobility and individual transformation could be achieved in the society. Everyone then began to position themselves to act on this reality created by the contractual colonial regime.

It was this position that the various nationalist leaders and the indigenous public servants, who were the few educated among the indigenous people, occupied in different capacities before independence. Invariably, they saw themselves as better than the rest of the society, closer to the colonial administrators and therefore in a position to act in their place as indigenous contractors to manage the affairs of the colony. They assumed this position fully upon independence with the contractor–colony interpretation of the newly independent state operated on a patron–client basis. Increasingly, more than for their colonial predecessors, and due to the dwindling economic fortune of the postindependence era, accumulation of wealth and hope of social mobility became heavily lined to the extent of access to the state treasury. For the people, those in government are the government, and there is no question as to the difference between their wealth and government treasury.[23] As such, an elected official is expected by his or her family and cronies to amass what could be called multigenerational wealth for his/her primordial base. Considering the intensity of the scramble for this access, the chance to be in the loop is seen as a onetime opportunity that needs to be taken full advantage of so as to keep reproducing oneself in that loop. People quickly and consistently accrue to themselves what they had not and could not reasonably earn in order to meet the de facto norms of governance and representation in the state and "secure" the future of their family and cronies in the societal contest. As contractors, like their colonial mentors, they are not bothered about the effects of their actions and inactions on the society.

Paradoxically, the same people deprived of opportunities through this process would find it ridiculous and consider it an aberration of the norm, for a public servant to have acted otherwise and for this reason been unable to fulfill some social obligation like building a private mansion in his or her community; paying for funerals, weddings, naming ceremonies, religious functions, and graduation fees; and feeding countless other families, at least within his or her constituency. It doesn't matter if the actual salary of the official is enough to capture these primitive de facto responsibilities expected of him or her. Depending on the position this individual occupies, failure to function within this structure casts him or

---

[23] Maira Martini, *Nigeria: Evidence of Corruption and the Influence of Social Norms* (Berlin: Transparency International, 2014), 2–4, www.u4.no/publications/nigeria-evidence-of-corruption-and-the-influence-of-social-norms.pdf.

her in a bad light in the society; and could be tagged frugal, devilish, and irresponsible. And such perceptions don't win elections in Nigeria, nor are they favorable for political appointment – two glorifications and medals consistently sought after by the political elites. The value of the people in the elections is not really because the elections actually count in choosing the people's representatives, but because those who manipulate and grant legitimacy to the theft are among this constituency. Public servants, including political office holders and the political elites, must then be able to live beyond their legitimate means to gain and sustain relevance in their constituencies. Since the political institution controls and shapes other state institutions, it is only expected that this culture spreads to other arenas of the state where it is a norm for one to gain what has not been earned. In any case, these individuals are products of this same environment.[24] Therefore, through this process and structure, there are replications of this idea of a contractual Nigerian state across all social boundaries in the country. Money rituals, scams (internet and analog, including examination malpractices, public procurement abuse, and electoral fraud), kidnapping, terrorism, banditry, armed robbery, theft, bribery, embezzlement, and sex-for-marks in the tertiary institutions, are among the common trends that manifest the rot in the system. Owing to the recurrent and ubiquitous manifestation of this in Nigeria, the country could rightly be described as corruption personified.

The political elites seek to outdo one another not on the performance scale but on the scale in which they are able to gain what they've not earned, without consequences. The people also seek to outdo one another not in lawful practices and actions that aid social cohesion but in the extent to which they could sabotage these two for personal gains. Overall, Nigeria represents one of the many locations of hope in the world for those who have the capacity to struggle to gain what they have not earned or cannot earn through legal means. The Babangida template has become instrumental in this evolution. In a bid to ensure that no one with the "voice" could speak against his government and to gain legitimacy, Babangida further entrenches corruption as a norm and ensures its elasticity as it is known today.[25] The template in which government is operated by a retinue of aids and staff, parastatals, ministries, agencies, and

---

[24] As retired General Ishola Williams rightly observed, "A leader does not come from heaven; if the people are good followers, they will choose the right leader." Quoted in Maier, *This House Has Fallen*, xxvii.

[25] See, for example, Paul K. N. Ugboajah, "Babangida Administration and the Crisis of Civil-Military Relations in Nigeria (1985–1993)," in *The Dynamics of Intergroup Relations in Nigeria Since 1960: Essays in Honour of Obaro Ikime At 70*, eds. C. B. N. Ogbogbo, R. O. Olaniyi, and O. G. Muojama (Ibadan: Department of History, University of Ibadan, 2012), 127–140.

committees is still in use today to "settle" patronage networks, and others who could cause trouble for the government and its patrimonial structure. Recruitment into the civil service also serves the same purpose. Apparently, efficiency of state institutions is not guaranteed in this respect. Those who could not fit into any of these categories of prebendal structure are to be covered by the award of contracts – phantom and/or inflated. Where such contracts exist, they are done in the most pathetic and unprofessional way. The grand effect of this when they deal with infrastructural development, aside from the possible loss of lives, is the persistent infrastructural deficit that beggars believe when compared to the tune of funds channeled toward this purpose.

A practical instance of this, among a plethora of others from the power sector[26] to other infrastructural development scams,[27] is the recent development in the Niger Delta Development Commission (NDDC) that is raging across the country. The NDDC was established on June 5, 2000, by the Obasanjo regime pursuant to the NDDC Act 2000, passed to stem the tide of agitations and violence in the Niger Delta region of the country and its effect on the nation's economy. However, this later became known as the usual network of patronage meant to give some elements in this area special access to loot and share state resources, rather than a service delivery to the Niger Deltans.[28] Consequently, both the Commission and the Ministry of Niger Delta Affairs were considered corrupt.[29] Meanwhile, Nigerians currently are observing another crisis in which the supervising

---

[26] See, among others, Olugbenga Adanikin, "Investigation: Jonathan, Buhari Spent N1.164 Trillion on Power in 8 Years, Yet Nigeria Remains in Darkness," *Premium Times*, October 14, 2019, www.premiumtimesng.com/investigationspecial-reports/357448-inv estigation-jonathan-buhari-spent-n1-164-trillion-on-power-in-8-years-yet-nigeria-rema ins-in-darkness.html.

[27] Kemi Busari, "Shocking: Buhari's Minister, Other Officials Spent N12 Million to Inspect Ghost Projects – Audit Report," *Premium Times*, September 8, 2017, www.premiumtimesng .com/news/headlines/242677-shocking-buharis-minister-other-officials-spent-n12-million-t o-inspect-ghost-projects-audit-report.html; Babatunde Akintunde and Ijeoma Okereke, "How Nigerian Agency Mismanaged N1.3 Billion on Abadanoned Projects, 'Non-Existent' Vehicles, Others – Audit Report," *Premium Times*, October 20, 2018, www.pre miumtimesng.com/news/headlines/291420-how-nigerian-agency-mismanaged-n1-3-bil lion-on-abadanoned-projects-non-existent-vehicles-others-audit-report.html.

[28] The present supervising Minister of the commission, who became enmeshed in the crisis that rocked the agency, noted on a TV program that the commission "had been a place for election matters before he assumed office. If you want to contest elections, all you need is to get into the NDDC; make money there and contest elections." Gboyega Akinsanmi, "Akpabio: Corruption, Lack of Patriotism Crippled NDDC for 19 Years," *This Day News*, July 12, 2020, www.thisdaylive.com/index.php/2020/07/12/ akpabio-corruption-lack-of-patriotism-crippled-nddc-for-19-years/amp/.

[29] *Punch News*, "Students Protest, Say NDDC Is Not Functioning In Bayelsa," *Punch News*, September 15, 2017, http://punchng.com/students-protest-say-nddc-is-not-functioning -in-bayelsa/; *Sahara Reporters*, "Six Years of Waste: How Niger Delta Ministry Blew N800b Between 2009 and 2015," *Sahara Reporters*, August 28, 2016, http://sahararepor

minister of the commission and the head of the Ministry of Niger Delta Affairs, Godswill Akpabio, has been accused of contract scamming and other corrupt practices by the Managing Director of the Commission, Dr. Joi Nunieh.[30] Here is a typical example of how the government, under the pretense of addressing the agitation of the Nigerian masses, opens networks of rent seeking. These networks come to further serve the patron–client structure of the polity, which is the "original sin" that birthed such agitations in the first place. The vicious cycle of corruption in Nigeria becomes conspicuous when this trajectory is clearly understood.

This cosmetic approach to issues of nation building has been consistent in the history of Nigeria. Ostensibly, in search of an efficient polity in the Second Republic, the country moved from a parliamentary to a presidential system of government. Before this time, the country had dismantled its regional structure for a state structure that has culminated in thirty-six federating states and a Federal Capital Territory, Abuja, in recent times. But none of these restructuring efforts addressed the fundamental issues that generated the first military coup of January 15, 1966, or the 1967–70 civil war, which both reforms tended to appeal to. If anything, the presidential system has proven to be more expensive and a better conduit for corruption, while the creation of states has been turned into an appeasement meal for disgruntled patrons with enough political clout to have their own estate of exploitation.[31] The former indeed weakened the state the more in that the figure of the president stands for a demigod to be worshipped by all, something that is very unlikely in the parliamentary structure.[32] Whoever occupies the presidency in Nigeria occupies a "throne" of power only synonymous to that of an emperor – but not really the responsibilities. For this reason, as an emperor, the president needed to be shielded from the reality of the society in order to not embarrass him and diminish his rank as the penultimate power after the

ters.com/2016/08/23/six-years-waste-how-niger-delta-ministry-blew-n800b-between-2 009-and-2015; *AllAfrica*, "Nigeria: Save Niger Delta Ministry from Corruption," *AllAfrica*, September 2, 2016, http://allafrica.com/stories/201609020657.html.

[30] Ignatius Chukwu, "NDDC Crisis: Court Restrains Police, Akpabio from Arresting, Intimidating Joi Nunieh," *Business Day News*, July 17, 2020, www.businessday.ng/lead-story/article/nddc-crisis-court-restrains-police-akpabio-from-arresting-intimidating-joi-nunieh/amp/.

[31] See how this has aided the looting and sharing of state resources in Bolaji Akinyemi, "Nigerian Exceptionalism: Nigerian Quest for World Leadership" (convocation lecture, the University of Ibadan, Ibadan, Nigeria, November 16, 2016), 2–19; see also Vande Philip Terzungwe, "Ethnicity and the Politics of State Creation in Nigeria," *European Scientific Journal* 8, no.16 (2000), https://doi.org/10.19044/esj.2012.v8n16p%p.

[32] Adebanwi and Obadare succinctly referred to this as the "Baba-rization of power." Wale Adebanwi and Ebenezer Obadare, "Introduction: Excess and Abjection in the Study of the African State," in *Encountering the Nigerian State*, eds. Wale Adebanwi and Ebenezer Obadare (New York: Palgrave Macmillan, 2010), 4.

gods. Accordingly, he is to be worshipped by all and must be surrounded by praise singers because his ego must be massaged every minute. Any aid, assistance, or appointee of the president who cannot serve this de facto responsibility more effectively than his or her official primary assignment risks being accused of sabotage and being an enemy of the state (which is Mr. President).

Aside from the long trajectory of this structure from the precolonial to the colonial times,[33] the current economic structure of Nigeria parochially skewed toward oil-rent collection controlled centrally by the federal government. And, the footprint of the various military regimes in which the Babangida and the Abacha regimes were instrumental, are, in fact, significant to be considered in search of the bedrock of the godlike posture of the Nigerian president. With every other sector of the economy comatose and there being very limited economic opportunities, corruption of varying magnitudes and implications survives as the alternative medium of escaping the economic trap and social deficits that characterize the Nigerian state.[34] This structure is reproduced at all levels of governance in the country. If it fails at any level, the government collapses, giving way to system reform – none of which is a good handwriting on the wall for the status quo. Take this template to Denmark or Switzerland, two of the least corrupt countries of the world, and it breeds fertile corruption.

Collective Mess: The Anatomy of Corruption

It is an understatement, and yet almost a cliché, to repeat here that corruption is endemic in Nigeria. Relatively, untold however, is that corruption is a perpetual odor that oozes out of a rotten system or entity – biologically or socially constructed. Depending on the magnitude, it pollutes the environment and begets an uneasy ambience. To adapt to this condition in an endemic and normative situation is to be polluted. In Nigeria, where it forms the de facto norm of social, political, and economic relations, it is hard not to be polluted; you can't escape it. As

---

[33] Keith Somerville, *Africa's Long Road since Independence: The Many Histories of a Continent* (London: Penguin Random House, 2017), 1–48.

[34] Lending some empirical fact to this, Kew and Oshikoya observed: "As Nigerian per capita incomes dropped from roughly $1,000 in 1980 to $250 in the early 1990s, and as structural adjustment gutted the nation's public infrastructure and social safety net, government largesse proved increasingly irresistible to political leaders and some civil society actors, and corruption boomed, allowing the military to lengthen its rule." Darren Kew and Modupe Oshikoya, "Escape from Tyranny: Civil Society and Democratic Struggles in Africa," in *The Handbook of Civil Society in Africa*, ed. Ebenezer Obadare (New York: Springer, 2014), 15. In the same manner, the so-called leaders of tomorrow engage in examination malpractices and sex-for-marks arrangements in order to meet societal pressure and expectations.

mentioned earlier, corruption can be acted upon and felt by the virtue of its impact. The impacts, as the foregoing has shown, have not amounted to any fundamental change in the act, rather, they have caused it to penetrate the remote corners of the state. The deodorant and insecticide analogy of a former Nigerian senator, Shehu Sani, is instructive here for two reasons not necessarily implied by the former senator but germane and informative in understanding the intricacies of corruption in Nigeria.[35] Basically, successive governments in Nigeria have been "fighting" corruption using what one might call the deodorant/insecticide approach.

This approach seeks – or so it seems – to treat the result but not the cause of the phenomenon. In other words, it seeks to suppress the odor while maggots feed fat on the rot. This is a common practice in cases where corruption has been weaponized as a political tool. The deodorant, when in use, seeks to justify an action deemed corrupt by others, deny it altogether, or keep silent about it. Conversely, when adopted, the insecticide serves the purpose of condemning the person and not rectifying the act or preventing future occurrence. It is worth mentioning that this approach is, in fact, the conventional prism within which corruption is generally seen and understood in Nigeria. However, this becomes destructive when put to use by those with the authority to prosecute the social menace. Corruption operates in the form of terrorism in Nigeria: one man's corruption is another man's pragmatic innovation. It all depends on to which side the benefit of the act swings. This has made it hard to have a consensus on the social menace. Ethnicity, religion, political party, and other affiliations that key into the primordial, are factors that determine if the action taken by a public servant is corrupt or not. In the current governance structure of Nigeria, since 1999, the deodorant has always been reserved for the allies (the praise singers and loyalists) of Mr. President. This is the case whether the accusation is at the federal, state, or local level, because in Nigeria, only the president has the "glove and the training to fight corruption."

State governors might attempt to tap into this arena to settle political scores in their states, but the demeanor of the Mr. President in the matter is essential to the outcome. Meanwhile, the deodorant does its work appropriately by shielding the accused from prosecution. However, it seldom washes off the public stain, which, in any case, is not a stigma of rejection for public appointment, holding elective positions, or whatever.

---

[35] Leke Baiyewu, "Buhari Uses Deodorants to Fight Corruption in Presidency – Shehu Sani," *Punch News*, January 24, 2017, https://punchng.com/buhari-uses-deodorants-to-fight-corruption-in-presidency-shehu-sani/?amp=1.

The insecticide, on the other hand, is used when there is a real or perceived threat to Mr. President and a subsequent need to protect his interests. These interests might be in the question of legitimacy, depleting the oppositions' treasury, settling political scores, or mere intimidation of the opposition. [36] Nothing speaks to this more than the current structure through which corruption is supposedly being fought in the country and the progress this structure has made so far.

Realizing the nature of corruption in Nigeria, and how the responsibilities of a designated anticorruption commission are relatable to the constitutional orders of other state domestic security institutions like the NPF, SSS, and others, those who framed the ICPC and EFCC Acts gave ample opportunities for interagency coordination and collaboration mechanism. [37] In addition to the chairmen of these commissions, there is a board, in theory, of seasoned and experienced professionals, that straddles areas of prosecution, criminology, philosophy, and administration. Moreover, the commissions are to conduct research and advise government institutions on ways to prevent acts of corruption, be it bribery, embezzlement, and all of that. However, none of these areas that promised to inoculate and induct the operations of the commissions in a unique manner and ensure their success have been activated appropriately. The EFCC, which is the most active agency of the two, operates more or less like other state security outfits; as if the media subscription of the ICPC is in the balance, it keeps fluctuating on the media radar, and so is the shifting public perception about its activities. This is not unconnected to its capacity limit, which is defined by its input to the interests of the president.

This has affected, greatly, the success of the commission (EFCC) as it reflects on the quality of its investigation, research, and cases presented for prosecution. For instance, between 2010 and 2015, the commission had worked on about 15,124 petitions, which constitute less than half of the petitions it received during this same period. Out of this, it filed about 2,460 cases for prosecution and won 568 convictions, which represents a mere 3.75 percent of investigated cases and a conviction rate of 23.09 - percent. [38] Additionally, the majority of these cases were of low-level corruption. More testimony to this was the Ikoyigate, in which

---

[36] Onyema et. al., "The Economic and Financial Crimes Commission," 8–9.

[37] Economic and Financial Crimes Commission (Establishment) Act 2003, A Bill for an Act to Repeal the Financial Crimes Commission (Establishment) Act, 2002 and Enact the Financial Crimes Commission (Establishment) Act, 2003; and for other Matters Connected therewith; and Corrupt Practices and Other Related Offences Act, 2000, Explanatory Memorandum.

[38] Onyema et al., "The Economic and Financial Crimes Commission," 4.

Ambassador Ayodele Oke (former Director General of the National Intelligence Agency, [NIA]) and his wife were implicated by a whistle blower in a N13 billion money-laundering scam in 2017.[39] The accused had claimed that the money found in an apartment at Ikoyi, Lagos state, was meant for some undercover security purposes. As if to lend their voices to this claim, the DSS and the NIA prevented the EFCC from arresting Mr. Oke and his wife.[40] To date, nothing is heard of the money, the case, or the accused. Ordinarily, meanwhile, within the interagency working instrument of the EFCC provided by the establishing act, this shouldn't have failed as it did, as the heads of these agencies or their representatives were supposed to be part of its operations. Even though the commission has won some high-profile cases recently, it has lost many more such cases at the same time.

Also, Nigeria is a federation of thirty-six states and the Federal Capital Territory (FCT), but these two anticorruption agencies only have a presence in less than half of these states with varying degrees of capacity and efficiency. It is even worse in the case of the ICPC, which is incapacitated by the overlapping reality of its responsibilities vis-à-vis the EFCC.[41] Corruption, in light of this, is cynically seen and treated as a federal government issue, rather than the local issue that it is. The federal government is a convergence of states, and the states are a conglomeration of several localities, all of which are infected by corruption in their daily social production and reproduction. As such, the federal level is only a convergence of the social maladies from the various localities, implying that the current structure is not only deficient, but also a fertilized bed for corruption. As pointed out earlier, the presidential system of government currently practiced in Nigeria is an effective repellent to any form of effective anticorruption initiative. Insofar as "Mr. President" has political and other interests to protect, it is only expected that the minimal capacity of the ICPC and EFCC would be devoted to monitoring and servicing these interests, like every other institution of government. This is even more so when one considers the

---

[39] Adelani Adepegba, "N13bn Money Laundering: EFCC Declares Ex-NIA DG, Oke, Wife Wanted," *Punch News*, March 24, 2019, www.punchng.com/n13bn-money-laundering-efcc-declares-ex-nia-dg-oke-wife-wanted%3famp=1.

[40] Channels Television, "Face Off as DSS, NIA Operatives Prevent EFCC from Arresting Oke, Ekpeyong," YouTube video, 1:17, November 21, 2017, www.youtube.com/watch?v=wczb_NHm-54.

[41] Hence, for a clear regulatory procedure, and effective use of the anticorruption commissions, Arowolo argued that the ICPC should be challenged to "change the focus of its regulatory activity from prosecution to prevention through the adoption of forensic strategies that would strengthen private and public institutions and reduce opportunities for corruption." Foluso Arowolo, "In the Shadows of the EFCC: Is the ICPC Still Relevant?" *Journal of Money Laundering Control* 9, no. 2 (2006): 203–213.

appointment of the heads of these agencies. Theoretically, they are nominated by the president to the highest chamber of the National Assembly, the Senate. In reality, however, they are appointees of the president considering that the nomination to the Senate is only a charade to depict wide consultations and acceptance of the nominated candidate.[42]

The appointment of the heads of these important agencies is not very different from how others are chosen. The passing of a candidate nominated by the president to any capacity in the country through the Senate is considered as a favor that needs to be reciprocated appropriately. Here, the favor goes two ways: between the president and the Senate, and between the nominee and the Senate. Consequently, the passing of a nominee depends on the nature of this relationship at the material time. On the whole, the process is not necessarily a measure of the capacity of the candidate to hold the position, but rather of these primitive considerations. The agency is thus compromised even before executing any assignment. With the ministers, as well as other heads of government institutions, departments, and agencies, the heads of this agency work for the president as his trusted allies to protect his interest. Also, the extent to which these individuals hold their positions, as mentioned earlier, depends largely on the extent to which they are able to keep Mr. President's trust.

Frankly, if corruption is to be prosecuted in the current form, then all past and present public office holders, including civil servants from the very least cadre to the peak, would have to be hounded. Simultaneously, those in the private sector, both formal and informal, would have to follow this purification train. This was not too hard to see when, in 2015, the Buhari administration came in with the anticorruption mantra. Genuine or not, the first few months of the administration were a litmus test on the nature of corruption in Nigeria. In less than a year in office, the administration threw the Nigerian economy into recession partly because of its clampdown on financial corruption. Within this period, it was clear that virtually all sectors of the economy, formal and informal, survive on pervasive networks of corruption. The banks went on massive retrenchment with the arguably knee-jerk implementation of the treasury single account (TSA) initiative. As a result, contractors were jobless as their clients became afraid of spending their ill-gotten wealth. Furthermore, hotels and car dealers witnessed a massive cut in their profit margins.

---

[42] As seen in the case of Ibrahim Magu, who acted in the capacity of the chairman of the EFCC for over four years, the refusal of the Senate to endorse the nomination does not stop the candidate from acting.

Indeed, this cycle continued to affect many households and families.[43] The effect of this bite was all the more intense as the government failed to complement its supposed reform with viable economic policies. On top of this, there was the global drop in crude oil price. Due to the continued economic woes of the country under the administration, things never remained the same. However, things became better as the political undercurrent of the anticorruption policy of the government became clear to all in positions of power who engaged in corrupt acts and wanted to spend their loot.[44]

The government's anticorruption mantra later became known as sabre rattling for legitimacy and settling political scores. The energy it garnered at the early stage was then torpedoed as its activities, in regards to fighting corruption, increasingly came under scrutiny.[45] This notwithstanding, the message was clear from this experience that corruption in Nigeria is not a federal issue; rather, it is endemic in a wide range of prebendal and patronage networks. It represents an immorality that is groomed on, and at the same time groomed by, the irresponsiveness and inefficiency of government institutions. From recruitment exercises to the award of contract, admission processing to teaching, and learning experiences as well as other bureaucratic and everyday life engagements of the people, corruption is the norm in Nigeria.[46] Not many experts are of the view that corruption is a disease best prevented than cured. And considering corruption's nature in Nigeria, there is no question that the only way to address it is through the adoption and strengthening of preventive mechanisms across governmental institutions. A taste of this approach was felt by the country in 2014 when the government discovered about 60,000 "ghost workers" in the Nigerian civil service and, by flushing out this scheme, saved around N170 billion in its annual expenditure.[47] However, considering the relooting galore in the current crisis bedeviling the

---

[43] Bolaji Akinyemi, *Nigerian Exceptionalism*, 21-23.

[44] Such was the boldness that made an All Progressive Congress (APC) Chieftain order for two bullion vans in his Ikoyi home during the 2019 elections. See, Gabriel Ewepu, "CSOs Call on EFCC to Investigate Tinubu over Alleged Money Conveyed in Bullion Vans," *Vanguard News*, October 25, 2019, www.vanguardngr.com/2019/10/csos-calls-on-efcc-to-investigate-tinubu-over-alleged-money-conveyed-in-bullion-vans/.

[45] *Sahara Reporters*, "Heavy Knocks for Buhari's Anti-Corruption War," *Sahara Reporters*, October 31, 2015, http://saharareporters.com/2015/10/31/heavy-knocks-buhari's-anti-corruption-war.

[46] Fakoyeje Olalekan, "Senate to Probe NPA, FCC over Alleged Job Scam," *Nairametrics*, February 25, 2020, https://nairametrics.com/2020/02/25/job-scam-rocks-npa-fcc-as-job-seekers-pay-n3-million-for-appointment-letters/.

[47] NSE Anthony-Uko, "Nigeria: FG Uncovers 60,000 Ghost Workers," *AllAfrica*, October 22, 2014, https://allafrica.com/stories/201410220230.html.

supposed corruption efforts of the current administration,[48] it remains to be seen how these gains have been maximally utilized for the people.

Conclusion

All of the above speak to the common trends that have existed since Transparency International began to conduct its corruption perception survey in 1995, which shows that the more disorganized a state is, the more organized its network of corruption. Concomitantly, virtually all the lowest-ranked countries on the reports have been well governed. Therefore, the level of corruption in a country tells a lot on the structure of governance and the social norm of relations. While this is true, it has to be reiterated, as this chapter has shown, that corruption – in both act and impact – is a human agency that surfaces wherever social relations among two or more people exist. Consequently, it is not limited to illegal material aggrandizement, but it is relevant to the discussion on accruing other undue privileges to oneself and one's cronies, illegally. Individuals and groups accrue to themselves what they could not have or cannot reasonably attain or earn. And, none of these is in short supply in Nigeria.

With all of the above in view, it will be safe to surmise that, left in its present structure, any effort at combating corruption and corrupt practices in Nigeria will consistently fail to win the appeal of objective and interest-laden observers alike. It will remain political and ineffective as often alleged because the ocean is bigger than the shore.

---

[48] John Owen Nwachukwu, "Ibrahim Magu: Fresh Facts on Relooting of Recovered Funds Emerge," *Daily Post*, July 11, 2020, https://dailypost.ng/2020/07/11/breaking-ibrahim-magu-fresh-facts-on-re-looting-of-recovered-funds-emerge/.

12   The Political Economy of Oil

Introduction

James Fennell's 2006 paper, "Nigeria: Democracy or Unity? A Conflict Analysis," questions how the practice of democracy in Nigeria, under the influence of petrodollar politics, has maintained colonial structures and functionality within the region.[1] Fennell expressly stated that the only force holding Nigeria together in its current form is Niger Delta oil. Take this away, and the Nigerian state would collapse, like a fragile calabash, into several irreparable parts. This undisputable fact about the Nigerian state requires careful observation and analysis of nuanced issues to be fully understood.

Many within Nigeria's borders, especially members of the political class who survive through the state's rentier structure, would not want to admit that Abuja is not holding the country together. The oil produced in the Niger Delta ensures national cohesion, and Abuja is a convenient device for those who want the country to continue in its current form, enabling further exploitation. As a rentier state, this is true in theory and in practice. The region's politics are the politics of oil, and oil politics have always been at the heart of every move in Nigerian politics – whether undertaken by political, market, bureaucratic, or other actors in the state.[2]

Oil politics is the soul of policy formation, the heart of its execution, and the breathing lungs through which state processes flow; it sustains the fragile body of the state, its handlers, and society. The experience of every living and nonliving thing in Nigeria depends on how the system functions.[3] Any

---

[1] James Fennell, "Nigeria: Unity or Democracy? A Conflict Analysis," December 2006, 10, www.academia.edu/4457697/Nigeria_Unity_or_Democracy.
[2] Ibid., 10–11.
[3] Etiosa Uyigue and Matthew Agho, *Coping with Climate Change and Environmental Degradation in the Niger Delta of Southern Nigeria* (Benin: Community Research and Development Centre (CREDC) Nigeria, 2007).

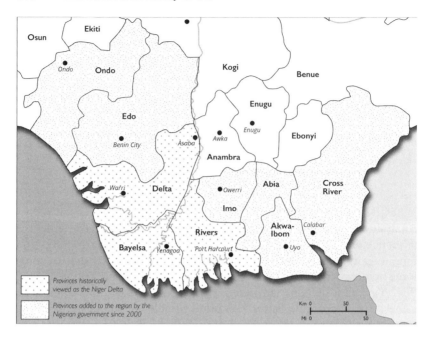

Map 12.1 Nigeria, Niger-Delta.

complication in this system creates complications for the state and its citizens. A food vendor's ability to sell a bag of rice within months, weeks, or days, and the price for which it is sold, depends on the "health" of this fragile entity. When it falls ill, the bricklayer is affected along with the contractor, the carpenter, the entrepreneur, the civil servant, and others. Directly or indirectly, every entity in the polity feeds on the decomposed organic material oozing from beneath the nine states collectively known as Nigeria's Niger Delta region.[4] This explains why different administrations have scrambled to curry favor with its local power brokers.

Activities in the Niger Delta determine the living conditions of the Nigerian state, and the government's management of these activities affects society's well-being. Challenges arise based on groups jockeying for position within the space through which oil is distributed, and their creation and resolution are driven by what Peter M. Lewis has described as

---

[4] According to the NDDC Act 2000, the Niger Delta area of Nigeria consists of Abia, Akwa-Ibom, Bayelsa, Cross-River, Delta, Edo, Imo, Ondo, and Rivers States. Niger-Delta Development Commission (Establishment etc.) Act 2000, Act No 6, Laws of the Federation of Nigeria, www.commonlii.org/ng/legis/num_act/ndceu504/.

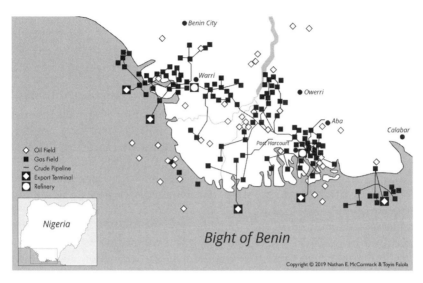

Map 12.2 Location of oil and gas resources.

"selective patronage and populist redistribution."[5] Individuals and groups
in the Niger Delta states have consistently positioned themselves to be seen
as both a threat to stability and as an asset for securing peace in a constantly
shifting terrain. Several ethnic and social bodies have been created, such as
the Oodua People's Congress (OPC), the Arewa People's Congress, the
Bakassi Boys, the Movement for the Emancipation of the Niger Delta
(MEND) – and the various Niger Delta militant groups – the Movement
for the Actualization of the Sovereign State of Biafra (MASSOB), the
Movement for the Survival of the Ogoni People (MOSOP), the Middle
Belt Elders Forum, and the Pan-Niger Delta Forum (PANDEF). These
groups advance and protect factional interests; their operationality and
functionality are each of the regions are very strategic.

Some of these bodies use outright violence as an instrument of power
and others use collective diplomacy to engage the state. More often
than not, both tactics are applied to gain the attention of those at the
helm of the state's rentier distribution system. The diplomatic clusters,
commonly occupied and controlled by the political elite class in each
region, can sometimes be seen encouraging or even sponsoring the
activities of violent groups. These groups prey on vulnerable youths –

---

[5] Peter M. Lewis, *Oil, Politics, and Economic Change in Indonesia and Nigeria* (Ann Arbor:
The University of Michigan Press, 2007), 9.

who are mostly found in the violent category – who have been frustrated by a system that doesn't represent or work for them. These disaffected individuals, and their struggle to access state resources, have made violence and insecurity prevalent in the Nigerian state and every other resource-rich state in Africa.[6]

Such practices precede the advent of oil politics in Nigeria, although oil politics exacerbated and shaped the formation of special interest groups and their demands. So-called nationalist leaders have not disguised their words on this; Obafemi Awolowo declared that Nigeria was a mere geographical expression in 1947.[7] In the same spirit, Sir Tafawa Balewa addressed the House of Representatives the following year and stated, "Many deceive themselves by thinking that Nigeria is one . . .. This is wrong. I am sorry to say that this presence of unity is artificial and it ends outside this chamber."[8] This mindset, nurtured by political leaders who lack the commitment to build any structure other than those that enable their rent collection, has shaped the Nigerian polity. Decades later, this view of a country with many interests and identities has been reinforced by scholars and close observers of Nigerian society who ask whether there is truly a Nigerian state and Nigerian citizens.[9]

The Willink Commission of 1958 set the tone for the ethnic rivalries that would play out in Nigeria after its 1960 independence. The commission, together with the mainstream nationalists of the time who were representing the interests of their own ethnic groups, established a pattern of mutual suspicion and competition for limited resources; national cohesion was an afterthought for the would-be-independent country. These attitudes were a continuation of the hierarchy imposed by the colonial administration; less powerful cultural groups were relegated to the status of second- or third-class citizens. Because status determines who gets what, when, and how, each cultural group uses every available method to proclaim their own superior status. The issue of minority groups and the rights available to them, reinforced during the independent debates on the Willink Commission in the 1950s, has

---

[6] Ray Bush and Morris Szeftel, "The Struggle for Resources in Africa," *Review of African Political Economy* 18, no. 51 (1991): 2–8.

[7] Obafemi Awolowo, *Path to Nigerian Freedom* (London: Faber, 1947), 47–48.

[8] See James S. Coleman, *Nigeria: Background to Nationalism* (Sweden & Nigeria: Broberg and Winston, 1958), 320.

[9] Taiwo concluded, expressly, "beyond phrase mongering, there are no citizens in Nigeria, only citizens of Nigeria." Femi Taiwo, "Of Citizens and Citizenship," *Constitutionalism and National Question, Lagos* (2000), quoted in William O. O. Idowu, "Citizenship, Alienation and Conflict in Nigeria," *Africa Development: Economy of Conflict in Africa* 24, no. 1/2 (1999): 33.

persisted to the present day. This influenced the formation of the Movement for the Emancipation of the Niger Delta (MEND) in 2005.

The MEND began with an attack on two Shell Petroleum Development Company (SPDC) facilities: pipelines at Okrika and Andoni axis, Rivers State, in November and December 2005. This group was an extension and continuation of the struggles of activists that included Isaac Adaka Boro and Ken Saro-Wiwa in the Niger Delta area. Although no group within or outside the region claimed responsibility for the attack, it appeared to be the perpetrators' first attack on SPDC and the Nigerian government.

The attacks were carried out by people whose government had sold out to corporate imperialist multinationals, keeping the region impoverished by failing to provide important infrastructure such as schools, hospitals, roads, health facilities, and stable sources of clean water. Land, water, and air in the region had been polluted, rendering it uninhabitable.[10] The population suffered from increased unemployment, high mortality rates, diseases, poverty, economic stagnation, massive underdevelopment, discontentment, resentment, aggression, and resistance that led to violent conflict between the communities and the multinational corporations (MNCs).

The complex matrix of the Nigerian state intertwines facets of ethnicity, imported governance models, unhealthy competition, nepotism, cronyism, marginalization, prebendalism, patronage systems, discrimination, and insensitivity to function as a rentier state controlling resources in ways that increase violence and conflict in the Niger Delta area.[11] This emphasizes the political economy of oil, which generates about 95 per cent of Nigeria's foreign exchange earnings and 85 per cent of the country's export products. By considering the concepts of identity, conflict, and security, and also noting the general and specific perspectives on politics leading to the manifestation of the MEND group, it becomes clear that successful nation building in any state depends on the creation of an effective institutional frame that is occupied by purposeful, growth-oriented leadership.[12] National culture is an imperative that must be conceived with support from all, regardless of the ethnic cultural differences in a pluralistic society like Nigeria. Such an approach could save the country from future insurgencies, economic sabotage, ethnic agitations, and the pervasive marginalization,

---

[10] *ESRI*, "Ogoni People vs. Shell," *ESRI*, n.d., www.arcgis.com/apps/Cascade/index.html? appid=a43f979996aa4da3bac7cae270a995e0.

[11] For a comprehensive historical review, see Bola Dauda, "Corruption, Nepotism, and Anti-Bureaucratic Behaviors," in *The Palgrave Handbook of African Social Ethics*, eds. Nimi Wariboko and Toyin Falola (London: Palgrave Macmillan, 2020), 317–338.

[12] Daron Acemoglu and James A. Robinson, *Why Nations Fail* (New York: Crown Publishers, 2012).

discrimination, oppression, and injustices that emanate from the parochial rentier economy currently powering the state.

How to Successfully Create a State without Guaranteed Security

In a discussion of identity, security, conflict, and nation building, some scholarly thoughts are important for summarizing the variance of ideas that abound in analyses. The African Centre for Development and Strategic Studies (ACDESS) recognized the prevalence of insecurity in Africa by sorting the countries of postindependence Africa into three dominant categories: countries engaged in armed conflict or civil strife; countries in several and prolonged political crises and turbulence; and countries enjoying a relatively stable political condition.[13] Few states exist in the final category, and most of them are still affected by countries in the other two categories. The impact of conflict on African states is overwhelming, especially when considering development on the continent.

Nelson Goodman has noted that "there can be no security in traditions that failed us; there is no black market in truth,"[14] and American philosopher John Dewey has observed that insecurity originates from the quest for certainty.[15] Wendell Bell has stated that in the face of insecurity, "we are faced with great decisions about what future we want. What do we prefer? For what reason do we prefer it?"[16] These ideas consider the importance of survival and the development of human capacity that can be undone by the threats that conflict, crises, and instability pose to every human society. Nelson Goodman and A. I. Asiwaju have pointed out that government disdain and conscious neglect of human dignity and respect leads to unending crises in the polity.[17] Bringing this to a more conceptual conclusion, Adda Bozeman has described conflict as follows:

---

[13] ACDESS Conflict Monitoring System, quoted in Adebayo Adedeji, *Comprehending and Mastering African Conflicts: The Search for Sustainable Peace and Good Governance* (London & New York: Zed Books, 1999), 31.

[14] Nelson Goodman, quoted in Philip Ogo Ujomu, "The Bounds of Security Theorizing: Envisioning Discursive Inputs for the Rectification of a Post-Colonial Situation," in *Rethinking Security in Nigeria: Conceptual Issues in the Quest for Social Order and National Integration*, eds. Dapo Adelugba and Philip Ogo Ujomu (Dakar: Council for the Development of Social Science Research in Africa (CODESRIA), 2008), 6.

[15] David Sidorsky, ed., *John Dewey: The Essential Writings* (New York: Harper and Row, 1997), 153.

[16] Wendell Bell, "The World as a Moral Community," *Society* (1994): 17–22.

[17] See A. I. Asiwaju, "Challenges of Regional Integration in Africa," in *The African Union and the Challenges of Cooperation and Integration: Proceedings of the National Seminar, the Ministry of Cooperation and Integration in Africa (the Presidency)* (Ibadan: Spectrum Books, 2002), 196; Nelson Goodman, quoted in Ujomu, "The Bounds of Security," 6.

on the plane of biography it usually stands for inner stress and tension, as when the self evolves from childhood and dependency; when choices between rival moral challenges or course of social action have to be made; or when competitive ideas intrude upon the mental process of seeking certainty and truth.[18]

All forms of revolt in human society are triggered by a sense of injustice. Regardless of their stated causes, these agitations always include the issue of inclusivity. Similar sentiments are seen in the nationalist period of countries in various parts of the world, including Africa. Bennie Khoapa furthered this argument:

it is a mystification to preach universal (national) brotherhood in a situation of oppression ... it is too soon to love everybody. History has charged us with the cruel responsibility of going to the very gate of racism (ethnicity) in order to destroy racism (Ethnicity) – to the gate, no further.[19]

This outlines the sentiment behind Nigeria's incessant agitations and crises, including the herdsmen–farmers crises, communal conflict, or the Niger Delta insurgencies.[20]

The question of identity lies at the root of these discussions. The issues of human survival, human capacity development, and the attendant nation-building processes are meshed with the question of the area's identity and that of the people within it – how they view these identities and how they are managed. Identity either unifies or divides people of identical preference-(s), vis-à-vis color, culture, tradition, language, sex, gender, and the like. Most of these differences are reinforced to suit specific, artificial purposes such as the sharing of resources. When they are not well managed, differences in identity lead to mutual suspicion, strife, rivalry, unhealthy competition, resentment, conflict, war, and other malignancies that arise from group classification.[21] Individualism also plays a role, because there are individual variances in the manifestation of group identity.[22] As much as culture is believed to be fluid, so also is identity.

---

[18] Adda B. Bozeman, *Conflict in Africa: Concepts and Reality* (Princeton: Princeton University Press, 1976), 3.

[19] Bennie Khoapa, quoted in David Hirschman, "The Black African Consciousness Movement in South Africa," *The Journal of Modern African Studies* 28, no. 1 (1990): 5.

[20] Cf. O. Otite and I. O. Albert, eds., *Community Conflicts in Nigeria: Management, Resolution and Transformation* (Ibadan: Spectrum Books, 1999).

[21] Olayemi Akinwunmi et al., eds., *Inter-Group Relations in Nigeria during the 19th and 20th Centuries* (Makurdi: Aboki Publishers, 2006).

[22] Billikopf argued that the differences between individuals are greater than the differences between groups in any given entity or culture. He identified some social variables, like education, social standing, religion, personality, belief structure, past experience, affection shown in the home, and others as factors necessitating (and as such, influencing) individuals' identity in society. Gregorio Billikopf, "Cultural Differences? Or Are We Really That Different?" www.cnr.berkley.edu/ucce50/ag-labour/7article/article01.htm.

After independence, political elites continued the divide-and-rule socio-political formations that had been established by their various colonial lords, which perpetuated the absence of national cohesion and identity. The question of nation building itself has become an abstract at best, and a mere cacophonic illusion at worst.[23] Idowu, while interrogating the term citizenship in Nigeria argued, "where different attitudes are expressed by individuals and groups in a particular geo-polity on the idea of citizenship, this seems in a sense bound to lead to the generation of conflict."[24] Idowu's argument sums up the nature of virtually all recorded violence and insecurity in the postindependent Nigerian state, including the MEND agitation. The coercive, domineering posture and presence of the federal government in the Niger Delta area – ever since the exploration and discovery of oil resources in the area – speaks to the rentier state it represents under the military and the "autodemocratic" dictatorships.

A rentier state only caters to the desires of a powerful minority, which fosters misgivings, anxiety, and suspicion along ethno-religious lines. To address the anti-national posturing that can negate the process and principles of nation building, many scholars have advocated for power-sharing options to ensure a stable polity. This is particularly relevant for pluralistic societies.

To placate the fears of the many cultural and religious entities found in a pluralistic society, power-sharing mechanisms are proposed to allow short-term political pacts, cultural protection, and more inclusive formulas for sharing state resources. Components of the power-sharing doctrine, from "consociationalism to various other integrative/accommodative/centripetalist approaches," are said to challenge the patronage systems and the distributive parochial economy that asphyxiates productive efforts within society.[25] Some question whether such power, which is retained by the political elites even after its diffusion, can meaningfully address the concerns of the broader population in a polity of conflicting identities. These concerns are reinforced by the supremacy of individual identity, which does not necessarily bring about justice. Neither does the mobilization of group

---

[23] For more on this intriguing identity of Nationhood in Africa, particularly in relations to Nigeria, see Tunde Decker, *Matrix of Inherited Identity: An Historical Exploration of the Underdog Phenomenon in Nigeria's Relationship Strategies, 1960–2011* (Ibadan: University Press, 2016).

[24] Idowu, "Citizenship, Alienation and Conflict," 31–55.

[25] Maren Milligan, "Fighting for the Right to Exist: Institutions, Identity, and Conflict in Jos, Nigeria," *Comparative Politics* 45, no. 3 (2013): 313. Other examples on the subject of plural society and peaceful coexistence include Leonard Wantchekon, "Credible Power Sharing Agreements: Theory with Evidence from South Africa and Lebanon," *Constitutional Political Economy* 11 (2000): 339–352; Donald Horowitz, *Ethnic Groups in Conflict* (Berkeley: University of California Press, 1985); Arend Lijphart, *Democracy in Plural Societies: A Comparative Exploration* (New Haven: Yale University Press, 1977).

identity necessarily bring about justice: institutions formed along these lines prior to colonial domination and reconfiguration of states in Africa were not always mindful of human rights or group interests.[26] This skepticism questions the feasibility of building effective institutions, developing growth-oriented leadership, and completing the sociocultural shift that could put the state on the path of development.

In Nigeria and many other states in Africa, power sharing is used as a pretext to extend the hand of prebendalism and enlarge the patronage system without any real reform or change that impacts ordinary people.[27] In a "resource curse" economy, where an abundance of natural resources paradoxically prevents national development, power-sharing measures bestow greater privilege on political elites to the detriment of everyone else. The resource curse theory explains that instability is the defining characteristic of politics in states that are rich in natural resources; those resources are used to create prebendal and patronage structures in their various forms. Ross, a scholar who writes on oil politics, has explained that the likelihood of conflict, and the duration of that conflict, depends on the "lootability" of the resources involved.[28]

The resource curse idea and its connection with conflict explains Nigeria's situation, which Richard A. Joseph has called "the politics of affluence" and which Kapucinksi, a Polish journalist and Nobel laureate, described as an illusion dream of endless auto-wealth.[29] As it stands today, this "black gold" is the darkest curse that people in the Niger Delta region, and the totality of the Nigerian people by extension, have to bear.[30] It is troubling that information and files related to the activities

[26] See Keith Somerville, *Africa's Long Road since Independence: The Many Histories of a Continent* (New York: Penguin Random House, 2017), 1–48, as he lays credence to this position. See also Lijphart, *Democracy in Plural Societies* for varying degrees of how this played out in different societies.

[27] No sooner had South Sudan seceded from the Republic of Sudan than the people began to face poverty, death, disease, and life-threatening conditions caused by their elites. They remained suspicious of one another, despite their power sharing formula, leading the country into another protracted war of supremacy for personal gains. Cf. Winnie Byanyima, "One Last Push to End South Sudan's Deadly Civil War," *Aljazeera*, December 14, 2017, www.aljazeera.com/indepth/opinion/push-south-sudan-deadly-civil-war-171214071246774.html.

[28] Ross, quoted in Elias Courson, *Movement for the Emancipation of the Niger Delta (MEND): Political Marginalization, Repression and Petro-Insurgency in the Niger Delta* (Uppsala: Nordiska Afrika Institute, 2009), 11.

[29] Richard A. Joseph, "Affluence and Underdevelopment: The Nigerian Experience," *The Journal of Modern African Studies* 16, no. 2 (1978): 221–239; Kapucinksi, quoted in Rob Nixon, *Slow Violence and the Environmentalism of the Poor* (Cambridge: Harvard University Press, 2011), 71.

[30] As Emmanuel Addeh noted after field work in the area, "to the people of Oloibiri, Otuogidi, and Otuabagi, they can't wait to witness that day when they will laugh heartedly again and dry the tears brought about by the black gold which has, as it seems,

of the multinational oil corporations (MNOCs) are classified as top secret, which allows the government to conceal the damage that these imperialist corporations have done to the people of the Niger Delta. It has made justice, recuperation, and reparations an uphill task when trying to resolve violence caused by the resource curse.[31]

Comatose without Oil

In 2015, the Jonathan administration handed over power to Buhari following an unprecedented loss to the opposition. Nigeria's new government responded to the economic threat of Niger Delta militants by turning the region into a military zone, although keen observers realized that this knee-jerk response would soon be replaced by dialogue. Less than five months into the standoff, accompanied by other governmental inaction and missteps, the Nigerian economy entered recession. This was followed by a massive retrenchment of workers, rising unemployment rates, inflation, destabilized foreign exchange markets, depleted foreign reserves, and abysmally low levels of foreign direct investment.[32] The government response followed the spirit of previous administrations, with the exception of Yar'Adua's and Jonathan's.

In fact, the militant threat had arisen due to the revocation of surveillance contracts between the militants and the previous administration that covered the pipeline and other oil facilities, along with the administration's decision to suspend the amnesty program initiated by the Yar'Adua government.[33] By the time the economy entered into recession, crude oil extraction had plummeted to less than a million barrels per day – less than half of average daily production. By the time the economy recovered from the recession, the impasse between the government and the militants had been resolved and oil production had returned to normal.

The government's action to stabilize Niger Delta politics and repair the economy involved some measure of patronage for those who had proven

become a curse." Emmanuel Addeh, "Oloibiri: A Story of Neglect," *This Day Live*, August 28, 2017, www.thisdaylive.com/index.php/2017/08/28/oloibiri-a-story-of-neglect/.

[31] See, for instance, Cletus Ukpong, "Ogoni Nine: Shell's Lawyers Refusing to Hand over 'Critical' Evidence–Amnesty International," *Premium Times*, September 8, 2017, www .premiumtimesng.com/regional/south-south-regional/242757-ogoni-nine-shells-law yers-refusing-hand-critical-evidence-amnesty-international.html.

[32] *Reuters*, "UPDATE 3-Nigeria's economy shrinks in 2016 for first time in 25 years," *Reuters*, February 28, 2017, www.reuters.com/article/nigeria-gdp/update-3-nigerias-economy-shrinks-in-2016-for-first-time-in-25-years-idUSL5N1GD2MJ.

[33] Emma Amaize and Brisibe Perez, "Avengers: The New Face of Niger-Delta Militancy," *Vanguard*, May 8, 2016, www.vanguardngr.com/2016/05/avengers-new-face-niger-delta -militancy/.

themselves to be influential in the region, which neglected the real issue.[34] The region's volatility affects the mood of the entire country, breeds perpetual uncertainty in the polity, and scares investors away. Stability in the region restores confidence in the government's ability to implement economic policies, encouraging outside investment and national development. The Amnesty Program that was introduced by the Yar'Adua administration and continued by its successor, along with the skilled economic teams employed by both administrations, led to an unprecedented rise in foreign direct investment in Nigeria.[35] Regional stability and global oil prices had massive effects on every other aspect of Nigeria's economy during this period. However, since the government was still operating patronage systems within a prebendal framework, the effects of growth were only felt by political elites and their cronies. For everyone else, it was only reporting on statistics.

Some effects, such as employment opportunities and infrastructure development, did trickle down to the rest of the country, but these minimal developments did not reflect the economic indices of this period. Paradoxically, the oil that helped stabilized the economy during the Jonathan administration's era was also responsible for the collapse of that administration; the administration's subsidy removal policy was criticized as insensitive to the plight of the people.[36] More importantly, because "politics and economic competition were overwhelmingly oriented to the capture and distribution of state-mediated rents,"[37] neither the state's privatization efforts nor private sector productivity could endure in Nigeria. In a bid to reform the economy, the Obasanjo government – and the government of Babangida, his military predecessor – attempted to

---

[34] Despite the Buhari administration's promise to clean up the environment, the rules for oil exploration remain unchanged in the region; no evidence of the project's commencement is visible. Cf. *Business & Human Rights Resource Centre*, "Nigeria: President Announces Cleanup of Oil Pollution Sites in Ogoniland," *Business & Human Rights Resource Centre*, June 1–3, 2019, www.business-humanrights.org/en/nigeria-president-announces-cleanup-of-oil-pollution-sites-in-ogoniland; Neil Munshi, "Graft and Mismanagement Claims Taint Nigeria Oil Clean-Up," *Financial Times*, December 29, 2019, www.ft.com/content/33485e22-104e-11ea-a225-db2f231cfeae; Mojeed Alabi, "INVESTIGATION: How Buhari Administration Awarded Ogoni Cleanup Contracts to Unqualified Firms," *Premium Times*, May 5, 2019, www.premiumtimesng.com/investigationspecial-reports/32 8460-investigation-how-buhari-administration-awarded-ogoni-cleanup-contracts-to-unqu alified-firms.html.

[35] Frederick Mordi, "Nigeria Is Top FDI Destination in Africa," *African Business Magazine*, March 20, 2013, https://africanbusinessmagazine.com/country-reports/nigeria-is-top-fdi-destination-in-africa/.

[36] Yemisi Akinbobola, "Bid to End Subsidy Stirs Protest in Nigeria: Unrest Highlights Problems of Mismanagement and Corruption," *Africa Renewal*, April 2012, www.un.org/africarenewal/magazine/april-2012/bid-end-subsidy-stirs-protest-nigeria.

[37] Lewis, *Oil, Politics, and Economic Change*, 254.

privatize some government assets to enhance their efficiency and reduce government liabilities. These ideas were only good on paper; companies and establishments were bought by cronies and legitimate investors were chased away. Instability and uncertainty were signaled by the very process of privatization,[38] and virtually all of these businesses quickly collapsed.

On the one hand, privatized businesses could not be run with the familiar rentier methods, and on the other hand, unstable government policies and wavering commitments to private sector development had negative consequences. Various power sharing measures also took their toll; Nigeria changed from having 12 states to having 36 states in less than three decades, with 774 Local Government areas. These measures did not stem the cries to properly share the "national cake," and while patronage politics served the needs of some, many others felt neglected. This was the case with the incessant rivalry between Ijo and Itsekiri groups in the Niger Delta area. Other ethnic nationalities engaged in wars of supremacy and rivalry, which were often instigated by the state to control regions and resources without encountering organized resistance from the people.[39] The system is skewed toward rent collection, access to the machinery of extraction is carefully controlled, and the patronage proceeds are distributed unequally. Aggravating the resource curse is the centralized system for administering this lazy, parochial economy. It has created a dearth of creative, pragmatic, and ingenious governance, enabling the state's desperately dangerous, manipulative, and self-centered political culture.

Poor governance has bastardized the allegedly federal state structure; the latest democratic transition has weakened the productivity and competitiveness of the state's component units. A developmental mindset was absent from the political machinations of Nigerian policy makers. Observers, commentators, political elites, and market actors viewed Abuja as important as an inhaler for an asthmatic patient – money from Niger Delta oil activities flowed to Abuja, and from there it flowed to other corners of the country and the world at large. The mad rush for Aso Rock, positioned as the hill through which pass the patronage, rentier, and prebendal systems, became a disgraceful struggle that has almost rendered the hope of a democratic state meaningless. Attention has been drawn to the activities of the federal government, but neither the fiscal accounts of the central authority nor those of its less-observed components are subject

---

[38] Edlyne E. Anugwom, "Review from Babangida to Obasanjo: The State, Rent-Seeking Behaviour and the Realities of Privatization in Nigeria," *International Journal of Sociology and Anthropology* 2, no. 7 (2011): 204–216.

[39] Meredeth Turshen, "The Warri Crisis, the Niger Delta, and the Nigerian State," *ACAS Bulletin*, no. 68 (2004).

to either accountability or transparency. Budgets are opaque and the fiscal frame of the state in general is grotesque. Through the patronage system, political elites see themselves as demi-gods not meant to be questioned by mere mortals.

Any attempt by Civil Society Organizations or other concerned citizens to introduce transparency and accountability – efforts to make politicians answer to the people who have "elected" them – is met with either stiff resistance or manipulative measures that disguise the real issue. This is unsurprising because electoral processes always reflect the governance of the state.

Political party candidates are predetermined by party chieftains, which is a refined term for those who fund the party. Alternative candidates are either bought or coerced to go along with the process. The Independent National Electoral Commission, saddled with the responsibility of regulating party affairs and conducting elections in Nigeria, neither scrutinizes the parties' sources of funding nor supervises campaign spending. Party activities that involve candidate nominations, campaign spending, and party funding are all shrouded in a secrecy that undermines the electoral process. When these parties get hold of state power, it is deployed to "settle" these patronage networks and bolster their own finances, carving a niche for themselves in the state's political arena. This process expands their patronage networks, although it is often perceived as a betrayal by their political supporters.

The system only benefits a small minority, and if a new group receives benefits, it is because another group has lost them. This makes the fraught political environment difficult to change. Elections are generally considered a civil matter, but civil matters are not always civil in Nigeria; the desperation of political elites trying to retain control leads to rent collection. Elections often involve every part of Nigeria's security forces, including the Army, Navy, Air Force, State Security Services, and the so-called Special Anti-Robbery Squad Unit of the Nigerian Police Force – their shocking involvement in armed robbery and kidnapping suggests that they are the official patrons of armed robbers and kidnappers. It's often the atmosphere of a state at war with itself.

The mobilization of armed forces, and the manner in which they behave, is a symbolic representation of Nigerian politics; it is literally how the system operates. The patronage and distribution systems have weakened all elements of professionalism and reinforced mediocrity in government. When political elites cannot use their thugs to disrupt elections and manipulate figures, the security services come in handy.

Nigeria's armed services are used to intimidate voters, especially in opposition strongholds. Apart from the legality of deploying the military for a civil election, it is unclear what their involvement has accomplished. Despite the deployment of 300,000 police officers for the presidential elections, and 95 percent of the Nigerian Army, along with thousands of other security personnel in the 2019 general elections, local and international observers considered the results to be among the worst in terms of intimidation, violence, and manipulation.[40] Because life must continue, the people ignore the conspicuous manipulation of election results – and the denunciations of the process made by outside observers – allowing the winners of this charade to claim the titles of the offices that they have forcibly occupied.

When people demand action from these officials, they receive more repression and manipulation. The process that brought these figures to power has emboldened them; either they choose to use force against the people or manipulate them and alter their demands. They are certain, according to one informant, that "in my country, life moves on so fast from the hardest situation that time doesn't even know it." These beliefs are exercised during the electioneering stage and in governance because the country is imprisoned by the largesse flowing from the hills of Aso Rock. The government's opposition is prone to leave the right and live the wrong, positioning themselves to be among the minority few who can access this prebendal cycle. What could have been a dissenting unit of the state is broken and left voiceless.

A former president of the country once admitted that the state's current economic structure made it hard to achieve any meaningful reform.[41] The political parties, as the only organizations that can produce political leadership, are a microcosm of the state's failure. Through them, violence is nurtured and festers. Those who get their daily bread and build up their bank balance are those who instrumentalize violence, either as a service, as with the thugs found among the National Union of Road Transport Workers (NURTW), or in response to state politics, as with the Niger Delta militants. As Claude Ake succinctly observed, "the elites in government having captured power, monopolizes it and finally regard the state

[40] Adelani Adepegba, "Police to Deploy over 300,000 Operatives for Presidential Election," *Punch News*, February 10, 2019, https://punchng.com/police-to-deploy-over-300000-operatives-for-presidential-election/; *Nigeria Civil Society Situation Room*, "The Nigerian Army Will Deploy 95 Per Cent of Its Troops for Elections," *Nigeria Civil Society Situation Room*, February 20, 2019, www.placng.org/situation_room/sr/the-nigerian-army-will-deploy-95-per-cent-of-its-troops-for-elections/; *Nigeria Civil Society Situation Room*, "Press Statement on the 2019 Elections Report of the Nigeria Civil Society Situation Room," July 30, 2019, www.placng.org/situation_room/sr/wp-content/uploads/2019/07/SITUATION-ROOM-STATEMENT-ON-LAUNCH-OF-ELECTION-REPORT.pdf.
[41] James Emejo, "Jonathan: Pay Taxes, Hold Govt Accountable," *This Day (AllAfrica)*, October 11, 2010, https://allafrica.com/stories/201010120384.html.

as an instrument of plunder and brutality; while the populace find solace in ethnic and primordial identities."[42]

"Resource Curse Violence": The Case of the Movement for the Emancipation of the Niger Delta (MEND)

Oil was discovered in 1956 at Oloibiri, a tiny community in the Niger Delta area, before the Nigerian entity gained independence. Shell explorers confirmed that the quantity and quality of the reserves were marketable, and this was the precursor to the resource curse that would be inflicted on the area by government officials and foreign companies. Independent Nigeria had initially based its national and sovereign survival on agro-economics and petty industrial outputs; these activities were abandoned with the commencement of oil exploration and the oil boom of the 1970s. Greater-than-expected oil reserves were found at Oloibiri after oil was discovered in other Niger Delta locations, and the global rise in oil prices meant that other economic activities were abandoned, especially in Nigeria's agricultural sector.[43] Oil dollars eventually generated about 95 percent of the country's foreign earnings and 80 percent of federal revenue, leading the "Giant of Africa" into the malignant web of a parochial economic monoculture.

The Niger Delta region is the epicenter of foreign attention and politics because it holds the largest oil deposits in Africa,[44] and oil is the foundation of the concept that is present-day Nigeria. The extent of the government's budget deficit or surplus is determined by oil production in the Niger Delta.[45] And the people who live in the nesting grounds of this golden goose are starved, alienated, and brutally condemned when they take action to protect their environment. Ken Saro-Wiwa, an Ogoni poet and environmental activist – the leader of the Ogoni Nine who was executed by the rogue Military Judicial Panel of 1995 – argued that "the environment is man's first right: the absence of a safe environment makes

---

[42] Claude Ake, *Democratization of Disempowerment*, quoted in Chris Ekene Mbah, "Is It Always the Economic Stupid?: Movement for the Emancipation of Niger Delta (MEND) and Petroviolence in the Niger Delta of Nigeria," Master's thesis, University of Toronto, 2013, 4.

[43] Cf. S. O. Tomori and O. W. Tomori, "Revisiting the African Alternative Framework to Structural Adjustment Programmes for Socio-Economic Recovery and Transformation (AAF-SAP) in Contemporary Nigeria," in *African Development and Governance Strategies in the 21st Century, Looking Back to Move Foreword: Essays in Honor of Adebayo Adedeji at Seventy*, eds. Bade Onimode et al. (London & New York: Zed Books, 2004), 30–46.

[44] See, for example, Bruce Malogo, "War of Bakassi? France Takes on Nigeria over Oil-Rich Peninsula," *African Guardian* (1994); 17.

[45] T. Abdulraheem et al., "Nigeria: Oil, Debts, and Democracy," *Review of African Political Economy*, no. 37 (1986): 6–10.

it impossible for man to fight for other rights: be they economic, social or political."[46] Residents are left with two choices: coastal fishing or subsistence farming on what little arable land remains for cultivation. Their economic activities are dictated by their natural environment, as with all other cultures and societies. However, the covetous nature of superior powers, similar to those of the exploitative colonial administration, work to incapacitate the people and degrade their existence so that profiteering can continue without interference from the region's indigenous people.[47]

As water supplies became polluted through oil spills and pipeline leaks, residents not only became vulnerable to sickness, but their livelihood was also taken away. Fishing became impossible when no live fish remained in the waterways. Gas flaring polluted the air. Scientists have established that emission practices in the area, connected with oil exploration, pose an existential threat to the area's rainfall.[48] Water becomes acidic before touching the ground, leaving residents unable to obtain fresh water either from existing groundwater supplies or new rainfall.

The Movement for the Emancipation of the Niger Delta (MEND) was influenced by previously existing currents in Nigerian politics, especially those concerning minority representation and ethnic favoritism, which had been issues since the so-called nationalists pushed for independence. The first disturbance in the Niger Delta area was Isaac Adaka Boro's Twelve-Day War of Independence in February 1966. After democracy returned to the Nigerian political space in 1999, the massive corruption of the military regimes had already led to a calamitous national economy and the ongoing alienation of several groups within the state; the incoming government was expected to address several pressing issues.

A full-blown crisis was only partially averted when the new democratic government – headed by Olusegun Obasanjo, who was a former military leader – attempted to address the issues on ground. Instead of resolving the problems, they were postponed by continuously issuing threats, deploying soldiers, and making empty promises to the people and their communities. In a rentier state under a dictatorial military regime, the opportunities for patronage payouts are more limited than in a state operating as a democracy. With the advent of the fourth republic in 1999, political gladiators came out of hibernation to regroup, build alliances, and position themselves for the

---

[46] Ken Saro-Wiwa, quoted in Elias Courson, *Movement for the Emancipation of the Niger Delta*, 10.

[47] Scholars have compared the situation in the Niger Delta with the colonial–native exploitation model, in which the wealth of one community is used to feed and develop another, leaving the producing communities impoverished. Cf. Ben Naanen, "Oil-Producing Minorities and the Restructuring of Nigerian Federalism: The Case of the Ogoni People," *Journal of Commonwealth and Comparative Politics* 33, no.1 (1995): 46–78.

[48] Ibid.

opportunities ahead.[49] Several militants and cult groups in the Niger Delta and elsewhere also took part in this "trade."[50] In the Niger Delta area specifically, state control by political parties meant control of the economic engine room. Many ethnic groups engaged in extortion, execution, and the localization of politics in their respective areas with varying degrees of intensity. Political elites forged alliances with groups that encouraged assassination, vandalism, illegal oil bunkering, intimidation of political opponents, and other lethal activities.

Nigerian military battalions have been marched to the creeks on several occasions,[51] and groups like MEND built up expertise, networks, and resources to organize and stage their attacks as a form of protest. The proliferation of weapons was largely due to the state's haphazard democratization, particularly in the Niger Delta region, which saw the emergence of violent conflicts shortly after the inauguration of the new government. The issue of arms proliferation had been experienced in other parts of the country, but the situation was more manageable in places of less strategic interest where oil politics were less influential.

The federal government's incarceration of Ijo leaders, perceived as an attempt to control the soul of the region through intraparty and interparty rivalry and competition, encouraged the fusion of different militia groups in the Niger Delta.[52] Issues reached a peak in the run up to the 2003 general elections – in March, just one month before the polls, violent conflict broke out between ethnic militias in the region. Fifty deaths were recorded and eight communities in and around the Warri petroleum complex were leveled to the ground. Staff and expatriates working for major oil companies in the area were evacuated. Oil operations were shut down and output reduced by more than 750,000 barrels per day, almost half of the national output.[53] Kenneth Amaeshi put the Niger Delta situation into a historical context:

---

[49] Kenneth Omeje, "The State, Conflict & Evolving Politics in the Niger Delta, Nigeria," *Review of African Political Economy* 31, no. 101 (2004): 426.

[50] The Environmental Rights Action described the period around the 2003 general elections as "a low intensity armed struggle." See Environmental Rights Action/Friends of the Earth, quoted in Courson, *Movement for the Emancipation of the Niger Delta*, 16.

[51] The Odi ground invasion of 1999, the Odioma massacre of 2005, and the Agge saga of 2008 are some of the many military assaults on protesting communities in the Niger Delta. Cf. Omeje, "The State, Conflict & Evolving Politics," 429–435.

[52] Ebitimi Banigo, an Ijo businessman, was targeted toward the end of 2005 and arrested by the Nigerian government; D. S. P. Alamieyeseigha, the governor of Bayelsa State, and Asari-Dokubo, NDPVF leader, were also arrested for money laundering and treason. Every security outfit in the country was deployed to crush agitations and protests against MNOCs, allegedly to protect pipeline installations and other oil facilities in the area.

[53] Oronto Douglas et al., "Oil and Militancy in the Niger Delta: Terrorist Threat or Another Colombia?" Niger Delta Economies of Violence Working Papers, Institute of International Studies, University of California, Berkeley, USA; The United States

Figure 12.1 A group of female demonstrators protesting environmental degradation due to oil spillage and pollution.

These large companies (i.e., the MNCs and their indigenous colleagues), together with the UAC, were as ruthlessly competitive as the local towns themselves and frequently engaged force to compel local trading partners to comply with the terms of exchange. Occasionally, however, the slave raiding instinct prevailed and these merchants resorted to outright banditry. In other words, banditry characterized the initial strategy of colonial firms in their dealings with the indigenous people of Nigeria. The case of the Niger Delta versus the Nigerian State and foreign oil corporations, therefore, has a rich historical antecedent.[54]

The situation is complicated by the state constitution, which provides legal backing for MNC activities in the area. The ambiguity and inadequacy of the Nigerian Constitution cannot protect the interests of its communities when dealing with either multinational or domestic corporations. The laws governing companies in Nigeria establish them as private actors; they only need to serve the interests of their shareholders, regardless of their effects on their host communities.[55] The more that these

Institute of Peace, Washington DC, USA, and Our Niger Delta, Port Harcourt, Nigeria, no. 4 (2004), 16.
[54] Kenneth M. Amaeshi, Bongo C. Adi et al., "Corporate Social Responsibility in Nigeria: Western Mimicry or Indigenous Influences?" *The Journal of Corporate Citizenship*, no. 24 (2006): 86.
[55] Ibid.

companies degrade their host communities, the more they can maximize profit to satisfy the greed of shareholders and the state. The matter is intensified by the dynamics of doing business in Nigeria. The National Economic Empowerment and Development Strategy noted that:

Businesses wishing to operate in Nigeria face many constraints, including poor infrastructure, particularly road networks and electricity supply; inadequate physical security; corruption; weak enforcement of contracts, and the high cost of finance. These factors have deterred foreign entrepreneurs from investing in Nigeria and induced many Nigerians to take their money and skills abroad.[56]

Companies operating within an entity such as Nigeria are empowered by the state authorities' indifference to constitutional obligations. These organizations assume the role of almighty entities within the state, prioritizing their own survival in an arena where the government has failed to provide any support.

Recognizing its own failings, the state competes with companies to exploit the area's major stakeholders – the people who must endure the brunt of harmful "externalities" that companies impose on the land, water, and air. Public and private organizations continuously reward shareholders at the expense of stakeholders. This marginalization, exploitation, and degradation did not stop with the pollution of the environment; it also involved confiscating the scarce arable land that remained along with the destruction of crops and plants. Agitation for control of the region's wealth, and adequate reparations for the region's people, became the focus of those who engaged in violent guerilla tactics.

Before the eventual emergence of the MEND, ethnic Ijo militants had forced several oil companies in the region to shut down operations. Oil production in Nigeria had declined by 40 percent ahead of the 2003 elections, and the government's response was to increase its military presence in the Delta region.[57] The MEND formed in 2005, when the region had already become a place where the state nurtured violent conflict.

The MEND was a resurgence of longtime grievances and discontent. Previous resistance to the rentier state's oppression, fighting the alliance between state and multinational corporations, involved a mix of peaceful and violent protests. Two examples were the 59-man Niger Delta Volunteer Force (NDVF), led by Isaac Adaka Boro, and the "resistance-

[56] National Economic Empowerment and Development Strategy (NEEDS), Nigerian National Planning Commission, Abuja, 2005, xv.
[57] *Reuters*, "FactBox-Facts on Nigerian Militant Group MEND," *Reuters*, July 23, 2008, www.reuters.com/article/nigeria-delta-militants/factbox-facts-on-nigerian-militant-group-mend-idUSL23100520320080723.

pen, letters and speeches" of Ken Saro-Wiwa and his eight comrades.[58] The MEND learned from and improved on these struggles, particularly their militant tactics. The movement's cluster of leadership drew from oil-rich communities across the Niger Delta area, which made it difficult for the state to target any individual as the group's leader. The MEND intensified their agitation with attacks at different strategic oil properties, with different commanders carrying out actions for a single body. The movement's collective strategies, aims, and goals were projected to the Nigerian government, and the MNOCs in particular, through a single channel.[59]

The MEND focused on the Nigerian oil industry, whose operations could be disrupted with a minimum of human casualties when compared to other encounters with militant groups. Local oil workers and expatriates were taken as hostages, primarily for funding, and the group's coordinated efforts slowed the exploration, production, and transportation of oil. They also engaged in oil bunkering to secure foreign currency that could build their arsenal.[60] It was a local resistance that affected the global space, due to its adverse impact on the world's supply of crude oil. A man known as Jomo Gbomo was the group's spokesman, claiming responsibility for attacks and issuing other statements. Known members of the cells that made up the MEND were Asari Dokubo, Ateke Tom, Government Ekpemupolo, Charles Okah, and Henry Okah. The fluid structure of the group allowed these cells to stage attacks without being aware of each other's activities.

Several oil companies, including Chevron, ExxonMobil, and Agip, suffered varying degrees of losses due to the MEND militants. The Royal Dutch Petroleum Development Company was hit the hardest, probably because it was the biggest player in Nigeria's oil politics. The militant group announced its modus operandi to the Nigerian state, the MNOCs, and the world with an initial attack that targeted two pipeline facilities belonging to the Royal Dutch Petroleum Development Company in the creeks of Rivers State at the Okrika and Andoni axis in a November/December 2005 incident. On January 11, 2006, the group

---

[58] See T. Tebekaemi, cd., *The Twelve-Day Revolution* (Benin: Umeh Publishers, 1982); Mbah, "Is It Always the Economic Stupid?" 3.

[59] Kimiebi Imomotimi Ebienfa, "Oil, Militancy and Political Opportunities in the Niger Delta," PhD. thesis, University of Ibadan, 2010, 10.

[60] Their activities can be summarized by a statement credited to the Amnesty program's presidential adviser during his interview with the BBC in 2009. Mr. Timi Alabi is quoted saying, "Until now, they have lived in militant camps, carrying out kidnappings, blowing up oil pipelines and stealing massive amounts of crude oil." Caroline Duffield, "Will Amnesty Bring Peace to Niger Delta?" October 5, 2009, http://news.bbc.co.uk/2/hi/afri ca/8291336.stm.

followed up with devastating damage inflicted on an oilfield located about 20 km off shore. In this attack, four expatriates who worked for the company were abducted by militants after a fierce gun battle with Nigerian military forces that guarded the oil-field.[61] Four days later, the group chose to attack Benisede's Shell Petroleum facility in Bayelsa state.

The attacks were an embarrassment to the federal government and its security echelons. In retaliation, communities sympathetic to the struggle were targeted and attacked by Nigerian Army and Air Force soldiers in February 2006, killing twenty residents and destroying properties around Gbamaturu kingdom less than a month after the Benisede incident. The Nigerian government and the MNOCs, with logistical support from foreign countries, increased their military presence in the area. Militants struck back a few days later, on February 18, to show their commitment to halting oil activities. They attacked the Forcados oil export terminal and took nine expatriate hostages.[62]

On April 20, 2006, the MEND detonated bombs at Port Harcourt's Bori camp military barracks and at a petrol tanker garage in the city. The group's shift away from attacking oil installations was well received by the Nigerian government and their oil-thirsty partners. Following the attacks, the government established Council on Social and Economic Development of Coastal States (COSEDECS) in 2006. The committee was responsible for ensuring peace in the region through dialogue with stakeholders; the government had previously considered this approach to be weak and unnecessary. The committee was meant to fail, and it collapsed within months due to mutual suspicion and mistrust. The people of Niger Delta, particularly the Ijo, refused to consent to the council's formation and working model. The government had proposed recruiting Niger Delta youths into the Nigerian army as part of the measures to enhance the committee's work toward peace, but it soon resulted in military engagement when fifteen Ijo were ambushed and murdered by government forces on their way back from Letugbene on August 20, 2006.[63]

On June 5, 2000, the government created the Niger Delta Development Commission (NDDC) to monitor and implement federal government

[61] *World Security Network*, "Intelligence Brief: M.E.N.D. Escalates Instability in Nigeria," *World Security Network*, April 27, 2006, www.worldsecuritynetwork.com/Africa/no_author/Intelligence-Brief-M.E.N.D.-Escalates-Instability-in-Nigeria.
[62] Mikhail Kashubsky, "A Chronology of Attacks on and Unlawful Interferences with Offshore Oil and Gas Installations, 1975–2010, Perspective on Terrorism," 5, no. 5–6 (2011), www.terrorismanalysts.com/pt/index.php/pot/article/view/offshore-gas-and-oil-attacks/html.
[63] The attack was staged by the Nigerian military after the release of Shell hostages held by the MEND.

projects and programs meant to ensure lasting peace. In reality, the problem was never a lack of government agencies, but a lack of effectiveness in a state where institutions are mired in politics. One can only wonder what the COSEDECS was meant to achieve apart from the NDDC, other than proliferating the state's prebendal network. The government's hypocrisy and policy inconsistency, simultaneously pursuing diplomatic and military solutions to stabilize the area, was further undermined by corruption among those heading the NDDC.

Average citizens of the Niger Delta had little or no hope. Many scholars have described the MEND as a child of necessity,[64] and people in the area who supported the militant struggle agreed with the group's goals. Although there was danger posed by the actions of the MEND and its militias, they saw it as a risk worth taking to protect their environment – nothing suggested that their state and corporate oppressors would do any less damage to their lands.

Because the people had nothing else to protect, the further degradation of their own environment was a sign of frustration and hopelessness, and a necessity to transmit their grievances. When Jasper Adaka Boro was addressing his men in 1966, charging them to fight for the independence of the Niger Delta, he said:

Let us examine with some latitude whether the state of development is to any extent commensurate with a tint of the bulk of already tapped mineral and agricultural resources ... Therefore, remember your seventy-year-old grandmother who still farms before she eats; remember also your poverty stricken people; remember too your petroleum which is being pumped out daily from your veins, and then fight for your freedom.[65]

These words remain an example of the length to which people would go to resist state and corporate domination. Ibaba has written that "MEND took a total of 119 hostages between 2006 and 2008, while 300 deaths were recorded in the course of attacks."[66] Such deaths were mainly those of the military engaging the militants in combat – the civilian losses could be described by the military as collateral damage. Several studies have emphasized, to the Federal Government of Nigeria and to the world, that

---

[64] This analogy is premised on the failure of all peaceful avenues for demanding environmental rights and opposing the militarization of the process by successive Nigerian governments (military and civilian alike). See, among many others, Shadi Bushra, "Nigeria Wages War for Its Own Oil," originally published in *The Stanford Progressive*, 2009, www.worldsecuritynetwork.com/Africa/no_author/Intelligence-Brief-M.E.N.D.-Escalates-Instability-in-Nigeria.

[65] Tebekaemi, *The Twelve-Day Revolution*, 116.

[66] Ibaba Samuel Ibaba, "Terrorism in Liberation Struggles: Interrogating the Engagement Tactics of the Movement for the Emancipation of the Niger Delta," *Perspectives on Terrorism* 5, no. 3–4 (2011).

rising insecurity in the Niger Delta area and government corruption have
allowed it to become a breeding ground for terrorism and violent acts in
the region.[67] After the government's reelection in 2003, several concerned organizations noted the danger of instability in the region, including the Centre for Strategic and International Studies in the United
States.[68] As usual, the warnings were mere reports to a government that
decided to criminalize the agitation and militarize the whole region as if it
were an enemy state.

The government's non-military response was to form a shoddy committee to execute the predetermined agenda of corporations and the state.
The various reports about turbulence in the Niger Delta region were
reviewed with imperial profit-making calculations and anxiety over the
global oil supply chain. Nigeria holds a strategic position in the global oil
market as the sixth largest exporter of oil in the world, holding the largest
oil deposits in Africa. The country has a stake in Western oil consumption, especially in America, which was importing 14 percent of its petroleum from the country at the time.[69] Aaron noted that Nigeria holds
20 billion of Africa's 66 billion barrels of oil reserves and more than 3
trillion cubic meters of gas reserves.[70]

Nigeria became more important to the industrialized (and industrializ-
ing) nations of the world in the post-9/11 politics that reconfigured
international security and the global oil supply chain. Nigeria and other
West African oil-producing states were referred to as the New Gulf Oil
States. As increasing global industrialization made crude oil the nucleus
of industrial outputs, several militant groups merged, including cult
groups in the Niger Delta area, which was significant for Nigeria's oil
politics. Their united forces attacked oil facilities that had been touted as
beyond the militants' reach. After the Obasanjo administration's failed
attempt at a third term in office, the government changed its approach.

In 2007, the new Yar'Adua/Jonathan administration attempted
a peaceful resolution to the crisis by releasing Asari-Dokubo and DSP
Alamieyeseigha, which was a landmark concession to one of the group's

[67] The Center for Strategic and International Studies in Washington, DC, issued a policy
brief titled "Alienation and Militancy in Nigeria's Niger Delta," which discussed the
"... more profound national challenges that are now facing the re-elected President
Obasanjo and his government. In their view, the recent conflicts in the Delta mark
a watershed, distinguished in particular by the prospects of an upward spiral of violence."
Douglas et al., "Oil And Militancy," 2; Similar warnings were included in the US
Department of State report in 2000, www.state.gov/s/ct/rls/pgtrpt/2000, and the CIA
report of the same year, www.eia.gov/emeu/cabs/nigeria.html.
[68] Ibid.   [69] See Douglas et al., "Oil and Militancy in the Niger Delta," 3.
[70] K. K. Aaron, "Perspective: Big Oil, Rural Poverty, and Environmental Degradation in
the Niger Delta Region of Nigeria," *Journal of Agriculture Safety and Health* 11, no. 2
(2005): 127.

major demands. Asari-Dokubo was a leader of the militant group, and Alamieyeseigha was a former governor of Bayelsa, a tiny state in the Niger Delta area with large oil deposits. Alamieyeseigha had been accused of corruption by the Obasanjo government as part of its war efforts.

Alamieyeseigha cannot be considered innocent of the charges, but in Nigeria's political climate the proceedings were seen as a victimization of not only the man but also the Niger Delta people, whose land produced the wealth he allegedly misappropriated: he was seen as one of the Niger Delta supporters persecuted by the federal government. The Alamieyeseigha case is symptomatic of Nigeria's consociationalism: corruption and incompetence are legitimized and recast as the actions of someone supporting a cultural or religious group and supposedly representing them in the consociation. Due to the mutual suspicion infesting the country's political space and the continuous efforts to prevent ordinary citizens from exerting any power, cultural and religious groups rally around their chosen representatives regardless of the cost to the larger polity. This not only promotes mediocrity and ignorance, but it also leads to the sycophancy that maintains the status quo and prevents meaningful reforms.

In Nigeria's government, mutual suspicion is justifiable. The organization that allegedly fights the war against corruption is heavily politicized, and the decisions to investigate and prosecute cases are made by an appointee of the president. In many cases, the Senate is merely a rubber stamp for executive appointments; candidates know how to play their political game. The anti-corruption body, like others created during Obasanjo's administration, is seen as an extension of the patronage system, regardless of whether its actions are legitimate.

The peace process between the federal government and the militants continued until Henry Okah – one of the militia leaders who had formed the MEND – was arrested, detained, and repatriated from Angola, where he was reportedly involved in gun running.[71] This was a major setback for peace in the Niger Delta. The militants soon resumed attacks on oil facilities and installations, demanding Henry Okah's release along with their previous demands for resource control and a cleanup of the Niger Delta's environment. The group staged attacks on Shell's facility at the Bonga oil platform on June 20, 2008, under the codenames Hurricane Barbarosa and Hurricane Obama. This was a coordinated attack by the MEND naval forces, shutting down 10 percent of Nigeria's daily oil production in a single strike, and deadlier than the attacks of November–December 2005.

---

[71] Estelle Shirbon, "Nigerian Rebels Say Leader Extradited from Angola," *Reuters*, February 15, 2008, www.reuters.com/article/idUSL151538.

Shell oil authorities revealed the extent of the damage when they announced that they were shutting down one of their main offshore facilities in Nigeria.[72] This was a flagship oil facility, located about 120 km off shore, in an area considered to be fortified. The attack also involved the abduction of an American expatriate.[73] With diplomacy falling apart between the two parties, the Yar'Adua administration returned to the previous government's inconsistent policies of diplomacy and force. The Ministry of Niger Delta was created for the development of the Niger Delta, and the NDDC was to be a parastatal. In the early months of 2009, the federal government sent three battalions of the Nigerian army to Rivers, Bayelsa, and Delta states, reinforced by twenty-four gunboats and four jet fighters.[74]

At this time, the government began to identify key components of the MEND. The battle for the soul of the Niger Delta targeted Government Oweizide Ekpemupolo, popularly known as Tompolo, at his shielded Gbamaturu kingdom. Other targets included Kurutie, Oporoza, Okerenkoko, Goba, Abiteye Beniku-rukuru, and Kunukunuma,.[75] Within a month, rapid retaliation from the militants had reduced oil production in the Nigerian state from 2.6 million barrels to 1.8 million barrels.[76] This established that militant forces were well trained, funded, inspired, and more familiar with the local terrain than the Nigerian military. The attack roused the international community – mostly because the greedy MNC agents of industrialized countries hoped that the government's military tactics could restore their business interests.

The Nigerian government was pressured to find a lasting solution to the crisis. In June 2009, the Yar'Adua government recalibrated to pursue peaceful diplomacy in the Niger Delta with specific goals: restore the flow of oil in the Niger Delta, continue the business of exploitation as usual, and stabilize the national economy. Negotiations released Henry Okah from prison, and the federal government declared amnesty for militants

---

[72] *BBC*, "Nigerian Attack Closes Oilfield," *BBC*, June 20, 2008, http://news.bbc.co.uk/2/hi/africa/7463288.stm.
[73] The Nigerian Navy had confirmed the abduction of an American oil expatriate, who was released hours later, from a vessel in the path of the returning militants. Ibid.
[74] Elias Courson, *Movement for the Emancipation of the Niger Delta*, 23.
[75] The details of the havoc wreaked by the Nigerian Military is well documented by many scholars and reputable media outlets. It involved the destruction of a palace at Oporonza, hotels, and other properties in an attack corresponding with a holiday in the kingdom. Cf. *Sahara Reporters*, "Femi Falana Sues Yar'adua on Behalf of Indigenes of Gbaramatu Kingdom," *Sahara Reporters*, June 22, 2009, http://saharareporters.com/2009/06/22/femi-falana-sues-yaradua-behalf-indigenes-gbaramatu-kingdom.
[76] Nick Tattersall, "Nigerian Rebels Hit Shell Site Despite Amnesty," *Mail and Guardian*, June 26, 2009, https://mg.co.za/article/2009-06-26-nigerian-rebels-hit-shell-site-despite-amnesty.

who put down their weapons and promised to reintegrate into their communities.[77] This was followed by a sixty-day ceasefire allowing the program to be implemented. Although the government had wanted to follow this path earlier, the MNOCs and their home countries would not have supported such an initiative. The amnesty program became a way for the government to expand its patronage system in the Niger Delta beyond the elites in the region. As before, symptoms were addressed without affecting the disease.

MNOCs were encouraged to resume business as usual in the Niger Delta region without reforming their activities. The status quo for oil exploitation and the archaic, incoherent Business Act Laws were upheld, leading the state-supervised palliatives to become as riddled with corruption as the rest of Nigeria's government.[78] Regulatory bodies with the responsibility of overseeing MNOC activities and addressing the region's challenges quickly became politicized. As the disease festered, armed conflict between Niger Delta militants and the Nigerian Armed Forces remained on the radar of state oil politics. The MEND has been disbanded through the amnesty program, but other militant organizations remain, and the narrative propelling violence has remained unchanged. Groups have threatened and carried out coordinated attacks on Nigerian oil facilities, affecting oil production and national revenue. Since the relative success of the MEND, and the life-transforming deals secured by its leaders – they became some of the richest and most influential individuals in the region – the threat of violence has become the preferred medium for communication between aggrieved youths and the Nigerian government.[79]

Protests that oppose MNOC activities and the Nigerian government's alleged marginalization of the people have been organized through

---

[77] Daniel Idonor, "Yar'Adua Grants Militants Unconditional Amnesty ... Frees Henry Okah," *Vanguard*, June 25, 2009, www.vanguardngr.com/2009/06/yaradua-grants-militants-unconditional-amnestyfrees-henry-okah/.

[78] Government ministries, managements, and directorates responsible for the well-being of the Delta have been enmeshed in several corruption scandals. See *Punch News*, "Students Protest, Say NDDC Is Not Functioning in Bayelsa," *Punch News*, September 15, 2017, http://punchng.com/students-protest-say-nddc-is-not-functioning-in-bayelsa/; *Sahara Reporters*, "Six Years of Waste: How Niger Delta Ministry Blew N800b between 2009 and 2015," *Sahara Reporters*, http://saharareporters.com/2016/08/23/six-years-waste-how-niger-delta-ministry-blew-n800b-between-2009-and-2015; *AllAfrica*, "Nigeria: Save Niger Delta Ministry from Corruption," *AllAfrica*, September 2, 2016, http://alla frica.com/stories/201609020657.html.

[79] See, for instance, Friday Amobi, "Rivers Communities Shut Oil Well, Protest Abandonment," *Punch*, September 14, 2017, http://punch.com/rivers-communities-shut-oil-well-protest-abandonment; Rosaline Okere, "Oil Production Dips to 1.3mbd over Vandalism, Says NNPC," *Guardian*, September 14, 2017, https://m.guardian.ng/news/oil-production-dips-to-1-3mbd-over-vandalism-says-nnpc/.

peaceful, diplomatic means. However, the violent engagements of the Niger Delta's youths have been more effective at provoking a response. The militants' opinions of the amnesty program were not lost on the government. The BBC, in its report on the launching of the program, quoted militant leader Farah Dagogo as saying "there are still thousands of people willing to continue fighting in the creeks." Bonny Gaeei, another leading figure, outlined his opinion of the arrangement: "Let them do as they say. If they don't? Then, I will bust pipelines again."[80]

Economic sabotage, carried out against the oil pipeline networks in the Niger Delta, has never ceased. It has become a standard activity for militant youths in the region, just as cash or crude deals have characterized the government's quick-fix responses. This pendulum swings across a shallow political terrain. However, the amnesty program is a functional method for responding to Niger Delta agitations; it promotes peace in the region and boosts the national economy, creating space for economic diversification. Training programs for youths, in what one could call life after camp, are constructive for their reorientation. However, their newfound sense of responsibility is quickly abandoned when there is cause to carry a gun or sponsor new attacks on pipelines.

Instabilities in the Niger Delta call for true constitutionalism and sincere dialogue with stakeholders in the region. The people should not be denied their natural and primordial connections to the territory where they have been situated for ages, and from the experience so far, an extension of the patronage system is not and cannot be the long-term answer. The shareholders who exercise influence over the Nigerian oil industry must recognize their humanity and stop the ongoing cycle of poverty and violence in the Niger Delta area. Their influence is needed when we consider the ambiguity, incoherence, and chameleonic aesthetic of the principles in the country's 1999 constitution.[81] Nigeria is a country with many complexities, and it is common sense for the government to engage these complexities in their various forms – it is an opportunity to support equality, unity, and purpose to enhance humanity, human production, and human dignity.

The first duty of any corporation should be the safety of its host community. A rentier state will ignore that duty in favor of helping MNOCs maximize their profits, from which the political elites are paid. The consistent "divide-and-rule" approach, which has marked Nigerian

---

[80] Duffield, "Will Amnesty Bring Peace to Niger Delta?"
[81] Among many works on this, see Godwin N. Okeke, "The Ambivalence of the 1999 Nigerian Constitution in Matters Relating to Secularism: A Case for a Constitutional Review," *International Journal of Humanities and Social Science Invention* 2, no. 3 (2013): 65–69.

politics since the colonial days, will not help construct a viable nationhood for the country. It will only increase the rapid deterioration of societies and human development that is detrimental to the nation-building process.

Conclusion

Nigeria, like Venezuela and other oil-dependent states, is at the mercy of the powerful oil-broker states such as Saudi Arabia, Russia, and the United States. As long as the country depends on oil, these nations can take action on the global stage to affect the supposedly sovereign state of Nigeria; their decisions can make or break the long- and short-term policies and plans of the government. The dependency has created a rentier state in which all problems are resolved through a patronage network funded by crude oil. Maintaining this network and diversifying the country's economy are opposing goals. The latter has always been the sacrificial lamb, which explains the failure of manufacturing, textile, steel, and other industries in Nigeria. At the microeconomic level, agriculture and small- and medium-scale enterprises (SMEs) have been placed on hold so that the state can expand its patronage network. It is too early to assess the impact of the Buhari administration's efforts to diversify the economy with agriculture and other industries.

Nigeria's current government institutions are avenues that enable the flow of illicit wealth and unbridled power to the political elites. The longer the state remains in a quagmire of uncertainty – driving away meaningful progress, such as equality for all and greater opportunities for human development – the more this small number of elites garners strength and remains influential in the polity. Maintaining Nigeria's socioeconomic and political status quo means increasing the wealth and influence of the power brokers, compradors, and political elites in the country. A seismic shift is required in the state's sociopolitical calibration to stem the tide that is drowning individual and collective efforts to change the economic realities and social narratives that are weighing down the region.

The MEND is only a microcosm of how individuals and groups have been engaging with the system, demanding big changes in the polity. Regardless of whether they are made through violent or diplomatic channels, these demands have always been considered a threat to the status quo, and they are treated as such. After the state's instruments of force are applied, a dramatic charade pretends to remedy the issue at hand. This approach has seen remarkable success in state relations and negotiations between different entities in the country, including academia. This approach will remain the hallmark of Nigeria's democratic practice for as long as these entities are comfortable accepting their existence in a patronage system. Instead of "sharing the national cake," they must stand firm and demand more opportunities for individuals to contribute and create a larger cake – although that would require the state to do things differently.

13   Environment and Sustainable Development

> ... development that meets the needs of the present without comprom-
> ising the ability of future generation to meet their own needs.
>
> – Brundtland Report, 1987[1]

Introduction

The opening epigraph supplies a consensus definition agreed to by many
countries on what sustainable development means, relating human progress to how people also relate to nature.[2] Sustainable economic development is often touted as a key principle of a modernized national economy.
For many developing countries, however, the quest for a modernized
economy is self-sabotaging and ends up damaging the progress it seeks
to obtain. With the notable example of the oil industry in the Niger Delta,
large-scale industrial projects in such nations have endangered millions of
lives and neglected to manage the environmental crises that emerge as
a result of their rush to obtain capital. In its attempt to seek economic
modernization, Nigeria has faced issues of resource depletion, environmental degradation, and highly unbalanced wealth distribution.

This gulf between economic development and responsible environmental principles is all too common, and points to larger failures in
reconciling the need for economic development and modernization with
interwoven environmental, organizational, and cultural concerns that are
often trampled underfoot by irresponsible business practices. Nigeria has
neglected these concerns, compromising the well-being of both present
and future generations of its citizens. Speaking on May 29, 2015, at his
inauguration, President Muhammadu Buhari of Nigeria readily admitted
the nation's failure in this regard:

---

[1] World Commission on Environment and Development. *Our Common Future: Report of the
World Commission on Environment and Development* (Oxford: Oxford University, 1987), 43.
[2] Part of this paper was presented as a Keynote Address at a conference on sustainable
development, Ladoke Akintola University, Ogbomoso, Nigeria. The Keynote was widely
reported by the media, with excerpts appearing in a number of newspapers.

My appeal for unity is predicated on the seriousness of the legacy we are getting into. With depleted foreign reserves, falling oil prices, leakages and debts the Nigerian economy is in deep trouble and will require careful management to bring it round and to tackle the immediate challenges confronting us, namely; Boko Haram, the Niger Delta situation, the power shortages and unemployment especially among young people. For the longer term we have to improve the standards of our education. We have to look at the whole field of medicare. We have to upgrade our dilapidated physical infrastructure.[3]

While President Buhari's speech points to a mismanagement of Nigerian domestic policy and economic concerns, it would be untrue to make the sweeping generalization that the government has completely neglected efforts to formulate and implement policies toward sustainable economic development modernization. Since the 1950s, the Nigerian government has made extensive political promises, held conferences to discuss national issues, and tried implementing policies aimed at improving the lot of its citizens, with mixed results. In spite of these efforts, the largest economy in Africa remains one of the world's poorest nations.[4] On the bright side, Nigeria overtook South Africa as the largest economy on the continent in 2014, becoming the twenty-sixth largest in the world with a growth rate of 7 percent per annum. Its GDP was valued at $510 billion in 2015, seemingly an indicator of successful economic development and prosperity for the entire nation.

In reality, bad politics, gross mismanagement, and corruption have stifled human development and sustainable economic progress. Nigeria is rated as one of the ten most corrupt governments of the world, crippling the likelihood for effective and sustainable policy.[5] Lackluster environmental policy in cities has resulted in hazardous levels of pollution and a lack of green spaces. Poverty is on the rise, sometimes afflicting up to 70 percent of the total population. Recent data indicates that around 50 percent of the population lives below the poverty line, 33 percent are

[3] President Muhammadu Buhari, "Inaugural Speech," *Vanguard*, May 29, 2015, www .vanguardngr.com/2015/05/read-president-buhari-inaugural-speech/.

[4] For some works on the Nigerian economy since independence, see, among others, Toyin Falola, *Economic Reforms and Modernization in Nigeria* (Kent: Kent State University Press, 2004); Charles Jarmon, *Nigeria: Reorganization and Development since the Mid-Twentieth Century* (Leiden: E. J. Brill, 1988); Jeremiah I. Dibua, *Modernization and the Crisis of Development in Africa: The Nigerian Experience* (Aldershot: Ashgate, 2006); K. Aaron Kiipoye and Dawari George, eds., *Placebo as Medicine: The Poverty of Development Intervention and Conflict Resolution Strategies in the Niger Delta Region of Nigeria* (Port Harcourt: Kemuela Publications, 2010); Nwafejoku Okolie Uwadibie, *Decentralization and Economic Development in Nigeria: Agricultural Policies and Implementation* (Lanham: University Press of America, 2000); and Tom Forrest, *Politics and Economic Development in Nigeria* (Boulder, Colorado: Westview Press, 1993).

[5] Ayodele Jimoh, *The Nigerian Governance and Corruption Survey* (Ilorin: University of Ilorin, 2004).

Figure 13.1 A small-scale village market where fresh farm produce is sold on a daily basis.

Figure 13.2 A young girl hawking solid pap (eko) wrapped in leaves for breakfast consumption.

in abject poverty, 85 percent of urban citizens live in over-crowded spaces, 40 percent of the population lacks access to clean water, and 60 percent of youths are unemployed. Nigerian politicians have not only shortchanged future generations through reckless disregard for the environment but have neglected the basic needs of the present generation by failing to sufficiently address widespread poverty and malnutrition.

Nigeria is part of the geographic space of underdevelopment, often termed the developing or underdeveloped world, or more generically as the Third World. Developing countries such as Nigeria continually face the dual challenges of political instability and economic underdevelopment, which obstruct the fulfillment of their citizens' basic human needs, the foundation upon which the modernization of society and enhancement of living standards is based.[6] Nigeria's economic progress in the 1970s and following decline in the 1980s demonstrate the elusiveness of sustainable growth for nations in its position and the struggle to create enduring policies that can sustain a sense of modernity.

In response to these challenges, the Nigerian government has throughout its history promoted a fabricated image of a stable and successful nation, massaging data and statistics that go against its carefully constructed narrative of prosperity. Since Nigeria attained independence in October 1960, this narrative has been consistently centered around covering up economic hardships, social injustice and inequality, massive corruption, military infractions, and the deaths of thousands resulting from poor living conditions and unchecked violence.

Moreover, the government has also struggled to create and maintain cohesive leadership driven by public service. Divisive religious and ethnic identities produce starkly conflicting viewpoints that have complicated the nation's fractured politics and collectively threaten its stability, resulting in politically and religiously motivated assassinations and internal violence such as the Biafran War and repeated campaigns of terror by groups such as Boko Haram. The government must deal with political disparity and insurgency on a near-daily basis, creating a nationwide sense of uncertainty and despair.

To combat this despair, the Nigerian government has repeatedly attempted to engender hope in the populace by creating plans of action codified within the template of sustainable development. The Nigerian Constitution even specifies the protection of the environment as a special concern in Article 20: "The state shall protect and improve the environment

---

[6] T. M. Yesufu, *The Human Factor in National Development: Nigeria* (Ibadan: Spectrum Books, 2000); and Volker Treichel, *Putting Nigeria to Work a Strategy for Employment and Growth* (Washington, DC: World Bank, 2010).

and safeguard the water, air and land, forest and wildlife of Nigeria."[7] By paying lip service to constitutional principles and providing data on the expansion of agricultural, industrial and service sectors, the increasing number of universities, and reduction of rates of illiteracy, governments such as Nigeria's obfuscate the gravity of national issues. To the contrary, news media, critics and analysts continue to point to poverty, authoritarian leadership, and corruption as participants in a tug-of-war over truth.

The Global Dimensions

A brief history of sustainable development as a concept is necessary, if only to stress why the environment became its central platform, and how it has become both a national and a global concern. In practice, it has existed for over two decades. A report by the World Commission on Environment and Development published in 1987, titled *Our Common Future*, argued that governments can improve the standard of living of their people, boost relations between countries, and meet their current needs without compromising the abilities and needs of future generations to also benefit from the environment.[8] The report, now known as the Brundtland Commission Report, touches upon poverty, gender inequality, human rights, local economies, agriculture, industry, health care, global economics, and environmental concerns such as climate change.

As a follow-up to the 1987 report, the United Nations in 1992 convened the Earth Summit, comprising 116 heads of state or governments in attendance, 8,000 official delegates, and representatives from the private sector, who gathered to discuss the key issues in Our Common Future. The question of globalizing the concept of sustainable development and making it both a national and a global priority was the main concern of both the Earth Summit and later the Rio+20 Summit in 2012. In both summits, delegates discussed strategies to overcome poverty, reduce unemployment, and fight pollution. The formulation of the Millennium Development Goals (MDGs) in 2000 also highlighted criteria for sustainable development that included gender equality, eradication of poverty and hunger, primary education, reduction of child mortality and maternal health, control of disease, and environmental sustainability.[9]

---

[7] World Intellectual Property Organization, *Nigeria: Constitution of the Federal Republic of Nigeria (Third Alteration) Act of February 22, 2011*, www.wipo.int/edocs/lexdocs/laws/en/ng/ng042en.pdf.

[8] World Commission on Environment and Development, *Our Common Future* (Oxford: Oxford University Press 1987).

[9] Robert Maduand and Shedrack Chinwuba Moguluwa, "Will the Social Media Lenses Be the Framework for Sustainable Development in Rural Nigeria?" *Journal of African Media Studies* 5, no. 2 (2013): 237–254; and Barnes Anger, "Poverty Eradication, Millennium

These summits indicate that the ideals of sustainable development have a global dimension, including the shared idea that nations must show solidarity on issues such as economic growth, poverty, global interaction between nations, and social inequality. This global dimension finds expression in Jeffrey Sachs' definition: "As an intellectual pursuit, sustainable development tries to make sense of the interactions of three complex systems: the world economy, the global society, and the Earth's physical environment."[10] To Sachs, there are normative, ethical issues at stake:

[S]ustainable development calls for a world in which economic progress is widespread; extreme poverty is eliminated; social trust is encouraged through policies that strengthen the community; and the environment is protected from human-induced degradation ... .To achieve the economic, social, and environmental objectives of the SDGs (that is, Social Development Goals), a fourth objective must also be achieved: good governance.[11]

At the 2002 UN World Summit on Sustainable Development held in Johannesburg, over a hundred heads of state and their officials worked together with many NGOs to draft clear-cut expectations for every nation's role in promoting sustainable development. The declarations that delegates signed stated the following:

1. We recognize that poverty eradication, changing consumption and production patterns, and protecting and managing the natural resource base for economic and social development are overarching objectives of, and essential requirements for, sustainable development.
2. The deep fault line that divides human society between the rich and the poor and the ever-increasing gap between the developed and developing worlds poses a major threat to global prosperity, security and stability.
3. The global environment continues to suffer. Loss of biodiversity continues, fish stocks continue to be depleted, desertification claims more and more fertile land, the adverse effects of climate change are already evident, natural disasters are more frequent and more devastating and developing countries more vulnerable, and air, water and marine pollution continue to rob millions of a decent life.
4. Globalization has added a new dimension to these challenges. The rapid integration of markets, mobility of capital and significant

---

Development Goals and Sustainable Development in Nigeria," *Journal of Sustainable Development* 3, no. 4 (2010): 138–144.

[10] Jeffrey D. Sachs, *The Age of Sustainable Development* (New York: Columbia University Press, 2015), 3.

[11] Ibid.

increases in investment flows around the world have opened new challenges and opportunities for the pursuit of sustainable development. But the benefits and costs of globalization are unevenly distributed, with developing countries facing special difficulties in meeting this challenge.

5. We risk the entrenchment of these global disparities and unless we act in a manner that fundamentally changes their lives, the poor of the world may lose confidence in their representatives and the democratic systems to which we remain committed, seeing their representatives as nothing more than sounding brass or tinkling cymbals.[12]

Other prominent topics for scholars of sustainable development involve maximizing income, maintaining resilience in the ecosystem, and generating stability in social and cultural systems.[13] One particular area of concern is conflict over natural resources, including strategic minerals such as diamonds, gold, and timber that have been the basis for wars in Central Africa, Sierra Leone, and Liberia, as well as conflict over water use that affects the half of the world's population living within river basins. Four critical questions have developed on this subject:

1. Will the currently wealthy countries, and groups within them, be willing to reduce their consumption of the planet's resources and also be willing to reduce the environmental effects associated with the current use of resources?

2. What are the political, social, and economic mechanisms that could be used to facilitate these compromises?

3. Will these compromises have to be enforced by multilateral (UN) actions, or can they arise out of negotiated agreements among the wealthy countries themselves, or between the wealthy and the poor countries?

4. What is to be expected of the poor countries? To what extent will their economic growth be reduced by the need to compromise on the environment?[14]

---

[12] Quoted in Jennifer A. Elliott, *An Introduction to Sustainable Development*, 4th ed. (New York: Routledge, 2013).

[13] Mohan Munasinghe, "Global concerns are not misplaced and should be put in the context of increasing population, urbanization and pressure on resources. In anticipation of a population explosion, three scholars have posed a series of questions which have been summarized thus: Will we have sufficient natural resources for the survival of our burgeoning population throughout this century?; Will we have enough resources to enable the growing populations to live a wealthier and healthier lifestyle?; Even if we have sufficient basic resources will we be able to survive the environmental consequences of their use?" Environmental Economic and Sustainable Development, *World Bank Environment Paper No. 3* (Washington, DC: World Bank, 1993).

[14] Rogers, Jalal, and Boyd, *An Introduction to Sustainable Development*. New York: Earthscan, 2008, 380.

Discussions of sustainable development have not been without dissenting opinions over its importance and controversy. Peter P. Rogers, Kazi F. Jalal, and John A Boyd have grouped counterarguments by critics of sustainable development into four concise clusters[15]:

1. Future generations are likely to be much better off than the present generation ... This is primarily the contribution of modern technology ... Critics therefore conclude that the greatest favor that the present generation can make to the future is to establish peace and security on earth and the principles of human rights and democracy.

2. When any natural resources, be they fossil fuels, water, or any others, become scarce, economic forces come into play; such scarcity is always related to a certain price, existing technological expertise, and substitutes ... the world will not run out of natural resources.

3. The real state of the world is much better and healthier than many environmentalists claim.

4. Sustainable development can be damaging for the poor. Some critics believe that, on the pretext of promoting sustainable development and environmental protection, many rich countries are adapting protectionist policies by restricting imports of agriculture, forestry, fisheries, and other products from poor countries ... They believe that resources released by not adopting such precautionary principles could otherwise be utilized to satisfy the basic needs of the poor in developing countries.[16]

Literature on the subject of sustainable development has exploded, covering diverse subjects including doubts and hopes, expectations and failures, national and global challenges, transformation of rural areas, food supplies, livelihoods, ecotourism, organizing people in cities, using resources, reducing poverty, and creating peace.[17] As a result, Nigerian politicians, policy makers and scholars now have a substantial body of work from which to draw ideas that can aid them in meeting the needs and requirements of their nation.

---

[15] Among the most famous critics are Ester Boserup, *Population and Technological Change: A Study of Long-Term Trends* (Chicago: University of Chicago Press, 1981); Julian L. Simon, *The Ultimate Resource* (Princeton: Princeton University Press, 1981); and Wilfred Beckerman, *A Poverty of Reason: Sustainable Development and Economic Growth* (Oakland: The Independence Institute, 2003).

[16] Ibid., 382.

[17] Oft-cited works on these subjects include: Jeffrey D. Sachs, *The End of Poverty: Economic Possibilities for Our Time* (New York: Penguin, 2005); Elliot, *An Introduction to Sustainable Development*; Sachs, *The Age of Sustainable Development*; Stephen Wheeler and Timothy Beatley, *The Sustainable Urban Development Reader*, 3rd ed. (New York: Routledge, 2014); Martha Honey, *Ecotourism and Sustainable Development: Who Owns Paradise?* 2nd ed. (Washington: Island Press, 2008).

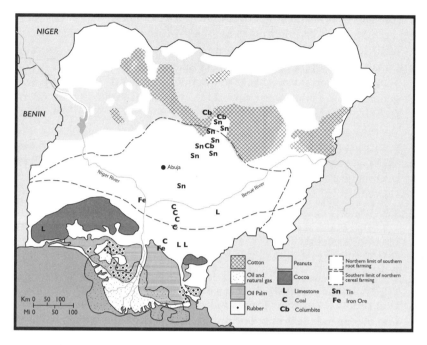

Map 13.1 Nigeria, natural resources.

The Nigerian Experience

As ideas of sustainable development gained worldwide visibility, different countries and regions began to envisage means of applying the ideas of sustainability to their own situations. To support that end, the United Nations held a conference devoted to Nigeria in 2012, and its conclusions were published in *Nigeria's Path to Sustainable Development through a Green Economy* later that year.[18] In his contribution to the book, President Goodluck Jonathan of Nigeria borrows from the typical presidential playbook by making impassioned promises to eradicate poverty, improve the nation's climate for investors, and contribute to economic growth. As a consequence of the conference, the Nigerian government accepted the conclusion that sustainable development was needed to fight

---

[18] Federal Government of Nigeria, *Nigeria's Path to Sustainable Development through Green Economy: Country Report to the Rio + 20 Summit* (Nigeria: Federal Government of Nigeria, June 2012), https://sustainabledevelopment.un.org/content/documents/1023nigeriana tionalreport.pdf.

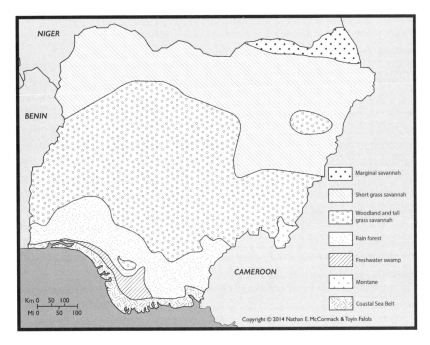

Map 13.2 Nigeria, vegetation.

environmental pollution, flooding, desertification, droughts, and the spread of diseases.

Nigeria affirmed its commitments to the United Nations by agreeing to the implementation of the framework of the Millennium Development Goals (MDGs) and by formulating the National Economic Empowerment and Development Strategy (NEEDS), a policy intended to eradicate poverty and subsequently implement policies supporting sustainable development.[19] Nigeria Vision 2020,[20] a major development policy paper, asserted that Nigeria has one of the fastest-developing economies and will reach a major economic milestone by the year 2020. This document also emphasized sustainable development, drawing ideas from *Our Common Future* (the Bruntland Report). Nigeria has passed various reforms in the last fifteen years, all presented as efforts to create

[19] Akintoye Victor Adejumo and Opeyemi Olubunmi Adejumo, "Prospects for Achieving Sustainable Development through the Millennium Development Goals in Nigeria," *European Journal of Sustainable Development* 3, no.1 (2014): 33–46.

[20] Federal Government, *Nigeria's Vision 2020: Economic Transformation Blueprint* (Abuja, 2009).

sustainable development: curbing petro-industrial influence on the overall economy, privatizing public enterprises, reforming civil service, and passing forestry legislation. Various federal and state agencies have been created to oversee environmental protection alongside the emergence of a number of NGOs and academic centers on university campuses.

Nevertheless, the practice of sustainable development in Nigeria has been paradoxical and complicated, with government agencies mired in controversies and corruption and little substantial evidence of progress resulting from new policies.[21] The Central Bank of Nigeria has attributed the failure of sustainable development to a deterioration in fiscal discipline, corruption, political instability, poor coordination, the absence of a comprehensive and consistent policy framework, excessive political interference, leakage of benefits to unintended beneficiaries, and an unregulated scope of programs which caused resources to be thinly spread across too many projects.[22] In spite of government commitment to sustainable development even at the highest level, optimistic predictions for Nigeria's future have proven illusory.

Sustainable development attempts to distinguish itself from preexisting labels in how it stresses reorganization of economic and social systems to improve resource gathering and management. It combines the enhancement of socioeconomic issues and concerns over a wide range of environmental issues.[23] There are two core elements: (1) taking care of the basic needs of those in poverty and prioritizing their well-being in economic development; and (2) imposing limits on technology and social organizations that are destroying the environment. The World Commission on Environment and Development views sustainable development as "the development that meets the needs of the present without compromising the ability of future generations to meet their own needs," underscoring the need to conserve nature, care for the environment, and plan carefully in order not to deplete natural resources.[24] A careful balance must be maintained between both core elements of sustainable development, as demands for rapid development can often result in neglecting pro-environment principles.

While sustainable development has become an enduring concept, various aspects of it are no different from preceding notions of economic underdevelopment, and discussions concerning sustainable development

[21] Ngozi Okonjo-Iweala, *Reforming the Unreformable* (Cambridge: MIT Press, 2012).

[22] Adejumo and Adejumo, "Prospects for Achieving Sustainable Development."

[23] Bill Hopwood, Mary Mellor, and Geoff O'Brien, "Sustainable Development: Mapping Different Approaches," *Sustainable Development* 13, no. 1 (2005): 38–52.

[24] W. M. Adams, *Green Development: Environment and Sustainability in the Third World* (New York: Routledge, 1990).

tend to be similar to previous discussions focused on concepts of under-development and "backward economies." The approach favored by many African scholars has been to relate sustainable development to virtually all aspects of underdevelopment, and sustainable development is now anchored to four pillars: economic, social, environmental, and political.

For Nigeria and other developing countries, emphasis is placed on the environmental and economic pillars of sustainable development. For these countries, rapid development is desired to meet goals of modern-ization, but often imperils environmental issues.[25] For example, meeting the consumption needs of a growing population that is increasingly moving to urban areas leads these countries to construct irrigation and drainage systems, use fertilizers and pesticides, and clear forests for agriculture, all of which place great stress on the ecosystem.

Nigerian economic development has been fraught with inequality since the 1970s, during which it "grew drastically due to the rapid expansion of petroleum sector."[26] This oil boom brought Nigeria wealth that created a sharp socioeconomic divide, as government officials and "people who had access to state power" were the sole benefactors.[27] Concentration on the boom in the petroleum industry resulted in a "neglect of other sectors in that is necessary for a stable and balanced economy."[28]

A rapidly increasing global population necessitates the consumption of more and more nonrenewable resources, leading to abusive trade rela-tionships that can damage sustainable development on a global level.[29] Industrialized countries such as the United States consume enormous quantities of raw materials in order to maintain their status and generate further economic growth, relying on less-industrialized countries such as Nigeria to supply their needs by depleting their natural resources. Nigeria and other developing countries cannot accept these conditions and must

---

[25] A number of Nigerian scholars have devoted attention to various components of this issue. See Adekunle Afolayan, *Agriculture and Economic Development in Nigeria: A Prescription for the Nigerian Green Revolution* (New York: Vantage Press, 1983); J. F. K. Akinbami, A. T. Salami, and W. O. Siyanbola, "An Integrated Strategy for Sustainable Forest-Energy-Environment Interactions in Nigeria," *Journal of Environmental Management* 69, no.2 (2003): 115–128; Victor I. Lukpata, "Culture, Tourism and Sustainable Development in Nigeria," *Journal of Good Governance and Sustainable Development in Africa* 2 (2014): 41–47; and Layi Egunjobi, "Issues in Environmental Management for Sustainable Development in Nigeria," *The Environmentalist* 13 (1993): 33–40.

[26] Toyin Falola and Matthew Heaton, *A History of Nigeria* (Cambridge: Cambridge University Press, 2008), 181.

[27] Ibid.   [28] Ibid., 183.

[29] Robin Attfield, Jophan Hatingh, and Manamela Matshabaphala, "Sustainable Development, Sustainable Livelihoods, and Land Reform in the South Africa: A Conceptual and Ethical Inquiry," *Third World Quarterly* 25, no. 2 (2004): 405–421.

develop to assert themselves on the world stage, compete with wealthy nations, and create structures and institutions that can withstand global exploitation.

Sustainable development is always set in a comparative context, such as the juxtaposition between developing countries and developed ones. In this particular comparison, it is a common mistake to not account for historical disadvantages including colonialism, imperialism, and the corrosive effects of globalization when criticizing a lack of progress in developing countries. Historically, British colonial rule resulted in the exploitation of Nigeria's natural resources and the extortion of human resources, and the lingering effects of colonialism – such as destructive ethnic rivalries – have stalled the industrialization process that is necessary for modern economic development. For developing countries, having an abundance of highly valuable resources does not necessarily lead to great financial gains, thanks to outside exploitation, and so Nigeria has not had an equal opportunity to develop, when compared to European colonizers that now profit from trade with it. As a result of this history, the process of sustainable development for developing countries such as Nigeria must reconcile idealistic goals with the necessity of playing catch-up with developed countries.

While not diminishing the gravity of the issues facing sustainable development in Nigeria, it is important to note that commitments to sustainable development in other countries have faced their own controversy and difficulties. Around the world, persuading the general public not to misuse and waste resources has been difficult. When alternative products are not available, people regularly choose the most expedient options, which tend to be among the least environmentally friendly. Finding a balance between environmental preservation and economic growth has never been easy, especially in countries that seek rapid development without a care for sustainability. Compounding issues of waste production is the problem of highly uneven distribution of food resources: while nations in Africa and the Middle East face crippling famine, the United States, Canada, New Zealand, and Australia waste 52 percent of fruits and vegetables, 38 percent of grains, and 22 percent of meat products, according to a 2011 survey by the Food and Agriculture Organization.[30]

Other obstacles for global sustainable development include differences in agenda between nations of varying levels of wealth. Developing nations seeking rapid economic development are not always easily persuaded to slow down for the sake of the environment, and developed nations want to

---

[30] *Statista Research Department*, "US Food Waste – Statistics & Facts," *Statista*, March 19, 2018, www.statista.com/topics/1623/food-waste/.

preserve their wealth, seeking to discourage competition that will undermine them or thwart their power. As evident in the case of China's economic involvement in Africa, countries that involve themselves in the affairs of the developing world often have economic objectives that override any humanitarian objectives.

The UN recognized the need to measure progress balanced against established obstacles of global inequalities when it created the Human Development Index (HDI) in 1990, widely used to measure how "developed" countries are based on income, education, and life expectancy.[31] Although fraught with limitations, the HDI carries weight as an indicator of how well a country's economy is faring compared to the rest of the world. It is a standard more aligned to Western interpretation of development and progress, and unsurprisingly, it ranks Western countries among the most successful, wealthiest, most powerful, and most developed while accounting for global inequalities. In 2014, the HDI rank for the United States was 5 and for Nigeria was 152 (out of 187 countries) on the HDI scale.[32] By the standards of the HDI ranking, Nigeria is severely lacking and measures to bridge the gap in HDI have so far been unsuccessful.[33]

The update at the core of this chapter focuses primarily on the inadequacies of sustainable development, and the resulting multifaceted environmental, economical, and social challenges. The lack of political will to address environmental issues is a serious problem that is evident in the case of oil spillage in the Niger Delta region, where unchecked oil drilling inflicted tremendous damage on both the ecosystem and the health and livelihood of people living in the region.[34] Oil companies operating in developing nations have done little or nothing to address the negative effects of their drilling in the region, and corporations operating mainly in unregulated markets outside government-approved guidelines present a significant challenge for advocacy of sustainable

---

[31] Yakeen A. Sanusi, "Application of Human Development Index to Measurement of Deprivations among Urban Households in Minna, Nigeria," *Habitat International* 32, no. 3 (2008): 384–398.

[32] *United Nations Development Programme*, "Human Development Reports," *United Nations Development Programme*, January 1, 2014, http://hdr.undp.org/en/data.

[33] Robert Madu and Shedrack Chinwuba Moguluwa, "Will the Social Media Lenses Be the Framework for Sustainable Development in Rural Nigeria?" *Journal of African Media Studies* 5, no. 2 (2013): 237–254; Victor Adejumo and Olubunmi Adejumo, "Prospects for Achieving Sustainable Development through the Millennium Development Goals in Nigeria," *European Journal of Sustainable Development* 3, no. 1 (2014): 33–46.

[34] Adedeji Daramola and Eziyi Ibem, "Urban Environmental Problems in Nigeria: Implications for Sustainable Development," *Journal of Sustainable Development in Africa* 12, no. 1 (2010): 124–145.

development.[35] Local and multinational businesses have demonstrated a lack of concern about the consequences of their practices, and the Nigerian government's enforcement of regulations and policy has shown little commitment to keeping corporations in check.

Worryingly, Nigeria is continually losing indigenous knowledge that can aid in creating a non-Western path to sustainability. For centuries before colonial conquest, these agrarian communities accumulated wisdom and proficiency in living off the land without damaging the ecosystem. This knowledge can potentially be used to sustain endangered communities and cultures, even in the face of looming multinational interests. An important quality of sustainable development is ensuring that local populations have the sustainable ability to make meaningful choices and influence their own circumstances for the better.[36]

This, then, is Nigeria's essential dilemma: on the one hand, all the necessary resources are present to create sustainability, yet on the other, the obstacles are many and no system of sustainable development has found success. Despite the vast supply of valuable natural resources that the country is capitalizing upon, it still ranks among the poorest countries in the world.[37]

Discussion of the Nigerian economy and its development centers largely around oil. Since the oil boom of the 1970s, extraction and export of crude oil has greatly diminished the nation's agrarian economy. Between 1970 and 2000, agricultural exports decreased from 7 percent to a mere 3 percent of gross exports, while oil exports increased from 35 to 96 percent during the same period. As a consequence, over 75 percent of revenue to finance government expenditure comes from oil exports, and the economy is dangerously dependent upon oil, presenting several concerns for sustainable development. Fluctuating oil prices result in a volatile economic atmosphere, and rapid development of cities thanks to oil wealth has resulted in limited urban infrastructure. Neglect in developing agriculture has caused it to lose its capacity as a meaningful

---

[35] E. Ire Uwem, "Multinationals and Corporate Social Responsibility in Developing Countries: A Case Study of Nigeria," *Corporate Social Responsibility and Environmental Management* 11, no. 1 (2004): 1–11; and Daniel Gberevbie, Adeola Opeyemi, and Nchekwube Excellence-Oluye, "The Challenges of Good Governance, Accountability of Governmental Agencies and Development in Nigeria," *Acta Universitatis Danubius* 6, no. 2 (2014): 80–97.

[36] United Nations, *Innovation for Sustainable Development: Local Case Studies from Africa* (New York: United Nations Publication, 2008).

[37] Michael Baghebo and Samuel Edoumiekumo, "Public Capital Accumulation and Economic Development in Nigeria: 1970–2010," *International Journal of Academic Research in Business and Social Sciences* 2, no. 6 (2012): 213–237.

agent of economic change, and reliance on oil makes environmental reform nigh impossible to enact without disrupting the economy.

The government allocation of oil revenues has historically promoted corruption and had a large impact on the outcome of sustainable development programs and policies. Between 1973 and 1999, around 600 state-owned enterprises in telecommunications, transportation, banking, and electricity consumed so many resources with such limited benefit to the country that policy thereafter shifted toward liberalization of all these failed enterprises. The potential long-term impact of a privatized economy in Nigeria is still under assessment, but attempts to modernize through industrialization have not yielded substantial results.

Another important context for discussing Nigerian development is the trend of declining efficiency in governance. Nigeria inherited good civil servants at the time of its independence in 1960, though at the time government emphasis was focused on means of disbursing greater profit from exports. The quality of civil service has since degraded, supervised by a series of politicians mainly concerned with lining their pockets with public funds.

Sustainable development must not only address the current conditions of poverty, but also tackle the injustice and corruption that caused it in the first place. In a 2015 speech, President Muhammadu Buhari spoke on economic inequality that most Nigerians are intimately familiar with:

> The current administration has created two economies in one country, a sorry tale of two nations: one economy for a few who have so much in their tiny island of prosperity; and the other economy for the many who have so little in their vast ocean of misery ... We also have one of the highest rates of inequalities in the world.[38]

Challenges for sustainable development often arise when concerns of poverty and the environment intersect. Poor people are the least equipped to live within new ecological limits, and mismanagement of land in Zimbabwe and South Africa serve as reminders of how easily both concerns may arise. Gender inequality is another factor as Nigeria has historically failed to recognize the full labor potential and value of women in bolstering economic development.[39]

Without sustainable energy, there can be no truly sustainable development. This is problematic because Nigeria has the tenth largest reserve of crude oil and some of the largest gas reserves in the world.[40] From 2007 to

[38] Buhari, "Inaugural Speech."

[39] A. Boyi Abubakar, "Gender Studies and Sustainable Development in Nigeria," *Mediterranean Journal of Social Sciences* 4, no. 8 (2013): 147–152.

[40] Sunday Olayinka Oyedepo, "On Energy for Sustainable Development in Nigeria," *Renewable and Sustainable Energy Reviews* 16, no. 5 (2012): 583–598.

2012, crude oil contributed to an average of 25 percent of Nigeria's gross domestic product, and short-sighted economic policy has arguably made the nation dependent upon the oil industry to keep its economy afloat. Ideally, Nigeria's wealth of natural resources can power the economy enough to make a shift toward alternative sources of clean and renewable energy viable.

A functioning electrical grid is a necessary framework for modern economic development, and Nigeria, with an estimated 60 to 70 percent of the country lacking access to electricity, is facing a developmental roadblock. To cite President Buhari's inaugural speech in 2015:

No single cause can be identified to explain Nigeria's poor economic performance over the years than the power situation. It is a national shame that an economy of 180 million generates only 4,000MW, and distributes even less. Continuous tinkering with the structures of power supply and distribution and close on $20b expanded since 1999 have only brought darkness, frustration, misery, and resignation among Nigerians.[41]

Many parts of the country that do have access to electricity often experience shortages due to poor energy allocation and urban planning.[42] Families are constrained to either rely on generators and thus contribute to environmental noise pollution, or to cope with long periods of darkness at night. On a broader scale, inadequacies in electricity generation damage nighttime economies, diminish productive capacities, increase production costs, and limit the use and innovation of new technology. Companies pay exorbitant amounts for oil or diesel to power their generators, transferring the cost to consumers and reducing profit margins. Medical facilities, education, and important governmental functions are also hindered or halted by a lack of power. Current reliance on diesel fuel is not cost effective, wastes revenue, and produces enormous carbon emissions.

Given the energy situation in Nigeria, the challenges facing environmentalist efforts are gargantuan.[43] An estimated 2.5 million cubic feet of gas is flared each day, equivalent to 40 percent of the total gas consumed in the entire African continent. Close to 70 percent of its population lives in rural areas where burning wood for fuel is the primary energy resource, contributing to destructive emission levels and creating issues of deforestation. In order to renew and preserve Nigeria's forests before it is too

[41] Buhari, "Inaugural Speech."
[42] Oyedepo, "On Energy for Sustainable Development in Nigeria."
[43] Olayinka Oyedepo, *Energy and Sustainable Development in Nigeria: The Way Forward* (New York: Springer, 2012); O. Davidson and D. Sparks, eds., "Developing Energy Solutions for Climate Change," *South African Research at EDRC, Energy and Development Research Centre, Cape Town* (2002): 145–152.

late, reliance on wood as a source of fuel must be cut significantly. Multiple reports have warned that without rapid efforts toward this preservation, devastating consequences should be expected.[44] The Niger Delta is a particularly important example, as the country relies on the region for much of its revenue but has severely damaged the environment and placed the area in jeopardy.

As the most populous country in Africa, Nigeria is in urgent need of renewable energy sources to provide accessible, reliable, and affordable services that can meet the basic needs of the people and ensure a healthy manufacturing and industrial capacity. Energy distribution must be more equitable, and reward those in rural areas in order to revitalize national agriculture. To this end, Nigeria must further develop renewable resources such as animal waste, wind, and crop residue. Greater technological innovation is in order to make renewable sources of energy more affordable.

The advantages of renewable energy sources include the protection of the environment and the preservation of wood and other life-sustaining resources. The use of solar energy has also been proposed, with claims that 0.1 percent of the solar energy capacity of the country is sufficient if converted to an efficient resource.

Renewable energy sources must be developed in a practical manner based on resources available locally in order to generate greater development in rural areas, but the infrastructure necessary to sustain rapid development has yet to be created. Most Nigerian roads are of poor quality, and many rural areas are badly integrated with existing transportation networks. Travel within big cities such as Lagos often takes long hours because of massive traffic congestion.

Nigeria is regarded as a country with a climate of insecurity, in the sense that many houses are fenced off with barred windows and doors.[45] Tourists are afraid to visit, and as a result the tourism industry has suffered in spite of the abundance of appealing sites and ecosystems. Nigerian politicians cannot sacrifice peace and stability and expect prosperity or hope to generate development while the country is vulnerable to a myriad of crises and insurgencies such as Boko Haram. Given the current economic consequences of government neglect, security issues must be treated as part and parcel of sustainable development.

---

[44] See, for instance, Michael S. Asante, *Deforestation in Ghana: Explaining the Chronic Failure of Forest Preservation Policies in a Developing Country* (Lanham: University Press of America, 2005).
[45] I. Robert-Okah, "Insecurity in Nigeria: Implications for Sustainable National Development in Nigeria," *International Journal of Academic Research* 6, no. 4 (2014): 242–250.

Environmental issues have received scholarly attention as one of the primary concerns of sustainable development in Nigeria.[46] Farmlands are experiencing a host of strains due to overuse, and deforestation at one of the highest rates in the world, diminishing nutrients in the soil, and fears of desertification in northern regions have recently emerged. Other problems include poor solid-waste management and water contamination.[47]

An awareness that science and technology are the foundation of modernity and are key to societal progress has become deeply embedded in communities around the world, and justifiably so. All aspects of modernity require the use of technology to function, from domestic spaces, to mass communication, to the education sector, to the workplace. The wealthiest and most powerful nations have historically thrived upon technological advancement, leading the wave of imperialism and later controlling the forces of globalization. European colonialism of African nations was made possible largely because of military technology that overpowered Africans' weapons of war. Nigeria's long-term sustainability will ultimately require a significant investment in technology that benefits not only the rich but the entire population.

One of the most significant differences between developed countries and developing countries such as Nigeria is the issue of the education gap. In 2006, the national literacy rate in Nigeria was 56 percent for females and 72 percent for males, demonstrating an unsustainable gender disparity.[48] A significant component of the HDI measurement is the level of education of a country's population, drawing a connection between well-developed education systems and overall prosperity. Gender disparity in education increases economic problems by excluding a large part of the population from learning valuable skills and contributing to a nation's GDP. Therefore, a sustainability-minded Nigerian education system that will contribute to overall advancement of society must give due focus to all subjects, teach practical skills, revamp technical training, and integrate vocational and entrepreneurial training. Lessons focusing on government institutions, civil practices, gender sensitivity, and environmental consciousness should be regarded as a necessity.

There can be no good economy without good politics, and there is a consensus among researchers and policy makers that good governance,

---

[46] Gozie Ogbodo and Ngozi Stewart, "Climate Change and Nigeria's Sustainable Development of Vision 20: 2020," *Annual Survey of International & Comparative Law* 20, no. 1 (2014): 16–34; Tade Aina and Ademola Salau, *The Challenge of Sustainable Development in Nigeria* (London: Sage Publishing, 1992).
[47] Daramola and Ibem, "Urban Environmental Problems in Nigeria."
[48] Mabel Oyitso and C. O. Olomukoro, "Enhancing Women's Development through Literacy Education in Nigeria," *Review of European Studies* 4, no. 4 (2012): 211–217.

efficient and effective public administration, and accountability of governmental agencies are necessary conditions to achieve sustainable development. Nigeria's rough political history includes the collapse of republican systems, civil war, and the rule of military regimes, all of which have been stumbling blocks in the way of economic progress. A democratic governmental structure has been in place since 1999, but lingering ethnic and religious divisions still plague the country. Corruption and ineffective policies are pervasive, and the government has shown no sense of urgency in rectifying these issues. Better governance is necessary to create an economic climate in which policies of sustainable development are possible, and to police the rampant corruption and inefficiency present in many agencies. The government must use oil revenue responsibly to generate gainful employment not directly dependent upon the oil industry, supported by superior social and economic infrastructure.

Conclusion

Nigeria has not been idle in its pursuit of greater economic prosperity, with mixed degrees of success. Impressive changes in overall quality of life, growth in the GDP, new manufacturing methods, and expansion in the service industry, have come hand-in-hand with rising unemployment rates and greater poverty. The government understands the concept of sustainable development and why it is necessary for the country's well-being, but rampant corruption has foiled many social initiatives, and plans to limit depletion of natural resources have failed. In addition, the populace cannot be sufficiently mobilized to commit to the ideas of protecting the environment while infrastructure and education are so limited.

Nigeria must rise to the challenge of meeting the needs of the present without bankrupting the future of both the people and the land. While short-term measures are important to avoid violence and political strife, long-term planning must be treated as a critical investment and balanced fairly in relation to immediate contingencies.

Drawing from the previous analysis, I would like to close with a dozen recommendations for modernizing the country:

1. Policies and economic growth must pay attention to environmentally sound policies and safe practices, aim to create stable ecological systems, and develop agriculture in order to implement massive national poverty alleviation programs that can supply food at affordable prices to the majority of the country's population. While figures of growth such as the GDP and GNP are

important, numbers have no feeling, need no food, and cannot quantify desperation and anger.

2. Meeting the needs of the poor by relating options to the durability of resources must be an overriding priority, especially the provision of clean water, health care, sanitation, and energy to cook. The distribution of wealth from oil has historically excluded poor rural populations, and the overall wellness of the poor should be the primary determinant of measuring the country's economic progress, rather than impersonal mathematical formulas of the inflow and outflow of cash.

3. Energy must become the topmost priority: without uninterrupted power supply, Nigeria cannot diversify its economy or advance technologically, and overall quality of life is diminished.

4. A steady and stable bureaucracy is needed to overcome the perennial crises generated by the instability of political offices and changes in political parties in power. Politicians think in terms of popular self-serving agenda, and they have contributed to the deficiencies in governance as well as to reckless and inefficient extraction of resources.

5. Corruption undermines the integrity of government and respect for leaders and is interrelated with many other national crises. By mitigating political corruption, all other issues become easier to manage.

6. The spatial organization of cities needs considerable improvement and better infrastructure in order to maintain a good economy, environment, and society.

7. Nigeria must thrive economically in the long term to eradicate poverty, create disposable income and leisure time, provide access to computers and the Internet, improve living conditions in rural areas, and engage the youth through constant job creation.

8. Security and the need to strengthen the institutions of governance to prevent conflict are paramount but must be balanced with promotion of peace and human rights.

9. A new sense of discipline within government must curb and curtail corruption; the strong hand of the government must produce the sanctions to punish those who break the rules.

10. Nigeria must improve quality of education in order to allocate the best talents to each sector, look for innovators, increase knowledge regarding generation of finite resources, utilize technology to meet basic needs, and generate scientific knowledge that will bring advancements toward true modernity.

11. Both the public and private sectors must enter into a coordinated sustainable partnership on relating business practices to sustainable

development, ensuring that natural resources are not over-extracted and preventing practices that will further destroy the environment.

12. Youth must be guided toward becoming "leader-preneurs" with the capacity to stand up and challenge corrupt leadership and take control of their future. Youths should not be encouraged to remain in unstimulating rural labor, but rather tasked with infusing enterprises with innovative technologies and developing entrepreneurial skills that will benefit the entire country.

Introduction

According to the United Nations' Food and Agriculture Organization (FAO), about 10.7 percent of the world's population is chronically hungry.[1] That is 815 million out of the 7.6 billion people who inhabit the world.[2] This number is about two-and-a-half times the population of the entire United States.[3] The United Nations sees hunger and malnutrition as greater health risks than even malaria, AIDS, and tuberculosis combined. Nigeria is one of the victims of the hunger crises.

Despite the numerous campaigns against hunger from national governments, intergovernmental organizations (IGOs) such as the United Nations and the exponentially increasing number of nongovernmental organizations (NGOs), this number continues to grow.[4] There was an increase of about 11 million hungry people from 2016 to 2017 alone.[5] Out of the current 815 million hungry people in the world, about 233 million live in sub-Saharan Africa (SSA): this is the second-largest population of hungry people in the world after Asia. Asia has the largest population of chronically hungry people,

---

[1] An earlier version was presented as a Convocation Lecture, Federal University of Agriculture, Abeokuta, 2018. The media that covered the event published various segments of it in the Nigerian newspapers, while the University posted a long section of it on its website. This chapter locates Nigeria as part of a larger continental problem.

[2] Food and Agriculture Organization, International Fund for Agricultural Development, UNICEF, World Food Programme, and World Health Organization, *The State of Food Security and Nutrition in the World 2020: Transforming Food Systems for Affordable Healthy Diets* (Rome, FAO, 2020), www.fao.org/3/ca9692en/CA9692EN.pdf.

[3] World Population Review, "United States Population," *World Population Review*, June 18, 2018, worldpopulationreview.com/countries/united-states-population/.

[4] Food and Agriculture Organization, International Fund for Agricultural Development, UNICEF, World Food Programme, and World Health Organization, *The State of Food Security and Nutrition in the World 2017: Building Resilience for Peace and Food Security* (Rome: FAO, 2017), www.fao.org/3/a-i7695e.pdf.

[5] Food Security Information Network, *Global Report on Food Crises 2018*, Food Security Information Network, 2018, www.fsincop.net/fileadmin/user_upload/fsin/docs/global_re port/2018/GRFC_2018_Full_report_EN_Low_resolution.pdf.

but SSA has a higher prevalence of hunger. Sub-Saharan Africa also has had the least regional progress in hunger reduction when compared to Asia or Latin America.[6] While cumulative statistics for Nigeria are not available, reports at various levels of government indicate the depth of the crisis.

Many examples illustrate human manifestations of the desperate conditions Nigerians are facing. In August 2016, a man broke into his neighbor's apartment in Abuja to steal a pot of rice and stew to feed his family. That same year, also in Abuja, a schoolteacher was beaten because he stole food. That November, foreign and local media reported that a fifteen-year-old was lynched in Lagos for stealing food. A woman in Ekiti was caught stealing a pot of amala, claiming that she had to feed her children. In September 2018, there was another report of a woman thoroughly beaten for stealing a pot of food from the fire. There are many other cases between 2016 and now that I could mention. Even if some of them were exaggerations, you get the point: there is hunger in the land that has to do with food in the physical and the abstract senses.

Given these examples, I ask: How could people improve themselves, their community, their nation, or their continent when they are overcome with hunger? In this chapter, I examine the way in which the food crisis limits human capabilities on a societal level. I explore this relationship through the philosophy of food, nature of the global food system and related food crisis, and the sociology of food and nutrition. In the conclusion, I offer a layered model for understanding the nature of food crisis as well as a few possible interventions.

Section A: Jesus Christ, Karl Marx, and Food: Conversations on Food and Humanity

The Universal Declaration of Human Rights Article 25 Section 1 states that a right to eat is inherent to every human.[7] Food is vital to human life, and it has significant cultural value. Throughout history, eating has been a major source of community and social interactions. Many religions center their rituals around harvests and times that celebrate the continuation of life. Food's importance and the religious, spiritual conversations around it have been with us since the Stone Age. Two divine figures – the religious and the secular – illustrate the relevance of this conversation,

---

[6] World Hunger Education Service, "Africa Hunger and Poverty Facts," *World Hunger Education Service*, August 2018, www.worldhunger.org/africa-hunger-poverty-facts/.
[7] The United Nations, *Universal Declaration of Human Rights*, 1948.

showing how food connects with our beings, our histories, our policies, and our politics.

Jesus' Last Supper is one of the most famous examples of a religious meal. During the last supper, Jesus encouraged his disciples to appreciate the bread and wine they drank as his own flesh and blood. This moment created the tradition of communion, where eating bread and drinking wine is ritually symbolic of Christ's death and the resurrection.[8] Theologians say that the message of the Last Supper was not about the physical food present; wine and bread are symbols for the spiritual connections between God and man. In that sense, food becomes both a necessity and a metaphor.

The Last Supper is indeed a good example of a religious meal. Also, notice the concern of the Bible that physical hunger must be assuaged first because man cannot serve God in hunger: the feeding of the 5,000 (Matthew 14:14–21), the feeding of the 4,000 (Matthew 15:32–38), the appointment of seven deacons to oversee the distribution of food to the needy in the early church (Acts 6:1–7). A classic example in the Old Testament is the feeding of the Israelites with manna and quail (Gen. 16:1–19).

In the Bible, food is thematic: God continually provides for his people. He provides manna for his children, those fleeing Israel, to show He supports their plight.[9] Hunger is portrayed as God's way of humbling His people. Eating gives His followers an opportunity to praise Him. Food as instrumental, not intrinsic, value is apparent by the status of gluttony as a sin. Food is a necessary condition of life, but it should be treated as a gift God provides so humanity can cultivate a relationship with Him.

Although food is venerated as God's gift in the Bible, Jesus says "Man shall not live by bread alone."[10] Food is necessary for life, but the teachings of Jesus are also necessary for humans. Jesus emphasizes that even though animals can live by consuming food alone, men are higher beings that require further subsistence. This common idea is expressed by the English idiom, "we eat to live, not live to eat." Jesus specifically meant that eating allows humans to live through a spiritual connection with God. This connection is not a luxury that is only available to the wealthy; Jesus sees it as a necessity for all human beings. Rituals such as communion allow food to serve as a spiritual tool. As a foundation for life, food is also a spiritual necessity. Without food, an individual cannot pursue a relationship with God, making food security an important component of Christian religion. In contexts where hunger is not an issue, the

---

[8] Luke 22:19–20 (ESV).   [9] Exodus 16 (NIV).   [10] Matthew 4:4 (ESV).

spiritual comes before the material. But where hunger is a problem, the material obstacle is first dealt with before spiritual issues are addressed.

Karl Marx, a religious critic, negated this statement with his claim that "man shall live by bread alone." Like Jesus, Marx acknowledged that men were different from animals. Jesus thought that this was a spiritual difference, but Marx viewed the difference as more practical.[11] In short, Jesus saw food as a means to religious connection while Marx viewed food as the goal in itself. Marx's quote is best understood within his framework of dialectical materialism. While animals adapt to survive in their environment, men require tools. For example, a bear's thick fur coat may help it survive in the winter, but man must make a blanket. To Marx, this dependence on tools meant that humans were inherently materialists.[12]

Marx saw society based on the division of labor involving producers and consumers. These distribution relationships lead to different social relationships, which is especially true for food, the most basic human good.[13] Social relationships established by distribution ultimately drive the consuming class to get the most possible work from the producing class. This conflict creates what Marx called a class struggle, and he viewed class struggle as the driving agent in historical change.[14] When Marx says, "man shall live by bread alone," he is making an ethical statement that food security for all should be the first issue addressed in society. The ethical problem that arises in a capitalist economy is food can be denied to certain individuals based on class, labor, and ability. Jesus, on the other hand, saw religious enlightenment as a priority to which food would follow. In his writings, Marx further explores issues of human fulfillment beyond food – but always under the assumption that human fulfillment is dependent on access to food.

Marx especially did not see religion as a form of human fulfillment. He described religion as the "opium of the people," something to distract and soothe the working class from the oppression of the consuming class.[15] He thought that humans served a higher purpose than animals, but that purpose was expressed through their labor. As a system of production, capitalism forced lower classes to sell their labor for food. Their ability to

---

[11] Oliver Brett, *A Defense of Liberty* (New York & London: G. P. Putnam's Sons, 1921).

[12] John Bellamy Foster, "Marx's Theory of Metabolic Rift: Classical Foundations for Environmental Sociology," *American Journal of Sociology* 105, no. 2 (1999): 366–405.

[13] H. P. Adams, "Karl Marx in His Earlier Writings," *The Journal of Philosophy* 38, no. 7 (1941): 188.

[14] Mark Tilzey, "Reintegrating Economy, Society, and Environment for Cooperative Futures: Polanyi, Marx, and Food Sovereignty," *Journal of Rural Studies* 53 (2017): 317–334.

[15] Karl Marx and Joseph J. O'Malley, *Critique of Hegel's "Philosophy of Right"* (Cambridge: Cambridge University Press, 1970).

use their labor at their own will, which would have defined their human-ity, was lost in that transaction.[16]

Marx argued that exploitation of the lower class would continue as production became more efficient, and eventually, fewer laborers would be needed. The higher supply of laborers relative to demand would lead to a "starving wage" – the few laborers who found employment would not make enough money to sustain themselves, but they would have more than the unemployed. Marx used arguments such as the "starving wage" and the selling of labor to advocate for lower-class rebellion. But his arguments are based on the materialist idea that men cannot live solely on jobs or religion, but only through the tangible substance of food. He equates the distribution of food with the distribution of power and life.[17]

In Nigeria, traditional Yoruba adherence to food as a religious and sociological necessity is underscored in Ifá literature. In its exposition of ẹbọ (sacrifice) in the Yoruba belief system, Odù Òwónrín Méjì tells the myth of a farmer: in spite of his generous offerings to the gods and the ancestral spirits, the prognostication remained negative. The farmer went back to the diviners, and Ifa revealed that any sacrifice failing to put food in human mouths was an exercise in futility. It would never work, regard-less of how many gods were appeased. And so, the esẹ Ifá concludes:[18]

> Njẹ́ kín l'à ń bọ n'Ífẹ̀.
> Ẹnuu wọn.
> Ẹnuu wọn l'à n bọ n'Ífẹ̀,
> Ẹnuu wọn.
> Mo fín'gbá,
> Mo f'áwo.
> Ẹnuu wọn kò mọ̀ lè rí mi bá jà.
> Ẹnuu wọn.
> Mo wálé,
> Mo wánà.
> Ẹnuu wọn.
> Ẹnuu wọn kò mọ̀ lè rí mi bá jà.
> Ẹnuu wọn.
>
> (I ask, therefore, what do we offer sacrifice to in Ifẹ?
> It's their mouths.
> It's their mouths we offer sacrifice to in Ifẹ,
> It's their mouths.
> I gave to the calabash,

[16] Victor Cathrein, *Socialism: Its Theoretical Basis and Practical Application* (New York: Benziger, 1904).
[17] John Bellamy Foster, "Marx as a Food Theorist," *Monthly Review* 68, no. 7 (2016): 1.
[18] Wande Abimbola, *Ijinle Ohun Enu Ifa, Apa Kiini* (Glasgow: Wm. Collins, Sons and Co.), 74–75.

And I gave to the bowl.
It's their mouths.
Their mouths can no longer mount warfare against me.
Their mouths.
I searched at home,
I searched on the pathway.
Their mouths.
Their mouths can no longer mount warfare against me.
Their mouths).

Abraham Maslow was another philosopher who argued for the importance of food. Maslow created the pyramid model ordering man's hierarchy of needs. At the bottom of the pyramid, he put the basic needs of food, shelter, and water. On top of this foundation, he placed safety, love and belonging, esteem, and then self-actualization.[19] From both religious and secular perspectives, food is foundational for life. Jesus saw food as essential for a religious relationship, something that would be provided by God. Marx saw food as necessary for life and central to class relationships and cyclical class struggle. Jesus and Marx had different ideas of what "self-actualization" looked like, but both agreed that access to food was a step toward achieving it.

Karl Marx said, "hunger is hunger; but the hunger that is satisfied by cooked meat eaten with a knife and fork differs from hunger that devours raw meat with the help of hands, nails and teeth."[20] A right to food is included in the International Declaration of Human Rights because food not only provides life but is also the key to human dignity. Humans require food to move beyond their nature as animals and work toward achieving any higher purpose.

Section B: Global Food Networks: History, Hunger, and Politics

Colonialism historically depended on colonies exporting raw materials to the West. These resources, crops, and minerals were sent to Europe or the Americas for processing, which distorted Africa's economy. Despite the transition of these colonies to sovereign nations, colonialism's global economic patterns continue. Neocolonialism describes the economic and political influence that Western nations wield over their former colonies. Neocolonialism's most obvious presence in Africa is the economic dependence on exports.

---

[19] Abraham Maslow and Karen J. Lewis, "Maslow's Hierarchy of Needs," *Salenger Incorporated* 14 (1987): 987.
[20] Karl Marx, *Grundrisse* (London: Penguin, 1973), 92.

The problem is, crops grown for export in Africa often do not offer reliable economic returns.[21] African governments create short-term policies to support high-demand export crops, neglecting investment in long-term resources and policies for staple crops.[22] The 2008 global market crash and subsequent food shortages were a manifestation of this larger pattern. Much of Africa's food security depends on the exportation of cash crops to purchase imported food. This leaves the future of hunger in Africa vulnerable to fluctuations in the global market.

Neocolonialism's patterns and the modern global economic network are rooted in the philosophy of neoliberalism, which is often described as extreme capitalism. It is the idea that the global markets should be completely unrestrained, with little government regulation. Neoliberalism's application means that poorer nations cannot protect themselves from corporate influence or unfair prices.[23] Neoliberalism has created the "global factory," benefitting some regions to the detriment of others. This idea of a global factory describes the separation of economic activities within a country, outsourcing some activity to other countries with lower costs. The global factory means that Western corporations can influence the economies and politics of African nations.[24]

Ellen Gustafson analyzed the global food economy in a TED talk. She argued that global health epidemics of both obesity and hunger are "two sides of the same coin." Gustafson explained that the global factory and its global food network encourages the creation of processed food. She analyzed two effects of this development. First, importing food to create processed food makes healthy food more expensive for Americans. Processed food replacing locally grown food causes obesity and malnutrition, because micronutrients have been replaced by fatty calories. In African nations, food exportation leads to economic dependence and famine. Gustafson proposes focusing on locally sourced foods and sustainable, socially, and nutritiously conscious farming methodologies to address both issues.[25]

Food waste is another similarity between developing and developed nations. Both sides of the global food network waste significant amounts of food every year, for different reasons. The high affluence of developed nations means that more food is wasted at an individual level, thrown away

[21] Russell L. Lamb, "Food Crops, Exports, and the Short-Run Policy Response of Agriculture in Africa," *Agricultural Economics* 22, no. 3 (2000): 271–298.
[22] Ibid.
[23] Lawrence Busch, "Can Fairy Tales Come True? The Surprising Story of Neoliberalism and World Agriculture," *Sociologia Ruralis* 50, no. 4 (2010): 331–351.
[24] Philip McMichael, "A Food Regime Analysis of the 'World Food Crisis,'" *Agriculture and Human Values* 26, no. 4 (2009): 281.
[25] Ellen Gustafson, "Obesity + Hunger = One Global Food Issue," TEDxEast video, 9:23, May 2010, www.ted.com/talks/ellen_gustafson_obesity_hunger_1_global_food_issue.

Figure 14.1 A buyer in a rural food market sampling the quality of the farm produce.

by sellers or consumers instead of farmers. In Africa, the largest causes of food waste are transportation and storage.[26] Underdeveloped infrastructure can make food transport take longer than necessary, causing food to spoil. Food storage facilities are often insufficient because of low capital investment and lack of advanced technological skill.[27] Most transported food in Africa, including food aid, spoils in either transport or storage. The United Nations recognizes food waste's role in the global food crisis, and their Zero Hunger Challenge includes a goal of "zero food waste" from all countries.[28]

[26] H. Charles et al., "Food Security: The Challenge of Feeding 9 Billion People," *Science* 327, no. 5967 (2010): 812–818.

[27] Esther Ndichu, "Hunger Isn't a Food Issue. It's a Logistics Issue," TED@UPS, video, 11:41, September 2015, www.ted.com/talks/esther_ndichu_hunger_isn_t_a_food_is sue_it_s_a_logistics_issue#t-1564.

[28] United Nations, "Zero Hunger Challenge," *United Nations*, n.d., www.un.org/zerohun ger/.

Africa's role in the global economy means that regions with low agricultural productivity can import food to combat famine, but this is only true if the imports are food aid, or if they are affordable.[29] In reality, food aid is not a sustainable solution for agricultural deficits. Imported food is almost never affordable for individuals living in poverty. Neoliberal arguments expect the market to use Africa's human resources to provide jobs, and that the market will invest in agricultural productivity to meet local demand. These patterns might happen eventually, but the market would need time to adjust. The cost of waiting is human suffering from hunger and poverty. This human cost is too great to delay while the global economy equalizes; the government must take action.[30]

Africa's history and unique role in the global marketplace explain its place in the global food chain and the problems that it entails. Malnutrition's cost on society is about 3.5 trillion dollars a year for the global economy.[31] Hunger is increasing globally. While Latin America and Asia have improved their agricultural production, a perfect storm of variables has contributed to Africa's agricultural decline since the 1970s. The Green Revolution increased Latin America's and Asia's ability to feed their people, but Africa's agricultural sector has just regained the productivity level it had in 1961.[32] This lack of productivity causes mass human suffering and perpetuates poverty, and it hurts the global economy.

Measuring Hunger

Hunger is a complex issue with multiple definitions. Hunger statistics can fluctuate significantly, depending on who is defining it and how. I will use three terms to define a population's inability to obtain food: food security, hunger, and famine.

Food security describes the ability of families to access the nutritious food that they need to live healthy lives. It requires access to this food without economic, social, or physical barriers. Hunger is a more general term, describing the physiological sensation resulting from a lack of food security. The term famine describes widespread death in an area due to hunger.[33] During famines, most people do not die from hunger directly,

---

[29] Charles et. al., "Food Security."   [30] Ibid.

[31] Food and Agriculture Organization of the United Nations, "Understanding the True Cost of Malnutrition," *Food and Agriculture Organization of the United Nations*, n.d., www .fao.org/zhc/detail-events/en/c/238389/.

[32] Charles et al., "Food Security."

[33] Vicky Hallett, "What's the Difference between Famine and Hunger? A Food FAQ," *NPR*, June 13, 2017, www.npr.org/sections/goatsandsoda/2017/06/13/532277316/wha t-s-the-difference-between-famine-and-hunger-a-food-faq.

but from disease. One of the effects of undernutrition and malnutrition is a weakened immune system.[34]

Data about food security often uses nutritional statistics, although nutrition is also a complex variable that can be misinterpreted or over-generalized. For example, an article titled "Calories Count" in National Geographic represented hunger on a map of the world that labeled the average number of calories consumed in each nation.[35] The article stated that the average adult needed about 2,300 calories per day. The suggestion that calorie intake indicates nutritional health makes Tanzania's average intake of 2,120 calories seem like a minor deficit. At the same time, United Nations data states that over 35 percent of children in Tanzania face compromised development due to poor nutrition.[36] The UN statistic describes nutrition's impact on health more accurately than the National Geographic article. The National Geographic article does not provide data to account for nutrient deficiencies, while the UN data provides a more meaningful representation.

International Hunger Eradication Efforts

The global food crisis intensified when food prices began rising in the early 2000s. Prices climaxed in 2008, with a sharp increase due to a global economic recession. The price spike meant that poorer nations were unable to purchase the food they needed, creating famines. This revealed the new global food market's power to devastate impoverished nations. In response to this crisis, the United Nations created a high-level task force for food security in 2008.[37] It marked the beginning of the United Nations as a key factor in international collaboration to reduce hunger.

The UN has continued to prioritize food security, making it the second pillar in its Sustainable Development Goals to "end hunger, achieve food security and improved nutrition and promote sustainable agriculture."[38] The Zero Hunger Challenge was based on this goal, launched in 2012 and aimed to eliminate hunger by 2030.[39] It is a lofty goal, especially with its 2030 deadline. The UN's previous development goal program, the Millennium Development Goals, began in 2000, with an end goal of

---

[34] Ibid.

[35] Kelsey Nowakowski, "Calories Count," *National Geographic Society* 232 (2017).

[36] World Food Programme, "10 Facts about Hunger in Tanzania," *World Food Programme*, May 13, 2016, www.wfp.org/stories/10-facts-about-hunger-tanzania.

[37] United Nations, "Food," *United Nations*, n.d., www.un.org/en/sections/issues-depth/fo od/.

[38] United Nations, "Sustainable Development Knowledge Platform," *United Nations*, n.d., https://sustainabledevelopment.un.org/?menu=1300.

[39] *United Nations*, "Zero Hunger Challenge."

2015. The first goal was to eradicate extreme poverty and hunger, and the UN touts the MDGs as history's greatest coordinated global effort to reduce hunger. But the number of people experiencing chronic hunger has continued to increase. The 2018 UN report on hunger attributes this increase to conflict and environmental issues.[40]

Historically, the UN has spent much of its budget for hunger reduction on food aid. This is unsustainable because it does not encourage the growth of agriculture or the reduction of poverty.[41] Food aid is frequently unable to reach its destination due to conflict, political barriers, or inadequate infrastructure. Much food aid spoils before reaching its destination, due to logistical and infrastructural storage issues.[42] When food aid does reach its destination, it is often distributed unfairly, or it is insufficient for the population.

Foreign aid reduces the ability of local organizations and governments to provide for their people, weakening the local aid infrastructures in existence. Food aid is not the only UN initiative to reduce hunger; their humanitarian efforts have many other pieces. Several branches of the UN, and other global organizations, collaborate to reduce hunger internationally. These organizations include the World Food Program, the World Bank, the FAO, and the IFAD.

The most recent food crisis is the famine in Southern Sudan. Conflict, poverty, and geographical barriers prevent food aid from reaching critical regions, and it is likely that the famine will continue.[43] Donations to the United Nations for humanitarian aid are reliable but insufficient. In February 2017, the UN Secretary General warned that a million people would fall into famine unless $4.4 billion could be raised by March 20 of that year. The United States, historically the largest donor to the UN, donated $277 million. Altogether, the UN raised less than a tenth of its goal by the end of March, falling short by billions of dollars.[44] Ambitious goals and underfunding have been a recurring pattern for the United Nations.

With its limited resources, the UN cannot bring sufficient famine relief to areas such as Southern Sudan. Sustainable solutions require coordination

[40] Food Security Information Network, *Global Report on Food Crises 2018.*
[41] Mukhtar Diriye, Abdirizak Nur, and Abdullahi Khalif, "Food Aid and the Challenge of Food Security in Africa," *Development* 56, no. 3 (2013): 396–403.
[42] Ndichu, "Hunger Isn't a Food Issue. It's a Logistics Issue."
[43] Joanne Lu, "'Unimaginable' Suffering in Southern Sudan. Is There Any Hope?" *NPR*, July 5, 2018, www.npr.org/sections/goatsandsoda/2018/07/05/620184859/unimagin able-suffering-in-south-sudan-is-there-any-hope.
[44] Somini Sengupta, "U.N.'s Famine Appeal Is Billions Shy of Goal," *The New York Times*, March 23, 2017, www.nytimes.com/2017/03/23/world/africa/un-famine-nigeria-somalia -south-sudan-yemen.html.

between governments and well-funded, well-analyzed solutions. The new wave of humanitarianism, aimed at reducing the global effects of poverty, has seen limited success. Africa's environmental and colonial history has set the food economy up for failure. The dynamics of the modern global economy perpetuate that position. The future of hunger in Africa cannot depend on UN humanitarian aid, which has made small but insufficient progress. Instead, the cycle of hunger in Africa must be addressed from a multilateral approach.

Section C: Food, Nutrition, and Human Capabilities

In the previous section, I discussed the issue of the food crisis in the global sphere, including historical, economic and political dimensions. In this section, I want to look at the local sphere and how food relates to individuals, families and communities. I'm interested in demonstrating the instrumental role of food in unlocking the human potential and the implications of this for society.

Food Distribution and Sociology

Africa has the highest rate of population growth as a continent.[45] In 1950, the people of Africa made up about 7 percent of the world's population. In 2050, they will be about 22 percent, despite the rest of the world's exponential population growth. Population growth puts additional pressure on the already high constraints of Africa's agricultural sector. It must not only catch up to feed Africa's current population but increase to feed the future population. A sufficient domestic food supply is necessary for equal distribution. Population growth accompanies sociological changes in society, and these can be barriers to food distribution – especially geographical changes, the growth of a middle class, and an increasing young population.[46]

The urban population has been neglected thus far in this chapter. Africa's urban growth is expected to increase by about three-fold from 2015 to 2050, while the rural population is predicted to increase by only 58 percent over same period.[47] Population growth is highly concentrated

---

[45] United Nations, "Population," *United Nations*, n.d., www.un.org/en/sections/issues-depth/population/.

[46] John Cleland and Kazuyo Machiyama, "The Challenges Posed by Demographic Change in Sub-Saharan Africa: A Concise Overview," *Population and Development Review* 43 (2017): 264–286.

[47] Ibid.

in cities, which provide unique challenges to hunger. Urbanization is associated with economic shifts to nonagricultural jobs, but this market does not exist in many African cities, resulting in large unemployed populations. And these urban poor cannot support themselves with subsistence agriculture.[48]

Cities pose the challenge of the "urban food desert." A food desert is an impoverished area in a city that experiences food insecurity. There may be a lack of supermarkets, or the existing food infrastructure is too far away or too expensive. The urban poor resort to eating a large amount of processed or other cheap, carbohydrate-rich foods, resulting in malnutrition. An analysis of urban planning in Uganda found that food infrastructure is rarely a factor in urban planning.[49] A lack of supermarkets usually creates a demand for informal food markets that are harder to accommodate in urban planning. Their pricing and taxation are also difficult to control. The urban poor are unlikely to receive national food aid in African nations. Food aid through systems like food stamps are impractical because of poor infrastructure and informal markets.

Another issue, related to food security and the urban poor, is the growth of the middle class. The African Development Bank has identified the growth of the middle class as essential for Africa's economic growth.[50] The middle class is expected to purchase more consumer products and services, providing jobs that lift the poorer class out of poverty. In Africa, the middle class is a very diverse category that includes those living just above the poverty line and those making a comfortable living. The international poverty line is about two dollars a day; individuals living just above this line are defined as the vulnerable middle class. This vulnerable middle class makes up about 60 percent of Africa's middle class. It does not act as a middle class "should" act, living very close to poverty and lacking the middle class's expected economic activity or political engagement.[51]

A topic of debate is whether the middle class will demand local or imported food. The vulnerable urban middle class is one of the fastest growing groups, which affects national economies. To promote food security and sustainable environmental and economic development, this class must purchase locally grown foods; imported foods leave them

---

[48] Jonathan Crush and Jane Battersby, *Rapid Urbanisation, Urban Food Deserts and Food Security in Africa*, 1st ed. (Cham: Springer Verlag, 2016).

[49] Ibid.

[50] David Tschirley et al., "The Rise of a Middle Class in East and Southern Africa: Implications for Food System Transformation," *Journal of International Development* 27, no. 5 (2015): 628–646.

[51] Ibid.

vulnerable to fluctuations in global markets. The middle class purchases more meat and produce than the poorer class, giving them more influence over the food market. Analysts have found that the vulnerable urban middle class is not more likely to purchase imported processed food than the urban poor – there is not an innate preference for the market to focus solely on imported food.[52] Middle class growth is compatible with sustainable food networks. Governments must get involved in mindful urban planning and consider food infrastructure to avoid urban food deserts.

Gender is another demographic factor contributing to unequal food distribution. Women in many African nations do not have equal educational opportunities, land rights, or access to resources. In rural areas, women managing farms are likely to be less productive than men for these reasons. They are less likely to have capital or invest it in land, because of uncertain land rights. They are less likely to have information about agricultural techniques because of exclusion and a lack of education.[53] Women in agriculture are less likely to share information due to social and political restrictions. Families in urban areas, led by single mothers, are twice as likely to have issues with food security because women do not have fair employment opportunities.[54] Programs such as African Women in Agriculture Research and Development (AWARD) are necessary for gender inclusion and better agricultural information and resources for women.[55]

Increasing fertility rates in African nations also affect women in the economy. Women are less likely to find employment in areas with high fertility rates, because they are needed to raise children. Children may be able to work to a limited degree, but they are less productive until they reach maturity. Note that I use the term child *work*, not child labor, referring to unharmful ways children contribute to the household through limited agricultural work, housework, or simple chores. These children also require investment in education and healthcare to grow into healthy adults who can contribute to the economy.[56] Having many children puts a high resource strain on families and limits the labor capacity of mothers. Therefore, nations should invest in family planning education for

[52] Ibid.
[53] Ruth Oniang'o, "Women Are Still the Key in Agriculture and Food Security in Africa," *South African Journal of Clinical Nutrition* 18, no. 2 (2005): 150–154.
[54] Crush and Battersby, *Rapid Urbanisation, Urban Food Deserts and Food Security in Africa*.
[55] Africa Research Bulletin: Economic, Financial and Technical Series, "Women in Agriculture," *Africa Research Bulletin* 49, no. 10 (2012): 19743B–19743C.
[56] Cleland and Machiyama, "The Challenges Posed by Demographic Change in Sub-Saharan Africa."

sustainable development, especially in urban areas where resources and employment are limited.

Agriculture investment must focus on more than improving productivity. The equal distribution of food must also be emphasized, which can be done through economic policies that improve the condition of the middle class, especially in urban areas. It must include solutions for the unique challenges of urban areas, and it must increase women's rights to land, employment, and education. Working toward economic and environmental sustainability will allow African nations to consume less imported food and increase their ability to access local food. The result means more independence from global food markets and less vulnerability to market crashes and famine.

Nutrition, Health, and Society

Undernutrition is a type of malnutrition where an individual does not consume enough daily calories over time. Individuals who suffer from malnutrition are consuming the right number of calories that their body needs, but they are not getting the micronutrients they need. Micronutrients include vitamins and minerals such as zinc, copper, and B12. Malnutrition often occurs when agricultural or economic limitations lead to a diet that is mostly carbohydrates.[57] Malnutrition, like undernutrition, poses serious health problems, and these various definitions of hunger must be considered when evaluating global data. Data based on caloric intake alone provides an incomplete picture of food insecurity's effects. Both malnutrition and undernutrition have negative impacts that go beyond starvation.

Malnutrition's effects are extensive, including diseases such as pellagra, scurvy, and anemia. Malnutrition also prevents individuals and communities from defending themselves against diseases. Malnourished populations have a weakened immune system, decreasing their ability to recover from illness such as HIV, malaria, and cholera. This is why malnutrition, either directly or indirectly, is a significant factor in about half the deaths of children in SSA.[58] A poor maternal diet during pregnancy, indicated by a low birth weight, causes delayed child development. Africa is noted to have a low-birth-weight rate of about 14 percent, getting as high as

---

[57] Justus Ochieng et al., "How Promoting Consumption of Traditional African Vegetables Affects Household Nutrition Security in Tanzania," *Renewable Agriculture and Food Systems* 33, no. 2 (2018): 105–115.

[58] Roy J. Hillocks, "Farming for Balanced Nutrition: An Agricultural Approach to Addressing Micronutrient Deficiency among the Vulnerable Poor in Africa," *African Journal of Food, Agriculture, Nutrition and Development* 11, no. 2 (2011).

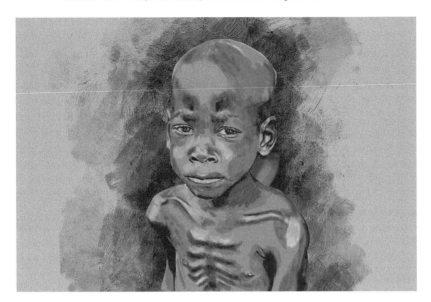

Figure 14.2 A portrait of a child shrunken by starvation.

24 percent in Senegal.[59] Compromised early development makes children more vulnerable to delays or permanent damage to their physical and developmental health. Breast milk production that is also compromised by malnutrition can worsen these delays.

Growth that is compromised by nutritional deficiencies is called "stunted" growth, which is a well-known phenomenon in biology and public health. Stunted growth means that hunger is not a temporary state but a trauma that impacts lifelong development. It not only affects the lives of individuals and families, it also has a cost on society. Recall the figure that I gave earlier on malnutrition's cost to society: about 3.5 trillion dollars a year.[60] Healthcare for stunted children and the economic loss caused by their poor health contributes to this cost significantly. Stunted growth degrades the quality of a nation's human capital. The large youth population is one of Africa's greatest untapped potentials; maintaining the quality of this human capital should be the top priority of nations. Public policy must fight malnutrition to promote economic development.

---

[59] World Health Organization, "Low Birth Weight: Data by Country," *World Health Organization*, June 3, 2019, https://apps.who.int/gho/data/node.main.LOWBIRTHWEIG HT?lang=en.
[60] FAO, "Understanding the True Cost of Malnutrition."

Epigenetics is a growing field of biology studying how the environment affects an individual's genetic expression. An individual's DNA, or genotype, stays the same throughout their life. Yet DNA has alleles, or multiple traits for different phenotypes, physical genetic expressions. The dominant allele in DNA is usually expressed while the recessive allele stays dormant. Recessive alleles are prevented from forming the proteins needed for expression because they are surrounded by a methyl group that acts as a cushion, keeping the recessive trait from being expressed. Epigenetics has found that environmental factors such as hunger can cause demethylation of DNA, expressing genes that were previously unexpressed.[61]

There are a wide variety of causes and effects to this process, many of which are under intense debate, but epigenetics has found conclusive evidence that malnutrition causes altered gene expression. This establishes that stunting not only impacts a child's physical development at time of malnutrition, but it also alters lifelong development.[62] There is evidence that the effects of epigenetics are intergenerational, meaning that the child of a malnourished individual may experience stunting even if they receive proper nutrition.[63] Malnutrition is a type of trauma, causing peak levels of stress hormones, cortisol, and impacting demethylation. Trauma can also be intergenerationally transmitted through psychological processes in families and communities.[64] Epigenetic and psychological mechanisms are just examples of how malnutrition can negatively affect individuals and communities.

A common intervention to combat the epigenetic and physical consequences of malnutrition is the use of nutritional supplements. These nutritional supplements are often given out by organizations such as the UN, containing the correct macro and micronutrients that an individual requires. They are prescribed like medicine to individuals who are sick or children who are malnourished, and they have been found effective in getting children and sick individuals back on track to a healthy life. One innovative nutritional supplement is called Plumpy'Nut, which has been

[61] What Is Epigenetics, "DNA Methylation," *What Is Epigenetics*, n.d., www .whatisepigenetics.com/dna-methylation/.

[62] E. Susser et al., "Maternal Prenatal Nutrition and Health in Grandchildren and Subsequent Generations," *Annual Review of Anthropology* 41 (2012): 577–610.

[63] Lucia L. Lam et al., "Factors Underlying Variable DNA Methylation in a Human Community Cohort," *Proceedings of the National Academy of Sciences of the United States of America* 109 (2012): 17253–17260.

[64] Gregory E. Miller, Edith Chen, and Karen J. Parker, "Psychological Stress in Childhood and Susceptibility to the Chronic Diseases of Aging: Moving toward a Model of Behavioral and Biological Mechanisms," *Psychological Bulletin* 137, no. 6 (2011): 959–997.

on the news as an innovative solution for providing food aid. It does not expire easily and is very rich in nutritional content.[65] Issues with nutritional supplements are their unsustainable model as well as the tendency for families to share them. Plumpy'Nut has been criticized for its bland taste and incompatibility with local cultures; promoting diverse agriculture is a better long-term nutritional intervention.[66]

Food, Well-Being, and Human Capabilities

Often, the investment in food and nutrition for a nation's population has been framed as an investment in human capital. I've included this idea in the previous section to support economic investment in better food systems and hunger interventions.

One problem that arises is that the human-capital theory is based on a specific value, that of the capitalist economy. This is problematic for two reasons. First, not all societies value a capitalist economy. In Africa, several influential leaders have denounced capitalism as unable to work in Africa as it did in the West. Second, human capital theory reduces people to their ability to make money. This underestimates their ability to contribute to society in other ways, including through religion, altruism, human rights, or politics.[67] It further devalues the intrinsic value of human dignity, the human right to food.

Instead of using human-capital theory to explain the benefit of investing in the individual to society, I will utilize the theory of human capabilities. This theory is a type of welfare economics that seeks to measure the capabilities of individuals to achieve their desired functioning based on their resources and individual conversion factors. Simply put, human capabilities measure the ability of individuals to reach their goals. It serves as a process to identify barriers to their success. This theory is more internationally applicable because it does not assume that income is the desired goal.

One idea key to human capabilities is human well-being. Amartya Sen claims that humans' ability to achieve their goals are limited by every aspect of their well-being, including physical health.[68] In our context, we are interested in the instrumental value of food as a resource that allows for other capabilities as well as access to food as an intrinsic desired

---

[65] Kate Klonick, "Peanut Paste Saves Starving African Children," *ABC News*, October 1, 2016, https://abcnews.go.com/Health/story?id=2497593&page=1.

[66] Ochieng et al., "How Promoting Consumption of Traditional African Vegetables Affects Household Nutrition Security in Tanzania."

[67] Steven J. Klees, "Human Capital and Rates of Return: Brilliant Ideas or Ideological Dead Ends?" *Comparative Education Review* 60, no. 4 (2016): 644–672.

[68] Amartya Sen, "Reason, Freedom and Well-Being," *Utilitas* 18, no. 1 (2006): 80–96.

functioning. In the previous two sections, I've analyzed the negative individual and intergenerational impacts of poor nutrition. Lack of access to food affects an individual in every aspect of their health, moving on to affect their overall well-being. I've also addressed the sociological factors that limit access to food. For policymakers, improving the social and physical institutions that perpetuate mass malnutrition will greatly increase citizens' human capabilities. This is the duty of a government that answers to the well-being of its people and the longevity of the state.

Section D: Possible Interventions

This chapter has described some of the complexities of the Nigerian-cum-African food crisis. There is no one direct cause, but a combination of factors layered on top of each other. The following model visually represents how factors trickle down to influence individual families. Global factors, such as the global economy and international policy, contribute to national food shortages. National economies and land policies affect the health of the agricultural sector. The agricultural sector influences community food shortages through poor productivity and inflation. Community factors, such as job availability, infrastructure, and wealth distribution affect family food security. Each layer of influence has problematic aspects contributing to Africa's food shortage. This model provides an introduction to the complexities of the food crisis in Africa and critical points for intervention.

There is no single cause of Africa's food crisis; it developed over time through complex historical and economic circumstances and a layered problem requires a layered solution. The solution should apply interventions on macroscopic and microscopic levels. Many creative, innovative solutions have been proposed to create sustainable change in African food systems. Here are a few recommendations that scholars and international policymakers have proposed.

Global Interventions

Global interventions in the African food system usually originate with the United Nations. It is not a perfect organization, but the UN has facilitated international communication and collaboration. Many Pan-African organizations, such as PAFO,[69] also invite the innovation and collaboration of multiple nations. For global interventions that would aid in solving the

---

[69] Panafrican Farmers' Organization, "Mission PAFO," *Panafrican Farmers' Organization*, September 14, 2017, http://pafo-africa.org/spip.php?article26.

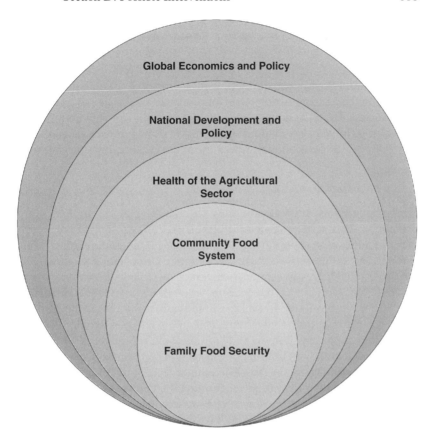

Figure 14.3 Visual model of the layered factors which influence food security in Africa.

African food crisis, I have four main recommendations. First, an international entity must hold nations accountable for their commitment to hunger. At present, no entity measures nations' commitment to hunger reduction. Creating a scale that ranks nations by their commitment to hunger reduction would provide humanitarian groups with the necessary information to make effective investments. Such a scale would include factors such as national policies toward hunger reduction and relative amounts of money spent on hunger reduction. Food or money donated to nations that actively implement plans toward hunger reduction would be spent more efficiently.[70]

---

[70] Te Lintelo et al., "Measuring the Commitment to Reduce Hunger: A Hunger Reduction Commitment Index," *Food Policy* 44 (2014): 115–128.

My second recommendation is for continued work to reduce global emissions. Carbon emissions are the primary factor in global warming, which has had and will continue to have significant impact on African agriculture. This is a global concern – the negative effects of climate change are global, and the large majority of carbon emissions aren't coming from Africa. My third recommendation is for more sustainable global trade solutions, such as limits on how much food can be exported from countries in a food crisis. Finally, international intervention should invest education and capital in the African economy, especially for the livelihood of small farmers.

National Interventions

National policy is difficult and slow to change. Nations in Africa are challenged with a heterogeneity of ethnicity, religion, and class, which causes conflict when combined with inequality. It is tempting for nations to focus on export crops to make more money immediately. But dependency on exports leaves an economy vulnerable to global fluctuations, which has grave consequences. In Africa, poverty leaves individuals unable to purchase imported food, and all the home-grown food has been sold for profit. I recommend that governments support national agricultural policies encouraging small farmers and limiting cash crops. Agricultural policy should also include environmental protections, equal land distribution, and limits on foreign land grabs. Governments must invest in agricultural research; each nation has unique environmental conditions and crops that require information sharing for best practices. Governments must also pursue gender reform by investing in women's education and property rights. Finally, they must invest in education to promote better economic growth and the implementation of best agricultural practices. Investment in education is best paired with school feeding programs, which both reduce malnutrition and encourage children to go to school.

Community and Family Interventions

Many different community intervention programs have been successfully implemented to aid in times of food crisis. The most widely known is the use of microcredit – small loans that enable small businesses or farmers to get started. These loans allow farmers to purchase seeds or agricultural technology, increasing their productivity.[71] Microcredit is often organized

---

[71] Rosemary E. Isoto, Abdoul G. Sam, and David S. Kraybill, "Uninsured Health Shocks and Agricultural Productivity among Rural Households: The Mitigating Role of Micro-Credit," *The Journal of Development Studies* 53, no. 12 (2017): 2050–2066.

in a community setting, where an existing community organization can regulate the partitioning of this capital. Another proposed intervention is to provide free food at schools.[72] This would allow children to get the nutrition and education that they need, although it requires either NGO or government funding, which is not always available.

Community involvement is a critical component of food security interventions. In Africa, different communities within nations have distinct values and religions. Communities often value the insight of elders, and they want to work together to do what is best for the community. Promoting shared traditional values and stories can help promote food sustainability: African religious values often focus on respecting the Earth and providing for the community, promoting eco-friendly practices.[73] Traditional medicine that includes food may help promote a more diverse diet. Instead of teaching nutrition and healthy eating through imported foods, interventions must focus on the available, traditional crops that provide the required micronutrients.[74]

The education of women is another important piece of intervention. Educating women early, especially on economic and health matters, allows them to be educated mothers. Educated women are more likely to use birth control, allowing them to control population growth and offering them more economic opportunities. Educating women would allow single-mother households to access economic opportunity and escape food insecurity. Mothers are often in charge of their children's eating patterns, and their nutritional health affects the development of their children in the womb and while breastfeeding. The World Health Organization estimates that around 800,000 lives could be saved globally each year through consistent breastfeeding, showing the powerful effects of educating mothers on best health practices.[75]

[72] Josette Sheeran, "Ending Hunger Now," TEDGlobal, video, 19:03, 2011, www.ted.com/talks/josette_sheeran_ending_hunger_now.

[73] Lancaster University, "Traditional Beliefs Promote Sustainability in West Africa," *Science Daily*, March 4, 2015, www.sciencedaily.com/releases/2015/03/150304110252.htm.

[74] Monica Samuel Chipungahelo, "Knowledge Sharing Strategies on Traditional Vegetables for Supporting Food Security in Kilosa District, Tanzania," *Library Review* 64, no. 3 (2015): 229–247.

[75] World Health Organization, "Increasing Breastfeeding Could Save 800,000 Children and US $300 Billion Every Year," *World Health Organization*, n.d., www.who.int/maternal_child_adolescent/news_events/news/2016/exclusive-breastfeeding/en/.

15 Women's Marginalization

Introduction

The marginalization of women is a global phenomenon; however, in developing countries like Nigeria, the situation is accentuated and can be traced to several colonial, sociocultural, religious, and constitutional factors in the society. This chapter aims at evaluating the marginalization of women in postcolonial Nigeria. This chapter further provides an overview of the position of women in Nigeria and examines the role of colonialism in promoting women's marginalization in the country. It considers the role of the patriarchal religions of Islam and Christianity as impediments to the full expression of women in major spheres of the society. Also, I identify women's financial incapacity as one of the reasons for their underrepresentation in politics. The predominant patriarchal culture in the country fosters the subordination of women, and therefore encourages placing women on the margins of society. Several constitutional provisions have been linked to the pervasive gender inequality in the country, while the chapter also explores the implications of women's marginalization in a developing economy like Nigeria's. However, the chapter notes that although the nation has ratified and promulgated many policies and laws with the intention of eradicating gender inequality, the situation has persisted and seems to be waxing stronger.

Overview of Women's Marginalization in Nigeria

Marginalization refers to a prejudicial relegation of a group of people or concepts in all or certain spheres of human society on the basis of insignificance or inferiority.[1] Therefore, with reference to women, the perception of subordination or secondary existence can be seen as a global challenge. However, in countries like Nigeria with its colonial history

[1] Mandy Jollie Bako and Jawad Syed, "Women's Marginalization in Nigeria and the Way Forward," *Human Resource Development International* 21 (2018): 425–443.

and its cultural and religious ideologies grounded in patriarchy, there are startling reports of women's continued marginalization in different areas of development. In other words, in the sociopolitical, economic, and educational spheres, women have experienced and continue to experience discrimination and underrepresentation on the basis of gender, which places Nigerian women in disempowered positions.

In the nation's economy, following a 2008 gender matrix for economic activities in Nigeria as evaluated by Okeyezu et al., women's participation in the labor market constituted about 43.1 percent, as against 56.9 percent of male participation.[2] They note however that although the aforementioned statistics do not present a cry for help, in reality women occupy highly underpaid sectors while the high-income-yielding economic sectors are largely inaccessible to them; for the few women who make their way to these income-yielding sectors, top administrative positions are beyond their reach. Although several factors have been attributed to the economic marginalization of women in Nigeria, the truth remains that there is no justification for the alienation of women from the nation's economic activities.

A more recent study conducted by the National Bureau of Statistics (NBS) shows that the trend of women's marginalization in the economic sector continues, and not much improvement has occurred since the time of Okeyezu et al.'s evaluation. The NBS report shows that the percentage of men employed by the state civil service from the year 2014–15 is about 68.84 percent for both the senior and junior positions, as against 38.16 percent for women, which reflects the economic situation of women in the country.[3] To corroborate this evaluation, Bako and Syed are of the opinion that women constantly face marginalization in all areas of the nation's economy. More specifically, they argue:

Marginalization of women is persistent in Nigeria in almost all spheres of the economy ... women constantly facing massive inequalities in the labour market. In working life, women meet with higher rates of unemployment, fewer possibilities for a career, and lower wages. Even highly educated women or those trying to attain higher education face marginalization in Nigeria.[4]

Politically, the marginalization of women has a long history, dating back to the colonial period when women were exempted from political

---

[2] Chinwe R. Okeyezu, P. Egbo Obiamaka, and J. U. J. Onwumere, "Shaping the Nigerian Economy: The Role of the Women," *Acta Universitatis Danubius, Economica* 8, no. 4 (2012): 15–24.

[3] National Bureau of Statistics, *Statistical Report on Women and Men in Nigeria* (Abuja: National Bureau of Statistics, 2018).

[4] Bako and Syed, "Women's Marginalization in Nigeria and the Way Forward," 422.

affairs as a result of the evident European bias against women.[5] This era, as noted by Ingyoroko et al., introduced the long-standing marginalization of women in the Nigeria's politics.[6] According to Olatunde, by the 1950s, after the incursion of colonialism, the contribution of women to governance began to diminish.[7] Consolidating previous opinions, Anunobi states that colonialism was introduced at a time when women's marginalization and restrictions on women's roles were the norm in Victorian England, which helps explain British bias against women and their exclusion of women from political concerns.[8] Yet the marginalization of women in politics has continued since the end of colonialism and is still a topical issue in local and international discourses on gender.

Women constitute about half of Nigeria's electorate, but according to recent political reports by the National Bureau of Statistics, since the emergence of the democratic administration in 1999, women have been underrepresented in all three arms of government. The positions of the president and the vice president seem to have been specifically carved out for men because, since 1999, no woman has occupied those positions. With reference to the appointed federal ministerial positions, the NBS shows that out of the 341 ministers who served from 1999 to 2015, 47 were women, for a total of 14 percent female representation. In the national parliament, from 2007 to 2011, the NBS reports that the highest levels of women's representation is about 7.2 percent at both the Senate and House of Representatives.[9] This, therefore, gives credence to Bako and Syed's opinion that "women's fate in politics has worsened."[10]

This situation has led to the implementation of affirmative action to encourage women's participation in all governing processes. However, in spite of these efforts, Omenka states that the height of women's political participation so far is the 16.7 percent attained in 2007 as deputy governors.[11] Unfortunately, the percentage continues to dwindle with

---

[5] Diane Olatunde, "Women's Participation and Representation in Nigeria's Politics in the Last Decade (1999–2009)" (thesis, University of the Witwatersrand, 2010).

[6] M. Ingyoroko, E. T. Sugh, and Alkali Terfa, "Nigerian Women and the Reformation of the Political System: A Historical Perspective," *Journal of Socialomics* 6, no. 2 (2017) :2–8.

[7] Olatunde, "Women's Participation and Representation in Nigeria's Politics in the Last Decade (1999–2009)."

[8] Fredoline Anunobi, "Women and Development in Africa: From Marginalization to Gender Inequality," *African Social Science Review* 2, no. 1 (2002): 41–63.

[9] National Bureau of Statistics, *Statistical Report on Women and Men in Nigeria.*

[10] Bako and Syed, "Women's Marginalization in Nigeria and the Way Forward."

[11] Nicodemus Omenka, "Appraising Nigeria's Implementation of the National Policy of 35% Affirmative Action for Women, 1999–2016" (thesis, Ebonyi State University, 2017), www.eajournals.org/wp-content/uploads/Appraising-Nigeria%E2%80%99s-Implementation-of-the-National-Policy-of-35-Affirmative-Action-for-Women-1999–2016.pdf.

more elected positions, a clear sign of the nation's aversion to women's participation in politics. It is therefore necessary to examine other likely factors that could have brought about this age-long marginalization of women in the nation's politics.

In the education sector, as noted by British Council reports in 2014, the marginalization of women – especially in the northern rural areas of Nigeria – is very apparent, and women constitute the population least likely to attend school at any level.[12] This reality sheds light on the regional disparities in women's access to education in Nigeria, implying that several regional factors affect women's education in different parts of the country. According to the statistical reports presented, 50 percent more young men in the southeast are literate compared to young women in the northwest, approximately 96 to 46 percent.[13] Also, the council's situational analysis on women and education in northern Nigeria shows that girls are less likely to attend primary school than boys. In their reports from research conducted in 2009–10, only 58 percent of girls attended primary schools as against the 64 percent of boys from the ages of four to sixteen years.[14] In the southern parts of the nation, the net attendance rate revealed that the number of girls who attended schools in the same academic session was above 90 percent.[15] The rate of school drop out is noticeably higher among girls; according to the Council's reports, 12 percent of girls are more likely to drop out of schools toward the end of their primary education compared to 10 percent of boys. This situation is often seen in the rural parts of the north-eastern and north-western parts of the country.[16] However, the regional disparities notwithstanding, women's marginalization in the education sector is a national phenomenon, especially considering that the Council's report attests that there are more literate men than women in the country.

The aforementioned overview is not merely to quote statistical reports, but rather to acquaint the reader with the extent of women's marginalization and their status in the major spheres of the nation's development. It will equally produce the much-needed interest for an in-depth evaluation and exploration of the current marginal position of women in Nigerian society. Nigerian society has gone through several eras in its development – the precolonial eras, the incursive colonial regimes, and the

[12] British Council, *Girls' Education in Nigeria: Issues, Influences and Actions: Report 2014* (London: British Council, 2014), www.britishcouncil.org/sites/default/files/british-council-girls-education-nigeria-report.pdf.
[13] Ibid.   [14] Ibid.   [15] Ibid.
[16] *Education for All: Global Monitoring Report*. Teaching and learning for all. Paris: UNESCO.

current postcolonial experience – and in all these eras, women have faced marginalization in different areas and in several ways. This study therefore intends to explore the marginalization of women in postcolonial Nigeria and its persistence, irrespective of the various efforts put in place to eliminate it, while also examining its implication for Nigeria's development.

Women's Marginalization in Various Areas of the Nation's Development

The pervasive marginalization of women in modern Nigeria, as earlier noted by Anunobi, can be traced to the nation's contact with the European colonizers, who, at the time of colonization, were already used to women's secondary positions in their home countries.[17] It was only logical for them to view the debatable inclusivity enjoyed by Nigerian women at the time as inappropriate, hence their exclusion of women from core societal affairs like politics. Pereira considers the colonial government as authoritarian, taking over traditional authority and replacing it with a supreme legal and political authority, therefore enabling them to impose their Victorian ideologies of women's alienation on Nigerian soil.[18]

Economic Marginalization of Women

Economically, colonialism superimposed men on women, eliciting a gender dominance that was more or less absent in the precolonial society. Before colonization, women and men were said to have played complementary roles in the overall development of the society, and no party's power seemed to outweigh the other so glaringly. Women were noted to have participated socially, economically, and politically, and still held domestic authorities. However, the colonial regime offered men the upper hand in the nation's economy, giving room to a long-term postcolonial imbalance and inequality in gender. Therefore, it can be stated that the engineering of a colonial economy on the basis of a bias against women led to the marginalization of women in Nigerian society. As noted by Dennis, the colonialists brought with them what they perceived to be appropriate social roles for men and women, and therefore created separate work segments on the basis of gender. Men were encouraged to the cultivation of cash crops for the international market, which yielded

---

[17] Anunobi, "Women and Development in Africa."
[18] Charmaine Pereira, "Domesticating Women? Gender, Religion and the State in Nigeria Under Colonial and Military Rule," *African Identities* 3, no. 1 (2005): 69–94.

massive returns, while women were confined to food crops with scantier yields. She also notes that the importation of manufactured goods affected the area of crafts and skills, which was an area rather dominated by women.[19] Therefore, as stated by Pereira:

Elite men worked as import-export merchants, colonial servants and professionals. These were occupations that brought them influence with Europeans, authority over other people and wealth in the form of privately-owned capital, real estate and luxury goods. Elite women on the other hand, toiled in the home and community to spread Christianity and civilization for fewer tangible rewards. Colonial rule brought about complex and contradictory effects on the material conditions and status of the woman. The growth of international trade under colonialism worked to the detriment of most West African women.[20]

Also, combined with missionary influences, Nigerian women were taught the concept of exclusive domesticity, especially since the eighteenth-century Victorian ethos preserved a place for women within their husbands' homes where they were shielded from the toil and bustle of the outside world. These women were expected to be pious, moral, subservient, and caring, which therefore led to Pereira's conclusion that the marginalization of women from core societal affairs stems from their role as "guardians of virtue."[21] This Victorian ideology of women's domesticity and silence, and the attendant patriarchy, has therefore permeated people's ideologies in the current postcolonial Nigerian society. This conception continues to play a role in gender power relations in all spheres of the society. However, Dennis opines that the changes Nigeria underwent with the advent of colonialism and the eventual independence led to the relegation of women, and their dominance in menial jobs, petty trading activities, and small-scale food production.[22]

The economic marginalization of women in the country has however persisted and is often manifested in unequal access to land in postcolonial Nigeria. Women's limited access to land – a major income-generating asset and a huge source of economic empowerment – has contributed to the financial vulnerability of women in the country. According to Oriaghan, there is a huge gender gap in land ownership in the country; in his opinion, 2 percent of women in comparison to 17 percent of men own land within the country.[23] There is, however, a strong connection

---

[19] Carolyne Dennis, "Women and the State in Nigeria: The Case of the Federal Military Government 1984–1985," in *Women, State and Ideology*, ed. Haleh Afshar (London: Macmillan Press, 1987).
[20] Pereira, "Domesticating Women?" 74.   [21] Ibid, 75.   [22] Ibid.
[23] Izehi Oriaghan, 2018 "A Quick Look at Women's Land and Inheritance Rights in Nigeria," *Landesa*, July 30, 2018, www.landesa.org/a-quick-look-at-womens-land-and-inheritance-rights-in-nigeria/.

between the gender disparity in land ownership in the country and the pervasive poverty amongst women. In other words, since men have the upper hand in income-generating assets like land, they also have the power to tilt the society's economic situation in their favor. Therefore, the absence of that form of power for most women places them on the bottom of the economic scale, kept in disempowered positions thus making them targets for exploitation.[24] This situation is primarily influenced by the economic implications of land, which Attah describes as follows:

> Real estate (land) whether developed or undeveloped is economically prized in Nigeria; it is a most important element of both group and individual ownership. This may be because, apart from being an important means of securing shelter and livelihood (primarily through farming), it has since the colonial period been central to trade and commerce as means of securing credit.[25]

Due to certain cultural practices in the country, very few women have access to lands for agricultural and credit purposes. On the other hand, land is important for economic growth; the lack therefore – as in the case of women – is a major generator of inequality in power, resources, and ultimately wealth. These cultural practices allow excluding women from land ownership, which therefore makes it impossible for women to acquire lands for farming – a major source of income for women in rural areas. It also makes it impossible for women to raise capital from the sale of valuable assets like land, and they also cannot provide collateral in the acquisition of loans for the initiation of businesses. Gender discrimination in land ownership is thus one of the leading causes of women's subjugation in Nigeria.[26] In other words, financial capacity is the bedrock of all forms of power; since that initial financial base has been withheld from women, their secondary position has persisted.

Political Marginalization of Women

In politics, women were initially denied franchise in different parts of the country; franchise for men was a norm, and therefore women had to fight for theirs. The exclusion of women in Southern Nigeria from voting until

---

[24] John E Roemer, "What Is Exploitation? Reply to Jeffrey Reiman," *Philosophy and Public Affairs* (1989): 90–97.

[25] Micheal Attah, "Divorcing Marriage from Marital Assets: Why Equity and Women Fail in Property Readjustment Actions in Nigeria," *Journal of African Law* 62, no. 3 (2018): 427–446.

[26] Taiwo Ajala, "Gender Discrimination in Land Ownership and the Alleviation of Women's Poverty in Nigeria: A Call for New Equities," *International Journal of Discrimination and the Law* 17, no. 1 (2017): 51–66.

eleven years preceding independence shows that women were sidelined from political decisions for that period of time. In the North, the situation of women has always been relatively tougher than that of the South. Women in that region, as noted by Pereira, gained franchise well after the attainment of independence.[27] Therefore, as the case may be, the colonial Nigerian woman had to fight for women's rights in order to participate in basic societal functions, and sadly the postcolonial woman continues to have to do the same.

According to Olabode et al., women in postcolonial Nigeria have given a lot of support and political patronage to the various governments and regimes the country has experienced since independence. However, sadly, women have hardly benefitted from their devotion toward the ruling parties and governments.[28] In the early years after independence, only a handful of women participated in the nation's governance; they were mostly from the South, as a result of their earlier franchise in 1958 compared to their counterparts in the North. Therefore, 1960 ushered in Wuraola Esan from the West as the first female member of the Parliament, and, in 1961, Margaret Ekpo contested elections under the National Council of Nigeria and the Cameroons (NCNC) political party in the Aba North constituency. She won the elections and became a member of the Eastern Nigerian House of Assembly. This era also produced women like Jane N. Mokelu and Ekpo A. Young, also members of the Eastern House of Assembly.[29]

Though hardly proportionate to the size of the female population in the country, the South conferred a little regard on women in their regions in comparison to the seclusion and total exclusion of women from political affairs that was pervasive in the North. In northern Nigeria, women were granted franchise in 1976; this was however followed by a series of anti-women statements in the National Assembly.[30] As noted by Pereira, given the national independence in 1960, the northern part of the country gained a majority rule at the federal level. This was partly due to the repressive gender practices of the region that was in alliance with the colonial conception of women's alienation. Therefore, the northern ruling party Northern People's Congress (NPC) used their assertion of patriarchy and their religious ideologies of "controlling" their women – which was in congruence to their religious beliefs – to garner regional support and maintain a Hausa/Fulani/Muslim alliance.[31]

[27] Pereira, "Domesticating Women?"
[28] Kolawole Taiwo Olabode, Abubakar M. Bashiru, and Owonibi Elizabeth, "Gender and Party Politics in Africa with Reference to Nigeria," *International Journal of Politics and Good Governance* 3, no. 3 (2012): 1–26.
[29] Ibid.   [30] Ibid.   [31] Pereira, "Domesticating Women?"

The seclusion of women in the northern parts of the country is a clear indication of the impact of religious fundamentalism on the position and situation of women in those regions. Women's seclusion in northern Nigeria dates as far back as the fifteenth century, at which time it was common among women from the upper echelons of society.[32] This period, as noted by Pereira, saw an increase in the recognition of women's formal roles. However, with the formation of the Sokoto Caliphate in the eighteenth century, free women were denounced in an attempt to institute a new order with a focus on moral purity. Therefore, all women who were not under either their husbands or fathers were denounced.[33]

Prior to the eighteenth century, women were noted to have occupied positions of power and were not secluded from society, as they were often spotted mingling freely and conducting farming and trading activities outdoors.[34] Women's activities gradually began to fall within the confines of domesticity, childbirth, and child rearing. There was also an implementation of a gendered division of labor, with women's activities restricted to homesteads, and at some point, this became so restrictive that the women rarely emerged from their homes. No doubt, the seclusion took away the women's voices from societal affairs and totally marginalized them in sociopolitical and economic activities within their various communities. Toward the end of the nineteenth century, their political and formal authority had completely vanished.

This seclusion continued well into colonialism and postcolonial society, giving justification to the late attainment of women's franchise in the region even after independence. Cited in Pereira, Waziri Ibrahim in 1965 in the National Assembly appealed to the general public in response to women's agitations for political rights to leave their women in peace because they were perfectly happy with their subservient position.[35] Pereira also asserts that before the year 1979, the former grand Qadi of the Northern Region, Sheikh Mohammcd Gumi, had expressed his opinion quite specifically on women's unsuitability in political activities, stating that Muslim women should not be allowed to vote or be voted for.[36] This therefore resulted in the inability of prominent female politicians from the North like Hajia Gambo Sawaba to vote and be voted for.[37]

Also, religion constitutes one of the biggest obstacles to women's participation in politics. Islam sees the headship and authority of a woman as

---

[32] Ibid.   [33] Ibid.

[34] Ingyoroko, Sugh, and Terfa, "Nigerian Women and the Reformation of the Political System."

[35] Pereira, "Domesticating Women?"   [36] Ibid.

[37] Olabode, Bashiru, and Elizabeth, "Gender and Party Politics in Africa with Reference to Nigeria."

Figure 15.1 A group of young ladies at a cultural festival.

offensive, and the Christian religion advocates for male superiority and female subordination; this is often expressed in the inability of women to attain certain religious positions in some orthodox Christian churches. This situation is justified by Bible injunctions such as Paul's admonition in his letter to the Corinthians, in the book of Corinthians 14:34–35, where he stated:

Let your women keep silence in the churches for it is not permitted unto them to speak; but they are commanded to be under obedience, as also saith the law. And if they will learn anything, let them ask their husbands at home, for it is a shame for women to speak in church.[38]

Consequently, the ideology of submissiveness in women and male headship impacts the nation's conception of the woman's secondary position. Domesticity is championed by both religions, which is, however, why

---

[38] Book of Corinthians 14:34–35 (KJV).

women are practically hounded to be homemakers and men pleasers. Very specifically, Pittin states that the *Sunday Triumph* newspaper, in a bid to commend the actions of the Kano state government in their efforts to stop girls from hawking, stated that, "Sharia provides that a woman should not be despised upon, a woman is not filth ... Islam provides that a woman should be respected as a daughter, as a mother and as a housewife."[39]

This excerpt from the *Sunday Triumph* reiterates the religion's opinion on the position of women and their restrictions in the modern society. In other words, the concept of authority for women is alien to Islam, and therefore constitutes one of the core factors for women's marginalization in politics and other areas in the nation's development. Politics is a concept reserved for male sensitivities as women are often thought to have no interest, and, quite frankly, very few show interest. The religious conditionings of female temperance, dependence, submission, piety, and morality make it almost impossible for women to reserve any thoughts for political ambitions, let alone actually pursue them. To make matters worse, the very few women who are courageous enough to indulge their political ambitions get little or no support from the Nigerian populace.

Generally, as observed by Olabode et al., since the 1950s, irrespective of female agitations led by Funmilayo Ransome Kuti and Magaret Ekpo, women's participation in the political landscape of the country has been very scanty. During the Second Republic, only three women won positions in the federal House of Representatives: Mrs. J. C. Eze from the Nigerian People's Party (NPP) representing the Uzouwani constituency; V. O. Nnaji also from the NPP; and Mrs. Abiola Babatope from the Unity Party of Nigeria. However, only a few women won elections into the state House of Assembly. Two women were appointed federal ministers, while a number of women were appointed commissioners and a handful of women contested elections in local government councils. In the Third Republic, following the 1990 elections, few women became councilors, while only Titilayo Ajanaku became the chairperson of a Western local government council.[40] No female emerged as governor in that year, and a similar situation continued right into the Fourth Republic. Although the number of female political appointees increased, the same cannot be said for the elected positions, as the nation has not recorded any female president to date. However, this is not to state that there have not been any improvements in women's political positions so far; it is rather to state

---

[39] R. Pittin, "Women, Work and Ideology in Nigeria," *Review of African Political Economy* 52 (2015): 38–52.

[40] Olabode, Bashiru, and Elizabeth, "Gender and Party Politics in Africa with Reference to Nigeria."

Figure 15.2 A woman with her four children hawking mangoes on a street in Lagos as a means of livelihood.

that the marginalization of women within the political terrain is more apparent than in any other area in the country.

The monetization of politics in the country is one of the contributory factors to women's marginalization in politics. Money is a major factor in the Nigerian political terrain. Asking aspirants to pay a sum of five million naira to collect nomination forms is a clear indication that the most financially incapacitated groups in Nigerian society are automatically excluded from the political offices available in the country.[41] According to Usman, going by recent statistics, most Nigerians live below the poverty line in the country, and, since women constitute more than half of the nation's population with the least access to well-paid jobs, they are therefore the highest victims of the pervasive poverty.[42] Poverty in this context is a product of several factors: women's limited access to

---

[41] Ibid., 4.
[42] Umar Shehu Usman, "Women and Poverty in Nigeria: Agenda for Poverty Eradication," *Developing Country Studies* 5, no. 3 (2015): 122–126.

education – especially in the northern parts of the country – is a major contributory factor to the impoverished status of most Northern Nigerian women.

Limited access to education can be traced to several religious and traditional norms in the region. The concept of child marriage is prevalent amongst the Muslim people of northern Nigeria; the early introduction of these Northern Muslim girls into household domesticity, childbearing, and financial dependence automatically takes away their interest in education as well as their chances for one. This, therefore, populates the scene of women petty traders with little or no academic qualifications or skills, and therefore very little income to cater for themselves let alone to purchase political forms. Therefore, the absence of a strong capital base amongst these women translates to little or no female representation in Nigerian political offices.

Women are therefore marginalized in the scramble for the nation's political offices and its financial benefits. Arguing that early marriage promotes women's marginalization in Nigeria, the government signed and ratified a Child Rights Act in 2003. This act put a ban on child marriage, therefore all marriages of those under the age of eighteen were declared void, and betrothals by guardians or parents for children were also considered a contravention to the provisions of the Child Rights Act. The act places a fine of five hundred thousand naira, or a five-year imprisonment on any man who marries a child, or parents or guardians who betroth underage children. However, there has been a lot of backlash from most of the northern states and Islamic leaders such as Imam Sani, who blatantly opposes the implementation of the Child Rights Act stating that in the occasion of its implementation by the government, there will be violence and conflicts which will most likely lead to the deaths of many.[43] In the defense of many Islamic contestations of the Act, most Muslim clerics and the general Muslim public share Sabattou's opinion that "this practice existed before I was born and there is no use complaining about it. My daughter, listen to me; I married your mother at the same age."[44]

However, some states in Northern Nigeria have adopted the Child Rights Act, although there have been self-serving manipulations to the Act. For instance, in Jigawa state, a child, in their opinion, is a person below the age of puberty, which therefore provides varied opinions on the definition of a child. More outrageously, the state reduces the sentence for

---

[43] Ngozi Oluchukwu Odiaka, "The Concept of Gender Justice and Women's Rights in Nigeria: Addressing the Missing Link," *Journal of Sustainable Development, Law and Policy* 2, no. 1 (2013): 190–205.

[44] Cited in Ngozi Oluchukwu Odiaka, "The Concept of Gender Justice and Women's Rights in Nigeria," 195.

defaulters to a fine of five thousand naira and one year imprisonment, or both. Also, the Borno state government finds a loophole in its implementation of the act by stating, "No person under the age of 18 years is capable of contracting a valid marriage unless the Law applicable to the child majority is attained earlier." However, quite conveniently, the Islamic law applicable to the child does not put any age to marriage; while the state puts a fine of ten thousand naira and a prison sentence of six months, or both.[45] As the case may be, the act is almost as good as useless in cases of Muslim girls bound by Islamic injunctions, while it is apparent that these regions have no intention of eliminating child marriage.

Party primary elections in the country are one of the major reasons women are largely under-represented in the nation's politics, as party members usually exhibit a preference for male aspirants.[46] However, this blatant display of male power makes patriarchy a dominant factor in the nation's politics. A good number of Nigerian traditional systems are founded on gender roles and hierarchy, most of which place men at the top of the cadre, and women at the secondary levels. Most of the Nigerian cultural systems uphold male superiority, promote family structures that place the male child above the female, and make husbands the lords of their households. These family structures and gender preferences have been internalized by the Nigerian populace, and find expression in politics. Men automatically take the superior position, expecting the women to follow. The struggle to eliminate women's marginalization and gender discrimination in the country is constantly being contested by "age long cultural practices and belief systems."[47]

Nigeria has come a long way from the supposed precolonial inclusivity in male and female relations in the society. Currently, and as acclaimed by Bako and Syed, women are perceived as weak, only suitable for domestic activities and male gratification. So far, these patriarchal notions frustrate the operations of female activists against the subordinate position of women in the Nigerian society. Patriarchal belief systems are ingrained in the array of ethnic groups in the country. These ethnic subcultures are often represented in the corridors of power, hence the continued operations of patriarchy in the Nigerian political space.

Also, these ethnic paternalistic notions are expressed in many cultural practices in the country. The practice of female genital mutilation was founded on the desire to repress women's sexual expression, but no such

[45] Ibid.
[46] Olabode, Bashiru, and Elizabeth, "Gender and Party Politics in Africa with Reference to Nigeria."
[47] Bako and Syed, "Women's Marginalization in Nigeria and the Way Forward."

measures were put in place for men. Most traditions celebrate male sexual voraciousness and often consider sex as a psychological and physical necessity for the men. This explains the misplaced belief that men are naturally polygamous and, therefore, are not sanctioned in the case of infidelity or promiscuity. The woman is often shamed and resented on such occasions, encouraging the impression that women are property owned by men. These traditional conditionings go a long way to influence women's perceptions of self and the society's action toward women. Most likely, the feeling of being regarded as second-rate human beings affects women's attitude toward positions of power.

Women's Marginalization in the Media

The role of the media in a democratic society like Nigeria cannot be overemphasized. The media is used to inform, educate, influence, and mobilize the public on sensitive issues in the society, hence the need to explore the role of the media in promoting patriarchy and women's marginalization in politics. During elections in the country, the mass media is usually utilized by all political aspirants to create awareness of their political ambitions, and the media achieves this by emphasizing and elaborating their ambitions on their various platforms. However, to elucidate the impact of the media in the society, Egbon states the following in relation to the press:

The press possesses the potential power to influence, not only the people, but also the society as a whole, and this influence can be for the political, socio-cultural and economic good or to the detriment of the country and by logical progression, this could extend to global issues and actions of great concern and magnitude.[48]

Therefore, the mass media – whether print or broadcast – have very massive impacts on the society's political activities. No wonder Endong and Obonganwan are of the opinion that the mass media "enjoys immeasurable powers of socialization, mass mobilization and advocacy."[49] In other words, it has power to sway public opinion on delicate matters, which therefore proves that they can be effective tools in framing the ideologies and opinions of the masses. The media serve as agents of social change and mediators of societal discourses; in other words, they serve as the meeting point between the public and the political aspirants. Therefore,

---

[48] M. Egbon, *Problems of Ethics in the Mass Media: In the Line Editor as Gatekeeper* (Lagos: Nigerian Press Council, 2007), 81–88.
[49] Floribert Patrick Endong and E. Obonganwan, "Media (Mis) Representation of the Nigerian Woman as a Product of the Society," *International Journal of Gender and Women's Studies* 3, no. 1 (2015): 101–106.

they have the power to influence voters through their formation of political understanding and political contexts.[50]

The marginalization of women in Nigerian politics is reflected in media coverage. There is inadequate reportage of female political aspirants in comparison to their male counterparts. In other words, the media in Nigeria plays a huge role in fostering gender inequality by creating a notion of absolute male dominance in all spheres of the nation's development. In politics, inadequate coverage of female politicians tends to encourage the perception of female inadequacy for political affairs. The media presents an androcentric predisposition through their relegation of women's political issues at the expense of the male political jamboree. This therefore influences and shapes public opinion on women and their position in the nation's politics. There is massive underrepresentation of women in politics, as well as chronic gender inequality, but this does not imply that there has been a complete dearth of female political aspirants and some other women who have fought their way into reputable political offices.

In fact, according to Ette, since the end of military dictatorship in 1999, women have taken more active interest in the political arena. They continue to struggle for spaces on newspaper pages, as well as television and radio airtime – which are competitive during elections and often sold to the highest bidder. However, if the media was more concerned in promoting women's visibility and in encouraging female participation in the nation's politics, they would offer women airtime and spaces irrespective of their low budgets. Given the capitalist and commercialized position of the media in the society, the women without massive budgets will continue to be invisible in the media and have little or no chance in winning elective positions in the country, mostly because the media has the power to promote people's images using their ability to elaborate, emphasize, and project positive images of their clients, which in turn sways people's opinions and therefore influences elections in the country.

Because it is inadequate, media coverage open to women has been unable to change social perceptions of the position of women in politics,[51] instead reinforcing conceptions of women being fit for domestic spaces instead of political arenas. Also, the sociocultural constructions of gender roles in Nigerian society influences media coverage and opinions on women and their political ambitions. After all, the media is said to reflect the society in which it operates. Given Nigeria's religious notoriety

---

[50] Mercy Ette, "Where Are Women? Evaluating Visibility of Nigerian Female Politicians in News Media Space," *Gender, Place and Culture, Journal of Feminist Geography* (2017): 1–18.

[51] Ette, "Where Are Women?"

and cultural perceptions of women's subordination, it is therefore not surprising that the nation's mass media reflects the invisibility of women, especially in politics. Oyewole and Olisa report that in 2003, the People's Democratic Party (PDP) female aspirant in Imo state was said to have been denied airtime to campaign on the state's radio, while being requested to get state government approval, which is in itself a clear violation of her freedom to express herself.[52]

According to Oyesomi and Oyero, in the 2011 elections, Nigerian newspapers – particularly *Punch* and *Guardian* – did not grant women adequate coverage compared to the male political aspirants. In a content analysis derived from their study, out of the 464 stories analyzed, only 62 reports were on female participation in the elections.[53] This limited visibility is therefore problematic and continues to reinforce age-long theories of female subordination, therefore influencing the portrayal of women – especially with reference to politics – as helpless and devoid of agency. However, the media strengthens this situation by the continued stereotypical representation of women in Nigeria. This informs the view of Administration and Cost of Elections Project (ACE):

Men are more visible and dominant in both media and elections and gender stereotypes prevail in both. These differences are mutually reinforcing in the sense that less visibility of women in the media impacts their political success; and fewer women politicians means fewer news stories focusing on women leaders.[54]

Representation of women as merely sexual beings or domestic home-makers contributes to the trivialization of their political ambitions. In other words, most people cannot reconcile the image of the sexual woman the media presents and a political office.

Culture in Property Marginalization

Aside from economic, political, and media marginalization, women are equally culturally marginalized in terms of legal acquisition and owner-ship of properties and inheritance. The practice of inheritance and inheritance rights within the country are majorly influenced by the existing cultures and norms of the communities involved. This conception

---

[52] John Oyewole Ayodele and Saheed Damilola Olisa, "Media, Politics and Gender Marginalization in Nigeria: Is There Still a Way Out?" *International Journal of Media, Journalism and Mass Communication* 3, no. 1 (2017): 20–26.

[53] K. Oyesomi and O. Oyero, "Newspaper Coverage of Women's Participation in the 2011 General Elections in Nigeria," *The Journal of the African Council for Communication Education* 10, no. 1 (2012): 136–156.

[54] *ACE*, "Media and Elections," *ACE*, 2012, https://aceproject.org/ace-en/topics/me/onePage.

therefore gives credence to Ashiru's opinion that culture is a major player in dictating the operations of gender with respect to gender roles, and legal and economic structures as they affect gender.[55] Women's access to land and the acquisition of certain properties is usually on the basis of inheritance. However, as stated by Oriaghan, the inheritance of properties such as land usually tilts in favor of the men.[56] This is a result of the inherent patriarchy existent in the customs of the people, as well as the patrilineal system of land inheritance among several ethnicities within the country.

Among the Igbo of the south-eastern part of the country, property inheritance under the customary law is primarily patrilineal, as the inheritance of properties such as land are considered a man's birthright. Land and all forms of landed properties, as noted by Ifemeje and Umejiaku, are passed on to males with the exclusion of the wives and daughters. Land inheritance practice amongst the Igbo is usually primogeniture, and this also applies to many ethnicities in the country including the Benin people of Edo state. In other words, ownership of land and landed properties are passed on to the first son upon the death of the father.[57] The woman is not eligible to inherit her father's landed properties, or those of her husband. In the event of a father's death, the son who is considered the head of the home inherits his father's properties automatically; in the absence of a male child in the family, the properties customarily belong to the man's male siblings. Also, where the husband's relatives are lenient enough to let the wife and daughters utilize their husband's or father's properties, they do not possess absolute rights and therefore would have to obtain the family's permission to perhaps sell or rent out such properties.[58] If there are no offspring, the woman is usually left with nothing and made to return to her natal home. The customary laws of the Igbo are gender discriminatory and show little or no regard for the woman. These laws, however, violate the provisions of section 42 and 34 of the 1999 Nigerian Constitution, which clearly stipulate an entitlement to the freedom from discrimination and the rights to the dignity of the human person.[59] However, irrespective of the provisions of the

---

[55] M. O. A. Ashiru, "Gender Discrimination in the Division of Property on Divorce in Nigeria," *Journal of African Law* 51 (2007): 316–331.

[56] Oriaghan, "A Quick Look at Women's Land and Inheritance Rights in Nigeria."

[57] Bioye Tajudeen Aluko and Abdul Rasheed Amidu, "Women and Land Rights Reforms in Nigeria" (paper, 5th FIG Regional Conference, Accra, Nigeria, March 8–11, 2006), www.fig.net/resources/proceedings/fig_proceedings/accra/papers/ts09/ts09_04_aluko_a midu.pdf

[58] Chika Sylvia Ifemeje and Nneka Umejiaku, "Discriminatory Cultural Practices and Women's Rights among the Igbos of South Eastern Nigeria: A Critique," *Journal of Law Policy and Globalization* 25 (2015): 18–27.

[59] Ibid.

Constitution, these discriminatory customary practices continue. On several occasions, there have been widows and daughters who have been disinherited and left helpless by greedy relatives. Ifemeje and Umejiaku are also of the opinion that so many of these cases that have made their ways to the courts of law have been ruled in favor of the customary provisions.

This situation has therefore engineered and sustained a preference for the male child among the Igbo people. There exists an unconscious desire for male children for social security, in case of a father's or husband's death. This preference is clearly seen in the displays of happiness in the occasion of childbirth – the birth of a son usually calls for extravagant celebrations from both parents; for the man, his ego and male pride are boosted, while the woman gains an assurance of social security. The consecutive birth of a female child usually attracts raised eyebrows and is often considered a very serious problem. With the preference of male children comes the introduction of gender roles. The male child is often treated with a subtle reverence and allowances are made for some of his actions. In contrast, the girl child is often made to assume domestic roles, and as Ajala opines, "the manifestation of gender discrimination begins from the household."[60] The home therefore becomes the first place for the expression of women's marginalization, which eventually finds its way into the rest of the society and permeates all spheres of human development. The outcome of this male preference and gender roles is a patriarchal society with entitled men, and women with psychological conceptions of inferiority. As sad as the situation seems, it is more unfortunate to realize that women are often the custodians of patriarchy and women's subordination in Nigerian society.

In the Yoruba community in western Nigeria, women also experience marginalization in property acquisition. Aluko opines that although women are entitled to their parent's properties, they have no inheritance rights from their husbands under the customary law:

Under the Yoruba custom and culture, women can inherit from their parents, brothers, or sisters, but often not from their husbands-because women have ownership and inheritance rights under statutory law, but these rights do not hold under customary law. This occurs because there is no concept of co-ownership of property by couples in traditional Nigerian culture. The presumption being that all substantial property, including the land, belongs to the husband; and the woman herself is virtually considered a form of property – thus widows have no inheritance rights under these traditional norms.[61]

---

[60] Ajala, "Gender Discrimination in Land Ownership and the Alleviation of Women's Poverty in Nigeria," 53.
[61] Yetunde Aluko, "Patriarchy and Property Rights among Yoruba Women in Nigeria," *Feminist Economics* 21, no. 3 (2015): 56–81.

However, Igbo and Yoruba women share a custom-approved disinheritance; the difference therefore lies in whose properties they have access to. Aluko presents a rather progressive picture of the customary Yoruba inheritance laws, which presents the woman with liberty to inherit her family's wealth. In reference to her husband, Aluko specifically states that these laws are not absolute; that is, several situations influence the implementation or nonimplementation of the cultural mandate. This however does not reduce a widow's vulnerability, and sometimes economic incapacity, in the cases where she had dedicated herself to catering to the family's needs. After all, Aluko is clearly of the opinion that "the highest value is given to women as mothers."[62]

The concept of submissiveness, however, applies most significantly to families in the Yoruba cultural space, given that the husband is termed to be the master and crown of his wife and therefore the woman's subservience is demanded by the culture. This situation therefore gives an edge to her in-laws, who are often unscrupulous with self-centered agendas in terms of property rights and access, and they find justification in customary laws. However, in both cultures, the vulnerability of women's property rights is increased upon the occasion of their husband's deaths. Generally, women's access to land is tied to their relationship with men through marriage or parentage, but there is no culture in the country where men's access to land is tied to their relationship with women.[63]

In the northern part of the country, given its religious affiliation to Islam, Sharia law controls the inheritance of properties. As noted by Abdullah and Ibrahim, Sharia grants the woman access to land inheritance. They however note that in spite of this, women have not had access to land and landed properties. In their opinion, this situation emanates from the claims of the Maliki School of Sharia Law that Islam was imposed on Nigeria by conquest and therefore, some allowances of preexisting customs would be made.[64] It is however very surprising that where the religion grants women access to land ownership, the people suddenly recognize that Islam was imposed on them. Yet, sadly, the people sanction all forms of repressive practices on women in defense of religion.

Divorce and Women's Marginalization

In the cases of ended marriages and divorce settlements in the country, women's marginalization is still predominant. Legal provisions of divorce

---

[62] Ibid., 60.   [63] Aluko and Amidu, "Women and Land Rights Reforms in Nigeria."
[64] Hussaina J. Abdullah and Ibrahim Hamza, "Women and Land in Northern Nigeria: The Need for Independent Ownership Rights," In *Women and Land in Africa*, ed. L. M. Wanyeki (New York: Zed Books).

are still discriminatory against women. Ashiru opines that there are three types of marriages recognized in Nigeria: customary marriage, which is under customary law; Islamic marriage under Islamic law; and statutory marriage under statutory law. However, in all these marriages, gender discrimination and patriarchy are still dominant. In the cases of dissolution of these marriages, there are appropriate and necessary judicial processes. In customary marriages, as noted by Ashiru, the verdict for property division or acquisition in the case of a broken marriage differs from ethnicity to ethnicity. However, there is a common principle that the man and woman married under the customary law are considered two "separate entities."[65] In other words, the concept of co-ownership of properties is not recognized, and the wife has the liberty to own her own properties, which is commonly applicable to the Yoruba ethnic group.

Ashiru also states that the case is different with the Idoma. Although the Idoma people recognize woman's property, property as provided by customary law belongs to her husband and his heirs. However, in cases of dispute or divorce, the woman is expected to apply for ownership and the court is licensed to determine such ownership. Among the Igbo people of eastern Nigeria, Ashiru explains that the woman can only acquire landed property through her husband. However, the court also recognizes her property, and in the case of a divorce, neither of the parties involved can lay claim to each other's properties acquired in the course of the marriage. The woman is usually more disadvantaged because in the case of a divorce, her family is made to refund her bride price and in cases of joint property ownership, the property is usually in the man's name and it is often a herculean task for the woman to prove her contributions to the acquisition. This is primarily because the court does not recognize the woman's contributions but usually assumes that landed properties and big projects were undertaken by the man and, therefore, he is most often awarded rights to the property even when the woman had made substantial contributions to the acquisition.[66]

Theoretically, in Islamic marriages, women are recognized as legal entities, at liberty to own and control property during and after their marriages. Ashiru is of the opinion that in the case of divorce, Islamic law permits the woman to take everything she brought into the marriage and whatever she acquired in the course of the marriage. The law even goes as far as demanding compensation from her husband in the case of divorce or separation. However, as observed by Ashiru, this is just in theory because practically, Muslim women – particularly in the northern

---

[65] Ashiru, "Gender Discrimination in the Division of Property on Divorce in Nigeria."
[66] Ibid.

parts of Nigeria – are too dependent on husbands or male relatives to own or control property; they are highly dependent on their spouses and other male figures like their fathers and brothers. To put it succinctly, he states "they do not enjoy independent land rights even though Islam recognizes them as legal entities."[67] Despite these Islamic provisions for economic independence and fairness, women still suffer significant economic loss in divorce cases since they often have nothing to fall back on. Several issues like seclusion and restrictions, as discussed earlier in this work, contribute to the high dependence rate of Muslim women in northern Nigeria. Therefore, one can confidently state that the provisions of Islamic law are made impractical by the demands the men make on women as a result of the authority the religion confers on men.

As noted by Attah, given land ownership's economic implications and viability, it usually constitutes a subject of conflict for the parties involved.[68] In statutory marriages, in the division of assets as the case may be, the court is granted full discretion to achieve fairness for both parties involved. Therefore, the court takes into consideration all properties owned by the couple either jointly or separately, which sounds relatively well defined and fair. However, Attah is of the opinion that the court is usually faced with the problem of exercising this jurisdiction.[69]

Therefore, the court excludes properties registered under formal names from the "equity jurisdiction." In other words, properties in formal names are not declared for equal division. Rather, sole ownership is granted to the party under whose name the property is listed. However, this ruling is usually not in the best interests of the woman, who is usually not a title holder in land and estate dealings; also, her disadvantaged position, given the traditional and religious expectations of submission and reverence in her relationship with her spouse, is hardly taken into consideration. The inherent patriarchy in property succession and ownership in the country implies that the man's name is usually used as title for land ownership between husband and wife in Nigeria, and the wife is hardly ever entitled to land ownership even from her natal family except for a few cultures like the Yoruba.

Attah observes that, in marriage, the property Nigerian women own is expected to be managed by her husband and his kin as a sign of deference to his position as the head of his wife. Most women, in his opinion, give in to these demands because of the social backlash they would receive in situations like that, or in cases where they decide to purchase landed property in their names or without the husband's consent, especially considering the fragile egos of men raised with patriarchal notions.

[67] Ibid., 325.   [68] Attah, "Divorcing Marriage from Marital Assets."   [69] Ibid.

Therefore, in the event of separation and divorce, women are frequently cheated out of their rightful property. This adjudication rarely takes into consideration the indirect contributions of women in the acquisition of land and landed property. If there is no proof of direct financial engagement in the acquisition, the woman in question has no share in the properties and the proceeds from them. To validate this assumption, Attah states specifically:

> [T]his approach ignores the socio-cultural underpinnings, orientation and environment of marriage that support patriarchy in Africa and generally disable women in relation to property rights. The ramification is that equity, the objective of the jurisdiction, fails and women are further deprived of property rights.[70]

This is why Attah states that, given the nature of court rulings in property settlements pertaining to divorce in Nigeria, "Critics agree, and judicial decisions show, that this equity jurisdiction has generally failed in Nigeria."[71] Although Attah does not state a bias on the part of the judges, this critical appraisal infers a bias. However, given that the operations of the top echelons of the country are often governed by patriarchal notions, it is unsurprising to see that the concept of male supremacy has seen to it that jurisdiction is still restricted to formal titles, which are usually in favor of men.

Attah additionally identifies the unfavorable position of women in cases of divorce in Nigeria. For one, he argues that there is no statutory definition for matrimonial property, and so the court searches for title listings of properties that are often jointly owned by the couples involved. For Attah, to achieve this, a definition of matrimonial properties should be made, and this definition should be able to take away discretion from the court. It should also take into consideration the sociocultural significance of marriage and its implications in property acquisition. In other words, the direct and indirect input of the couples in the acquisition of the properties should be taken into consideration, and adequate compensation should be awarded as well.

Attempts to Eradicate Women's Marginalization

There is no benefit to restating that women are marginalized in several areas in Nigerian society. This sustained marginalization is primarily a result of many sociohistorical, cultural, and religious ideologies of female subordination ingrained in the nation's structures and its people. Having recognized this situation in the country, the Nigerian Constitution, women's movements, international trends in women's

---

[70] Ibid., 429.   [71] Ibid.

emancipation, and feminism have given rise to many steps and actions put in motion to eradicate the marginalization of women in Nigeria. It is necessary, however, to evaluate the measures geared toward this goal, so as to examine their successes, identify their shortcomings, and make recommendations to improve these efforts.

The Nigerian Constitution makes provisions against all forms of gender discrimination in the country. In Article 17 of the 1999 Constitution, the following are stipulated in relation to fostering equality and eliminating marginalization:

(1) The State's social order is founded on ideals of freedom, equality and justice.
(2) In furtherance of the social order:
   (a) Every citizen shall have equality of rights, obligations and opportunities before the law;
(3) The State shall direct its policy toward ensuring that:
   (a) All citizens, without discrimination on any group whatsoever, have the opportunity for securing adequate means of livelihood as well as adequate opportunity to secure suitable employment;
   (b) Conditions of work are just and humane, and that there are adequate facilities for leisure and for social, religious and cultural life;
   (c) The health, safety and welfare of all persons in employment are safeguarded and not endangered or abused;
   (d) There are adequate medical and health facilities for all persons;
   (e) There is equal pay for equal work without discrimination on account of sex, or on any other grounds whatsoever.[72]

With these stipulations, it is apparent that the constitution frowns on some forms of discrimination and marginalization, which therefore lends justification to the claims that cultural and religious ideologies that endorse women's subjugation are to blame for the underrepresentation and marginalization of women in public and economic life.

With reference to important international laws on women's emancipation and inclusion, in 1985 Nigeria ratified CEDAW (Convention for the Elimination of all Forms of Discrimination against Women). Nwankwo describes CEDAW as the most comprehensive human rights treaty on the elimination of discrimination against women.[73] However, according to Anyogu and Okpalobi, the ratification implies the full

---

[72] Constitution of the Federal Republic of Nigeria, "Chapter 2: Fundamental Objectives and Directive Principles of State Policy," 1999.
[73] Oby Nwankwo, "Domestication of CEDAW" (briefing, Civil Resource Development and Documentation Centre, 2009).

implementation of the provisions of the treaty and has also led to constitutional amendment in the countries that ratified it, Nigeria inclusive. In their opinion, the Convention identifies gender roles as one of the impediments to gender equality, and therefore advocates for a change in traditional roles that tend to foster gender discrimination. The Convention, in Article 1 defines discrimination thus:

> Any distinction, exclusion or restriction made on the basis of which has the effect or purpose of impairing or nullifying the recognition, enjoyment or exercise by women, irrespective of their marital status, on a basis of equality of men and women of human rights and fundamental freedoms in the political, economic, social, cultural, civil or any other field.[74]

Therefore, the adoption of the treaty by the Nigerian government is proof of its intention to eradicate the prevalent discrimination against women in the country. However, as noted in a report about Nigeria's ratification and application of the treaty, Nigeria is yet to domesticate the CEDAW, which simply means that the impact of the treaty on national laws is limited.[75] Therefore, there is still a need to invalidate several laws and practices that are discriminatory against women, as there is not very much the treaty has achieved.

Also, in a bid to reduce poverty and empower women in the country, several international organizations as well as the government have launched programs and policies aimed at equipping women with the necessary resources, skills, and education for financial independence and economic growth. This includes the UN's launch of the Millennium Development Goals (MDGs), which advocate for women's economic empowerment and view it as a way to eliminate gender inequality and the marginalization of women in the world. Therefore, in line with the MDGs, some organizations and empowerment initiatives have sprung up. According to Okechukwu et al., some international organizations like the International Monetary Fund (IMF), African Development Bank Group (AfDBG), United States Agency for International Development (USAID), International Finance Corporation (IFC), African Development Bank (ADB) Economic Community of West African States (ECOWAS), World Bank, Department for International Development (DFID), and many

---

[74] Felicia Anyogu and B. N. Okpalobi, "Human Right Issues and Women's Experiences on Demanding Their Rights in Their Communities: The Way Forward for Nigeria," *Global Journal of Politics and Law* Research 4, no. 1 (2016): 9–17, 10.
[75] NGO Coalition, *Shadow Report to the 7th & 8th Periodic Report of Nigeria on Convention on the Elimination of All Forms of Discrimination against Women (CEDAW)* (Geneva: UN CEDAW Committee Submitted to UN CEDAW, June 2017).

more have played huge and remarkable roles in women's empowerment and poverty reduction worldwide.[76]

However, aside from these international organizations, the Nigerian
government at federal and state levels has initiated a number of programs
with the aim of eradicating women's marginalization in the nation's
economy. Some of these programs are geared toward supporting female
entrepreneurs with financial assistance and offering the requisite skills for
financial independence and economic opportunities. The 2006 National
Gender Policy was reviewed by the federal government in collaboration
with the Federal Ministry of Women Affairs and Social Development,
which led to the implementation of policies that were aimed at women's
economic empowerment and the infusion of gender in several sectors
such as agriculture and rural development, and environment and natural
resources – which was financed by the Central Bank of Nigeria in collaboration with other banks within the country to provide easy access to
funds.[77]

There are also microfinance initiatives aimed at ensuring women's
access to financial assistance such as the Microfinance Development
Funds, which support women-based lending and other initiatives.
However, their sole aim is to eradicate gender inequality and equip
women financially.[78] The Central Bank also focuses on several strategies
such as "the creation of [the] Micro Small and Medium Enterprise
Development Fund (MSMEDF)" to promote gender inclusion, and
also see to it that matters of women's development and financial inclusion
are top priority.[79] Also, in 2012, the Central Bank of Nigeria (CBN)
created the National Financial Inclusion Strategy (NFIS), which, as
stated by Bala-Keffi:

addresses factors constraining financial access, financial literacy and application
of financial services in a specified time frame for groups that are excluded,
especially women. The objective is to ensure that by the year 2020, the proportion
of women that are financially excluded would have been reduced from 54 per cent
to 20 per cent.[80]

There have also been attempts and initiatives by the Bankers' Committee
in Nigeria to promote women into high-ranking decision-making roles in
the banking sector. In other words, there have been several initiatives

---

[76] Uzoamaka Elizabeth Okechukwu, Gerald Nebo, and Jude Eze, "Women Empowerment:
Panacea for Poverty Reduction and Economic Development in Nigeria," *Journal of Policy
and Development Studies* 10, no. 2 (2016): 31–41.

[77] Ladi R. Bala-Keffi, "Women Economic Empowerment," *Central Bank of Nigeria,
Understanding Monetary Policy Series* 54 (2015).

[78] Ibid.   [79] Ibid., 19.   [80] Ibid.

developed with the aim of eradicating women's marginalization in the nation's economy.

In 2013, the federal government launched a program known as the "Smart Woman Nigeria Initiative" as well as the "1000 Girls in ICT" and the "ICT Girls Club." These programs – initiated by the Federal Ministry of Communication and Technology – are aimed at ensuring women's education in information communication technology (ICT), and other areas of human endeavor. This is primarily because of the alarming gender disparity or digital gap in the expertise of science and technology. The Smart Woman Nigeria initiative is designed to improve the knowledge of women in communication, finance, and banking, as well equipping them with other necessary skills to ensure their independence and financial security. On the other hand, the "1000 Girls in ICT" initiative is aimed at equipping young women with skills in ICT for financial stability and development. The young women are trained on "Telecommunication Networks, Transmission Network and GSM, LTE, WCDMA and other ICT skills."[81]

Furthermore, the "ICT Girls Club" intends to motivate and encourage women to take up courses and jobs in technology-related fields so as to bridge the gap between men and women in that area.[82] However, with the many programs and initiatives enacted and implemented by several economic sectors at the state and federal levels of government, it is surprising that the nation still records a high rate of women's marginalization in several sectors of the economy. This sheds light on the many challenges these initiatives and programs have experienced since their inception and implementation.

The politicization of some of these projects has taken away from their aims and objectives and has robbed the marginalized women in Nigeria of access to some of the opportunities offered by these initiatives. These initiatives have had very limited practical reach, to the extent that implementation of the policies and programs has been merely theoretical. In cases of actual implementation, there has been a problem of poor implementation, which plagues most of the projects initiated in the country. Also, mismanagement of public funds, corruption, and the absence of transparency are still major problems in Nigerian society that challenge implementation of women's development projects in Nigeria. The religious and cultural ideologies that promote patriarchy also influence the implementation of these programs. Pervasive illiteracy among women, particularly those in rural areas, prevents them from accessing available opportunities. These factors and many more generate problems for the

---

[81] Ibid.   [82] Ibid.

implementation of empowerment programs for women and sustain the marginalization of women in the country.

Many policies and programs have been put in place to eliminate the political marginalization of women around the world. In Article 7 of the Convention on the Elimination of All Forms of Discrimination Against Women (CEDAW), the United Nations makes provisions for female representation in democracies around the world. In its provisions, all countries that have ratified the treaty should ensure the following with reference to women's participation in politics:

[E]nsure to women, on equal terms with men, the right to vote in all elections and public referenda and to be eligible for election to all publicly elected bodies . . . and to participate in the formulation of government policy and the implementation thereof and to hold public office and perform all public functions at all levels of government.[83]

The Nigerian Constitution frowns on discrimination of any kind. It stipulates and endorses the principle of equality in Article 17 of the 1999 Constitution, where it is clearly stated that; "every citizen shall have equality of rights, obligations and opportunities before the law."[84] In Article 15, the nation specifically discourages all forms of discrimination by stating that "accordingly, national integration shall be actively encouraged, whilst discrimination on the grounds of place of origin, sex, religion, status, ethnic or linguistic association or ties shall be prohibited."[85] This shows that the marginalization of women in politics is unlawful, and Nigerian women are entitled to equal political rights and opportunities in politics and other spheres of the nation's development.

Locally, the National Gender Policy (NGP) launched in 2007 sanctions the adoption of a 35 percent affirmative action for women's participation in all processes of governance, appointive and elective, in conjunction with the declaration at the Fourth World Conference on Women in Beijing, where a 30 percent affirmative action was advocated.[86] There has also been the establishment of the women's political empowerment office, an INEC gender policy, Nigerian women trust funds, women's lobby groups, and a great many others. The INEC gender policy that was launched in 2014 aims at improving female participation both in elective positions and within the agency itself.

[83] Mervis Zungura et al., "The Relationship between Democracy and Women Participation in Politics," *Journal of Public Administration and Governance* 3, no. 1 (2013): 168–176, 170.

[84] Constitution of the Federal Republic of Nigeria, "Chapter 2."   [85] Ibid.

[86] Oloyede Oluyemi, "Monitoring Participation of Women in Politics in Nigeria" (paper, National Bureau of Statistics, Abuja, Nigeria, October 2016), https://unstats.un.org/unsd/gender/Finland_Oct2016/Documents/Nigeria_paper.pdf.

Irrespective of these efforts aimed at eliminating gender disparity in the nation's politics, women are still extremely marginalized in Nigerian politics. Several factors can therefore be attributed to the operational failure of these constitutional provisions, policies, and programs. The nation's constitutional provisions clearly discourage all forms of discrimination and marginalization on the basis of sex. However, upon a closer look and analysis of the stipulations of the Constitution, one can detect that the Constitution itself is inherently discriminatory and partial in its provisions. The Constitution is written in exclusively masculine language and contains some discriminatory clauses in its stipulations. For instance, in section 26 subsection 2, the Constitution states the following: "any woman who is or has been married to a citizen of Nigeria can apply to be registered as a citizen of Nigeria." The gendered language gives away the Constitution's bias toward women. Given the provision of that section, citizenship can only be granted to a foreigner on their status as female, and on the basis of their marriage to a man in the country. In other words, the same cannot be applied to a foreign man who marries a Nigerian woman. Also, stated in section 29 subsection 4, "full age" means the age of eighteen years and above. In other words, recognition of adulthood or "full age" is granted to persons of eighteen years and older. However, in section 4b, the Constitution also states that; "any woman who is married shall be deemed of full age."[87] This means even if she is married at the age of fourteen, she is of full age. This section of the Constitution indirectly validates the practice of child marriage prevalent in the country, and therefore encourages the deprivation of women's education as well as their fundamental human rights. All these factors show the true perception of women by the Nigerian laws, and this perception and treatment affects the political expression of women in the country. These constitutional provisions simply encourage patriarchy and female subordination, and also discourage women from taking up relevant political offices.

Furthermore, the actualization of the 35 percent affirmative action is hampered by many sociocultural factors. As much as the government lays emphasis on the need for women to participate and run for elective positions in the country, religious and cultural factors will continue to serve as impediments to women's free political expression. Other factors like illiteracy and poverty also play major roles in the continued marginalization of women. The absence of accountability and the corruption that is at play in the country makes it

---

[87] Constitution of the Federal Republic of Nigeria, "Chapter 3: Citizenship."

impossible to implement the policies that have been initiated for the benefit of women in the country.

With reference to women's land rights, the Land Use Act of 1978 was introduced with the fundamental objective to guarantee equal access to land in the country. This is however necessary given the initial monopoly of lands and exclusive control of lands by certain members of the society. After independence, Aluko and Amidu observe that the land-holding system gave room to problems such as "inaccessibility of land to government, and private individuals for development projects, land speculation leading to exorbitant land prices in the cities, fraudulent sales."[88] This therefore led to the promulgation of the Land Use Act in 1978 by the then-military regime to provide equal access to citizens irrespective of gender, and also to provide a uniform land tenure system in the country. They also state that section 1 of the Act entrusts land ownership on the state and shall be granted for the use and benefit of all Nigerians with respect to the provisions of the act.[89] Therefore, with reference to this Act, women are entitled to land use and ownership in the country.

However, like other promulgations and policies, the country has been unable to effectively implement the provisions of the Act, which is why Ajala opines that the original families who exercised land monopoly pre-independence continue to do the same; they sell lands and backdate purchase receipts to a time prior to the promulgation of the Land Act in 1978.[90] The dangers of this situation are that land ownership still operates within the provisions of the customary law that are mostly patriarchal, hinging women's access to lands on their relationship with men. Without effective implementation of the Land Act, women are still exempted from land ownership and robbed of the economic benefits therein.

Also, in an attempt to eliminate the marginalization of women in the cases of divorce and property settlements, Nigeria adopted the Married Women's Property Act of 1882 from England. The Act makes it possible for women married under the statutory law; "to acquire, hold, and dispose of property acquired before or after marriages."[91] It is also within her rights to apply for title to a property. However, in the case of divorce, the Act grants the court the authority to enforce the woman's rights. Also,

---

[88] Aluko and Amidu, "Women and Land Rights Reforms in Nigeria," 5.   [89] Ibid.
[90] Ajala, "Gender Discrimination in Land Ownership and the Alleviation of Women's Poverty in Nigeria."
[91] Food and Agriculture Organization of the United Nations, "Gender and Land Rights Database: Nigeria: Women's Property and Use Rights in Personal Laws," Food and Agriculture Organization of the United Nations, n.d., www.fao.org/gender-landrights-database/country-profiles/countries-list/national-legal-framework/women%E2%80%99s-property-and-use-rights-in-personal-laws/en/?country_iso3=NGA.

under the Marriage Act of 1990, married women are given equal rights to family assets acquired in the course of the marriage. However, given the limited fairness of these Acts to women, they have hardly been useful in the Nigerian legal system. As noted by Ashiru, the judge has been given sole discretion to pass judgment as he sees fit, and women have only been granted proprietary rights occasionally.

Implications of Women's Marginalization

Having established existent marginalization of Nigerian women in various spheres, it is therefore needful to explore the implications of this marginalization on the nation's development. Nigerian women constitute about half of the nation's population. Therefore, the alienation of women from participating in significant aspects of development is logically a waste of human resources and an impediment to the nation's economic, social, and political growth. This marginalization implies a sustained financial incapacity that often finds expression in the number of women and children with little or no access to the necessities of life such as good health, good education, proper food, clothing, and hygiene. This will ultimately affect the psychological well-being of the society and will encourage the crime and corruption already prevalent in Nigeria.

The culture of patriarchy and women's subordination is one of the major factors limiting the nation's development, which is why Bako and Syed opine that research proves that the promotion of gender equality improves performance in many areas in a society, and is ultimately to the benefit of the society involved.[92] Encouraging women's participation in politics is a necessary development that promises an introduction of various and diverse ideologies that are set to put the nation on the right track. In terms of education, emphasizing women's education in the country is a worthy investment for every nation with hopes of advancement and development. It will improve the nation's economy by providing more skilled manpower that will in turn alleviate poverty and crime in the country. The inclusion of women and elimination of marginalization will also bring about equitable distribution of the nation's resources that will be put to good use by every citizen of the country to achieve financial independence and economic growth, and result in a positive image that will provide an international edge and advantage in global negotiations. The relevance of women's involvement and the eradication of forms of structural enablement to marginalization in the country cannot be overemphasized.

---

[92] Bako and Syed, "Women's Marginalization in Nigeria."

Conclusion

The postcolonial Nigerian woman has been marginalized in several areas of society; in the nation's labor force the study reveals a gaping gender imbalance in high paying sectors, while women have also been unable to attain top administrative positions in formal institutions where they are employed. Statistical reports reveal that women occupy the major under-paid sectors of the economy, while for several reasons the various economic sectors that generate maximum income are inaccessible to women. Factors like illiteracy and poor educational backgrounds play huge roles in sustaining the underemployment and financial incapacity of women. The practice of child marriage, particularly in the Northern Region, is a gross violation of their fundamental human rights, which denies them access to basic education and puts them at several health risks. The same applies to women's political participation in the country; they are obviously marginalized while several socioeconomic, cultural, and religious factors contribute to their underrepresentation and outright marginalization in the nation's political space. Several discriminatory laws, customs, and practices serve as impediments to women's inheritance and land rights, which therefore contributes immensely to the marginalization of women in property acquisition and land ownership.

Notwithstanding, the nation has promulgated and ratified several policies and laws aimed at eliminating the marginalization of women in the society, but the trend has persisted. This proves that the continued thriving of women's marginalization in the country is a product of several socioeconomic, legal, religious, and customary factors inherent in Nigerian society. This study therefore recommends the steady involvement of the Nigerian government in social affairs, especially as they pertain to gender. It is also not enough to ratify and promulgate policies and laws; it is expedient to see to the strict implementation of and compliance to these policies and rules. The image of the woman in the media should be improved upon as this will go a long way to impacting the psychological perceptions of society regarding women. Women's achievements should be emphasized by the media, while enlightenment on the value and relevance of women in the various sectors of the society should be embarked upon. Also, the government and society in general should advocate for the eradication of customs and religious practices that deny women their rights and subjugate women in various areas of society. In other words, to achieve a society of equal rights and opportunities, all hands must be on deck.

16   Human and Minority Rights

Introduction

Societies contain different groups of people who are defined by their social status in relation to their environment. This status determines how they are viewed, treated, and integrated into society. The environment plays a role because human societies have learned, over the years, to build a suitable, sustainable social milieux in response to their surroundings. Culture could be defined as the totality of experience for a cluster of people; society is the residual manifestation of the culture.[1] Although individuals react to their environment differently, individual responses are overshadowed by the larger picture of societal practices.[2] There is no culture without collectivity, because culture breeds a sense of collectivity and the sense of collectivity establishes the abstract concepts of in-groups and out-groups. The out-groups are best explained as the mirror of the Other.[3]

Culture is an evolving pattern of experience and ideas, and the most durable component of the pattern resides in the practices and beliefs that survive as a group's traditions. The essence of a culture is in the traditions it embodies. Traditions appeal to the sentiments and emotions of in-group members, which has been used to sustain cultures for generations. The traditional practices and beliefs of a culture only morph when a better alternative arises to sustain the culture through the evolving milieu.[4] Even then, these changes always take a long time to

---

[1] See, Toyin Falola, *The Power of African Culture* (New York: University of Rochester Press, 2003).

[2] See, for instance, the dynamics of cultural perception about disability in Chomba Wa Munyi, "Past and Present Perceptions towards Disability: A Historical Perspective," *Disabilities Studies Quarterly* 32, no. 2 (2012): 11.

[3] For more discussion on the making of in-group and out-group identity and classification, see Tajfel Henri Tajfel, "Social Psychology of Intergroup Relations," *Annual Review Psychology* 33 (1982): 1–39.

[4] See, for instance, Karin Barber, *The Anthropology of Texts, Persons and Publics: Oral and Written Culture in Africa and Beyond* (Cambridge: Cambridge University Press, 2007), 24.

materialize fully. With change comes societal reformation, consistently redefining those regarded as the minority.

Minority groups, living with their own differences and levels of social perception, are the social constructs of those without dominant voices. To be deemed irrelevant or voiceless is to be dismissed as a passive member of society whose choices, desires, and opinions do not shape the evolution of the society and its social space. In contemporary discourse, the existence of this social status raises the issue of fundamental human rights and the enforcement of human dignity.

Persons with Disability and the "Unknown Space"

Disabled persons have always been part of society, and persons with disabilities must occasionally deal with terror that stems from the social perception of their personhood – mostly due to cultural interpretations of their physiological and/or psychological condition. Whyte's idea of a "social looking glass" has existed as a common truth for ages, changing through the social milieu in which these persons live. The theory, which seeks to understand how persons with disabilities act and see themselves in society, explains that persons with disabilities tend to lose their innate form and skills when faced with society's overwhelming disposition toward them; they are rarely seen beyond their immediately apparent physiological or psychological conditions. This can render them useless, dependent, and despondent in society, to the point where they perpetually see themselves in this light.[5]

In Nigeria, persons with disabilities are often viewed as monstrous beings, regardless of whether their condition is a recent development or has been present since birth. There are several interpretations for this condition along cultural lines, and they vary based on the specific disability. A person with a hunched back might be viewed as a special being sent by the gods, while a person with a mental health disorder might be seen as a nuisance. In general, persons with disabilities are viewed with pity, violence, discrimination, rejection, and stigmatization in Nigeria. This treatment deprives them of their human dignity, including freedom of movement, association, and education, along with the ability to pursue their goals and have control over their own bodies. Persons born with these conditions are seen as suffering for the atrocities committed by their parents, especially their mothers. A survey conducted by Onu and his

---

[5] For more on this, see Edwin Etieyibo and Odirin Omiegbe, "Religion, Culture, and Discrimination against Persons with Disabilities in Nigeria," *African Journal of Disability* 5, no.1 (2016): 2–3.

colleagues found that various cultures in Nigeria view the causes of disability as "a curse from God; ancestral violations of societal norms; offenses against the gods of the land; breaking laws and family sins; misfortune; witches and wizards; and adultery, among others."[6]

Persons with disabilities commonly suffer from violence in society, which can include rape, exploitation, and forcible eviction. Rape is usually committed for ritual purposes, mostly against women and girls with mental impairments – an individual seeking power or financial gain might be instructed by his ritualist to engage in sexual intercourse with a mentally impaired woman to achieve his goal. Persons who "have genetic mutations that affect the production of a pigment called melanin,"[7] commonly known as albinism, are also at risk. They are less likely to be raped for ritual purposes, but they are at risk of being killed so that their body parts can be used in rituals.[8] Other females with disabilities can be victims of sexual abuse, and the perpetrators seek to exploit their vulnerability.

Measuring the prevalence of these practices is a daunting task; no reliable data exist for this endeavor. The persons whose rights have been violated lack the means or power to report the crime. Their situation is compounded by the fact that those who could report such cases to the authorities are either complicit or unconcerned. Given the sociocultural views that shape public perception of these persons, the people who are willing to report cases of abuse are often intimidated by the stigma of being associated with disabled persons, or frustrated by the response from authorities. The experiences of rejection and dejection leave disabled persons residing and operating in a different space within their societies. Just as the interpretation of persons with disabilities can vary in cultural perception, so can the condition that qualifies them as members of this social category. It is difficult to assemble a complete list of perceived disabilities without considering patterns of stigmatization, marginality, discrimination, seclusion, and additional consequences of the Other that afflict persons with disabilities in regions, states, and communities.

Even more varied are the individual experiences associated with disabilities. Although albinos and mentally disabled people are all considered to have disabilities in Nigeria, the disabled spaces in which they

---

[6] United Nations: Department for Social Policy and Development and the Department of Economic and Social Affairs, *Toolkit on Disability for Africa: Culture, Beliefs and Disability* (New York: United Nations, 2016), 13, www.un.org/esa/socdev/documents/disability/Toolkit/Cultures-Beliefs-Disability.pdf.

[7] Coco Ballantyne, "What Is Albinism?" *Scientific American*, February 18, 2009, www.scientificamerican.com/article/killing-albinos-tanzania-albinism/.

[8] Channels Television, "Albino Foundation Condemns Killing of Albinos in Nigeria," YouTube video, 2:34, May 3, 2013, www.youtube.com/watch?v=31_uzJ67EYY.

reside are different. Similar variations are experienced by women without the ability to conceive children, people who have more or fewer than five fingers, and others, even though they can all be found in the disabled space of stigmatization in Nigeria. These people are regarded as persons with disabilities in the country, but the degree and methods by which they experience discrimination, stigmatization, neglect, and dependency can differ from person to person and from place to place.

Persons with disabilities might have had them since birth or received them through damage caused by an accident or medical complications. In all cases, a person's ability to navigate through the ordeal of the "unknown space" to the "known space," through financial independence and profitable engagement with the known space, can change that person's identity. They move from the margins of society to its core, existing alongside persons considered normal in society.[9]

In the Nigerian environment, profitably engaging the "known space" is not an easy task, even for those without disabilities – people with and without disabilities scramble to survive. For those living with disabilities, survival is mostly found through what Whyte called "distributive labor."[10] This includes various methods such as collecting charitable donations and generally depending on the disbursement of gifts from society, which relates to the condition described by the phrase *kosi ona miran*, "there is no alternative." This creates an opportunity for moving between the unknown space and what could be called an alternative space. Through this medium, persons with disabilities can enjoy an existence that may be better than that of others in their families who are not physiologically or psychologically challenged.

Disability studies conducted over the years – in social sciences, humanities, and even the health sciences – take two different perspectives. One group could be called the orthodox school of disability studies, also referred to as the ableist school, viewing persons with disabilities as those who need to be repaired to ensure their (re)integration into society.[11] The other group could be referred to as the progressive school of disability, interpreting disability as a social construct, not a biomedical one. This latter school champions the social model approach, asserting

---

[9] Examples of this are seldom seen in the country, but not entirely absent. These few excel in the music industry and as entrepreneurs, without government sanctions. See, for instance, Youngstars Foundation, "Cobhams Asuquo Story," Youngstars Foundation, n.d., www.youngstarsfoundation.org/my_story_cobhamsasuquo.html.

[10] Susan Reynolds Whyte, "In the Long Run: Ugandans Living with Disability," *Current Anthropology* 61 (2019): 5.

[11] See, for instance David M. Turner, "Introduction: Approaching Anomalous Bodies," in *Histories of Disability and Deformity*, eds. David M. Turner and Kevin Stagg (New York: Routledge, 2006), 7–12.

Figure 16.1 A male paraplegic receiving alms from a passerby.

that the body of the individual does not need to be reconstituted – society itself should adjust to the reality of these persons.[12] This school asserts that society, through the construction of the social space and abstract ideas of normal and abnormal, has done more to disable these persons than any physiological or psychological condition.[13]

While the ableist school focuses on the biomedical structure of disablement, the progressive school concentrates on acquired and innate skills that can be used productively. This allows disabled people to become less dependent and play more active roles in society's economic activity. The progressive school asserts that the inability to contribute to society's productivity and economic evolution is what leads people to be seen as liabilities and dependent members of society and inhabitants of the "Other space." The ableist school asserts that no matter what one does to help people sustain themselves and become independent, they will remain hopeless without a biomedical reconstruction of their condition.

[12] Rob Imrie, "Ableist Geographies, Disablist Spaces: Towards a Reconstruction of Golledge's Geography and the Disabled," *Transactions of the Institute of British Geographers* 21, no. 2 (1996): 398.

[13] See, for instance, B. J. Gleeson, "A Geography for Disabled People?" *Transactions of the Institute of British Geographers* (1996): 388.

These two schools of thought birthed the two dominant frames through which society addresses the condition of persons with disabilities. The traditional logic of the ableist school leads to a charity-based approach for integrating these persons into society; disabled persons are to be pitied, surviving off networks of charity and goodwill. This approach is denounced by the progressive school, which seeks to integrate persons with disabilities through a developmental approach based on human rights. The consensus among member states of the United Nations and other experts is that the issue of development should be seen as a fundamental human right; the amelioration of the hydra-headed, problematic condition of persons with disabilities should be approached as a right, not as an option.

The 2006 United Nations Convention on the Rights of Persons with Disabilities (UNCRPD) suggested that the human-rights-based approach (HRBA) should overturn the charity-based approach and uphold the rights of persons with disabilities. However, legal frames in Africa are limited by the social status of the right-bearer – mainly their educational and financial status. This factor, influenced by the preponderance of socioeconomic and political conditions in which these rights are expected to operate in Africa, has been at the forefront of criticism against the promotion of a HRBA.[14] If there are no adequate media through which these rights could be pursued, or their implementation monitored, then the bearers of the rights would be left more vulnerable than they had been previously.[15]

To rectify UNCRPD issues, the African Union was encouraged to domesticate this declaration within the African context. It was adapted into the 2018 Protocol to the African Charter on Human and Peoples' Rights on the Rights of Persons with Disabilities in Africa,[16] which has yet to come into effect. As an entity whose work primarily rallies support for "sovereign states" in Africa, without any coercive power, it remains to be seen how the organization will achieve the Africanization of the UNCRPD better than what was achieved under the 1999–2009 African Decade of the Disabled Persons.

---

[14] See Rachel Kudakwashe et al., "The Africa Network for Evidence-to-Action on Disability: A Role Player in the Realization of the UNCRPD in Africa," *African Journal of Disability* 3, no. 2 (2014); Malcolm MacLachlan et al., "Facilitating Disability Inclusion in Poverty Reduction Processes: Group Consensus Perspectives from Disability Stakeholders in Uganda, Malawi, Ethiopia, and Sierra Leone," *Disability and the Global South* 1, no. 1 (2014): 107–123.

[15] Whyte, "In the Long Run," 8.

[16] See United Nations, "African States Affirm the Rights of Persons with Disabilities in a New Landmark Protocol," United Nations, February 15, 2018, www.ohchr.org/EN/NewsEvents/Pages/DisplayNews.aspx?NewsID=22661&LangID=E.

Nigeria was part of a decade-long, collective approach to improve conditions for persons with disabilities, but like the ratification of other international treaties and obligations, the state has been unable to domesticate this in ways that achieve meaningful impact. In 2019, the Muhammadu Buhari administration ratified the UNCRPD, thirteen years after the convention was held, under intense pressure from civil society organizations. The World Health Organization's 2011 World Disability Report noted that "about 15 percent of Nigeria's population, or at least 25 million people, have a disability."[17] Considering the atmosphere in which the convention was ratified, it remains to be seen how this will be translated to tangible action.

Social Defiance or Natural Evolution? Discussing the LGBTIQ Community in Nigeria

A prominent minority group in Africa is the LGBTIQ community, consisting of lesbians, gays, bisexuals, transgender and intersex individuals, and queers. They do not suffer from physical or mental disability, but they are a minority group because of the controversy that they elicit through their social identities and sexual preferences. Debate in Nigeria rages over this community: one side believes that members of this community are social deviants whose inclinations oppose nature and the natural composition of society, and the other side argues that members of this community are, indeed, part of the natural state of being as part of natural human evolution.[18] The first group assumes that the lifestyles of the LGBTIQ community developed from conscious choices made by the community's members – this group declares that LGBTIQ community members must either be persecuted for their choices or subjected to spiritual cleansing to be rid of evil possession. This orthodox interpretation of the community emanates from prejudicial conclusions about its practices.

Members of the LGBTIQ community reside in the Other space, or unknown space, similar to that of persons with disabilities. Society has constructed an image of the "normal," implying that anything outside of this social construct is abnormal. Practices, activities, and beliefs outside the normal cast people into a different space in society; their level of integration is limited until they fulfill the criteria of self-reconstruction for full (re)integration, returning to the "known space."

---

[17] Anietie Ewang, "Nigeria Passes Disability Rights Law: Offers Hope of Inclusion, Improved Access," Human Rights Watch, January 25, 2019, www.hrw.org/news/2019/01/25/nigeria-passes-disability-rights-law.

[18] Stephen O. Murray and Will Roscoe, eds., *Boy-Wives and Female Husbands Studies of African Homosexualities* (New York: Palgrave Publishers, 1998), 26.

A second level of analysis challenges the notion of heteronormativity at the base of this school, seeing members of the community as victims of the social construction of the normal. This normal has never been consistent across cultures and time. Instead, it is a subject of the social milieu in which one lives.[19] Like the social model of disability, or the "progressive school of disability studies," proponents of natural evolution do not find it productive to persecute members of this community. Instead of attempting to force them back in line with the "normal" rest of society, the known space of society should adjust to accommodate this community. This line of thinking is largely found among the community of those who have undertaken scientific enquiry into the practices: this submission sparked another debate as to the trajectory of the practices within the community of Africa.

The conservative school of thought argues that all the practices found among the LGBTIQ community in Africa are imported cultures from Arabs and Europeans who had contact with the people of Africa. Their view is that homosexuality in Africa is as white as the visiting Arabs and Europeans, not any part of African traditions. Based on this argument of tradition and culture, homosexuality is criminalized in many African countries, including Nigeria. The other school's scientific approach refutes these claims with historical evidence from different parts of Africa. Oral literature scholars, historians, sociologists, anthropologists, and others have studied African cultural practices. These investigations and archeological inquiries propose that homosexuality is as black as the people of Africa.[20] It is generally agreed that the exact beginning of the practice is impossible to pinpoint in time, but the antiquity of homosexuality is not in question. Amory and Gevisser suggest it existed about 2,000 years ago, based on evidence found in rock paintings in Southern Africa.[21]

It is difficult to accept a foreign origin for the phenomenon when there are more than seventy indigenous words for homosexual practices across Africa. Evidence of homosexuality predates the period in which foreign cultures began to influence the continent. In the case of Nigeria, Sinikangas' study of the northern region showed that the practices were well entrenched in the pre-Islamic cultures and traditions of the Hausa – the majority group populating this region.[22] If anything, the various

---

[19] Ibid.
[20] See, for instance, Maarit Sinikangas, "Yan Daudu: A Study of Transgendering Men in Hausaland West Africa" (thesis, Uppsala University, 2004).
[21] Deborah Amory and Mark Gevisser, "Homosexuality in Africa," in *Encyclopedia of Africa*, Vol. 1, eds. Anthony Appiah and Henry Louis Gates (Oxford: Oxford University Press, 2010), 566.
[22] Sinikangas, "Yan Daudu."

practices found among the LGBTIQ community in Africa were criminalized after the incursion of foreign religions and cultures. This explains the root of current attitudes toward homosexuality in Africa.

The "imported" explanation for Africa's LGBTIQ community began with the colonial administrators and their dozens of ethnographers and anthropologists; they gave themselves the responsibility of studying the cultures and practices of the colonized peoples. The limitations of their endeavor are well known and well documented in academic circles. Their efforts supported racist views of Europeans that saw themselves as sophisticated societies encountering primitive African cultures. Part of the alleged sophistication of European and the Arabic cultures was their ability to grow beyond that which was deemed natural to develop new social behavior and sexual relations.

Homosexual practices were interpreted as a negative evolution of humanity, and condemned in Europe and the Middle East under the ideological leadership of Christianity and Islam. Colonial ethnographers encouraged the idea that Africans were not capable of such "deviancy," because they were closer to the natural state of humanity. To support their narrative, they concluded that the manifestation of these practices in Africa developed through contact with Arab invaders.

As the Arabs became scapegoats in some circles, Europeans did as well. It was decided that homosexual practices should be criminalized, as in Europe, to realign those who had adopted "foreign" cultural ideas. This gave rise to the colonial penal code in 1901 that prohibited "unnatural desire" in the Northern and Southern protectorates of the British colonial territories in Nigeria. This law was upheld in the Nigerian state for more than five decades after independence. In 2014, the Jonathan administration reinvigorated this act in the contemporary state without any meaningful difference from the 1901 code.[23] Today, the practice continues to be blamed on European cultural imperialism through western media. Foreign religions have profoundly influenced the cultures of Nigerian people, and the social status of homosexuals in the country has shifted dramatically.

Before the end of the colonial era, Islamic and Christian doctrines became the primary influence on public perceptions, conduct, and expectations. The condemnation, discrimination, segregation, hate, retribution, seclusion, and marginality inflicted on the LGBTIQ community were based on what was alleged to be the true interpretation of the Quran and the Bible. Homosexuality in Nigeria and other African countries was seen as the behavior of infidels, which was used to justify the violence they faced.

---

[23] Carla Sutherland et al., *Progressive Prudes: A Survey of Attitudes towards Homosexuality & Gender Non-Conformity in South Africa* (Johannesburg: The Other Foundation, 2016), 9.

Detractors assert that the LGBTIQ community and relationships among its members are based solely on sex. However, this is not entirely true. Sexual preferences form part of the practice that sets the community apart in the "Other space," but the community provides alternative discursive patterns to address gender and gender roles, personhood and identity, body and body functioning, and varieties of the psychological expression of the self. That is why the "I" and the "Q" were added to the community's acronym: to include community members whose social behavior and innate construction of the self could not be easily grouped under other labels.

Given the often-derogatory connotations associated with being gay, lesbian, bisexual, and other, the term "Queer" has become the most acceptable reference term for the community. When not interpreted as queer, the Q stands for variables like Queen and Questioning; the latter accommodates those who are still exploring where they belong in the community,[24] and the former stems from the rejection of the transgender title by members of GALZ in Zimbabwe.[25] The criminalization of these practices have made them punishable by a minimum of four years in prison, up to a maximum sentence of fourteen years in prison.[26]

In a country with overzealous religious adherents, the queer community faces devastating oppression. Nigeria's core northern region, where Sharia law has been adopted as the code governing state affairs, is the most dangerous part of the country for members of the LGBTIQ community. Under the region's ostensibly Islamic law, the mere suspicion of queer behavior is enough to confront a person with the ultimate penalty of death. Members of their society, especially restless youths, take it upon themselves to police the population looking for alleged violators of these laws to lynch or turn over to the authorities.[27] After handing suspects to the police or the *hisbah* police, they follow up to ensure that those who are accused pay the ultimate price.[28]

---

[24] Emanuella Grinberg, "What the 'Q' in LGBTQ Stands for, and Other Identity Terms Explained," *CNN*, June 14, 2019, https://edition.cnn.com/interactive/2019/06/health/lgbtq-explainer/.

[25] Marc Epprecht, *Hungochani: The History of a Dissident Sexuality in Southern Africa*, 2nd ed. (London: McGill-Queen's University Press, 2013), x.

[26] Mojisola Eseyin, "Same Sex Marriage Prohibition Act of Nigeria, 2013: A Still Birth?" *Journal of Law, Policy and Globalization* 36 (2015): 46.

[27] Makmid Kamara, "Happening Now: LGBT Nigerians Jailed after Passage of New Anti-Gay Law," Amnesty International, n.d., www.amnestyusa.org/happening-now-lgbt-nigerians-jailed-after-passage-of-new-anti-gay-law/.

[28] Adams Nossiter, "Nigeria Tries to 'Sanitize' Itself of Gays," *The New York Times*, February 8, 2014, www.nytimes.com/2014/02/09/world/africa/nigeria-uses-law-and-whip-to-sanitize-gays.html.

Members of the LGBTIQ community face challenges finding housing, employment, and access to appropriate health care. They experience difficulty securing IVF treatments, surrogate support, mental health services, and other treatments.[29] In response, queers in Nigeria and elsewhere in Africa began to form a kind of bio-sociality through which they could express solidarity, steer public discussion and perception of the community, and document the various experiences of the group's members.[30] This level of organization, which started in the 1990s, allowed queers in Nigeria and other parts of Africa to feel as though they belonged to a community; it was the evolution of the queer community in the country.

This community has not completely changed public perception or allayed the fears of its members, but bio-sociality has encouraged community members to stay safe – many were frustrated, suffering from depression, and in extreme cases, taking their own lives. Within the community, they were able to better understand themselves outside of the public's noise. Due to the hostile environment in which they reside, attempting to organize meetings involves the risk of getting lynched, arrested, molested, or brutalized by state authorities for violating the country's Same-Sex Prohibition Act. The community holds in-person meetings such as seminars, lectures, and conferences, and its members also use several online platforms, including designated web sites and social media outlets.

The low level of internet penetration in Nigeria means that the impact of these efforts is minimal. Other factors, including the cost of maintaining websites and accessing their content, deep-seated cultural perceptions that view such practices as immoral, and the coverage that the community receives in the media, have impaired efforts to change public perception.[31] However, online and in-person platforms serve as places where members of this community can express themselves freely – without fear of prejudice, hate speech, or denigration – to get support and archive their experiences.

Among the organizations that provide support for the LGBTIQ community in Nigeria are NoStringsNG, Nigeria's Queer Alliance Rights Group,

---

[29] A leading member of Nigeria's community referred to this as the moralization of health care access in the country, leaving queers at the risk of sexually transmitted diseases, depression, and other afflictions. Shannon Marie Harmon, "Nigeria's Anti-homosexuality Laws Block Access to Care," *SciDevNet*, January 24, 2017, www.scidev.net/global/human-rights/news/nigeria-s-anti-homosexuality-laws-block-access-to-care.

[30] See Tiffany Kagure Mugo, "African Queer Women Tackling Erasure and Ostracization: Love, Lust, and Lived Experience," in *The Palgrave Handbook of African Women's Studies*, eds. Olajumoke Yacob-Haliso and Toyin Falola (Cham: Palgrave Macmillan, 2019), 12.

[31] See, for instance, Vincent Desmond, "How the Internet Is Helping Queer Nigerian Youth Push for Pride," *Dazed Digital*, June 28, 2019, www.dazeddigital.com/life-culture/article/culture/article/45073/1/nigeria-lgbtq-queer-youth-pride-2019.

Initiative for Equal Rights (TIERS) Queer Alliance for Nigeria, Bisi Alimi Foundation, and Women's Media Center. Outside of these platforms specifically organized for the queer community, members are vulnerable to online assaults and threats on social media platforms such as Twitter, Instagram, Facebook, and others. Many queers delete their public accounts to avoid harassment.[32] The attacks on queers in Nigeria are perpetrated by strangers and family members alike. Indeed, many of the negative experiences they must endure begin at the family level.[33] Declaring one's queer status in Nigeria is to deliberately exclude oneself from every conceivable right under state laws and international human rights declarations.

For members of this community, as with disabled persons, the right to life, a good quality of life, and access to health, education, employment, and housing are taken from them. A queer who dies as a result of public lynching or injury related to their sexual preference is ignored, dismissed as a self-inflicted and justifiable consequence. At least nine out of every ten Nigerians support the government's position on the queer community.[34] Given homosexuality's controversial nature in Nigeria, these surveys are unlikely to measure the public's true perception, but instead they reflect an idea of what is considered normal and moral.

The easiest option for individuals is to condemn those who are already considered outcasts in the court of public opinion. A queer interviewed in a public space, in the presence of others who are less tolerant, may feel pressured to conform with public opinion and avoid controversy. To oppose popular sentiment is to draw suspicion, if not outright criticism. In the same vein, it will amount to a mere guesstimate to survey the extent of same-sex activities or homosexuals in a country where the majority of homosexuals live in hiding. The community's efforts to change the prevailing sociocultural and political milieu is a herculean task.

Sexuality and Female Genital Mutilation/Cutting (FGM/C)

African society prides itself on a collection of cultural practices founded on morality and honorable conduct, and sexuality is one of the many social constructions through which African civilization was built. Hierarchies set

---

[32] Ibid.

[33] See, for instance, Mark Schoofs and Augustus Olakunle, "In Nigeria, a Bill to Punish Gays Divides a Family," *The Wall Street Journal*, January 12, 2007, www.wsj.com/art icles/SB116855583547274450.

[34] Pew Research Center, "The Global Divide on Homosexuality: Greater Acceptance in More Secular and Affluent Countries," Pew Research Center, June 4, 2013, www .pewresearch.org/global/2013/06/04/the-global-divide-on-homosexuality/.

limitations and restrictions on the conduct of each member of society, along with expectations for social relations. For matters such as sexuality, physiological and psychological behaviors were cast into idealized roles for everyone to live by. The image has since been accepted as normal, or the core of the culture and traditions of the people of Africa. A man is expected to be more sexually active than a woman. A sexually active woman is deemed to be promiscuous, seen as a shame to her family and likely to be unfaithful to her husband.

A sexually active man is considered strong, a good carrier of family tradition, and virile – he can even be hailed for his accomplishments in praise poems. In this social construct, sexual intercourse is only meant to be procreational for a woman. They are not expected to enjoy sex, or use it to relieve stress, or hold any of the other sexual attitudes that are considered ideal for men. For women in traditional African settings, discussing sex is committing a social transgression.[35]

Ostensibly, the only way to avoid this form of "perversion" for women is to tame their sexual urges through physical alteration. To do this, parts of the vagina are cut as deeply as culture or family tradition demands. This is the practice of Female Genital Mutilation/Cutting, a process that can involve cutting and repositioning the labia minora and the labia majora. Similar practices involve cauterizing, incising, pricking, scraping, and piercing the genital area.[36] According to the World Health Organization, the countries of Egypt, Ethiopia, and Nigeria are where these customs are most frequently practiced.[37] In Nigeria, at least one in every four women between the ages of fifteen and forty-nine has undergone this process.

Although attitudes toward sexuality dominate discussion of FMG/C in Africa, other traditional justifications are used to defend the practice. These include aesthetic arguments claiming that the ritual seeks to beautify the female genitals, that it is a rite of passage, a mark of progression into womanhood, a sign of marriageability or fertility, and others.[38] Attempts to justify female circumcision as a traditional practice are based on

---

[35] For more on this, see Deevia Bhana, "Girls' Sexuality between Agency and Vulnerability," in *The Palgrave Handbook of African Women's Studies*, eds. Yacob-Haliso and Falola (London: Palgrave Macmillan, 2020), 2–11.

[36] World Health Organization, "Female Genital Mutilation: Key Facts," World Health Organization, February 10, 2020, www.who.int/news-room/fact-sheets/detail/female-genital-mutilation.

[37] Onyinye Edeh, "It's Tradition: Female Genital Mutilations," Institute of Current World Affairs, September 20, 2017, www.icwa.org/its-tradition-female-genital-mutilation-in-nigeria#_ftn2.

[38] Lawrence A. Adeokun et al., "Trends in Female Circumcision between 1993 and 2003 in Osun and Ogun States, Nigeria (A Cohort Analysis)," *African Journal of Reproductive Health* 10, no. 2 (2006): 49.

cultural assumptions, without any scientific proof or health considerations for the females involved.

In cultures where it is used as a rite of passage for a child, FGM/C is often
performed on adult women, usually before they give birth to children of
their own. Tradition prohibits the clitoris of the mother to touch the head of
the baby during labor – it is believed that this threatens the baby's survival.
The clitoris is seen as a curse manifesting on the woman's body that must
be removed. During the procedure leading to the FMG/C, materials such
as herbal mixtures, cow dung, hot ashes, and unsterilized sharp objects are
used on the victim, who would not be given anesthetics to reduce the pain,
as is done during a surgical operation. Experts use the term "genital
surgery" to describe the process, because the term "circumcision" was
rejected by scholars and medical practitioners.

A surgical operation cannot be medically certified when it is being
performed by traditional doctors, local midwives, community leaders,
family heads, or an experienced female elder. The search for a better
term to qualify the practice hoped to explain its hazardous consequences
for women and girls, not to polish the image of an act they were trying to
abolish. That is why the term mutilation has been used, but it may not
translate into impactful measures within society; the point is to assist the
process of advocacy and to raise awareness of the damage to women's
bodies and sexuality caused by the procedure.

Local communities – key stakeholders in the eradication of the
procedure – felt that the term mutilation suggested prejudice, and
so the word "cutting" became a comprise term between them and the
medical experts/scholars/policy makers discussing female genital cutting.[39]
The community of experts still refers to the practice as mutilation in their
official communication to emphasize the urgency required from relevant
bodies. Sometimes it is referred to with the combination of terms, FGM/
C, as used here.

Damage caused by this practice, depending on the extremity of the
tradition, can include complications during marriage, sexual injury,
uneven sexual satisfaction between couples, and other physical and psychological damage such as depression and neglect. The 1995 Beijing
declaration described the practice as a crime against women.[40] It has

[39] Bettina Shell-Duncan and Ylva Hernlund, "Female 'Circumcision' in Africa:
Dimensions of the Practice and Debates," in *Female Circumcision Africa: Culture,
Controversy, and Change*, eds. Bettina Shell-Duncan and Ylva Hernlund (Colorado:
Lynne Renner Publisher, 2000), 6.
[40] United Nations, *Report of the Fourth World Conference on Women: Beijing, September 4–15*
(New York: United Nations, 1995), www.un.org/womenwatch/daw/beijing/pdf/Beijing
%20full%20report%20E.pdf.

also been denounced by the Convention to Eliminate All Forms of Discrimination Against Women (CEDAW), the Convention on the Rights of the Child (CRC), the African Charter on the Rights and Welfare of the Child (ACRWC), and other organizations. The World Health Organization (WHO) prohibits medical practitioners from performing the procedure.

At the national level, anti-FMG/C movements have been active in Nigeria even before independence, beginning in the 1950s with Nigerian medical practitioners raising awareness of the issues with pregnant women and nursing mothers at the community level.[41] Records show that public perception of the practice has changed over time, but it has not led to a meaningful decrease in the number of cases of FMG/C. Meaningful change will require not just laws, treaties, and declarations, but a focus on novel ways to change this cultural attitude.[42]

As a public health challenge, the WHO leads the campaign for the eradication of FMG/C. After recognizing the effort required to achieve this goal, the organization changed its approach in 2008 to adopt a holistic approach that includes education, justice, health, and women's affairs.[43] Beyond its traditional supporters, FMG/C has created a means of economic survival for the custodians of this tradition, and their support will be needed to curb the practice in Nigeria and elsewhere. The practice also affects the marriageability of a female child – in some cultures, undergoing this process launches her into the realm of womanhood, and without it she may not get a suitor, depriving her parents of their right to her bride-price.

Protecting the Leaders of Tomorrow: The Nigerian Child and the Nigerian State

Children are regarded as the leaders of tomorrow, hence the need to prioritize their interests and secure their future today. This axiom has become a cliché in Nigeria, where it is used as political rhetoric. Children are among the most vulnerable groups in the country, with the government making little strategic investment in their future. Despite extant laws and international declarations seeking to protect the dignity of children, secure their future, and prepare them for leadership roles, Nigeria remains party to child labor exploitation, child marriage, and other forms of domestic

---

[41] Francis A. Althaus, "Female Circumcision: Rite of Passage or Violation of Rights?" *International Family Planning Perspectives* 23, no. 3 (1997): 130.
[42] George C. Denniston et al., eds., *Bodily Integrity and the Politics of Circumcision: Culture, Controversy, and Change* (New York: Springer, 2006).
[43] World Health Organization, "Female Genital Mutilation."

violence against children. These forms of violence against children in Nigeria, as in every other African state, are somewhat cultural and standard societal practices. Children in these societies have virtually no say in the decisions made about their present and future. In some cases, ostensibly for the purpose of discipline, Nigerian children often suffer from physical and psychological domestic violence, which has negative effects on their personality and development.

Children who experience domestic violence develop low self-esteem or aggressive attitudes. In some cases, the violence is indirect and stems from the environment in which the child grows up. In a hostile environment, where parents fought each other or a spouse suffered domestic violence, the child can retain trauma throughout his or her life. Direct or indirect violence against children can take the form of physical abuse or psychological punishment. Sexual abuse is often suffered by girl children and women in general, and it can include both physical and psychological forms of domestic violence. Victims of sexual abuse often suffer brutalization, suffering from psychological disorders that can lead to a loss of interest in healthy sexual activity.

Emotional support is essential for children. It allows children to be emotionally stable, helping them to concentrate their minds on things that are relevant and productive for their future. When emotional support is missing, especially from family and loved ones, they are left in a wild, cold long night. They can seek alternatives in the company of friends who lure them into insidious and detrimental practices like substance abuse, theft, prostitution, thuggery, and other criminal activity.

Children who live with stepparents or members of their extended families, or who serve as domestic labor, are more vulnerable to domestic violence. Child labor occupies a popular space in the political economy of African states. Children are used as domestic labor, street hawkers, industrial laborers, *agbero* (bus conductors), and they hold many other jobs in formal and informal economic sectors. Children have been used in typical African settings to strengthen a family's economic standing. Traditionally, they are a social investment for their parents and a return is expected from them.[44]

What took place during precolonial times was not considered child labor, aside from the use of enslaved children, who were deprived of the emotional ties and affection of their parents. The global body responsible for labor affairs, the International Labor Organization (ILO), describes

---

[44] Deji Ogunremi, "Economic Development and Warfare in Nineteenth Century Yorubaland," in *War and Peace in Yorubaland 1793–1893*, eds. I. A. Akinjogbin, A. A. Adediran, and G. A. Adebayo (Nigeria: Heinemann, 1988), 696.

child labor as that which includes "all forms of work by children under the age laid down in ILO standards (normally 15 years or the age of completion of compulsory schooling subject to some exceptions)."[45] During precolonial times, schooling was part of everyday practice. After a child was old enough to walk and talk properly, they joined the family labor force.

These practices prepared a child for the future. Child labor became prevalent in Nigeria and elsewhere in Africa following the colonial period's reorganization of labor and the economic morphology of society. The extreme and "moderate" forms of child labor identified by the ILO spread rapidly in Nigeria during this period, with around 50 percent of its child population currently living within this web.[46] This is a minimum, and it is not surprising when we consider that Nigeria has the highest rate of out-of-school children in the world.[47]

Children between the ages of five and eighteen are working on job sites that include quarries, mines, and other industrial fields. They are also forced into prostitution and other conditions of servitude, in most cases after falling victim to child trafficking. Child soldiers are not uncommon among the Boko Haram terrorist sects, just as they are engaged in less extreme but time-consuming activities such as hawking, apprenticeship, running shops, begging, and domestic servitude. It is seen as proper and conventional for children to help their parents or caregivers in household chores and to reduce the family's financial burden. Time and intention are important factors in identifying child labor.

In cases where children are engaged in apprenticeships, running shops, hawking, and participating in other labor that affects their educational development, it is child labor.[48] Conventional activities can border on

---

[45] International Labour Organization, "Child Labor in Africa," in *Focus Programme on Promoting the Declaration on Fundamental Principles and Rights at Work: Work in Freedom*, International Labor Organization.

[46] *Vanguard*, "50% of Nigerian Children Engage in Child Labour – NBS," *Vanguard*, February 13, 2018, www.vanguardngr.com/2018/02/50-nigerian-children-engage-child -labour-nbs/amp; Anadolu Agency, "Nigeria: ILO Says Least at 43% of the Children Population Trapped in Child Labour, Including in Private Businesses," Business and Human Rights Resource Centre, May 13, 2019, www.business-humanrights.org/en/nig eria-ilo-says-least-at-43-of-children-population-trapped-in-child-labour-Including-in-p rivate-businesses.

[47] *VOA*, "UN: In Nigeria More Than 13 million School-Age Children out of School," *VOA*, December 11, 2018, www.voanews.com/africa/un-nigeria-more-13-million-scho ol-age-children-out-school#:~:text=English%20voanews.com-,UN%3A%20In%20Nigeri a%20More%20Than%2013%20Million%20School,age%20Children%20Out%20of% 20School&text=ABUJA%2C%20NIGERIA%20%2D%20A%20survey%20con ducted,the%20highest%20in%20the%20world.

[48] International Labour Organization, "What Is Child Labor," International Labour Organization, n.d., www.ilo.org/ipec/facts/lang–en/index.htm.

mild forms of child labor, but the extreme cases that affect the mental, social, and physical development of children share no link with socially accepted roles for children. In most cases, they are the last options for Nigerian children after they have been pushed to the wall by neglect and servitude.[49] Basic education, health care facilities, and decent standards of living are difficult for Nigerian children to access, making them vulnerable to human traffickers who promise comfort, or they can be prone to disease that can cost them their lives or render them permanently handicapped.[50]

The prospects are even more bleak for girl children. They are not merely denied the opportunity to live and enjoy their childhood with appropriate support; that childhood can be cut short through child marriage or teenage pregnancy. In most cases, this perpetuates a cycle where the girl is faced with the prospect of raising a child that she is neither old enough nor competent enough to care for on her own. Child marriage violates the freedom of female children, and it can result in physical, sexual, or psychological harm that can include violence, marital rape, and other domestic violence and exploitation.[51] It increases their vulnerability to sexually transmitted diseases such as HIV/AIDS and sexual injuries such as vesico vaginal fistula (VVF). The latter condition is said to be prominent in areas where poverty and ignorance prevail, but child marriage itself is linked with both of these unfortunate conditions, making VVF prevalent in northern Nigeria, where the practice is ubiquitous.[52] A report from the United Nations Children's Fund (UNICEF) disclosed that around 3,538,000 girl children in Nigeria are victims of the child marriage tradition, ranking the country as having the third-largest number of child brides in the world and having the eleventh highest rate of child marriage globally.[53]

---

[49] Rory Carroll, "Child Labourers Rescued from Nigerian Quarries," *The Guardian*, October 16, 2003, www.google.com/amp.theguardian.com/world/2003/oct/17/childpro tection.uk; *The New Humanitarian*, "Children Crushing Stones into Gravel to Get through School," *The New Humanitarian*, June 29, 2005, www.thenewhumanitarian.org /report/55172/benin-children-crushing-stones-gravel-get-through-school.

[50] Michael Eli Dokosi, "Meet Geoffrey Asadu, Visually Impaired Nigerian Lawyer Who Hasn't Lost a Case in 25 Years," *Face2face Africa*, March 9, 2020, https://face2faceafrica .com/article/meet-geoffrey-asadu-visually-impaired-nigerian-lawyer-who-hasnt-lost-a-c ase-in-25-years.

[51] All of these and many more, the Beijing declaration described as violence against women. United Nations, *Report of the Fourth World Conference on Women*.

[52] See Suzan Edeh Buchi, "12,000 Women Develop VVF Every Year in Nigeria," *Vanguard*, July 20, 2012, www.vanguardngr.com/2012/07/1200-women-develop-vvf- every-year-in-nigeria/.

[53] Girls Not Brides, "What's the Child Marriage Rate? How Big of an Issue Is Child Marriage?" Girls Not Brides, www.girlsnotbrides.org/child-marriage/nigeria/.

More than half of these numbers come from the northern part of the country, where the tradition is connected to Islamic doctrine. Under the guise of religious sanctioning, neither the Convention on the Rights of the Child nor other global declarations have been domesticated into the country's Child Rights Act (CRA). Contentions often surface over the ambiguity of the Nigerian constitution and its operationality vis-à-vis the Sharia law of the northern states. On the other hand, the Convention's position on adulthood is hazy – it was declared as age eighteen, but the same document gives exceptions for specific practices in UN member states.[54] This ambiguity was rectified in the Africa Union Charter on the Rights and Welfare of the Child, which expressly insisted, "Child marriage and the betrothal of girls and boys shall be prohibited and effective action, including legislation, shall be taken to specify the minimum age of marriage to be 18 years and make registration of all marriages in an official registry compulsory."[55]

But one year after this declaration, core northern states in Nigeria began to adopt Sharia legal codes. Complications with the Federal constitution, particularly in relation to Sharia law, mean that it remains to be seen how this declaration and others protecting the dignity of the child, as ratified by the Nigerian federal government, can take effect. Eighteen years old is recognized by Nigeria's Federal Government as the age of adulthood (with complications in relation to marriage),[56] but in Islamic law this is replaced by the attainment of puberty, which can be as early as age twelve. This practice breeds poverty and it is sustained by poverty. Among the Becheve people of Cross River state in Nigeria, where the practice is common and cultural, girl children are reared like livestock meant to be sold.[57] A girl child can be sold in the money-marriage tradition, as it is called, as early as the age of seven. The family that sells the girl in exchange for money and other material gifts from the buyer-husband does so to stave off poverty.[58]

---

[54] For more on these legal dynamics, see Kayode Olatunbosun Fayokun, "Legality of Child Marriage in Nigeria and Inhibitions against Realization of Education Rights," *US-China Education Review* 5, no. 7 (2015): 460–470; Enyinna S. Nwauche, "Child Marriage in Nigeria: (Il)legal and (Un)constitutional?" *African Human Rights Law Journal* 15 (2015): 421–431; Tim S. Braimah, "Child Marriage in Northern Nigeria: Section 61 of Part I of the 1999 Constitution and the Protection of Children against Child Marriage," *African Human Rights Law Journal* 14 (2014): 474–488.

[55] Protection against Harmful Social and Cultural Practices, Article 21(2), African Charter on the Rights and Welfare of the Child.

[56] See Section 29(4) A & B of the 1999 Constitution of the Federal Republic of Nigeria.

[57] Franklin Adegbie, Stephanie Hegarty, and Mayeni Jones, "Money Wives: The Nigerian Girls Sold to Repay Debts," BBC, September 17, 2018, www.bbc.com/news/av/world-africa-45514154/money-wives-the-nigerian-girls-sold-to-repay-debts.

[58] Mudiaga Affe, "Agony of Cross River Community Girls Married Off at Infancy by Indebted Parents," *Punch News*, May 13, 2018, https://punchng.com/agony-of-cross-river-community-girls-married-off-at-infancy-by-indebted-parents/amp/.

The money-wife who becomes property of a buyer-husband can be sold to another buyer-husband if she fails to meet expectations. In a situation where she gives birth to children for her buyer-husband, her daughters will suffer the same fate. This characterizes the living conditions for around 50 percent of Nigerian children. No special insight is necessary to perceive how this pattern will affect the country's future.

Conclusion

Persons with disabilities, the LGBTIQ community, and Nigerian children are vulnerable to cultural practices, conventions, and societal norms that affect their daily lives. To varying degrees, they live at the margins where they have few choices and almost no rights at all. Like every other member of society, they are protected by a larger body of rights – fundamental human rights. Groups are seeking to build on these rights at the global and national levels, but these individuals remain vulnerable to cultural practices that define their place in the social space. The hardest links to break are the oppressive practices and beliefs that survive as cultural traditions.

All these groups reside in what is referred to as the "unknown space" and the "Other space." The difficulties of their experiences may be temporarily cushioned by creating an alternative space, but they could be permanently transformed by successfully shifting cultural behavior within their society. As much as policies and laws are good steps to change the narrative concerning minority groups in Nigeria and Africa in general, they must be linked with an implementation mechanism that involves rigorous local campaigns meant to change society's cultural perception. If anything can be drawn from the efforts to change the minority and human rights narratives so far, it is that an unbreakable grip on culture and tradition means the death of effective laws and policies.

17   Political Violence

Introduction

In a heterogeneous society, where many opposing ideologies are prevalent and clashing, destructive acts are usually unavoidable. When destruction becomes an indispensable part of a society's day-to-day reality, it requires insight into the root causes of such antisocial engagements, demanding actionable plans to eradicate or contain them. Humans, as animals with ambitions to dominate others, are bound to lock horns when their contrasting ideologies meet on the field of interest.

People are bound to protect their own interests when clustering with others, regardless of their preferred philosophy's feasibility. They are not normally concerned about their ideas' potential to inflict discomfort on others – their focus is to remain a nucleus of concern around which the rest of society revolves. This can breed violence as long as personal ambition is linked with a quest for supremacy. The reality is that humans are wired with an urge to dominate and it makes it difficult to avoid clashes of interest.

The plural nature of Nigerian society has produced repeated instances of violence that stand in the way of its collective growth. Deeper scrutiny reveals that the violence is arranged by people looking to gain political profit, score cheap religious points, or strike fear in the heart of the people, all to promote their interests above others. It puts a dangling question mark on the ability to administer governance free of prejudice; people always go to extremes when pursing their interests. Recent events in the country have cast doubt on whether its leaders are capable of holding the heterogeneous society together. It springs from the fact that countless violent attacks, damaging lives and property, have devastated the collective outlook and psychology of the country. Reports of outrageous occurrences compel observers to doubt whether the country has everything under control. The temporary, peaceful interludes between periods of violence do not guarantee the total effacement of destructive action.

Nigeria has included variegated regional and cultural expressions from its very beginning, when it was created by Lord Lugard in 1914. Since then, it has carried the potential for internal strife – the different nationalities within the country were unable to reach mutual agreement around shared interests before they were compacted by European interests. They had no recourse for avoiding the adverse consequences resulting from the imposed marriage. More than a hundred years after this merger, they remain under the influence of Europeans because they have been unable to develop workable philosophies that enable a formidable country to support all of its internal groups without prejudice.

The absence of unity has allowed people to commit evil deeds with impunity. The country's pattern of complicated existence leaves no escape from the anomalies that breed violent behavior and attacks on

Figure 17.1 An armed political thug standing against the Nigerian flag with a hijacked ballot box.

the vulnerable and helpless. A group's vulnerability is determined by the amount of political power that it wields, which is in turn shaped by different factors that include the resources and economic value under their control.

Some helpless ethnic communities bear the brunt of the trauma inflicted by Lugard's unnegotiated marriage. The occasional violence marring the country today is a way of actualizing the looming danger of bringing together people from varying linguistic and cultural philosophies before they can find a common ground. The United States, which is normally held up as a heterogeneous society that maintains relative peace, has a key element that is missing from Nigeria. Apart from each state's autonomy to administer its governance under moderate influence from the White House at the center, even the most insignificant parts of the United States possess a shared sense of belonging. Without this component in Nigeria's political space, the country rests on a gunpowder keg waiting for a spark. The violence ravaging the country will remain with Nigerians until these background issues of nation-state formulation are addressed.

Social scientists, philosophers, and others have offered solutions to the violence that has held the country for ransom, but the challenges of civil unrest, which breed continuous violence, have defied every remedy. The price for nationhood, paid by the innocent Nigerians who become victims, forces us to ask what must be sacrificed before we can have a peaceful country. There appears to be no end in sight; people continue offering provincial justifications for actions that inflict painful consequences on the country. The root of the matter deserves careful attention, instead of the manufactured patriotism pervasive among Nigerians who discuss national issues. An enduring solution must be proposed to address the myriad of challenges confronting the country. The continuous reports of violence have strong foundations.

Political Dimensions of Violence

The various ethnic nationalities that converge within Nigerian society fuel a struggle for political power, which is always accompanied by its own resultant violence, no matter how minimal. This has become a perennial custom in the country's political business; many differing interests struggle for supremacy in bids to secure or retain power. Unsavory underground moves are orchestrated by those seeking power, and the people at the bottom rung of the social ladder are their collateral sacrifices. Lives are considered to have little or no value outside of their immediate social circles. When an ethnic or political group acquires power, it enacts a sequence of punishments against opponents who will eagerly return the gesture once they are back in power. It defies logic to think that these sensibilities would vanish as if by magic. Politically motivated violence can take different forms, but it has devastating effects in every situation.

Professor Patrick Lumumba has stated that violence is not merely the presence of war, but also the absence of justice. This explains the issues that provide the foundations for the violence pervading society. Nigerian society does not produce citizens who can be called patriots, in the actual sense of the word,[1] which paves the way for the growth of inequality that eventually leads to chaos. It also explains why people pursue factional interests over national ones.

At first glance, one might condemn the relentless pursuit of self-interest as wrong from every angle, but deeper consideration shows that the nature of the unity governing Nigerians gives room for a porous identity that remains an unending source of unrest in Nigeria. The concepts of nationhood found among the English, the Dutch, or the Arabs are missing from Nigeria, which contributes to the challenges that confront the people. Unity only occurs within the country when corrupt interests gather to feast on Nigeria's resources. It has led to the metaphor of a "national cake," referring to the rot plaguing the country.

Ethnic groups or political parties flex their strength, using the backing of numbers to dominate the country's political social space. In the spirit of sectionalism, parochialism, and provincial loyalty, these people are emboldened to perpetuate evil when they control the country's power structures. This explains the unceasing regional terrorism, tacitly supported by the members of their clans holding the country's highest political offices. The silence of their representatives worsens the situation, and it becomes more alarming with each successive political dispensation.

It is becoming evident that these attitudes are a permanent part of the country's political landscape. People automatically formulate an army of dissidents primarily focused on frustrating the person in the seat of power who does not share their ethnic or regional bonds. A National Bureau of Statistics report showed that conflict was higher in 2016 than in 2010 in each of the North-East, North-Central, and South-South zones.[2]

A cursory look at events reveals that these major zones produced the country's last two presidents. It becomes more interesting after understanding the country's polarization along ethnic lines and the political

---

[1] Obafemi Awolowo, *Path to Nigerian Freedom* (London: Faber and Faber, 1947), 47–48.

[2] Abdul Azad, Emily Crawford, and Heidi Kaila, *Conflict and Violence in Nigeria Results from the North East, North Central, and South Zones* (Washington, DC, and Nigeria: World Bank and National Bureau of Statistics, 2018), http://documents1.worldbank.org/curated/en/111851538025875054/pdf/130198-WP-P160999-PUBLIC-26-9-2018-14-42-49-ConflictViolenceinNigeriaResultsfromNENCSSzonesFinal.pdf.

dynamics that are responsible for such an outcome. The growing security concerns raised by Fulani herdsmen sporadically seizing Nigerian space, for example, can only be interpreted as an arrogant abuse of power from those who expect that their supporters at Aso Rock will provide them with complete immunity from the consequences. People in authority have remained silent when it was time to condemn or appraise minority affronts. Similar deafness, bordering on outright disrespect, was shown to government authorities during the reign of President Goodluck Jonathan, current President Muhammad Buhari's immediate predecessor. These actions invite violence that is felt across the nation. In a nutshell, violent attacks are enabled, if not masterminded, by political interests.

Other factors can motivate violence as people unleash immoral behavior under the canopy of politics. When resources are unevenly distributed among the political class, they rush to invoke every divisive tool that could shift the balance in their favor, encouraging their constituents to generate conflict. This problem persists because Nigeria does not have a working political philosophy that allows factional sentiments to be put aside when addressing national issues. Among Nigerians, politics is not seen as an end in itself, but a means to an end. This attitude makes it difficult to exterminate the violence that benefits the practitioners of discordant politics in the country. The political superstructures are rarely the target of violent attacks inside the country, and their inhabitants are free to incite aggression for any cause that will benefit them. The nature of the heterogeneous society called Nigeria enables lopsided systems of governance and their attendant eventualities.

The country's heterogeneous composition gives room for ethnic politics, where people are appointed and compensated based on ethnographic quotas, even when they are not the best hands for the job. The nature of ethnic consideration for political offices blurs the chance for transparent leadership, which enables further unspoken violence that ravages the country. Violence does not require the physical involvement of combative citizenry; when injustices are perpetrated and go unpunished under the umbrella of ethnicity, they are a form of violence that wreaks physical and emotional damage on those who suffer the consequences. For example, when a project is awarded by a government parastatal and the funds have been appropriated, the citizens face gradual harm that matures with time if the project fails because of corruption. When they are confronted with that harm, they either show resistance or resort to violence.

The clause called political forgiveness is prone to be unjustly invoked; we have seen it in different capacities across Nigeria's political landscape. When these actions are the order of the day, they breed future controversies, particularly, in national issues. A multiethnic country can perpetuate conflicts that come to dominate its sociopolitical landscape. It becomes inevitable when strong institutions are not in place to shield national interests from factional concerns. Nigeria's traditional social justice system is inherently forgiving of faults, and the people's collective memory erases the immoralities perpetrated by their political class. Sadly, the country's diverse ethnic makeup does not seem to help the issue. Careful study shows that from the very beginning, the people engaging in violence have done so under the certainty that they would be supported by members of their clans who hold political power.

Another political dimension of the common violence in the country is the lack of a distinct separation of powers among the agents of democracy. The people who we expect to oversee community affairs do so without regard for the traditional structure of the society that they rule. The outright disregard for the traditional structures breeds violence. Each unit of the country has been ruled for ages by political philosophies that answer to the immediate exigencies of the people. This had been happening for centuries, until the people were suddenly alienated by another, non-native philosophy. Colonists from the West arrived and introduced their preferred style of government from Europe, which had worked for their own culture. However, their dismissal of local governance was done without considering whether western democracy could work in societies that had different approaches to life, different customs, and disparate philosophies. Would such an imposition have worked in Europe without first considering the systems in place?

Let us imagine a setting where the monarch had been installed by the social law and ethics of that society, and whose tenure was attached to his existence on earth. If that sovereign violates the rules of the land, to what extent would other political actors carry out their statutory duties without the direct involvement of the monarch? Bearing in mind the unstable nature of democratic indulgence, and the reality that there is no continuity when opponents rise to power, how could there be infrastructural stability, economic growth, or effective social institutions? At the abstract level, would there be a collectively stable psychology? How can violence be avoided when these are the prevailing realities of the country's political landscape? We have witnessed various political stunts that seem more like personal vendettas than actual leadership from the people in power. In 2017, the Oyo State government, under the leadership of Senator Isiaka Ajimobi, elevated forty-eight chiefs, to kingly status.[3] Months later, the

---

[3] Bisi Olawunmi, "Ajimobi, the Constituted Kingmaker," *The Nation*, September 19, 2017, https://thenationonlineng.net/ajimobi-constituted-kingmaker/.

governor of Kano State made a similar decision.[4] The tenure of Ajimobi is over, and the same fate awaits his philosophical counterpart in Kano. Provided that they succeed, how does society contain the eventualities?

Economic Angle to the Issues of Violence

Karl Marx, when viewing the various struggles in society, saw every form of violence tied to the economy. Economic distribution determines the predominant values of the society. This makes it possible to link every problem of violence to the country's economic struggles. People will go to any lengths to ensure their survival, and everyone is looking to put food on the table. The man angling for political appointment, or seeking promotion at work, or developing a network of contacts is looking for ways to ensure his social safety and survival. It is inevitable that there are clashes in our collective bids to actualize these individual goals. The complex composition of the country makes it difficult to pursue objectives without ruffling feathers in the process. The various ethnicities within the country engage in different businesses, and each finds ways for their own group to prevail.

In the north, the predominant population of Fulani migrate to support their business of herding cattle. Other groups raise large quantities of cash crops. In the south, agricultural activities involve cocoa, palm oil, and kola nut. Within these regions, individuals have migrated in search of greater productivity. As a result, people from different cultural backgrounds are found across the country, performing jobs and enjoying their profits. However, clashes of interest occur when groups of diasporic minorities pursue their preferred form of business without considering how the businesses of others will be affected. When a herdsman invades a farm to find new grazing land for his cows, his actions are met with resistance from the affected group. It can be the starting point for internal strife if the separate groups engage in a war of ego and a battle for dominance. The government's customary silence, failing to condemn the dispute or mediate a solution, can allow minor disputes to grow into major internal conflicts.

Nigeria's heavy reliance on imports, and sparse internal production, aggravate the impact of these challenging situations; ordinary people are always the ones who bear the brunt. It can create needless inflation and ethnic suspicion. Violence is not kept at bay, and the incessant conflicts

---

[4] *Sahara Reporters*, "EXCLUSIVE: How Governor Ganduje Plans to Oust Emir of Kano Sanusi," *Sahara Reporters*, May 7, 2019, http://saharareporters.com/2019/05/07/exclusive-how-governor-ganduje-plans-oust-emir-kano-sanusi.

driven by opposing interests speak to the divisive internal politics that dominate Nigeria's social and political space. The struggles of Nigerians confirm these assertions. The media contributes to the bloated numbers of ethnic clashes, but we cannot overlook the fact that the country has witnessed increasing numbers of violent attacks. Instead of opening dialogue to settle perceived injustices, continuing violence remains the preferred tool. It is wielded without any recourse to peace.

Religious Reasons for Violence

Multiethnic and multicultural societies house multiple religious interests, requiring high levels of tolerance to avoid clashes over faith. Nigeria is an amalgam of different cultures that were maintaining unique belief systems before the West's intervention merged everything together. These opposing religions have become involved with and used by different power brokers, serving parochial interests in a bid to overrun national affairs. Logic is the first casualty when religious conflicts arise, and people give undue credence to their biases to help them feel that they are in the majority. Economic inequity remains the battleground where other conflicts are resolved, and the masses cannot escape it easily; their emotions are tied to it. An average member of society defends religious doctrine jealously and physical pressure could not make them relinquish their burning loyalty. People at the bottom of the social ladder usually view their belief system as the only way to enjoy affluence, even if it is in the afterlife.

Religiously motivated violence in Nigeria is all encompassing. One cannot escape a daily, existential war for souls, as "rescuers" crusade vehemently to win "lost" souls for their own God, ignoring how their activities invade the religious space of others. Even within the same faith, different denominations wage verbal assaults to boost their numbers and intimidate others who are not perceived to be on the way to salvation. The two most populous religions are notable in this struggle. People must resolve internal conflicts when making sense of the different religious sermons that bombard them on a daily basis. Just as physical violence disrupts social activities, religious violence perforates the mind with varying interpretations each day in Nigerian public space. People undergo personal torture as their minds are driven to nurse hate or affection for their neighbors. Contradictory religious messages, garnished with fear, pave the way for physical violence.

Lives have been lost in different religious wars, and cruelty is inflicted on innocents in the name of religion. Sensitive religious philosophies dictate how people must administer their lives, regardless of prevailing circumstances. Based on their regard for religion, many people indulge in extreme actions as a bid to appear faithful. This means that there are bound to be clashes between members of the two most popular religions in the country. Many people merge this conflict with their own religious convictions to forge an identity on that basis. Sadly, this happens most often among people on society's lowest rung of economic power. Religion can afflict the Nigerian mind the way poison harms a human body. Ordinary people are at risk of ill treatment based on the religion they profess. Choices are made under the cover of religion to justify lopsided appointments in government, business, and the nation in general. The country's division along religious lines provides more reasons for faith to be used as a potent tool for the people who are willing to abuse it for their own advantage.

Ethnic Coloration of Violence

Different ethnic groups in Nigeria often lock horns for various reasons. Conflicts are fueled by competition over the highest positions in the land, so that they can be used for personal or factional advancement. And people have unlimited capacity to pursue evil intent when the chance presents itself. The violence that is motivated by the need to prove ethnic supremacy usually arises from inadequate internal security policies. People are determined to break statutory rules in any ethnic clash. The violence built around the political power plays of different ethnic groups is informed by the unequal distribution of national benefits. Nigerian society's heterogeneous nature permits an identity grounded in religion and ethnicity, and each region has a specific religion that makes it simple to escalate conflicts from ethnic rivalries to religious ones. In the Southwest Region, Islam, Christianity, and traditional religions have similar numbers of adherents, but the dominant religions in other areas of the country allow internal strife to take on religious overtones.

Even before independence, Nigeria experienced cross-cultural migration as Hausa–Fulani in the Northern part of the country searched for greener pastures to the south.[5] Nigeria's historical undercurrents of violence are like an iceberg; the clear frame above the water does not display the true complexity of the full mass beneath. What becomes clear is the idea that people become emboldened by the assurance of political backing, which has led to increased violence attached to ethnicity. It has risen exponentially since the postindependence era. Although harsh climatic

---

[5] A. G. Adebayo, "Of Man and Cattle: A Reconsideration of the Traditions of Origin of Pastoral Fulani of Nigeria," *History in Africa* 18 (1991): 1–21.

conditions in the North have encouraged their unchecked migration, as explained by some analysts,[6] the reality is that intruding into the social space of others while refusing to adhere to their preexisting rules and regulations is an affront on their regional sovereignty. It is a potent recipe for violence that explains why the record of ethno-religious conflicts has been increasing to unprecedented levels since 1993.[7] People who accommodate the settlement of these herders feel more heat, living in daily fear of violent attacks from them.

Lack of state autonomy compounds the problem of violence in Nigeria. It allows unjust acts to be perpetuated without punitive measures in response. In many instances, the government's attitude does not show genuine intent to build a bond that can enhance solid democracy.

Political power in Nigeria is always deployed to satisfy ethnic emergencies, undermining the country's political system – it erodes the maturity that people have developed over time to build a united country that is free from internal strife and suspicion. One example of ethnic intimidation happened in Ile-Ife, the cradle of the Yoruba race, on March 21, 2017, in a clash between the Hausa people and their host Yoruba community.[8] Under state jurisdiction, arrests were made from Abuja and the parade of suspects showed injudicious deployment of federal might. This affront was difficult to dismiss as a mere mistake, and a Yoruba group by the name of Afenifere denounced the parochial view and double standards of the Nigerian government.[9] In a true democracy, the case would be justly handled by an autonomous state that had full jurisdiction.

These issues are a potent ground for hatching future violence; precedent has been used to justify similar actions. People live in daily fear of invasion or intimidation. Ethnic supremacy and internal imperialism, enabled by the political backing of sympathetic groups, make it difficult to resolve violence without a workable blueprint. These events have created fear in the minds of the people, and harm the mental well-being of people living in affected areas. If people are unjustly treated when issues demand transparency, their humanity is shattered. They would find it difficult to forge a common identity with others. This has been the case in Nigeria today. Ethnic considerations are the nucleus of violence around which other factors revolve, including religion, politics, and the

---

[6] Olakunle Michael Folami and Adejoke Olubimpe Folami, "Climate Change and Inter-Ethnic Conflict in Nigeria," *Peace Review* 25, no. 1 (2013): 104–110.
[7] Ibid.
[8] Kingsley Omonobi, "46 Killed, 96 Wounded in Ile-Ife Yoruba-Hausa Clash – Police," *Vanguard*, March 21, 2017, www.vanguardngr.com/2017/03/46-killed-96-wounded-ile-ife-yoruba-hausa-clash-police/.
[9] Ibid.

economy. The lasting effect is that the country's regressive politics force people to accept their ethnic identity instead of the national one.

The damaging effect of violence in Nigeria has jammed the gears of national progress, and people are locked in a worrying stagnation. There are many layers to the scourge of violence that torments the nation, and the country's shattered solidarity blurs every effort made on political and social fronts. Despite the efforts of different groups, violence and its corrosive effects continue to act as powerful deterrents to unity. Different groups, especially those that do not occupy decisive political positions in the country, have known abuse and suffering under the asymmetrical relationship known as One Nigeria. The various, devastating effects of violence have painted a picture of punctured togetherness.

Unstable Political Philosophy

Any developing civilization has a stable and defined political philosophy. In America, despite its population surge, political views are grouped under two major camps: Democrats and Republicans. Political parties in England are grouped around similar ideas. These parties have recognized philosophies that are respected by people who choose to follow parties based on their agreement with the values embedded in each group. Instead of seeing the parties as a path to holding the nation for ransom – like Nigerian politicians do – people protect the convictions of their parties with a sense of altruism that allows for durable nation building.

Nigeria is ideologically different because political offices are the inspirations that create political parties. Within the logic of a Nigerian mind, a political party can be created as a visa to negotiate valuable positions in the country's national businesses. The absence of a strong political philosophy makes it easy for people to launder the wealth of the country, creating and exploiting internal confusion along ethnic and economic lines for their own gain.

The background of internal strife is predominant in politics because, until now, there has not been a genuine reason to forge a national identity. People act as Nigerians only when it profits them. The political understanding of a simple majority vote does not break the attitude of parasitic deference that people expect from the nation. People rarely, if ever, believe in making personal sacrifices for the greater good. Different cultures, compacted under diverse ethnic and cultural dissimilarities, must consciously engage in talks to foster oneness and address the sensibilities of different cultural groups. Meanwhile, Nigerian leadership assumes that the country's union is watertight and that occasional negotiations are unnecessary.

Figure 17.2 A young man smoking an illicit substance.

A defective philosophy dominates the country, and it has permeated the tools used to build the nation. Such a method for birthing a country defies conventions of nation formation and policy development. On the surface, problems of bland mutual suspicion could be seen as unavoidable in a diverse and heterogeneous country. But the feigned readiness of the political class, and the insincerity of the populace, are persistent enemies of national unity.

Controversies driven by constant struggles for power are a signal of violence and the cause of endless internal wars among the people. Even within a single political group, opposing interests engineer social disturbances to jockey for power among members from different ethnic backgrounds. Despite eventual efforts at reconciliation, divisions continue to grow. The political effects of violence take different shapes as people find it easy to dismantle the false union upon which the country stands. Reports are common of powerful individuals sponsoring violence within and across parties to retain power or negotiate with the government of the day.

This can only happen when people do not trust the country's political system. An erstwhile head of state in Nigeria, some time ago, admitted that his cabinet had been infiltrated by members of the Boko Haram sect and that he believed they were there for sinister purposes.[10] The incident shows the nature of the political hide-and-seek that occurs in Nigeria. Former President Goodluck Jonathan, coming from a minority group, encountered this situation because of the true reason for political formation in Nigeria: personal interest. His administration was infiltrated because factional goals outweighed national concerns.

By failing to address the political skulduggery occupying the citizens' collective psychology, it becomes difficult to forge a common identity that can work toward a united future. The country concentrates too much of its power at the center, tacitly endorsing racial politics where those with higher population numbers use their strength to retain power or to allocate positions in government. It is natural for parts of the country to feel marginalized, giving them reasons to resist an un-negotiated union. A reliance on goodwill suggests that equality will remain elusive for many minorities. The lack of strong political institutions that could address their discontent further compound the reasons for political violence. The stark reality is that the delegation of power, allocation of national assignments, and many other government decisions are steered by ethnic and political affiliation; growing political despondence threatens to destabilize any vestige of unity that the country's founding fathers had fought to acquire. Politics in Nigeria increasingly emboldens outrageous indulgences that beneficiaries describe as national cake. It throttles the image of a unified nation that has taken long years to build.

The country's peace is disrupted by political machinations from bad actors who know that they can flout national conventions without facing consequences. Often, the cultural neighbors of politicians become pompous, capitalizing on their allies ascending to government offices and instigating trouble that bears an imprint on national life. Because people have been grouped into structures without considering either their geography or their cultural identity, the further divisions over incompatible ideologies make violence unavoidable. The Northern part of the country, for example, is a strong advocate of Sharia Law and would find it easy to practice it implicitly within its domain. Problems arise when these advocates are in a position to determine things for the entire country, or when they can impose conditions on cultures that do not share their genetic affiliation.

A northern judge might see no irregularity in maiming criminals as punishment for misdeeds, but the southern part of the country would

---

[10] *Premium Times*, "Boko Haram Has Infiltrated My Government," *Premium Times*, January 8, 2012, www.premiumtimesng.com/news/3360-boko-haram-has-infiltrated-my-government-says-jonathan.html.

definitely condemn such practices. Someone from the western part of the nation might refuse to perform religious rites, believing that the decision should be made by the individual practitioner, and that attitude may irk others from the North. There is no collective cohesion in the ideologies we practice.

Deserting Economic Glory

Economic growth thrives in a relatively peaceful environment; no investors would make large financial commitments in areas plagued with violence. Peace has a huge impact on a nation's economy, and its absence invites stagnation and unproductivity. Social and economic progress are not possible in unsettled environments, and there is little hope for sustained wealth in areas full of discordant politics.

In Nigeria's political atmosphere, wars and uprisings are a living characteristic of the people that typically impairs how the rest of the world perceives the nation. In a world where it is cheap and easy to access information, news stories about kidnapping, robbery, high unemployment, aimless citizens, and blatantly unproductive leadership impair economic growth. Nigeria is a country that has witnessed a steady, progressive economic boom due to foreign businesses investing in the country. In 2014, it experienced a pathetic downturn when Boko Haram threatened the country's economic outlook.[11] Investors were forced to withdraw when violence was the order of the day.

Violence never improves the economic climate of a country. About a decade ago, Nigeria saw increasing numbers of incidents where pipes were vandalized, along with increasing numbers of terror attacks in the eastern and southern regions of the country. People carried out violent demonstrations to protest the perceived injustices that they had suffered. The violence damaged the economy and the production of crude oil plummeted. The national income was also affected. At a time when the global price of oil was greatly affected by different factors, the country was exposed to further economic dangers – its hopes were dashed by acts of vandalism. In 2017, pipe vandalism lowered the country's production from around 2.2 million barrels per day down to 1.3 million barrels per day.[12] The usual blame game was played, disturbing the political atmosphere and disrupting national progress.

[11] Matt Egan, "Boko Haram Threatens Nigeria's Economic Future," *CNN*, May 12, 2014, https://money.cnn.com/2014/05/12/investing/nigeria-kidnapping-investing/index.html.
[12] Roseline Okere, "Nigeria: Oil Production Dips to 1.3mbd Over Vandalism," *AllAfrica/ The Guardian*, September 14, 2017, https://allafrica.com/stories/201709140086.html.

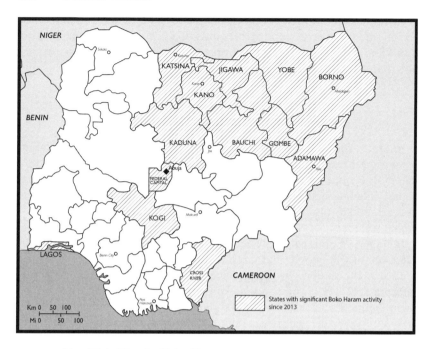

Map 17.1 Nigeria, Boko Haram.

Delicate macro and micro economies in Nigeria are threatened by the violence that pervades the country. Inflation usually skyrockets during the severe economic conditions created by civil unrest. Previously affordable goods and services become difficult to acquire during times of social and political unrest – violence shapes the economic condition of the people, and the vulnerable masses suffer from the pressure. The economic fluctuations resulting from internal strife prevent measurable growth in the country.

The widespread problem of terrorism has devastating effects on economic growth. Every person is focused on providing shelter, food, and other basic necessities – this impulse for survival supplies the driving force for violent acts and indulgences. The layers can be difficult to untangle once violence escalates, because they become shrouded by a web of complexities. On many occasions, leaders of Boko Haram sects have demanded money from the government in exchange for ceasing their raids and public disturbances; when their demands are met, tensions de-escalate for a short while. People prioritizing their safety have explained the reduced economic activity that takes place when violence is the order of the day. The relationship between violence and economic stagnation, which has been established repeatedly, means that a country grappling with adverse conditions cannot compete effectively in the global marketplace. International relationships are severed, which has further negative effects for the country.

The psychologically disruptive effects of violence prevent citizens from applying their creativity in ways that could advance economic development. Recent reports of kidnapping have paralyzed the minds of many who would normally make efforts at economic improvement. The overriding drive for self-preservation makes it impossible for many to conduct business, due to the fear of imminent violence that could affect their activities at any time. National violence has been a continuous challenge to economic prosperity, which has a negative bearing on the country's political outlook.

By failing to provide lasting solutions for this scourge, Nigeria has lost financial opportunities to other countries that made peace a national concern and demonstrated their commitment to nation building. The problem is more daunting, and continues to challenge Nigerians, because many are stuck in stagnation. The fortune that the country loses to inadequate security measures, on a yearly basis, questions its ability to measure up to other developed nations.

Religio-cultural Dents

The diverse religious beliefs that guide spiritual philosophies are affected by the same violence that has unbearable consequences on the political community. At the height of the Boko Haram strikes in northern states, many decided to take drastic measures to ensure their own safety, after their hopes of relying on the government for protection had been dashed. Some congregants attended religious gatherings with guns and other weapons to guarantee their safety. Not only do these actions display a lack of trust in the government's ability to provide security, it also shows the extreme measures that people will take when they are incessantly ravaged by violent attacks.

Worshippers bringing weapons to religious services suggests a country that is on the brink of collapse. It shows people fearing that anarchy will reign supreme, with pronounced disregard for existing rules and regulations. In some places, believers remained indoors as they felt it was too risky to openly practice religion. This atmosphere has created pressure within religious camps that do not provide a stable atmosphere to pursue the serious business of leadership, and they do not foster the trust that people must invest in their government.

Growing violence has created a form of ethnic profiling that breeds mutual distrust among Nigerian citizens. By believing that specific ethnicities are ready to destroy lives and properties at the slightest provocation, the Nigerian people now maintain a psychological distance that strains any attempted relationships. The attitudes engender cultural sabotage, setting the people into national confusion.

The mutual cultural suspicion created by stereotypes is a barrier to productive engagement; it provides a space to apply unwarranted stigma on persons or groups, making it difficult to attain any type of development. Under these conditions, there can be no end to ethnic cleansing – different cultural communities are ready to take up arms against the people they already suspect, open to the idea of obliterating other humans from the face of the earth. When coupled with political language that suggests indecision or indifference to violence, if not outright endorsement, the attacks can escalate as people feel more emboldened.

Intercultural conflict generates fears among minorities who cannot define the best way to be a Nigerian. They are pushed to the margin of irrelevance at best, or they are dismissed as collateral damage. In the process, many defenseless people give up, becoming displaced by the growing influence of violence in their country. Continuous Hausa–Fulani demands, asking the Yoruba people to cede their lands and enable unrestricted grazing, is considered ecological colonialism;[13] it is an extension of the conquer-them-all mentality in the country. The kidnap-for-ransom incidents and day-to-day torments inflicted on the Yoruba are recognized as psychological warfare. It is meant to apply pressure, and the number of violent attacks has escalated. Peace is becoming elusive and anomie is common in contemporary Nigerian society. If Nigeria is not involved in discussions about climate change, if it does not consider how technology can be used to become globally competitive, and if it ignores intercultural occupation of ethnic territories, the signs are ominous.

The intractable nature of violent attacks illustrates the thick cloud surrounding the political and social landscape of the people. The glorification of internal miasma, through silence and inaction, makes it difficult to forge a national identity where prosperity can thrive. People in power display an obvious parochialism that suggests there is an imbalanced benefit to being a Nigerian. The implicit message is that some Nigerians are considered more important than others, and their status is determined by their cultural affiliation.

---

[13] Bámidélé Adémólá-Olátéjú, "While Yoruba Land Sleeps!" *Premium Times*, June 25, 2019, https://opinion.premiumtimesng.com/2019/06/25/while-yoruba-land-sleeps-by-bamidele-ademola-olateju/.

Various episodes in recent history show the lopsided, jaundiced conception of the Nigeria project. It took no time for the government to react to the indigenous people of Biafra, mobilizing men in khaki under the auspice of Operation Python Dance. The same zeal is missing in the face of reports that the Hausa–Fulani are holding the country by the jugular. Instead, every resource is deployed to engage them in dialogue, persuade them, and even allocate money from the federal government to silence them. Sadly, this is unsuccessful in most cases, and the investments are wasted.

Apart from the southwest region, where there are roughly equal numbers of Christians and Muslims, the country is polarized along religious lines. The increasing number of Christians in the northern region suggests that there is hope for religious tolerance, but the fact remains that there are many cases of violent attacks among people of differing beliefs. It wreaks psychological and religious havoc on worshippers in the region. The failure to tame these raging outbreaks of violence is responsible for the changing attitudes that make it impossible for opposing ideologies to coexist. It causes economic harm, and it plants a seed of discord that will be harvested in the future.

A heterogeneous society like Nigeria cannot erase awful experiences, carried out by any group, from its collective memory. People may temporarily suppress their urge to retaliate, but they will always revisit past grievances whenever they have the power to enact vengeance. Whatever union the country enjoys today will be haunted in the future if there are no measures in place to curb growing threats. The collective effects of violence on the people are destructive, and should be given national attention so that peace can be restored.

There are workable solutions to the scourge of violence. Solutions require pragmatism, because careful enforcers of extreme actions are at the roots of these challenges. Actionable plans are necessary to counter their disingenuous machinations. One reason for the continuous attacks on nationhood is that its leadership views the country's unity as nonnegotiable. Even amidst many homogeneous communities, the people deserve timely assurance of their citizenry; they are known as the bedrock of society, without which it would be impossible to form a nation. The continuous reminder that these people matter has an inherent capacity to give them a sense of belonging. It encourages them to accept a common identity, needed to promote peace and set the quest for national development in motion.

It would be folly to assert that a heterogeneous society like Nigeria does not need to have occasional discussions about its unity. A conglomerate of different civilizations, with their own ideological beliefs and cultural peculiarities, should appreciate dialogue as a national necessity. Not only does it cement the lukewarm bonds among the various cultures within the country, it also fosters rapid development and relegates mutual suspicion to the past. It would create a fair environment for maximum growth, and people would engage in their business with a fair mindset and an assurance of success.

National dialogue would provide an avenue for the different nations that make up the country to express their fears, voicing the uncertainties that shroud their existence. Providing a space for those perceived as minorities to decide the country's political direction would build their confidence and ignite their own passion for togetherness; they would have no reason to feel unsafe amidst dissimilar people. Nations across the world have shown the potency of negotiation and dialogue in building a formidable national family. A heterogeneous society requires conscious efforts to ensure stability, given the propensity toward instability when appropriate measures are not in place. Attracting the required forces would propel progress of unimaginable standards.

No country has simultaneously experienced the ravages of violence and the growth of economic prosperity. Even England was crushed economically and financially during their participation in World War II; the country would later defer to the United States after it provided assistance during the war. To avoid economic decapitation, the country needs national dialogue to save its economy from total obliteration. If the interest of the people is duly secured, there would be no reason for internal violence.

Inherent in national dialogue is its potential to establish an understanding that national politics should not be seized to serve factional purposes. People must understand that using the presidency to dish out provincial favors contaminates the very essence of nationhood and ridicules the idea of purposeful leadership. When people are dissuaded from unwholesome actions by the fear of tarnishing the country's image among the community of nations, it will send an important message to the perpetrators of evil: their interests do not supersede the need for national peace and stability.

When people relate to each other in ways that are not based on ethnic affiliations, but instead on the basis of merit and transparency, it has ripple effects on the country's physical and emotional make-up. In a country where states have autonomy and the exclusive freedom to decide what transpires within their sovereign settings, there would be no need to flex political muscle and override decisions to satisfy parochial interests. The case of internal strife between the Hausa and the Yoruba communities, which resulted in arrests from Abuja, the Federal

Capital Territory, says a lot about the pretentious nature of Nigerian nationhood.

Political parties in Nigeria were built on ethnic foundations. Nigeria's political evolution began when different ethnic communities organized themselves into groups to occupy national offices, making themselves the primary beneficiaries of national dispensations. This motivation retains significant influence over the thinking of many Nigerians; it is the cornerstone of philosophies that have developed political mercenaries in place of true patriots who are capable of building a nation. A national dialogue is long overdue to shift the mindset of the Nigerian people. To rescue the country from imminent doom, conscious effort must be made to forestall the formation of political parties that lack strong moral and ideological standards. Instead, parties must have standards that can be shared by all members, regardless of their social and economic status. In a situation without stringent guidelines, people will claim to be political saviors even when their primary aim is to use their platform for personal gain.

Nigerian elections are marred by violence because people are not held accountable for inflammatory comments or for organizing activities that disrupt the peace within the community. The compounding number of the political parties provides an avenue for dissidents to engage in violence. The fact that they usually escape punishment displays the country's porous political philosophy. An examination of party composition and their followers can identify the uprisings motivated by political machinations. At the most recent presidential election, seventy-three political parties registered their interest,[14] although it was obvious that only five of them would attract national attention. This excessive activity drains the country of its hard-fought wealth and makes a mockery of its electoral process.

A national dialogue is urgently required to discuss institutional infrastructure that can avoid the pull of ethnic sentiments. Countries are only as stable as their institutions, and the survival of the people depends on the institutions available to them. Weak institutions yield to pressure from personalities who wield powerful social networks and alliances; they can be undone by external influences. When the rules of engagement for specific institutions are transparent, understandable, and followed by every faction within the country, it sends important signals to the citizenry that makes them understand the urgency of nation building. When no individual is seen to be "above the law," fairness would become the

---

[14] *Sahara Reporters*, "At a Glance: The Final Positions of All 73 Parties That Contested Presidential Election," *Sahara Reporters*, February 27, 2019, http://saharareporters.com /2019/02/27/glance-final-positions-all-73-parties-contested-presidential-election.

bedrock of national values, encouraging growth beyond expectations. State pardons, deployed to excuse offenders who have committed crimes that cut deep into the heart of the country, can create a precedent that encourages future violators. Ethnic politics that enable this behavior should be addressed through negotiation, and ongoing occurrences should be discontinued and brought to redress.

It is a national necessity that every president should make rigorous efforts to dissuade his or her own ethnic group from using the presidential office as an excuse to ignore the law. The president's public messaging is an important part of this effort. On many occasions, silence is interpreted as endorsement. It emboldens minority groups who have cultural representatives in a seat of power; silence is interpreted as permission to perpetrate greater evils with more confidence. Evil thrives in an environment where people take no action to resist it – a show of silence extends the influence of people engaged in criminal behavior. Government inaction, especially when the government shares genetic bonds with the people disrupting the peace, portends danger for the country as a whole. National stability should be prioritized above all if the country is serious about the business of nation building. Violence should be condemned, regardless of the perpetrators.

It is not difficult to understand that cultural and geographical boundaries require mutual respect, and that making cross-cultural bonds among this country's diverse set of people is a compulsory exercise. Although cultural factors are not mutually exclusive, their inclusivity must be a conscious decision that is duly respected; otherwise, any attempt at unity would break apart. If Nigerians are not given enough reasons to maintain the marriage of unified nationhood, each group will solely pursue their own interests: group identity would be their watchword and their proud finality. The cultural boundaries of each nation within the country should be prioritized in a conscious attempt to disperse the power concentrated at the center.

Before the merger that Lord Lugard imposed in 1914, each of these cultures administered their affairs amicably, maintaining their sovereign integrity without recourse to violence. They would defend their cultures and their values as necessary. By doing this, they all showed their capacity for self-reliance, which is the common way for every known civilization to develop and endure. The external imposition of foreign powers did not change the fact that they would protect their own integrity when faced with external threats.

Nigerian leadership should build on these positive attributes to facilitate an atmosphere where territorial integrity is not threatened by individuals from outside people's sociocultural environment. Forcefully taking land through political power infringes on the rights of the people, and it is a subtle invitation to violence. People do not easily give up their legal rights to land in any nation of the world; in African countries the land is linked with ancestry.

To an average African, the issue of land is more important than money. Kenyans, dispossessed of their lands, sparked a rage that led to violent resistance against the West. Black South Africans still struggle to reclaim their land from the colonialist brutes who took possession through political force. The unjust seizure of land is a time bomb that will eventually detonate. We may not know when the explosion will occur, but it is certain that people will fight to protect their territory. Recent calls to cede lands for Hausa–Fulani grazing in other parts of the country should be handled carefully. The issue has the capacity to launch the whole populace into chaos.

History shows that any relative peace within the country is marked by mutual suspicion. People are automatically suspicious of any process that undermines their sovereign integrity. The people of Nigeria must strengthen their bonds and secure mutual trust to avoid carrying out such affronts on their neighbors. In the meantime, people should see their diverse nature for what it is, respecting it and promoting mutual understanding to avoid ethnic uprising. All stakeholders should come together and develop ways for the country to make progress and remain suitably competitive in the global economy. With a booming economy and technological advancements, the country would take its place on the map of reverence, and its lost glories would be restored in the process. Instead of being hindered by issues that stem from internal strife, the country could focus on areas needing improvement to offer lasting solutions.

Conclusion

Violence in Nigeria has many underlying influences that must be carefully examined to fully understand the best approaches for resolution. The combination of different cultural realities under the canopy of a single nation-state is bound to result in various struggles that can be tied to the quest for internal supremacy; individual groups will struggle just to avoid being relegated to the margin of national affairs. Occasions of internal violence cannot be avoided, and the universal rule of survival applies in politics as it does in nature: those deemed fit are the ones that can adapt and survive under the pressures of the environment. Diverse approaches are necessary for adaptation and survival, meaning that each culture's or ethnic background's perspective is helpful. However, the current environment is one where those in control determine which attitudes are helpful for attaining their goals, and political power is allocated in accordance to the degree of helpfulness. This arrangement is occasionally challenged by others who feel unduly usurped by the process, and the rollercoaster of struggles ensures that the violence continues.

Without finding common ground and creating a structure for peaceful coexistence, it is difficult for a heterogeneous society like Nigeria to avoid the uprisings that have engulfed the country at every tier of government. A country with no clearly defined political philosophy will encounter the irregularities characterizing Nigeria today. A country that practices federalism on paper while maintaining a centralized and unitary political institutions and bureaucracies cannot be serious about designing a better nation.

Excessive concentration of political power in the center weakens individual states. It renders them practically impotent in the administration of state autonomy. By failing to uphold the conventional standards of federalism while operating without a clear-cut blueprint for government strategy, Nigeria has increased the potential for violence. Its structure accommodates things that cannot naturally be reconciled with progressive governance. When states are incapable of exercising autonomy, and unable to act in full capacity regarding matters under their jurisdiction, things cannot be in order. Such is a recipe for violence – political violence.

The composition of Nigeria's political parties is a conduit for draining the country's economic strength. Seasoned politicians create parties not to advance a convincing philosophy that can trigger a revolutionary breakthrough for the people, but because of the calculated understanding that those parties can negotiate concessions from other parties in exchange for their endorsement. Instead of operating as groups that are genuinely patriotic and supportive of the country's true cause, these parties serve predetermined political interests to the detriment of the common good. These parties will employ any method available to serve personal interests, doing so at the expense of the people. It is an established fact that there is no limit to their underhanded methods when their personal goals are involved – this includes organizing violent attacks against civilians, trying to force the government into a position of vulnerability, and opening negotiations only to make demands.

Violence and its related damage poison an environment that could otherwise allow the national economy to grow and develop. National advancement happens at a slow pace because of the harsh conditions. The economy of the people is the first victim in a system plagued by violence; the people who must endure this hardship live in the most severe conditions without any peace of mind.

Knowing the economy's tremendous influence on virtually all aspects of life, it says much about the priorities of those who allow – or actively engage in – activities that disrupt it. Our many years spent living together should have taught us that our collective survival depends on our ability to tolerate each other. Nigeria's major source of income is oil revenues, and it is logical to avoid violence and embrace dialogue whenever there appears to be mismanagement or deliberate misrule. Trusted institutions must be put in place to aid this and to enhance fairness in national issues. However, things will remain unchanged if specific components of our political system wield unchecked power and influence.

Dialogue enhances mutual trust and builds formidable relationships. No one can dismiss the undeniable influence of dialogue in nation building. There is no thing as an un-negotiated relationship. Even in a marriage, a union that is not negotiated from time to time is abusive; it holds no advantage for one party in the relationship. A culturally diverse country like Nigeria, particularly, one whose citizens share similar histories of colonial hardship, needs to consciously engage in dialogue. People must come together and air their views about national matters, given the assurance that their demands can be heard and that compromise is possible. It would go a long way in strengthening bonds across cultures, and Nigerians would be happy to identify as a single, strong family. There is no limit to what the country can achieve in unity, due to its interminable list of natural and human resources. These resources have not been harnessed yet because there has not been a single continuous decade of peace among the people, even after they survived being merged together and endured colonial strangulation.

Everything hinges on the inherent distrust fueled by a baseless fear of others. When people show trust in others and accept their philosophies, the peaceful atmosphere triggers an energy that allows them to maximize their potential and share it with the world. Talents have frequently been mismanaged under the twisted canopy of politics, fostering distrust in the government and increasing the number of people who abandon their country to pursue opportunities in other places. Brain drain has negative consequences on the country; our best minds and hands leave for other countries instead of staying to develop their homeland with our own human resources. Dialogue would have astounding impact on the union: it must be employed any time that the country is on the verge of collapse through violence.

18   Challenges of Western Education

Introduction

From time immemorial, what constitutes a society is the combination of the population and different interrelated institutions that drive the conduct of the population. This is why, to the functionalists, the society exists on the interactions of these institutions that include familial, religious, economic, state (political), and educational systems. It is only through the agency of these institutions that one could begin to properly fathom the society.[1] Although all of these institutions are essential to the development and progress of any civilization in view, the educational system in practice remains the nucleus of designing the path this would take.[2] This is more so in that it remains the "process of training and teaching, the impacting of acquisition of skills for a specific trade or profession – a set of systems that can be implemented by community and government for their people."[3] It defines the composition of the family, the nature of the religion, the path of the economy, the structure of the political institution, and generally, the social relations among the production forces in the society. In light of this, the institution could rightly be described as the incubator of civilizations. The acquisition of knowledge is indispensable to every human civilization, and it is through that which is passed down through generations that humankind is significantly different from other animals.[4] The primary paradigm by which this is cultivated is through observation, contextualization, and elaboration. Through observation, humankind responds to its environmental needs and challenges as they

[1] Olakunle A. Ogunbameru, *Sociology: Origin, Development and Uses* (Ibadan: Penthouse Publications, 2008), 168.
[2] Vusi Gumede, "Exploring Thought Leadership, Thought Liberation and Critical Consciousness for Africa's Development," *Africa Development/Afrique et Développement* 40, no. 4 (2015): 91–111.
[3] Toyin Falola, *The Humanities in Africa: Knowledge Production, Universities, and the Transformation of Society* (Austin: Pan-African University Press, 2016), 161–162.
[4] Jared P. Taglialatela et al., "Communicative Signaling Activates 'Broca's' Homolog in Chimpanzees," *Current Biology* 18, no. 5 (2008): 343–348.

surface in different forms and different times; contextualization aids humanity's ability to put the observations in a proper perspective, either in mythical or scientific form; and elaboration prepares the acquired knowledge for dissemination and transformation into practical use.

To this extent, all acquired knowledge, either in art or the sciences, is ordinarily problem solving. The problems in the arts and sciences may be different, but collectively, acquired knowledge in the arts and sciences forms a dialectical relation that supports the purpose of one another and one body: the society. Thus, the science of a civilization works in tandem with its arts; a disconnect between the two implies a dwindling civilization at the edge of a precipice. Meanwhile, like every other state in Africa, the modern Nigerian state, and by implication in this context, the educational system, is a creation of three epochs: the precolonial, colonial, and postcolonial.[5] Events and evolving trends during each period culminated into the characterization of the state and its educational system. But of all these periods, the postcolonial state shares the resemblance of the colonial structure in functionality, purpose, and effect. As noted elsewhere, the challenges facing the educators and the educational system in Nigeria are closely linked to the challenges faced by the nation.[6] The failure of the state to decolonize its political economy is definitely at the root of faltered efforts at decolonizing the educational system created for the purpose of administering and sustaining the colonial state. In what follows, the chapter attempts an overview of the introduction and nature of Western education in Nigeria and the challenges this has posed to the nation-building process of the state.

Understanding the Nigerian Educational System

The debate over the vitality of the African past before the colonial period is a long-concluded one with the works of many notable Africanist historians like Kenneth O. Dike.[7] The body of knowledge produced by these scholars, has established that knowledge production systems long existed in different parts of Africa, making Africa the residual place of knowledge advancement before the modern era, through its capitals in Egypt, Morocco, and Mali.[8] To some extent, these cities produced the modern

[5] Keith Somerville, *Africa's Long Road since Independence: The Many Histories of a Continent* (London: Penguin Random House, 2017), 1–48.
[6] Falola, *The Humanities in Africa*, xiv.
[7] J. F. Ade Ajayi, ed., "Towards a More Enduring Sense of History," in *History and the Nation and Other Addresses* (Ibadan: Spectrum Books, 1991), 40–41.
[8] Gloria Ndisha Mbogoma, "Julius Nyerere's Education for Self-Reliance in Post-Colonial Tanzania: A Reconsideration," PhD thesis, University of Pretoria, 2018, 49.

structure of what is today known as Western education. Until the colonial period, the primary mode of conducting educational processes in Africa was through oral documentation and transmission. This accorded the people an opportunity to learn beyond enclosed walls of any of the institutions that drove the society, including that of the family. Learning was tailored toward self-reliance as every acquired knowledge had a ready vacuum to fill for societal progress.[9] As such, those trained in hunting, blacksmithing, farming, carving, weaving, dyeing, and many more, were gainfully employed, and there was no issue of underemployment or unemployment. Being gainfully employed in the skills one has acquired is invariably the practical aspect of the educational process. Before this time (that is, the colonial period), the family and the entire society through religious, political, sociocultural, and economic engagements, took charge of this process. Even though knowledge came from different cultures outside the society, the educational system was never alien to the people, their culture, or their everyday living experience, owing to the fact that borrowed systems were acculturated into the existing larger structure of the society.[10] The somewhat communal bearing of the society was also very integral as children learnt cognitively and instructively from older individuals in the community.[11]

Of course, all of these were made possible by various factors that include the population and the socioeconomic milieu of the time – all of which did change with the colonial experience of the cultures and peoples that made up the Nigerian state.[12] Expectedly, the significance of education in the society never changed. The British colonial government brought about fundamental changes to the sociocultural, religious, economic, and political fabrics of the peoples and cultures that made up the Nigerian colony. It should be recalled that the traditional system – or rather, the precolonial educational system of the people – was predicated on these very structures. Not only was the structure lost to the colonial frame, but also the history of the people was designed to be equally whitewashed. Events before this time had laid the groundwork for the eventual collapse of the traditional structure for the Western taxonomic

[9] Dama Mosweunyane, "The African Educational Evolution: From Traditional Training to Formal Education," *Higher Education Studies* 3, no. 4 (2013): 50–53.

[10] Toyin Falola, *The Power of African Culture* (New York: University of Rochester Press, 2003).

[11] Toyin Falola, *Cultural Modernity in a Colonized World: The Writings of Chief Isaac Oluwole Delano* (Austin: Pan-African University Press, 2020), 20.

[12] Damilola Osunlakin, "Educational System and the Challenges of Restructuring Nigeria for Sustainable Development," in *Humanities and Challenges of Development: Interrogating Nigeria's Nation Building Project since 1960*, eds. Abdullahi M. Ashafa, Gaius Jatau, and Ayemga Tor (Kaduna: Kaduna State University, 2020), 53.

modernity. Like Islam did through the trans-Saharan trade,[13] which included trade in slaves – from the Atlantic slave trade to the so-called legitimate trade – the European culture began to penetrate first the coastal cities and then the hinterlands in later stages.[14] Through European commodities and trading patterns, indigenous production began to face the Atlantic, and the people began to look West for their social form. The essential commodities were beginning to look Western, and all was bound to take a new form with the return of the ex-slaves in the Americas following the industrial revolution that began in Britain, as well as the eventual abolition of the slave trade – all before the twentieth century. While European commodities were already occupying the elite and luxury spaces, the coming of the ex-slave returnees exacerbated the Westernization process of the society.[15]

Bringing them with a variation on European civilization in religion, language, and general orientation, these ex-slave returnees began to assume leadership roles and, more importantly, they became the catalyst to the colonial enterprise in the society. As collaborators, they helped introduce and entrench Christianity, Western education, fashion, and Western taxonomic modernity into the social fabrics of the society. As dissidents, they helped fashion the revivalist mission of indigenous cultures and laid the groundwork for eventual independence in 1960.[16] Here, we see Western education playing a core part in the collapse of the traditional structure of the society and attempts at rejuvenating this structure in light of the emerging social milieu. This speaks to the fact that Western education is not intrinsically bad in itself; its bane is how it was incorporated into the society. Tellingly, Western education cannot be discussed in isolation from Christian missionary activities. Both missions facilitated one another in that they came through the same instrument of Westernization and the "civilizing" mission of the Europeans. Wherever the Church went, the school also followed and vice versa. Like the precolonial educational system that survived on the other traditional institutions in the society, most importantly the religious, Christianity played a huge role in the spread and form of the educational system introduced by the colonial government.[17] As instruments of civilization,

[13] Toyin Falola and Matthew M. Heaton, *A History of Nigeria* (Cambridge: Cambridge University Press, 2008), 16.
[14] Ibid., 40.
[15] See, for example, Rev. Michael Thomas Euler Ajayi, "A General History of the Yoruba, Country: Part 3," *Lagos Standard* (1905).
[16] James S. Coleman, *Nigeria: Background to Nationalism* (Sweden & Nigeria: Broberg and Winston, 1958).
[17] J. F. Ade Ajayi, ed., *General History of Africa VI: Africa in the Nineteenth Century until the 1880s* (Paris: UNESCO Publishing, 1998), 18.

the missionaries brought Western values and promoted the universality of the Christian ideals, while degrading indigenous structures and values.

The society was supposed to be transformed into modernity, and everything African was to be relegated for European taxonomic modernity.[18] Both Christianity and Western education championed this message and supervised the seismic shift in the social fabrics of the society. Neither the religious nor the socioeconomic basis of the society could be incorporated into the emerging educational system. Whereas the indigenous missionaries were able to rebel and refute the Europeanization of the Christianity that was offered them, as they took charge of the idea,[19] this could not be replicated at the educational level. The Christianity taught in schools and churches deemed African inventions backward and without value in the modernity to be pursued by the society. Because the educational system was closely supervised by the colonial government, there was no room for flexibility in the school curriculum and the general educational system as it took the colonial form envisaged for its creation. The missionaries needed men and women who could read the Bible, as well as write and communicate in English; the colonial government needed colonial officials to be drawn from the local population so as to fill the shortage of British staff. But this population needed to be indoctrinated into the path of the civilization that would make them cope with the responsibilities of documentation, executing instructions of the colonial government, and functioning within the nascent modern bureaucratic structure of governance. They were not meant to question but rather obey instructions dogmatically. A different approach amounted to sedition and other serious charges related to criminality and treason, being considered an enemy of the state (the colonial formation).

These skills were similarly needed by the Christian missionaries. Whereas the missionaries needed those skills for the spread and growth of Christianity, the colonial government needed them for effective colonial administration. In addition, the colonial government needed people with basic arithmetic knowledge to balance the accounts of the administration from the Districts to the Divisions, and right down to the provincial levels. It was toward this purpose that colonial education was introduced: how to read, write, and communicate in English; identify and categorize; maintain the colonial bureaucracy; and aid the Christian mission. Productivity was never the issue; it was the maintenance of the existing order that was the primary concern. It was Western education in structure, but colonial education in form and what it hoped to achieve. This structure and the form later produced doctors, lawyers, teachers,

---

[18] Toyin Falola, *Cultural Modernity in a Colonized World*, 57.   [19] Ibid., 250–253.

accountants, and many more. The meaning and implication of being educated changed fundamentally with Western education becoming the basis for the identification of the educated and uneducated classes in the society. Whether relevant to societal and individual progress or not, an educated person must pass through one of the existing institutions of learning that prepared people for bureaucratic responsibilities.

Through their training, the educated population was disconnected from the rest of the society, yet these people constituted the societal standard that everyone, particularly the youths, wanted to attain. They had the best paying jobs, usually with the government and its multi-national friends (the two entities sucking local production dry), and they had better hope of steady social mobility. Social mobility networks were largely restricted to this formal setting as the government, through its economic structure and policies, now reinforced capitalism and a formal and informal economy. The former was promoted by the government at the detriment of the latter, which received neither government incentives nor recognition beyond the collection of taxes. To avoid misrepresentation, it would be well to mention that the colonial administration did take some moves toward aiding artisans and craftsmen. Such institutions as the Hussey Charity Institution were situated in major cities like Lagos, Onitsha, Abeokuta, and Bonny, where students were taught carpentry, masonry, tailoring, and many other skills.[20] None of these efforts could materialize as local artisans had problems competing with the foreign products that were already flooding the market.[21] Reviving local production in an environment where local products could not compete favorably with foreign products can always be an idea dead on arrival. Western education together with Christianity and the colonial economy opened a new paradigm in the social order by creating new social stratification based on faith, education, and employment status.

Among the class of educated persons at this time were the educated elite, some of whom would later drive Nigeria into independence, though others were religious bigots and opportunists.[22] An independent Nigerian educational system was birthed in this ambience. One of the victims was the late pioneer Africanist historian, Kenneth O. Dike, at the then University College, Ibadan, in 1966.[23] The many universities and other

---

[20] J. F. Ade Ajayi, "The Development of Secondary Grammar School Education in Nigeria," *Journal of the Historical Society of Nigeria* 2, no. 4 (1963): 519.

[21] E. A. Ayandele, *Missionary Impact on Modern Nigeria 1842–1914* (London: Longman Group, 1966), 296.

[22] E. A. Ayandele, *The Educated Elite in the Nigerian Society* (Ibadan: Ibadan University Press, 1974).

[23] Ajayi, "Towards a More Enduring Sense of History," 43.

institutions of higher learning became things of other considerations aside from filling the intellectual vacuum in the society. Acquiring Western education and being educated became synonymous with university education. This testifies to the preponderance of the linkages between the socioeconomic composition of a state and its educational sector in the functionality of the latter. In the socioeconomic formation of the precolonial period, education was synonymous with the acquisition of skills and principles for responsible daily living; colonial education was characterized by the ability to attain, at least, a certificate equivalent to the contemporary secondary-school leaving certificate; and postcolonial education shifted this from all tertiary institutions to a university degree. These are reflections of the emphasis placed on the qualifications for social mobility opportunities during each period.

The university system was thus under intense population pressure without commensurate facilities in quality and quantity. In lieu of strengthening the lagging latter, successive governments have responded to the former by creating more universities without adequate facilities. As it turned out, the government couldn't cope with the rising demand for university education. Private investors soon joined in this proliferation of universities, many of which are mere walls rather than a citadel of learning. Like every other discipline, the Departments of Medicine teach Western medicine without contextualizing it within their social environment. The universality of Western education – trimmed to its colonial form – persisted perpetually.

Figure 18.1 A group of students in a junior secondary school.

Therefore, in less than three decades to the independence of the country, history as a stand-alone subject was removed from the school curriculum from the elementary to senior secondary level.[24] This somewhat confirmed the "no history, no past" narrative of Eurocentric writers about Africa because what existed in the past was full of darkness. Whereas the colonial government only sought to relegate or substitute local history with European history, the postcolonial government shut down everything relating to history altogether.

This shows the continuous disconnect between the educational system and the society because history shapes the self-perception of a nation and "the interaction between the nation and its past is an unending one."[25] The educational system and the intellectual community, just as in the days when they began to emerge, are positioned to be productive members but passive members sustaining the status quo.[26] The current educational system in Nigeria was introduced as a colonial project as it became part of the institutions that emerged for the effective administration of the colonial state. It doesn't require a whole lot of sources to describe Nigeria in its current form as the colonial creation that it was till the 1960s. Like every other institution and template set by the colonial government, the Nigerian educational system is still skewed at maintaining the colonial structure.

The Failed Promises

Tóo bá kà'wé rẹ, bàtà rẹ á dún ko ko kà ...[27]

In surmising the nature of the colonial state and characterizing the educational system it introduced for its perpetration and reproduction, two things come to mind: first, the colonial government emphasized "subservient attitudes and white-collar skills"[28] as it was skewing the socioeconomic

---

[24] Since teachers are not expected to teach it, it didn't feature in their N.C.E. program either and historical studies generally suffered setbacks as it became unpopular at the university level. See the Historical Society of Nigeria, "The Place of History in Nigeria's School System and the Nation," to the Hon. Minister of Education of the Federal Republic of Nigeria, January 21, 1987.

[25] J. F. Ade Ajayi, ed., "History and the Nation," in *History and the Nation Valedictory Lecture, University of Ibadan, 1989 and Other Addresses* (Ibadan: Ibadan University Press, 1990), 2.

[26] So, over fifty years after independence, Nigerian civil engineers don't construct roads; they either work in the bank or perform other daily routines that keep them off the site. Likewise, scientists are kept in the office rather the laboratory and researchers don't produce any innovation but consume all the consumables.

[27] A popular school song taught in colonial and postcolonial Nigeria, telling your kids that if they faced their education, they would have worthy formal jobs with shining shoes.

[28] E. Lema et al., eds., *Nyerere on Education*, Vol. 1 (Dar es Salaam: Haki Elimu and E & D Ltd.), 69, quoted in Mbogoma, "Julius Nyerere's Education for Self-Reliance," 49.

condition of the society against blue-collar workers who would later become the vast majority of employed Africans in Africa; second, the colonial government created the epistemological and ontological paradigm of thought in the society.[29] Through these two mechanisms, it isn't the colonial specter that keeps tormenting the state, but rather the living and continued exertion of colonial systems. Since the political institution dominates other institutions of government and the autonomy of the universities is within the reach of this institution as well, there emerges a disconnect between the education system and the society. In terms of skills and other essentials, graduates are seldom prepared for the job market. The story they were told while growing up about the acquisition of Western education and its efficacy in determining a brighter and highly elitist future did not add up.[30] Rather, many count the years spent studying engineering, history, political science, tourism, law, and others, as a waste. This is even more so when they eventually find themselves preparing for another skill entirely after graduating so as to secure a place in the available job market.

The reality that dawned on a vast majority after acquiring this formal education is that, if what they were told was once valid, it has become delusional and has out-lived its relevance when considering its practicality in the present socioeconomic milieu. The students can as well ask their teachers why the shoes of an illiterate bricklayer look and sound the same as theirs. To be sure, the message is as much a literary expression as it is a metaphor. However, both implications have since lost their relevance to the bastardization of the economy, abysmally low educational budgets, shrinking employment opportunities (especially from the government, which used to be the largest employer), increasing numbers of graduates, unequal access to opportunities, inability of the education system to respond appropriately to the development through introduction of noble policies (including in the school curriculum), and all myriads of challenges that limit the quality of graduates, teachers, and the educational system itself. Indeed, as the late erudite scholar Ali Mazrui perfectly puts it, "Behind the individual tragedy was the wider tragedy of frustrated skills acquired in college from which there were no appropriate jobs in the wider society. The Owl of Minerva was flying without a sense of direction, without a sense of purpose."[31] In this case, education – particularly

---

[29] Toyin Falola, *The Toyin Falola Reader on African Culture, Nationalism, Development and Epistemology* (Austin: Pan-African University Press, 2018), 889–910.

[30] Agency Report, "Nigeria's Unemployment Rate Hits 33.5 Per Cent by 2020 – Minister," *Premium Times News*, May 2, 2019, www.premiumtimesng.com/news/top-news/328137-nigerias-unemployment-rate-hits-33-5-per-cent-by-2020-minister.html.

[31] Ali A. Mazrui, "A Fragment: Africa between the Baobab Tree and the Owl of Minerva: A Post-Colonial Educational Narrative" (lecture, McGill University, Montreal, Canada, April 30–May 4, 2011), 10.

Western education – is likened to the Roman goddess of knowledge, wisdom, science, art, and war; and the owl is described as the accomplice of the goddess. Implicitly, Mazrui was equating the educated youths in Africa to the owl that always seeks to dine and wine with Minerva, as well as share from the wisdom of Minerva, only to later find out that the acquired knowledge has no place in their "real world." Failure to reinvent themselves outside of what Minerva created within their educational system is a letter to self-induced injustice.

It is not that the knowledge acquired from Minerva is totally devoid of opportunities and relevance in the society where they reside (which is the nest of the owl); the challenge, rather, is that this knowledge occupies a restricted space in the society. At least, if the knowledge had been useless, we will not be debating on the question of brain drain.[32] The language of Minerva is English; any other thing communicated in indigenous languages is rarely wisdom. So, medicine is devoid of local contexts, and African medicine has become "alternative medicine." The death of the language policy of the government on education cannot be discussed in isolation of the socioeconomic conditions of the society. Why would a Hausa female student study Igbo as an alternative Nigerian language when her parents would not allow her to marry out of her culture due to ethnic prejudice, let alone convert to Christianity because of animosities?

If anything, there is the issue of limited demand and excessive supply on the one hand, and the preponderance of anti-intellectual culture of the state governance on the other hand. In 1963, the total population of Nigeria was estimated to be around 58 million, and the total number of people speaking English, which has remained the official language of common communication and instruction in the acquisition of Western education, was roughly 10 percent of the total population.[33] It is worth telling that not all of the population that made up the 10 percent were graduates from the existing higher institutions. The socioeconomic conditions of the society at this time still had enough space for this limited quota of the total population. The inadequacies of the system were not yet an issue, until the population began to burgeon, the numbers of universities increased (not for service delivery, but for primitive political goals), the quota of higher-school graduates rose, and economic opportunities decreased at an unprecedented level. It is not an easy task trying to

---

[32] See, for example, Donald P. Chimanikire, "Brain Drain: Causes and Economic Consequences for Africa," Lecture, 27th AAPAM Annual Roundtable Conference, Livingstone, Zambia, December 5–9, 2005.

[33] Abiodun Adetugbo, "The Development of English in Nigeria up to 1914: A Socio-Historical Appraisal," *Journal of the Historical Society of Nigeria* 9, no. 2 (1978): 89.

Figure 18.2 An overpopulated classroom.

conduct research on the current number of English-speaking populations in Nigeria, let alone the number of graduates – now that the total population is over 200 million. This notwithstanding, the population is expected to double within the next four decades.[34] The numbers of higher institution graduates are bound to skyrocket as well. This takes us to the other side of the discourse: the dwindling opportunities and the anti-intellectual culture of the state.

Since the turn of the present democratic dispensation, successive governments have been talking about the need for diversification of the economy to no effect. The oil boom of the late 1970s and the concretization of the rentier system structure afterwards, which successive governments have been trying to sustain,[35] have metamorphosed into the

[34] United Nations, "World Population Projected to Reach 9.8 billion in 2050, and 11.2 billion in 2100," United Nations, June 21, 2017, www.un.org/development/desa/en/news/population/world-population-prospects-2017.html.

[35] Tajudeen Abdulraheem et al., "Nigeria: Oil, Debts, and Democracy," *Review of African Political Economy*, no. 37 (1986): 6–10; S. O. Tomori and O. W. Tomori, "Revisiting the African Alternative Framework to Structural Adjustment Programmes for Socio-Economic Recovery and Transformation (AAF-SAP) in Contemporary Nigeria," in *African Development and Governance Strategies in the 21st Century, Looking Back to Move Foreword: Essays in Honor of Adebayo Adedeji at 70*, ed. Lawrence Agubuzu (London & New York: Zed Books, 2004), 30–46.

bogeyman intimidating talks of diversification from materializing into reality.[36] The anti-intellectualist posture of the government has thus met the patronage-seeking proclivity of the academics, which has compromised its autonomy and interests. Academia, which should ordinarily be regarded as the soul of the society, is instead a captive of the society. The unproductive nature of academia and the general intellectual community in Nigeria are equally proportional to the economic formation of the state, which is unproductive but rent seeking. In simple terms, the educational system seems to have nothing to offer as it holds little or no place in the state governance structure.[37] Productive or not, like the civil servants, teachers – especially at the higher institution level – expect to be paid their salaries. Since renumeration of a supposed member of the intellectual community of the state is not in any way connected to his or her productivity, healthy competition among scholars for rigorous scholarship is not promoted – just as competence and productivity are not rewarded. This invariably leads to lethargy, complacency, and mediocrity in academia. A simple testimony to this is the common practice of teaching students from a note prepared many years back – as far back as a decade. Some, in addition to this, mandate students to repeat this same note "verbatim" while answering examination questions. Following this is the sexual harassment culture pervasive in these institutions. The teacher is either demanding sex to give away marks, or the student is pleading for the same.[38] Intellectual growth is basically stampeded in this process. The socioeconomic realities of the state have conditioned academics not to be problem solving but rather rent seeking.

The relationship between the government and members of this community hardly goes beyond the patronage level, in which, for instance, the former is positioned to access the state treasury and used it to execute its hatchet agenda.[39] Aside from the centralization of the educational system

---

[36] Peter M. Lewis, *Oil, Politics, and Economic Change in Indonesia and Nigeria* (Ann Arbor: The University of Michigan Press, 2007), 9.

[37] A clear revelation of this is the measure of the average annual budget allocation going into the educational sector. Records put this at 6.7% in the current year, 2020. See Abdulssalam Amoo, "Nigeria Allocates 6.7% of 2020 Budget to Education Ministry," *Education Statistics*, October 11, 2019, www.google.com/amp/s/educeleb.com/nigerian-2020-budget-education-ministry/amp/. This was later reduced, together with the health budget, as the government needed to cut the year's budget due to the COVID-19 outbreak. See Abdullateef Salau et al., "Nigeria: Revised Budget – Anger over Cuts in Health, Education Votes," *AllAfrica*, June 4, 2020, https://allafrica.com/stories/202006 040446.html.

[38] Minabere Ibelema, "Explaining Sex-for-Marks," *Punch News*, October 28, 2018, https://punchng.com/explaining-sex-for-marks/.

[39] See, for example, Paul K. N. Ugboajah, "Babangida Administration and the Crisis of Civil-Military Relations in Nigeria (1985–1993)," in *The Dynamics of Intergroup Relations*

in Nigeria, the forgoing is often the fertile ground upon which the autonomy of the universities has been compromised. Like the colonial government before them, successive Nigerian governments have abused the autonomy of their universities, in order to facilitate their grip on power. The identity and cultural incubator of the society – the educational system – is faced with the crises of cultural and religious differences.[40] Some of these institutions became the center of religious violence, and ethno-religious considerations feature hugely in their admission, appointment, and general regulation processes. The so-called intellectual community has thus failed to unite the fractured society it was supposedly established to consistently amend and shape.[41]

The oil boom of the late 1970s further led to the centralization of the Nigerian educational system. The government took over the administration of many schools during this period, only to later realize how irrational this was as it began to face dwindling economic fortune. The educational sector suffered a lot from this. In what seemed like a deliberate attempt at bringing to life the fear of the Nigerian students when they rejected the introduction of the Nigerian school certificate in 1929 by the colonial government, the commercialization of education from the 1990s onward reduced the opportunities for potential students, particularly at the higher education level, to achieve their dreams of being educated. Worse still, the abysmal level of funding going into the system truncated the dream of attaining quality education by the others privileged to take part in the limited opportunity. The effect of government regulation of the educational sector in Nigeria, like every other institution of government, is in many inter-related folds: quality of teachers, teaching method (quantity of) facilities and graduates, global competitiveness, and the synergy between the education sector and national cohesion which comprises, in a broad sense, the relationship between the town and the gown.

The socioeconomic dynamics of the postindependent state prioritizes having a university degree. This increased the relevance of holding a degree certificate in the country. The pressure witnessed by the universities and the abysmal government allocation further brought the institutions to this point. The condition of the universities, in spite of their popularity, negatively impact upon other tertiary institutions that enjoy

in Nigeria since 1960: Essays in Honour of Obaro Ikime at 70, eds. C. B. N. Ogbogbo, R. O. Olaniyi, and O. G. Muojama (Ibadan: University of Ibadan, 2012), 127–140.
[40] Ajayi, "Towards a More Enduring Sense of History," 43.
[41] See, Joseph Ki-Zerbo, "African Intellectuals, Nationalism and Pan Africanism: A Testimony," in African Intellectuals: Rethinking Politics, Language, Gender and Development, ed. Thandika Nkandawire (Dakar & London: CODESRIA & Zed Books, 2005), 92.

less status – the technical schools that remained as unattractive as they were since the colonial days, for instance. Already, there is an over-centralization burden on the educational system and structure, especially at the university level. Now, in what constitutes the current ASUU-FGN (Federal Government of Nigeria) standoff, the introduction of Integrated Payroll and Personnel Information (IPPIS) to the university system promised to further toll the already gasping institution into oblivion.[42] The Academic Staff Union of Universities (ASUU) is the umbrella body of Nigerian academics in the public sector. Established to demand better conditions of service, improved funding, and university autonomy, it remains one of the most vibrant unions in Nigeria. The ASUU has developed a reputation for consistent criticisms of the condition of Nigerian universities in the bid to meet its established goals.

Ordinarily, the ASUU is the union of the community of the country's intellectuals. However, this intellectualism has not been applied in dealing with the government and achieving its set-out goals. The union perpetuates the colonial response of the railway union workers and others. It trivializes the importance of education in the nation-building process so badly that it finds strike action as the only means of "enforcing" and communicating its will. This, in a way, is like the police using strikes to gain government attention; the government, as all are aware, doesn't really care. Hence, the student is faced with the reality that a four-year degree needs an additional year planned. The ASUU should realize its linkage to the society and realize that an ASUU strike that doesn't shut down the economy with it is less effective. The union has the capacity to work closely with the NLC and TUC and to unite other civil society organizations (CSOs) in reforming the base of the system that keeps driving it into collapsing what it is purportedly building, but it has yet to explore this. Unlike the private universities, the digital drive of publicly owned so-called citadels of education has been indecisive and drawn-out. The question might be asked: What does Nigeria's educational system champion in the course of the nation-building process, and how has this impacted the society?

Conclusion

In a quick overview, the previous captures the nature and challenges of the Nigerian educational system in its current form and the place of major

---

[42] Innocent Odoh, "FG, ASUU Move to Resolve IPPIS, Others as Talks Continue," *Business Day*, March 18, 2020, https://businessday.ng/education/article/fg-asuu-move-to-resolve-ippis-others-as-talks-continue/.

stakeholders in saving the situation. This should be extended to students and parents through their various bodies at this point. Culture and development are unquestionable companions.[43] There will remain a tale of failures if this paradigm is not understood and taken into action – reconstructing the curriculum to reflect cultural realities. A degree in medicine and other related fields should not be complete without taking courses in Traditional African medicine. The current university structure cannot even incubate a pluriversal world, like the Europeans created the universal, let alone pass this reality on to the society. Repositioning this sector of the state to be productive is an essential task that needs to be pursued by all stakeholders if it is to assume its place in the society. As has been likewise shown, this can only be done as an integral part of decolonizing and reordering of the socioeconomic paradigm of the state.

---

[43] Toyin Falola, "Technology, Culture and Society" (University Distinguished Lecture, First Technical University, Ibadan, Nigeria, July 4, 2019).

Part V

Reforms and Revolutions

19   Change Agents: Youths and Politics

Introduction

The active participation of youths in a society is unarguably a determining factor in the economic, sociocultural, and political growth of such societies, and Africa, with about two-third of its population being youth, has been regarded as the most youthful continent; it is upon these premises that the "African Youth Charter" is formulated to "strengthen, reinforce and consolidate efforts to empower young people through meaningful youth participation and equal partnership in driving Africa's development agenda."[1] The natural heirs of any country are its population between the ages of eighteen and thirty-five. No matter how gerontocratic a country may be, the young will someday take control of it. With a gradual but definite shift, the young become custodians of the cultural, ethical, financial, social, and familial structures and preferences that older generations have used. Young people are variously described as strong, virile, and teachable, and they generally have a longer lifespan. In any nation, they are seen as its energy and future. Many well-coordinated countries use various innovative approaches to keep their population youthful and active.

The education, health, and sociocultural integration of young people are arranged to guarantee that they develop the ability to seamlessly take over governance and national administration. A country with a larger youthful population is seen to possess the opportunity for great economic prosperity – provided that they invest in that population, especially in the health, education, and human rights sectors. The quality of those investments is shown in their sporting exploits, inventions, and military capacity.

---

[1] African Union Commission, *African Youth Charter* (Addis Ababa: African Union, 2006), www.un.org/en/africa/osaa/pdf/au/african_youth_charter_2006.pdf.

451

Governments on the macro-level and parents on the micro-level plan education, health, social well-being, and cultural integration. To varying degrees, societal structures are fortified to ensure that youths who excel get resources and attention, pushing them closer to leadership positions at all levels. Youths are always an important component of a country's population. They keep the country politically and economically vibrant. Even at the international level, a country with optimally engaged youths is easily distinguished from its peers. In wartime, youths are selected for conscription into the army and other essential duties. In peacetime, they bring glory to their countries through international competitions in areas such as sports, music, and science. They bring vibrancy to their activities, and their strength, freshness, and eagerness get more done than the older population can manage. As more enhanced technology and better health-care systems become more widely available, African societies are seeing declining mortality rates and continuing high fertility rates increasing their youthful populations. The United Nations' 2015 Population Facts Sheet projects that the youth population in Africa will increase from 19 percent to 42 percent by 2030.

Figure 19.1 A group of young Nigerians reading dailies at a roadside vendor stand and discussing topical issues of the day.

The present organization and policies of most countries recognize the need for strong structures ensuring that the young have access to sound education and healthcare. These will help them become national assets, well equipped, willing, and able to replace those who are inevitably taken by death. Effective investment in the young ensures that countries never have a shortage of human resources. It provides a stable base for the country's continuity and guarantees personal fulfillment through the resulting upward social mobility.

Parents and governments share the responsibility for this education and care. However, the government has long taken over formal education and healthcare systems in a bid to make them available for all classes of people. Even when such institutions are set up by private bodies or individuals, they are subject to government rules and regulations; the government maintains administrative oversight to varying degrees.

The advantage of providing standard education and healthcare for the young cannot be overstated. The social and economic returns are many, but most importantly, it is their right. According to Article 4 of the 1989 UN Convention on the Rights of the Child, national governments have the legal obligation to ensure the realization of children's economic, social, civil, political, and cultural rights to the maximum extent of their available resources.[2]

Structured care and training for the young also yields profit in the form of self-actualization for the individual, and growth and stability for the family unit and the country. When youths are strengthened with the necessary education, healthcare, and other interventions for optimal growth, they become young adults willing and able to use their strength for the progress of the country. The relationship between an individual's enterprise and the country's economic growth is obvious. If there are youths that excel in the area of technological innovation, they will attract most of the investment in that sector, and Nigeria will become the technological capital of the world within a few years. If a great percentage of the Nigerian youths excel in sports, the nation will top the charts by receiving gold medals in all sporting competitions. If the youths focus on manufacturing, Nigeria will have an economy that exports finished products. Such is the immediate reward for providing and maintaining educational and healthcare systems for a country's youths.

Countries with a large youthful population are expected to be vibrant and strong in all facets of national life, although the dividend can only be realized when there is sufficient investment in the growth of that

---

[2] UNICEF, "What Is the Convention on the Rights of the Child?" *UNICEF*, n.d., www.unicef.org/child-rights-convention/what-is-the-convention.

population segment. The East Asian economies are a perfect example of this: they invested in their young people in the 1970s and became the "Asian Tigers." Their economies showed the reward of having a large number of young, well-educated youths when their GDP rose by 6 percent, and in some cases, their per-capita income increased threefold.[3]

Despite the consistently rising population figures skewed toward the young, the same benefit cannot be claimed for African countries. There are now 1.8 billion people aged between ten and twenty-four. More than 500 million young people live on less than $2 a day, and 73.4 million people between the ages of fifteen and twenty-four are jobless.[4] These are cases of abject poverty and high unemployment. These situations are not likely to change, even if the population growth declines, because it is estimated that the population of Africans between zero and twenty-four years old will double by 2050. At the same time, 86 percent of the world's extreme poor will live in sub-Saharan Africa.[5] There could be hope that the "Africa Rising" dream will soon manifest like the Asian Tiger example, but how much is Africa investing in its young? Not much.

Nigeria had an estimated GDP of over US$481 billion in 2015, almost inexhaustible natural gas and crude oil reserves, arable land, and uncollected mineral deposits across the country. Yet, the nation has failed to optimally convert these resources into lasting socioeconomic benefits: shortcomings have been its focus on quick income from crude oil, and enjoying imported goods that do nothing for economic growth. Unlike the Asian Tigers, Nigeria (like the rest of Africa) continues to favor short-term solutions and projects that only glorify personalities above long-term, sometimes bitter, solutions.

Alexander Chikwanda, Zambia's finance minister, was quoted by the United Nations calling the population situation "a ticking time bomb."[6] That is how bleak the predictions are – the levels of investment in

---

[3] According to the report: "In the 1970s, East Asia invested in its young people's human capital, it enabled the region to realize its demographic dividend, contributing to a 6% surge in GDP and a quadrupling of per capita income in some countries. That is why we ended up with what we call the 'Asian tigers' and that's how Asia has been the point of growth since then." Mark Anderson, "Sub-Saharan Africa's Youth Population Offers 'Enormous Potential'," *The Guardian*, November 18, 2014, www.theguardian.com/glo bal-development/2014/nov/18/sub-saharan-africa-youth-population-potential.

[4] Ibid.

[5] Mariama Sow, "Figures of the Week: Africa's Growing Youth Population and Human Capital Investments," *Brookings*, November 20, 2018, www.brookings.edu/blog/africa-in-focus/2018/09/20/figures-of-the-week-africas-growing-youth-population-and-human-ca pital-investments/.

[6] Kingsley Ighobor, "Africa's Youth: A 'Ticking Time Bomb' or an Opportunity?" *Africa Renewal*, November 20, 2018, www.un.org/africarenewal/magazine/may-2013/africa%E 2%80%99s-youth-%E2%80%9Cticking-time-bomb%E2%80%9D-or-opportunity.

education, healthcare, social services, and other safety nets for families are either non-existent or in dire need of upgrades. This is seen in the low level of return the country receives from its youths.

Nigerian Youths and the Fight for Independence and Development

Nigeria is yet to become the "Giant of Africa," even after more than half a century of independence from foreign domination. Yet, the country did not start like this. Nigeria's independence was fought for, and won, by its youths. Most of those at the forefront of politics and the push for Nigeria's independence from Great Britain were less than forty years old in 1953, when the first motion was formally moved through legislative chambers. Youths at countless times have been actively involved in the rise and fall of political powers in their society; their unison is unarguably a force with volatile and limitless possibilities, which is the reason why the older generation keeps putting checks in place to disunite them.

From the liberation of African states to Pan-Africanism and several military uprisings, African youths have always had an active engagement with the political movements and development of African states. When Chief Anthony Enahoro moved a motion for "self-rule" in 1953, he was thirty years old. Chief S. L. Akintola, who would follow it up with a motion for independence four years later, was forty-three years old. Chief Remi Fani-Kayode, whose motion for independence was success-fully accepted, was thirty-two years old. And Sir Abubakar Tafawa Balewa, who moved to amend the date of independence, was forty-one years old. These are four examples from Federal Parliament that included well-educated and internationally recognized achievers like Chief Bode Thomas, who was already a Queen's Counsel (the equivalent of today's Senior Advocate of Nigeria), and the Balogun of Oyo at the age of thirty-four. Many of them had successful careers and businesses, able to hold their own anywhere in the world, despite the relative bias hindering black men.

From the time of amalgamation, young Nigerians sought to work for, with, and against the British Imperialists. They understood the need to regain control of the country, and they knew there would be no returning to clannish arrangements and traditional monarchies. Their West Africa had changed forever, and they took an active role in shaping the new Nigeria.

Northern youths, led by Sir Abubakar Tafawa Balewa and Sir Ahmadu Bello, desired a little more time before independence. Afterward, they desired a Nigeria governed as decentralized units, evidenced by the demands they made in return for not seceding from Nigeria.[78] The South had different desires; they protested via the pages of newspapers that the British powers had not achieved the "UNITY of the North, East and West they (had) promised us." Protectionist demands made by each side reveal their level of thoughtfulness and ability to play politics according to Western dictates.

Their vigor and strong desire to represent the interests of their localities caused rancor and debates over Nigeria's independence that led to the Kano riots of 1953. This pattern of rioting, over grievances real and imagined, continues today.

The southerners seemed more concerned about social and governance issues, showing little hostility to the white man's spread of Christianity across Nigeria. The northerners were concerned about the imposition of Christianity along with social and governance issues. If they seemed reluctant to support the southerners' demands for independence, it was more about strengthening their position in the postindependence government and less about being comfortable with British Imperialism. They were just as hostile – if not more hostile – to the British and their tendency to treat other cultures and religions with disdain and contempt; the northerners tried to put up stronger resistance.

In 1901, The Emir of Kano tried to explain why two foreign missionaries were not welcome in Kano. He was recorded saying to them, "We do not want you: you can go; I give you three days to prepare a hundred donkeys to carry your loads back to Zaria and we never wish to see you here again."[9] In contrast, the southerners were more interested in trade, knowledge, power, and anything else they could gain by associating with the British. These outlooks were reflected in their responses to the independence question. Whether they were taking these positions in the interests of the younger generation, or out of nationalist pride and positional obligation, their preferences became obvious shortly after the reality of independence.

The nationalists continued pressing for independence until it was inevitable, and a final date was set. October 1, 1960, is not only the date of Nigeria's independence; it was an epoch of Nigeria's glory and strength, driven by an active, knowledgeable youth population.

---

[7] Igho Natufe, "The Amalgamation of Nigeria and the Quest for a Nation," in *Federalism in Africa: Problems and Perspectives*, ed. Russian Academy of Sciences. (Canada: MeaBooks Inc., 2016), 106–109.

[8] Yinka Odumakin, "As It Was in 1953," *Vanguard*, www.vanguardngr.com/2016/07/as-it-was-in-1953/.

[9] W. R. Miller, *Walter Miller, 1872–1952: An Autobiography* (Zaira: Gaskiya Corporation, 1953), quoted in J. Kenny, "Christian-Muslim Relations in Nigeria," in *Islamochristiana* 5 (1979): 171–192.

The Nigerian Youth Movement was a multiethnic organization that sought to improve the situation and fortunes of young Nigerians. It started mildly in 1936, with concerns about the quality of education that colonialists intended to offer students at the newly built Yaba College of Technology, and grew into a nationalist movement of youths, run by youths. Professor Eyo Ita, Samuel Akinsanya, Ernest Ikoli, Nnamdi Azikiwe, Dr. Kofo Abayomi, and Chief Hezekiah Oladipo Davies are some of the prominent members and officers of the movement, which later ran as a political party and mounted strong opposition to British indirect rule through traditional rulers.

There was also the Federation of Nigerian Women's Societies, which started as a women's charity body, the Abeokuta Ladies Club. It metamorphosed into a group that was concerned about improving the situation that women had to cope with in Abeokuta, and then it grew to have a national outlook. After several name changes, the Club dropped its elitist look and objectives, opening membership to market women and adopting populist and feminist objectives. The Union, started by Funmilayo Anikulapo-Kuti when she was in her thirties, grew to lead resistance to price controls and unfair treatment of market women. It campaigned for better educational opportunities for girls, enforcement of sanitary regulations, and the provision of health care and other social services for women. In 1947, they led campaigns and demonstrations against local policies, especially the direct tax on women. They were so fierce that the ruler, the Alake of Abeokuta, Sir Ladapo Ademola II, abdicated the throne the following year until 1950. Funmilayo Anikulapo-Kuti, later ran for a parliamentary position.

The vibrancy of Nigerian youths was also obvious in trade. Prince Samuel Akinsanya, later the king of Isara, was the Organizing Secretary of the Nigerian Produce Traders Union (N.P.T.U.) and President of the Nigerian Motor Transport Union from 1932 to 1940. He was in his thirties. During that time, he led union protests against Cadbury Brothers and other expatriate firms involved in antitrust activities; the firms tried to form a buying agreement to suppress the price of cocoa, a cherished cash crop. Union influence was so powerful that they agreed to destroy crops rather than allow the companies to enact their plans, and the government had to wade in.

These youths were educated and most of them received higher education in the West. Some found it easy and others did not, but none of them could endure the ongoing discrimination that they suffered under the British colonialists. They desired upward mobility, and they were not afraid to work for it. Those with easy access to international education made use of it. Even those who found it hard to access would strive to get it. Obafemi Awolowo sold firewood to earn his school fees, and Nnamdi Azikiwe tried to attend school in the United States, traveling by ship as a stowaway. Many of them knew they wanted to end British rule. Their success was converted to active nationalism that earned self-determination for the country.

Those with athletic ability were also finding their feet in the world. Teslim "Thunder" Balogun was the first Nigerian footballer to become a professional international player when he signed with Peterborough in 1950. Hogan "Kid" Bassey raised the Nigerian flag when he became a world boxing champion in 1957. Nojeem Maiyegun earned bronze in Boxing at the 1964 Tokyo Olympic Games, and it was Nigeria's first Olympic medal. Richard Ihetu, known as Dick Tiger, was in his twenties when he knocked out his opponent in the ring in Liverpool, UK. Back then, there was also the national football team, nicknamed the "red devils." The sixties were glorious years for Nigeria and its energetic youths. The discovery of crude oil within the country's borders made them even stronger, increasing their international regard.

Their zeal was not totally altruistic, nor did it envision Nigeria as one indivisible unit. Some favored a decentralized system, even as minority groups cried out against oppression under the Yoruba, Igbo, and Hausa–Fulani. Some were already enriching themselves, some played their politics along ethnic lines, and others used religion as their measuring stick. Pressing issues were handed over along with independence – the politicking was unfriendly, and the politicians were not always concerned with their people's welfare, although indigenous peoples were ruling the country, the economy was booming, the indigenization policy was just around the corner and basic infrastructure was on ground.

The Action Group (AG) was one of the three main political groups that existed before Nigeria's independence; the others were the Northern People's Congress (NPC) and the National Council of Nigerian Citizens (NCNC). They all had ethnic associations that would become more pronounced as politicking grew fierce. In postindependence jostling for power and superiority, there were several realignments. New political parties formed from the carcasses of old ones, carpets were crossed, and badges constantly changed from foe to ally and back again. Special interests determined political decisions.

The military quickly became interested in politics. As a power bloc within the organs of state, they had watched former classmates, play-mates, and neighbors become bloated from inordinate riches. Their salaries remained unchanged for years while they watched the limitless flow of oil wealth. About five years after independence, twenty-two politicians were dead at the hands of murderous military officers. The youthful officers easily legitimized their abandonment of the barracks with the blatant corruption and patronage politics in full effect.

They tried to force changes, but they were overthrown by another coup. The accusation of one-sided killings during these coups triggered the country's free fall into civil war in 1967: it would run for three years, destroying millions of lives, livelihoods, and properties before a truce was declared. Two military coups d'état and the resultant persecution of Igbo people are cited as the war's immediate cause, but oil wealth from the Niger Delta region was an underlying issue.

Nigerians did not rise above ethnic and religious considerations before or after independence. After the departure of their common enemy, the British, they had to face themselves – the education, social sophistication, and international exposure that had helped them fight the colonialists were less useful for keeping them united. Their divergent views split along many lines, such as religion, leadership ethos, preferred systems of governance, relationships with other West African countries, and the enduring problem of corruption that had crossed over into their new republic.

Obafemi Awolowo, Premier of the Western Region, favored a patriarchal, pseudo-socialist state. Under the dominance of the Action Group as the party of the southwest, his policies offered free education and free healthcare for all. However, the other regions were not so keen to follow suit. Northern region leaders were protectionists in their outlook and activities, preferring to keep their cultural and religious legacies intact through a gradual introduction of Western education into existing Islamic schools. The eastern region encouraged indigenous entrepreneurial activities to stay independent and the ability to "boycott the boycottable." There would be bickering and in-fighting within political groups in the southwest and southeast, but the north would always present a united front. The strong youths leading the nascent democracy had a chink in their armor, and it quickly led to their undoing.

The breakdown of control over the new nation was predictable. No matter how avoidable the civil war may have been, something equally sinister would have happened. No one had experience in leading a multiethnic, multireligious, and geographically diverse polity like Nigeria. Nor was there any country similarly birthed from an administrative union, and almost no other shared quality or experience to use as a case study. Within six years, matters had come to a head; the strength and vibrancy that reclaimed the country from the British was turned to destructive ends.

The theatre of war was mainly the eastern parts of Nigeria, although infrastructural development had begun stagnating in every other part of the country. Rot had infected all the amenities provided by the government, such as water, electricity, education, healthcare, housing, and transportation, because of corruption and a widespread refusal or inability to maintain their investments. The gap between electrical supply and demand was already wide enough to merit deliberations on privatization in 1988. It was an established fact that telephone lines would not extend to common people; they were only available to powerful individuals who could exert their influence and pay multiples of official rates. The protracted military administration extending from the 1980s into 1998, which was marked by heavy restrictions on speech, made things worse. By the end of the war, the East required rebuilding in the spirit of "no victor, no vanquished," and all of the government's social and infrastructural development activities, in every part of the country, needed to resume as the rural–urban migration continued.

Before the first military incursion into Nigeria's political life, the roles and contributions of Nigerian youths changed dramatically. They had to express resistance and criticism of indigenous politicians, which was unlike the pre-independence resistance against foreign hegemony and the struggle for self-rule. A new crop of youths joined those choosing to resist self-serving activities and policies in the government.

In between the many military coups and counter-coups, the National Association of Nigerian Students (NANS) moved into issues beyond education and campus life. Universities had been unable to maintain their initial standards of campus life and tutoring as established pre-independence. Increasing enrollment and decreasing or absent government funds required university administrators to manage the unmanageable. NANS started in the seventies as the National Union of Nigerian Students (NUNS), which evolved from the West African Students' Union (WASU) that was founded in London in 1925 to protect the interests of West African students who were facing discrimination and financial problems. NUNS was proscribed in 1978 after a protest against increasing school fees had turned deadly; around twenty students were injured or killed, mostly due to the heavy-handed response from police and army units dispatched to control the protests.

In 1980, NANS was different only in nomenclature from the banned NUNS, becoming involved in more dissents over the years. In May 1986, more than a dozen Ahmadu Bello University students were killed by the police during protests over the punishment of student leaders who had honored the students killed in the 1978 demonstration. Later, they became a strong force protesting increases in fuel prices and calling for the removal of university administrators, telling the military government to take itself back to the barracks.[10] It is presently a shadow of its former self, weakened through a combination of violent government responses, graft, bribery, and emasculation by university authorities.

The Nigeria Labour Congress and the Academic Staff Union of Universities were also populated by young professionals struggling against military regimes during the 1980s. They were mostly concerned with the welfare of their members and the ways that the military government's actions and policies would affect them. These groups were dissolved and proscribed at different times during the military years. Their major weapons were strike actions and work boycotts, although some of the protesting staff were dismissed, meetings were disrupted, and labor leaders were frequently arrested. There were some allegations that leaders received bribes to call off strikes, but they tried to remain strong and act above board.

Fela Anikulapo-Kuti stood out as a youth, who converted his livelihood into an act of protest against government corruption. As a musician, he dedicated several albums and tracks to speaking out against corrupt administrations that impoverished ordinary Nigerians. He called out nepotism, bribery, decaying infrastructure, the underfunded educational system, and the elite's preference for Western culture over Nigerian culture. He also criticized election rigging and coups that produced sit-tight military heads of state that brutalized civilians and enriched their personal bank accounts.

Fela was a radical, and proudly Pan-African. He sang in pidgin to reach more people, and his music and lifestyle attracted many jobless, demoralized, and excluded youths. He suffered for his "yabis sessions"; the Nigerian state responded with frequent raids on his concerts and on his house. People were beaten, and his instruments and recordings were destroyed. Fela was arrested more than 200 times, for various unsubstantiated charges, and he was sentenced to 20 months in prison. An attack on his home in 1977, carried out by about 1,000 "unknown soldiers," led to his mother being thrown from the two-story building – medical complications from the fall ultimately led to her death. From the 1970s until around 1993, Fela was a fierce campaigner for an equitable and just society. Music, his preferred medium, spread his voice worldwide.

Ken Saro Wiwa was killed in 1995 by the military administration led by General Sani Abacha. He was the president of the Movement for the Survival of the Ogoni People (MOSOP), which organized nonviolent

---

[10] Photius, "Nigeria Student Organizations," Photius, March 27, 2005, www.photius.com /countries/nigeria/national_security/nigeria_national_security_student_organiza tion~10049.html.

campaigns against the environmental degradation of Ogoniland, his hometown. The degradation was caused by crude oil extraction, which the government was reluctant to control. After several intimidating arrests and detainments, he and eight other members of MOSOP were accused of killing conservative members of the group. They were detained for a year before they were tried by a military tribunal and hanged.

The combination of the individual and collective resistance efforts brought down the military government after the death of General Abacha in 1998. The political class was tired of being excluded, the unions and youth organizations were taking an aggressive stance, and the international community was threatening further sanctions and trade boycotts. The military organized rapid elections to birth Nigeria's Fourth Republic, thirty-nine years after independence.

The Paradoxical Shift: Nigerian Youths and Political Apathy

> Youth participation in elections and governance processes is character-ised by high levels of apathy. Young people, whilst being the most affected by democratic processes, are the least interested in them.[11]

Despite its large numbers, Africa is not at the top of the charts in any international indices. As much as we love football, we rarely excel at it on the international stage. A deliberate refusal to invest, and decadent cor-ruption sucking up what little investment is made, means that Nigeria does not have the best facilities for training, or the best processes for identifying and encouraging the best football players at a young age. And this is just a subsector of sports; there are many other sectors in which the country is failing its young population. The best outputs from youths in economic, political, social, and sports leadership are not obtained because the leaders of the country are not providing adequate inputs into their growth.

Nigeria, bursting at the seams with over 62 percent of its population under twenty-five years old,[12] has been particularly unable to care for its young. While the elites and the educated acted out decades of misrule, military rule, and a nasty civil war with corruption conducting the mass choir, millions of children were born and grew up with scant or nonexist-ent resources to prepare their bodies and minds for a technologically

[11] Hillary Jephat Musarurwa, "Closed Spaces or (In)competent Citizens? A Study of Youth Preparedness for Participation in Elections in Zimbabwe," *Commonwealth & Comparative Politics* (2018): 1.
[12] Indexmundi, "Nigeria Demographics Profile 2019," Indexmundi, December 7, 2019, www.indexmundi.com/nigeria/demographics_profile.html.

advanced, hyper-connected world. Many were schooled under tin roofs, without chairs, and probably with half the number of teachers that were required.

Many grew up malnourished. Some were raised in conditions of semi-slavery, in the homes of relatives who only took them in because they could not afford paid help. A lot of them are grown and unable to find or assert their voices in a world that has moved on from what they are used to. Many still grow up that way. The ones lucky enough to get some schooling will probably be taught on a syllabus that even Samuel Ajayi Crowder would condemn. The luckiest ones will attend expensive private schools, only to find themselves jostling to be underemployed in public service or at private companies.

Military uniforms might have left the nation's executive offices, but corruption still occupies the head table. Even before the election of Olusegun Obasanjo's administration, the political class had started acting as though they had not just suffered oppression under the military. The People's Democratic Party bought and rigged their way into power,[13] staying there for sixteen years before their candidate was unseated by a combination of protest votes and deft political maneuverings made by their closest rivals, the Alliance for Democracy and the Congress for Progressive Change.

The two parties merged with two other parties to become the All Progressives Congress, running a campaign that tapped heavily into the citizens' collective abhorrence of corruption in politics and in the country generally. They also heavily tapped into youth culture, infiltrating their gathering spots online, mainly Facebook and Twitter, to project the opposition party and their candidate as incurably corrupt and lacking the resolve to change the country. Anyone who tried to call attention to Muhammadu Buhari's antecedents as military head of state – his dismal human rights record and his inability to control the economy's rate of inflation – was shouted down and dismissed as an agent of corruption.

Youths have always been instrumental in political, social, and economic activities in Nigeria, but not always in an ideal way. They have been used as thugs, as minions, and as convenient buffers between murderous extremists and those wielding political and economic power. They were unplanned oversights, seen as nuisance figures used to downgrade score cards issued by international bodies like the UN, UNICEF, WHO, and others like ASUU. After being used, what do these youths get? They get to die as soldiers, when they are told to face

---

[13] Julius O. Ihonvbere, "The 1999 Presidential Elections in Nigeria: The Unresolved Issues," *Issue: A Journal of Opinion* 27, no. 1 (1999): 59–62.

extremists with better weaponry, like Boko Haram. They get to endure harrowing lives after being wounded or captured and made to serve extremists. They get kidnapped and killed, so their organs can be harvested for the rich. And they get to live unfulfilled lives, regardless of their education. There is always some rich person's family who is considered better for good jobs.

Poverty, which defaces the country in its third-world glory, is both a weapon of oppression and a tool for control. Rulers wield it as they strike deals on rotational power, holding on with a twisted oligarchic bond broken only by death. This, combined with the sheer number of young people – those who have been left behind, excluded, and those who are regressing daily – weighs down all the occupants of government seats in the country. Their efforts are like a spoonful of water in an empty bucket. We hear the sound, but where is it, and what has it achieved?

Despite international pressure, a negligible percentage of the national budget goes to core areas like education, healthcare, and economic empowerment. Although youth's welfare is vital, they are left to cope with unemployment and the challenges of insufficiently equipped tertiary institutions. They fall for the lure of quick money through crime, religious fundamentalism, internet fraud, kidnapping, and militancy. And the youths seem to have acclimated to it. They have become used to the poverty that emasculates them from before birth, gifting them with the undesirable effects of malnourishment. They have become accustomed to overworked and probably undernourished parents in slum houses. And they have become familiar with neighborhoods that have half-built schools covered with corrugated iron sheets, protecting them from the sun but transmitting all the heat straight down into brains that are supposed to be alert enough to grasp concepts taught in a language that is only used in school.

Children born into poverty with no hope of a safety net from the government go on to live lives full of denied needs and untapped potential. Many of them mindlessly repeat the cycle, taking refuge in religion, alcohol, music, drugs, and any other coping mechanisms that make life a little easier to bear.

Poverty's evils are multi-faceted, showing up in various forms. It creates a vicious cycle keeping generations subservient to the wealthy, much like the feudal, precolonial societies that democracy was supposed to replace. The economy is structured so that the vulnerable do not receive any special consideration. The strong must strive extra hard just to keep themselves fed, ensuring that they do not have the energy or desire to participate in politics.

Many cannot even see the correlation between corrupt public practices and the deprivation that binds them. The right to participate in politics, freedom of speech, and freedom of association are concepts they cannot understand or apply because their social well-being and education did not unlock the true meaning of democracy; their reality does not interpret it, either. Having neither experienced a truly participatory democracy nor experienced governance at the grassroots level in a way that reflects the ideal on paper, they expect nothing but rare trickles of money or noodles from the government. They resent the time it takes to obtain the Voter's Card, and some see Election Day as a time to sleep off the weariness in their bones.

A lot of Nigerian youths, especially the larger rural populace, are unused to associating the "big man" politicians with "service." They do not see the convoys of big, speeding black SUVs as the forces making life so difficult for them. Preoccupied with the search for food to eat, and the struggle to avoid getting evicted by equally needy landlords, they do not associate the pittance that they receive from politicians with the millions that do not get invested in roads, schools, and hospitals. Instead, the money keeps appearing in the pages of newspapers as "misappropriated."

Many youths do not advance beyond primary education. Even when they are apprenticed to learn skills, they must learn by practicing with outdated instruments at a subsistence level. Too many doors of opportunity are closed against them before they are even fifteen years old. Nigerian youths may not have been intentionally relegated to the background by the political class, but it certainly serves their purposes. Politicians and rich people exploit the situation. They love having servants, housemaids, gatekeepers, gardeners, laundrymen, and shop assistants working for a pittance. Even the little children from disadvantaged homes that they offer to send to school or train are only turned into househelp. They engage the frustrated, drug-addicted, aggressive, rough, and dangerous youths who are willing to help them intimidate and attack their opponents.

They will always need youths to follow them on the campaign trail for the price of a plate of food, serving as thugs to help them steal ballot boxes and execute their political opponents. The political class cannot dissociate itself from the constant political violence in Nigeria; they apply "Godfather" tactics, desperation, and money politics to retain control over the machinery of the state. As long as they do not provide training for each Nigerian child to explore their potential and assist them in finding positions that put that potential to use, they continue sending signals that they do not mind the hopelessness or powerlessness felt by most youths. It is believable because it is a favorable situation for them. Ironically, from Zimbabwe, Angola, Libya, Malawi, Cameroon, Uganda, and Zambia to Gambia, African youth (usually militias or youth wings of political parties) are exploited by political elites to attain political power and leadership roles. As a result of their selfishness, illiteracy, ignorance, poverty, and unemployment, they are known across the continent as the same force that ejects these leaders from the political system, usually in a violent manner; while these might be a misdirected or misguided act of political participation, it establishes the force that lay within the premise of the youths' participation in politics and other societal activities.[14]

This has been costly, and it will continue to cost the youths in the long run; the offspring of the same families look to continue in the footsteps of their forebears, while the excluded set are busy continuing to look for daily sustenance. Claude Ake normalized this situation when he asserted, "it is patently absurd for a starving peasant to be chasing after these abstract rights instead of attending to the stomach."[15] The situation remains the same as when he wrote in 1996.

Perhaps the most painfully wasted reform opportunity in recent memory is the circumstantial president, who was also the youngest president since the start of the Fourth Republic. Hopes were very high when he assumed power, and he had as much support as any politician could hope to get from the many groups in the country. However, his administration was as ineffective and as corrupt as its predecessors. But should we really expect much from any candidate delivered by the same party machinations that produced the previous leaders? What can PDP offer Nigeria and its youthful population that it could not deliver during sixteen years of rule at the federal level? And the APC, the present ruling party at the federal level, is populated with the same career politicians and political jobbers who have been on the scene since the announcement of the Fourth Republic – if not for centuries before that.

This brings to the fore the subjugation of the youths by the older generation. Mamadou Faye observes that "[the] African continent is still plagued by a gerontic political cast, which lacks the dynamism, moral integrity and creativity that the youth embodies and could contribute to the political landscape of the continent."[16] This persistent subjugation itself is a largely responsible friction due to ideological dissonance between the old and young generations, as well as the increasing political apathy among the youths in Africa. Africa, with the exception of the pro-independence leaders, lacks transformational leaders who are willing and ready to mentor the younger generation on the role of leadership and

[14] See Obediah Dodo and Jesca Majaha, "African Youth's 'Whirl-wind' Allegiance to Leadership," *International Journal of Modern Anthropology* 2, no. 11 (2018): 108–124.

[15] Claude Ake, *Is Africa Democratizing?* (Lagos: Malthouse Press Limited, 1996), 23.

[16] Mamadou Faye, "African Youth Integration in Politics," *Argumente und Materialien der Entwicklungszusammenarbeit* 21 (2017): 31.

include them in their leadership; rather, the African public and political space is dominated by recycled and authoritarian leaders who seek self-gratification in continuously holding tight to the reins of power at whatever cost.

Student Unionism in African tertiary institutions has been a stronghold of political participation by the youths. Kgosidintsi documents how student activism continues to be a shaping force not only in the political domain of Botswana, but how it has also prompted socioeconomic and cultural agitations that benefit the general populace and Africa as a whole. Sadly, the crop of leaders that enjoyed the democratic and emancipatory benefits of this unionism in their youthful days are the one stifling it, further suppressing the available avenues for the youths in various Nigerian tertiary instituitions to be actively involved in the political activities of their immediate society. It is common practice among the administrative leaders of Nigerian tertiary institutions to suspend active Student Union leaders who are bold enough to speak on issues affecting the welfare of the entire student body. Two recent examples at the University of Ibadan are the four-semester suspension of Ojo Aderemi, a few months after being elected the Student Union president, "for leading a protest in 2017 over the school's inability to provide identity cards for students,"[17] and the suspension of Adekunle Adebajo, a final-year law student, for two semesters for his scathing article that highlighted poor management of the school's facilities, especially the halls of residence.[18] In even worse cases, students' leaders/activists are rusticated and the union banned from operating within the school premises to further consolidate the institutes' domination of power.[19]

A strategic approach that has been adopted by the older generation to constantly subject the youths under their control, yet "be seen to be accommodating youth participation,"[20] is to allocate positions with little or no decision-making significance to the youths: "youth wings" is a manifestation of this at the party level. Such popular expressions as "the young shall grow" and "youths are the leaders of tomorrow" are symbolic indices employed by the older generation to continuously defer and marginalize the role and relationship of the youth with politics.

[17] Adejumo Kabir, "University of Ibadan Suspends Student for Leading Protest," *Premium Times*, April 11, 2019, www.premiumtimesng.com/news/headlines/324992-university-of-ibadan-suspends-student-for-leading-protest.html.

[18] Fisayo Adekunle Adebajo, "UI: The Irony of Fashionable Rooftops and Awful Interiors," *The Guardian*, April 20, 2016, https://guardian.ng/features/ui-the-irony-of-fashionable-rooftops-and-awful-interiors/.

[19] See Resego Natalie Kgosidintsi, "Student Activism and Youth Agency in Botswana," *BUWA! A Journal on African Women's Experiences*, no. 8 (2017): 36.

[20] Musarurwa, "Closed Spaces or (In)competent Citizens?" 6.

Hence, the older generation assumes an intangible and indefinite role of custodian of the state while the youth keeps awaiting "tomorrow" or when they shall grow; hence, "uncertainty beclouds the agency and identities of 'youth'."[21] Such is the manifestation of the African Union Agenda 2063 that promises to attend to the present realities that challenge the African Youth; such a far-future-oriented agenda "denies them [the youths] the opportunity to have their issues addressed with the urgency they demand."[22]

Aside from the gerontocratic nature of Nigerian cultural and political space, which to a large extent is a contributing factor to the exclusion of youths from active political activities, there is also the younger generation's seeming insufficiency of social capital (as in trust, loyalty, respect, etc.), which doesn't give the older generation enough confidence to trust the youths with leadership responsibilities at whatever level, coupled with their greed to maintain the reins of authority. For example, the young and vibrant 2019 Nigerian presidential candidate of the African Alliance Congress (AAC), Omoyele Sowore, like Julius Malema of South Africa and Bobby Wine in Uganda, regardless of his popularity among Nigerian youths, as well as the proposed brilliant ideas and visions, didn't do very well at the polls. This was partly because of what has been tagged by the older generation as his rude and arrogant behavior, and partly because of the limited capacity of his political party which emerged barely a year before the election.

The long years of turmoil experienced in the political space in Nigeria – from very violent protests to coups and then full-scale civil wars, all which have youth at the center of the activities – is a negative testament to the perception of youth engagement with politics. It has also been a major factor contributing to the lack of trust in the leadership of a vibrant but naïve young generation. However, ironically, it should be noted that the youths responsible for this perception are still holding political positions at different levels in the nation. Therefore, there is the need, on both parts, to demonstrate a considerable level of trust to ensure a successful democracy through active political participation and reverse the narrative that "politics is the affair of corrupt and immoral people."[23]

But more importantly, the older generation has a lot of restitution to make to overturn the youths' misgivings on issues of immediate concern.

---

[21] Taiwo A. Olaiya, "Youth and Ethnic Movements and Their Impacts on Party Politics in ECOWAS Member States," *SAGE Open* (2014): 3.

[22] Douglas Gichuki, "Leadership in Africa and the Role of Youth in the Leadership Milieu," *Mandela Institute for Development Studies* (2014): 12.

[23] Faye, "African Youth Integration in Politics," 33.

This reversion would help to re-awaken the youths' zeal, trust, and passion to be actively involved in the governance of their society as it undoubtedly affects their well-being. As elaborated by Sommers, "'Trust' here refers to the significance of building relationships with members of your target group and those who work with them. This is done through positive engagement: establishing both a focused interest in the lives of youth and determined efforts to make programming participatory, and then following through."[24]

Among the counterarguments against the disengagement of youths from political participation in Africa is the detachment of the political class and institutions themselves from the youth. An active relation between the citizens and the political class is marked as an essential component of political participation; hence, what has largely been perceived as the withdrawal of the youths from political activities is, to a reasonable extent, a recoil of the political powers from the youth – fundamentally or deliberately. There is need for a reconnection between the political class and the governed, especially the youths, in terms of representation, mentorship, and deliberation. This helps to establish the Nigerian youths as more than a political tool of thuggery and violence.

Another determent is the ideological construct of political system/ parties in Nigeria, and Africa at large, which are mostly outdated, abstract, or unrealistic. By and large, the ideological dispensation of the present generation is more pragmatic and realistic as a result of their engagement with the technologically advanced world and modern challenges which give credence to the polemics of youth's engagement with politics in Nigeria; as reiterated by Livingston et al., "Young people are not necessarily any less interested in politics than previous generations but rather that traditional political activity no longer appears appropriate to address the concerns associated with contemporary youth culture."[25] Ironically, Africa is home to the largest number of youth in the world and the population is enormously dominated by them as well, and Nigeria claims a sizeable chunk of this population, yet the various government policies and political systems do not reflect this reality, thereby marginalizing what is supposed to be the stronghold of the country: "In the real sense, the only strength for the youth is

---

[24] Marc Sommers, "Creating Programs for Africa's Urban Youth: The Challenge of Marginalization," *Journal of International Cooperation in Education* 10, no. 1 (2007): 22.
[25] S. Livingstone, N. Couldry, and T. Markham, "Youthful Steps towards Civic Participation: Does the Internet Help?" in *Young Citizens in the Digital Age: Political Engagement, Young People and New Media*, ed. B. Loader (London: Routledge, 2007), 1.

the huge number, which is certainly not enough to cause a fundamental change in the bastion of power and economic control in the region."[26]

It is no surprise that the youth wings of Nigerian political parties are even dominated by old people who constantly use their age and power to suppress the youths. By default, the setup of these political parties is not youth inclusive. Mostly, political posts in Nigeria can only be attained through nominations by existing political parties, who tend to prefer an older person over a youth, and the influence of these political parties to dominate elections is overbearing due to a strong support system and an availability of funds, which makes it almost impossible to be defeated by new political parties formed by youths to ensure their active involvement in political parties.

The legal frameworks of most African states do not permit the involvement of youths in active political duties as a result of age (dis)qualification. Only recently, when vigorous agitations are being made by African youths (the example of "Not Too Young to Run") for inclusion in the political activities of their societies, did African states start reducing the age-qualification barrier, and even at that, its applicability is only theoretical: "Adopting a youth-inclusive legal framework is an essential and primary step in mainstreaming the youth in the political aspects of a country. It would allow youth to participate formally and improve their political roles in their societies."[27] A sound recommendation made by Mengistu to ensure the inclusion of African youths in the governance of their society is that "[c]ountries should also frame a quota or any kind of means to enable youth to have a representative from the local assemblies to the national parliament."[28] Similarly, an age quota should enabled; it is only logical that a nation with an average life expectancy of fifty-five should have at its governance system and other leadership positions a sizeable number of competent youths. The financial implication of engaging in politics is overwhelming, and this discourages a very large percentage of the Nigerian youths who are already confounded by the challenges of poverty and mass unemployment from either nurturing political ambitions or involving themselves in political activities.

In Mike Ushe's study of the interrelation of Christian Youths and politics in Africa, using Nigeria as a case study, he sums up the prevalent menace that characterizes the political landscape in Africa, which broadly accounts for the seeming departure of the youths in politics, in his view:

---

[26] Olaiya, "Youth and Ethnic Movements and Their Impacts on Party Politics in ECOWAS Member States," 11.

[27] M. M. Mengistu, "The Quest for Youth Inclusion in the African Politics: Trends, Challenges, and Prospects," *Journal of Socialomics* 6, no. 1 (2017): 4.

[28] Ibid.

The non-involvement of youths in politics, monetization of politics and prebend-alism (popularly known as God-fatherism and God-son syndrome), violent behaviors of youths such as political thuggery, political motivated assassinations, molestation of innocent citizens, seizure of ballot boxes, and wanton destruction of properties (ARSON), intimidation of political opponents, political syco-phancy, looting, prevalence of cult's activities and incitement of religious crisis in the name of politics, are negative behaviors exhibited by the youths in the name of politics in Nigeria.[29]

The withdrawal of the youth from political participation is partly caused by the deliberate marginalization by the system which has excluded the youths from the vital decision-making process or its failure to put into consideration such decision-making contributions that emerge from youths' perspective. Youths then often resort to violence and pro-tests as a consequence of their exclusion from governance and politics, a manifestation of the menace the Nigerian society has degenerated into, and as demonstrative acts against their noninclusion in the political activities of their society, especially on matters very germane to their survival and well-being: as collaborated by Mengistu, "As a result of lack of political participation of youth in the continent, most of the younger population is disorganized, unemployed, and vulnerable to rad-ical ideas."[30]

The overall unfavorable challenges plaguing the Nigerian society have rendered its youth very vulnerable and easily recruited for insurgent and illegal activities. The lack of proper education and vocational skills, the growing increase in poverty, and mass unemployment are what limits not only against the society's advancement but also the resourcefulness of the youths. This destabilization that characterizes the life of youths is what Honwana describes as "waithood," which is a "period of suspension between childhood and adulthood. It represents a prolonged adolescence or an involuntary delay in reaching adulthood"[31] that, if not adequately managed or utilized, erupts into events as violence, crime, depression, etc.

On the engagement of African youths with political violence, Ojok and Acol emphasized the misconception and often misleading political under-play of valid agitations as violence:

It is important to understand that the discourse on youth in Africa cannot and should not be dominated by narratives of political violence which oftentimes tend to be too narrowly focused on youth as threats while the underlying

---

[29] Mike Ushe, "Christian Youths and Politics in Nigeria: Implications for Sustainable Development," *Journal of Sustainable Development in Africa* 16, no. 8 (2014): 16.

[30] Mengistu, "The Quest for Youth Inclusion in the African Politics," 1.

[31] Alcinda M. Honwana, "Youths," in *The Time of Youth: Work, Social Change and Politics in Africa* (Boulder: Kumarian Press, 2012), 4.

socio-economic and political meanings of violence, for instance with regard to legitimate claims against an authoritarian and incapable state, are ignored.[32]

It has been sixty years since independence. Nigeria's population has increased by almost 300 percent, and despite almost consistent revenue sources, the country isn't planning to capitalize on the opportunity inherent in the massive number of youths within its borders. Unlike China, with its Asian Tiger phenomenon, Nigeria does not have a disciplined central authority making constructive decisions for the young and relaying them to effective ministries and institutions for implementation. Yet, these transitions are needed for the advancement of the nation. Lack of discipline feeds corruption, weakening even the most devout person.

However, the perceived withdrawal of the youth is not only limited to political participation; it cuts across the different structures of the socio-political institutions, including participation in religious or sociocultural activities. This disengagement is, sometimes, a result of the shift in time and the harsh realities of modernity, which the youths, even the society at large, are inadequately prepared to overcome. As Bincof indicated, "in Somalia, for instance, decades of unrests, conflicts, and instability left many in the current generation with deep psychological wounds"[33]; that makes engagement with political activities unappealing and seem unhealthy.

The Youth and the Fight for a True Nigerian Independence

Young people today understand that the struggle to overcome their predicament requires radical social change. No longer defined by political parties' ideology yet rejecting being cast as apathetic, they are engaging in civil society organizations and using popular culture as well as new technologies of information, communication, and social networking to confront the status quo.[34]

As it has been pointed out by, among others, Uche Kalu's[35] numerous studies on the sociocultural dynamics of religion in Africa, there is the increasing awareness created by religious bodies for their followers to be actively involved in the political affairs of their society, especially the

---

[32] Donnas Ojoka and Tony Acol, "Connecting the Dots: Youth Political Participation and Electoral Violence in Africa," *Journal of African Democracy and Development* 1, no. 2 (2017): 96–97.

[33] Mohamed Omar Bincof, "The Role of Youth in Political Participation in Somalia," *IOSR Journal of Humanities and Social Science* 23, no. 10 (2018): 65.

[34] Honwana, "Youths," 7.

[35] See Wilhelm J. Kalu, Nimi Wariboko, and Toyin Falola, eds., *African Christianity* (Trenton: Africa World Press, 2010).

youths, and how and why they should avoid being manipulated by the political class for their selfish gains. This political awareness is molded into sermons in churches and mosques usually by finding correlating illustrations of young spiritual leaders in their Holy Scriptures who can be seen as role models of how spiritual-minded individuals can be part of the political affairs, as leaders, followers, voters, or conscience of their society and not "be as onlookers, passengers or passive participants in the political affairs of the nation."[36]

Also, these religious bodies do not only conscientize their political youths on the need to actively engage themselves in politics and the act of good and effective governance, but also serve as rallying points to support, ensure their success as a political leader, and also provide adequate criticism/advice on a regular basis when the expected moral standard is being derailed: "indeed, religious groups may be the only organizations that are targeting marginalized urban youth for positive development."[37]

A noticeable paradoxical relation between the Nigerian youth and political activities is the almost total withdrawal of the youth from the arena of legal active politics as a voter, member of a political ideology, or political candidate but nevertheless are the most engaged in political violence, thuggery, protests, and demonstrations, which becomes a "counterweight to democratic development" and "continues to reinforce and sustain the dominance of the aged in the political sphere as the youth take the position of mafias and mechanism for the execution of the inordinate ambitions of the in articulate old men in the system."[38]

Political participation in modern times has shifted from the single and dominant perspective of election to include multiple other facets of politics and governance which are likewise vital to the collective sustenance of democracy in a given society as they are "intended to influence either directly or indirectly political choices at various levels of the political system."[39] Hence, such activities as political analysis and criticism, political protest and demonstration, campaign activities, and political education and awareness are also essential contemporary dimensions of political participation, in which the active involvement of youth are needed to consolidate their representation and inclusion. While there

---

[36] Ushe, "Christian Youths and Politics in Nigeria," 24.

[37] Sommers, "Creating Programs for Africa's Urban Youth," 23.

[38] Samuel Okey, "Youth Involvement in Political Violence/Thuggery: A Counter Weight to Democratic Development in Africa," *Journal of Political Sciences and Public Affairs* 5, no. 3 (2017): 3–4.

[39] H. Brady, "Political Participation," in *Measures of Political Attitudes*, eds. J. P. Robinson et al. (San Diego: Academic Press, 1999), 737.

might be restraint voicing their opinions on political policies and issues, newspaper stands, and social media platforms are filled with fierce voices of Nigerian youths dutifully engaging the older generations on political matters and other socioeconomic issues.

A continuous and active relationship, for instance, between the political activities of a country and its mainstream popular culture (as in dance, music, movies, industries) would ensure the engagement of youths in politics.[40] For instance, the popular Ajegunle musician, African China, severely engaged the Nigerian political system and leaders in his songs, offering true criticism of the political landscape and thereby intimating the young generation about the political affairs of the nation. In recent times, popular musicians as Falz, 2 Face, Burna Boy, Tekno, etc., have made political discourses the center of their songs; criticizing the government, admonishing the youths to vote and avoid violence, and bringing the attention of both the government and citizens to topical issues:

[M]usic becomes a powerful means to generate social action. Whether through calming anxieties, raising awareness, or moving people to oppose an apparent inequality, songs assist in forming communities proclaiming common desires: desires to attain certain rights draw attention to certain problems.[41]

Another perspective of the interrelation of popular culture, youth, and politics in Nigeria is the increasing declaration by popular artists to represent their people in various levels of government positions, capitalizing on their popularity and openness. In the past years, popular names as Desmond Elliot, Banky W, 9ice, RMD, etc., in the Nigerian entertainment industry have vied for political posts at different levels. Therefore, a proper scrutiny would reveal the huge participation of the youths in politics and governance in their society in new ways. In a similar vein, Perullo[42] made an irrefutable case for this in his extensive study of East African youth and their engagement in politics and governance through popular music, which creates the viable opportunity to express their concerns, establish their understanding of the present political scape as well as engage the larger population.

Whatever young people have achieved under Nigeria's Fourth Republic, they have achieved in spite of the government, not because of it or with its support. They are carving new paths to achieve their aims and

---

[40] For years, popular cultures and their custodians have been adopted (and sometimes manipulated) by politicians during elections to appeal to their younger audience. Therefore, continuous engagement of this kind would see to the gradual involvement of African youth in politics.

[41] Alex Perullo, "Politics and Popular Song: Youth, Authority, and Popular Music in East Africa," *Journal of International Library of African Music* 9, no. 1 (2011): 88.

[42] Ibid., 87–115.

breaking new grounds to do what the government has been unable to do. Youths are leveraging advances in communications technology, the increasing applications of information technology, and the growing global attention to the plight of women and children, and are achieving great things in their fields of interest. Youths are even working separately and in tandem politically, to shift away from the old and clear space for the new to come in and do better.

In politics, Bugdit works with other social impact organizations to push for the passage of the Freedom of Information Bill. It is arguably the best outcome of the Goodluck Jonathan administration, and it has pushed back the darkness shrouding Nigeria's public finances. The organization uses information to show people the relationship between the long figures leaving state accounts and the abandoned or completed projects in their localities. These activities increase awareness, serve as a stop-gap for projects being abandoned, and trigger and sustain conversations that keep public servants on their toes.

In 2012, youths sustained a two-week protest over an increase in the price of petrol at the pump. Nigeria Labour Congress and Trade Union Congress joined the protests, making them a complete success. The protest, which spanned Kano, Lagos, Abuja, and London, with Brussels, Washington, and South Africa following in the second week, was named "Occupy Nigeria." It signaled to youths nationwide that they have the power to control the country, if they would only unite and be well organized.

Professional activities are also receiving international recognition. Youths in the technology space are solely responsible for getting Facebook's tech billionaire founder into Nigeria in 2016. Iyinoluwa Aboyeji, a twenty-seven-year-old who co-founded two international companies, is the only Nigerian who has been named one of the World Economic Forum 2018 Young Global Leaders, which is a platform for young innovators and influencers around the world. He recently resigned to start canvassing for the teaching of history in primary and secondary schools in Nigeria. Lois Auta, an advocate for the rights of people living with disabilities in Nigeria, was the only Nigerian inducted into the group in 2017.

Nigeria participated in the 2018 Winter Olympic Games for the first time because youths decided they could do it, trained, and registered to do it. Their sense of nationalism compelled them to participate under the Nigerian flag. Four of them – bobsledders Seun Adigun, Akuoma Omeoga, and Ngozi Onwumere, and skeleton racer Simidele Adeagbo – were eager to represent their country in Korea. Following the footpath of Bash Ali, who is "the only boxer in the world to win every cruiser weight title conceivable,"[43] but with less or no support from the government, boxers like Anthony Joshua and Israel Adesanya are patriotic athletes who are proud of their Nigerian nationality.

Youth representation in Nigerian politics, though constitutional, had traditionally been limited to running errands and waiting to be given an appointment. Now, youths are picking up nomination forms and acting on their ideology and slogan, "Not Too Young to Run." Fine examples included Rinsola Abiola and Aisha Augie Kuta, both of whom wanted to become legislators in the House of Representatives and tried to contest in 2019.

These outliers are using their resources and privileges to serve the country. But youths are reawakening from the violence-induced lethargy of the military years. They are finding their voices and seizing opportunities, shifting away from a focus on white-collar employment to embrace entrepreneurship in all its forms. They are leveraging social media and real-life meet-ups to make their voices heard. Many youths are no longer content to knock on opportunity's door politely, waiting for it to be opened. Instead, they are crafting keys and knocking out walls where they can't find doors.

Nigerian youths are excelling, but not in the right numbers. Too many untrained minds and hands could be strengthened for the glory of the country, if only the present crop of leaders would rise above their base instincts and petty desires for self-enrichment and aggrandizement. Imagine a Nigeria that values honesty, equity, social justice, inclusiveness, equality, human rights, nondiscrimination, and the dignity of labor. Nigeria can fulfill its potential if corruption, nepotism, ethnicity, and injustice are wiped out from the litany and the system.

There is the need to ensure that children get the best education, in comfortable learning environments and at affordable costs, from the proper age. There is the need to protect them from conflicts, violence, molestation, and diseases. In order to get the best from the abundant numbers of young people who exist in the country, adequate preparations and implementation should be made. But how willing are the political leaders and the populace to ensure that Nigeria becomes a world leader in sports, military power, and economic strength?

Is Nigeria ready to pay for accelerated development? Cuba once rejected the low literacy rate scorecard that it received in 1959. It was estimated that the Cuban literacy level was about 60–76 percent, and investigations revealed that many people in rural areas were unable to access education, which was made worse by a general shortage of instructors. The government put everything into erasing the blight as fast as

---

[43] Silva N, "Top 5 Nigerian Boxers," *Lists*, n.d., https://lists.ng/top-5-nigerian-boxers/.

possible, naming 1961 the "year of education" and increasing the country's literacy rate to 96 percent.

Cuba focused on the most important needs of education – literacy and numeracy. The country shut down schools for one calendar year, from January 1 to December 22, 1961, forming students and instructors into "literacy brigades." They went into the countryside and built schools where none existed, trained new educators, and taught illiterate rural dwellers how to read and write. This twelve-month action helped 707,212 adults achieve literacy; that is, how far they were willing to go as a nation to achieve their collective desire.

The demands to actualize a preferable Nigeria is beyond meetings, seminars, committees, and policy documents. An earnest intent to invest in youths must be demonstrated through budgeting for education, healthcare, and youth empowerment. Beyond paltry, poverty-inspired "empowerment programs," Nigeria needs to budget substantially for these plans and implementations; not only disbursing the needed money, but also ensuring that the appropriate ministries and civil-service arms execute the plans faithfully. There is the need to nurture youths who are aware of their country's history and proud to be part of its present. Also, the youths must be willing and able to build a country that is greater than the one that raised them. But if the generations currently leading do not put the affairs of the country in order, how will the youth love it? If there is no investment in their minds and hands, how will the youth build improvements? If the current rulers do not display and talk about Nigeria with pride, why should the youth?

The youths must know that the nation is defended by more than its military. They must fight to defend it from thieving politicians and bribe-seeking civil servants, even to the point of organizing protests and civil disobedience. Nigerians must unite to repent and renounce actions that undermine and tear their pride and dignity as a nation. Nigerian youths must know how to engage government, infiltrate government, and change government from the inside out and from the outside in: "The youth fail to self-organise and rally together behind a few candidates from across the political divide who can champion for the prioritization of youth empowerment in policies and initiatives – thus tackling youth exclusion and ensuring that their concerns are addressed in government."[44] The disengagement of the youth from politics right after election is partly responsible for political leaders' increasing acts of corruption, fund misappropriation, and so on as youths energetic enough to hold them responsible for their acts are disinterested in the governance of their societies.

---

[44] Musarurwa, "Closed Spaces or (In)competent Citizens?" 6.

To achieve the long-desired preferable Nigeria, the people must reject ethnic division in all its forms because it only divides and belittles each group, but rather re-channel their energy to the task of building an all-inclusive nation where all residents are at peace and can conduct their business without fear. The desired Nigeria cannot be built by engaging in divisive politics, spreading hatred, reporting fake news, using social media platforms to fuel violence, or allowing corruption to continue its reign unchecked.

Nigerian youths are not adequately represented through available political positions, and the most alienated are the females. There is no Nigerian parliamentarian currently under the age of thirty, which is a hurdle that the "Not Too Young to Run" law seeks to overcome. But even political parties do not offer the needed recognition. Established power brokers are reluctant to ensure youth representation and to give young people the chance to act in meaningful roles. In 2012, the ruling People's Democratic Party (PDP) elected sixty-year-old Mallam Umar Garba Chiza from Niger State as their National Youth Leader, and the major opposition party, All Progressives Congress (APC), laughed at them. Two years later, APC appointed a fifty-two-year-old man as their own National Youth Leader.

Only a small number of well-educated and articulate youths are active within actual political parties, but this is somewhat balanced by their online political activities, where they tactically and passionately discuss the merits of candidates and their campaign promises, expose flaws, engage with politicians, seek donations for their candidates, and share information surrounding elections and politics. They even attempt to undermine the opposition with yellow journalism, which has been dubbed fake news. The "fake news" epidemic is the nasty, negative side of online political participation for democratic countries.[45]

Youth participation in politics is nonnegotiable, regardless of their preferred platform of engagement. Only the young can carry the weight of nation building, either in peacetime or wartime. And they are the ones who the country can influence, shaping the course of their history, their individual capacity, and their later achievements through policies and actions, especially in the areas of education and healthcare. The Nigerian youths must rise to this challenge, regardless of gender, and push Nigeria toward global dominance.

If Nigerian youths wish to actively shape their future, they have to take the opportunity. Thankfully, there is the precedent of those referred to as

---

[45] Darrell M. West, "How to Combat Fake News and Disinformation," *Brookings Institution*, December 18, 2017, www.brookings.edu/research/how-to-combat-fake-news-and-disinformation/.

"fathers of nationalism." They dared, back in the fifties, to demand Nigeria's sovereignty. They did what they could, even though it meant attracting the displeasure and wrath of the colonial overlords. They wanted to be the captain of their own ship. This should be the attitude of today's youths toward governance and politicians. The years of shrinking back are over. It is time to join ranks against the leeches sucking the country's lifeblood, ripping them off mercilessly.

Nigerian youths can be guided to use their energy for positive national development in various ways. The first things to put in place are quality education and healthcare: their importance cannot be overemphasized in building a great nation and the Nigerian populace cannot continue to ignore them and hope for the best. If the government cannot afford to fund these two areas, they must encourage private practitioners, making it easier to set up standard schools and hospitals and strengthening their monitoring agencies.

Vice President Yemi Osinbajo worked to encourage entrepreneurship by increasing the ease of doing business in Nigeria. If the ministries and relevant bodies meet this effort halfway by providing oversight and upholding rules, policies, and strategies that are already in place while refusing to be corrupted, many people will be positively affected.

More schools and more hospitals are needed to help Nigeria cope with the young population. The schools should be all-inclusive, accommodating those with disabilities and teenage delinquents. Everyone counts, and they should all be cared for. More youth-focused programs should be planned and strategically executed to train the willing in marketable life skills. The poor should be "empowered" with tools and equipment to create income for themselves. Academic programs should be enriched with classes in history and the civic process, ensuring that the young ones do not feel lost when listening to the news, and that they are equipped to engage with the political process later in life.

Beside enhancing the healthcare and education sectors, other factors, including better project planning, stronger technical partnerships, and high-quality, transparent financing arrangements are necessary to ensure infrastructure development in Nigeria. If business is booming and trade is increasing, more people will have the opportunity to work and live a dignified life.

Nigeria needs sincere, visionary leaders to achieve this: leaders who understand the need, and the present urgency, for wealth redistribution as a weapon to fight the country's pervasive poverty. Leaders who can use available resources, along with a large dose of (political) willpower to ensure that Nigeria has a highly educated, productive workforce in the shortest time possible. Resources must be directed toward faster industrialization and better economic growth. Nigerians need leaders who understand the role of mentorship, who can lead inclusively, and who are not afraid to take a back seat and let capable youths take over. Nigeria needs leaders who have abandoned the idea of monarchy, where power is held until death. Nigerians need leaders who do not care for sycophancy and who do not want to play anyone's godfather. Nigerian youths need leaders who are not afraid to stand with the young, protecting the interests of youths against the marauding hawks who care only for themselves. Nigeria can do with such leaders – Nigeria needs such leaders.

In addition to sincere, visionary leaders looking forward to a stronger Nigeria, youths should also be encouraged to think for themselves and act in the right ways. No matter how adequate the programs and implementations are, there will be the indolent, criminally minded, and selfish, along with those who will never work for a unified Nigeria. The hope for Nigeria's future glory rests on conscientious, right-thinking young Nigerians. The few who will think, speak, and take action to improve the country; youths who will not let the weight of daily challenges blind them from seeing the bigger picture. If youths focus, and if they shun the "I don't care" that has become the mantra of some, they can work together. They can make use of, and improve on, the achievements of pressure groups and civil society organizations like the Not Too Young to Run Movement, BudgIT, Enough is Enough, and others working to stop the rot, and place Nigeria on the path of accelerated development. They can demand, and achieve, all they desire for the good of the country.

In addition to leaders, Nigeria needs youths who believe in the dignity of honest labor and whose minds are decolonized. To take Nigeria to glory will require youths who believe in the equality of all ethnicities and genders that make up the country. Excellent youths, who have character and the simple virtues of truthfulness, diligence, humility, patience, kindness, and temperance; they will need to be liberal in accepting ethnicities, genders, religions, and regions. They will understand that they cannot afford to let the same schisms that held the older generations back at the start of independence continue to dog their heels. They will understand that even if their only option is civil disobedience, they must employ it to achieve their aims.

There are situations where democratic governments behave like autocratic ones, denying the will of their citizens. Governors behave like feudal overlords, and legislators forget that the Constitution says they can be recalled by the electorates who protest their uselessness. It is the youths who can be, and who must be, at the forefront of efforts to keep politicians and public officers on their toes, calling out bad behavior and unjust policies, laws, or actions. Youths are powerful in this regard; they can better plan, mobilize, and execute protests online and offline.

This is why politicians have largely relegated young party members to the role of canvassers, campaign rally organizers, and praise singers. Their willpower, freshness, and vigor will ensure the success of such protests, which must always be nonviolent in strategy and execution. Violent protests help no one. They only give security agencies a good reason to clap back even more violently. There are many options for nonviolent protests; even when a physical gathering of demonstrators is not possible, there are online methods to convey protest messages to the appropriate persons or bodies.

Youths must never forget or ignore this option when their elected officials seem to be making the wrong decisions or leading the country down the wrong path. They must explore combinations of tactics like demonstrations, workplace occupations, blockades, strikes, tax resistance, conscientious objection, sabotage, and sit-ins, as well as innovative, technology-enhanced digital civil disobedience tactics to expose corrupt practices, enforce justice, repeal unjust laws, and embarrass amoral politicians. Nigerian youths must take politics seriously – it is the single most important activity determining the trajectory of their lives and the lives of millions.

Conclusion

The "youth bulge" phenomenon and the alienation of Nigerian youths from political activities have been major issues of concern for political scientists and researchers as factors that would drive Africa into more democratic and political instability if proper measures are not taken. And the active engagement of the youths in political activities transcends the premises of politics and governance, and limitless socioeconomic benefits that would accrue from the meaningful participation of youths in politics. This active participation of the youths at the moment is not only crucial to the advancement of the present society, it likewise projects into the future of the society's governance and leadership as each generation has a unique conception of shaping and what defines these phenomena.

As revealed in this discourse, there is the need to make the political system more flexible to include the active participation of youths. The rigidity that shrouds politics and governance in Nigeria makes it unappealing to the youths whose generation is characterized by postmodernity and popular cultures. The distance maintained by political powers, leaders, and parties from the general and other aspects of life with which the youths are more engaged is a turnoff: the youths do not see a reflection of themselves in political activities nor the immediate (beneficial) relation of politics in their lives, at least in the simplest terms that would attract them to it. Hence, there is the need to refashion the political system to actively engage other spheres of life, which the youths find relevance in.

Therefore, the need for the government to intensify their political outreach programs to the youth especially cannot be overstressed, foregrounding how active participation in politics and governance of society holds a direct and immediate relation with youths' existence as well as the democracy of the society. There is the need to introduce the youths to civic duties and activities at a very young age, both in school curriculum and outside to instill the zeal, the necessity, and the process of engaging in nation-building activities. Political participation is spurred on and manifested by the advancement of political knowledge. Coupled with the traditional media, the technological media should be adequately utilized as a tool of political socialization to engage the youths in political participation.

The integration of youths as a political force would not only see to their adequate representation in political activities but would also help to ensure the vital issues concerning youths are adequately addressed. The availability and access to information via technological media is a formidable resource the Nigerian youths can utilize to harness themselves and propagate their political ambitions. However, there is the need to actualize online activism into real-life political engagement and criticism. During the 2019 Nigerian general election, the presidential candidate of the African Alliance Congress raised the bulk of his campaign funds and awareness through and on social media. Therefore, there is the need for the youths to capitalize on the power-altering dynamics[46] of the social media and other technological media to actualize their active inclusion in politics.

While there are no absolute or one-time solutions to the problem of youth disengagement with politics and governance, the need to attend to its underlying factors cannot be overstressed. The need to strengthen the educational system, increase economic empowerment, create viable economic opportunities, eradicate hunger and poverty, and provide basic medical care are some of the vital issues cutting across Nigerian states responsible for youth apathy and violent engagement with politics.

---

[46] Ojoka and Acol, "Connecting the Dots," 104.

20 Hashtags and Social Protests: Reformation and Revolution in the Age of Social Media

Introduction

Technology, from its earliest inception to its numerous inventions, has been a vital component of reformation and revolution that characterizes each age and period across the globe, actively or passively. Technology poses a threat to rigid tradition and autocracy, as the constant transformation of society is defined by it and vice versa. From printing technology to social media, the various manifestations of technology have established themselves as important agencies of development. Printing technology, both as a technological invention and a mass medium, particularly helped to suppress the domineering leadership of the Medieval European church on state control. As expressed by Renato Rosaldo: "Roughly during the first century after Gutenberg's invention, print did as much to perpetuate blatant errors as it did to spread enlightened truth,"[1] which opposed the conventional "reality" established by the church and papacy.

Manuel Castells argues that societal development is not directly anchored to the invention of new technologies, but rather that the creative adoption of communication technologies by humans is what restructures society,[2] and accordingly, "online social media have been found to be the most common gateway into digital activism, even though none of these electronic tools were created with activism in mind."[3] Technological inventions are meant to stir social change and social movements, which have found a stronger root in the transformational dimension of social media.

Social media is a vital manifestation of globalization, as well as its evolution and transformation. The most compelling feature, arguably,

---

[1] Renato Rosaldo, "The Cultural Impact of the Printed Word, A Review Article," *Comparative Studies in Society and History* 23 (1981): 508.

[2] See Manuel Castells and Gustavo Cardoso, eds., *The Network Society: From Knowledge to Policy* (Baltimore: Center for Transatlantic Relations, 2006).

[3] Summer Harlow and Lei Guo, "Will the Revolution be Tweeted or Facebooked? Using Digital Communication Tools in Immigrant Activism," *Journal of Computer-Mediated Communication* 19 (2014): 463.

of social media is its advanced modification of the availability of information; with the help of social media, information, constantly regenerating, is made readily available almost instantaneously to a large number of audiences in different places across the world, and each person has the autonomy to modify or mediate such information. This has contributed to the mass mobilizing effect of this technological media toward revolution and protest. In common terms, social media can be defined as the "Internet-based tools and services that allow users to engage with each other, generate content, distribute, and search for information online."[4] They are characterized by the alteration of the single and parallel approach to communication that defines most traditional media.

Social media represents a new generation of media and communication, especially among Millennials and Gen Z, which seeks to disrupt boundaries and the rigidity of information imposed by traditional media. Its boundless and constant regeneration of information is the central component that has enabled it to become relevant to all spheres of human life and endeavors and enabled its users to be simultaneously consumers and producers of information. Also, the ability of social media to blur the social divide between rich and poor has established it, perhaps, as a democratic tool that unites a large pool of people in solidarity regardless of class, gender, cultural, religious, language, ethnic, or regional barriers. The dimensions and scope of social media itself are revolutionary and reformative.

Social media is the only modern genre with communication integrated with the possibility to access information in audio, video, and text formats without one compromising the other; in situations where more than one format is adopted, one becomes a complement or exploration of the others, providing real-time evidence and (always available) coverage like no other media genre has been able to achieve in human history. Likewise, social media has established itself as a vital coordinating mechanism for the formation of social movements, as its dynamism cuts across various components relevant to the efficiency of such groups, among which are communication, organization, mobilization, and execution.[5] From revolutionary movements, reform movements, identity movements, reactionary movements, innovative movements, or conservative movements, social media has become a mechanism vital to the processes and all types of social movements. That the make-up of both social media and social movements are revolutionary is no mere coincidence; it indicates

---

[4] Onyedikachi Madueke et al., "The Role of Social Media in Enhancing Political Participation in Nigeria," *IDOSR Journal of Arts and Management* 2, no. 3 (2017): 48.

[5] See Clay Shirky, "The Political Power of Social Media," *Foreign Affairs* 90, no. 1 (2011): 28–41.

the mutual complementarity of both phenomena toward the progress of society.

On the other hand, social media helps to create the immediate awareness needed to prevent social movements from escalating into violence, as the various responsible security and government agencies are alerted almost instantaneously about planned or ongoing incidents. For example, immediate statements or responses can be released by the responsible government or leader to douse the heat being generated by a planned or ongoing protest with updates on social media, which helps to keep the citizens calm and reassures them that the government is interested in their well-being, compared to the silence and alienation that characterize the delay associated with traditional media. This offers both the people and the government a flexible democracy to check the excesses of one another without sacrificing the collective peace and development of society.

The deliberate refusal or inability of governments to attend to socioeconomic and political issues triggers anger and frustration among its citizens which gradually develops into protests and, in extreme cases, revolt. There is the need for a mass mobilizing catalyst to transform the raging anger of the masses into protest or some other form of social action to effect change. The traditional media used to be an effective channel of social-movement mobilization until their efforts and activities were clamped down by totalitarian authorities who suppress all voices that oppose or challenge their governance. Also, as communication agencies owned and controlled by the elites, the traditional media retains its old-age tradition of being partisan in view and does not always express the outbursts of the masses. However, with the advent of social media, social movements not only find a mass-mobilizing agent but a time- and cost-effective platform to drive the desired changes in society, which has placed it at the center of reformation and revolution in society.

Social Media and Social Movement

Social media is important not only because it is a medium through which information spreads, but also because it provides an opportunity, responsibility, and choice for the receptor as to what an individual will do with the information. It is in this capacity that people maintain agency and categorize themselves as passive bystanders or active participants.[6]

Social media helps to build a strong social network relevant to the success of a social movement. By garnering enough awareness and strengthening

---

[6] M. Alam, "Weighing the Limitations against the Added-Value of Social Media as a Tool for Political Change," *Democracy and Society* 8, no. 2 (2011): 19.

solidarity and trust ties among various political or identity groups, social media creates a hub of experiences common to everyone, which intensifies the objective of the movement and drives the strong will for collective action. Also, social media as a social movement tool gives the masses the added advantage to suitably frame the available information to achieve optimal results as against government interference, or even blockage, in traditional media. Collectivism is paramount to social movement, and social media as an activist tool enables it, from identity to framing and action.[7]

The limited control governments have over social media platforms affords multiple understandings of events or issues to a wide audience, thereby garnering the necessary audience. Of course, the counter-discourses that would be offered by state authorities and their supporters further establishes social media as a true agent of reformation, as it affords everyone the fundamental principle of democracy – the right to speech and expression. In principle, social media does not only help to strengthen solidarity, it can also (though not always) help to distill facts from fiction and therefore enable everyone to make the right decision. As identified by Jasper: "Participants in social movements constantly face choices. It is in those choices that we see the cultural meanings, moral sentiments, emotions, and forms of rationality of groups and individuals."[8] This free will to choose between discourses and narratives is what social media concretizes into strong will to execute an action.

The framing theory suggests that structural appeal guides the coordination, goal, and perception of a social movement, without which the actions and cause of the movement are bound to fail. The framing of a social movement through social media not only explains the issue that is of concern, but also provides the general audience with enough information to make a "personal frame" of the issue, either in solidarity or opposition. The accessibility of this tool of documentation and truthtelling by the general populace, "create linked activists who can contest the narrative crafting and information-controlling capabilities of authoritarian regimes."[9] This framing attempt through social media presents both the problem and the suggested solutions to it. Therefore, social

---

[7] Huma Haider, "Helpdesk Research Report: Social Media and Reform Networks, Protests, Social Movements and Coalitions," *Governance and Social Development Resource Centre* (2011): 1, www.gsdrc.org/docs/open/hd764.pdf.

[8] James Jasper, "A Strategic Approach to Collective Action: Looking for Agency in Social Movement Choices," *Mobilization: An International Journal* 9, no. 1 (2004): 10.

[9] Constance Duncombe, *The Twitter Revolution? Social Media, Representation and Crisis in Iran and Libya* (Cambria: Australian National University, 2011), 32.

media accomplishes the three tasks of the framing theory: diagnosis, prognosis, and motivation:

What is remarkable about protesting social movements in the age of CMC [computer mediated–communication] is that they frequently do not have a clearly identifiable leader or even set of leaders. The framing process that has almost always been top-down is more opaque in CMC.[10]

This, however, does not suggest lack of organization or disunity, but points to the fact that social media enables and promotes a democratic society where every voice is considered equal and can thrive in solidarity to achieve a common good. The collective spirit of equality and freedom harnesses the solidarity needed to drive the action of a social movement. The aim and effectiveness of social movement is to bring about social change by opposing the dominance, abuse of power, or ineffectiveness of certain social forces.

It is important to note that while the central agitations of a social movement are the most important to the cause of reformation and revolution, the immense contribution of social media to this cause is to help properly propel the direction and transform the built-up anger and frustration into a desired result without violence. In recent times, activists have capitalized on the mass mobilization of social media to stage protests, boycott government activities, criticize critical political issues, and organize rebellion as "these new technologies have brought down barriers to group action, which has allowed for new ways of gathering together and getting things done."[11]

Organizing protests of social movements through social media helps with resource mobilization theory, which states that there must be certain resources available to ensure the victory of a social action among which are mobilization and recruitment of new participants; leadership, which controls the direction of the movement, especially people with enormous influence to effect the desired change or garner the needed audience/ attention to do so; as well as funding, which social media not only helps to reduce, but also helps to gather through public funding when the need arises.

Social media has become a historical and sociological tool to organize and understand a social movement right from incipiency when a social challenge gains popularity; through coalescence, whence the problem

---

[10] Felix Tusa, "How Social Media Can Shape a Protest Movement: The Cases of Egypt in 2011 and Iran in 2009," *Arab Media and Society*, no. 17 (2013): 6.

[11] Haider, "Helpdesk Research Report," 2. It should be noted, however, that social movements are not always only about anger and frustration; some of them have also emerged in support of policy and action for government, and to frustrate opposing views.

becomes more foregrounded and the people become organized into a movement; to institutionalization, where both the movement and social issues gain the awareness of authorities; and to fragmentation and demise, which mark the end of a movement either due to partial or/full success, in the sense that it has achieved its aim, or due to the collapse of the movement due to lack of popular support among the people or suppression by authorities. This not only gives us a comprehensive view of a societal event and public history but helps us to better understand it and develop it. "Public history is constructed, not, in the main, for the purposes of posterity or objectivity, but for the aims of present action (conquest, social reform, building, political reorganization, economic transformation)."[12]

Alienation that often arises from participation in social movements, due to lack of information or time and space barriers, has been bridged by social media through its mass mobilization capacity and a sense of participation online, which not only aids the online mass mobilization but is also capable of influencing legitimization that can affect the desired change. The basic role of media in social movements is "to advance social movements by helping to deliver the movement's message and promoting actions to achieve its goals."[13] Hence, rather than focus on the argument of social media supplanting other communication agencies of social movement or its impact on the overall success/failure of the movement, as is in many studies, more efforts should be geared toward understanding the dynamics of social media in relation to social movements' agitations, as well as its tendency to increase solidarity and awaken true consciousness, particularly.

On the cohesive interrelationship between the technological media represented by social media and the traditional media, Brouwer and Bartel suggest that, "if we realize how social media is also embedded in mainstream media, such as television, then the multiplier effect of social media becomes even more apparent."[14] Aside from its mass mobilization effect, an often-underrepresented dimension of social media is its ability to identify and strengthen social capital (trust, loyalty, sympathy, solidarity, etc.). As suggested by Mario Diani, social capital is perhaps the most valuable outcome of social movement and should be the gauge of measurement for the success or failure of a social action:

[12] Charles Tilly, "Political Identities in Changing Polities," *Social Research* 70, no. 2 (2003): 613.
[13] Steven Gordon, "Fostering Social Movements with Social Media," *SSRN Electronic Journal* (2015): 1, http://ssrn.com/abstract=2708079.
[14] Lenie Brouwer and Edien Bartel, "Arab Spring in Morocco: Social Media and the 20 February Movement," *Afrika Focus* 27, no. 2 (2014): 15.

[T]he central problem is no longer whether and how mobilization campaigns, and cycles of protest determine specific changes at different levels of the political and the social system. It becomes instead whether they facilitate the emergence of new networks, which in turn allow advocacy groups, citizens' organizations, action committees, and alternative intellectuals and artists to be more influential in processes of political and cultural change.[15]

That is, the aim and process of a social movement does not terminate at the dying stage but continues at a revival stage that maximizes the social capital and guiding ideologies of the previous social movement. The intervention of social media enables exactly this as similar issues resurface after a period of time, which are then intensified by the background of the terminated movement that helps not only to drive the current issue toward a positive outcome but also to create an awareness of the need for a revolutionary movement to address the (multiple) replication of the same social problem in the future. Diani adds: "The impact of collective action will be stronger where permanent bonds of solidarity have emerged during the conflict."[16]

Where rage on social media does not lend credence or result in a social movement, social media becomes a coping mechanism which people resort to in order to express themselves and seek solace in the voices of others. Thus, social media has a position as a medium "to understand how society copes with crises and how communities leverage these tools for collective action."[17] Either way, it helps to curtail acts of violence that might ensue in the process of reformation and revolutionary agitation, as "social media have given social movements useful tools to coordinate and to undertake collective action."[18]

As identified by Gordon, the tactics of social movements aided by social media are awareness program, boycott coordination, fundraising, lobbying, negotiation, occupation, rally cry – use of symbols and street protests; while grievances leading to social movements as identified on social media are autocratic rule, lack of democracy, censorship, corporate greed and influence, corruption, economic inequality, electoral repression, government policies, general human rights, inflation, justice inequality, legal rights, living conditions, police brutality, poverty and hunger, racism repression, general secret detention, imprisonment, and unemployment.[19]

---

[15] Mario Diani, "Social Movements and Social Capital: A Network Perspective on Movement Outcomes," *Mobilization: An International Journal* 2, no. 2 (1997): 135.

[16] Ibid., 136.

[17] Munmun De Choudhury et al., "Social Media Participation in an Activist Movement for Racial Equality," *Proc Int AAAI Conf Weblogs Soc Media* (2017): 4.

[18] Regina Salanov, "Social Media and Political Change: The Case of the 2011 Revolutions in Tunisia and Egypt," ICIP working paper 7 (2012): 11.

[19] Gordon, "Fostering Social Movements with Social Media," 18–19.

Hashtags, Online Activism, and Social Protests

While public relations, social networking, and digital marketing have exposed social media as an efficient tool of communication and commercialization due to its immediate availability of information and wide audience, online protests and activism have revealed its capacity to engage in social movement activities as protests, polls, and criticism to drive society forward. The terrain and modus operandi of social movements have evolved with the interrelation of social media with the traditional media. The emergence of social movements and activism on social media owes its widespread origin to the so-called Arab Spring protests that took off from Tunisia in 2011, and which was a manifestation of the extent to which social media can mass mobilize and create global awareness without compromising the organization and effectiveness of physical protests either. It is on this premise that Brouwer and Bartel comment: "participating in a social movement, appropriating social media generates new meanings: it relocates the movement from a local, regional or national movement to one which is part of the global world, thereby uniting the local with the global."[20]

Hashtags have become the defining timeline of social media; they encapsulate the socioeconomic and political struggles that characterize a period and a society.[21] This online form of social movement has widely been regarded as "Hashtag Activism." This mechanism has been regarded as a "galvanizing tool for the otherwise voiceless, allowing such groups to effectively disseminate messages in a way and at a speed otherwise impossible with traditional media."[22] First introduced by Chris Messina in 2007, the hashtag is a metadata sorting mechanism on social media for proper categorization of information, preservation and easy accessibility, and, of course, attracting popularity, but it has evolved and gained prominence as an online social activism tool to drive the cause of a social movement/action by emphasizing the keyword, statement, or expression that defines the movement. Hashtags synthesize the power of language, technology, and social struggle to amass awareness for topical political and socioeconomic issues with the aim of effecting the desired change.

---

[20] Brouwer and Bartel, "Arab Spring in Morocco," 15.

[21] In a private communication, Farooq Kperogi pointed my attention to the limitation of hashtags, saying that they are not central to the architecture and effectiveness of all social media. "For instance, hashtags are ineffective on Facebook. Hashtags are important for discoverability of trends on kinds of social media platforms that are almost always public by default such as Twitter. Facebook's many privacy settings (private, limited, public, etc.) limit the utility of hashtags on it."

[22] Cynthia Igodo, "The Power of Social Media: Nigeria's Changing Feminist Movement," *The Republic* 3, no. 1 (2019), www.republic.com.ng/vol3-no1/the-power-of-social-media/.

Accordingly, Ofori-Oparku and Moscato observe, "Semiotically, hashtags mark the intended meaning of an utterance – what a statement is really about."[23] Hence, as a sorting mechanism, they become a method of identifying and synchronizing discourses and counter-discourses related to the thematic disposition they represent. As a technology-driven age antithetically characterized by the love for varieties, but with little patience for a catalogue of verbose information, social media and its tools like hashtags make the consumption of information (which is constantly being produced, from political, socioeconomic, religious, and cultural to environmental activism) easy, concise, and more accessible.

The most prominent genesis and successful trend of hashtag activism, undoubtedly, in Nigeria to date, is the #BringBackOurGirls movement founded by an Abuja-based lawyer, Ibrahim M. Abdullahi.[24] In no time, it received support from prominent activists such as Bukky Sonibare and Aisha Yusuf, and was championed by the former Minister of Education, Obiageli Ezekwesili. The movement is a solidarity of voices, led by women, to protest the kidnap of 276 Chibok Government Secondary School female students on April 14, 2014, in Borno State by the Boko Haram terrorist group. This campaign was not only spurred by the alarming increase of insecurity in the nation, but also due to the weakness of the mainstream media to give the situation the needed awareness and urgency. At the intervention of social media around the third week of the incident, it witnessed the support of Hillary Clinton and Michelle Obama calling for the Nigerian government to take quick and decisive steps to ensure the return of the abducted girls and curtail the reoccurrence of such incidents in the future.

As noted by Marissa Jackson, this movement is a manifestation of social media's reformative and revolutionary power: "[it] has thus far demonstrated the virtues of solidarity and grassroots international cooperation, within and beyond the African Diaspora. It has shed much meaningful light on how to make visibility and voice to the invisible and voiceless."[25] The "Bring Back Our Girls Movement" campaign is rightly reputed to be the most popular manifestation of hashtag social activism on the continent with regards to upholding human and women's rights. The transborder

---

[23] Sylvester Ofori-Parku and Derek Moscato, "Hashtag Activism as a Form of Political Action: A Qualitative Analysis of the #BringBackOurGirls Campaign in Nigerian, UK, and U.S. Press," *International Journal of Communication* 12 (2018): 2482.

[24] Kunbiti Nuoye, "Meet the Nigerian Lawyer Who Created #BringBackOurGirls Campaign," *The Grio*, May 9, 2014, https://thegrio.com/2014/05/09/nigeria-bringbackourgirls-twitter-missing-girls/.

[25] Marissa Jackson, "Nigeria: In Defence of Hashtags and #BringBackOurGirls," *The Guardian*, May 11, 2014, https://amp.theguardian.com/world/2014/may/11/Nigeria-bringbackourgirls-boko-haram/.

penetration of the online protest establishes social media's capacity to transform a reactionary movement from a national to a transnational movement to give it the needed attention. Being the first of its kind, donations and supports were pledged across the globe to seek the release and integration of the girls back into the community, using social media. Beyoncé dedicated a page on her website to solicit for funds for the movement under the caption "#ChimeIn and help bring back our girls."[26] Likewise, the campaign helped to solicit the political intervention and military support of foreign powers like Canada, the European Union, China, Israel, the United Kingdom, and the United States, etc., whose political leaders pledged intelligence and resources to ensure the release of the Chibok girls.

The campaign not only invalidated the usual criticism against online activism's failure to manifest as true-life physical protest, but it also partially achieved its aim – the return of some of the kidnapped girls, although 112 girls are still missing many years later. Thousands of people, notable entertainment celebrities, and political figures were photographed with placards and papers with signs of solidarity expressing support for the movement, usually with the movement's popular hashtag #BringBackOurGirls, or alternative hashtags like #TheChibokGirls, #RescueOurChibokGirls, #BBOG, or #StolenDreams, which render the same awareness and relevance to the movement and even help to create more awareness.

There have been other incidents which led to public campaigns. For instance, when the release of a captive, Leah Shaibu, was refused by the terrorist group as a result of her refusal to deny her faith, the hashtag #FreeLeahShaibu occupied social space in solidarity with her release and justice. #FreeCiaxon is yet another but similar movement to ensure the release of one Yusuff Siyaka Onimisi (@Ciaxon) who was detained for about two weeks for protesting online on the embarrassing jailbreak in Abuja.[27] Liberation campaigns are always directed at an opposing force that violates the exercise of human rights.

The effectiveness of hashtags and social media in fighting for human rights has stimulated a new wave of feminism popularly described as "hashtag feminism." Due to the privacy issues mass awareness, and social media as a coping mechanism, more women are turning to social media to express their anguish on the inhumane and unjust treatment they experience by virtue of being a woman, and in so doing, their hope to encourage

[26] Beyoncé, "#BEYGOOD, #BRINGBACKOURGIRLS," Beyoncé, May 8, 2014, www.beyonce.com/bringbackourgirls/.

[27] Cordelia Hebblewaite, "#BBCtrending: Lessons from Nigeria on Social Media Activism," BBC, April 12, 2014, https://www.bbc.com/news/blog-trending-27026755/.

others to voice out, seek solidarity and justice or equality, as the case may be. Unlike how the #BringBackOurGirls movement gained prominence from Nigeria to nations beyond, the #MeToo movement gained its vitality by soliciting for corresponding manifestations of sexual harassment experiences of women across all nations, all which are further subcategorized under the movement.

The #MeToo campaign, hence, is a hashtag feminist movement that seeks to ameliorate the unjust treatment and experiences of women by unburdening the victims from the trauma or stigma of the experience. As a feminist movement, it aims at a socio-psychological liberation of women across differences in age, class, space, and time. "[D]eveloped by American civil rights activists, Tarana Burke ... highlighting the prevalence of sexual assault and sexual harassment particularly in the workplace,"[28] it quickly gained awareness not only because of social media, but also because it attends to an often-neglected feminist concern: trauma and stigmatization of women.

In Nigeria, a popular manifestation of this is the #YabaMarch movement, which protests the indiscriminate sexual harassment of ladies at the popular Yaba market in Lagos, Nigeria, by sellers, and "this led to calls from women across Nigeria for a similar march in their cities."[29] Again, this online activism did not end with online rage and rants as social media activism critics would have us believe. A protest march was successfully organized as a physical manifestation of the campaign, which invariably helped to further create awareness about the issue as all activities in the market were at a standstill and, of course, helped to caution the sellers on the unmannered gestures (which oftentimes are intentionally sexual) toward potential customers. After the protest, social media platforms were filled with testimonies of women, many of whom were not even part of the activism, who corroborated the success of the protest.

The #MeToo movement witnessed a surge in rape narratives by traumatized women, accentuating the fact that "social media platforms have enabled a new crop of tech-savvy activists to emerge, energizing people through personal stories in a bid to create shared experiences and a sense of camaraderie."[30] As a larger online feminist movement, sympathy and solidarity are two key features of the movement, through which it set out to seek justice and equality in society. For example, #IStandWithBusola is a solidarity expression seeking truth and justice for Busola Dakolo, the wife of a popular Nigerian Gospel singer, who has levied rape allegations against one Pastor Biodun Fatoyinbo of the Commonwealth of Zion Assembly (COZA). Busola's testimony and narrative unleashed other

---

[28] Igodo, "The Power of Social Media."   [29] Ibid.   [30] Ibid.

sexual allegations against the same pastor, and established a previous case, by Ese Walter, as most likely true; hence, it "creates a sense of community for women"[31] on related feminist issues. Her narrative establishes the psychosocial aim of the #MeToo movement as an important feminist liberation ideology.

So, due to several narratives indicating the prevalence of sexual harassment in churches across the nation and even beyond, the hashtag #NotInMyChurch has been designated to protest further occurrence of such incidents in churches, which are assumed as places of fortification, redemption, and consolation.[32] Ironically, some have designated it to express the nonoccurrence of such incidents in their churches. While this seems a counter-discourse, it rather should be viewed as an alternative narrative, which still bears the same goal of the need to bar such atrocities from places of worship. Owing to limitless freedom of expression, issues, and discourses on social media quickly "escalate" into several anti- and counter-discourses.

Ettobe Meres notes that divisions arise, largely due to politics, from the use of hashtags on social media to protest an unwelcomed sociopolitical or economic event or act.[33] But what is more important is that these campaigns have unearthed several fault lines of our society, which is still deemed patriarchal, and has generated a worrisome level of misandry under the campaign #MenAreScum. These energized female voices are relentless, foremost, in psychologically liberating themselves, establishing communal bonds and solidarity with others, and seeking social justice for oppressed women. Hence, they have pledged to no longer be mute: #WeWillNotBeSilent.

The #SexForMarks campaign was prompted by a leaked audio detailing a conversation between one Professor Richard Akindele of the Obafemi Awolowo University with one of his female postgraduate students, requesting sex in exchange for marks. This campaign especially helps to draw long-overdue attention to the improper advances of Nigerian lecturers toward their students who look up to them as models

---

[31] Ibid.

[32] #FreeTheSheepies is an online campaign initiated by a popular on-air personality, Daddy Freeze, whose stance on religious issues continues to generate controversy among the Christians in Nigeria. He has fiercely attacked the domineering control of religions, especially Christianity, over the people, as the former hinders the people from facing reality, which is a contributing factor to the lingering backwardness of our society, according to him, including such issues as the payment of tithes, first fruits, prayers of ill wishes on one's enemy, etc.

[33] Ettobe David Meres, "Nigeria: A Nation Divided by Hashtags, Two Protests with Half Momentum," *The Nerve Africa*, February 4, 2017, https://the-nerveafrica.com/9902/Ni geria-a-nation-divided-by-hastags-two-protests-with-half-momentum.

and tutors, but are rather often coerced by threats of failure for sex in exchange for high grades or other favors.

These online feminist social movements are driven by the need to curtail the unfair harassment of women, especially the rape culture. #EndRape and #SayNoToRape are popular hashtags that encapsulate this protest. The increasing rate of child molestation in the country, and some other nations on the continent, has escalated the agitations for justice for raped women/girls and the need for stiff policies to end the malice. A popular example of such a campaign seeking justice for a child molestation is #JusticeForOchanya, a campaign requesting the prosecution of Andrew Ogbuja who repeatedly raped 13-year-old Ochanya Obaje Elizabeth, which later resulted in multiple health complications for her and her eventual death. Like the campaign demanding the release of Leah Sharibu, the image of the molested child and her abuser were widely circulated across the social media to create mass awareness on the increasing rate of female child molestations in society; to encourage other young girls to speak up if they have ever been sexually molested; to alert parents on the need to be cautious of their children's wellbeing, especially when they are not within reach; and to stimulate the responsible authorities to take necessary actions toward prosecuting the offenders. These campaigns and others like them have largely been successful, as they have been able to create the necessary awareness about the cruelty suffered by victims, seek justice for the offenders, as well as spur the legislators to formulate policies that would ensure the occurrence of such incidents are forbidden and their perpetrators well prosecuted.

Other prominent campaigns on social media around children's rights in Nigeria are #PenNotPenis, #StopChildMarriage, #GirlsNotProperty, #StopFemaleCircumcision, #WifeNotMaid, etc., which are agitating for the need to educate young children in Nigeria, especially females, as the level of illiteracy in sub-Saharan Africa keeps swirling; protesting the culture and practice of child marriage, which further contributes to the increasing levels of illiteracy, poverty, and health complications for such children; and agitating for gender equality between men and women in society to stop the unfair treatment of girls and women across all sectors of life, especially in the family as wives, mothers, or daughters. These movements aim for the delimitation of women's rights and capacities as equal humans in society.

Like #MeToo, the campaign #BlackLivesMatter is a global movement that originated from America but soon found solidarity and its manifestation across different places of the world. The movement began with a Facebook post of Alicia Garza on the random and reckless shooting of African American males by police in America. This hashtag-cum-movement resurfaces every time such an incident is repeated. Patrisse Khan-Cullors and Opal Tometi later co-originated the hashtag https:/blacklivesmatter. As corroborated by Gordon, "A number of hash tags, each appropriate to the purportedly unnecessary death of an African-American man at the hands of police, has been used in social media tweets and posts in support of the Black Lives Matter movement."[34] In addition to the transborder power and effectiveness of social media activism, the #BlackLivesMatter campaign indicates the continuous relevance of online activism.

In Nigeria, a similar movement protesting the indiscriminate shooting of young males by the Special Anti-Robbery Squad (SARS) is designated under the hashtags #EndSARS, #ReformSARS, #StopKillingUs, #StopKillingOurYoungMen, etc., all pointing to and creating mass awareness on the shooting of young men by the Nigerian Police force, especially the Anti-Robbery unit. Aside from random killings and shootings, Muneer Yaqub reported, "SARS, has over the years, earned a notorious reputation of a brutal agency following cases of extrajudicial killing, torture, ill-treatment of detainees, and extortion of suspects."[35] It is a common practice among the operatives of this police force to forcefully search the phones and other gadgets, even houses and rooms, of everyone they deem fit to be a crime suspect, especially young men (students), without the observing proper right nor with legal warrant to do so, and when such acts of intrusion are denied, they resort to violence. This online movement is responsible for several protest marches across the country, especially in Lagos and Abuja, against these harassments and acts of violence, and to seek justice for the victims of such crimes, both of which helped to drive the reformation of the police unit from SARS to FSARS (Federal Special Anti-Robbery Squad).

The youth population, like women, has been at the center of online activism across the globe, especially in underdeveloped and developing nations. In Nigeria, social media has been adopted as a safer channel of social and political revolutions among the youths whom Fela, the Afro-beats superstar, taunted as jittery and scared of death, and hence reluctant to revolt against their oppressive leaders for the fear of causing their parents and family sorrow. So, where outright physical revolts are repressed by government agencies, social media is adopted as a communication agency to gain broader audiences for their agitations. #LazyNigerianYouth quickly gained an ironical twist to the statement of the president on the slothfulness of Nigerians toward work and economic productivity. The Nigerian youths

---

[34] Gordon, "Fostering Social Movement with Social Media," 15.

[35] Muneer Yaqub, "SARS Has Turned Rogue: Nigeria Should End It Now," *African Liberty*, April 15, 2019, www.africanliberty.org/2019/04/15/sars-has-turned-rogue-nigeria-should-end-it-now/.

had seized the moment to further lament the terrible state of the economy which has failed to provide them gainful employment and, worse still, crumbled the little micro-businesses they invested in. Likewise, social media platforms were flooded with narratives and images depicting successful and hardworking Nigerian youth, captioned as #LazyNigerianYouth to downplay the seriousness and validity of the president's comment.

The increasing rate of suicide among Nigerian youths due to depression and economic hardship has resulted into the #SuicideIsNotAnOption campaign, which is a solidarity movement among the youth to proffer psychological and economic solutions to the challenges they often encounter. This movement seeks to bring the attention of the political leaders to the increasing rate of suicide among the youths, so they provide a more equitable society where the youth are empowered and can thrive and contribute. Largely, this movement is responsible for the proclaimed ban of Sniper products, which oftentimes have been used by victims to commit suicide. A similar campaign is #SayNoToDrugs, which addresses the prevalent menace of hard drug use and abuse among Nigerian youths.

Soon enough, demonstrations and protests are symbolized by hashtags across social media to further push their awareness and participation, and thus facilitate their effectiveness. In the alienation of the youths in Africa from active political participation, #NotTooYoungToRun gained massive awareness among the youths as its focus is central to the well-being of the youths and the masses. Also, youths' access to the Internet, new media, technology, and social media helped to actualize the aim of the movement by driving legislation reformation policies that would embrace the youths in political participation as political leaders. Additional social media campaigns directed at the youth toward ideal political participation are the #VoteNotFight and #VoteNotViolence hashtags. These aim to curb the rate and occurrence of violence during election periods – usually perpetrated by the political elites through the youths – to sensitize the youths and everyone on the benefits of a safe and fair election.

The increasing rates of terrorism and insecurity in the nation is another issue that has gained huge traction online in Nigeria and beyond. The menace was spotlighted by the #BringBackOurGirls movement, and other dimensions of the insecurity crises. As noted by Isa Sanusi, "if we situate it within the context of conflicts in Nigeria . . . it is only a symbol of how vulnerable life is for millions of Nigerians living in areas affected by such conflicts."[36]

---

[36] Darius Sadighi, "How Hashtag Activism Helped Raise Awareness about Boko Haram: It Started with #BringBackOurGirls," *Teen Vogue*, May 12, 2017, www.teenvogue.com/story/how-hashtag-activism-helped-raise-awareness-about-boko-haram/.

The #BokoHaram hashtag gained popularity from every terrorist attack perpetrated by the insurgency group, thereby compelling the government to take more security actions to ensure the safety and lives of its citizens as well as to sympathize with the victims of the several conflicts. This activism on insecurity in the nation also helped to highlight other security challenges in the nation, notably under the campaign #BeyondHashtags,[37] which has been responsible for the widening gyre of terrorism and insurgency in the nation. Among the challenges are lack of security intelligence and surveillance systems, weak defense/security budget, lack of modern-day weaponry and security equipment, incompetence and poor motivation among security personnel due to terrible welfare, etc. Citizens are concerned with how best to deal with the security challenge in the nation, from the active advocacy to end terrorism and the need for trauma centers to attend to the emotional shock and trauma of the victims and their families, to the provision of security infrastructures to allow them to alert the responsible security institutions during security challenges. These advocacy efforts are sub-categorized under the #CitizenSolutionToEndTerrorism campaign.

The continuous killings by Fulani herdsmen has prompted such campaigns as #BenueKilling and the #BloodOnTheFlag campaign to bring awareness to the havoc wreaked by these unfortunate incidents. Concerned Nigerians, especially celebrities, took to social media by uploading morbid images and videos depicting both the act and the horrors caused by the marauders, and hoping by so doing to appeal to the emotions of the people, especially those not directly affected in other regions of the country or outside it, to rise up and bring an end to the bloodshed. International solidarity and emotional sympathy are crucial to the success of these social movements, which have been described as "the public sense of shared grievance and potential for change [that] can develop rapidly through shared communication via the social media."[38] While these gruesome images and videos are censored on traditional media, even the unbiased/uncontrolled ones, thereby underplaying the severity of events and issues, social media channels motivate and aid citizen journalism which helps to provide broad and uncensored evidence and information on issues and events across time and space in real time.

It is no surprise that the traditional media outlets also take recourse to social media platforms to obtain some of this freely available information,

---

[37] Samuel Okocha, "Beyond the Hashtags: Nigerians Seek Lasting Solution to Boko Haram Insurgency," *Rewire News*, March 22, 2014, https://rewire.news/article/201/05/22/beyo nd-the-hashtags-nigerians-seek-lasting-solution-to-boko-haram-insurgency/.

[38] Ihediwa Nkemjika Chimee and Amaechi M. Chidi, "Social Media and Political Change in the 21st Century: The African Experience," *Glocalism: Journal of Culture, Politics and Innovation* 1 (2016): 19.

hopefully with more research to validate its authenticity. Felix Tusa agrees: "Technology [has] allowed people to share not simply information about how and when to protest, but more importantly, to share images and videos that contributed to a different interpretation of events than that which the authorities themselves wished."[39] #LightUpNigeria, #EndBankCharges, and #FuelScarcity are other popular hashtag campaigns that have been adopted by the masses to agitate for a better welfare system and an improved standard of living in the country.

Due to their massive popularity, the vital function of hashtags has shifted domain from sorting mechanisms in computation to the historical development of democracy and human rights in various communities across the globe. They can be used as historical nodes to trace the evolvement of a society from one point in time to another. For example, #BringBackOurGirls is a codification of a turbulent historical period in the socioreligious democracy of Nigeria, while #NotTooYoungToRun captures the sociopolitical wave against the denomination of power by the older generation and the alienation of youths from political participation and key governance decisions. Thus, these hashtags assume a techno-metaphoric state upon which the historical occurrence of the present or past can be understood, especially from multifarious perspectives.

Social Media and Global Petitions from Nigeria

Similarly, social media helps in raising awareness over topical issues of global concern that have evolved into petitions on online platforms. Unlike hashtags, these petitions usually require the signatures (names and email address) of thousands or millions of people globally to affect their aim. Change.org, GoPetition.com, IPetition.com, Petitions.net, Petitionsite.com, Openpetition.eu, and Avaaz.org are popular examples of online platforms that allow people to create petitions easily and at no cost. In Nigeria, among such petitions are ones against the marriage of female children at an illegal age, the circumcision of girls, the rape and sexual exploitation of women, the instability of power supplies, etc. These petitions across the sociopolitical and economic spectrum of national existence have helped to garner significant awareness and solidarity both within and outside the boundaries of the nation and necessitated certain steps to be taken in resolution of the raised issues. For example, there are ongoing deliberations in Nigeria on the severity of punishment for the rape of women and especially children, to maximally curb the

---

[39] Tusa, "How Social Media Can Shape a Protest Movement," 2.

crime and violence. This legislation has been driven by online activism and petitions.

Unlike hashtags, online petitions garner awareness and effectiveness from millions of people lending their voices to the movement by signing the petition and thereafter sharing it with their friends and families across several social media platforms. These petitions remain active till the desired aim or result is achieved. Sometimes, these petitions are meant to only create awareness. For example, the aim of the "#OpenGovtNG – I Promote Public Service Transparency & Accountability in Nigeria" petition started on Change.org by the Young African Leadership Initiative states: "We believe that this public commitment will serve as an accountability check and increase your consciousness, now and in the future to imbibe greater accountability and transparency in public service."[40] Activism to seek justice is also the forte of online petitions. Thousands of voices and signatures have been gathered on Change.org to petition the physical assault of a nursing mother by Senator Elisha Cliff Ishaku, who also happens to be the youngest senator in Nigeria; the goal is to condemn the unjust treatment of women and Nigerian citizens by the political elites.

In 2018, a petition on Change.org started by Jeremiah Shallangwa and signed by thousands of Nigerian youths protested the high cost of internet connections in Nigeria; this exorbitant cost strains their educational and entrepreneurial development, which creates a digital divide that further alienates them from accessing necessary information. "Titled 'End high internet subscription charges for Spectranet, Smile and Ntel in Nigeria'," Shallangwa said, "Internet providers charge too much for internet service, despite poor network coverage. They keep increasing the p1rize (price) of the internet without improving their service."[41] "Stop Child Marriage in Nigeria!," "Pay Former Nigeria Airways Staff and bring back Nigeria Airways," and "Stop the Violence Against Women in Nigeria" are all petitions pertaining to the socioeconomic welfare of Nigeria signed on GoPetition.com.[42]

Social Media and Political Participation in Nigeria

Accessible social media platforms offer ordinary citizens the opportunity to interact more directly and actively with their political systems. Social

---

[40] Young African Leadership Initiative, "#OpenGovtNG – I Promote Public Service Transparency & Accountability in Nigeria," www.change.org/p/nigerian-youths-opengovtng-i-promote-public-service-transparency-accountability-in-Nigeria/.

[41] Aderemi Ojekunle, "Nigerians Are Signing a Petition against the High Cost of Internet Subscription," *Pulse*, November 22, 2018, www.pulse.ng/tech-nigerians-are-signing-a-petition–against-the-high-cost-of-internet-subscription/h7sn64.

[42] See: www.gopetition.com/petition-campaigns.Nigeria/.

media tools also possess the potential to allow diaspora communities to get involved in social-political processes.[43]

Social media has, since its inception, established itself as a formidable medium of participation in global politics, especially in developing countries whose citizens aspire for better development and freedom of speech, amidst other fundamentals of true democracy. Hence, social media offers the dual benefit of effective participation in political activities with a reasonable measure of safety. As these media are global tools, it is impossible for the government of a region to effectively clamp them down, and the masses utilize this liberation to their advantage to express their struggles and pain. The first of the major interventions of social media in global politics is recorded during the 2008 presidential campaign of the former American leader, President Barack Obama. In this instance, social media gained relevance in creating political awareness and mass mobilization through social branding strategies. This techno-political participation has since changed the dimension of political engagement between political leaders and their followers, as well as between followers and political participation (governance). It has helped in "shaping political communication by segmenting its audience through diversification of coverage and exposure. By weakening the gate-keeping role in social media, political communications are formed and shaped."[44]

In recent years, active political participation promoted as the most effective revolution strategy for the masses to reform governance, drive development, and uphold democracy. Social media has not only made participation in politics easier and cheaper, but also more efficient and encompassing. Popular social media platforms like Facebook, Twitter, and LinkedIn are continuously breaking the regimented boundaries between the political leaders/elites and the masses, as they've become more accessible compared to the period of pre–popular social media. Political leaders not only have a broad avenue to reach out to their followers, but the platforms can also be utilized as well to garner popular opinion about issues and governance activities, and as such reform the system of governance and help cater to the immediate needs of the people. This medium of conducting opinion polling is not only convenient and affordable for both parties, as it requires almost no cost, but also renders

---

[43] Michael Aleyomi and Olanrewaju Ajakaiye, "The Impact of Social Media on Citizens' Mobilization and Participation in Nigeria's 2011 General Elections," *Centrepoint Journal* 17, no. 2: 39.

[44] Madueke et al., "The Role of Social Media in Enhancing Political Participation in Nigeria," 49.

an almost immediate result as individual responses are automatically collated by the technological media, which makes the process very credible.

In creating awareness, politics in Nigeria gained massive social media attention during the 2011 presidential election when Goodluck Jonathan announced his intention to run for the presidency. Madueke et al.,[45] note that from the moment of his declaration to the period of election, his followership increased from 217,000 to over half a million, while he gained 4,000 followers in the space of 24 hours of declaring his intent to run. While there is no actual connection between his social media followership and eventual victory at the polls, it does, however, highlight the potential that is latent in the use of social media in politics to drive massive and grassroots reformation. Aptly put: "Elections may not be won on social media but perceptions are shaped there. More often than not, these perceptions even influence and shape the mind of the social media users which are over 11.2 million Nigerians on the choices of their candidate."[46]

Interestingly, the social media that contributed to the popular choice of Goodluck Jonathan during the 2011 presidential election turned against him during the #OccupyNigeria campaign, which protested the removal of subsidies from petroleum products and the scarcity that prevailed thereafter. This wave of negative popularity, amidst other corrupt practices that thrived during his tenure, culminated in his loss in the 2015 presidential election to Muhammadu Buhari, who had quickly capitalized on the weakness of Jonathan's administration by promising Nigerians change. When suspicions were aroused due to election postponement, #March4Buhari became a political campaign to both express the solidarity for Buhari and condemn the undue postponement of the election.

The #Change movement started by the 2015 Buhari administration to provide a better living standard to Nigerian citizens, and more especially the agenda to end corruption, helped to start a new #ChangeStartsWithMe campaign to create awareness on the collective efforts of everyone to end corruption. When the life of a notable Nigerian scholar and activist, Pius Adesanmi, was lost to a plane crash – on top of the failure of the Buhari government to end corruption, as pledged during his election campaign – Nigerians creatively commenced the #PIUSMoreThanACountry campaign to achieve two things: mourn the death of Pius, and ridicule the failure of the government to deliver its agendas. Hence, citizens like Pius

---

[45] Ibid., 45.
[46] Emmanuel Obarisiagbon, Osagie Agbontaen, and Mohammed Gujbawu, "A Sociological Investigation into the Influence of the New Media on Political Mobilization: A Study of Nigeria's 2015 Presidential Election," *New Media and Mass Communication* 58 (2017): 12.

Figure 20.1 An anti-corruption crusader wearing a hashtag.

are more pious than a country with corrupt political leaders. Also, #WhereIsOurPresident and #BuhariMustGo are examples of social media campaigns that have been used to address vital issues since the victory of President Muhammadu Buhari in 2015.

A tangible correlation has been established between social media and political participation in Nigeria. Social media platforms serve as convenient and immediate avenues to make political contributions and likewise facilitate active involvement in "real-life" politics, as they catalyze and promote political activities. On the other hand, social media has not reduced nor can it eliminate the formal modes of political participation. Rather, it seeks to revolutionize them to conform with modern-day technological developments, and by so doing, make them more effective and appealing. Hence, political participation via social media should be considered an aid and component to broad spectrum political participation.

Contrary to the popular opinion that Nigerian youths are disengaged from political participation, active or passive, researches on the role of social media in enhancing political participation have revealed that quite a huge number of youths are involved in numerous innovative forums and platforms across the Internet, actively engaging in political discussion and making the necessary efforts to effect what they deem to be the solution to the sociopolitical menace ravaging the nation. As noted by Ezema et al., there is an upsurge in the "use of social networking media for participation in government programmes and policies"[47] in Nigeria, especially via Facebook, Twitter, and Google+, which are considered the most utilized social media platforms by Nigerian youths, "for a number of [whom], online participation is a gateway to meaningful engagement in political life"[48] and political participation is simply defined "as all voluntary activities that aim to influence political decisions at all levels of the political system."[49]

In addition to the aforementioned, an often-overlooked ingenious social network popular among the Nigerian youth (and even beyond the age group) to discuss vital economic and sociopolitical issues is *Nairaland*, founded by Oluwaseun Osewa in 2005. It should likewise be noted that the lack of proper information is also responsible for the inadequate participation in politics in general, which is not only particular to the youth, and this obstacle is what social media has helped to resolve, thereby increasing the rate of political participation across the country by encouraging the citizens to make more informed decisions on political issues and actions. Needless to say, "Youth today get their political information from Facebook rather than the legacy media such as radio, television and newspaper[s]. The information given is more interactive, user friendly, concise and easier to comprehend."[50]

It would not only be inaccurate but also uninformed to debate the involvement of youths in the current trends of political activities, given they have revolutionized the ideology of participating in politics to become a weapon by which they can shape and take charge of the development of the country. In the 2018 general elections in Nigeria, voting to rule became a popular ideology among the youth; hence the Permanent Voters Card (PVC) is accorded the power of a revolutionary tool. This revolutionary political ideology among the youths started such hashtag campaigns as #EveryPVCCounts to create awareness on the importance of voting as a political activity that shapes the well-being of everyone. This engagement is what Dogona et al., describe as "a form of pro-activism and its importance thus cannot be overestimated."[51] These

---

[47] Ifeanyi Ezema, Christian Ezeah, and Benedict Ishiwu. "Social Networking Services: A New Platform for Participation in Government Programmes and Policies among Nigerian Youths," *Libres* 25, no. 1 (2015): 45.

[48] Z. K. Dagona, H. Karick, and F. M. Abubakar, "Youth Participation in Social Media and Political Attitudes in Nigeria," *Journal of Sociology, Psychology and Anthropology in Practice* 5, no. 1 (2013): 3.

[49] M. Bello, H. Yusuf, and M. Akinola, "Social Media Usage and Political Participation among University Undergraduates for Political Stability in Nigeria," 3, no. 1 (2017): 71.

[50] Shamsu Abdu, Bahtiar Mohamad, and Suhaini Muda, "New Perspectives to Political Participation among Youth: The Impact of Facebook Usage," *The European Proceedings of Social & Behavioural Sciences* (2016): 131.

[51] Dagona, Karick, and Abubakar, "Youth Participation in Social Media and Political Attitudes in Nigeria," 3.

campaigns were soon supported by political parties and their contestants, election bodies, and corporate organizations to further foreground the aims of the movement. However, one must clarify that while there is increased involvement of youths in political activities, the fraction of those involved is relatively low compared to the huge population of youth in the country.

Reforms and revolution are necessary tools of political participation, regardless of the latter's negative associations. However, with social media, sociopolitical revolution has been rendered more efficient through mass mobilization and global awareness, and less violent by disengaging from physical confrontations. The ideology of protest has shifted from what obtained before the widespread usage of social media; hence, the fear expressed in Fela's lyrics[52] about Nigerians/Africans not willing to protest their suppression is increasingly absent in this age of social rage characterized by massive solidarity, the youth bulge, and far more horrendous modern realities. As put by Farid Shirazi, "[P]rovide citizens in repressed countries opportunities to participate in communication discourse by creating equifinal meaning which ultimately contributes to organized civil resistance and social actions."[53] The massive success of the Arab Spring testifies to the efficacy of hashtags and social media in engaging political issues. #OurMumuDonDo, #IStandWithNigeria, #EnoughIsEnough, #OccupyNigeria, #Otoge, and #IStandWithBuhari are a few among the hashtag campaigns that have attempted to reform and revolutionize the Nigerian political landscape. On the partial success of the #OccupyNigeria campaign that resulted in a 50 percent reduction of the fuel hike, Ojigho comments that the movement "represented a clear indication of the future of social advocacy and global movements."[54]

The ineffectiveness of the Nigerian government to end the numerous security threats, especially the Fulani herdsmen terrorism, has largely contributed to citizens' strong rejection of the government's plan to develop ranches and cattle colonies across the states to relieve the herdsmen of their challenges arising from nomadic pasturing. The #SayNoToRuga campaign is evidence of how social media has reconfigured the political terrain to include the voices of the marginalized and the masses on cogent issues pertaining to the collective development of their society, as well as to engage political representatives on

---

[52] Fela Kuti, "Sorrow, Tears and Blood," www.youtube.com/watch?v=pbhMnYyHnuE.
[53] Farid Shirazi, "Social Media and the Social Movements in the Middle East and North Africa," *Information Technology & People* 26, no. 1 (2013): 43.
[54] Osai Ojigbo, "Hashtag Activism Makes the Invisible Visible," *The Mantle*, November 16, 2017, www.themantle.com/international-affairs/hashtag-activism-makes-inisible-visible/.

issues particular to their well-being as members of society, which promotes all-inclusive governance.

In this age of social rage, the masses have transformed social media to replace town-hall meetings in local and traditional governance for deliberating on vital political and developmental issues. Because the political elites/leaders are present on social media, and the tools of social media are likewise accessible to the masses, the boundaries and bureaucracy alienating the political leaders from their followers are eradicated. Hence, social media has contributed to "government accountability, human rights activism, the development of civil society and practices of citizenship."[55]

Following several recommendations amidst agitations, it is necessary to recognize the new media technologies, especially the social media, as a "veritable tool for aggregating public opinion by public office holders, and should encourage free expression therein, and let such views guide their activities."[56] Such reformations can facilitate stronger democratic governance in the nation. Through active social media engagement, "the government is also better positioned than before to explain and enlighten citizens on government policies and programmes,"[57] which aids governance and the well-being of the citizens as they become more aware of vital information and issues than before.

To invoke Muse yet again, the "value of the communication experience has undergone a sea-change; from the need to share it, to the need to share in it. Technology and social media in particular have brought power back to the people; with such technologies, established authorities are now undermined and users are now the experts."[58] The relation of activism with social media has constrained the extent to which a dictatorial government can suppress the views and voice of the people, as it has no real or ultimate power over the people's access to such mobile facilities, like social media, which make information available in real time with pictorial or video evidence. The power of social media is global and no national government wields as enormous an influence. As indicated by Salanova, the resistance of social media to the "censorship and fierce state-control," as seen in the traditional media, contributed to tremendous success recorded by the protests as "they helped raise awareness about the regime's brutal practices that, although widely

---

[55] Haider, "Helpdesk Research Report," 2.
[56] Brenda Uji, "Social Media and the Mobilization of Youths for Socio-Political Participation," *New Media and Mass Communication* 42 (2015): 33.
[57] S. Muse, "Social Media and Public Participation in Nigeria: Challenges and Possibilities," *Advances in Social Sciences Research Journal* 17 (2014): 46.
[58] Ibid.

known by the population, had not had the coverage by traditional media."[59]

There is an ever-increasing relevance of social media to the political activities of the nations, as there is the rising need for a better and more effective electoral process to ensure electoral violence and malpractice are minimized in future general elections across all levels of governance. Over the years, social media has proven to be an indispensable tool of election monitoring in Nigeria. Constant updates are given on social media by electoral bodies and citizens on the processes, outcomes, and relevant information pertaining to the conduct of election. However, this has often generated misleading information that can cause conflict and disunity. Thus, the following suggestions by Aleyomi and Ajakaiye are more than relevant to ensure a safe relationship of social media intervention in electioneering in Nigeria:

1. The benefits of the use of social media outweigh its challenges; as such the civil society should adopt its use and equally encourage other election stakeholders to use social media in subsequent elections in Nigeria.
2. The Electoral Act should be enhanced to provide specific guidelines on the use of social media in Nigeria's future elections.
3. Independent National Electoral Commission (INEC) should establish guidelines for the use of social media as a political communication tool in Nigeria.
4. Security agencies should establish modalities to systematically verify information reported by citizen observers through the social media.
5. INEC should establish a social media tracking center to monitor, collate, and interpret trends and reports during elections.
6. Development partners should support domestic observer groups to utilize social media as a means of improving election observation in Nigeria.[60]

Conclusion

Unarguably, social media allows for flexible coordination of protests and social movements to drive desired societal change or development, and, like social media, "the efficacy of hashtag activism has been challenged and questioned, but critics are missing a crucial point: hashtag activism is only one tool in the advocacy circle and not a sole agent of change."[61]

---

[59] Salanova, "Social Media and Political Change," 29.
[60] Aleyomi and Ajakaiye, "The Impact of Social Media on Citizens' Mobilization and Participation in Nigeria's 2011 General Elections," 49.
[61] Ojigbo, "Hashtag Activism Makes the Invisible Visible."

From Morozov's *The Net Delusion*[62] to the ideology of "clicktivism" and slacktivism (a combination of slacker and activism), online criticism has often been criticized, especially through social media, as insincere solidarity to a movement with no real-life support or action.

However, at the heart of social media activism is mass awareness/ mobilization, solidarity, purpose, and efficacy. It has also helped to further blur the discrimination arising from geographical, gender, and age differences by uniting the globe in the advocacy of human rights, freedom, and true democracy. The point is not whether reformation and revolution will take place without social media (of course, it will!), but how social media helps to shape and direct the movement – understanding the contribution of the social media to the framing and objectives of a social movement. On its contribution to the political reformation in Egypt, Bhaiyal remarks, "Perhaps social media was not absolutely critical to the uprising in Egypt; however, it made protest possible sooner, and helped it develop in a way that would have been impossible without social media."[63] The same applies to online political campaigns such as #NotTooYoungToRun, #OccupyNigeria, and #EnoughIsEnough, which transformed to physical protests and have helped to reshape the political landscape of Nigeria.

Caution, however, should be taken to make the right connections between online activism and "real-life" activism to fully bring the efficacy of the mass mobilizing influence of social media to effect, as participation in online activism might mislead participants to appropriate online rhetoric with substantial political action, diverting their attention away from productive activities."[64] Social media, or other genres of technological media, will not operate solely to achieve the objectives of social movements at any point in the foreseeable future, but have proven to be indispensable with limitless possibilities in driving needed awareness toward a social movement; as observed by Haider, "social media's real potential may lie in supporting civil society and the public sphere."[65]

More than ever, there is the need for the existing labor unions, pressure organizations, and social movements in Nigeria to integrate social media as a vital part of their communication agency to create awareness, mass mobilize, and achieve their collective goals for the development of society and the people. In doing so, efforts should be channeled at curtailing

[62] Evgeny Morozov, *The Net Delusion*. London: Penguin Books. 2011.
[63] Serajul Bhuiyan, "Social Media and Its Effectiveness in the Political Reform Movement in Egypt," *Middle East Media Educator* 1, no. 1 (2011): 18.
[64] Sean Aday, *Blogs and Bullets: New Media in Contentious Politics* (Washington, DC: United States Institute of Peace, 2010), 9, www.usip.org/files/resources/pw65.pdf.
[65] Haider, "Helpdesk Research Report," 2.

misinformation by disclaiming and verifying the accuracy of information and events. Also, the digital divide – the inaccessibility of social media to a group of people within society due to various reasons – is a potential cause of disunity, inefficiency, and marginalization in the cause of social movements. With less than half the population of the country having access to the Internet, it is expedient that social media efforts are transformed into physical action, and that the available information is passed down to others at the grassroots level for better mobilization, solidarity, and unity.

While it has been established that social media contributes immensely to social movements and political participation toward progressive reformation and revolution in Nigeria, there is still a need to make the Internet and social media networks more accessible to the citizens in order to impact the continuous reformative progress of the nation. Hence, the relationship between social media and all-new technological media and social movements and political participation is symbiotic and should be further encouraged.

Ironically, the main constraint on the success of social media action is not really the inability to implement the organization and coordination of social movements on social media to actual protests, but the suppression of such movements both on social media and in actual life by state forces, often resulting in violence in the case of the latter or censorship and division in the case of the former. The same revolutionary contributions made by social media in communication and marketing are increasingly being driven toward politics, governance, and human rights activism, which portends better societal development, stronger democracy, and safer societies for everyone.

21 Reformist Option: Grassroots and Political Activism

All politics is local.

– Tip O'Neill, Speaker of the US House of Representatives

The only way that real change is going to take place is when millions of people get involved in the political process.

– Bernie Sanders, US Senator

Introduction

Political positions and administration have always been reserved for the elites while political struggle and several discourses of politics remain a lofty topic of conversation among most laymen. However, events in the political sphere affect every man, woman, and child in immense ways, regardless of ethnicity, race, gender, or creed. This raises crucial queries like: What is the overall importance of politics? And what is the importance of grassroots participation in politics? How does it shift the way we conceptualize, implement, and participate in politics? How does a grassroots approach to politics put individuals at odds with, sometimes threatening, the status quo of power? How do we, as active participants, prevent that from happening? And above all, how do we protect the voices of those who are most vulnerable? Looking at the Nigerian context, and Africa at large, this chapter examines these questions and provides some measure of elucidation.

Any meaningful aspect of politics may be conceived to usher in societal change. But, as former Democratic contender for US presidential nomination Bernie Sanders has observed, the only way for real change is when multitudes of people – in fact, millions – agree to be involved in the political process of any given environment. Political endeavors affect just about every aspect of our lives, from educational and economic policies to jobs, healthcare, and infrastructure. Politics is essentially the science of governing a body of people,[1] and this is an important part of life

---

[1] *Merriam-Webster*, "Politics" *Merriam-Webster*, n.d., www.merriam-webster.com/diction ary/politics.

for everyone who lives in a society. Educating ourselves to learn how governments operate will make us better participants in our civic duties, which highlights the significance of grassroots activism.

Grassroots activism is rooted in local, collective action. It has often been viewed as the "weapon of the weak,"[2] providing a platform for those whose voices have historically been marginalized. It is a mobilizing tool operating from a bottom-up approach, rather than a top-down one, to implement policies, effect change, and drive development. A defining factor of grassroots activism is its base engagement and direct accountability; those engaged in grassroots activism are responsible for their communities and attentive in ways that are impossible for governments. This chapter, divided into three parts for clarity and proper delineation, sees either grassroots or community power as the locus of the democratic essence. Through these parts, this chapter engages the narrative of Nigeria focusing on the existing grassroots structures and their formation, suggests how grassroots efforts can work in a global comparative context, and ends with a conclusion, identifying possible ways to move the country forward.

Repressed Localities, Suppressed Voices, and Submerged Spaces

Nigeria operates a three-tiered structure of government administration – the federal government, 36 state governments, and the Federal Capital Territory and 774 local governments – established by the country's constitution and other supporting laws. This arrangement is ostensibly in place to ensure that infrastructural and economic development permeates the country through democratic governance, that governance is truly representative, and that every village and hamlet feels a sense of belonging to every other constituent part of the country.[3]

The size of Nigeria and the pluralistic nature of its population makes this the ideal structure for balancing power without any region, ethnic group, or religion feeling left out. The federal, state, and local government structures all have their own powers, duties, and obligations as detailed in the national constitution. And the spread of power is meant to make the

---

[2] Meg Sullivan, "When Grassroots Activism Becomes a Commodity," *UCLA Newsroom*, May 29, 2014, http://newsroom.ucla.edu/releases/when-grassroots-activism-becomes-a-commodity.

[3] Ito Diejomaoh and Eric Eboh, "Local Government in Nigeria: Relevance and Effectiveness in Poverty Reduction and Economic Development," *Journal of Economics and Sustainable Development* 1, no. 1 (2010), https://iiste.org/Journals/index.php/JEDS/article/view/2143.

gains of democratic governance visible across the nation because local governments are better placed to assess and respond to citizens' immediate needs.

The Chairmen of the Local Government Areas (LGA) Council are administrative heads of elected positions that are restricted to eligible residents of the areas. They collaborate with elected local council members from wards making up the local government and serve three-year terms. Their functions have changed over the years, expanding, and contracting with the wisdom and exigencies of the time. The latest official records of all local government council functions are listed under the fourth schedule of the Nigerian Constitution (1999). They include various licensing and registration duties; property enumeration and identification activities; construction and maintenance of roads and cemeteries; primary, vocational, and adult education; and homes for the infirm.

Federalism was adopted in Nigeria in 1954. Since then, there have been changes in the administrative and fiscal characteristics of its component units, affected by factors like principles of derivation, national interest, and military incursion into politics. The fiscal arrangements, like the revenue-sharing formula, are constantly being renegotiated, with federal and state governments having more authority over the outcome.[4] The American scholar K. C. Wheare's concept of federalism argues that "powers are shared between central and regional governments so that each is in a sphere coordinate and independent."[5] This means that, ordinarily, federalism is the perfect method governing for a country with linguistic, ideological, and religious diversity.

However, power relations among Nigeria's three units keep the local government subservient to the other units, especially the state governments, reducing its ability to serve constituents. In several ways, local autonomy exists only as law and policy documents. In practice, local governments are merely appendages to the state government. Many scholars and social commentators have criticized the practice of federalism in Nigeria, claiming it falls short of the ideal,[6] with Odisu describing it as "a disguised unitary system."[7] In conception, each level of Nigeria's federal government system has clearly defined responsibilities, obligations, and

---

[4] Stuti Khemani, "Fiscal Federalism and Service Delivery in Nigeria: The Role of States and Local Governments," paper, Nigerian PER Steering Committee, Abuja, Nigeria, 2001, www.worldbank.org/publicsector/decentralization/march2003seminar/fiscalfedre port.pdf.

[5] K. C. Wheare, *Federal Government*, 4th ed. (London: Oxford University Press, 1963), 11.

[6] Leke Salaudeen, "Tragedy of Third Tier of Government," *The Nation*, August 16, 2017, http://thenationonlineng.net/tragedy-third-tier-government/.

[7] T. A. Odisu, "Federalism in Nigeria: A Critique," *Journal of Political Sciences & Public Affairs* 3, no. 3 (2015): 185.

rights with some areas of overlap.[8] In practice, Nigeria is more of a centralized federalism.[9]

The seed of today's state domination of the local government affairs was planted with the recommendation of Lord Hailey that "the varied responsibilities now placed on these authorities demand the exercise of close and continuous supervision by the administration."[10] Subsequently, since 1951, it was nurtured during the contest between colonial officials and the three giant Nigerian nationalists: Dr. Nnamdi Azikiwe; Sir Ahmadu Bello, the Sardauna of Sokoto; and Chief Obafemi Awolowo. Most of Chief Obafemi Awolowo's disagreements with the 1951 Macpherson Constitution were rooted in the convoluted relationship between the British colonial administration and the native administration system.

No other aspect of decolonization was more delicate and difficult to manage at the launch of self-government than the issue of native administration. The political importance of native administration in the process of decolonization, and its critical position as an instrument for local participation and self-government, meant that the new Nigerian regional leaders – who were reluctantly entrusted with self-government by the British colonial officials – had viewed the native administration system as coterminous with the British imperial administrative structure. They also saw it as a meta-government that must be overthrown if self-government were to have any meaning. Hence, Dr. Nnamdi Azikiwe, Sir Ahmadu Bello, and Chief Obafemi Awolowo, acting as political party leaders in their respective regions, chose to personally run each region's Ministry of Local Government.

Like most colonized African nations, Nigeria has not divested itself of the imperial military unitary governance system that it inherited. There is a single salary structure for the three tiers of government, a single university commission that approves appointments of full professors and courses for both private and public higher institutions, and all agencies of government have the same operational manual for appointments, compensation, and discipline of public officials.

---

[8] Many Nigerians argue that, on paper and in practice, the country does not have a federal system. Laws skew the constitutionally allocated powers and resources to give overwhelming power to the federal government. Look at the lengthy list of items in the exclusive list, including trivial matters that states can ordinarily deal with. Look at the provisions for control of revenue. Look at the overbearing powers given to states, which basically suffocate local governments and render them redundant. The construction pays lip service to being federal, and calls itself federal, but its provisions counter that claim.

[9] Rotimi Suberu, "The Nigerian Federal System: Performance, Problems and Prospects," *Journal of Contemporary African Studies* 28, no. 4 (2010): 459–477.

[10] Lord William Malcolm Hailey, *An African Survey: A Study of Problems Arising in Africa South of the Sahara* (Oxford: Oxford University Press, 1938), 538.

The federal government has appropriated increasing power for itself over the years, especially through oppressive military decrees that were not removed after the 1999 return to democratic civilian rule.[11] The state government controls the local government through fiscal and electoral manipulation, gagging local government Chairmen and often dictating which projects can be carried out within their jurisdiction.[12] The reality and practice of federalism in Nigeria is the opposite of the concept's original definition and spirit. Nigeria's political and administrative system has subverted the political and economic justifications for federalism.

The results are obvious in the various levels of infrastructural development between urban and rural areas, perpetuating the problems of excessive industry concentration along with population and housing problems in urban areas. Rural areas suffer from a lack of infrastructural amenities and job opportunities. Functional road networks, public schools, and general hospitals are all concentrated in the city centers, undermining decentralization. Rural–urban migration is a major problem for Lagos State, with over 20 million inhabitants and an 8 percent growth rate, meaning that the country's smallest state by land mass is harboring 36.8 percent of the total national population.[13]

Residents have no say in electing their local government representatives; political parties foist candidates on them through the influence of federal and state governments. This makes local government offices undesirable for upright, educated citizens and it disillusions the people at the grassroots level. Many do not embrace local governance because of the lack of engagement through healthy involvement in decision-making with elected officials.

Local government performance is notably poor across the nation, which is attributable to the methods that officials use to claim power – favors and patronage – and the excessive financial control wielded by state governments. The composition and power of many local governments are not prepared for Nigeria's ongoing population growth. For instance, Nigeria's population currently includes a substantial percentage of young people. Skillful planning and management would increase the budget for primary and secondary education, create more maternal and childcare centers, and develop higher education plans to cater to all

---

[11] Emmanuel Ibiam Amah, "Federalism, Nigerian Federal Constitution and the Practice of Federalism: An Appraisal," *Beijing Law Review* 8, no. 3 (2017): 141–158.

[12] Sunday Inyokwe Otinche, "Fiscal Policy and Local Government Administration in Nigeria," *African Research Review* 8, no. 33 (2018): 122–124.

[13] Budgit Foundation, *What We Know about Lagos State Finances* (Lagos: Budgit Foundation, 2018), http://yourbudgit.com/wp-content/uploads/2018/05/LAGOS-STATE-DATA-BOOK.pdf.

economic classes. Local governments cannot move decisively to tackle infrastructure gaps, improve planning, foster high-productivity job growth, and overcome other diseconomies due to persistent problems that they seem unwilling to tackle.

One of the stated intents of the 1976 Local Government Reforms was to strengthen governments and transform them into strong institutions by which democracy will be practiced inclusively in the country, from the grassroots up. It is important to consider what grassroots democracy means. Democracy itself is a concept carried over from ancient Greek city-states, where their means of governance was direct participation through voting. This has metamorphosed into representative government, where groups of people in a community vote for one or more people to represent their interests, especially when making laws.

Inclusive governance requires representatives to understand the needs and wants of the people they are representing in order to meet those needs and ensure that their communities receive democracy's dividends. After years of practice, many have observed that there is a disconnect in adequate representation in Nigerian governance. Representatives generally acquire positions of power only to execute their own agenda, or that of the political party. At the same time, the size of the states involved means that most infrastructure is developed in city centers and urban areas.

The local government tier is the most important level for the practice of inclusive governance. Governance cannot be inclusive if large segments of the population do not have a say, or if they remain uninformed except during election periods – when those seeking votes suddenly could reach even the most remote hamlets. Local government authorities were created to support people at the grassroots level, bringing governance close to them. They are supposed to ensure the provision of basic amenities, maintain orderliness in their communities, and ensure the collection of basic taxes.

One of the tenets of democracy is to guarantee active participation in public life, both political and civic.[14] Adopting democracy as a system of governance implies accepting it as the best form of government for us, meaning that we want to uphold its principles. Nigeria's disconnect between elected representatives and the electorate is thus an anomaly, one even more grotesque when observed at the local government level, which is the exact gap that the local government tier is supposed to bridge. Local government authorities are supposed to bring grassroots democracy into practice in Nigeria, but they have been unable to fulfill their mandate.

[14] Larry Diamond, "What Is Democracy?" (lecture, Hilla University for Humanistic Studies, Hillah, Iraq, January 21, 2004), https://diamond-democracy.stanford.edu/speaking/lectures/what-democracy.

Figure 21.1 Informed citizens following the news and events.

Grassroots democracy is a political and social process ensuring that ordinary citizens are invested in the administration of their geographical space with more relatable, more visible, and more accessible elected officers. It is supposed to result in adequate solutions and targeted budgeting for each local government, allowing state and federal governments to focus on their official duties. Grassroots democracy should be an avenue for people to experience total participation in the political space, influencing governance for the benefit of their communities. It is people-driven and community-driven participation in elections, governance, and decision-making.[15] Unfortunately, the phrase is simply a buzzword in Nigeria, becoming relevant only during election periods when political parties need to canvass for votes. This has stunted political participation at the grassroots level.

Instead of the bottom-up approach to governance that the Local Government Reforms were supposed to achieve, candidates are imposed on the populace through party machinations and state governor favoritism. Local government elections are organized by the state government in collaboration with the staff of the Independent Electoral Commission in each state, which means that any candidate that any governor does not like will not be viable. Some chairmen do not even live within the domains

---

[15] John Sunday Ojo and Godwin Chinedum Ihemeje, "Mushrooming Appointed Caretaker Committee: A Quagmire to Grassroot Democracy in Nigeria," *International Journal of Sociology and Anthropology* 6, no. 7 (2014): 217.

they govern; they show up to pay salaries and share other monies, only to disappear afterward.[16] Nationally, discussions on radio and social media show that people are more interested in presidential and state elections than local government elections. If a poll were conducted right now, I am certain that a large percentage of people could not name or identify their local government chairmen, not to mention the councilors. This does not bode well for grassroots democracy as a concept or as a practice.

Political participation is the act of citizens getting involved and taking ownership of the political process and apparatus in their country. Political participation is high in countries with healthy systems of governance that are characterized by rule of law, respect for human rights, strong judicial systems, and a free press.

The trend of local government official disempowerment has led to the populace's inability to take ownership of the local government apparatus. They are unwilling to take elected officials to task to ensure proper governance. Participation in political processes enables citizens to evolve their capacities, articulate their demands, and legitimize decisions.[17] Instead, the nation is experiencing voter apathy, a willingness to sell votes for a pittance, and a willingness to vote based on sentiment, religion, ethnicity, and every other motivation – except for confidence that the candidates will represent their interests. These can only make the country worse for the same set of people that local government is meant to protect and empower: the people at the grassroots, especially in the rural areas.

Community members express negative sentiment in response to federal and state government actions that weaken the local government structures. This indicates erosion of trust and growing resentment when the power imbalance manifests against local governments. Although people at the grassroots level – family, village, church group, guild, or economic unit – are the subject of "compensatory eulogy," society has been reorganized to disempower them. They have been rendered functionally insignificant and distant from the bureaucratic elites.[18] Instead of representative democracy, where inputs taken from the ground are used to inform policies at the upper tiers, it is the upper tiers deciding which interventions, infrastructure developments, and "gains of democracy" that communities need.

---

[16] Lambert Tyem, "N3.3Tr Squandered by LG Chairmen in 8 Years – EFCC," *Nigerian Muse*, 2008, www.nigerianmuse.com/20080827000403zg/nigeria-watch/official-fraud-watch-towards-fraud-free-governance-in-nigeria/n3-3tr-squandered-by-lg-chairmen-in -8-years-efcc/.

[17] Jan W. van Deth, "Political Participation," in *The International Encyclopedia of Political Communication* (Hoboken: John Wiley & Sons, Inc., 2015).

[18] Robert Alexander Nisbet, *Community and Power* (Oxford: Oxford University Press, 1965).

Political participation is central to development through good governance, and grassroots political participation should be the most crucial factor determining the extent to which citizens are invested and satisfied with their governance model. Local districts can be broken down into wards or communities that should have formal representation in their corresponding local governments. The present structures recognize and involve Community Development Association (CDAs) chairmen and their representatives. Legally, they make up part of the governance structures for different committees in the local government.

Lagos State has the Local Government Health Authority (LGHAs), Ward Health Committees (WHCs), and Health Facility Management Teams. They are made up of health officers and community representatives charged with improving the health-seeking behaviors of people in their communities, healthcare facilities management, and the level of available healthcare in the Primary Health Centers. New Primary Health Centers have been built in new Local Council Development Areas, and they are formally handed over to the LGHA in each local Council Development Area. However, this has not had the expected large-scale effect. Researchers report that there is poor coordination, poor funding, and poor implementation, low level of ownership and participation, dilapidated infrastructure, inadequate workforce in the Primary Health Centers, and lack of basic drugs. In some centers, there is an outright lack of Health Center structures.[19]

In this scenario, the local government is not funding activities and ensuring proper coordination of the Ward Development Committees. The committee members, made up of volunteers from the constituent communities, have lost interest in the arrangement. Calls from civil society bodies like Lagos State Civil Society Partnership, Budgit Nigeria, and individuals like barrister Ayo Ayobusoye have asked Lagos State government to expedite the inauguration of the LGHA.

All eyes are on the state government to allow or inaugurate bodies that will be operating for local government or local council development areas; it is another indicator of the continued erosion of local government power, leading to reduced interest in participating in political or administrative processes. Citizens will respond negatively because of the unfortunate but realistic perception of local government officials as powerless. They are seen as mere figureheads, not as active directors of their communal fate.

---

[19] Olayinka Akanke, Abosede Olugbenga, and Fola Sholeye, "Strengthening the Foundation for Sustainable Primary Health Care Services in Nigeria," *Primary Health Care: Open Access* 4, no. 3 (2014).

Local government administration in Nigeria was created by colonial authorities as a mere administrative appendage. However, it was strengthened in 1976 by the adoption of Local Government Reform.[20] The reform aimed:

[t]o] give the council substantial control over local affairs as well as institutional and financial powers to initiate and direct the provision of services and to determine and implement projects so as to complement the activities of the states and federal governments in their areas, and to ensure, through devolution of these functions to these councils and through the active participation of the people and their traditional institutions, that local initiative and response to local needs and conditions are maximized.[21]

The reform document recommended uniformity in structure and function across all local governments nationwide. It also accorded the power of effective grassroots governance to local governments.

Despite the lofty ideals and its backing by law and the 1979 and 1999 Constitutions, the reality and practice of local governance is different. Today, the revenue-allocation formula is a constant source of bickering among the three levels of government. At the inter-state level, The Governor's Forum is a pressure group used to influence the federal government's revenue decisions in favor of state governments. A famous example happened during Goodluck Jonathan's presidency; governors insisted on sharing the excess crude oil revenue and regularly pressured the federal government to distribute money from the country's Excess Crude Revenue Account.[22] The governors had the constitutional right to make their demands, but it was shortsighted of them to think oil prices would remain high indefinitely. When the prices dropped in 2016, the country was plunged into recession. The present revenue sharing formula among the three levels of government is 20.6 percent for local governments, 26.7 percent for state governments, 52.6 percent for the federal government – local governments that have the highest units get the least revenue from the federal purse.

This division suggests that the federal government, a single unit, does more work or has more responsibilities than the 36 state governments or 774 local governments. Can the most inaccessible layer of government,

---

[20] Chukwuemeka Okafor, E. O. Emma Chukwuemeka, and Jude O. Udenta, "Developmental Local Government as a Model for Grassroots Socio-Economic Development in Nigeria," *International Journal of Arts and Humanities* 4, no. 14 (2015): 49–50.

[21] Federal Republic of Nigeria, *Guidelines for Local Government Reform* (Lagos: Government Printer, 1971).

[22] Obo Effanga, "Time to Focus on State Governors," *Punch Newspapers*, November 14, 2016, https://punchng.com/time-focus-state-governors.

which is cut off from local communities, do more than the smaller parts? This negates the spirit of federalism and kills effective political participation. The issues contributing to the emasculation of local governments are ambiguous constitutional provisions, overlapping areas of responsibility among the three tiers of government, state governments positioning themselves as overlords dictating finances and activity, low political participation at the grassroots level, and corruption.

One anomaly of local government administration is its lack of autonomy in fiscal decisions. Legally, local government allocations from the Federation Account are paid into a Joint State and Local Government Account for each state, to be divided among the local government areas. This means state governors exercise absolute control over the accounts; they have been known to delay, deny, or reduce payments to local governments. Justifications include the execution of infrastructure projects that should have been done at the local government level, or explanations that it is easier to coordinate security and other issues at the state level.

It has also been observed that many local government chairmen and their councilors cannot initiate projects without approval from the state government. Local government chairmen and other elected officials tolerate outright disregard for their offices, and disregard for the laws guiding fiscal relationships between local and state governments, leading to reduced performance. Their offices are crippled by the same system that put them in place. Some receive their positions through a political patronage system entrenched and strictly guarded by political parties using offices as rewards for active party members. This binds them to party leaders and state governors, who already have constitutional oversight powers at their disposal to address local government chairmen, councilors, and their activities.

Because they are the appointees of governors and their parties, their loyalty is automatically and obviously to the system that enthroned them. They become unresponsive, or they cannot even comprehend local needs and wishes. This leads to an inability to initiate customized projects or programs that could solve the issues experienced by their respective communities. These encumbrances make local government ineffective at poverty reduction and the practice of true federalism.

The Lagos State situation is even more disconcerting. The Lagos State government, then headed by Bola Ahmed Tinubu, faced with the prospect of governing millions of people within a small area and coming out of the long years of oppressive military rule, made some critical decisions. Those decisions, which assisted the Tinubu administration, reduced government costs by returning government-administered schools back to the missionary organizations that they had originally been taken from.

By 2003, the state government had created thirty-seven additional local government areas to further reduce the pressures of administration. The constitution required a population-based factor for the creation of new local government areas, but the federal government refused to acknowledge them. Instead, it insisted that the state would need to revert to its previous twenty local government areas.

As a concession, the state government named its units Local Council Development Areas (LCDAs), backed by the state's legislative arm. Although a bill was passed into law to create them, the federal government subsequently withheld the state's LGA allocations, even after Supreme Court's intervention. The Federal government retained the allocations until a new president was sworn in; the late President Musa Yar'adua released the money to the Lagos State government when its new governor, Babatunde Raji Fashola, continued to stand his ground.

The Lagos State situation is interesting because the state government needed to exercise more discretionary power over its allocation from the federal government for the Joint State and Local Government Account after the additional LCDAs were created. Lagos State finances are some of the most opaque in the country and there is little information available. The budget breakdown and details of the cost of projects are kept far from scrutiny.[23]

In 2012, Governor Fashola officially delivered 114 security vehicles to the Inspector General of the Police Force, given as "donations" from the 20 LGAs and 37 LCDAs. At the handover ceremony, the State Commissioner for Local Government and Chieftaincy Affairs, Mr. Ademorin Kuye, stated that the donation affirms the unity of purpose between Local Government Councils, Council Development Areas, and the State Government. Is this really the case? Rationally and legally, the thirty-seven LGDAs are only funded through ticketing and licensing revenues.[24] This impasse is presently being ignored, but it will need to be addressed.

What if the people had been allowed to hold a referendum on the administrative division of the local governments? The results could have been accepted by local government authorities and ratified by the state House of Representatives. It would have shown the real practice of democracy, one that encourages the strengthening of the people's voices.

Corruption is another factor that contributes to the non-performance of local government authorities, affecting all the local government

---

[23] Budgit Foundation, *What We Know about Lagos State Finances.*
[24] Babatunde Raji Fashola, "Fashola Hands Over 114 Patrol Vehicles, Other Security Items to Police," *Babatunde Raji Fashola*, September 10, 2012, www.tundefashola.com/arch ives/news/2012/09/10/20120910N01.html.

councils in Nigeria. Even the staff are vulnerable to corrupt practices. This becomes evident at the grassroots level, inhabited by the poorest citizens. Elected officials and civil servants ensure that the government's financial affairs remain opaque, since financial impropriety cannot survive scrutiny. Financial services companies have been indicted for helping corrupt officials launder funds; even anti-graft bodies fall for the lure of easy money. Everyday citizens are also guilty of looking the other way, sitting on the fence, or accepting bribes in exchange for votes. It is as though we cannot defeat the monster called corruption.

Politicians behave in much the same way as they did in the 1960s and 1970s, which led to the development-freeze years of military rule. Media reports list various indictments, accusations, and evidently corrupt practices in the political domain, and the civil service staff is also implicated. Even the present administration, which rode in on an "anti-corruption" promise, has been unable to keep a clean sheet. It has been accused of human rights violations, disregard for due process, and ongoing graft. Local government chairmen, whether elected or part of Caretaker Committees, mostly see the positions as an opportunity to engage in misappropriation of funds, inflation of contract sums, over-invoicing of goods, unauthorized withdrawals, and outright embezzlement.[25]

A drive through the communities of the Niger Delta, with all the derivation-based funds and oil royalties they receive, shows the extent of local government corruption. Buffeted by poor quality education, almost non-existent primary healthcare facilities, no social safety net, poor housing, high unemployment rates, and an ever-moving inflation rate, Nigeria's poor have stopped expecting the government to provide basic amenities – although every campaign manifesto mentions them during election season. Impoverished citizens gratefully receive the cups of rice, noodles, plastics, money, and other inducements to vote for specific candidates. Then they look the other way when reports of financial impropriety are published in the press, on the radio, and through social media. Citizens at the grassroots level expect, accommodate, and even celebrate corruption in their own government. They must accept their portion of the blame and shun political apathy, ending the sale of votes and political patronage systems.

Local governments work their hardest fulfilling responsibilities that involve collecting from the populace, and they put the least amount of effort into providing for the populace. Revenue mobilization offices,

[25] A. Agbo, "Institutionalizing Integrity," *Tell Magazine*, December 2010, quoted in Oluwatobi O. Adeyemi, "Corruption and Local Government Administration in Nigeria: A Discourse of Core Issues," *European Journal of Sustainable Development* 1, no. 2 (2012): 194.

which receive taxes, grant licenses, and give out tickets, are the most active units in any local government area. They are in markets enforcing the payment of parking tickets; "lock-up shops," food, beverages, liquor, and medicine sales permits and licenses; the licensing of bicycles, wheelbarrows, carts, and trucks; birth, death, and marriage registrations; outdoor advertising permits; tenement rates; and radio and television licenses. But the construction and maintenance of roads, drainage, streetlights, parks, and gardens, along with proper sewage and refuse disposal, are apparently too much of a load for them to bear. We can imagine how these local government councils are perceived by people at the grassroots level, making minimal effort while the gap between the council and the people grows wider each year.

Accountability, effectiveness and efficiency, rule of law, responsiveness, transparency, and participation have been identified as characteristics of good governance.[26] The absence of good governance at the local level is lamentable, and it deserves urgent measures to rectify it. Citizens should be encouraged to take ownership of their local government processes through transparent fiscal, electoral, and administrative action so that people see themselves deciding the fate of their government. For example, people are interested and invested in the processes and outcomes at the Community Development Association (CDA) level or at the level of Landlords' Association meetings; they have a firm sense of belonging that should be present at the local government level.

A lot of CDAs and Landlords' Associations contribute money to grade roads, fix drainage, install security gates, hire private nightguards, and request police investigation into suspicious movements and inhabitants within their domains. Local governments would champion these efforts if there was true representation at the grassroots level; they should encourage the participation of the CDAs in their plans so that development solutions will directly impact the problems that people want resolved.

How Can We Make Grassroots Politics Work?

Grassroots activism is about mobilizing enthusiastic people and harnessing the power of their beliefs to advance specific causes. It often takes place within communities, relying on those willing to fight for change from the ground up. Grassroots politics rely on support from a community of like-minded advocates, pursuing a campaign that engages the masses and creates

---

[26] P. O. Oviasuyi, W. Idada, and Lawrence Isiraojie, "Constraints of Local Government Administration in Nigeria," *Journal of Social Sciences* 24, no. 2 (2010): 83.

a debate that will influence leaders and decision makers.[27] The power of a grassroots movement comes from the passion of the individuals involved; their enthusiasm and motivation combined with educational awareness is the best way to find support and make change for the better.

Education is an essential part of any grassroots campaign because people cannot support a cause that they do not understand. Campaigns must raise awareness about their issues, communicating them efficiently and effectively, making them more likely to garner support from individuals. It is also important for grassroots activists and their supporters to stay well-informed about their cause, in order to make persuasive arguments when addressing those in positions of power and influence. Communication can include quantitative data that supports the campaign and personal stories from those affected by the issues.[28]

Grassroots engagement has become a major part of any government relations or advocacy communication strategy, with the power to sway the hearts and minds of elected officials, regulators, and the media.[29] Spurred on by nonprofits, associations, and coalitions, as well as other individuals involved in the political process, grassroots movements have a greater capacity than ever to educate the masses and gain support. An examination of historical and current grassroots campaigns to analyze their tactics and strategies for gaining supporters, provides a better understanding of how grassroots politics works. This includes localized issues from all around the world and movements that have developed internationally or that stem from multiple places.

Modern globalization has increased the visibility and presence of landless peasant movements around the world. In countries like Brazil, Mexico, the Philippines, and South Africa, landless workers and farmers have come together to "demand access to land and new economic development policies that prioritize sustainable local communities and food sovereignty."[30] The South African Landless People's Movement (LPM) garnered considerable attention after its 2001 formation, mobilizing grassroots interests for agrarian reform. Land distribution, and the control of land, had been the backbone of colonial policies in South Africa. They remained an issue following the end of Apartheid. The LPM

---

[27] JoJo Swords, "Grassroots Activism: Make That Change," *Thought Works*, November 16, 2017, www.thoughtworks.com/insights/blog/grassroots-activism-make-change.

[28] Ibid.

[29] Joshua Habursky and Mike Fulton, "The Future of Politics Is Grassroots," *The Hill*, March 12, 2017, https://thehill.com/blogs/pundits-blog/campaign/323480-the-future-of -politics-is-grassroots.

[30] Brenda Baletti, Tamara M. Johnson, and Wendy Wolford, "'Late Mobilization': Transnational Peasant Networks and Grassroots Organizing in Brazil and South Africa," *Journal of Agrarian Change* 8, no. 2/3 (2008): 290–314.

attempted to force this issue into the national spotlight in the early 2000s; at one point they listed a membership of 100,000 people, which was an important strategy to gain attention.[31] The movement was influenced by the Movimento dos Trabalhadores Rurais Sem Terra (MST) campaign in Brazil, where rural farmers faced similar issues of racialized social hierarchies upheld by land ownership based on colonial policies. The MST gained national visibility during the mid-90s, and went from being a small, marginalized movement to one of the most powerful and well-organized social movements in the country. It includes approximately two million members today.[32]

Successful grassroots movements and reform strategies in Africa are based on building coalitions with several organizations and people. These may include a combination of communities, NGOs, organizations, and other institutions.[33] These coalitions can take many forms, often involving support from international organizations to bring light to specific issues or give people a platform to discuss their desired changes. Women's movements in Uganda and Botswana established relationships with external organizations that render various kinds of support, including money and personnel. Another important aspect of grassroots successes has been their autonomy. For example, NGOs have autonomy from donors, civil societies have autonomy from political influence, and scale-up efforts have autonomy from being co-opted by the state. One influential NGO is Ndifuna Ukwazi (NU), which has supported the South African campaign Reclaim the City (RTC), and their battle for affordable housing in Cape Town since 2016. NU exerts significant influence over the campaign, but it cannot actually make decisions for RTC.[34]

In recent years, the Internet has become a tool for political movements all over the world, presenting information and calling people to action on a global scale. The Occupy Wall Street movement was one of the first major efforts driven by social media. Beginning as a small political protest, it soon became an international movement, drawing awareness to the extreme concentration of wealth among a few "one-percenters." Members of the

---

[31] Ibid. [32] Ibid.

[33] Anindita Adhikari, Benjamin Bradlow, Patrick Heller, Rehan Rafay Jamil, Kristine Li, Chantel Pheiffer, Andrew Schrank, and Marcus Walton. "Grassroots Reform in the Global South." Paper, Research and Innovation Grants Working Paper Series, Washington, DC, September 21, 2017. www.usaid.gov/sites/default/files/documents/18 66/Grassroots_Reform_in_the_Global_South_-_Research_and_Innovation_Grants_Wo rking_Papers_Series.pdf.

[34] Lucy Valerie Graham and Malibongwe Tuku, "A Captured Occupation? On Ngos, Accountability, and Grassroots Movements," *Bulletin of the National Library of South Africa* 72, no. 1 (2018): 93–104.

campaign used Facebook and Twitter to spread their movement on a massive scale. It is arguable whether the movement created much change, but it was a notably successful mobilization.[35]

A more-recent grassroots phenomenon, which started in the United States, has been the #BlackLivesMatter (BLM) campaign. In 2013, three women created the movement in response to the acquittal of George Zimmerman, the man who murdered Trayvon Martin. Unlike other black liberation movements in the United States, BLM has sought to include women, queer, and transgender people of color and to give them a platform. The movement gained significant attention after Michael Brown was killed by Darren Wilson, a white police officer: hundreds of BLM protesters flooded Ferguson, Missouri, for weeks following the murder.[36] The BLM Movement has continued to demand that politicians and the public acknowledge the epidemic of violence toward women and people of color, particularly, transgender women of color. During the 2016 election, they actively questioned politicians, including Clinton and Sanders, about black lives. The movement continues around the United States today on national and local levels.[37]

The #MeToo movement has been another recent campaign that gained tremendous support and attention. Much like #BlackLivesMatter, it has caught on due to celebrity endorsement and the global scale of social media. Reportedly started by Tarana Burke in 2006, the phrase "me too" was used to support women and girls who had survived sexual violence. In October 2017, film producer Harvey Weinstein and several other celebrities and politicians were publicly accused of sexual assault and the campaign rapidly gained momentum. It set off a worldwide reckoning over sexual misconduct in the workplace, forming a community of support for sexual assault survivors. In just a few months, it gained enough attention for *Time Magazine* to recognize the "Silence Breakers" as People of the Year in December 2017.[38]

Despite its Hollywood focal point, the #MeToo movement has drawn support from around the world and continues to gain attention. Brett Kavanaugh's appointment as a US Supreme Court Justice in 2018 – despite sexual assault allegations that were not fully investigated – triggered

---

[35] Jonathan Moyer, "Political Activism on Social Media Has Grown Some Teeth," *Pacific Standard*, May 8, 2017, https://psmag.com/social-justice/social-media-activism.

[36] Jamilah King, "How Black Lives Matter Has Changed US Politics," *New Internationalist*, March 9, 2018, https://newint.org/features/2018/03/01/black-lives-matter-changed-politics.

[37] Ibid.

[38] Christen A. Johnson and K. T. Hawbaker, "#MeToo: A Timeline of Events," *Chicago Tribune*, October 11, 2018, www.chicagotribune.com/lifestyles/ct-me-too-timeline-201 71208-htmlstory.html.

another national outcry from survivors and #MeToo supporters. The episode shows how significant and widespread the issue remains, and how far we still have to go to transform politics to address sexual violence.

Empowering Localities and Governance in Nigeria

Two crucial queries come to mind: How do we get local governance back on track? How do we get from here to the stage where local government is an inclusive grassroots effort in Nigeria? The first and foremost solution is education. Primary and secondary education, for all children, is important to secure their economic future and realize their full potential. It is also important for developing their ability to grasp what governance is about, why they should engage with politicians, and how to relate the tolls collected on the streets with the social amenities that they may or may not receive.

Education is globally recognized as the path to a better future, since the educated person is equipped with the language of national and global communication. If education were prioritized in Nigeria, people would be less reluctant to call out politicians who do not get it right. Education is crucial for vibrant, politically aware, and unshakable grassroots participation. Better education ensures a better systemic environment, enabling people to believe in the power of their votes and giving them the chance to contribute directly to policymaking.

The current education indices in Nigeria are not completely gloomy, but they leave much to be desired. A country with education budgets as low as ours, in the face of educational needs as great as ours, is not positioning itself for better things. The 2014 figures from Proshare show that the student to teacher ratio is 40 to 1 in the public education system. A 100 to 1 ratio is not unheard of. It is not encouraging to know that we have millions of children out of school; the full classrooms mean that the infrastructure is not in place to serve millions of out-of-school children currently at primary school age.[39]

Education drives economic growth and development. It starts at the primary level, which is managed by local governments. However, ill-trained teachers, poor equipment, and outdated curriculum material hinders the provision of quality education. It needs to be changed as soon as possible if we want to see balanced, knowledgeable, and skilled citizens in our population. Millions of children are enrolled in primary schools as we speak. How many are going to graduate with relevant literacy and numeracy skills?

[39] National Bureau of Statistics & UBEC, *Education Data* (Abuja: National Bureau of Statistics & UBEC, 2016), www.proshareng.com/admin/upload/report/UBECData.pdf.

Early years' education being *the real structural foundation* for the nation, every local government must seriously address the task of increasing the number of children enrolling and completing their primary education so that they are well-prepared for secondary schools. Civic education curriculums should be strengthened to discuss the citizen's obligation to ensure the progress of the country. That is what participatory democracy is all about – not about leaving every decision in the hands of a few to do as they wish. Every child and adult must know that they should expect subpar results if they don't clarify their demands and make them known to their elected representatives.

In August, 2014, the federal government confirmed that Nigeria has the "largest number of children out-of-school" in the world. UNICEF puts the figure at 10.5 million. There is no outrage or widespread concern expressed by the populace; it is likely that the government will also pay cursory attention to it before moving on to address topical issues that are more likely to "heat up the polity." This is what citizens need to understand: The government doesn't want you to heat up the polity. When you complain and insist on what you want, they must get it done. This is one thing we will do well to understand and to teach the coming generations – the power of the electorate endures beyond election days.

To leverage the power of massive cooperation at the grassroots level and push for improvements in Nigeria's political and economic development, it is important to realize the full capabilities of local governments, including autonomy in practice, exactly as it is set out in the Constitution. Full exercise of their powers will expose weak areas that can be strengthened with legal amendments or reforms.

Nigeria returned to a democratic mode of governance in 1999. It was a relief for many, but a look at present political activities and the country's development indices show a cloud-covered economic and political landscape. The clouds are heavy with the promise of rain showers that can cool the harassed masses, but they never fall. Nigeria is a country with more problems than resolutions, full of citizens with the highest level of docility and endurance. Nigeria is not growing at the required rate, and it is not likely to. Under the 1979 and 1999 Constitutions, local governments hold a good degree of autonomy to bolster their administrative functions and fiscal responsibilities. Unfortunately, executive mismanagement and excessive state interference have meant that the dreams of the constitutional amendments cannot become reality.

Efficient rural development strategies require extensive financial outlay. Presently, that is beyond the financial capacity of local government councils, because state governments weaken local finances through delays, deductions, and fixed expenses. Local government officials worsen their own inefficiency through a lack of fiscal discipline. The "big brother" element, engendered by the Joint State and Local Government Account, will need to be removed by revisiting its structure. What was intended to be inter-governmental fiscal co-operation has become a master–slave relationship; it negates the spirit of cooperation that created the clause in the Constitution. The joint account arrangement should be rejected, in favor of an option that grants freedom of action to local government councils.

Nationwide, local governments should be allowed to conduct their own elections independent of the state government. The current arrangement, which allows state governments to conduct elections at their convenience, must be completely rejected. It empowers the patronage system ensuring that only "anointed" candidates hold Council posts, instead of the candidates who are known and trusted by community members. This is in opposition to the philosophy behind the creation of local governments and the amendments made to strengthen them. If council chairmen receive their posts for any reason other than the support of their communities, then it is a fundamental problem that must be resolved. Nigeria needs to produce an alternative to the present arrangement that leaves local election decisions in the hands of state governments.

The present arrangement is not ideal for democracy. Chuks Oluigbo identified what he called "sham elections" across the country; his examples show the pre-arranged, "winner take all" nature of politicking in Nigeria. For example, APC Governor Rochas Okorocha's party won all 27 chairmanship seats and 636 out of the 645 councillorship seats in Imo state, although 13 political parties were contending for these positions. It is not limited to Imo State; the PDP swept all 31 local government area seats and 329 councillorship wards in the December 2, 2017, local government election in Udom Emmanuel's Akwa Ibom State. The results were rejected by the APC, citing the state electoral commission's lack of independence.

In Ifeanyi Ugwuanyi's Enugu State, PDP won chairmanship positions in all 17 local government areas and all the councillorship seats in the 258 electoral wards in the November 4, 2017, local council elections. In Akinwunmi Ambode's Lagos State, APC won all 20 local government areas, 37 local council development areas, and all the councillorship seats in the July 22, 2017, local council elections. In Zamfara State, APC won all 14 chairmanship positions in the January 2, 2016, local council elections. PDP won all 15 chairmanship and 181 councillorship seats in Kwara State on October 26, 2013. These are just a few examples of the shenanigans called local government council elections in Nigeria.[40] The Nigerian Senate's bid to strip state governors of their power to conduct local government council elections was scuttled in 2017, when the House of Representatives voted 229/59 against it.[41] Further efforts should be made to ensure this error is corrected, especially when elections are conducted.

Some state governors simply institute "caretaker committees" that handle government administration for years. This happens for political reasons or to retain their grip on the affairs of the councils: for example, Ondo State did not conduct council elections under the governorship of Olusegun Mimiko. The governor worked with caretaker committees the entire time. The same happened in Oyo State for almost a decade.[42] We cannot continue like this – we already pay dearly for a lack of strong structures at the local government level. It may be better to give the powers to conduct local council polls to the Independent National Electoral Commission than to keep using the State Independent Electoral Commissions option.

Nigerian citizens must discard their apathy toward holding political officials accountable for their actions. If we are truly interested in making government work for us, from the most elite citizen to the most disconnected members of the grassroots population, then we need accountability for all government roles. The beauty of democracy is that it includes the people – the governance of, by, and for the people who embrace it. Each person must understand that their civic duties include asking questions about governance inputs, processes, and outcomes. Throwing up one's hands in defeat or choosing apathy is an abdication of responsibility; it is an informal legalization of trampling the rule of law, embracing corruption, and accepting declining development indices and decaying standards of living. This option is unacceptable, and it will not help anyone, least of all the people at the grassroots level who need governance gains the most.

Nigerian citizens may have to fight to insist that lawmakers ensure local government reform, removing the clauses that currently hinder the functionality of the councils. In section 8 of the 1999 Constitution, it implies that local government authorities are creations of the state governments.

[40] Chuks Oluigbo, "Sham LG Elections: The Blame Is on House of Reps," *Business Day*, September 2, 2018, www.businessdayonline.com/news/article/sham-lg-elections-blame-house-reps/.

[41] Ibid.

[42] Johnson O. Olaniyi, "State Independent Electoral Commissions and Local Government Elections in Nigeria," *Africa's Public Service Delivery & Performance Review* 5, no. 1 (2017): 133.

The national assembly must acknowledge that this hampers their ability to function, especially with regards to funding.

Another area that needs better interpretation and simplification is section 8 (13) of the 1999 Constitution, which grants state governments the power to create new local government areas. It also grants this creative power to houses of assembly at the state level. At the same time, the Constitution in section 8(13) also empowers the National Assembly to ratify such creations, leading to conflict between Federal and State governments over the creation and administration of local governments.

Enugu State Government relied on the provision of section 8 (13) to recreate fifty-two local government authorities from the initial seventeen local government authorities in the state, but the Federal Government refused to ratify the creation.[43] Lagos State later had a similar confrontation with the Federal Government over the same issue. They have the power to pressure law enforcement bodies, especially anti-graft agencies like the Economic and Financial Crimes Commission (EFCC) and the Independent Corrupt Practices Commission (ICPC), to enforce the present fiscal laws as they apply to public offices across the board.

How well-governed a country is depends on the amount of work that inhabitants are willing to put in, and the management of local government is the responsibility of everyone. Local governance should be the level that is the most important and feels the most familiar. The late Claude Ake indicted the present situation under postcolonial rule: "Indigenous leaders are responsible for a perverse alienation, the delinking of leaders from followers, a weak sense of national identity and perception of the government as a hostile force."[44]

Confucius links the ethical principles involved in administering the affairs of a state with an aggregation of the ethical principles belonging to its constituent units.[45] In this context, Nigerian citizens should show that they value justice and progress by ensuring that their representatives display these values. Public administration decisions should be challenged through peaceful protest methods, such as writing to lawmakers and expressing their viewpoints, rejecting money or other incentives to vote for the wrong people, showing up to vote, and calling out poor behavior in public officials. At the local government level, communities should insist on knowing what was budgeted and following the process

---

[43] Okafor et al., "Developmental Local Government as a Model for Grassroots Socio-Economic Development in Nigeria," 49–50.

[44] Claude Ake, *Democracy and Development in Africa* (Washington, DC: Brookings Institution Press, 2001).

[45] Miles Menander Dawson, "The Ethics of Confucius, Chapter V: The State," *Sacred Texts*, 2002, www.sacred-texts.com/cfu/eoc/eoc10.htm.

until all items are accounted for. For glaring cases of fiscal irresponsibility and outright theft, they should insist on following the due course of law. Anti-corruption laws are in place, and they can be enforced by the appropriate bodies, but the responsible agencies tire easily or fall victim to politicking. Only deliberate, focused, and insistent citizen demands can galvanize them into action.

Citizen Power

Grassroots activism should be a vital component of government institutions. It involves a vast number of marginalized people, addressing their concerns and needs. This makes policies more inclusive and more reflective of the constitution that they serve. The World Social Forum (WSF) is an annual meeting of civil society organizations that are focused on finding grassroots solutions to the issues plaguing countries, especially in the Global South.[46] It is a little large in scope, but it is considered, at its core, to be a collection of grassroots organizations because of the principles that it exemplifies: anti-Western hegemonic, anti-capitalist, self-sustainability, decolonization, environmental/climate justice, property, and human rights principles. The WSF hosts well-known leaders, such as Evo Morales of Bolivia and Lula da Silva of Brazil,[47] and countless others from West Africa. These conferences push heads of state to think through the question of what economic and social development looks like in their nations when it benefits the masses.

Grassroots activism allows individuals to find their own voices. When high government officials create policies, there is a disconnect between the concerns of the people and the policies that are implemented. Wangari Maathai's Green Belt Movement in Kenya is an example of successful grassroots organizing. The movement focused on re-cultivating and conserving the local environment by planting over 51 million trees in Kenya.[48] It was not inherently political, but it informed and empowered communities, allowing them to foster a more democratic space where the Kenyan government would take their concerns seriously. Grassroots organizers are reluctant to participate in political processes, because of their distrust of institutions that have continuously oppressed

---

[46] *World Social Forum*, "About the World Social Forum," *World Social Forum*, 2016, fsm2016.org/en/sinformer/a-propos-du-forum-social-mondial/.

[47] Claire Provost, "World Social Forum: Grassroots Africa Takes Centre Stage," *The Guardian*, February 18, 2011, www.theguardian.com/global-development/poverty-matters/2011/feb/18/world-social-forum-reflections-back-ahead.

[48] See www.greenbeltmovement.org/.

them. But these bottom-up approaches to democracy and development are the ones that enable the most radical reforms.

The late Burkina Faso President Thomas Sankara's socialist, community-oriented approach to politics and development is another example of large-scale grassroots organizing. The government was responsible for constructing and implementing various policies in Burkina Faso, and Sankara focused on the remnants of colonialism that deeply affected the lives of many regional communities, especially lower-class ones. He and his cabinet were concerned with the well-being of the whole country. Sankara's concern for the public good resulted in many programs improving public health,[49] gender equality,[50] and self-sustainability in the country, due to grassroots ideology working in conjunction with government institutions.

If these transformative, radical changes are a result of grassroots ideology and organizing, why don't more leaders employ a grassroots approach to politics, democratization, and development? Ultimately, Sankara was assassinated; these movements cause an incredible power shift in most governments. Privileged elites are rendered powerless in the face of mass organizing, and it is not a power dynamic they are accustomed to. These threats to power are generally why governments that are allegedly democratic end up employing violent, militaristic tactics, and suppressive policies that reinforce existing power structures.

The relevant questions are how the voice of the people can be amplified and how civic engagement can be encouraged through a grassroots framework. Incentivizing governments to collaborate with local communities – to understand the needs of those communities and potentially workshop solutions to their issues – could foster a sense of true democracy and empowerment. It would also decrease the disconnect between federal and local governments. Within these institutions, there is a need for more checks and balances to address corruption and nepotism and to hold the government wholly accountable to the people. Once these democratic institutions understand that their legitimacy is derived from their constituents, they will be incentivized to serve the people. Ultimately, the people need to recognize this as well. Any government's power over people is directly derived from people. They are the force behind government. Once that power is recognized and internalized, mass socioeconomic and political revolution is on the horizon.

---

[49] *Thomas Sankara: The Upright Man*, directed by Robin Shuffield (2006; San Francisco, CA: California Newsreel), https://search.alexanderstreet.com/preview/work/bibliographi c_entry%7Cvideo_work%7C3798038.
[50] Ibid.

Citizen power is the greatest force for actualizing political change. Citizen participation unlocks the gains of democracy for the benefit of everyone involved, raising the country's development indices. Health infrastructure will work for those who need it. Educational systems will be reengineered to serve all children comfortably, possessing the resources to prepare them for the post-millennial world of work. Industry will expand and benefit entrepreneurial and goal-getting employees. Social plans will protect those who are unable to fend for themselves and safety nets will catch those at risk of pauperization. The power supply shortages will become history, and our sports teams will have the ability to excel at international competitions because the structures and processes will finally be right. When we all resolve to participate in our governing processes, and insist on our right to participate, Nigeria will reach the heights that we presently desire but seem unable to achieve.

Just as this nation's governance process was wrested from the military through pockets of defense, defiance, and opposition, citizens must wrest the governance process from the present crop of political leaders that do not measure up to the judiciary's unbiased scrutiny. And it starts at the most accessible level: the local government councils. When communities deliberately request audiences with and participation from their local government officials, it will snowball into the actualization of needed reforms; the status quo persists due to a lack of accountability.

The inhabitants of every local government area must actively acquaint themselves with their elected officials, going to them for information on the roads, markets, drainages, and other issues. If they ask about the local government budget, and why or how it will be executed in a certain way, and if they are clear about which items or utility projects they would like included in the budget, the officials will understand that there are eyes on them. This understanding will keep their behavior in line, and they will try to pass the buck to the other levels of government, especially on financing issues, to take the heat off themselves.

Imagine that millions of citizens, instead of being tired and disinterested in maintaining good governance, started to pressure their state governors and state lawmakers, asking for audiences, and regularly airing their needs and grievances through radio and TV stations. In that environment, public censure and fear of imminent disgrace, especially at the voting stations, would prevent governors from dictating unlawful demands connected to LGA allocations, or even from refusing to conduct elections. All because the people are interested and willing to protest peacefully, to rally around and say, "do it the way it is written in the Constitution of the Federal Republic of Nigeria."

There can never be a vibrant democracy without a vibrant populace. People must realize that, even now, the power is in their hands. They have chosen not to wield it in some cases, or they have opted to outsource and sell it in some other cases. The perceived lack of power for citizens is a systemic issue that local government reforms were meant to address. Of course, the Big Men run a patrimonial state. If government is unresponsive, citizens lose their sense of political efficacy and abdicate the political space in favor of alternative spaces, such as churches.

The Nigerian experience has shown that it is not enough to create local government councils. Citizens must be encouraged to take ownership of local governance and contribute their ideas and perspectives. When they see their ideas being utilized, it will spur them to contribute more, volunteer for committees, and develop a partnership mindset that makes them protective of the system. Then, the encroachment of other levels of government will not be tolerated. In fact, their opinions, ideas, and decisions will form the basis of activity at those levels, since politicians love being popular.

The Nigerian Labour Organization (NLO), the Academic Staff Union of Universities (ASUU), and other professional bodies needed to resort to strike actions to make demands in their sectors. It was like a civil rebellion, and great for the country because it forced elected officials to do the right thing for their constituents. Communities can practice their own civil rebellions to push home their demands for the government. But first, there must be a perspective shift to understand the fact that good governance is impossible without their active input.

An apparent disconnect among the people, especially young people, makes them unable to link the oil revenues that the government collects with the millions or billions that go "missing" in any theft or misappropriation scandal. A combination of poor education, repression from the military years, and the unconscious perception that politicians are untouchable – which is perhaps a legacy from the concept of kingship in Nigeria – prevent the people from rising up against poor governance. They must speak out against undemocratic and outright criminal activities performed by the political elites. Their emphatic rejection of poor governance will keep politicians on their toes. It will allow disciplined and visionary leaders, and an active and involved populace, to work together for relevant socioeconomic projects that improve the country's indices in all sectors and improve the welfare of its citizens. This will give rise to unbridled national growth and development, and Nigeria will take its place of pride on the world stage as the giant of Africa.

Civil society organizations like Budgit, Follow the Money, SERAP, and Enough is Enough Nigeria are trying to achieve that perspective shift on a national scale. They use slogans, such as "Office of the Citizen of the Federal Republic of Nigeria," "Ask Questions," and "Get Involved," to galvanize the citizenry into action. These organizations understand the thrust of citizen participation and employ it in their communication – Educate, Engage, Empower. They educate the citizens, especially on social media.

Enough is Enough recently started using the WhatsApp platform, to engage with questions and answer inquiries, as a way of making itself more accessible to the people. The project empowers citizens with facts, figures, pictures, and other documented evidence. It is behind the successful Freedom of Information Bill, which has been passed into law; the bill allows citizens to compel government ministries and parastatal organizations to open their accounting books. These laudable activities, if sustained, will ensure that corrupt and inept politicians are flushed out of the system and made too fearful to run for public office.

In fact, social media conversations on politics and the country reveal some positivity. Some young people are becoming interested in party politics, and others are choosing activism routes. One example is the #EndSARS campaign, which addressed issues with the Special Anti-Armed Robbery Squad (SARS). The squad was the Nigeria Police Force's response to frequent, high-profile armed robbery cases, but its members began turning their guns on civilians. Any young person that the squad encountered, male or female, would be ordered to turn over huge sums of money if they didn't want to be arrested as armed robbery suspects. These encounters could become deadly, and reports began surfacing in the media. The issue grew viral on social media, and more people shared experiences of extortion, extra-judicial killings, and wrongful detention. Demands grew for the disbanding and disarmament of the Squad, using the #EndSARS hashtag.

Another example of successful youth participation is Budgit, an organization created by Oluseun Onigbinde, a young man interested in tracking budgeting and budget implementation nationwide. It also joined the push for the Freedom of Information Bill, and we hope that the ongoing push for open budgets from the National Assembly and the Lagos State governments will also be successful.

Budgit's 2016 Tracka report followed 852 projects, showing that 343 were not done and 118 are still ongoing. No one is complaining. Citizens rarely ask questions or engage their lawmakers and local government officials. If young people looked through these Tracka reports for projects in their areas and then engaged their lawmakers and local government officials, we would see a massive reduction in misappropriation. These positive results would help more people take ownership of the governance structures in their communities. We need more brave and relentless young people to join the effort to ensure good governance through grassroots participation across the nation, entrenching true democracy in Nigeria.

Growing political participation at the grassroots level requires enlightenment and ways to exchange views, information, and opinions to inform the programs and activities of local governments. This can be assisted by community radio stations. Community radio is a tool for enhancing development and participation, and it is owned, managed, and controlled by local communities.[51] It has the potential to develop broad-based participation within communities, encouraging idea sharing and bringing local governments closer to the grassroots with opportunities for easy information sharing between citizens and elected officials. Proponents of community radio have long pushed for the government to liberalize radio broadcast policies, moving beyond the "decentralized state radios" currently in operation in Nigeria. Communities can use it for nonprofit, cohesion activities engendering better communications between communities and their elected representatives.

Better communication flow means better understanding of issues. Politicians can tailor their programs to meet community needs. It will increase the community members' interest in governance, because they will feel heard, they will feel that their opinions matter, and they will understand that their contributions can change the trend of development. This empowers people to take charge of their own destinies, decide how their communities will run, and determine what happens even at the federal government level. It is crucial to build roads, hospitals, schools, and other amenities, but the level of empowerment brought about through participatory governance is also essential. As the channels of communication and feedback grow healthier, the governance grows more participatory.

The possibilities inherent in community radio can be seen in today's commercial radio stations; there are a few call-in programs that focus on citizen complaints. They hear complaints on abandoned projects, dilapidated roads, broken water pipes, and power generation issues, calling on the appropriate authorities to address them. The programs have seen some success, especially when community members with complaints provide adequate details. If a road project is abandoned, and an affected community member calls in with details – its location, the period the repairs started, the state of the road, and the contractor that was working

---

[51] Nigeria Community Radio, "Welcome to Nigeria Community Radio Website," Nigeria Community Radio, 2012, http://nigeriacommunityradio.org/faqs.php.

on it – then the program presenters can call on both the government ministry that gave out the project and the contractor that failed to execute the project. This has resulted in higher compliance levels and reduced corrupt practices. If this kind of system can operate at the community level, where people can talk about their street, farm, power transformers, water pipes, drainages, or refuse disposal and see results, then community radio deserves to be institutionalized.

Commercial radio stations are not a substitute for community radio. They focus on profits because they are highly commercialized and heavily levied by the government. They cannot afford to focus on development programs, especially when entertainment brings more money. Community radio is not-for-profit, and it will encourage citizen participation in politics. It should be encouraged in Nigeria as part of government's determination to ensure all-around development and participatory governance.

Local government authorities, the third tier of government, should actually be the most important and most interesting tier for citizens. That is where they can exert the most influence and access the other tiers of government. However, factors like corruption, ambiguous division of power, citizen apathy, and political patronage systems have turned the beneficial concept of grassroots governance on its head, and benefits to the citizens are severely limited.

To give power back to the people, which is essential for the practice of democracy, we must ensure the growth of grassroots organizing and reenergize the local government authorities to take their rightful position in governance and development, fulfilling all the conditions mentioned here. This requires the input of all stakeholders – all tiers of government, civil society, the media, and citizens everywhere. It may even require struggle and well-focused protests directed at dismantling a failed system.

22 Revolutionary Option: Social Movements and Power to the Citizens

In reflecting on solutions to Nigeria's problems, one is fragmenting a sin into so many others: the sin of modernity into its primordial components, its lingering anomies, even antinomies, a cultural root that grows into a huge tree but then falls and crushes innocent passersby. In this chapter, the entanglements between culture, ethnicity, and development, and the interfaces between development and historical events will be explored, as well as the place of social movements in the history and advancement of Nigeria. To do so, it will draw on three theoretical templates comprising three scapes and habitus that shape intellectual thinking and routine practices and form linkages and intersections between so many variables.

The "Scapes" and Habitus

The first is the culture scape, referring to how ideas from the past and conglomeration of traditions shape how we think, understand, and interpret events. For instance, cultural cognition – the beliefs that are in our minds – shapes how we see people, interpret the things around us, and even reach certain conclusions others not only disagree with but find amusing. Human beings process their day-to-day lives and realities based on inherited and acquired onto-epistemologies. Ideas, beliefs, and thought systems are processes of "scapes" that connect to our organization of the society; how individuals convert their "capital" into habitus, and how those aggregated habitus shape events in the process of human interactions.

Events are outcomes of decisions – those taken and those not taken – which cause tremendous consequences for nations and their people. Leaders constitute an elite, a political elite, but an elite operates on the basis of habits and behaviors that in turn affect the responses and behavior of the majority of the population in a political community. A set of elites may be morally upright, and this will reflect on institutions of society and how they are deployed. But an elite can also be morally bankrupt and, if they are thieves, the institutions they create will be corrupt. To illustrate:

Nigerian nationalism is a culture scape that contributed remarkably to the independence, development, and sustainability of Nigeria as a united nation-state. This scape is formulated by the accumulated necessity to end colonialism in Nigeria and achieve independence. Hence, it becomes an ideology to drive independence, not just politically and economically, but also socioculturally.

The second theoretical paradigm is the habitus of capital. What individuals do reflects their routine habits, drawn from the "capital" they have acquired – linguistic capital, erotic capital, intellectual capital, aristocratic capital, etc. The habitus of capital can in turn affect how the state is understood and responded to. For instance, one can complain that the Nigerian state is corrupt, but if the person has developed an aristocratic habitus, his desire may be to participate in that corruption so that he can become an aristocrat. An endomorphic habitus seeks more food and the means to acquire food, even to steal or allocate resources to acquire rice and bread; while the ectomorphic habitus may seek the opposite means of avoiding food. While the ectomorphic habitus generates a lean body, the endomorphic habitus becomes bigger and bigger till it hits the point of implosion. In the same way, a state too manifests endomorphic habitus, taking its resources and squandering it, even when the danger signs of trouble are visible, till it becomes unsustainable. Regarded as the pioneer of Nigerian nationalism, Herbert Macauley acquired and exhibited a high-level nationalist habitus, which prompted the struggle for the independence of Nigeria that challenged such culture scapes as that of colonialism. The interrelation between the habitus and scape becomes evidently intertwined at this level; the habitus can be likened to a system and the scape to a worldview. The internetwork of habitus strengthens or destabilizes a scape.

The state, described by Aristotle as *hexis*, can have a character, and the elements of that character can generate problems. Over time, this concept of *hexis* becomes transformed into habitus. By 1934, Mauss was already applying habitus to culture and society, arguing that an entire group creates habits, skills, tastes, and practices that define how they think and act.[1] By 1977, Pierre Bourdieu, one of the most preeminent sociologists, had turned the concept of habitus into a core aspect in the field of sociology.[2] As Bourdieu formulates the concept of habitus, a society or state can be divided into various clusters on the basis of religion, class, education, profession, race, ethnicity, language, etc. Each cluster creates

[1] Marcel Mauss, "Les Techniques du Corps," *Journal de Psychologie* 32, no. 3–4 (1936): 271–293.
[2] Pierre Bourdieu, *Outline of a Theory of Practice* (Cambridge University Press, 1977).

its own habitus, which is how it sees the world around itself, reacts to events, and relates to others. In this formulation, the rich and poor don't think alike and don't see things the same way. Muslims and Christians think differently. All these are possible because the people have acquired different habitus capitals, and a person can equally acquire multiple habitus capitals. Also, what holds the society from self-destruction from these varying levels of habitus is the intersectionality formed by virtue of human relation and association. Hence, while the habitus differs, there are shared conceptions that bring society to a border of a rather fragmented solidarity.

The third paradigm is the habitus of politics: how individuals within each cluster analyze the Nigerian nation in terms of different dispositions and beliefs. Ethnicity, for instance, as a habitus, shapes our bodies and minds and the actions we produce from them. Thoughts and social perceptions are organized around ethnic habitus; one's dispositions to politics may be shaped by ethnic locations. This brings to the fore the differing positions and the ultimate outcomes of Nigerian nationalism as a culture scape. While there is a consensus on the habitus of nationalism, (that is, the independence of Nigeria), other capitals and habitus such as that of ethnicity, religiosity, aristocracy, etc., create a dissonance that distort the proper and effective formation of the postindependent Nigerian nationalist scape. At the ethnic level, there is the contention for dominance and fear of alienation; at the aristocratic level, there is the acquisition of the nationalist habitus to acquire power for selfish gains or as an exhibition of class struggle. Similarly, these habitus and scapes are manifested in different dimensions and through different approaches, which reiterates the interaction of these phenomena.

The nationalist scape, for example, is manifested in the political habitus, literary habitus, religious habitus, etc., and the formulation of the nationalist scape is tempered by intellectual and ideological capitals/ approaches, as in the literary habitus; revolutionary, as in the political habitus; or violent and practical, as in the habitus occupied by the masses. The (partial) failure of these different conceptions and acquisitions to enhance the postindependent Nigerian scape spurred military interventions starting from the civil war. While this intervention would turn out to be a great distortion to the progress of the nation, it indicated the political habitus acquired by the military men, which is more violent and radical. As Pierre Bourdieu clearly formulates it, hexis – how we arrange our physical self and space – and the mental habits we cultivate that shape our actions are created. As he explains, one does not have to think anymore before acting or reacting, having been socialized into certain practices, ideas, and beliefs, thereby enabling social structures to be reproduced. To apply this concept, Nigerian habitus of politics has been constant since the country's formation as a colonial nation and the transition to postindependence.

The scapes and habitus, in combination, generate a system of meta narratives: the threads of discord over a prolonged period in the country's history. Current challenges have their roots in the past, consolidated by the scapes and habitus of the present. The colonial state was part of the orbit of global imperial forces that promoted territorial acquisition for the sake of extractive economies. The colonial state had the capacity to unleash repression. The colonial state had an offensive capacity that the postcolonial military adopted after independence. A state with an offensive capacity belittles the representation, rights, and well-being of those it governs. The tragedy is the failure of the various groups to respond appropriately, but instead to act confused. Internal cohesion of progressive forces has given way to division and to the expression of hate by one group for another. The acquired operating habitus and scapes can be deployed to analyze the political scenery of Nigeria during the 2015 presidential election. The perceived gross failure of President Goodluck Jonathan, and the accumulated unyielding outcome of democracy since 1999 (under the control of the People's Democratic Party), reignited a longing for a return to an authoritarian society governed by the military who could at least ensure security and control the mismanagement challenges that set back the country's progress. Also, these failures and challenges necessitated a desire for any other system of governance, as long as it promised a radical change. It is on these premises of expectations, failures, and desires that Muhammadu Buhari became a preferable alternative, not necessarily a better one. With dictatorship experience and a democratic present, he fulfilled the figure of "the benevolent dictator" that some hoped could make the proper policies and changes. This distorted conception and fragmented formation of improper habitus and scapes continues to hinder Nigeria's progress.

Critical challenges to the colonial state, and the belief that a better postcolonial state can emerge, began during World War II. If WWII gave room for the loyal support of the British and their imperialist project – masking the contradictions in society – the years after 1945 saw a deep hostility to colonial rule. A political upsurge followed after 1945, also accompanied by the desire for a democratic upsurge. During the same time, some radical and even violent expressions followed, especially in labor union quarters, verbalized as revolutionary anger. The British became the enemies: Sometimes radical groups framed capitalism as an enemy force as well. To radical union leaders, the British, and the capitalist forces they represented, exploited, dominated, oppressed, and enslaved

Nigerians. Nigeria's politics in the 1950s was dealing with challenges to the colonizers while building fresh imaginations of the future based on feasible and performative solutions to change the system they were criticizing.

The features of this continued in the 1960s. Radical elements began to express anger and to call on various segments of society to fuse democratic current with patriotic current so as to criticize politicians and members of the ruling class, culminating in the 1960s with the first coup when the planners criticized the political leaders as allies of imperial forces who were servile to capitalism.

In the 1960s, revolt turned away from the British to Nigerians in power. The federal government became the symbol of the ills of the nation. Virtually all ethnic groups had their grievances – to the North, the South wanted to dominate them; to the South, the North was retarding their progress. By the time the army took over in 1966, it quickly presented itself as a political messiah, an untested instrument of change and class consolidation; but by the time of such regimes as that of General Sani Abacha, the army had become a core apparatus of repression and oppression of the same people it purported to rescue from political disintegration and ethnic anarchy. The military engaged in violent repression of opposition forces. What is not always spoken about is that the military was also a key facilitator of ideological repression.

In spite of the scattered radical actions after 1945, the process of dismantling the colonial state in its government form was not accompanied by the creation of a new political structure and revolutionary institutions but by a series of upsurges – in labor union and its assertions; in the mobilization of the masses, consequently with ethnic coloration; in support of leading politicians and their political parties; and in the rising expectation of benefits that would come with independence. The internal upsurge was supported by big changes in geopolitics, global economics, and rising leftist ideologies. World War II produced serious outcomes: the colonial powers were weakened politically and militarily, capitalism was in crisis, and the repressive capacity of the colonial state was greatly attenuated. Ideologies of the left and radicalism grew in various ways: the stature of the Soviet Union was enhanced, and the Chinese revolution was declared a success. As the ideologies and their promises spread, many colonies began to witness radical and revolutionary upsurge. There were conversations about the people's war, conversion to socialism, expectations of support from China and the Soviet Union. In Asia, Africa, and Latin America, revolutionary masses began to develop ideas of revolutionary power. Concrete assertions were being made about the declining repressive powers of the capitalist world, including the ideology that sustained it.

Why did this expectation of the revolutionary moment fail? The answers to this question connect to the failure of the postcolonial state. To begin with, while there were conversations about radicalism and revolution in Nigeria, the country did not translate them into concrete action: the political parties that took over power from the British were not radical ideologically, with a very few exceptions. Second, at the global level, the rise of the United States after WWII was an obstacle. The United States was fiercely anti-socialist, anti-communist, and it did whatever it could to halt the spread of radicalism and revolution. The United States began to spread its tentacles in areas formerly colonized by Europe, and to even regard and present itself as the policeman of the world. The United States wisely anticipated that revolutionary movements would narrow capitalist markets and reduce profit.

The Nigerian leaders of the 1950s understood the politics of the Cold War. However, they calculated that strengthening people's democracy would undermine it, and their masses would challenge their exploitation. The leadership settled for the continuity of the institutions and practices of the colonial state that now favored US foreign policy goals. The weakness of the leadership that inherited power could not withstand the American offensive.

Fast forward: The current Nigerian state is able to get away with minimal development efforts not only because those who preside over it are not interested in development but that citizens behave as if they are powerless to oppose it. It appears as if there is a political lethargy, in spite of the constant expressions of aggravation with the status quo. There is an anti-state feeling, but there is also the prostration to power and a profound sociocultural disorientation. This dimension to the habitus of politics is fueled by the capital of political apathy and accumulated frustration. The sociohistorical timeline of Nigeria reveals little progress achieved by fierce opposition to the state, from Fela Kuti to Ken Saro-Wiwa. The forceful repression exhibited by the state has dismantled the leftover capitals of revolution and agitation. At best, what is left is doubt and uncertainty.

This cultural disorientation needs be underscored to the extent that it is unable to deal with anti-popular political leadership. Ethnicity tends to suggest that Nigerians have little in common, the *habitus of politics* earlier mentioned. The habitus plays out as in the construction of the tower of Babel that eventually collapsed: There is no agreement on the religion and rituals to sustain governance; there are divisions along religious, economic, and education lines. Since the collapse of colonialism, where is the common ideal to integrate the nation? The lines of division are multiple – religious, ethnic, social, and individual aspirational interests, cumulating in the *habitus of ethnicity*. There seems to be no institution, as in the army, to unite the vision of those elements seeking change. What movement or organization can mobilize the people and coordinate that agenda? The tendency for division is so strong in Nigeria that demonstrating against an unpopular government and corrupt state is difficult. Rather than coming together for political mobilization, they are evolving into a large network of a crisis-ridden society united by consumerism.

Challenges to the state are increasing, but not necessarily in ways that can create a better country, but rather further fragment it. Militant currents have developed at an alarming rate – kidnappings, the herdsmen crises, the Boko Haram insurgency, and an overall fear of insecurity. The militarist currents of ethnic nationalities, such as the agitation for Biafra, challenge the power of the state over them; those in the Niger Delta challenge the maldistribution of resources, as well as the growing clamor for a Republic of Oduduwa.

If the leadership is not doing well, would it be possible to turn to a segment of the civil society to become the agent of change and ultimately create the scape of development and the habitus of transformation? To interject the civil society into this discussion, the starting point will be to consider some of the legacies of the colonial past.

Modernity and the Locus of Struggles

After 1945, the prime target of nationalism was the British, the colonizers who conquered and controlled the country. The first locus of struggles was post/de/anti-colonization. For about the fifteen years between 1945 and 1960, this vibrant nationalism generated tremendous hope and optimism. It even delivered a temporary phase of welfarist ideology – deep thinking that connected power to development. The expectation, so strong in the 1950s, was that freedom from colonial rule would lead to development, a long-awaited paradise. The people placed their hope in indigenous leadership and transformational politics. However, this was not to be, and the period became the prelude to the deluge of depression and decadence.

Since the 1960s when Nigerians began to govern themselves, the critical space of resistance has been internal – anger and their manifestations produced coups, countercoups, a civil war, and a long period of military rule. Changes in government seem to always bring out a worse cast of leaders who stall even the small gains in the process of development, setting back the hands of the clock. It is as if the country always has to reset and begin again. The post-1960 struggles have exposed the limitations of the political system, the corruption of those who govern the country, and the bankruptcy of the vision of governance. To the poor, it is a story of hopelessness. The second locus of struggles became the efforts to reform leadership.

A third locus seeking positive changes has also been internal – changing the purpose of service in government from the intention to be rich to the intention to serve the public. This locus of attitudinal change is yet to be realized. This vision, which will transform the country, is yet to be created with any movement or solidity, although the need for it is always being discussed. This third locus, as is to be expected, will rethink the ideology of politics, the goals of civil society, and the tolerance of the populace for corruption. It will entail political mobilization of the poor, retooling cultures to service development. It will call for a new economic model different from that founded by the colonial state – production for export, based on profit and profitability to production for the masses, based on their needs.

Will this third locus ever materialize? There are assumptions that it won't on various grounds: that resistance will not come with the expected change; that millions of people are poor is true and should be taken for granted. But also taken for granted is that the poor will never unite. Class consciousness, some will argue, does not even exist as a unifying force. Violent revolutions don't produce positive outcomes, some would add, preferring instead the bloodless change that comes with electoral politics. The masses may also have been further paralyzed by the messages of Pentecostalism – a belief that faith and prayer will bring prosperity. Hope, in religious teaching, means that "no condition is permanent" – the person perceived as poor today may become rich a day after.

Devastating regimes such as those of General Sani Abacha which governed the country from 1993 to 1998, and highly corrupt ones such as that of Goodluck Jonathan (2010 to 2015) even supply some depressing evidence that authoritarianism of the former and the corruption of the latter did not trigger any large-scale rebellion. Nigerians, it is always argued, have an enormous capacity to endure poverty, to suffer, and to accept mismanagement. This capital of pseudo-endurance strengthens the political habitus characterized by apathy, which maintains the status quo of Nigeria as improperly managed and governed. Any regime that can bribe people with temporary cash, so goes the argument, can survive. These temporal succors become mechanisms to regulate the energy of the masses to protest all manners of unjustness. Sometimes, too, regimes are judged in relative terms, contrasting the depth of corruption of one as less intense than another; thereby accepting the lesser of two evils and leaving the more evil one/s to "God's imminent judgment."

Figure 22.1 A rally protest in Lagos against the high level of corruption in governance, unemployment, and poverty.

Yet, there is also contrary evidence to support the assertion that Nigerians do indeed protest and resist: for example, the peasant uprisings of the 1960s, revolts in the Niger Delta, the Boko Haram insurgencies, and countless student protests on university campuses. There is a history that has never been fully told – the various forms of overt and covert resistance against the state. Sites of resistance are also manifested in nonviolence, as in lamentations, daily curses, the angst, the search for alternative solutions outside of the state, and even apathy. Forces of repression may break some spirits, and the use of bribery and corruption may divide the ranks, but the masses are never deceived. Revolts, strikes, and protests might have failed, but not the desire to think of possibilities.

One may argue that Nigeria, like many other African countries, has not actually experienced the involvement of its people in deliberations on development and politics. In other words, the people have neither actually overthrown the political structures they dislike nor, even more import-antly, created alternative ones. In other words, the masses of Nigeria have not exercised the privilege of creating new forms of power, economy, and organization that can supplant those that fail. The habitus and scapes they have acquired and operate within are machinations of the political class that wants to hold on to power.

Complications of Politics

What can make the restoration of hope in Nigeria possible? If the leadership is not doing well, can civilian structures emerge to create a Pan-Nigerian solidarity? Would there ever be a crisis of conscience among the leadership and a crisis of confidence in the civil society? If the conflicts and crises of Nigeria are cumulated, they are all internal. Arguments can be raised, using the example of Israeli–Arab perpetual conflicts, as to whether it is not better to have an external enemy than an internal one. The unity of the Jews in Israel is in part grounded on the belief that they are surrounded by enemies, and whereas the division between European Jews and Oriental Jews may be deep, they all forget their differences and unite in the face of hostilities with the Palestinians and Arabs.

Patriotism in Nigeria has been forever weak. There has never been a moment in the country's history when a national-based political party has emerged to generate a collective nationalist orientation. In the absence of that patriotism, moments of grave threats to the country are greater than moments of collective unity.

A national movement is yet to emerge, whether generated by the Left or the Right. Successive governments have failed to create adequate socio-cultural and political national movements, despite attempts to use the national youth corps, federal university, and federal unity schools. With political instability in the first five decades after independence, militarization of power became adopted as a technique to build the nation. The military failed and no pro-Nigerian patriotism emerged. The technical infrastructure of the country is inadequate to transform the country and generate the security where and when needed. Even a kidnapper who uses a cellphone to collect ransom cannot be located in spite of the massive advances in tracking technologies. There is also evidence of technical paralysis in the management of airports, roads, and facilities to develop the state.

Infrastructure of training to acquire skills, capital, and resources continues to be degraded. Repressive regimes, as in the case under the military and corrupt governments witnessed after 1999, cannot generate any cohesive society; neither can their offensive power deal with insurgent forces. Whereas the state can muster larger police and army forces, it has been unable to deal with even the smaller forces of the Boko Haram and Niger Delta insurgency. The anti-state forces are grounded in nationalism and strong commitments to their fundamentalist causes. Lacking in authenticity, legitimacy, and relevance, the state is unable to eliminate or negotiate with insurgent forces.

The Nigerian leadership is always drawn into conflicts they are not prepared for. Irreconcilable forces have been created to discuss Nigeria. On the one hand are forces opposed to the federalist power that is over-centralized; these forces tend to be organized along ethnic and religious lines. Their representatives are organized and methodical, persistent, and trenchant; there are also the angry ones who complain about resource allocation. On the other hand, there are those who preside over the management of the Nigerian state, handicapped by corrupt tendencies and lack of patriotism. The state is incoherent in its political goal and aspirations. It lacks the proper scapes that can energize and actualize a truly developed Nigeria. It even lacks the moral power to mobilize its own citizens for counteroffensives against alternative sub-nationalities. Popular forces that want the country to be restructured along more democratic lines have been prevented from realizing their wishes.

There is too much concentration of analysis on the deficiencies of leadership, which seems appropriate as its members control and distribute resources. However, we need to spend more time focusing on the followership as well, which brings to the fore the values of the habitus as the building block of a progressive scape and society. In so doing, we must first identify the values of followership. We understand what the people want – leadership to deliver development in an atmosphere of peace and stability. There are positive values already in place: tolerance, cooperation, religiosity – to mention but a few. All of them allow the leadership to govern without much challenge. It can even be argued that Nigerians are not difficult to govern because of a high level of (in)tolerance. Pentecostalism and Sunni Islam are also religious enforcement of tolerance, even the traditional beliefs. The excessive hope-preaching in Pentecostalism supports the politics of tolerance – if God will ultimately bless you, what is your business in fighting power? Rather than assessing the possibilities of how it can be or ought to be, the notion of pseudo-endurance has reinforced the belief that "it is because it is meant to be." At these levels, human agency is discarded, surrendered to the fatalistic belief that "it is because it has been made to be."

On the other side of the coin are the negative values. The ultimate one is corruption, and complicity with corruption. Followers receive bribes just as officials do. There is the violation of regulations from building codes to obtaining driver's licenses. If followers are corrupt, then what we analyze is the scale of corruption; that is, those with power steal more than those without, or those without crave to do as much or worse than those with the power. As such, the basis for moral indictment is flawed and rendered non-functional in a society that operates a "fantastically corrupt"[3] political system, and expressions as *gbogbo wa ni ole t'ile ba da* (that is, "we are all thieves in the absence of everyone") are used to justify condemnable consciousness; increase in cybercrimes among the Nigerian youths is a pre-indication of the looming crisis that awaits the country if proper proactive measures are not taken to instill positive values/habitus.[4]

Many followers participate in politics for what they can get, even little crumbs. There is the worship of money and expectations of undue favors from the politicians, all embedded in the misleading ideology that those at the helm should give part of what they have allegedly stolen. Many even encourage their children to look for jobs or go to college to study in fields with high-yielding remunerations or work in places with high potential for accumulating bribes, charmingly called *egunje*. The sought-after careers are those with opportunities to collect bribes. It is not uncommon to find even the youngest in Nigeria striving for every (political) opportunity to mismanage public funds and resources, what would unashamedly be referred to as his/her own share of the "national cake."

In addition, there is the distorted notion of false reality and blame shifting. A popular mantra among the political class, especially during election, is how the past/present government has failed the people or how it is responsible for the present predicaments bedeviling the nation. A government employee who refuses to perform his/her duty will blame the government for not employing enough hands, the political leader will blame the past government for the misappropriation of funds which has hindered the inability to employ more hands, the past government would in return blame the present administration for incompetency, also blaming a past government, but more importantly justifying to the people why they should be re-elected to bring the desired change. This bottom-up spectrum blame shifting highlights the need for individual ascension to bring about desired development. So, admittedly, there is no need to fight over embracing evil or corruption.

---

[3] In 2016, during a conversation with the Queen of England and at an anti-corruption summit in London, David Cameron, the then British Prime Minister, referred to Nigeria and Afghanistan as "fantastically corrupt." See BBC News, "David Cameron Calls Nigeria and Afghanistan 'Fantastically Corrupt' – BBC News," YouTube video, 0:28, May 10, 2016, www.youtube.com/watch?v=yO_EekNnfjI. Accessed March 28, 2020.

[4] Turning the revolutionary logic of Fela on its head, the sensational Nigerian artist, Naira Marley – in a claim to refute the Economic Financial Crime Commission's accusation of his involvement in cybercrime – referred to as "Yahoo Yahoo" in the Nigerian *street lingo*, sang in "Am I a Yahoo Boy," summarily, that everyone, including the government, the bloggers, the religious priests, etc., are all criminals but rhythmically arguing that *eni ti ile ba mo ba ni barawo* (that is, "only those caught are the criminals"), again, manipulating the "not criminal until convicted" basis of legal justice, which, to start with, is lacking in Nigeria.

Social Movements

In recent times, not enough consideration has been given to either the historical significance of social movements or their present potential to drive reformation and revolution. Diverse groups of the masses – from artisans, traders, laborers to teachers – have always mobilized themselves under the solidarity of a common struggle to protest, to advocate for change, and to see a better life. At different points in the history of Nigeria, there have been alliances between various social movement to advance a common struggle.

As in every society, social movements in Nigeria since the precolonial period have been divided between the reformational and the fanatical. Eventual liberation of the country is important to counter the stiff challenges against colonial rule. Such movements as the Ekumeku (Niger River West)[5] witnessed the rise and participation of monarchs who confronted colonial raiders and utilized mercenaries and warriors to participate in actions for reformation and drive positive changes. The coalitions of these movements, shortly before and after independence, evolved into several political parties to contest the political powers and positions to manage the affairs of the country. The concerns of social movements can likewise be trans-border: a number of other groups, such as environmental and feminist groups, are called "new movements" because, unlike Sokoto and Niger Delta, they cut across tribes, ethnicities, and nationalities to focus on issues that may or may not be related with social class.[6]

The failures and escalations of previous social movement are, on the one hand, important to better plan the intricacies and processes to drive reformation, and, on the other hand, imperative to sustaining the stability and development of the nation by avoiding terrible and violent outcomes if not social movements are properly managed as a result of the negligence, indifference, and insensitivity of the political elites. Enough inferences from the nineteenth-century jihad and the formation of the Sokoto Caliphate, for example, could have been made to prevent the outbreak of the Biafra crises. The civil war proves the possible resistance of armed social movements to even a military dictatorship; this has also been seen

---

[5] Toyin Falola, *Colonialism and Violence in Nigeria* (Bloomington: Indiana University Press, 2009).
[6] The literature is extensive. Among others, see Graeme Chesters and Ian Welsh, *Complexity and Social Movements: Multitudes at the Edge of Chaos* (Abingdon: Routledge, 2006); Susan Eckstein, ed., *Power and Popular Protest: Latin American Social Movements*, updated ed. (Los Angeles: University of California Press, 2001); David Snow, Sarah A. Soule, and Hanspeter Kriesi, eds., *The Blackwell Companion to Social Movements* (Malden: Blackwell, 2004); and Suzanne Staggenborg, *Social Movements* (Oxford: Oxford University Press, 2008).

in the formation of the Movement for the Actualization of the Sovereign State of Biafra (MASSOB), the Ijo Youth Council (IYC), and a host of other associations in central Nigeria during the despotic rule of General Sani Abacha.[7]

The lack of food, good roads, an adequate supply of electricity, adequate health care, or any other basic amenities are abundant reasons to cause a social shift and massive uprising against the government, resisting even the usual violent state control. Displaced, alienated, and frustrated, social movements become attractive to the masses and are earnestly embraced as the power mechanism to articulate their opinions, to revert their unfortunate realities, and to enhance the society. Hence, social movements become a preferable alternative to governance and idyllic state formation. Evolving from dialogue, then to protest, and then to violence when the needs and demands of the movement are not met, social movements are continuously structured to agree to a set of demands, elaborate a set of wishes, make known a set of choices, regularize actions, and also offer new prospects and possibilities of how the society can develop.

As social movements fade away after either failing or achieving their goal, ethnicity, religious affiliation, and difference in goal are lingering factors that also affect the integration of social movement and overall achievement. The presence of an "adversary" and savior phenomenon, willing followers, and the chain reaction of events are factors that drive the creation and progress/success of a movement. An agent of resistance, which has suffered or hindered the well-being of the people, is established, and the state, capitalism, or the political elites can be depicted as the adversary, depending on the goal and formation of the movement. The formation of the movement, having identified and established the adversary, is led by a charismatic and often ideological leader who possesses the vision and astuteness to mobilize the masses to achieve a common good. The course of events and their reach determines the band of followership and the strength of the power that can be attained by a movement.

A successful social movement can be the beginning of a new political party, civil war, or resistance. A social movement can also influence an existing political party or an ethnic group to absorb a new social agenda. The jihadist movement in the north captured power and gained enormous influence, while the Niger Delta social movements aim to influence politics, most especially on how revenues generated from oil are shared

---

[7] Okpeh Ochayi Okpeh Jr., Ada Okau, and Sati Umaru Fwatshak, eds., *The Middle Belt in the Shadow of Nigeria* (Makurdi: Oracle, 2007).

and used for development. In either case, social movements cannot be overlooked; they have considerable ability to realign civil society, enlarge the democratic arena, challenge the relationship between the government and violence, and adjust the reactions of international companies and other areas of globalization that they stand for.

However, absorbing movement leaders into politics weakens and absolves the functionality of such movements, and that are consequently marginalized. At this point, civil recovery gives way to cynicism, thereby creating a vicious cycle. The framework of the civil society and social movements exposes the failures of the state, which necessitates the rehabilitative and reconstructive agendas of social movements. For any society to move forward, it must be willing to adopt and learn from social movements and the concerns of interest groups, which can be devoid of violence and insurgency. Instead, oral traditions, divination, music, story-telling, and other aspects of popular culture can be adopted to advance the cores of social movements. Recast as cultural history, the motifs of social movement become cultural expressions engrafted into unbecoming daily realities and struggles to manage the challenges of political margin-alization and instability. Cultural productions are creative responses to power, especially against violence and military terror.

Hence, there must be an end to the lack of trust and constant mutual suspicion among ethnic groups. Distrustful religious divisions need to be healed. When historical grudges fester, they deepen. Social movements get involved with nationalism, and the downtrodden look forward to becoming the oppressors. Nigeria's postcolonial journey into modernity must be accompanied by the ideals driving the formation of social move-ments: social justice, equity, development, political stability, democracy, and human rights. Because power is still linked with either ethnicity or the armed forces, naturally, resource control is connected to both. The distribution of power and resources will always be sources of disunity that eventually trigger centrifugal forces. High rates of unemployment will create youth movements. Economic challenges, political assump-tions, and instrumentalized tribalism, among other issues, will continue to guarantee the formation and the continuous existence of social move-ments that launch protests and can lead to revolutions.

The Scenarios of Radicalism

Radical orientation is necessary although some may think it is over-the-top or farfetched. Some may even regard radical statements as acts of treason, for example, Omoyele Sowore's clamor for revolution. A culture of developing opposition to abusive power and corruption must emerge with coherence, methodology, expansion, and offensive mechanism. Incoherent sporadic mobilization must give way to a long-lasting formula with absolute capacity to mobilize people for well-defined, coordinated, and protracted offensive to demand accountability and end corruption. While this may incite violence, it is not coterminous with violence.

There is the need to learn to replace defensive words with bellicose words against the corruption of power. An outwardly calm demeanor has to be replaced by a combative one and punctuated, when necessary, by demagogic statements to indicate deep moral intolerance to mismanagement and corruption. Of course, there should be the awareness that aggression has to combat repression as both are locked in opposition. Popular forces must assure themselves that they can break the fetters imposed on them by repressive governments.

Expressions of patriotic aspirations, combined with revolutionary orientation, can produce new democratic associations and combative struggles. The unnecessary violent struggles by Boko Haram and fringe groups must give way to a more popular approach based on positive orientations. Revolutionary resistance that is uncoordinated, builds on ethnicity, and relies on the charisma of one person or a few may not work in such a plural society as Nigeria. There is no guarantee for success in any revolutionary struggle, which means that those who engage in them must have the capacity for intellectual sagacity. Hence, there must be a thorough coordination between the appropriate capital acquisitions to drive the revolutionary habitus which would provide the enhanced Nigerian scape.

In linking radical positive movements to political mobilizations and actions, a set of future scenarios can be attempted here; none with the data to predict its possibilities, processes, and outcome but these can be inferred through a proper scrutiny of past antecedents in Nigeria and elsewhere:

1. If more people become politically active, with a positive transformational agenda, there will certainly be a qualitative transformation of the political spaces since forces in opposition will reach points of compromise if not of resolution. Despite the existing difference among the earliest Nigerian nationalist, their sociopolitical consciousness, driven toward the independence of Nigeria, is unshaken.

2. Contradictions will open up within the state itself, among the people, and between the state and its people as they all engage in combative activities either for or against the emergence of leaders committed to positive transformation and development.

3. Sources of weakness and strength will develop among people fighting for change, but their forms and outcomes are difficult to predict. Offensives and

counteroffensives will produce different results, each opening up new sets of contradictions. Sources of strength can become sources of weakness and vice versa, leading to the emergence of new strategies of mobilization and political thought. This means it is important to identify the points of strength and weaknesses with adequate plans to deal with them when they arise.

4. Anti-despotic, anti-oppressive, anti-development, anti-corruption statements and positions will gain currency as part of building political networks and concrete mobilization for action. Some will be sincere statements, and others will be to mask individual ambitions and desire.

5. Resistance is a form of political creativity that can become more energized. This creativity will find limitless space in music, Nollywood, dance, drama, and stories. The potency of art to drive transformation in a society cannot be overstated. The artistry of figures like Fela Anikulapo, Wole Soyinka, and the rest, helps to conscientize the people about their true social realities and serves as anchorage to mobilize revolution. Moreover, the audience of these creative outputs reaches across gender, age, class, region, or other barriers, which makes them appropriate for formulating solidarity.

6. Systematic anti-people offensives and repression will produce popular counteroffensives; and the state will respond, possibly not to negotiate but to repress. Because the state boasts more machinations and resources, it is somewhat assured of its ability to repress every form of offensive, from peaceful protest to revolution. Exploiting diplomacy and democracy, a call for negotiation or peace has always been a succor mechanism employed by the state to destabilize the foundation, agitation, and strength of a protest or uprising. The Academic Staff Union of Universities in Nigeria has been embarking on strike actions for more than a decade on the premise of the same issues. A call for negotiation and peace averted what could have been the victory of the Agbekoya revolt (1968–9) in the western region of Nigeria.

7. If initial popular offensives succeed, more and more people will join: millions can march in protest waves against corrupt government. The Arab Spring, for example, is a revolutionary struggle that started in Tunisia in 2010 but quickly escalated into a regional revolutionary wave in the whole of North Africa, pressing further into the Middle Eastern region. Should this happen, new combative forms of struggles can emerge taking the form of democratic organizations and militant forms of struggle. Unchecked, uncoordinated, and undisciplined, what started as positive may end up as anarchy. Following the overthrow and

demise of Muammar Gaddafi in October 2011, without well-thought-out plans and ideology, Libya plunged into a state of military anarchy from which it is yet to recover.

8. Whether they win or lose battles, as sketched in point (7), if defeated by repressive power of the state, popular forces can regroup with their fighters and propagandists.

9. This regrouping will produce theories, unleash greater creativity, and connect with major causes and motivations, sense of purpose, and sacrifices. Popular forces may become better able to understand success to surrender with dignity when necessary.

10. Defeat can produce positive results – greater ability to analyze a situation and to regroup, to regenerate commitment to seek a collective liberty, and emergence of new relationships among the members of the popular forces.

11. The confidence of the state in itself can be eroded as its army and police are overwhelmed and spread too thin to function. Popular movements and wars of harassment, in combination with guerilla warfare, can break down the defenses of the state. As balances of forces are created, the belief in the superiority of the army of the state can actually collapse.

However, none of the aforementioned scenarios will ever happen as long as the populace is divided by religion and ethnicity. The habitus of ethnicity will continue to shape and dominate the habitus of politics. The scenarios created here require revolutionary modifications to current scapes and habitus. Nigeria cannot move forward on any radical revolutionary path without genuine democratic values, mass heroism, radical fraternity, and revolutionary values. The strength of the state does not lie in any strong ideology; not even in pseudo-idealism. The essential element in the state is the force of corruption with a reactionary ideology that holds people in contempt. There is always an enthusiastic conversation to crush the reactionary ideology of the state, a heritage since the 1950s. If progressive values can spread, perhaps the recruitment of citizens to democratic and non-corrupt values can succeed. Who knows? The scenarios attempted here are about a possible teleology of the future, which can now be grounded in a more realistic narrative.

Crossroads: Challenges and Vision of the Future

The country is at critical crossroads as the government seems incapable of improving living conditions and resolving the controversies around the national question. Ethnic militias are creating havocs; Boko Haram in the North-East has visited its terrorism on innocent lives; pro-Biafra agitators want to secede; Arewa youth asked the Igbo to leave the northern region; some want the Yoruba to create an Oduduwa Republic. The minorities fear that the majorities want to perpetuate their superiority over them. Speaking ill about Nigeria has become the starter, the main course, and the dessert of daily diets.

Conversations on restructuring occupies pages of newspapers and forums on the Internet and social media: views on how to restructure the country and how to move forward are no different from the metaphor and mythology of the "Tower of Babel," which herein can be referred to as the "tower parable" that gives the central organizing principle to this part of the book. The original intention in the 1950s was how to create one strong nation state, the "tower." But as the politicians and their followers work in multiple ways and directions, and as the politicians seek different means to enrich themselves, not only do they not coordinate what they do, but they speak in different languages such that a tower cannot be constructed in the first instance, but indeed, the fear is that the very foundation, not even just the building, will collapse.

In the original rendition of the Tower of Babel, it was the stronger force of a superior spiritual figure that caused the calamity, scattering the people in different directions and seizing the capacity to communicate. In this discourse, reworked as a mythology of the Nigerian secular space, there is no stronger external force, but those of minions setting traps for one another. They do not speak the same language, and even when they use the colonizer's language to understand one another, they don't agree on what they mean, what they intend, and what they will do. It is high time resources and energies were channeled to building a new and better structure, a sphere and not a tower! A tower is what Nigeria is presently, laid vertically on the axes of ethnicity, class, regionalization, and other sociocultural differences. Therefore, to suggest a new tower is to revitalize the same structure that causes the problem, it is reverting to the past. Unlike the tower, the operation of the sphere is all-inclusive, interconnected and inter-dependent, and its horizontal dimension reinforces the images of collectivity, synchronism, equality, and equity.

When all the crises are summed up, a number of questions arise: Who should defend the Nigerian state? What should be the reasons to defend it? Must the defender be profiting from the state? If the poor are many and oppressed, can forces unite them so that they can be the agents of their own destiny? If that destiny will be tied to resistance, can we be sure that the capacity for repression will not be overwhelming to destroy the capacity for resistance? As Africa itself is within a global world system that is dominated by capital, how does it remove itself from the shackles of global domination and exploitation?

In posing these questions, the fragility of the Nigerian state to the extent that previous gains can be wiped out within a few months is realized. Events are fluid; politics is complex. Many are calling for changes to the constitution and political structures. Ethnic motivations are grounded in identity politics in addition to personal ambitions. Power relationships among ethnic leaders tend to dominate the nature and processes of politics. Ethnic leaders do not necessarily represent their people but rather their own personal interest in power and business.

Social antagonisms are emerging – social media is very critical of politicians, and messages of scandalous scales of corruption dominate Facebook and Twitter. It is now clear that oil revenues have not delivered the modernity that people hoped for. As one government after another makes it its only duty to identify the failure of the preceding ones, government itself has supplied the data of failure, the gross limitations of socioeconomic experience to deliver sustainable development. Leaders and failure, in people's minds, have become coterminous. The state has succeeded in using its agencies and institutions to reach those with access to it. Those with power, benefiting from the state, have not developed an appetite for profit based on production, but for greed and unproductive consumption on an unimaginable scale.

It is becoming clearer that there is no one who can arbitrate conflicts among warring ethnic factions or, at least, equilibrate the rivalries among ethnic majorities. And it is clearer still that there is no capacity to meet the demands of the poor. More dangerously, there are no institutions in place to reconcile the weak and poor with the government. There is the definite choice of a liberal economic ideology in place, allowing the informal sector to operate, but the infrastructures and energy supply are sources of limitation. It is only the state, as the prime collector of oil revenues, that can end the sequestration imposed on entrepreneurs by lack of electricity and access to capital.

Due in part to the divisive forces of ethnicity and religion, a national protest movement is yet to emerge. There is the solidarity of critical dialogue, as in media reports and analysis, and unbounded echoes of grievances – powerful words and routinized angry arguments. The criticisms of the state are contagious, especially on social media, with so many debates on the problems of the country and how to resolve them. Whether government officials read those things or not is one question; and whether they ever act on what they read is another.

While many doubt that democracy can deliver, it seems to be the only feasible option. A radical segment always insists on a war of liberation – that is, the transformation of politics itself to empower more and more people. Democracy must be grounded in accountability to reduce the scale of corruption. Economic forces must also deliver on production of food and seeing to the basic needs of the poor. Confidence in leadership has to be restored as many no longer believe in the promises made by politicians or in their capacity to deliver development. The immediate thing is to halt the decline of institutions, reduce the practices of supplementing salaries with bribes, and generate optimism in the economy to reduce the belief that one must migrate outside of the country to be able to make it.

Many layers of leverages have to be created in the years ahead. The country as a whole, has to leverage as a regional member of ECOWAS and the African Union to support both regional and continental power. The leadership has to leverage by building institutions that will provide political and economic stability: living conditions must not keep degenerating. Meeting the fundamental needs of Nigerians must be the primary preoccupation of leaders at all levels of governance. One way to do this is to restore preeminence to agriculture as the core engine of change – it will employ millions of people, reconnect rural areas to development agenda, combine economic goals with social realities, and generate an endless stream of production on a daily basis to make food available to all.

Voices that demand progressive change are many. A currency of experience has been created and acquired on how to criticize the state and fight. In various parts of the country, practical ways of confronting the state through violence have been tried and tested. Ideas about people's power are well-known. Ways to disturb levers of power have become ideas expressed on the pages of newspapers and the streets. When these struggles are no longer organized across ethnic and religious lines will be the beginning of a new day – a day when an Igbo will not be fighting to actualize Biafra, when the OPC will not be looking for an Oduduwa Republic, when the Ogoni will not want a separate state – that is, a day when all the poor and oppressed will unite to want Nigeria; that will be the day that Nigeria needs. That day, a democratic movement will be grounded in a patriotic movement with committed and selfless leaders who will create a revolutionary path, a new dawn. But that new dawn would be one in which the birthright of the Nigerian citizenship and equal access and recruitment to socioeconomic opportunities and political power would be determined by neutrality of merit and human right rather than by the primordial accident of birthplace, social class or caste, and religion.

This is not wishful thinking, but it will require leadership from the masses. It cannot be imposed by political elites; it must be enacted by real representatives of the people. The leadership of this movement will not think in terms of gains, but how to be part of how the people think, how they mobilize their thinking for change, and how their experiences will shape the politics and economy they envision. A few leaders, irrespective of knowledge and education, cannot replace millions of people or pretend to act on their behalf, but on collective initiatives, inspirations, and progressive worldview.

Nigerians should not be long on analysis and short on remedies. A good start is by affirming a commitment to Nigeria as a people and as a territory. Its current ideological foundation may be weak, but one can be created to ensure a strong future. Progressive elements must acquire the cohesion to attain legitimacy, giving the resistance an agency of morality that is superior to that of the state itself.

23 Nationalist Ethos, Collective Reformation, and Citizenry Power

> Arise, O compatriots
> Nigeria's call obey
> To serve our fatherland
> With love and strength and faith.
> The labor of our heroes past
> Shall never be in vain,
> To serve with heart and might
> One nation bound in freedom
> Peace and unity.
>
> (First Stanza, Nigeria Anthem)

Introduction: Nationhood and National Identity

The notions of nation and nationalism are modern in(ter)ventions that resituate the idea of identity around the perception of a defined geographical setting/boundary, an "imagined community," that defines a group of people as unique and united. A general consensus as to the origin of the two terms dates back to the end of the eighteenth century and the French revolution.[1] These Western ideological impositions of state and nation displace the prevailing ethno-cultural mode of identity that defined Africans in precolonial times. The "nationalist" idea of belonging and togetherness before the European scramble of Africa is fluid and permissible, which makes immersion and integration within African communities much easier.[2] Taiwo Olaiya notes that "[European] nationalism as a homogenizing and unifying factor did not take adequate cognizance of the diverse composition of groups on ground in most African nations."[3]

---

[1] John Plamenatz, "Two Types of Nationalism," in *Nationalism: The Nature and Evolution of an Idea,* ed. Eugene Kamenka (Canberra: Australian National University Press, 1973), 22.

[2] Olusola Olasupo, Isaac Olayide Oladeji, and E. O. C. Ijeoma, "Nationalism and Nationalist Agitation in Africa: The Nigerian Trajectory," *Review of Black Political Economy* 44 (2017): 269.

[3] Taiwo Olaiya, "Proto-Nationalisms as Sub-text for the Crisis of Governance in Nigeria," *SAGE Open* (2016): 4.

Therefore, the unpremeditated inclination toward ethnic identity and the imposition of national identity highlights the struggle of belongingness and identity or, better put, the double consciousness of belonging to both, by preference or by imposition, that shapes the identity formation of most Africans.

The complication that arises from the lack of a proper definition of national identity as a Nigerian, in many studies, is regarded as the "national question." In addressing the "national question," Abubakar Momoh traces this fragmentation of identity to "the (un)evenness in the distribution of, or access to power and economy in the context of deliverables and what advantage co-ethnics or a fraction of them take of one another in the process"[4] of national development. To others, this fragmentation of identity arises as a consequence of the lack of consent of the state members to be integrated into a nation known as Nigeria. Michael Levin stresses this when he notes that the statehood of Nigeria is not in question but "what national allegiance, identity, and patriotism means in Nigeria is deeply in doubt,"[5] despite existing for more than a century. Simply defined, a nation "connotes a collection of persons united as one people so as to form a cohesive social body."[6] In the case of Nigeria, the consent variable is absent; hence, the issue of the "national question" continues to pose a threat to the (ideological) existence of Nigeria as a nation in solidarity.

These ethnic identities "preceded the nation-building efforts by post-colonial governments"[7] but have also been identified as some of the "greatest obstacles to African nationhood."[8] Nationalism in pre-independent Nigeria quickly degenerated into ethnic-nationalism, peripheral nationalism or sub-nationalism after independence to this very day.[9] A tangible

[4] Abubakar Momoh, "The Philosophy and Theory of the National Question," in *The National Question in Nigeria: Comparative Perspectives*, eds. Abubakar Momoh et al. (Hampshire: Ashgate, 2002), 2.

[5] Michael Levin, "The New Nigeria: Displacement and the Nation," *Journal of Asia and African Studies* 32, no. 1–2 (1997): 135.

[6] Mojibayo Fadakinte and Babatunde Amolegbe, "Crisis of Citizenship and Nationhood in Africa: Reflections on Hegemony and the State," *Review of History and Political Science* 5, no. 1 (2017): 62.

[7] Maxim Ananyev and Michael Poyker, "Nation-Building in Sub-Saharan Africa and Civil Conflict: Theory and Evidence from Boko Haram and Tuareg Insurgencies," (2016): 4.

[8] Joseph O. Ajor, Julius S. Odey, and Louis A. Edet, "The Realism of Nigerian Nationalism and the Challenges of Nationhood, 1922–2015," *Journal of Good Governance and Sustainable Development in Africa* 4, no. 2 (2018): 14.

[9] It is important to note that while ethnic-nationalism or other variants of sub-nationalism still linger, their survival (if eventually established as a nation) is almost impossible due to the presence of the same variables that had resulted in them in the first instance. Within a given ethnic group, there can be a handful of language dialects, multiple religions, different political ideologies, and intangible border territory. Hence, with the implementation of necessary policies and programs, the continuous existence of Nigeria as a nation is in the best interest of everyone.

reason attributed to this nationalist degradation is the ideological pursuit behind the formation and integration of the nationalists during colonialism, which was to seek the inclusion and independence of the African people from colonial domination and not (necessarily) to form a sense of belonging as one, and since this supposed independence has been achieved, nationalism seems to have lost its enchanting magic. As indicated by Ali Mazrui, the homogenization of Africans is a result of the experience of constant subjugation and the common goal to be independent of colonial domination.[10] Consciousness as a common race with a shared past of colonial suppression is a binding force that integrates Africans into collective action, while ethnicism remains a divisive mechanism wherein larger nation-states like Nigeria with multiethnicities constantly struggle to remain indivisible. However, there is a need to perceive strength from the multicultural existence of Nigeria, and not concentrate on the divisive tendency of diversity. The spirit of inclusiveness fosters peace and development.

Nationalism as a patriotic allegiance to a national identity is central to the reformation and revolution interventions, yet the least explored or emphasized. The collective identification of a group of people as one is a needed impetus that drives national development, democracy, and empowerment. Defined as "a grand solidarity constituted by the sentiment of sacrifices which one has made and those one is disposed to make again," nationalism is characterized by the resilience of "an everyday plebiscite"[11] that surpasses the challenges that bedevil the society. The national anthem and pledge of Nigeria are summations of the expected allegiance and civic responsibilities of members of the nation to its stability and development.

There is a lot to be learned from the struggles and achievements of early African nationalists who fiercely fought for the independence of African states. In various African states, their struggles are strengthened by the sense of belonging and collectivism, and the need to be further unified, as expressed by Brian Barry: "[T]he people should have a sense of shared political destiny with others, a preference for being united with them politically in an independent state, and [the] preparedness to be committed to common political action."[12] Proto-nationalism and anticolonial nationalism best portray the ideologies of the early Nigerian nationalists

---

[10] Ali Mazrui, "On the Concept of 'We Are All Africans,'" *The American Political Science Review* 57, no. 1 (1963): 89.

[11] Ernest Renan, "Qu'est-ce Qu'une Nation?" in *The Dynamics of Nationalism*, ed. Luis Snyder (New York: Van Nostrand, 1964), 9.

[12] Brian Barry, "Self-Government Revisited," in *Theorizing Nationalism*, ed. Ronald Beiner (New York: SUNY Press, 1999), 287.

as their movement was a mobilization to resist colonial rule. Ajor et al. describe it as "the devotion of some elite groups (the nationalists) in advocating for the political emancipation of Nigerians from colonial yoke."[13] While the objective of putting an end to colonial dictatorship in Africa has been achieved, the evolution of the African states into a stable and full-fledged nation remains vague.[14]

The ideological differences in the political representations of the pro-independence nationalists has also been ascertained as a major factor complicating the national coexistence of Nigeria. These differences still linger to the present period; some have become worse. However, the ideological differences between pro-independence nationalists have the unifying focus of national development as "strong disagreement among these nationalists revolved mostly around issues relating to state structure and governance arrangements,"[15] while the differences between anticolonial nationalists have been based on corrupt ethnic and selfish prejudices. This inadequacy has culminated in structural deficiencies that impede proper national development and identity. Rather than enhance the integration of the nation, federalism, as it is practiced in Nigeria, further divides the nation across majority–minority and regional dichotomies.

It is no overstatement that Nigeria is a super-nation – a nation of nations, a multinational state whose existence is dependent on the compatibility of each constituent's nation-building process.[16] As a consequence of the forceful integration of Nigeria (and other African states) by the colonial powers, there is the lack of vital parameters that are pertinent to foster the development of a nation: neither was there a general consensus/consent among the people before the formation of Nigeria nor is there the presence of a common language, a common religion, a common custom or way of life, or the willingness to maintain their unity as one. An often-quoted expression by Obafemi Awolowo during the wake of nationalism in Nigeria is, "Nigeria is not a nation. It is a mere geographical expression. There are no Nigerians in the same sense as there are 'English', 'Welsh' or

---

[13] Kelechi Ubaku, Chikezie Emeh, and Chineye Anyikwa, "Impact of Nationalist Movement on the Actualization of Nigerian Independence, 1914–1960," *International Journal of History and Philosophical Research* 2, no.1 (2014): 55.

[14] Ajor, Odey, and Edet, "The Realism of Nigerian Nationalism and the Challenges of Nationhood, 1922–2015," 13.

[15] Michael Kpessa, Daniel Béland, and André Lecours, "Nationalism, Development, and Social Policy: The Politics of Nation-Building in Sub-Saharan Africa," *Ethnic and Racial Studies* 34, no. 12 (2011): 2116.

[16] Armin von Bogdandy et al., "State-Building, Nation-Building, and Constitutional Politics in Post-Conflict Situations: Conceptual Clarifications and an Appraisal of Different Approaches," *Max Planck Yearbook of United Nations Law* 9 (2005): 587.

'French.'"[17] Hence, parodying the words of Massimo d'Azeglio: Nigeria has been made, it remains to make Nigerians. Only the territory has been clearly defined, the people and the governments are at indeterminate extremes of national formation with insufficient integrating ideologies.

Just as the government is alienated from the people, the people are also alienated from the state by their utmost preoccupation: scrambling for survival. Such inadequacies are themselves dangerous prompts for succession and (ethnic)nationalism. In tandem, Plamenatz is of the view that nationalism (what we may herein refer to as ethnicism), reversely, is a derivative or "a reaction of peoples who feel culturally at a disadvantage."[18] Plamenatz further defines nationalism as the interest to protect an identity when "that identity is threatened, or the desires to transform or even create it where it is felt to be inadequate or lacking."[19] The dutiful provision of social goods and services to the people by the government renders the people more reliant on the stability of the government, which propels their belongingness and contribution to its continuous growth and survival. Ananyev and Poyker[20] have identified the increasing rate of insurgency in (African) nations as a threat and cause of decline in national identity as it indicates the state's loss of power and inability to coordinate the affairs of the state as well as protect the lives of those who identify as members of the state. Consequently, they are left with little or no reason to be associated as a member of such a state beyond residency as "construction of order and security within a territory" is identified as one of the actual parameters that define a nation.[21]

Contrary to the jubilation and high-spiritedness that characterized the immediate postindependent Nigeria, what exists now is a deliberate alienation from national identity and the unwillingness to belong to the collective. While this is an indication of the various setbacks that have plagued the nation over the years, it also points to the fact that little is being done to incorporate the citizens into the consciousness of belonging to the nation for its greater development. For example, the culture of reciting the national anthem in some schools (ravaged by insecurity) is no longer in practice. As insignificant as this seem, it indicates a step away from creating a strong bond, love, and patriotic spirit in regard to one's nation.

Active nationalist consciousness and collective nation-building efforts are viable reformative and revolutionary strategies to be adopted by the citizens to drive an effective democracy and development in Nigeria.

---

[17] Obafemi Awolowo, *Path to Nigerian Freedom* (London: Faber and Faber, 1947), 47.
[18] Plamenatz, "Two Types of Nationalism," 27.   [19] Ibid., 23–24.
[20] Ananyev and Poyker, "Nation-Building in Sub-Saharan Africa and Civil Conflict."
[21] David Abraham, "Constitutional Patriotism, Citizenship, and Belonging." *I•CON* 6, no. 1 (2008): 141.

National development is further enhanced by the obligations and duties of the citizens to the state. The low development witnessed in the nation is largely defined by the inefficiency of the government as well as the unpatriotic relationship of the citizens with the state. While the ineffectiveness of the government can be compensated for by the obligations of the citizens to the state and vice-versa, in a democracy where citizenship is only defined by rights and expectations with no civic duty or obligation in return to the state, development is largely hindered.

Contrasting the relationship between the people and the state in precolonial and (post)colonial Africa, Fadakinte and Amolegbe note that "the colonial experience led to a noticeable but remarkable shift in African politics, a development that upsets the traditional conceptions of citizenship and listed the following far-reaching unintended consequences of colonial ideologies on citizenship, that is, the encouragement of Africans to identify citizenship with rights and not with duties and taking the conception of civil duties, without any regard."[22] The roles and responsibilities of the father–son relationship[23] has been adopted to conceptualize the supposed ideal relationship between citizens and the nation to foster development and unity in Nigeria by explaining how the expectations of right and responsibility shape the relationship. As aptly put by Negedu and Atabor: "The father has duties and responsibilities to the son. The son also has duties and obligations to the father. And so the duty of one is the right of the other in this relationship of mutual responsibility."[24]

Challenges such as low tax payment that hinders national development are caused by the lack of conviction of belonging to the nation and the failure of the government, over the years, of ensuring and fostering various nation-building agendas. As the benefits of good governance become more distant to them, the people also become more distant to the consciousness that consolidates their national identity. One of Nigeria's fastest runners, Divine Oduduru,[25] declined to participate and represent the nation in an all-African game due to the negligence of the government to meet its obligations. This makes him, apparently (just like many other creatives in their various fields), feel less appreciated and unmotivated and captures the level of lethargy that has set in as a result of the failure that characterizes Nigeria's nationhood and nationalist orientation.

---

[22] Fadakinte and Amolegbe, "Crisis of Citizenship and Nationhood in Africa," 62.

[23] Ike Odimegwu, "Nigerian Nationalism and the Crisis of Patriotism: A Conceptual Dialogics in Philosophy and Africa," *World Philosophy* 1 (2006): 203–213.

[24] Isaiah Negedu and Augustine Atabor, "Nationalism in Nigeria: A Case for Patriotic Citizenship," *American International Journal of Contemporary Research* 5, no. 3 (2015): 74–79.

[25] TVC News Nigeria, "Divine Okorodudu [*sic*] – Africa's Fastest Man in 2019," YouTube video, 7:41, July 31, 2019, www.youtube.com/watch?v=44Mglzmqo-U.

While it is imperative for the citizens to cultivate the spirit of belonging and the preparedness to sustain it, it is also important for the government to intensify initiatives that promote peace and integration of society as well as the spirit of belonging among the people; hence, there is the need to adopt various state mechanisms (political, economic, cultural, and educational) to achieve nationalist ethos and collective reformation goals. It is the duty of the government to ensure that the citizens are believers and are confident in the growth of the nation by enabling transparent and all-inclusive governance. The postindependent African states are characterized by "the absence of hegemonic order that ought to catalyze and jumpstart the process of state formation that will create an acceptable level of homogeneity by institutionalizing and maintaining a social order that will eventually engender some high level of consciousness and a common identity."[26] The notion of nationalism is well-elucidated in the words of Ubaku et al. as "first, the attitude which members of a nation have when they care about their national identity; and second, the actions that the members of a nation take when seeking to sustain self-determination."[27] A nation exists by virtue of the people's consciousness of their nationality, and this in Nigeria has been hindered by the lack of adequate representation and the imbalance of resource distribution.

As identified by Alesina and Reich, the unwillingness of a democratic government or leaders to work toward the proper homogenization of their state engenders a sense that their effort "works against the other incentives of the ruler to homogenize."[28] Democratic reformation and revolution that is well-organized by citizens who communicate as one and for a common goal challenges the inadequacies and excesses of various autocratic leaders. Therefore, divisive variables such as ethnicity and religion are instigated to divide the people. Nigeria, as a national identity/boundary engineered by the colonialists is constructed to create classes and enhance control, and not for national integration and development. Tangri corroborates this view: "[A]t independence, African countries largely lacked a national identity, partly because colonial policy did much to strengthen ethnic, as opposed to national consciousness, and partly because the countries were too recent in existence to elicit a sense of common nationhood."[29]

[26] Fadakinte and Amolegbe, "Crisis of Citizenship and Nationhood in Africa," 62.
[27] Ubaku, Emeh, and Anyikwa, "Impact of Nationalist Movement on the Actualization of Nigerian Independence, 1914–1960," 55.
[28] Alberto Alesina and Bryony Reich, "Nation-Building," working paper, department of economics, Harvard University (2015): 5, https://dash.harvard.edu/handle/1/28652213.
[29] Roger Tangri, The Politics of Patronage in Africa: Parastatals, Privatization and Private Enterprise (Oxford: James Currey, 1999), 8.

There are multiple steps necessary in order to homogenize the Nigerian population, among them: state control of elementary education, the promotion of indigenous languages and cultures, history, the availability of social amenities that cut across the different geo-political regions of the country, equal representation of people from different backgrounds of the country in government, military foster nation building, and nationalism. These steps constitute the process of nation building in "an effort to develop the spirit of patriotism and solidarity to create a country whose people share a common identity."[30] As aptly put by Ananyev and Poyker, "the viability of national identity is anchored in the existence of a well-functioning state, the threats to state institutions, break up that coordination, and thus erode national identity."[31]

Yet, integration and development of Nigeria would remain a mirage until the ideas of nationhood, citizenship, and nationalism are properly defined, actualized, and made functional. However, the continuous existence of Nigeria, despite countless doomful prophesies of its dissolution and national struggles, is a testament to the (unconscious) willingness of the people to remain united and their "commitment to holding the country together."[32] Thus, nationalism in Nigeria follows the pathway identified by Plamenatz as "confined to peoples who, despite their rivalries and the cultural differences between them, already belong to, or are being drawn into, a family of nations which all aspire to make progress in roughly the same directions."[33]

Collective Reformation: Steps toward Nation Building and National Integration

The inability of a nation to be fully or properly integrated is a preindication of national failure and chaos, which can be averted by well-organized and well-executed social policies. The continuous process of enhancing the integration of a group of people regardless of ethnic, language, religious, and individual differences to ensure stable development and unity can be regarded as the act of nation building, "a process of collective identity formation with a view to legitimizing public power within a given territory."[34] From the government

---

[30] Okechukwu Eme and Tony Onyishi, "Federalism and Nation Building in Nigeria," *Arabian Journal of Business and Management Review* 2, no. 6 (2014): 4.

[31] Ananyev and Poyker, "Nation-Building in Sub-Saharan Africa and Civil Conflict," 3.

[32] Abdul Mustapha, "Ethnic Structure, Inequality and Governance of the Public Sector in Nigeria," *UNRISD Programme on Democracy, Governance and Human Rights*, Paper Number 24 (2006): 2.

[33] Plamenatz, "Two Types of Nationalism," 27.

[34] von Bogdandy et al., "State-Building, Nation-Building, and Constitutional Politics in Post-Conflict Situations," 586.

perspective, it has also been described as the act of marshalling state power and resources to ensure an established nation remains indissoluble and progressive. Alesina and Reich define nation building "as a process which leads to the formation of countries in which the citizens feel a sufficient amount of commonality of interests, goals, and preferences so that they do not wish to separate from each other."[35] Put differently, Egbefo and Shedrack conceptualize it "as a strategy that seeks to integrate ideology and create a functional state apparatus with a view to developing a unified and harmonious society."[36]

The Development and Enhancement of Education in the Nation

This cannot be overemphasized. Be it formal or otherwise, education has proven to be the most effective channel of transmitting the ideals and values of a society to a person or group of people, thereby preparing them to be dutiful and law-abiding members of such a society. The attainment of nationhood and nationalism, according to Gellner, is "based on deeply internalized, education-dependent high cultures," which are transformed in the process of homogenization.[37] The quality and level of education available in a society is an indication of the development of such society and the knowledge of its members toward an active and collective participation.

Highlighting the failure of the various programs set up by the federal government to imbue the spirit of national consciousness among Nigerians, and suggesting the intensification of citizenship education, Akuson remarks: "What is missing in all this programs is a lack of systematic education process of training the mind and the intellect to the orientation of the people from greedy, selfish, chaotic, dishonest and unjust living to that of seeing fellow Nigerians as equal members of the polity with a shared sense of responsibility."[38] The educational attainment of twentieth-century Nigerian nationalists is a testament to the centrality of quality education in driving the progress of the nation. The development of education in sub-Saharan Africa that coincided with the leadership of early nationalists has been noted by Kpessa et al. as "a tool aimed at improving human capital to increase

---

[35] Alesina and Reich, "Nation-Building," 3.
[36] Dawood Egbefo and Onyema Shedrack, "Terrorism in Nigeria: Its Implication for Nation Building and National Integration," (2007): 3, https://www.edouniversity.edu .ng/oerrepository/articles/terrorism_in_nigeria_its_implication_for_nation_building_and_ national_integration.pdf.
[37] Ernest Gellner, *Nations and Nationalism* (Oxford: Basil Blackwell, 1983), 48.
[38] Felicia Akuson, "Citizenship Education as a Creative Intervention Tool for National Development," *Journal of Teacher Perspective* 10, no. 2 (2016): 2.

productivity, open possibilities for innovation, and provide lifelong opportunities to reduce the number of people falling into poverty."[39] Strong and effective educational institutions can trigger "positive orientations that generate norms, values, beliefs, and attitudes"[40] needed to build progressive politics and sustainable development.

The knowledge of rights as members of a given society is as vital as the understanding of the same responsibility to such a society. Such comprehensive knowledge helps to uplift the status quo of the nation and helps to keep the citizens well-informed on the processes that are central to the stable and peaceful continuous existence of the nation. While lamenting the lack of good leadership, it is pertinent to note that leadership is as vital to governance as followership; hence, education creates the equilibrium to imbue everyone with both leadership and followership skills. In so doing, education leverages existing moral values that cut across the different ethnic groups to consolidate the spirit of fairness and equality in dealing with individuals and society. Loyalty, tolerance, honesty, and other sociomoral responsibilities are harnessed through education, which helps the people understand the values of such ideals, both to themselves and to society. Education is central to the integration of the diverse cultures that are present in Nigeria as it helps members of each culture to not only understand his/her heritage but also that of others so as to be able to affiliate with them properly, which is essential to the consciousness of nationalism.

Corruption and other examples of antisocial vices thrive in a nation whose members are uninformed about their sociopolitical rights, responsibilities, and processes. The sociopolitical and economic potentials inherent in a nation can only be unleashed with the enhancement of education that fortifies the ability of the members to make tangible contributions to the growth of the nation without overtly being dependent on the intervention of the state. Education affords the maximal utilization of the resources (natural, human, or otherwise) available in the nation, first, by equipping the members with the knowledge of such resources, and second, providing the modern skills needed to transform such resources.

The Development of Indigenous Languages and Cultures

The failure of the nation has several times been linked to the presence of multiple languages and cultures forcefully integrated by the colonialists,

---

[39] Kpessa, Béland, and Lecours, "Nationalism, Development, and Social Policy," 2123–2124.
[40] Uche Bright Odoemelam and Ebiuwa Aisien, "Political Socialization and Nation Building: The Case of Nigeria," *European Scientific Journal* 9, no.11 (2013): 237–253.

which makes a proper integration an almost impossible task. However, such factors as the non-promotion of these languages and cultures are at the base of this integration difficulty. Feelings of alienation often arise not only as a result of unequal distribution of national wealth, but also as a result of the noninclusion of the languages and cultures of the minority in the broad view of governance or social interrelation. The nonrecognition of an individual's cultural values and beliefs hinder his willingness to belong to a collective identity.

This feeling of selective exclusion develops into a perceived threat of language and culture extinction or dominance, which further widens the gap between the various ethnic groups as there is the presence of distrust. The challenge of ethnicism can be attended to by the constant exhibition and gradual integration of the positive values of these ethnic groups (as in language and culture) in the overall national identity and symbol of Nigeria. That is, it is not inclusive enough to regard the entirety of the over 250 ethnic groups as *wazobia*, which only represents the three dominant ethnic groups. This disregard for the multiethnicity of the nation stems from the arbitrary coalescence of the nation by the colonialists to aid their administration, and this malformation lingers on after independence with no proper scrutiny to understand and enhance the relations of these multiple ethnic groups. According to Olaiya: "The colonial rulers and successors in governments desired independence without properly interrogating the inter-territoriality and intra-boundary peculiarities of the people of banded communities, their identities, and ethnic idiosyncrasy."[41] Language and cultural values are symbolic institutions[42] that should be integrated into the framework of the nation, appropriating adequate recognition and respect for their significance. Hence, there is the need to invest more in our language and culture as national symbols, which are representatives of our unity as a diverse nation.

The Development of the Media and Press

In the past few years, under the guise of the right to free expression and press, the press has played a vital role in contributing to the ill repute of the nation by constantly constructing negative narratives about the country thereby deflating the pride of its members to be associated with Nigeria, both at home and abroad. While the aforementioned rights are crucial to the development of the nation as a democratic society and these narratives are largely

---

[41] Olaiya, "Proto-Nationalisms as Sub-Text for the Crisis of Governance in Nigeria," 4.
[42] Raphael Utz, "Nations, Nation-Building, and Cultural Intervention: A Social Science Perspective," *Max Planck Yearbook of United Nations Law* 9 (2005): 636.

true, although sometimes overblown, it is unfortunate that the tangible progress that has been marked both by the people and the nation are often under-narrated, or totally overlooked. Meanwhile, the press and media have been proven to be an effective tool to enhance nationalism and nation building. Jaffrelot opines that the growth of the press "gives the feeling of belonging to an 'imagined community' by arousing the same thoughts at the same time among members of a national culture whose borders are marked out on the basis of language."[43] The awareness of the citizens about the nation is regulated by the press and media, as channels of communication and relation between the people and the state; hence, true nationalist ethos and collective reformation, through the media and press, can either be actualized or aborted.

The press and media are the most available and immediate channels to conscientize the populace on the political culture of the nation, enlighten them on the collective history that unifies the nation as well as the knowledge about the multiple cultural and ethnic groups. There is so much to be exploited in adopting the press and media as strong integrating forces for nation building.

The Development and Promotion of the Historical Past

A sense of historical belonging and shared memory is central to the process of homogenization and nationalism. This "usable past" highlights the distinctiveness of the nation and its people,[44] and details the nation-building development/processes of a group of people, which reflects a common historical and cultural experience that fosters unity. Through good-quality education, the historicity of a people and a place is framed as a unifying tool, which indicates a shared historical past. In a nation where history as a fundamental aspect of the society is constantly suppressed and unappreciated, it becomes difficult to have a comprehensive understanding of oneself, others, and the society, and therefore individuals and groups become more alienated from the perceived diversification of others. A well-grounded historical lesson on the efforts of Nigerian/African nationalism would no doubt help to further strengthen the relationship between the diverse ethnic groups in the nation. A unified historical past plays a vital role in the Pan-Africanist and early nationalist struggles against colonialism and dictatorship in Africa. It is a shame that the value and significance of historical studies in Nigerian schools is worsening. How does one know where one is going when one has no understanding where one comes from?

[43] Christophe Jaffrelot, "For a Theory of Nationalism," *Research in Question* 10 (2003): 10.
[44] Utzm "Nations, Nation-Building, and Cultural Intervention," 616–627.

A proper knowledge of the past helps insure against past mistakes and suggests better ways to navigate the current challenges bedeviling the nation by drawing from historical antecedents. The historicity of a nation (highlighting the development and unification of the people) helps to beckon unto others (who are reluctant) to join and further shape the nation. There is the enlivening of the consciousness of nationalism in promoting the nation as a "culmination of a long past of endeavors, sacrifice, and devotion," which consolidate the identity of a group of people as one.[45]

Therefore central to nation building is the creation of a national history which (1) would prove the uniqueness of the nation. (2) Constructing a usable past by referring to particular aspects of history where there was some sort of social consensus or "political culture" that would serve as the foci of identification and loyalty, a display of political knowledge and expectations which are the product of the history of the people.[46]

The evidence of these is in "the labor of our heroes past" which "shall never be in vain."

Also, the enhancement of the historical past is vital to the task of reconciliation and rehabilitation for people who are victims of different national struggles and experiences. Since the formation of the country would help to foster integration and national development as proper restitutions are made, future chaos would be avoided and collective solutions would be preferred to the various current national challenges. Deserting history (significant to the present of a group of people) aggravates agony and bitterness, and this hinders unity and development. Ayokhai and Naankiel put it thus: "[T]he failure of the reconciliation, reconstruction and rehabilitation program of the post-civil war military governments ... among others, are further evidences of a leadership class wanting in nation-building ideas and strategies."[47] The continuous alienation from the past only results into more uprisings in search of it.

The Enhancement of Local Production and Development of Industrialization

This "involves a permanent growth of productivity" that "goes on to promote cultural homogenization at the end of a long process inherent

---

[45] Renan, "Qu'est-ceQu'une Nation?" 9.
[46] Williams Ahmed-Gamgum, "Nigeria at 100 Years: The Process and Challenges of Nation Building," *Public Policy and Administration* Research 4, no. 8 (2014): 126.
[47] Fred Ayokhai and Peter Naankiel, "Rethinking Pan-Africanism and Nationalism in Africa: The Dilemma of Nation-Building in Nigeria," *Historical Research Letter* 27, (2015): 8.

Figure 23.1 A young girl leading a parade, exhibiting pride in Nigeria.

in the economic logic of this society,"[48] which is another key element of nation building. The industrial and technological development of the society is interrelated with educational enhancement as one serves as a motivation for the other. The implication of a well-industrialized society is a good economy that necessitates a high level of literacy and educational attainment as a precondition to benefit from the material wealth of the society.

Nigeria, like most African states, needs to resuscitate and advance from the precolonial industrialization period during which it was rudely distorted. The industrialization of the nation (natural resources, agriculture, etc.) helps to create more interdependence and connection between the regions (ethnics) of the nation as each makes a unique and collective contribution to the development of the entire society, thereby establishing both their commitment to and the importance of

[48] Jaffrelot, "For a Theory of Nationalism," 13.

growth of the nation. The most felt impact of a government on the welfare of its citizens is the availability of a good economy as this cuts across all sectors and classes. The intervention of the government, in past years, in improving the economy of the nation has been subverted to serve the few who have converted "the state's patrimony in core sectors of the economy to private wealth as rapacious entrepreneurs in control of the government and big-business for top government officials, thus exacerbating hopelessness and poverty," and offsetting the balance of distribution of the nation's wealth.[49]

The promotion and enhancement of locally manufactured goods, products, and services is an overlooked but key aspect to the development of the nation as well as to uplifting the spirit of nationalism among the people as products and services made in Nigeria are proudly consumed and demanded. Also, the overall impact of this on the economy cannot be overstressed: consumption and patronization of "made in Nigeria" is a strategic socioeconomic and psychological nation-building policy that should be implemented.

The Development and Promotion of a Nationalist Political Ideology

The failure of Nigeria, and other African countries, to attain a maximum level of democracy, development, nationhood, and nationalism has often been associated with the lack of good leaders who possess true visionary goals to transform their counties and unite their followership. A more crucial reason is the lack of a strong nationalist political ideology that guides the governance of the nation and the orientation of the general populace. A strong political will and ideology is central to the success of achieving true reformation in the nation. Likewise, the success of a nation-building process (which spans "social, institutional, intellectual, ideological, and political processes"[50]) is contingent on the relentless commitment and endeavor of political leaders: [T]he notion of nationalism describes a collective state of mind or consciousness in which people believe that their primary duty and loyalty is to the nation, with a lot of emphasis placed on national superiority and glorification of certain national cultural virtues.[51]

Unfortunately, the existing political parties are created and divided along ethnic and religious lines with no irrefutable ideology to champion

---

[49] Olasupo, Oladeji, and Ijeoma, "Nationalism and Nationalist Agitation in Africa," 280.
[50] Utz, "Nations, Nation-Building, and Cultural Intervention," 618.
[51] Olaiya, "Proto-Nationalisms as Sub-text for the Crisis of Governance in Nigeria," 2.

the development of the nation to form a strong and sufficient political culture that can be transmitted from one generation to another. Identifying this political inadequacy, Ayokhai and Naankiel trace the origin to the political thoughts upon which the liberation of the nation is achieved: according to them, these political ideologies are "not only fundamentally flawed in the necessary nationalist ideology of statecraft but also strongly skewed in favor of ethno-regionalism and religious sectarianism on which the Nigerian post-colonial nationhood project was founded."[52]

In the words of Odoemelam and Aisien, "political parties in Nigerian society [are characterized to] have 'manifesto' that are not philosophically and ideologically tailored. This phenomenon has resulted to lack of sense of direction. Consequently, these phenomena are believed to be responsible for the problem of 'Nation Building in Nigeria.'"[53] The deficiency of true political vision and the ineffectiveness of the political leaders are largely responsible for the growing level of political apathy in Nigeria, especially among the youths and the poor who feel unrepresented and alienated from the political and governance dynamics of the nation, and therefore have resulted in nonparticipation in the political processes of the nation as they feel, albeit erroneously, that it has no tangible or positive implication on their welfare and general existence. Also, the observance of true democratic principles is vital to the process of nation building.

The political articulation and aggregation of the early nationalists harnessed the concerns of the masses to drive their political will to put an end to colonial rule, and the ideology to create a self-sustaining government.[54] Only such political ideology – with the genuine interest of the people and a true vision to develop the society – is capable of ensuring the active and mass participation of the citizens in the governance and politics of the nation just as the Garvey Movement, Pan-Africanism, and West African Student Union, etc., had impacted the political experience and ideology of the early nationalists. Culmination of the political vibrancy and ideology of the early nationalists helped to achieve the independence of Nigeria and a true political ideology could help ascertain the second and true independence of Nigeria and enhance national growth. The misrule and mismanagement that has hindered the

---

[52] Ayokhai and Naankiel, "Rethinking Pan-Africanism and Nationalism in Africa," 6.
[53] Odoemelam and Aisien, "Political Socialization and Nation Building," 240.
[54] A partial reason for the lack of true political ideologies in the current orientation of political parties in Nigeria is as a result of the failure of the early nationalists to fully evolve their political ideology from the fight for the Nigerian independence to that of essential political ideology needed for the development and integration of Nigeria after independence, which has further aggravated the lack of direction and craving for absolute political authority that characterize the present political culture.

progress of Nigeria is a result of lack of well-defined sociopolitical ideology. Indeed, as Helen Keller quipped, "the only thing worse than being blind is having sight but no vision."

The Development of Social Programs

The characteristic poverty and poor levels of development and health in Nigeria since independence are major factors influencing the weak development of nationalism. Partly, ethnic-nationalism thrives in Nigeria as a result of the government's inability to attend to the basic needs of the people, especially the minorities who feel marginalized and those who are directly affected by the unequal (under)development in the rural areas, as well as the gap between the rich and the poor. Hence, recourse is made to ethnicity to seek solidarity, belongingness, and solace in times of socioeconomic dissatisfaction: "[I]t projects the phenomenon that the more incompetent the state, the wider has grown the gap between the state and society."[55] Reversely, this alternative allegiance often disturbs the stability of governance and the economy as it hinders collective development and integration.

Healthcare, housing, security, food, education, economic and social empowerment, etc., are among the social programs that should be established by the government to improve the standard of living of the people and thereby enhance their feelings of nationalism. In the submission of Kpessa et al., drawing from the social policy efforts of the early nationalists in sub-Saharan Africa states to unite their people, it is highlighted that "social programmes are likely to become a direct component of ethnoterritorial mobilizations and nation-building projects."[56] The ability of the government to cater to the needs of its members not only improves the obtainable standard of living in such a society but also helps as the "government gains credibility and citizens tend to align their individual goals with those of the state or government harmoniously,"[57] which helps to enhance the level of nationalism among the members, and subsequently achieve a well-integrated and developed society.

---

[55] Ejovi Austine, Ataine Stephen, and Akpokighe Raymond, "Ethnicity and Nation Building in Africa," *Journal of Political Science and Leadership Research* 2, no. 2 (2016): 4.
[56] Kpessa, Béland, and Lecours, "Nationalism, Development, and Social Policy," 2116.
[57] Odoemelam and Aisien, "Political Socialization and Nation Building," 245.

24 Popular Culture and Politics

Introduction

Nigeria's popular culture can transform the country's sociopolitical future: as a social institution that arose from the forces of colonization, popular culture has a specific social role to play in that process. Shared culture, formed through a blend of indigenous songs, dances, performances, and other practices that came into contact with the Western world can revolutionize existing cultural ideas. Popular culture is a massively influential force when it provides entertainment to communities, easing their tensions and teaching them values; it gives opportunities for opposing voices to make their own contributions to the development of Nigerian society.

Entertainment industries around the world provide similar services, and they are recognized as important stakeholders for making desirable changes in society. Popular culture in Nigerian society has shown an elastic capacity to instigate social ideas. Recording and distributing these ideas can bring about transformational changes and revolutionary thinking that can shape the Nigerian environment.

Various cultural influences are measured through the reactions they generate. Citizen responses at every level – shared in social gatherings and expressed through individual behavior – are significant for shaping human society. In general, people act in predetermined ways that draw on the information they receive through the media, populated by popular culture artists; the messages they access through different mediums are retained differently. The majority of people in the twenty-first century depend largely on various types of media because popular culture survives better on these media. The entertainment industry's reliance on the media emphasizes the importance of popular culture and its ability to reduce the burdens of a society struggling through difficult experiences. In Nigerian society, the welfare of the masses has always been of secondary concern to its leadership: popular culture plays an important role providing emotional relief for the general public.

Nigeria's politics have an overwhelming influence on its people, but popular culture can be used to inspire Nigerians and encourage them to manifest the future of their dreams. Step-by-step analysis reveals the different approaches that can actively target a better Nigerian future. Although the general belief is that popular culture serves as entertainment with no significant social benefits, that is not entirely the case. Nigerian popular culture can use its transformational capacity to inspire desirable changes in the country's political trajectory. When the people who create cultural materials understand the power that they wield as a social institution, and when they use that power objectively, they can enact a revolution without violence.

Being the Conscience of Society

Pop culture artists have a unique social responsibility: they must serve as the conscience of society. Throughout history, individuals who enact revolutionary ideas always understand their roles in instigating and enforcing them. Accepting this role satisfies the initial requirement of changing the sociopolitical environment, which comes into effect as soon as these individuals have a clear definition of purpose. When film writers, singers, actors, and others become aware of their roles in building society, and they assume an uncompromising dedication to identifying social ills, they activate a sentiment within the people that demands accountability from their leaders.

Being the conscience of a country requires unfailing commitment, because it comes with substantial challenges. Nigeria's political class wields so much power that they are normally feared by ordinary citizens. This fear compels undeserved adulation and commendations delivered, especially from people in the entertainment industry. In extreme cases, the praise is mere sycophantic behavior that illustrates the compromised nature of the issuers.

The people who are the custodians of popular culture in Nigeria continually show that they fail to understand their role in the country's development. This has led to the production of philosophically delinquent content that does not relate to the social exigencies of the country. Products of the music and entertainment industries clearly indicate that the political class can continue to lounge in their pool of irresponsibility, breeding poor foresight and irresponsible leadership while misappropriating public funds remains their primary goal. These leaders are mostly spared from the criticism, satire, or calling-out that would compel them to take purposeful transformative action.

As a result, social ills thrive in Nigerian society, especially those enabled by political ineptitude. For productive, healthy changes, the creators of popular culture should mirror society's actual events, regardless of whose ox is gored. By joining the majority's camp, they would be instigating revolutionary action.

Nollywood can expose societal ills that were encouraged by the proliferation of morally reprehensible behaviors that have enabled corruption and are sustained through moral decadence. Corruption's effects on Nigeria have been devastating. In the corridors of power, it has led to the misappropriation of state funds that could build useful infrastructure such as hospitals, schools, and roads. Numerous development opportunities continue to be squandered. On the global stage, Nigerians are ridiculed because their leaders lack foresight, which is also a result of inadequate anti-corruption activist struggles.

Stealing public assets, abusing the public's trust, and showing no concern for public welfare are the default attitudes of Nigeria's leadership, but the consequences for politicians are minimal. Despite seeing the results of these behaviors in their day-to-day lives, people are generally unreceptive to progressive messages and efforts. Popular culture can be an instrument of change when those who create public works accept their role as society's conscience, revealing these ills in ways that reach their targeted audience: the political class.

Artists who contribute to Nigeria's popular culture can collaborate to accurately depict leadership failings – unfurling the shortcomings inherent in their political philosophy and sensitizing society in the process. They could link harsh social realities with irresponsible leaders, showing how continued mismanagement is holding the society back. Nigerian leadership pays little attention to the public's well-being, believing that they will never be held accountable for either action or inaction. Public institutions have failed to receive necessary support because leaders believe that their own positions are insulated from the effects of their unproductive choices. The medical system has been left unattended, the justice system is in shambles, and necessary transportation infrastructure has been completely neglected. The multiplier effects of such behavior can be overwhelming, especially when the environment is under dire threat.

The entertainment industry should take a role on the front line, interpreting government policies and how they affect the masses. The public should be informed about the competence of their representatives and be encouraged to monitor these leaders more closely, making sure they arrive at productive decisions. Adequate information is necessary for informed choices – during the electoral process, the people usually have little opportunity to study the candidates' mental capacity, their philosophy, or the soundness of their judgment. Citizens cannot afford to waste their votes backing inappropriate candidates.

Popular culture can come to the rescue because its institutions are close to the people; its artists and producers must educate and inform the public, assisting the decision-making process by allowing people to support representatives based on their behavior and their ability to deliver improvements. Raising public awareness is good political behavior in a democratic environment. It can prevent undesirable outcomes by allowing the people who understand the effects of a poorly led administration to support appropriate politicians.

Corruption degrades the standards of living for society at large, and it is a companion of irresponsible leadership. Corruption's virulent effects stand stubbornly in the way of progressive ideas, taunting every effort at improvement. The economic and political lockdown, courtesy of the global COVID-19 pandemic, has revealed how individuals involved in Nigeria's popular culture have not accepted their social responsibility. Nigeria's political elite have ignored the country's institutions, diverting national resources toward personal gains for many years. Their inability to imagine a future where those institutions would be needed – a future where those entities are capable of rescuing the public from a global health crisis – has inadvertently forced the country to its knees. The superficial policies and empty projects that have occupied the political class for decades have come back to haunt the entire country and victimize innocent people. Citizens must be made aware of this tragic history through music, films, and clothing.

The importance of popular culture has grown over the years, and modernity has expanded the reach of popular culture components such as films, music, dancing, clothing, and artwork. These creative forces can transform Nigeria into something magnificent. To do so, creators must immerse themselves in social activities, drawing material from local contexts that help their messages resonate with every part of society. They should primarily target the political elites with their messages because the elite class must lead the efforts required for transformation. Great leadership establishes worthwhile social institutions that anchor societies in times of emergency and rescue people from impending doom. Corruption and mismanagement have encouraged an unprecedented exodus of Nigerians, leaving the country suffering from brain drain as its brightest minds depart other countries. Popular culture would be an effective method of social sensitization, interpreting the predictable shortcomings of the country's policies.

Human society is vulnerable when its safety nets have been systematically removed, and playing politics to serve the interests of an exclusive few leads to disastrous results. Although the emasculation of different social

Figure 24.1 A collage of music superstars: Sunny Ade, Fela Anikulapo, and Lagbaja.

institutions has been felt for a very long time, music can set the country's leadership on a new trajectory. Music, as a component of popular culture, can stem the ongoing damage done to public institutions and affairs. Apart from consoling the masses, music serves an important purpose by circulating information. In the neocolonial Nigerian state, elites do not hide their aversion to being criticized for their shortsightedness. They are average in their thinking, and their inability to prepare for the future has required expensive, last-minute efforts to keep the country functioning in times of crisis. The custodians of popular culture have avoided calling attention to these failures; they seem to fear draconian retribution from leaders who are capable of putting them out of business.

Nigerian musicians have successfully spread their music beyond the country's borders to earn international recognition. Through music, they have introduced styles and techniques of dancing that have been widely adopted by the public. If they can invent a dance that is internationally popular, they are equally capable of igniting revolutionary action. They must not ignore their ability to inspire the public, or to inform them of bad leadership's effects. Their creativity can be brought to bear on the challenge of inventing a dance style or pattern of dress that broadcasts society's deteriorating state to the political elite and the public. Their power should not be compromised in exchange for state recognition; they cannot become another instrument used to enable the unproductive leadership that has undermined society for so long. Nigerian popular culture wields considerable power: its authority must be used to support the masses and strengthen the future of the country.

By Serving as a Liberation Media

Popular culture's strength as an institution can be seen in its ability to instigate social movements. Historically, popular culture has emerged as a medium to address the struggle for liberation from oppressive forces. Popular culture has been employed in countries around the world to undertake similar liberation struggles as part of correctional and structural narratives. American society was swayed by the influence of popular music when pop icons Michael Jackson and Lionel Richie produced "We Are The World." The song was released on March 7, 1985 to raise funds for Ethiopians struggling against famine.[1] The electrifying influence of this popular culture production was unprecedented; it single-handedly drew the world's attention to the struggle of Ethiopians.

Such events are clear indicators of popular culture's massive influence. Its cross-cultural import has the ability to affect peoples' political understanding. Looking at Nigeria's situation, the popular culture industry can have a notable influence over the public perception of the country; the government would be compelled to recognize the bond created by people united to unselfishly highlight the issues challenging Nigerian society. We cannot underestimate the impact of collective voices working to overcome challenges – it pierces the hearts of those leading the people and the country. A musical arrangement, from an ethnically varied assembly of artists, would send a clear signal to the political class, encouraging them to undertake socially impactful programs. This could change the lives of the people and correct existing social anomalies.

The combination of popular culture artists versed in singing, acting, performing, and other cultural components would have an undeniable impact on the sociopolitical lifestyle of Nigerians. As noted by Florian Zappe, in her contribution to *Unpopular Culture*, "pop culture has provided an enduring and ever-adjustable myth of liberation around this rebellious outsider and sold it (in any sense of the word) to its audiences in various guises."[2] Fela Anikulapo Kuti, who was popular in the Nigerian space from the 1960s to the 1980s, is an example of popular culture's power in Nigeria. Fela became an unrepressed voice using music to criticize the political class. His notoriety required personal sacrifices, enduring arrests, torture, and the harassment of his loved ones, but he

---

[1] Jaap Kooijman, *Fabricating the Absolute Fake* (Amsterdam: Amsterdam University Press, 2013), 1, www.jstore.org/stable/j.ctt6wp7ck.6.

[2] Florian Zappe, "'When Order Is Lost, Time Spits': The Abject Unpopular Art of Genesis (Breyer) P-Orridge," in *Unpopular Culture*, eds. Lüthe Martin and Pöhlmann Sascha (Amsterdam: Amsterdam University Press, 2016), 129–46.

did not break under the pressure. He ultimately became a hero of the people, which brewed more extreme hostility from the government.

Popular culture can instigate movements to change oppressive systems. Nigerians are victims of irresponsible and high-handed leadership, applied deliberately to create a directionless populace. In most cases, people are deprived of basic amenities because their well-being has never been their leaders' primary concern. Nigeria is blessed with responsible citizens who are predominantly interested in working, contributing their quota to the system, and enjoying the dividends of democracy. However, these desires have been thwarted by a government that is either disinterested in collective progress or actively working to loot the public treasury. Popular culture has a responsibility to keep the government on its toes, providing content that sends liberation messages and educates the people about the importance of their collective decisions.

Within African societies, popular culture has been used to instigate a revolution. African life has experienced instances of political absurdism that were countered by resistance through popular culture. In January 2011, the Tunisian Revolution exposed the country's leadership to a backlash of criticism from global society through the compelling influence of popular culture.[3] Popular culture's successful campaign to inspire new waves of leadership and social change proves its importance as an institution. All institutions can be compromised by fear, or a lack of willingness to hold people accountable for mishandling public affairs. But industries connected to popular culture have the power to enhance revolutionary action by constantly engaging the public and the political class in arenas where change is needed. Without such a forum, there would be an absence of criticism; people would grow unaware of matters that affect them. Popular culture provides an opportunity to act, allowing people to register their voices in the process of developing society, which gives the government a chance to comport itself in a mature fashion.

It is possible for society's institutions to compromise their duties, but popular culture has different dynamics. Every individual musician cannot be oppressed by a corrupt government in the same way that other institutions can be oppressed. Individuals who are committed to liberation endure the government's displeasure, sending a message of unity to the people through their public resistance. It makes perfect sense that Nigerian youths, like young people everywhere, would look to popular artists as role models because of their unwavering dedication to the people.

---

[3] Glasius Marlies and Geoffrey Pleyers, "The Global Movement of 2011: Democracy, Social Justice and Dignity," *Development and Change* 44, no. 3 (2013): 547–567.

Preserving Culture as a Source of Economic Growth

Nigeria's political class has caused national complications, sometimes deliberately and sometimes inadvertently, since the beginning of the postcolonial period. Their choices have limited the country's options for economic survival. The entertainment industry could become a major part of the national economy if it receives initial investments in the form of government funding. Nollywood is already an important component, providing employment opportunities for a growing number of young Nigerians. Immediately after receiving their university education, these individuals awaken to the rude shock of irresponsible leadership, and they still manage to generate economic benefits for their industry and contribute to the country's international standing: this is done without any support from a government that remains largely unaware of the immense benefits they have to offer.

Little of the film industry's content draws from the country's bank of precolonial reserves; they are often unable to research original cultural material. This shortcoming is due, in part, to the lack of funding to embark on such projects. Some films end up mixing fact with fiction to produce deprecatory results, but they manage to generate considerable financial profits.

If the elite class invested in popular culture, they could accurately research the country's cultural heritage and history, producing content that attracts international audiences. In some cases, this could create opportunities for tourism. In many parts of the world, the film industry receives government attention and support, making it easy to pursue goals and achieve comparative success. Nigeria's popular culture gets minimal financial attention from the government; sometimes the government poses severe challenges to them. Despite this, the presence of popular culture is felt in the country and around the world.

Creators of cultural content can influence the country's politics by serving as reliable sources of employment and income generation. This can be achieved by creating material that attracts global attention, which would also draw investments into Nigerian industry. By enhancing Nigeria's national image, investors will be encouraged and people will become interested in the country's advancement. Popular culture can improve Nigeria by actively bolstering the reputation and managing the image of the country.

Nigeria's popular culture can generate national income once its artists abandon the Westernized aesthetic that permeates their content. Their Western-centric perspective has harmed the country's image, but linking the politics of the people with their way of life may not be as difficult as we expect. The country's political life and the content produced by its film industry are similar; the fact that Nigeria's political landscape reflects Western political values explains some of the country's inadequacies. The Nigerian political landscape is unsuited for the country's actual needs, but leadership continues to appropriate Western ideas without considering their practicality. It is another reason why conditions have steadily worsened. The Nigerian film industry, which mimics these attitudes, likewise reflects Western ideas and attitudes in the content it produces. Nigeria's film industry has failed to attract global attention because of its imitative tropes.

The international community appreciates originality, especially when it draws from unique indigenous content. Nigerian culture needs to stop copying Western concepts and start being original, which could have a profound influence on Nigerian politics. People producing work that relates to the country's moral and social goals would bring about a synchrony between film, music, dance, and the political world. The country's political aim is to discourage immoral action, and popular culture would do well to reinforce this message with its content. Movies should discourage behavior that the majority of the public consider appalling, while not encroaching upon the human rights of innocent people. There are more people consuming popular culture than there are following the latest policy updates from the government; cultural products can be adapted to align with the positive goals of political leaders and, at the same time, to criticize corruption, mismanagement, and state failure. If the producers of popular culture understood the power that they wield in determining society's development, they could structure their productions in ways that benefit the entire country.

The Nigerian government has plans for decolonization, but the various ways that this policy can be pursued quickly confuse the issue. Nigeria's environment must be developed to suit philosophical arrangements that prioritize African or Nigerian identities. The government lacks the will to impose these arrangements, but this task can be taken up by artists working in cultural industries. Their work provides the medium through which people can be persuaded to take up a certain behavior. The responsibility of instilling appropriate moral behavior in the younger generation is the work of different social groups; the popular culture industry has an important role to play in this effort. The cultural system of the Nigerian people has useful lessons for the world, and it should be explored for meaningful content that can simultaneously repair the country's decaying moral system and attract attention from international audiences.

Children imbibe from culture and model their actions on behaviors they witness in the media. They repeat songs from their favorite artists and select attitudes that reflect situations from their favorite programs. Even the political class picks up ideas from cultural productions. When the industry endorses a culture of materialism, members of the political class become more concerned with materialist culture than with public service. It is important for popular culture to promote equity, condemn excessive materialism, and refrain from encouraging morally condemnable clothing and behavior that are a negative influence on impressionable minds. By guiding society away from corrupt and criminal activities, sound governance would become less challenging. As elements of a powerful institution, artists involved with popular culture have a social responsibility to lead the country and encourage positive social and economic developments to improve their country.

Exploring Indigenous Political Social Structures

The transformational capacity of Nigeria's popular culture is enormous, given its ability to explore areas that could yield knowledge for the country's political actors. One reliable way to educate Nigeria's political elite and to encourage a different approach to leadership is to produce stimulating content that attracts their interest. Leaders must be educated about styles of political administration from past generations, seeing how they had maximum impact on grassroot politics. As a multiethnic country, Nigeria is proud of its vast cultural diversity and distinct political philosophies, working proactively and patiently to develop its people prior to the arrival of Europeans and their forced merger of the country. Right now, politicians appropriate contextually unworkable political philosophies and increase the distance between the leaders and the led. The country's political class is either unaware of or disinterested in the fact that a country as diverse as Nigeria must consider political philosophies that can include a majority of the people.

The ignorance exhibited by the highest echelons of power can be mitigated through the production of educational movies, songs, and dances that highlight existing social practices from different cultural and political systems. The political class can be educated about the potency of these indigenous social structures and their value in developing society. Foreign political systems and philosophies have not shown positive results for Nigeria. The country's popular culture should dig into the history of the people and excavate important political views along with the corresponding results of their historical application. Where necessary, more mature and appropriate concepts should be developed for contemporary needs. This will redefine the Nigerian political landscape and adequately represent a wide range of interests. Even if the current political class was minimally influenced through such productions, we cannot underestimate their impact on succeeding generations. The content must not focus on the promulgation of modernist culture and politics; that would have minimal influence on the future and the environment.

Nigeria's diversity will not suddenly disappear because it has applied a new political philosophy; the system inherited from the colonial powers is deeply entrenched. However, these different cultures would receive appropriate recognition when consolidated in musical productions that appreciate them, movies that celebrate them, and dance culture that corroborates them. Instead of investing energy in the denigration of precolonial African cultures, there are limitless numbers of cultural values that can be explored to examine political styles and systems from the past and these could benefit the entire country. It is incumbent on the institution of popular culture to begin actively investing in the African past. It could inspire changes in society merely by finding cultural legacies that readily add value to the development of the people.

Popular culture must make a profound demonstration of interest in social values and systems, encouraging their revitalization and urging a revamping of the existing political system. This will be difficult in a capitalist environment focused on making money, which is why producers must resolutely dedicate themselves to improving the country. This approach has benefits for the entire country, improving other aspects of society. Human culture and political systems are inseparable, and popular culture can be used to reach the political class. Through popular culture's relentless education of the public, leaders would be compelled to abandon the ineffective approaches that have been favored by politicians of the past. When cultural productions have charged the social atmosphere, the political class will recognize that the public is aware of their duty to make contributions to society's development. Change might not be initiated by the elites; society itself has a role to play. The reality is that Nigeria's political elites are scarcely concerned about ideas like this.

Popular culture must make a social impact by being imaginative. The power of imagination allows individuals to use existing and available materials in creative ways. This type of imaginative exercise is easier when it draws from the experiences of the people. Nigeria's situation offers more than enough material to evaluate the seriousness of the country's political elite. Movies, songs, and dance culture would be useful methods of evaluation, expressing the shortcomings of current political philosophies and the dangers that they pose to the nation's future. Political alternatives could be provided by Nollywood, the music industry, and others working with popular culture to pinpoint areas where the country can adopt political philosophies or systems that engage with the various ethnic identities that exist within the country and this diversity can be harnessed to build a formidable nation state. At the local level, grassroots politics would offer benefits for the people because it can accommodate the needs of different groups.

The politics of inclusion, which characterized African life before the arrival of the colonists, would play an important role in the production of cultural works. Many notable Nigerian musicians, who prioritize the indigenous systems of the past, attract local and international audiences. They are deliberate in their commitment to cultural redemption, and they believe that inclusion offers an avenue for instigating political revolution. That makes popular culture an important instrument for changing the narrative of politics in Nigerian society. People's ideas are shaped by what they consume through the media, which has the capacity to redefine policies in the political sphere. Participants within Nigeria's popular culture barely understand that their institution has the potential to change many things. In various civilizations across the world, film and music industries influence the political systems of their host countries. This includes Nigeria, but the country has not fully explored the traditional politics of various ethnic groups, evaluating them for lessons that can be taught to the political class.

The Idea of Being Predictive

Nigeria's political future can be projected through calculation and objective predictions. The current situation is the result of repeated actions from history; the present reflects the decisions and lifestyles chosen by people of the past. In Nigerian society, people who are familiar with the indifference of its political leaders can show the country how those decisions and attitudes will affect the future. Creators who work in industries connected to popular culture must understand their assignment: use these forecasts to rebuild Nigeria's societies and remodel them for a global existence. The consequences of bad decisions – whether acting or failing to take action – can be scripted as plays, set to music, and commemorated in styles of dress that signal society's awareness to the political class. These cultural materials will indicate that the people are aware of their leaders' philosophical impotence and inability to craft sound policies that can improve their future. When elected representatives pursue their own needs instead of aiding the struggling masses, dire uncertainties loom in their society's future.

The advantage of cultural artists is that their creativity can be brought to bear during difficult times; the political shallowness of leaders can be mined for content to produce something meaningful for society. A general economic challenge can easily reveal that political leaders are unprepared, and during especially dire periods, it becomes evident not only that Nigeria failed to prepare for trying times, but it also cannot respond effectively in times of unexpected crisis. Popular culture has a social contract to assist the masses with plays, music, and dance that reflect the costs of this willful ignorance within the political class. These important observations would establish the importance of their creative roles, attracting support from local audiences and international observers. Leadership is a responsibility, not an opportunity to milk the state dry, and cultural contributors who have the courage to recognize this can make a greater contribution to nation building than many politicians today.

During the COVID-19 global pandemic, Nigeria felt the effects of poor leadership with painful consequences. The lack of foresight, inability to prepare for the future, and unwillingness to address corruption and unproductive leadership resulted in a quagmire. Nigerian elites were grossly ill-prepared because their reluctance to provide basic amenities needlessly magnified the impact of a global crisis. They failed to recognize that their lackadaisical attitude to healthcare services weakened Nigeria's ability to address a public health crisis and left it with no resources to deploy during an emergency. There must be an institution that is committed to revealing the danger that accompanies neglect for institutions that are the bedrock of society. The artists, creators, and producers who are active in popular culture must uncompromisingly confront these concerns.

Hunger and poverty continue to drive people away from Nigeria. Professionals face daunting economic challenges because they are either underpaid or unable to advance in their chosen careers. For those who are employed, their contributions to the development of society are overlooked as the political class undermines their efforts or discredits their contributions. This persistent disparagement, degradation, and dismissal leaves many people seeking better working conditions elsewhere; they lack confidence in Nigeria's future and their own place in it. It is difficult to say whether Nigeria's political elites are interested in addressing this problem because they are all busy acquiring private wealth at the public's expense.

Nigeria is completely unprepared for a national health crisis. The enormity of the damage done to Nigeria's healthcare sector cannot be understood without realizing that the whole country – about two hundred million people – does not even have 500 ventilators[4] available to deal with the COVID-19 crisis. It is a national embarrassment that the popular culture industry has not deemed it interesting enough to explore these shortcomings or discuss the dangers that they pose to the country's future. By calling out poor decisions and identifying recklessness that threatens the country, popular culture can serve the national interest and remind the public about the dangers of unpreparedness. Music and movies can raise awareness of the risks inherent in bad leadership. Calling out the political class is a civic responsibility that can sanitize public institutions for everyone's benefit.

Hunger is another national emergency that should be addressed as a thematic focus for cultural productions. Leadership comes with responsibility, and when people fail to uphold that responsibility by failing to provide basic amenities, it blocks the nation's progress. Nigeria's economy cannot withstand a prolonged lapse in activity because it is predominantly driven by macroeconomics. People depend on their salaries to feed themselves, and furloughs, layoffs, or other interruptions in their employment mean unpredictable chaos for society. During emergencies, especially ones that have been created by sudden global turmoil like the COVID-19 virus, the Nigerian public is hit very hard. Popular culture should reflect these conditions and recommend ways to proactively address their concerns.

Avoiding Partisanship

Popular culture's influence stretches to accommodate the politics of a nation, and this is no different in Nigeria. Its transformational impact should not be underestimated when considering its effects on Nigeria's sociopolitical environment. As a social institution managed outside political influence, popular culture must be devoted to national progress and not to the government officials who happen to be holding office. No matter how much power political representatives accumulate while in office, the responsibilities of their position must be transferred to the next person assuming the role. It is understandable that some individuals develop a dedicated bloc of support from the people while in power, but this closeness should be terminated after their time in office expires. They must avoid abusing public affection to influence the affairs of the country. If film makers, musicians, and other practitioners involved with popular

---

[4] *Punch News*, "Nigeria Has Less Than 500 Ventilators for Coronavirus Patients – Sources," *Punch News*, March 24, 2020, www.google.com/amp/s/punchng.com/nigeria-has-less-than-500-ventilators-for-coronavirus-patients-sources/%3famp=1.

culture have preferences for specific politicians, they must separate their emotions from their professional obligations – otherwise, the results can be devastating.

In compromised political climates, objective criticism and evaluation are sacrificed on the altar of personal interest and cultural materials become biased. The position held by artists who work with popular culture is very sensitive, and if they do not realize how their interpretations of social realities shape the society in which they exist, the situation can quickly deteriorate. Partisan politics have the capacity to divide a country like Nigeria that is already struggling with differences in ethnicity, religion, and political affiliations. When producers of cultural products encourage these disagreements, the fragmentation of the country harms everyone.

In an environment like Nigeria's, social and political events must be interpreted without the slightest tinge of personal bias. Commitment is necessary to clearly separate an individual's social responsibility from their personal agenda. In every society where popular culture encourages partisan politics, national development is impossible.

Nigeria's multiethnic composition leaves it vulnerable to divisive factional politics. However, its people have shared constitutional responsibilities that encourage them to view collective progress and togetherness as goals that are greater than personal concerns. With this mindset, individuals who understand the primacy of political transparency can embark on projects that transform Nigerian society. Custodians of popular culture must understand that their role in shaping society cannot be compromised; otherwise, politics will quickly become poisonous. An unbiased mindset is necessary to avoid this outcome; cultural content must not attack political opponents for superficial differences and personal vendettas. This is an important responsibility for people who hold a sensitive role in the country's development.

Divisive content can be omitted from the public discourse to avoid factional politics from running wild. Popular culture industries should be subject to appropriate regulations, preventing them from participating in partisan activities that unravel the fabric of society. Against this backdrop, the government can concentrate on building a society where the spirit of nationalism is dominant and individuals understand their roles in developing the society. Partisanship has been a notorious impediment to Nigerian progress for a long time.

Nigeria's popular culture includes anti-government content that reflects an inherent disunity, in extreme cases, calling the country's survival into question. Popular culture is one of the public's tools for national development, and their input cannot be ignored. They must also uphold their social responsibility and refrain from activity that encourages disunity.

Nigeria's music industry has undertaken a duty of spreading messages of love and affection for everyone, regardless of their ethnic affiliations. The media has already distributed content that can strengthen bonds among the people. These efforts must continue because they allow the government to focus its efforts on meaningful change. If society does not cooperate, the government must fight to accomplish the simplest tasks. Government representatives are individuals drawn from their societies, and they make judgments based on the country's sociocultural situation. A president who is disturbed by materials from popular culture that are unapologetic in their promotion of factional, divisive behavior becomes vulnerable to emotional shock. Ultimately, it could lead to backlash from the government. Even when different groups engage in factional squabbling, popular culture should steer clear of exhibiting bias.

The government has its own role to play in shaping popular culture; content producers are motivated by the prospects of financial gain. Most of the sensationalist media outlets that peddle unsubstantiated rumors and unfounded claims are driven by profit motives. Their prioritization of personal gain to the detriment of national stability can be curbed by government intervention that is untainted by favoritism. Although the people in power provide tacit approval for organizations that encourage factionalism and divisive behavior, regulatory bodies must serve the national interest above other priorities and regulators must have the autonomy to act free from political interference. Nigeria has experienced many situations where artists are silenced by government power applied to satisfy a personal vendetta. Impartial regulators would discourage the worst excesses of partisan culture exploited for personal profit.

Identify with the Masses

Producers of popular culture must identify with the masses. They should not blindly follow the crowd in defiance of common sense, but ordinary people are led by their emotions in many situations. In difficult times of national tension, the country could be plunged into chaos without some mechanism for keeping emotions in check and this is when the entertainment industry can come to the rescue. Good music can be therapeutic. Good governance is easier when the public is focused on good citizenship. Happiness puts people into a mental state where they can function at their best. If the mental state of the public is unhealthy, the government has difficulty enacting meaningful change. Society grows when everyone is carried along in a collective agenda and common expectations.

Popular culture can perform important work to assuage public fears and address despair. Every society experiences challenges and the responsibility to address these situations does not rest exclusively with the federal government or the political class. The duty of educating the public is a collaborative effort requiring the government to work with various institutions and agencies to distribute necessary information and relevant facts in times of crisis.

Today, access to popular culture is ubiquitous. Custodians of this culture can use it to its full effect by ensuring effective and reliable communication with the public providing ongoing reassurance that individuals and groups are being included in the government's plans and have not been left behind.

Greater organization in the music industry could help make it accessible and able to deliver messages more effectively. It would transform political life in Nigeria by properly educating people about how to vote, who to vote for, and why voting is important. It is a challenge to identify and support effective leaders because political discourse is full of empty rhetoric; Nigerian leaders are quite effective at executing schemes to cajole the majority into voting against the public interest. Politicians mostly use the music and movie industries to sway public opinion for personal gain.

Popular culture has the power to control the direction of public opinion. This role has been compromised in the past, normally when individuals satisfy their own greed instead of performing a public service by holding government representatives accountable. If the industries that affect popular culture are organized as a coherent unit, they can work together for common progress instead of being exploited for parochial purposes.

Popular culture can initiate various educational, entertaining, and appealing programs to connect the public with the political class. This intermediary role is accompanied by a responsibility to produce content that delivers clear, accessible, and accurate messages. It is no coincidence that people, especially the younger generation, rely on artists as role models for inspiration, moral values, and social attitudes. The people within this creative circle provide the public with the content necessary to ease their emotional burden and reduce the workload of the Nigerian government in communicating the collective aspirations of the citizens.

Nigerians are regarded as a special breed in the international community because they are seen as happy people. They have earned this reputation through their adaptability and their persistent good nature, even in the face of the most challenging hardship. Nigeria's popular culture, which includes music, movies, and dance, has played an important role in supporting these attitudes.

When a country is overwhelmed by sudden tragedy, especially one that is wrought by an unusual pandemic such as Ebola or COVID-19, national tensions increase exponentially. In situations like this, the popular culture industry has an important role to play easing tensions and soothing fears. The government's response to the crisis must deal with the logistics of emergency management, allocating resources to places in need. Meanwhile, people must find emotional assistance in the therapeutic power of popular culture which can identify with the masses, provide them with entertainment, settle their tormented minds, and give them reassurance and confidence. In the absence of such efforts, the government would be facing an unimaginable challenge. Public fear is antagonistic to great ideas, and leaders are unable to craft effective policies in an environment of panic. When public fear is managed effectively by popular culture, the government can focus on its tasks with undivided attention.

Music, dance, movies, and other examples of popular culture can change existing narratives. When an industry or institution strengthens the public's mental health, the burden of leadership becomes lighter. The institution of popular culture is capable of making substantial changes and contributions that affect public conditions, and the government must understand this role and demonstrate its commitment to supporting those efforts – the government must uphold its side of the social contract by funding and supporting industries that are part of popular culture.

The Nigerian government is currently indifferent to the existence of popular culture, but it cannot assume that society is formed by mere coincidence or forces of nature. Government agencies must stop undermining the efforts of popular culture institutions that can ensure normalcy and promote social ethics in Nigeria.

For National Integration

In addition to its other sociological roles, popular culture can become an important tool for national integration. Differences in religious and ethnic affiliations have always been a recipe for disunity in Nigerian society, and they are normally exploited by any individual who stands to gain from those divisions. However, Nigeria is not the only multiethnic country in the contemporary world, and other countries have successfully responded to the conflicts that can arise from different ethnic affiliations.

Nigeria's case is unique because its heterogeneity has always been used to obstruct progress, although this could change if concerned institutions take the necessary steps. Popular culture can work toward national integration: it holds immense potential to shape events and spearhead revolutionary action to rebuild national unity. The relationships between the multiethnic groups of Nigeria can be solidified and validated through conscious efforts to promote and reinforce them.

Creativity is required to craft an avenue for voices to address issues that are causing disunity. Nollywood must take up a daunting social responsibility, forging a shared identity and common ground to ignite the passions of the majority; they must conceive of the nation as an indivisible entity. With a single voice, the Nigerian public would be able to build a better nation and hold government leaders accountable. Disunity has stood in the way of good governance because individuals use the lens of their ethnic background to interpret the actions of public officials: instead of asking how government leaders have supported a single Nigerian identity, people seek advantages for members of their own group. Popular culture can reverse this trend by redefining and reshaping national identity to encourage unity within the country.

Nigerians do not encourage intercultural or interreligious marriages because of mutual suspicion. Despite their allegedly forward-looking attitudes, people secretly foster mistrust for outsiders and this has harmful effects on national politics. Groups should find it easier to tolerate differences if they all accept themselves as members of a truly indivisible nation. When the politics of difference remain at the center of national attitudes, it strains relationships and endangers cooperation. Popular culture can address this challenge and use its transformational ability to mend these fractures. The persuasive ability of popular culture can use songs and movies to help people understand the need for genuine integration. Maintaining a nation founded on truly democratic structures is continuous work: the fact that Nigeria has struggled with this shows that popular culture has important work to do.

Educating the Masses

Popular culture must embrace its educational responsibility to provide civic knowledge. Most people are uneducated about their civic rights and responsibilities, and this increases the number of social crimes that blatantly challenge national advancement. Political apathy is easy to spot in Nigeria and this attitude stems from ignorance: people must understand how governance, in its positive and negative senses, influences their own way of life from ensuring stability to developing society and economic advancement. Sadly, most people are unaware of this. The public displays this ignorance by selling their votes and commodifying their values. People underestimate their collective power and believe their government representatives when they are told that nothing can be done without them.

The Nigerian government should view these attitudes as an environmental threat, but instead they exploit them and benefit from the public's ignorance. The absence of civic education has brought additional challenges; the political class remains comfortably indifferent and convinced that they have nothing to lose. However, this mindset is dangerous. Complacency in times of plenty leads to disaster in times of crisis when the government is not able to coordinate a public response to emergency situations because ignorance stands in the way of genuine cooperation. In Nigeria, many people downplayed the threat of COVID-19 and erroneously believed that the entire public health emergency was a government ruse to carry out economic and religious sabotage.

The prevailing mindset of Nigeria's public discourages them from following government recommendations unless accompanied by drastic action. The existing system does not encourage people to engage in self-reflection or access information independently. Without the ability to make informed decisions and exercise sound judgment, the public's ignorance prevented the government from controlling the spread of disease during the COVID-19 outbreak. Similar situations play out in other aspects of national life. People cannot be bothered to select effective representatives who will practice purposeful leadership, and the results are devastating for the country. The entertainment industry must use its influence over popular culture to educate people and encourage politics driven by active, effective leaders.

The educational work of popular culture industries is necessary on several levels. Nigerian intellectuals currently sing the praises of leaders who do not share the dividends of democracy: this has been a coping mechanism to adapt to the reduced attention that they receive from the political class following a long denial of the country's economic and financial expansion. Public intellectuals have adjusted to the system by aggressively pursuing their own financial interests, and collective well-being has been sacrificed for personal gain. The political class banks on this sycophantic attitude, accepting cheerful praise and pretending that it is public approval.

Public intellectuals understand that being truthful with the government can cost them their freedom. Honesty can ruin a person's career because of the massive influence that the government commands in every aspect of society. Instead, public discourse elevates bad leaders, sacrificing true democracy in the process.

Popular culture, which can blend indigenous African cultures with Western styles, has the ability to challenge this trend. Artists can craft messages that are accessible to everyone and which reveal the corruption and bad practices at every level of society. The responsibility for cleaning up society does not rest exclusively on them, but they should take bold steps to correct the porous social values that encourage moral delinquency. The media is an important tool for instigating actions in the modern world, and popular culture predominantly uses media. Many components of popular culture could be mustered to perform important duties, reminding people that every institution must be up and running to advance Nigerian society. Objective criticism is the only instrument that can keep the government in check and prevent it from abandoning its responsibilities – these ideas must be reinforced through popular culture.

Songs are necessary to send clear messages to the people. In some cases, the language of colonial power undermines the intended messages, but cultural artists can employ local languages to remain faithful to the spirit of their work. The absence of an educated citizenry will obstruct the progress of the people, and politics can make exponential advancements to improve people's lives. However, the government has failed to educate the masses because of an inherent fear of change. The people deserve to know what effective governance looks like and how it behaves. As one of society's institutions, popular culture can provide this education.

Conclusion

Popular culture emerges from unique historical realities. Jarula Wegner, in his contribution to the book, "A Poetics of Neurosis,"[5] explains that rap culture is a product of struggle and the dehumanizing experience of colonialism that African Americans endured in the Americas. It is an example of popular culture identifying with the suffering masses who have been deprived of basic amenities and rights. Popular culture has the capacity to transform Nigerian society because it wields the power to represent people who have been victims of bad government policies and it can channel their grievances into appropriate outlets and deliver their messages effectively. The role of popular culture cannot be underestimated; it provides people with a medium for airing their views, calling the world's attention to their situation and provoking an overhaul of the system.

Artists and industries that serve as the curators of popular culture can use their social influence to provide people with the education necessary to become more effective citizens. Elections and their importance could

---

[5] Jarula Wegner, "Reading Rap with Fanon and Fanon with Rap: The Potential of Transcultural Recognition," in *A Poetics of Neurosis*, eds. Elena Furlanetto and Dietmar Meinel (Bielefeld: Transcript Verlag, 2018), www.jstore.org/stable/j.c tv6zdbtz.6.

be understood by the public and made accessible to the majority, and in turn they could understand the consequences of choosing bad leaders to conduct state affairs. By doing this, artists would perform their duty as the conscience of society. They must show unwavering commitment to constantly placing society within a framework of exceptional leadership. They must identify purposeless leadership through the interpretation of government policies and actions, working to inspire social changes. Through this work and their objective criticism, citizens can make their own contributions to society's development.

The custodians of popular culture can also add value to Nigerian society by discouraging partisanship. Excessive allegiance to cultural and ethnic affiliations can compromise the entire country, especially when criticism of government policies is driven by parochial interests that are devoid of objectivity. By prioritizing national integration, factional politics can be avoided and the country will be in an appropriate state to encourage sustainable development. Nigeria clearly needs national unity – the absence of that binding force continues to undermine advancements that could otherwise have been easily achieved. Popular culture artists in the Nigerian environment have shown how their institution can identify with the masses and value togetherness. These forces could transform the country and guide the political system of the people.

Part VI

Conclusion

Conclusion: Pathways to the Future

This book has revealed different components that are responsible for – and have compelling influence on – the development of Nigerian society. Ethnicity remains a strong factor that is critical to the country's advancement due to the nation's heterogeneous nature. This heterogeneous nature has sometimes been considered a benefit, and at other times it has functioned as one of the abysmally cantankerous obstacles hindering national growth because it allows the political elites that steer the country to exploit ethnic weaknesses for their own parochial advantage. This is not exclusive to Nigeria, or even African countries alone. Across the world, members of the political class have always held the masses hostage within their countries, using every opportunity to divide people and retain their grip on power.

An outsider observing Nigeria's political progression following independence, or even its development before the expulsion of colonialism, would marvel at narratives showing travails and triumphs, tribulations and jubilations, and temptations and redemptions that simultaneously display the country's strengths and weaknesses. Despite their increasing ethnic differences, Nigerians have collaborated to overcome common challenges and emerged with impressive results.

The early nationalists' call for independence from colonial rule is a good example of various ethnicities working together to reject a gross and improper domination that undermined them and threatened their collective well-being. It was obvious that their ethnic and religious differences could weaken their sturdy collectivism in the (postindependence) future, but they forged an alliance to achieve their desire at a critical moment. Despite pessimistic forecasts, such collaboration continues to surprise brilliant sociopolitical experts.

Untold narratives of unity were shrouded by nationalist enthusiasm, downplaying differences to fight a common imperial enemy and to promote shared values and interests. In the 1950s, an impasse on negotiations for self-rule was overcome through a nexus of agreements on regional fiscal and political autonomies, different dates for regional independence, and the adoption of the principles of confederal consociationalism. Things began to unravel after civilian and military political elites hijacked the process and steered the course of Nigerian government from true federalism to prebendal unitary kleptocracy.

Other challenges have threatened relationships and progress within the country, and events have revealed that Nigeria's unity rests on an unstable foundation whose destruction could erase the country's advancement. Nigeria's ethnic heterogeneity, which can serve as a source of strength, has been exploited by members of the country's political class for divisive and destructive goals. This has compelled political analysts, sociocultural experts, astute writers, stakeholders, and other committed people to chart various paths toward a Nigerian future that considers the interests of every citizen. This work reflects the important steps necessary to actualize a desirable future: these arguments are not presented as an exhaustive list, but rather fundamental approaches to achieve common goals for national development.

One of the disquieting challenges continuing to make a mockery of Nigeria's progress has been the appropriation of inadequate political ideas. Nigerian political elites seem unaware of the essential role of values in good governance, especially in a country that is diverse in culture, religion, and ideology. This failure of national leaders to understand or employ adequate political ideology has prevented them from harnessing the country's potential. Nigerian elites remain grossly uninformed regarding the damage caused by this willful ignorance. Although a homogeneous society could become successful – in the long run – by applying methods embraced by Nigeria's elite, it would be difficult, if not impossible, for a heterogeneous country. Nigeria's history of shared hardship, which was suffered at the hands of colonial imperialists who were unconcerned about their subjects' genuine advancement, makes it essential to develop a philosophical roadmap to run the country's affairs.

Nigeria's aversion to a strong, beneficial philosophy for governance reflects its poor understanding of the challenges inherent in managing a culturally diverse society. The country, which is the most populated nation in Africa, has a volatile history from being one of the most complex emerging countries developed through the "trial and error" experiments that colonial powers conducted. It would have been difficult for a colony, founded by an imperialist power, to establish different systems of self-administration among various ethnic groups that were capable of continuing as a strong entity after independence. When the country was fused together by Lord Lugard in 1914, it was a pilot project to study the formation of a sovereign state. Colonial powers never imagined that the multiethnic colonies comprising Nigeria would experience a centenary without separation. Africans have managed diversity far beyond the dreams and expectations of their European conquerors. However, Nigeria's experience proves that managing diversity and preventing it from succumbing to divisive forces does not guarantee that it will transform into a strong, sovereign entity.

Nigerians have remained together as a country for more than a hundred years, but they have not attained progress similar to that of Japan, India, China, or other developing countries. This is in spite of the country having human and natural resources that are similar to or greater than those of its peers. There must be a fundamental explanation for the country's flat trajectory, and it appears that its declaration of war against philosophy may be to blame. It is possible for a person to attain some level of happiness through sheer luck, but it is not possible to remain lucky and relevant without any effort. Nigerians have been blessed with abundant natural resources, but this has not translated to success because there are no unifying ethics or applied will to manage their natural, human, political, and intellectual properties. This is why they continue to squander potential while their contemporaries achieve great success.

If Nigeria is to claim its true place on the global stage, it must embrace a tradition of federalism. "True" federalism, as a political ideal, would allow different regions or ethnic groups to move at a consistent pace, encouraging constructive competition among the people. Africans in general would be more successful with political philosophies that can relate to their needs, prove contextually useful, and accommodate change as new ideas develop. Federalism, if appropriately domesticated, has limitless capacity to become useful and productive. States and ethnic groups could draw on their innate strengths and environmental advantages to aid their development. A sense of competition among the people would quickly allow them to realize their potential and achieve success. Nigerian progress is reportedly in decline because haphazard central planning is inadequate for organizing the activity of more than 190 million people.

The progressives genuinely rooting for Nigeria's development must support concerted efforts to return to true federalism – the nation's current system of government is a distorted federalism. Political elites seem to think that their access to the country's resources and wealth makes them immune to the consequences of purposeless leadership. Their disregard for the effects of flawed leadership and misconduct sets an example for future leaders who commit further atrocities. These actions fail to recognize that the unsafe environment created by their reckless indifference jeopardizes the security of society for everyone, including their own children. Nigeria requires appropriate political ideologies and attitudes to ensure the safety and protection of everyone. Another challenge is that the country's political arrangement does not provide opportunities for minority groups; comprehensive development is not possible for the country without sincere and genuine representation for all people.

When the political class decides to utilize functional political philosophy, they are halfway to actualizing a developed Nigeria. Democracy applied to the wrong political principles can be devastating; democracy's beauty lies in its ability to apply philosophy that brings about the collective transformation of the people. Too much centralization of power limits the ability of the people. Nigeria's past successes were achieved during a time when its government permitted every region to develop at its own pace, and the notable improvements that occurred within this relatively short period prove that Nigeria's future lies in applying the appropriate political principles for collective progress. Differences in ethnic identity should not be seen as a threat. Instead, they can be applied to create a national advantage.

The future of every serious country depends on its education system and Nigeria is no exception. The light of education drives back the darkness of ignorance and sharpens the intellect of the people. By empowering people's minds, they can re(de)fine their thinking and become useful to themselves and society at large. Education is not merely studying facts in books, it is training the mind to think uniquely. People who receive a thorough education are aware of problems and seek solutions to address the challenges ravaging society. Educated minds understand their social responsibilities and strive fervently to make contributions that advance society. Productive education deters people from pursuing ambitions that jeopardize public interest. It is not that education limits a person's capability for evil – instead, the notion is similar to that of Plato's philosopher kings whose years of rigorous education led them to act in the public interest because they understood that good education influences the ability to make sound decisions, preventing people from pursuing interests that threaten the safety of others.

One might ask whether a lack of basic education is the reason why Nigerians engage in questionable activities. A considerable percentage of people are denied access to quality education – the country's education system has faltered because the necessary resources have not been allocated to maintain it. The challenges faced by Nigeria's education system have been felt in different capacities. Education is the bedrock of every social institution in all societies, and its absence means that such institutions cannot stand. The rot that is prevalent in politics, the increased moral decay, and the ubiquity of corruption are all symptoms of an ailing educational system. The public institution has been weakened while elite groups collect endless profits from the ignorance of the masses; uneducated citizens are less likely to challenge the shortcomings of their society.

While youths in other developing countries receive opportunities through their educational systems that give them a sense of belonging, Nigerian youths are not receiving a high-quality education; the government has demonstrated that it does not consider education to be a primary concern. The country's development has excluded this demographic, and when youth are deliberately disempowered, the future is under serious threat. People who do not engage with educational opportunities – either deliberately or due to government efforts to marginalize them – become hostile to valuable ideas that could propel society to greater heights. A person's decision to either inspire change or discourage it depends on whether they have access to education that can enhance the mind. The country's dysfunctional education system does not support the many innovative ideas that young Nigerians could nurture.

What will a country rely on for self-development when it has been negligent about educating its youth? Such country is destined to consume foreign products that could have been produced locally and conveniently by the demographic that was neglected. South Africa commits around 16 percent of its budgetary plans to education,[1] and Ghana committed more than 20 percent of its budgetary allocations to education[2] for the year 2020. In Nigeria's case, only 6.7 percent of its budget has been committed to education.[3] These figures demonstrate the government's attitude toward national education. It is apparent that Nigeria's government, unlike its counterparts in Africa, is not interested in educational investments and the result is devastating. Discouraging the country's youngest demographic cohort from attaining knowledge – and demotivating it from applying knowledge to transform itself and society – will cripple national development.

The absence of financial support for national education provides insight into the government's preferred policies. It is not surprising that

[1] UNICEF, *2018/19 Education Budget Brief: South Africa* (New York: UNICEF, 2018), www .unicef.org/esaro/UNICEF-South-Africa-2018-Education-Budget-Brief.pdf.
[2] PwC Ghana, *2020 Budget Highlights: Consolidating the Gains for Growth, Jobs and Prosperity for All* (Accra: PwC Ghana, 2019), www.pwc.com/gh/en/assets/pdf/2020-budget-highlights.pdf.
[3] Yushau Shuaib, "SDGs: 2020 Budget and Education in Nigeria," *Blueprint*, November 18, 2019, https://blueprint.ng/sdgs-2020-budget-and-education-in-nigeria/.

the education sector has encountered challenges from teachers who take a lackadaisical attitude toward discharging their duty, organized labor actions, and researchers who are discouraged from pursuing great innovations that could turn the country around. These problems are made worse by the fact that Nigeria's tertiary educational curriculum needs an emergency overhaul. Many of its course specializations are outdated; some have become irrelevant and need to be revisited – they have endured because the government is not receptive to new ideas. Course contents must be adapted for contemporary needs, and all specializations should be reviewed for relevance. It is expensive to equip science laboratories with modern technology and to provide the technical materials necessary for studying machine learning and artificial intelligence. This is why public and private universities specialize in finance, banking, and mass communications.

Problems persist because the Nigerian government does not recognize its leadership role in reviving the indigenous African educational system as a counterweight to balance the Western educational methods still touted by Africans almost a century after their purported independence. It is not only sad that colonial education systems do not fit contemporary educational needs, but it is also complicated and complex because Africans show no interest in revamping their inherited educational system. Sadly, Nigeria is not leading in that respect. Education should reflect the urgent needs of the people, answering their development goals. The production of graduates who have studied courses that are out of step with modern society makes Nigeria's case even more pathetic. To save the country from this unbridled and unguarded leadership behavior, Nigeria must make deliberate commitments to recognizing the financial value of education.

Once the political system stops undermining ethnic minorities, Nigeria's diversity can be harnessed for the benefit of everyone. The country is known for its diversity in culture, ethnicity, and religion, and these must all be included in constitutional and political arrangements. The founding of the country was driven more by the greed of colonial imperialists than by any authentic pattern of state formation. If a nation is a group of people unified by common history, culture, language, and religious philosophies, then the multiethnic country of Nigeria consists of different nationalities bound together by European imperialists. This is the source of the divisive politics that are still pursued to fulfill personal and provincial agendas. Ethnic disparity continues unabated in the country, and every ethnic group seeks to wield power so they can remain relevant in socioeconomic, sociopolitical, and sociocultural discussions. This explains why Nigeria struggles with overwhelming challenges in its efforts for national development.

The formation of Nigeria's political parties reveals the country's pattern of ethnic disparity. The inherent philosophical lopsidedness is evident in the creation of political parties that threaten Nigeria's present and future by operating like interest groups. Citizens who are persuaded to belong to political groups based on ethnic affiliation further compound the problem within Nigeria, for various reasons. They encourage the belief that a person's primary loyalty lies with their ethnic group, due to shared opinions and convictions within the group. They also give a disproportionate advantage to groups that have the most members. This unconsciously plants seeds of discord – instead of seeing political parties as vehicles for advancing national interest, development, and progress, members begin nurturing ambitions to use their political parties for selfish ends.

Individuals placed at a disadvantage by this arrangement face difficult situations. They are often compelled to align with other groups to pursue their own goals, meaning that loyalty becomes negotiable and people and parties undermine national development. One who is versed in Nigerian politics, or who has examined political behavior for any amount of time, would understand that the betrayal of party principles, or "crossing the carpet," thrives in the country's political climate because ethnicity is valued above party membership. Two political parties have always appeared popular since the return to democratic elections – until one realizes how people switch between these two parties, depending on which one is in charge. The underpinnings of these so-called parties remain dictated by ethnic affiliation. It is not beneath the dignity of Nigerian politicians to plant moles and spies in other groups to retain their grip on power.

Party members conceal suspicion, distrust, and grievances as they jostle to retain power. In cases where different ethnicities belong to a single party, it is normally because the various groups are plotting to hijack that party's political structure for provincial gains – this is the primary political philosophy of the various parties and groups. The president's position is the most coveted because people seek federal power to advance the interests of their preferred ethnic group. This is usually done to the detriment of others, especially ethnic minorities that lack the strength of numbers necessary to compete for leadership. Nigeria's political system oppresses many ethnic groups who do not have the power to contest this situation. The country's highest office has been used to hunt down people from the opposition's camp, punishing them for having different philosophies or belonging to a different political party. The position of president is seen differently.

Social groups have been created to support various presidential candidates based solely on ethnicity. The Nigerian political system has endured the creation of unconstitutional groups established with mischievous intentions – the tacit approval of these groups, given by some Nigerian presidents, indicates that the issue of ethnicity still plays an important role in the country's sociopolitical engagements. During the era of President Goodluck Jonathan – the first individual from the Ijo minority group elected to the office – the Niger-Delta Militant Group arose from his home region. This group served no national function other than to issue demands, threatening the country's peace over concerns that they were missing their share of the "national cake." These groups form barriers to progress, preventing the country from achieving its fullest potential. It has set a horrible precedent; a similar group, called the Miyetti Allah Association of Nigeria, was formed immediately after President Mohammadu Buhari's inauguration.

Such social groups might have been in existence before some of their members assumed power, but they are now holding the country to ransom. This raises questions as to why they should exist. What about the minority groups that cannot produce presidents? If they cannot garner enough support to put a candidate in office, are their members less important than other Nigerian citizens? Without members of their group in power, they are unable to claim the expected benefits: these groups are paid from the national treasury whenever they threaten to bring about violence. The fact that such groups can openly challenge the country's constitutional framework, implicitly supported by presidential inaction, puts the nation's future in jeopardy. Rather than making genuine contributions to advance the country through their human resources, each group sees an opportunity to milk the country's treasury whenever their members hold office. Militant interest groups or violent social groups must be constitutionally prohibited from taking felonious action when their members assume power.

It is appalling that the misapplication of religion is one of the factors keeping Nigeria in perpetual stagnation. Religion is expected to guide people toward purposeful lives, but it has been manipulated to accomplish the opposite in Nigeria. As a country with diverse religious beliefs, the nation's various religions often interfere with government to affect rulers and subjects alike. For the former, religion is used as a tool for political purposes and leaders play the religion card to mobilize support or attack an opponent. For the latter, religion is the only consolation in a life of unending difficulty. There are few countries that validate Karl Marx's disdainful description of religion as an opiate quite so completely. In Nigeria, the masses avidly cling to religion for consolation; it has become a solace that offers distractions from bad governance and provides an escape from society's daunting socioeconomic realties. Failures of government officials are seen as acts of God, and individuals would rather seek spiritual remedies than hold their leaders accountable for poor performance.

Nigeria's religious dynamics are another consequence of the deliberate neglect of the country's education system, one of the ways that people are kept ignorant in order to accommodate corrupt government officials. Religion is a multidimensional challenge contributing to the regression of the country. For the teeming masses, all national activities are first viewed from the perspective of religion, regardless of the benefits they could bring. It encourages an unhealthy national attitude, rendering the economy irrelevant and viewing businesses as unproductive. Sanusi Lamido Sanusi, the former governor of the Central Bank of Nigeria, attempted to introduce an Islamic banking system as a means of harnessing the financial sector for productive national purposes.[4] Instead, it was met with fierce opposition from different religious groups, fearful that it was an attempt to "Islamize" the country. The mutual suspicion arising from religious radicalism continually stifles new opportunities.

Religion poses an alarming threat to Nigeria's future because it has been combined with volatile emotions in ways that damage national unity. The nature and intentions of many so-called "moral" imperatives have harmful effects. People are afraid to migrate to other parts of the country because they assume that by having different religious or cultural backgrounds from their new neighbors, their lives will be in jeopardy anytime a religious controversy surfaces. There have been tragic incidents of assault and executions of people who hold different beliefs, worship different Gods, or follow different religious philosophies. The accompanying silence from religious leaders and government officials is interpreted as concessions to the violence. Extreme cases have victimized National Youth Service Corps (NYSC) members, and the evils continue.

The country's meager economic resources have been squandered on religious frivolity. While government policy supports the country's two major religions, using state funds to sponsor people on pilgrimages, the country's other religions are consistently treated with arrogant indifference. Non-Islamic and Christian groups in the minority suffer blatant disrespect and are undervalued in favor of the two preferred religions. Such conduct is incapable of fostering the unity necessary for comprehensive development and is a worrying impediment to both their realization and their actualization. The funds dedicated to the religions that

---

[4] *Lotus Capital*, "Sanusi Tasks Islamic Banks to Impact Financial System," *Lotus Capital*, November 27, 2013, www.lotuscapitallimited.com/index.php/media-centre/press-releases/87-press-release/127-sanusi-tasks-islamic-banks-to-impact-financial-system.

receive preferential treatment could be applied to more productive national efforts. In a country where the masses lack quality education and modern infrastructure, the allocation of state resources to fund personal pilgrimages is nothing short of a wasteful extravagance.

How can Nigeria reverse this state of affairs to strengthen its future prospects? Identifying the answer is not as difficult as implementing it: Nigeria must return to the secularist philosophy that should guide the conduct of a multiethnic, multireligious, and multicultural community. In a religiously diverse society, it is only logical for people to separate religious convictions from state governance. Bringing exclusionary religious beliefs and philosophies into the public domain leads to divisiveness and the dismissal of collective ideas, posing challenges for national development. Using religious philosophy to dictate the rules for public engagement and activity prompts internal strife; individuals imposing their religious beliefs on others will always be met with heavy resistance. The separation of the religious and the political will help the country advance and explore the potential for collective growth. People who violate social rules must be punished according to secular law, not religious edict.

Nigeria has experienced numerous challenges from religious groups that are quick to hide behind their faith. People who cling to religious doctrine while serving in public office end up considering issues from emotional angles before applying objective lenses. Justice is bound to be subverted in an environment where religion is given primary importance. Nigeria's history has seen murders that were inspired by various religious beliefs; they have been absolved or swept under the carpet by people in power who share similar convictions. The country's future would be secure if religious issues were separated from political affairs: people must understand that such a combination has always resulted in the kinds of unbearable outcomes that Nigeria seeks to avoid. Other countries in the world have integrated varied religious beliefs and opinions without allowing them to interfere with national development and political progress. If this were the case in Nigeria, it would be relatively easy to form a national identity and people would feel secure visiting different places with diverse local culture.

The obvious insecurity displayed by Nigeria's political leaders is adding to the existing problems. It is pitiful that postcolonial leaders are still fearful of handing the baton over to the younger generation. This attitude, which is prevalent in all African countries, reflects a lack of confidence in what the younger generation has to offer. Seats of power across the continent are occupied by gerontocrats who are out of touch with contemporary reality. Nigerian leaders are making it especially difficult for youths to access platforms that can exhibit their ingenuity. The younger generation is denied chances to apply their knowledge and perspectives. Leaders always argue that controlling the youths is in the country's best interests, but they continue to marginalize and reduce the representation and importance of youth in sociopolitical issues. The younger generation's contributions are not only discouraged and misunderstood, they are also denied. This alienation has its consequences as virtually all aspects of life in Nigeria today show clear signs of government incompetence.

Some argue that youths are not necessarily discouraged by participating in the political process, but their absence from the political arena reinforces the idea that they are irrelevant to national governance. Discouraged, they turn to other activities that are mostly detrimental to Nigeria's progress. Youth involvement in criminal behavior, morally condemnable actions, intellectually deficient activities, and other delinquency can be seen as reactions to the country's indifference. In other parts of the world, youths secure important positions running society's affairs, including leadership positions in governments. We must understand why such youths engage with their nations' values to collectively move their countries forward. Nigerian youths are normally excluded from government planning, raising concern about their demographic's role in developing the country.

Youths are discouraged in several different ways. Nigeria's political system does not provide opportunities for them, and this stance is supported by the constitution. Various political positions, opened to them after years of agitation and protest, appear more like burdens than official involvement. Youths are expected to raise money and purchase tickets to run for office, even though their sources of income are negligible and infrequent. This barrier is used as an excuse to dismiss them as incapable or irrelevant for addressing important issues that concern the people's progress. Youths may have contagious energy, be filled with ideas and brimming with zeal and hope, but they are prevented from taking action. After graduation, most of them join the ranks of the unemployed and associate with groups of questionable moral character. There, they are tempted to use their youthful energy and intellectual proficiency to perpetrate all manners of delinquent behavior. By squandering their talents on antisocial behavior, they simultaneously harm present-day society and undermine its prospects for the future.

The alienation of youth occurs because basic amenities are not provided and their needs go unmet, preventing people from maximizing their potential and denying them the opportunity to serve in political positions. Their demographic's discouragement is apparent in the country's neglect of their well-being. Government assistance, enabling them to produce services and amenities for the modern world, could become a profitable arrangement. It could reduce the number of youths engaged in morally delinquent and antisocial behavior because they would have worthwhile opportunities to earn income and become useful for society's advancement. In other words, the government's mishandling of its youth programs is making the situation more difficult and disastrous for the entire country.

Many youths escape to other countries, believing their skills could be honed, harnessed, and used for constructive purposes elsewhere. This is a national concern, even when those abroad send remittances, which minimizes the losses at a personal level for their kinship groups. Many Nigerian youths go on to make landmark achievements in their chosen fields, setting an important pace for development and making an overwhelming impression. It is Nigeria's loss, allowing its best minds to seek greener pastures in other countries and environments. In their new surroundings, these driven individuals use their human resources to turn the tide. Some may question how this could become a threat to Nigeria's future, but remember that the development of a country, state, or province is the duty of the younger generation. When they are not applying their talents to improve their environment, it becomes a disadvantage – the inaction cedes the opportunity for improvement.

Nigeria's development relies on the engagement of the younger generation who must be given a sense of belonging, assuring their position in society. They must not be offered adjunct, disposable positions that undermine their usefulness. They are excited to hold important positions in politics and other national endeavors where they can apply their intelligence and ingenuity for the country's benefit; their place cannot be ignored in the developmental process. Their energy can drive results and inspire changes. When they have the opportunity to represent and be represented in various capacities, they are almost guaranteed to make immense contributions to national development. With the necessary support and encouragement, these same youths who are advancing international communities could revolutionize Nigeria's economy, education, politics, and infrastructure, putting the country back on the map of global relevance with impressive contributions.

Nigeria's challenges come from the inability to make effective use of its resources, both natural and human. The government does not display the interest and activity necessary to develop the economy, demonstrating complacency when it should show ravenous hunger. This has eroded the economy and undermined national efforts over the years. The Nigerian government's over-reliance on oil over the last five decades, has come to haunt them. Other resources have gone unattended when they could have become reliable sources of income, which has left nothing in reserve and no safety net in the event of disaster. Oil has proven very useful for strengthening the Nigerian economy over an extended period of time, but the sad reality is that the world is quickly diversifying away from a total reliance on oil. This should warn Nigeria's political leaders that they must take different measures and stand firm. Otherwise, the economy risks a continued downward trajectory.

Prior to the discovery of oil, Nigeria was thriving on agriculture, cashing in on vast tracts of arable land that provided limitless agricultural produce. The country built important and impressive social institutions through agricultural development, sustaining them without much difficulty. National affairs were run this way for a very long time. This economic model was not invulnerable because it was based on exporting cash crops whose demand fluctuated on the world market,[5] which was the bane of the Western Region's austerity government in the 1960s. It was a model upon which national activities were built, and Nigeria was popular for making pioneering strides, making Africa globally recognized.

These development trends deteriorated immediately after the discovery of oil, which reconfigured the national focus. The success of the oil boom changed the narrative, and the frenzy of economic growth in the oil era encouraged complacency among the political class, drifting away from effective economic policies. The inability to develop other sectors during this period had long-lasting results; people were overtaken by greed and national development was no longer a priority.

The end result of this unsustainable trajectory was a disaster, affecting the economy and almost every aspect of society. The Nigerian population grew at an alarming rate while the elites remained unconcerned, presumably believing that they could remain unaffected. Risks built up that could instigate a financial crisis capable of threatening the nation's economy and destroying the country. In the halls of power, leaders satisfied their personal ambitions by impounding public properties. Others squandered government resources at every opportunity, increasing their wasteful habits and encouraging a culture of negligence in public affairs.

These trends continued unabated, accumulating woes that would plague Nigeria's future. This future was concealed by a flimsy veil of

---

[5] It is virtually impossible for Nigeria to compete in global agriculture today because the country's lack of industrialization has left low levels of mechanization in farming, a lack of scientific research and development (R&D) to improve agricultural practices and crop/animal yields, and an inability to address the increasing environmental impact of agricultural activities. Other challenges include the lack of market roads and storage facilities, the loss of agricultural skills between generations, and unfair agricultural policies in developed nations that cannot be matched by developing countries.

indifference until it was finally revealed by the soft breeze of oil revenue depletion – Nigeria was quickly mired in economic problems and financial crises. By failing to diversify its economy, the nation became enmeshed in financial difficulties after a few years of extravagance.

A straightforward solution is readily available: the teeming masses of Nigerian people confront hunger, unemployment, and underdevelopment that can be addressed through government investment in the agricultural sector. The government must provide an environment for agricultural engagement. Without suitable infrastructure, farmers cannot realize their fullest potential. It is incumbent on the government to create a network of roads between farm production sites and urban markets to enhance agricultural engagement, guaranteeing economic and financial success. Through its work enabling agricultural development, the government could collaborate with domestic farms and farmers, encouraging them to grow specific crops for purchase and export by the government. The government and its citizens would benefit immensely.

These actions would benefit the Nigerian people and reduce the country's reliance on oil. The diversification of Nigeria's economy can address economic, social, and political problems. When people are gainfully employed, there is less social unrest and fewer individuals stirring up discontent. It is disheartening that most Nigerians cannot access materials that would aid their successful engagement in agricultural activities. People in rural environments largely depend on farming, but their inability to access essential materials hinders their efforts and keeps them trailing behind their contemporaries in other countries and societies. Despite its abundance of resources and arable land, Nigeria still relies on imported materials. Import costs are a crippling burden, and the fact that Nigeria does not have domestic industries producing most of the materials needed for routine survival proves that the country still has a long way to go.

Development is not possible without economic diversification. The global economy is shifting from oil dependency to becoming knowledge based, which is why many countries have taken to industrialization. These trends clearly indicate that Nigeria will be left behind if it does not update its thinking about economic prosperity. Recent events have demonstrated the fragility of an economy that depends on a single source of income. The global COVID-19 pandemic is an example of civilizations made vulnerable through the emergence of an unexpected disease. Dependence on foreign industries for domestic production can wreak untold havoc on not only economies, but also on populations during times of crisis. The consequences of relying on imports can be overwhelming. Nigeria must develop an economic blueprint to support its population during unanticipated global crises.

The current, ongoing expansion of globalization means that security determines the viability of businesses. Each business relies on supporters who believe that their investments are capable of fending off threats and thriving in various environments. If a society is troubled by war or social unrest, it cannot attract the necessary attention from investors, no matter how promising their business models may be. People are primarily interested in the stability of an environment that will ensure the safety of their investments. A location that is threatened by social collapse is a bad environment for any business, which discourages people from investing the resources necessary for development. Nigeria has been identified as a terror zone, bearing the persistent reputation of being an unsettled society that does not respond to outside intervention. The assumption that businesses would struggle to survive reduces interest in investment; potential investors fear total loss in the absence of government support.

The last two decades of Nigeria's history have been challenging. Parts of the country have been set ablaze by various insurgent groups. In their drive to satisfy personal interests, these groups have made those places uninhabitable, ungovernable, and toxic for business. When these challenges overtake local affairs, social interactions are completely halted. This has ripple effects on the economy that can be outright devastating. People flee for their lives in response to perceived threats and businesses cannot flourish when people are afraid. The reality is that human lives under threat cannot achieve any degree of progress. Businesses in Nigeria remain unstable because poor security means lives under threat, properties seized by hoodlums, and falling chances for survival. Insecurity is unhealthy.

Violence in Nigeria is driven by various factors, including social, religious, cultural, and sometimes ethnic reasons. These are the major components of division in the country, and the government appears to be incapable of addressing these concerns. Individuals who perpetrate evil are shielded from justice because of their powerful connections. The failure of the justice system means enduring political violence, ethnic unrest, robbery becoming normalized, kidnapping becoming commonplace, and acts of terrorism increasing exponentially. These are all indices of insecurity that impede every attempt at progress across the world. There cannot be true progress or development when the government fails to address these shortcomings.

The project to set Nigeria on the right path must provide a welcoming atmosphere for business. When the environment is stable, and free from insurgent attacks, people will see opportunities for investing in the economy, which would bring about massive benefits for citizens and the government. The survival of businesses would create employment opportunities for youths, keeping them away from antisocial activities that threaten society.

Security goes beyond providing physical safety for individuals. Physical safety guarantees other dimensions of safety to a certain extent, but there are important requirements for true and comprehensive safety and stability. Financial insecurity must be addressed through investments that provide economic incentives in exchange for participating in specific activities. Many Nigerian youths are brimming with ideas, but they lack the ability to make the investments necessary to transform their ideas into reality. If there are systematic plans to offer government funds that can support their profitable ideas, the rate of crime will be reduced dramatically. Such a plan would need to be supported by government transparency and availability. Nigeria has demonstrated how it can derail beneficial programs for personal reasons: incumbents do not want people who have the economic ability to challenge the government or oppose the status quo. This mindset has killed many dreams within the country.

Emotional, psychological, and economic security also depends on a reliable supply of electricity. The Nigerian government must ensure the generation and steady distribution of electrical power as reducing energy insecurity will dramatically decrease the challenges that face the country. Recommendations already exist for such a project. Currently, the government cannot meet the energy needs of an expanding population, partly because many individuals could not pay for services without a reliable source of income. However, the government can power industries that pay for the energy they consume, generating funds to create additional opportunities for people through job creation and other benefits. The majority of the population could purchase electricity from private companies that serve customers who can afford their services. When the government creates job opportunities, it offers additional incentives.

Citizens must also demonstrate that they are ready to support government projects with an equal amount of effort. Government officials are not imported from afar; they come from the people themselves, suggesting that they can identify with the masses, understand their own weaknesses, and recognize areas in need of assistance. Citizens must do their part to create an atmosphere for growth. Their insecurities can be addressed by cooperating with the government. In the past, citizens had sabotaged the government's development projects, inspired by the ethnic politics that characterize the nation's history. There are many instances of youths destroying public assets to protest actions taken by presidents who do not share their ethnicity. What they fail to recognize is that they will bear the brunt of the hardship created by their actions.

Nigeria's development has been impaired because political leaders refuse to harness the country's diverse cultural resources. This shameful neglect of the country's diversity may be due to complacent feelings of self-sufficiency that come from relying on oil as the sole source of income. Many Nigerians are unaware that their cultures could offer limitless potential if the country developed a receptive attitude to cultural revival. National leaders either do not understand how impactful this issue could be, or they are indifferent because their fortunes have been acquired through other sources. Culture and its redefinition have been left in the care of interested passionate individuals, but on their own they are incapable of creating a broad national movement for cultural transformation and preservation. Government support is required to create the synergies necessary for any worthwhile revitalization.

Many countries generate handsome revenues from branding and trademarking their cultural properties. Globalization provides limitless chances to enable intercultural and cross-cultural trade in ideas, making it easy to profitably market a culture to others. Several Asian countries have shown the immense benefits of marketing their cultural heritage to the world. The reality is that the multidimensional nature of Nigeria's cultures could hold many economic benefits. The country's numerous cultural variations can be harnessed to serve another purpose of national integration. Regrettably, the Nigerian government has failed to explore this potential. Creativity is essential for branding and merchandizing cultural items, and there are fundamental steps that must be taken by the government and the people for the best results.

Nigeria should recognize cultural icons from different groups who can be used to craft marketable narratives. People who have spent their lives making positive cultural contributions and are recognized for their impact on society, should become figures that advance the nation's cultural economy. Museums can be created to accommodate statues of these icons, and tourist centers should feature them, attracting and increasing the interest of the people. Countless African descendants in diaspora retain strong emotional ties to their ancestral heritage; they would embrace opportunities to visit historical reference points and experience cultural events at their sites of origin. Not only would this attract interest from the international community, investing resources into Nigerian tourism, but it would also encourage international businesses and bring greater financial benefit to the people. This would open employment opportunities for the people, building additional businesses to grace the Nigerian space. We cannot overestimate the level of financial development that would be possible if the government taxed these activities appropriately and reinvested the proceeds into national advancement.

Cultural revival offers the promise of future development if Africans themselves begin a massive campaign for decolonization. Nigeria must understand that revitalizing these cultural heritages cannot only help the nation financially, it can also support a process of decolonization and integration. By strengthening Nigeria's cultural heritages, the people's attention can be redirected to their values, creating a strong connection to their roots over the long term. Most African people in the contemporary world are unaware of their cultural background because they were not introduced to these values during their formative years. The reintroduction of these values can both serve an economic purpose and open minds to the full expanse of Nigerian culture. Placed alongside other cultures of the world, it has the ingredients to transform into an international standard, which would be of immense importance for the country's future.

The government must be aware that there are daunting tasks to overcome before cultural revival and revitalization is possible. Conscious efforts are required to educate people who could profit from producing cultural activities for international and domestic audiences. People who market cultural material for profit are often culpable in propagating negative, disastrous stereotypes of the African people. The capitalist quest for domination leaves little room for concern over tarnishing the image of Nigeria, or Africa at large, through misrepresentation. Their consistent blurring of boundaries between African precolonial experiences and colonial realities has been harmful – it de-markets African cultural heritage and displaces objects from their historic contexts. The Nigerian entertainment industry could play a significant part in rebranding the country, but at present these obligations are being subverted to continued debasement of the culture itself and as well as the erosion of positive values.

There must be collaboration between the people, the government, and other stakeholders. The people must recognize that they should be wary of the information they receive through the media, especially the movie industry. They should understand the creative liberties taken with history that frequently result in misrepresentation of their cultural backgrounds. Every culture of the world has its dark side, and most of them have questionable origins, including our own. It is not that early people committed heinous crimes or possessed crude mindsets – cultural shifts over time highlight the beauty of evolution. Every society evolves from its initial practices and understanding this would assist people trying to process the negative information about their culture in the media. People get the wrong impression about their cultural heritage based on misinformation from the media, and cultural icons and activists should identity their place in this struggle, engaging in activities that foster national development.

The eradication of corruption, across parastatals and private companies, is another requirement for Nigeria's future growth. The country is not merely overwhelmed by the inadequate allocation of resources, it is harmed by acute mismanagement, blatant misappropriation of public funds, and other corrupt practices including the allocation of funds to nonexistent projects. The results are devastating. Nigerian leaders are notorious for diverting national resources for their personal benefit. Many are vain, materialistic, and crass opportunists. They regularly demonstrate that they are unequipped to plan a clear path out of poverty, hunger, and sickness and have consistently shown that they have little or no idea how true development works. Sadly, they are unconcerned about the consequences of failing to prepare for emergency challenges.

It is difficult to work toward a clean slate when corruption is prominent. But Nigeria's social critics have given up on curbing corrupt practices; instead, they compete to outdo one another often ending up blinded by their parochial interests, sabotaging their attempts at development. This condemnable situation has existed since the time of independence. Nigeria was advancing far ahead of other countries in the world, including South Korea, Malaysia, and Singapore, about a decade after independence. The country has since been overtaken by these others and left far behind. Statistics reveal that other nations were serious about committing their resources to progress and development, and Nigeria's leaders quickly became complacent after experiencing the brief euphoria of temporary economic progress. One of Nigeria's past leaders had a famous statement credited to him: "Money is not the problem, it is how to spend it."

This pronouncement might well have been the open admission of a decadent philosophy; his successors regularly demonstrate that they are incapable of spending money to make social progress. Their actions display unmistakable support for the statement, in practice and in character. Examples abound of African leaders, especially in Nigeria, regularly spending public funds on lavish material possessions and luxury items. Even when the country is confronted with daunting challenges, they never prioritize the welfare of the people. This creates an unpredictable, uncertain, and unstable situation. Most Nigerians face daily challenges from hunger and unemployment while their politicians enjoy considerable wealth. This has eroded public trust in the country's moral foundations; people are following the example of their leaders and amassing private wealth without considering how their actions affect others. As more people internalize this attitude of personal gain above national interest, national development becomes more difficult.

The challenges are daunting, but they can be addressed with serious leadership. Corruption thrives where social institutions are weak: Nigerians must prove their support for democratic governance by rehabilitating the country's existing institutions. This requires conscious collaboration between the people and their government representatives. The government must initiate corrective measures to address the inherent pitfalls in the system, steering clear of corruption and its associated vices. Government officials must clearly disclose their emotional and cultural attachments. Many times, these relationships compel representatives to abuse public office for personal gain. Ethnic sympathies can encourage opportunists to serve in any capacity that allows them to claim collective property for their own use. The people who work hardest to whip up ethnic sentiment are often connected to clan members who are guilty of treacherous allegations and practices.

Instead of funding nationally beneficial projects, politicians siphon off federal allocations to purchase cars and houses that generate no financial returns for the country. Future generations must do something revolutionary to inspire fundamental change. Substantial funds are committed to maintaining Nigerian democracy – hardly any civilization in the world spends as much as Nigeria to sustain and maintain officials who are supposed to represent their constituents. Regrettably, those constituents receive little in exchange for this extravagant spending. The interests of the nation must be given primacy. China reduced the shockingly high percentage of people living in poverty within its borders over a thirty-year period, and Nigeria's resources offer no excuse for allowing such large numbers of its own people to struggle. China's path, which wasted 70 million lives, should be avoided, but Nigeria must find a way out of its current predicament. Politicians could turn the tables by imposing a self-austerity program, reducing their own personal expenses to improve the national economy.

Nigeria's corruption is enabled by the country's culture of godfatherism, allowing the structure of society to decay. Patronage systems discourage merit-based appointments, spreading the rot that permeates public activity. People are selected for public positions based on their affiliation with powerful patrons, even when they clearly lack the qualifications for the role. It is unlikely that such opportunists would perform well in any capacity. Affirmative action is necessary to bridge the gaps in the socioeconomic and political development across the country, but the Nigerian Constitution must expunge its "federal character" clauses. The quota system should be replaced by a merit system that allows public positions to be filled by competent individuals who have clearly demonstrated their capacity to deliver.

Nigeria must embrace a culture of merit-based appointments. With equitable social justice and equality of access ensuring fair treatment – regardless of one's birth, ethnicity, religion, or social class – people will be encouraged to put greater effort into developing their society. It would reduce the unprecedented rate of expatriation, stemming the brain drain that is prevalent in Nigeria today. There is nothing wrong with migrating to other countries and exploring other opportunities, but migration should not be driven by frustration and the absence of opportunity. If the number of people emigrating from Nigeria keeps rising, it will be devastating for the country.

Nigeria's shambolic justice system is not immune to the corruption that runs rampant through the country. The legal system is so riddled with graft and corruption that it is difficult – if not impossible – for ordinary individuals to receive justice without having connections to highly placed benefactors within the system. Legal restrictions are relaxed for wealthy individuals, justice is subverted for the minority that can afford it, and the common people suffer injustice and inequity through a poor democratic system and visionless leadership. The problem of injustice impairs development and makes stability impossible. A social institution is necessary to protect the fundamental rights of every citizen; the justice system represents their interests and prevents them from being victimized. When this institution is compromised, their defenses are also compromised.

Nigerians must fight injustice and corrupt practices to improve their society and restore confidence in the country. The institution of justice is the backbone of other government agencies, determining how they are run and restoring sanity whenever those agencies depart from their assigned roles. The government must not be allowed to act as if it were above the law, freely trampling on justice, manipulating the electoral system, exploiting parliamentary offices, and committing other atrocities without consequence. By setting that example, others within the country follow suit and reflect those attitudes in all their social engagements. If it goes unchallenged, anomie would infect the environment and halt all social progress. Youth involvement in antisocial groups is a symptom of this kind of social disorganization.

No one desires a future where governments endlessly deliberate over electoral justice without reaching a conclusion, or one where political parties constantly file lawsuits to challenge the victories of their opponents. The process creates added hostilities and manipulations that delay justice, inflicting unwanted consequences on the people. Nigerian leadership must craft new policies to create alternative or adjunct courts specifically to respond to electoral issues and their many complications. This would address the ongoing subversion of justice and pave the way for an effective democracy. A multiethnic and multicultural democracy such as Nigeria's must be supported by transparent institutions that are above suspicion to promote justice and fundamental human rights and help the people to reach their collective goals. To ensure the beautiful future envisioned by the country and its people, fairness must be integrated into the character of the Nigerian justice system.

Bibliography

Adamu, Saidu H., and Yahaya A. Abdullahi. "Rural Economy and Society in Nigeria Since 1900." In *Seminar on Nigerian Economy and Society Since the Berlin Conference*, Vol. 2, edited by Musa Adamu Mamman, Enoch Oyedele, Kabiru Sulaiman Chafe, Hannatu A. Alahira, Idris Sha'aba Jimada, J. O. Agi, A. Z. Ibrahim, Hussaina J. Abdullah, and S. M. Zubairu. Zaria: Ahmadu Bello University Press Limited, 2005, 57–78.

Abdul, Shamsu, Mohammad Bahtiar, and Suhaini Muda. "New Perspectives to Political Participation Among Youth: The Impact of Facebook Usage." *The European Proceedings of Social & Behavioural Sciences* (2016): 128–134.

Abdullah, Hussaina J., and Ibrahim Hamza. "Women and Land in Northern Nigeria: The Need for Independent Ownership Rights." In *Women and Land in Africa*, edited by L. M. Wanyeki. New York: Zed Books, 2003, 119–135.

Abdulraheem, Tajudeen, Abedayo Olukoshi, Abdul R. Mustapha, and Gavin P. Williams. "Nigeria: Oil, Debts and Democracy." *Review of African Political Economy* no. 37 (1986): 6–10.

Abimbola, Wande. *Ijinle Ohun Enu Ifa, Apa Kiini*. Glasgow: William Collins, Sons and Co., n.d.

Abraham, David. "Constitutional Patriotism, Citizenship, and Belonging." *I·CON* 6, no. 1 (2008): 137–152.

Abubakar, A. Boyi. "Gender Studies and Sustainable Development in Nigeria." *Mediterranean Journal of Social Sciences* 4, no. 8 (2–13): 147–152.

Achebe, Chinua. *Things Fall Apart*. London: Penguin Books, 1994.

ActionAid. *Corruption and Poverty in Nigeria: A Report*. Garki, Abuja, Nigeria: ActionAid Nigeria, 2015. www.actionaid.org/sites/files/actionaid/pc_report_content.pdf.

Adams, H. P. "Karl Marx in His Earlier Writings." *The Journal of Philosophy* 38, no. 7 (1941): 188.

Adams, W. M. *Green Development: Environment and Sustainability in the Third World*. New York: Routledge, 1990.

Aday, Sean. "Blogs and Bullets: New Media in Contentious Politics." Washington, DC: United States Institute of Peace. 2010. www.usip.org/file s/resources/pw65.pdf.

Adebanwi, Wale, and Ebenezer Obadare. "Introducing Nigeria at Fifty: The Nation in Narration." *Journal of Contemporary African Studies* 28, no. 4 (2010): 379–405.

Adebayo, A. G. "Of Man and Cattle: A Reconsideration of the Traditions of Origin of Pastoral Fulani of Nigeria." *History in Africa* 18 (1991): 1–21.

Adediji, Daramola, and Ibem Eziyi. "Urban Environmental Problems in Nigeria: Implications for Sustainable Development." *Journal of Sustainable Development in Africa* 12, no. 1 (2010): 124–145.

Adejumo, V. Akintoye, and Opeyemi O. Adejumo. "Prospects for Achieving Sustainable Development through the Millennium Development Goals in Nigeria." *European Journal of Sustainable Development* 3, no. 1 (2014): 33–46.

Adémólá-Olátéjú, Bámidélé. "While Yoruba Land Sleeps!" *Premium Times*, June 25, 2019. https://opinion.premiumtimesng.com/2019/06/25/while-yoruba-land-sleeps-by-bamidele-ademola-olateju/.

Adeokun, Lawrence A., Modupe Oduwole, Frank Oronsaye et al. "Trends in Female Circumcision between 1933 and 2003 in Osun and Ogun States, Nigeria: A Cohort Analysis." *African Journal of Reproductive Health* 10, no. 2 (2006): 48–56.

Aderibigbe, A. B. *Lagos: The Development of an African City*. Lagos: Longman, 1975.

Adetugbo, Abiodun. "The Development of English in Nigeria up to 1914: A Socio-historical Appraisal." *Journal of the Historical Society of Nigeria* 9, no. 2 (1978): 89–103.

Adeyemi, Oluwatobi O. "Corruption and Local Government Administration in Nigeria: A Discourse of Core Issues." *European Journal of Sustainable Development* 1, no. 2 (2012): 183–198.

Adeyemo, Ademola Morakinyo. "Environmental Policy Failure in Nigeria and the Tragedy of the Under-Development of the Niger Delta Region." *Inaugural Lecture Series*, no. 64. Port Harcourt: University of Port Harcourt Press, 2008.

Affe, Mudiaga. "Agony of Cross River Community Girls Married Off at Infancy by Indebted Parents." *Punch News*, May 13, 2018. https://punchng.com/agony-of-cross-river-community-girls-married-off-at-infancy-by-indebted-parents/amp/.

Afigbo, Adiele E. "Background to Nigerian Federalism: Federal Features in the Colonial State." *Publius: The Journal of Federalism* 21, no. 4 (1991): 13–29.

Afolabi, Abiodun. "The Colonial Taxation Policy among Yoruba of Southwestern Nigeria and Its Implications for Socio-economic Development." *Journal of the Historical Society of Nigeria* (2010): 63–92.

Afolabi, Oluwaseun O. "The Role of Religion in Nigerian Politics and its Sustainability for Political Development." *Journal of Social Sciences* 3, no. 2 (2015): 42–49.

Afolayan, Adekunle. *Agriculture and Economic Development in Nigeria: A Prescription for the Nigerian Green Revolution*. New York: Vantage Press, 1983.

Africa Research Bulletin. "Women in Agriculture." *Africa Research Bulletin: Economic, Financial and Technical Series* 49, no. 10 (2012): 19743B–19743C.

African Development Bank Group. "Democratic Elections in Africa: Opportunities and Risks." *African Development Bank Group*, April 24, 2012. www.afdb.org/en/blogs/afdb-championing-inclusive-growth-across-africa/post/democratic-elections-in-africa-opportunities-and-risks-9117/.

African Health Observatory. "Low Birth Rate." *Health Situation Analysis*, n.d. www.aho.afro.who.int/profiles_information/index.php/AFRO:Low_birth_weight.

African Union Commission. *African Youth Charter*. Addis Ababa: African Union, 2006. www.un.org/en/africa/osaa/pdf/au/african_youth_charter_2006.pdf.

Agbiboa, Daniel Egiegba, and Benjamin Maiangwa. "Corruption in the Underdevelopment of the Niger Delta in Nigeria." *Journal of Pan African Studies* 5, no. 8(2012): 108–132. www.researchgate.net/publication/2542590 40_Corruption_in_the_Underdevelopment of the_Niger_Delta_in_Nigeria.

Agency, Anadolu. "Almost Half of Nigerian Children Trapped in Forced Labor, Int'l Labor Org., Says." *Daily Sabah*, May 3, 2019. www.dailysabah.com/af rica/2019/05/03/almost-half-of-nigerian-children-trapped-in-forced-labor-i ntl-labor-org-says.

Agency Report. "Nigeria's Unemployment Rate Hits 33.5 Per Cent by 2020 – Minister." *Premium Times News*, May 2, 2019. www.premiumtimesng.com/ news/top-news/328137-nigerias-unemployment-rate-hits-33-5-per-cent-b y-2020-minister.html.

Agubuzu, Lawrence O. C., Bade Onimode, and Adebayo Adedeji. *African Development and Governance Strategies in the 21st Century, Looking Back to Move Forward: Essays in Honor of Adebayo Adedeji at 70*. London & New York: Zed Books, 2004.

Ahazuem, J. O. "Nigeria: Gowon Regime, 1966–1975." In *Encyclopedia of African History*, edited by Kevin Shillington. New York: Routledge, 2004, 1113–1114. http://ezproxy.lib.utexas.edu/login?url=https://search.credoreference.com/con tent/entry/routafricanhistory/nigeria_gowon_regime_1966_1975/0? institutionId=4864.

Ahmed-Gamgum, Williams. "Nigeria at 100 Years: The Process and Challenges of Nation Building." *Public Policy and Administration Research* 4, no. 8 (2014): 114–140.

Aina, Tade, and Ademola Salau. *The Challenge of Sustainable Development in Nigeria*. London: Sage Publishing, 1992.

Ajala, Taiwo. "Gender Discrimination in Land Ownership and the Alleviation of Women's Poverty in Nigeria: A Call for New Equities." *International Journal of Discrimination and the Law* 17, no. 1 (2017): 51–66.

Ajayi, J. F. Ade. *Christian Missions in Nigeria, 1841–1891*. London: Longmans, 1969.

"The Development of Secondary Grammar School Education in Nigeria." *Journal of the Historical Society of Nigeria* 2, no. 4 (1963): 517–535.

ed. *General History of Africa VI: Africa in the Nineteenth Century until the 1880s*. Abridged ed. Paris: UNESCO Publishing, 1998.

History and the Nation and Other Addresses. Ibadan: Spectrum Books, 1991.

ed. *History and the Nation Valedictory Lecture, University of Ibadan, 1989 and Other Addresses*. Ibadan: Ibadan University Press, 1990.

Ajayi, J. F. Ade, and Robert Smith. *Yoruba Warfare in the Nineteenth Century*. London: Cambridge University Press, 1971.

Ajayi, Rev. Michael Thomas Euler. "A General History of the Yoruba, Country: Part 3." *Lagos Standard* (1905).

Ajor, Joseph, Julius Odey, and Louis Edet. "The Realism of Nigerian Nationalism and the Challenges of Nationhood, 1922–2015." *Journal of Good Governance and Sustainable Development in Africa* 4, no. 2 (2018): 13–20.

Ake, Claude. *The Feasibility of Democracy in Africa*. Dakar: CODESRIA Books, 2000.
  "Dangerous Liaisons: The Interface of Globalization and Democracy." In *Democracy's Victory and Crisis*, edited by Alex Hadenius, 282–296. Cambridge: Cambridge University Press, 1997.
  Democracy and Development in Africa. Washington DC: Brookings Institution Press, 2001.
Akinbami, J. F. K., A. T. Salami, and W. O. Siyanbola. "An Integrated Strategy for Sustainable Forest–Energy–Environment Interactions in Nigeria." *Journal of Environmental Management* 69, no. 2 (2003): 115–128.
Akinkuotu, Eniola. "Leave Nigeria Now or Suffer, Police Tell Homosexuals." *Punch News*, January 22, 2019. https://punchng.com/leave-nigeria-now-or-suffer-police-tell-homosexuals/.
Akuson, Felicia. "Citizenship Education as a Creative Intervention Tool for National Development." *Journal of Teacher Perspective* 10, no. 2 (2016): 1–7.
Alam, M. "Weighing the Limitations against the Added-Value of Social Media as a Tool for Political Change." *Democracy and Society* 8, no. 2 (2011): 1–19.
Alesina, Alberto, and Bryony Reich. "Nation-Building," working paper, Department of Economics, Harvard University (2015): 1–42. https://dash.harvard.edu/handle/1/28652213.
Aleyomi, Michael, and Olanrewaju Ajakaiye. "The Impact of Social Media on Citizens' Mobilization and Participation in Nigeria's 2011 General Elections." *Centrepoint Journal* 17, no. 2: 31–52.
Ali, Merima, Odd-Helge Fjeldstad, Boqian Jiang, and Abdulaziz B. Shifa. "Colonial Legacy, State-Building and the Salience of Ethnicity in Sub-Saharan Africa." *The Economic Journal* (2015).
Alkali, Abdul-Majeed. "Federalism and the Creation of Sub-national States in Nigeria: Appraising the State-Creation Exercise under Babangida Administration." *Journal of Humanities and Social Sciences* 22, no. 1 (2017): 1–8.
Althaus, Francis A. "Female Circumcision: Rite of Passage or Violation of Rights?" *International Family Planning Perspectives* 23, no. 3 (1997). doi:10.2307/2950769.
Alubo, Ogoh. *Nigeria: Ethnic Conflicts and Citizenship Crises in the Central Region*. Ibadan: PEFS, 2006.
Aluko, Yetunde. "Patriarchy and Property Rights among Yoruba Women in Nigeria." *Feminist Economics* 21, no. 3 (2015): 56–81.
Amaechi, Ikechukwu. "In Defence of Muhammadu Buhari (1)." *Iyke*, May 24, 2011. https://ikechukwu.wordpress.com/2011/07/16/in-defence-of-muhammadu-buhari-1.
Amah, Emmanuel Ibiam. "Federalism, Nigerian Federal Constitution and the Practice of Federalism: An Appraisal." *Beijing Law Review* 8, no. 3 (2017): 141–158.
Amalu, N. S. "Impact of Boko Haram Insurgency on Human Security in Nigeria." *Global Journal of Social Sciences* 14 (2015): 35–42.
American Historical Association. "Biafran Declaration of Independence." *American Historical Association*, n.d. www.historians.org/teaching-and-learning/teaching-resources-for-historians/teaching-and-learning-in-the-digital-age/through-the-le

ns-of-history-biafra-nigeria-the-west-and-the-world/the-republic-of-biafra/biaf
ran-declaration-of-independence.

"England's Indirect Rule in Its African Colonies." *American Historical
Association*, n.d. www.historians.org/teaching-and-learning/teaching-resou
rces-for-historians/teaching-and-learning-in-the-digital-age/through-the-le
ns-of-history-biafra-nigeria-the-west-and-the-world/the-colonial-and-pre-
colonial-eras-in-nigeria/englands-indirect-rule-in-its-african-colonies.

Amnesty International. "Nigeria: Oil, Poverty, and Violence." *Amnesty International*,
August 1, 2006. web.archive.org/web/20070819155442/www.web.amnesty.or
g/library/Index/ENGAFR440172006?open&of=ENG-NGA.

Amoo, Abdulssalam. "Nigeria Allocates 6.7% of 2020 Budget to Education
Ministry." *Education Statistics*, October 11, 2019. www.google.com/amp/s/e
duceleb.com/nigerian-2020-budget-education-ministry/amp/.

Amory, Deborah, and Mark Gevisser. "Homosexuality in Africa." In *Encyclopedia
of Africa*, Vol. 1, edited by Anthony Appiah and Henry Louis Gates. Oxford:
Oxford University Press, 2010.

Amuwo, Kunle. "Treetop Politics Versus Grassroots Democracy in Nigeria:
Some Theoretical and Methodological Queries." *Africa: Rivistatrimestrale di
studi e documentazionedell'Istituoitaliano per l'Africa e l'Oriente* 47, no. 4
(1992).

Ananyev, Maxim, and Michael Poyker. "Nation-Building in Sub-Saharan Africa
and Civil Conflict: Theory and Evidence from Boko Haram and Tuareg
Insurgencies." *Pac-Dev.* (2016): 1–30.

Añez, Luis M., Michelle A. Silva, Manuel Paris Jr., and Luis E. Bedregal.
"Engaging Latinos through the Integration of Cultural Values and
Motivational Interviewing Principles." *Professional Psychology: Research and
Practice* 39, no. 2 (2008): 153–159.

Anger, Barnes. "Poverty Eradication, Millennium Development Goals and
Sustainable Development in Nigeria." *Journal of Sustainable Development* 3,
no. 4 (2010): 138–144.

Angerbrandt, Henrik. "Struggles over Identity and Territory: Regional Identities
in Ethnoreligious Conflict in Northern Nigeria." *Nationalism and Ethnic
Politics* 22, no. 2 (2016): 172–192.

Annamalai, S. "Gandhi's Philosophy Led to Regenerative Agriculture." *The
Hindu*, November 24, 2015. www.thehindu.com/news/cities/Madurai/gand
his-philosophy-led-to-regenerative-agriculture/article7910982.ece.

Anunobi, Fredoline. "Women and Development in Africa: From Marginalization
to Gender Inequality." *African Social Science Review* 2, no. 1 (2002): 41–63.

Anyogu, Felicia, and B. N. Okpalobi. "Human Right Issues and Women's
Experiences on Demanding Their Rights in Their Communities: The Way
Forward for Nigeria." *Global Journal of Politics and Law Research* 4, no. 1
(2016): 9–17.

Archibong, Belinda. "Historical Origins of Persistent Inequality in Nigeria."
Oxford Development Studies 46, no. 3 (2018): 325–347.

Asante, Molefi Kente. *The History of Africa: The Quest for Eternal Harmony.*
New York: Routledge, 2019.

Asante, S. Michael. *Deforestation in Ghana: Explaining the Chronic Failure of Forest Preservation Policies in a Developing Country.* Lanham: University Press of America, 2005.

Ashafa, Abdullahi M., Gaius Jatau, and Ayemga Tor, eds. *Humanities and Challenges of Development: Interrogating Nigeria's Nation Building Project Since 1960.* Kaduna: Kaduna State University, 2020.

Ashafa, Muhammad, and James Wuye. "Warriors and Brothers." In *Peacemakers in Action: Profiles of Religion in Conflict Resolution,* edited by David Little. Cambridge: Cambridge University Press, 2007, 247–277.

Ashiru, M. O. A. "Gender Discrimination in the Division of Property on Divorce in Nigeria." *Journal of African Law* 51 (2007): 316–331.

Attah, Michael. "Divorcing Marriage from Marital Assets: Why Equity and Women Fail in Property Readjustment Actions in Nigeria." *Journal of African Law* 62, no. 3 (2018): 427–446.

Attfield, Robin, Jophan Hatingh, and Manamela Matshabaphala. "Sustainable Development, Sustainable Livelihoods, and Land Reform in the South Africa: A Conceptual and Ethical Inquiry." *Third World Quarterly* 25, no. 2 (2004): 405–421.

Austine, Ejovi, Ataine Stephen, and Akpokighe Raymond. "Ethnicity and Nation Building in Africa." *Journal of Political Science and Leadership Research* 2, no. 2 (2016): 1–9.

Awolowo, Obafemi. *Path to Nigerian Freedom.* London: Faber and Faber, 1947.
   "Presidential Address." Address, Fourth Congress of the Action Group, Calabar, Nigeria, April 8, 1958.

Ayandele, E. A. *The Educated Elite in the Nigerian Society.* Ibadan: Ibadan University Press, 1974.
   Missionary Impact on Modern Nigeria, 1842–1942. London: Longman, 1966.

Ayatse, Felicia H., and Isaac Iorhen Akuya. "The Origin and Development of Ethnic Politics and Its Impact on Post-Colonial Governance in Nigeria." *European Scientific Journal* 9, no. 17 (2013): 178–189. eujournal.org/index.php/esj/article/view/1165/1182.

Ayoade, John. "Party and Ideology in Nigeria: A Case Study of the Action Group." *Journal of Black Studies* 16, no. 2 (1985): 169–188.

Ayodele, John Oyewole, and Saheed Damilola Olisa. "Media, Politics and Gender Marginalization in Nigeria: Is There Still a Way Out?" *International Journal of Media, Journalism and Mass Communication* 3, no. 1 (2017): 20–26.

Ayokhai, Fred, and Peter Naankiel. "Rethinking Pan-Africanism and Nationalism in Africa: The Dilemma of Nation-Building in Nigeria." *Historical Research Letter* 27 (2015): 1–9.

Ayua, I. A. "The Nigerian Constitutional Scheme on the Sharing of Its Resources and Its Implementation: An Assessment." In *Major Issues in the 1999 Constitution,* edited by I. A. Ayua, D. Guobadia, and A. O. Adekunle, 130. Lagos: NIALS, 2000, 198–234.

Azad, Abdul, Emily Crawford, and Heidi Kaila. *Conflict and Violence in Nigeria Results from the North East, North Central, and South Zones.* Washington, DC, and Nigeria: World Bank and National Bureau of Statistics, 2018. http://documents1.worldbank.org/curated/en/111851538025875054/pdf/130198-W

P-P160999-PUBLIC-26-9-2018-14-42-49-ConflictViolenceinNigeriaRes
ultsfromNENCSSzonesFinal.pdf.

Azikiwe, Nnamdi. *My Odyssey: An Autobiography*. London: C. Hurst, 1970.

Babalola, Dele. "Nigeria: A Federation in Search of Federalism." *50 Shades of
Federalism*, September 04, 2018. http://50shadesoffederalism.com/case-
studies/nigeria-federation-search-federalism/.

Babatunde, Abosede Omowumi. "Environmental Insecurity and Poverty in the
Niger Delta: A Case of Ilaje." *African Conflict and Peacebuilding Review* 7, no.
2 (2017): 36–59.

Bako, Mandy Jollie, and Jawad Syed. "Women's Marginalization in Nigeria and
the Way Forward." *Human Resource Development International* 21 (2018):
425–443.

Bagga, Henna. "The Future of Europe: Is Europe Really Moving Forward to
Federalism?" *Jurist*, October 31, 2017. www.jurist.org/commentary/2017/1
0/sedef-topal-future-of-europe/.

Baghebo, Michael, and Samuel Edoumiekumo. "Public Capital Accumulation
and Economic Development in Nigeria: 1970–2010." *International Journal of
Academic Research in Business and Social Sciences* 2, no. 6 (2012): 213–37.

Baldwin-Philippi, Jessica. *Using Technology, Building Democracy: Digital
Campaigning and the Construction of Citizenship*. Oxford: Oxford University
Press, 2015.

Baletti, Brenda, Tamara M. Johnson, and Wendy Wolford. "'Late Mobilization':
Transnational Peasant Networks and Grassroots Organizing in Brazil and
South Africa." *Journal of Agrarian Change* 8, no. 2/3 (2008): 290–314.

Bandy, Joe, and Jackie Smith, eds. *Coalitions Across Borders, Negotiating Difference
and Unity in Transnational Struggles Against Neo Liberalism*. London:
Rowman and Littlefield, 2001.

Barber, Benjamin. *Strong Democracy: Participatory Politics for a New Age*. Berkeley:
University of California Press, 1984.

Barry, Brian. "Self-Government Revisited." In *Theorizing Nationalism*, edited by
Ronald Beiner. New York: SUNY Press, 1999, 144–163.

Barry, P. *Beginning Theory*. New Delhi: Viva Books Pvt. Ltd, 2010.

Barth, Fredrik, ed. *Ethnic Groups and Boundaries*. London: George Allen and
Unwin, 1969.

BBC. "Desertification: The People Whose Land Is Turning to Dust." *BBC*,
November 12, 2015. www.bbc.com/news/worldafrica-34790661.

Beck, Ulrich, Wolfgang Boss, and Christopher Lau. "The Theory of Reflexive
Modernization: Problematic, Hypothesis, and Research Programme."
Theory, Culture and Society 20, no. 1 (2003): 1–34.

Beckerman, Wilfred. *A Poverty of Reason: Sustainable Development and Economic
Growth*. Oakland: The Independence Institute, 2003.

Bello, M., H. A. Yusuf, and M. Akinola. "Social Media Usage and Political
Participation among University Undergraduates for Political Stability in
Nigeria." *Inquiry* 3, no. 1 (2017): 69–86.

Bennett, W. Lance, and Alexandra Segerberg. *The Logic of Connective Action:
Digital Media and the Personalization of Contentious Politics*. New York:
Cambridge University Press, 2013.

Bergan, Daniel E. "Grassroots: Movement or Campaign." *Encyclopaedia Britannica*. n.d. www.britannica.com/topic/grassroots.

Berger, Sebastien. "Madagascar's New Leader Cancels Korean Land Deal." *The Telegraph*, March 18, 2009. www.telegraph.co.uk/news/worldnews/africaan dindianocean/madagascar/5012961/Madagascars-new-leader-cancels-Kore an-land-deal.html.

Berman, P. S. "From International Law to Law and Globalization." *Columbian Journal of Transnational Law* 43 (2005): 485.

Bernstein, Henry. "Commercial Agriculture in South Africa Since 1994: Natural, Simply Capitalism." *Journal of Agrarian Change* 13, no. 1 (2013): 23–46.

Bhuiyan, Serajul. "Social Media and Its Effectiveness in the Political Reform Movement in Egypt." *Middle East Media Educator* 1, no. 1 (2011): 14–20.

Bincof, Mohamed Omar. "The Role of Youth in Political Participation in Somalia." *IOSR Journal of Humanities and Social Science* 23, no. 10 (2018): 64–74.

Bjorn, Wittrock. "Modernity: One, None or Many? European Origins and Modernity as a Global Condition." In *Multiple Modernities*, edited by Shmuel Eisenstadt. New Brunswick: Transaction Publications, 2002, 31–60.

Boahen, A. Adu, ed. *General History of Africa VII: Africa Under Colonial Domination 1880–1935*. Abridged ed. Paris: UNESCO, 1990.

Boden, T. A., G. Marland, and R. J. Andres. *Global, Regional, and National Fossil-Fuel CO2 Emissions*. Oak Ridge: Carbon Dioxide Information Analysis Center, 2011. https://cdiac.ess-dive.lbl.gov/trends/emis/tre_afr.html.

Borras Jr., Saturnino M., and Jennifer C. Franco. "Global Land Grabbing and Trajectories of Agrarian Change: A Preliminary Analysis." *Journal of Agrarian Change* 12, no. 1 (2012): 34–59.

Boserup, Ester. *The Conditions of Agricultural Growth: The Economics of Agrarian Change Under Population Pressure*. London: Allan and Urwin, 1965.

Population and Technological Change: A Study of Long-Term Trends. Chicago: University of Chicago Press, 1981.

Boyi, A. Abubakar. "Gender Studies and Sustainable Development in Nigeria." *Mediterranean Journal of Social Sciences* 4, no. 8 (2013): 147–152.

Braimah, Tim S. "Child Marriage in Northern Nigeria: Section 61 of Part I of the 1999 Constitution and the Protection of Children Against Child Marriage." *African Human Rights Law Journal* 14 (2014).

Brett, Oliver. *A Defense of Liberty*. New York and London: G. P. Putnam's Sons, 1921.

Brouwer, Lenie, and Edien Bartel. "Arab Spring in Morocco: Social Media and the 20 February Movement." *Afrika Focus* 27, no. 2 (2014): 9–22.

Brubaker, Rogers. "Religion and Nationalism: Four Approaches." *Nations and Nationalism* 18, no. 1 (2012): 2–20.

Bruce, Kapferer, and Bertelsen Bjørn Enge. "Introduction: The Crisis of Power and Reformations of the State in Globalizing Realities." In *Crisis of the State: War and Social Upheaval*, edited by Kapferer Bruce and Bertelsen Bjørn Enge, 1–26. New York: Berghahn Books, 2009.

Buchi, Suzan Edeh. "12,000 Women Develop VVF Every Year in Nigeria." *Vanguard*, July 20, 2012. www.vanguardngr.com/2012/07/1200-women-develop-vvf-every-year-in-nigeria/.

Buhari, Muhammadu. "Inaugural Speech." *Vanguard*, May 29, 2015. www
  .vanguardngr.com/2015/05/read-president-buhari-inaugural-speech/.
  "Prospects for Democratic Consolidation in Africa: Nigeria's Transition."
  Lecture, Chatham House, London, England, February 26, 2015. www.van
  guardngr.com/2015/02/chatham-house-buharis-speech-on-nigerias-transi
  tion/.
Busch, Lawrence. "Can Fairy Tales Come True? The Surprising Story of
  Neoliberalism and World Agriculture." *Sociologia Ruralis* 50, no. 4 (2010):
  331–351.
Butler-Adam, John, and Academy of Science of South Africa, Pretoria, South
  Africa."More Scientific Thinking Needed to Feed Society: The NSTF
  Tackles Hunger." *South African Journal of Science* 112, no. 7/8 (2016): 1.
Calderisi, Robert. *The Trouble with Africa: Why Foreign Aid Isn't Working*. New
  Haven and London: Yale University Press. 2015.
Calzadilla, Alvaro, Tingju Zhu, KatrinRehdanz, Richard S. J. Tol, and Claudia
  Ringler. "Economywide Impacts of Climate Change on Agriculture in
  Sub-Saharan Africa." *Ecological Economics* 93 (2013): 150–165.
Castells, Manuel. *The Internet Galaxy: Reflections on the Internet, Business and
  Society*. Oxford: University Press. 2001.
Cathrein, Victor. *Socialism: Its Theoretical Basis and Practical Application*.
  New York: Benziger, 1904.
Chakrabarty, Dipesh. *Provincializing Europe: Postcolonial Thought and Historical
  Difference*. 2nd ed. Princeton: Princeton University Press, 2008.
Charles, H., J. Godfray, John R. Beddington, et al. "Food Security: The Challenge
  of Feeding 9 Billion People." *Science* 327, no. 5967 (2010): 812–818.
Chepkemoi, Joyce. "What Type of Government Does Tunisia Have?" *World
  Atlas*, August 1, 2017. www.worldatlas.com/articles/what-type-of-
  government-does-tunisia-have.have.html#:~:text=The%20Republic%20of
  %20Tunisia%20is,Zine%20El%20Abidine%20Ben%20Ali.
Chimanikire, Donald P. "Brain Drain: Causes and Economic Consequences for
  Africa." Lecture, 27th AAPAM Annual Roundtable Conference,
  Livingstone, Zambia, December 5–9, 2005.
Chimee, Ihediwa Nkemjika, and Amaechi M. Chidi. "Social Media and Political
  Change in the 21st Century: The African Experience." *Globalism: Journal of
  Culture, Politics and Innovation* 1 (2016): 1–21.
Chipungahelo, Monica Samuel. "Knowledge Sharing Strategies on Traditional
  Vegetables for Supporting Food Security in Kilosa District, Tanzania."
  Library Review 64, no. 3 (2015): 229–247.
Clapp, Jennifer. *Hunger in the Balance: The New Politics of International Food Aid*.
  1st ed. Ithaca: Cornell University Press, 1963.
Cleland, John, and Kazuyo Machiyama. "The Challenges Posed by Demographic
  Change in Sub-Saharan Africa: A Concise Overview." *Population and
  Development Review* 43 (2017): 264–286.
Coleman, James S. *Nigeria: Background to Nationalism*. Sweden and Nigeria:
  Broberg and Winston, 1958.
Collier, Paul. *Wars, Guns, and Votes: Democracy in Dangerous Places*. New York:
  Harper Perennial, 2009.

Comas, Jordi, David Connor, Mohamed El Moctar Isselmou, Luciano Mateos, and Helena Gómez-Macpherson. "Why Has Small-Scale Irrigation Not Responded to Expectations with Traditional Subsistence Farmers along the Senegal River in Mauritania?" *Agricultural Systems* 110 (2012): 152–161.

Constitution of the Federal Republic of Nigeria (Third Alteration) Act. "World Intellectual Property Organization." February 22, 2011.

Cresswell, T. *Place: A Short Introduction*. Oxford: Oxford University Press, 2004.

Crowder, Michael. "Indirect Rule: French and British Style." *Africa* 34, no. 3 (1964): 197–205.

Crush, Jonathan, and Jane Battersby. *Rapid Urbanisation, Urban Food Deserts and Food Security in Africa*. 1st ed. Cham: Springer Verlag, 2016.

Dagona, Z. K., Haruna Karick, and F. M. Abubakar. "Youth Participation in Social Media and Political Attitudes in Nigeria." *Journal of Sociology, Psychology and Anthropology in Practice* 5, no. 1 (2013): 1–7.

Dapel, Zuhumnan. "Poverty in Nigeria: Understanding and Bridging the Divide Between North and South." *Center for Global Development*, April 6, 2018. www .cgdev.org/blog/blog/poverty-nigeria-understanding-and-bridging-divide-betw een-North-and-South.

Daramola, Adedeji, and Eziyi Ibem. "Urban Environmental Problems in Nigeria: Implications for Sustainable Development." *Journal of Sustainable Development in Africa* 12, no. 1 (2010): 124–145.

Dasylva, Ademola. *Songs of Odamolugbe*. Ibadan: Kraftgriots, 2006.

Dauda, Abubakar. "Ethnic Identity, Democratization, and the Future of the African State." *African Issues* 29, no. 1/2 (2001): 31–36.

Dauda, Bola. "Fallacies and Dilemmas: The Theory of Representative Bureaucracy with Particular Reference to the Nigerian Public Service 1950–86." *International Review of Administrative Sciences* 56(3) (September 1991): 465–490 (also published in French and Spanish).

Dauda, Bola. "Corruption, Nepotism, and Anti-Bureaucratic Behaviors." In *The Palgrave Handbook of African Social Ethics*, edited by Nimi Wariboko and Toyin Falola. New York: Palgrave Macmillan, 2020, 317–338.

Davidson, Cathy N., and David Theo Goldberg. "A Manifesto for the Humanities in a Technological Age." *Chronicle of Higher Education* 50, no. 23 (2004): B7.

Davidson, O., and D. Sparks. *Developing Energy Solutions for Climate Change: South African Research at EDRC*. Cape Town: Energy and Development Research Centre, 2002.

Davis, Thomas J., and Azubike Kalu-Nwiwu. "Education, Ethnicity and National Integration in the History of Nigeria: Continuing Problems of Africa's Colonial Legacy." *The Journal of Negro History* 86, no. 1 (2001): 1–11.

de Choudhury, Munmun, Shagun Jhaver, Benjamin Sugar, and Ingmar Weber. "Social Media Participation in an Activist Movement for Racial Equality." *ProcInt AAAI Conf Weblogs SocMedia* (2017): 1–27.

de Sousa Santos, B. "Law: A Map of Misreading towards a Postmodern Conception of Law." *Journal of Law and Society* 14, no. 3 (1987): 279–302.

Decker, Alicia C., and Andrea L. Arrington. *Africanizing Democracies, 1980–Present*. New York: Oxford University Press, 2015.

Decker, Tunde. *Matrix of Inherited Identity: A Historical Exploration of the Underdog Phenomenon in Nigeria's Relationship Strategies, 1960–2011*. Ibadan: University Press, 2016.

Dennis, Carolyne. "Women and the State in Nigeria: The Case of the Federal Military Government 1984–1985." In *Women, State and Ideology*, edited by Haleh Afshar. London: Macmillan Press, 1987, 95–109.

Denniston, George C., Pia Grassivaro Gallo, Frederick M. Hodges, Marilyn Fayre Milos, and Franco Viviani. *Bodily Integrity and the Politics of Circumcision: Culture, Controversy, and Change*. New York: Springer, 2006.

Dent, M. "Nigeria: Federalism and Ethnic Rivalry." *Parliamentary Affairs* 53, no. 1 (2000): 157–168.

Dewey, John. "Democracy and Educational Administration." *School and Society* 45 (1937): 457–467.

Di Maggio, P. "Culture and Cognition." *Annual Review of Sociology* 23 (1997): 263–287.

Diamond, Larry. *The Spirit of Democracy: The Struggle to Build Free Societies Throughout the World*. New York: Henry Holt and Company, 2008.

Diani, Mario. "Social Movements and Social Capital: A Network Perspective on Movement Outcomes." *Mobilization: An International Journal* 2, no. 2 (1997): 129–147.

Dibua, Jeremiah I. *Modernization and the Crisis of Development in Africa: The Nigerian Experience*. Aldershot: Ashgate, 2006.

"Ethnic Citizenship, Federal Character, and Inter-Group Relations in Nigeria." *Journal of Historical Society of Nigeria* 20 (2011): 1–25.

Dickson, Del. *The People's Government: An Introduction to Democracy*. New York: Cambridge University Press, 2014.

Diejomaoh, Ito, and Eric Eboh. "Local Government in Nigeria: Relevance and Effectiveness in Poverty Reduction and Economic Development." *Journal of Economics and Sustainable Development* 1, no. 1 (2010). https://iiste.org/Journals/index.php/JEDS/article/view/2143.

Dike, K. O. *Trade and Politics in the Niger Delta 1830–1885*. Oxford: Clarendon, 1956.

Dimelu, Mabel Ukamaka, Edward Danjuma Salifu, and Edwin M. Igbokwe. "Resource Use Conflict in Agrarian Communities, Management and Challenges: A Case of Farmer-Herdsmen Conflict in Kogi State, Nigeria." *Journal of Rural Studies* 46 (2016): 147–154.

Diriye, Mukhtar, Abdirizak Nur, and Abdullahi Khalif. "Food Aid and the Challenge of Food Security in Africa." *Development* 56, no. 3 (2013): 396–403.

Dodani, Sunita, and Ronald E. LaPorte. "Brain Drain from Developing Countries: How Can Brain Drain Be Converted into Wisdom Gain?" *Journal of the Royal Society of Medicine* 98, no. 11 (2005): 487–91.

Dodo, Obediah, and Jesca Majaha. "African Youth's 'Whirl-Wind' Allegiance to Leadership." *International Journal of Modern Anthropology* 2, no. 11 (2018): 108–124.

Dovere, Edward-Isaac. "Bernie's Army in Disarray." *Politico*, May 21, 2018. www.politico.com/story/2018/05/21/bernie-sanders-democrats-2018-599331.

Drafor, Ivy, Glen Filson, and Ellen W. Goddard. "Cereal Producers and the Structural Adjustment Programme (SAP) in Ghana: A Welfare Analysis of the First Decade of SAP." *Development Southern Africa* 17, no. 4 (2000): 489–499.

Dudley, B. J. *An Introduction to Nigerian Government and Politics.* Bloomington: Indiana University Press, 1982.

Duncombe, Constance. *The Twitter Revolution? Social Media, Representation and Crisis in Iran and Libya.* Canberra: University of Queensland, 2011. https://espace.library.ug.edu.au/view/UQ:269526.

Dywer, Colin. "Here's the Story Behind That Trump Tweet on South Africa – and Why It Sparked Outrage." *NPR*, August 23, 2018. www.npr.org/2018/08/23/641181345/heres-the-story-behind-that-trump-tweet-on-south-afric a-and-why-it-sparked-outra#reform.

Ebegbulum, J. C. "Federalism and the Politics of Resource Control in Nigeria: A Critical Analysis of the Niger Delta Crisis." *International Journal of Humanities and Social Science* 1, no. 12 (2011): 218–229.

Edeh, Onyinye. "It's Tradition: Female Genitals Mutilations." *Institute of Current World Affairs*, September 20, 2017. www.icwa.org/its-tradition-female-genital-mutilation-in-nigeria/#_ftn2.

Edewor, A. P., A. Y. Aluko, and F. S. Folarin. "Managing Ethnic and Cultural Diversity for National Integration in Nigeria." *Developing Country Studies* 4, no. 6 (2014): 70–76.

Egan, Matt. "Boko Haram Threatens Nigeria's Economic Future, 2014." *CNN*, May 12, 2014. https://money.cnn.com/2014/05/12/investing/nigeria-kidnapping-investing/index.html.

Egbe, Robert. "Inside the 'Risky' Life of 'Nigerian Male Barbie' Bobrisky." *The Nation*, October 19, 2019. https://thenationonlineng.net/inside-the-risky-life -of-nigerian-male-barbie-bobrisky/.

Egbefo, Dawood, and Onyema Shedrack. "Terrorism in Nigeria: Its Implication for Nation Building and National Integration." *Edo University Journal of History and International Studies*, (2007): 1–24.

Egbo, Obiamaka, Ifeoma Nwakoby, Josaphat Onwumere, and Chibuike Uche. "Security Votes in Nigeria: Disguising Stealing from the Public Purse." *African Affairs* 111, no. 445 (2012): 597–614. doi: 10.1093/afraf/ads060.

Egunjobi, Layi. "Issues in Environmental Management for Sustainable Development in Nigeria." *The Environmentalist* 13 (1993): 33–40.

Ehrensaft, Philip. "The Political Economy of Informal Empire in Pre-Colonial Nigeria, 1807–1884." *Canadian Journal of African Studies/La Revue Canadienne des étudesafricaines* 6, no. 3 (1972): 451–490.

Ehwarieme, W., and N. Umukoro. "Civil Society and Terrorism in Nigeria: A Study of the Boko Haram Crisis." *International Journal on World Peace* 32, no. 3 (2015): 25–48.

Eisenstadt, Shmuel N. "Social Change and Modernization in African Societies South of the Sahara." *Cahiers D'études Africaines* 5, no. 19 (1965): 453–471.

Ejobowah, John C. "Political Recognition of Ethnic Pluralism: Lessons from Nigeria." *Nationalism and Ethnic Politics* 6, no. 3 (2000): 1–18.

Ekechi, Felix K. *Missionary Enterprise and Rivalry in Igboland, 1857–1914.* London: Cass, 1972.

Ekwe-Ekwe, Herbert. "Biafra 1966–1970." *Combat Genocide Association*, n.d. combatgenocide.org/?page_id=90.

Elaigwu, Isawa J. "Federalism in Nigeria's New Democratic Polity." *Plubius: The Journal of Federalism* 32, no. 2 (2002): 73–95.

Elliot, A. Jennifer. *An Introduction to Sustainable Development*. 4th ed. New York: Routledge, 2013.

El-Rufai, Nasir Ahmad. *The Accidental Public Servant*. Ibadan: Safari Books, 2013.

Eme, Okechukwu, and Tony Onyishi. "Federalism and Nation Building in Nigeria." *Arabian Journal of Business and Management Review* 2, no. 6 (2014): 1–14.

Emeghara, E. E. "Brain Drain as A Clog in the Wheel of Nigeria's Development." *International Journal of Development and Management Review* 8, no. 1 (2013): 110–121.

Encyclopedia Britannica. "Pluralism: Politics." *Encyclopedia Britannica*, n.d. www.britannica.com/topic/pluralism-politics.

Endong, Floribert Patrick, and Edim Ekpenyong Obonganwan, "Media (Mis) representation of the Nigerian Woman as a Product of the Society." *International Journal of Gender and Women's Studies* 3, no. 1 (2015): 101–106.

Enwerem, Iheanyi. *A Dangerous Awakening: The Politicization of Religion in Nigeria*. Ibadan: IFRA-Nigeria, 1995.

Enwezor, Okwui. "Modernity and Postcolonial Ambivalence." *South Atlantic Quarterly* 109, no. 3 (2010): 595–620.

Epprecht, Marc. *Hungochani: The History of a Sexually Dissident in Southern Africa*. 2nd ed. London: McGill-Queen's University Press, 2013.

Ette, Mercy. "Where Are Women? Evaluating Visibility of Nigerian Female Politicians in News Mediaspace." *Gender, Place and Culture: A Journal of Feminist Geography* (2017): 1–18.

Ewang, Anietie. "Nigeria Passes Disability Rights Law: Offers Hope of Inclusion, Improved Access." *Human Rights Watch*, January 25, 2019. www.hrw.org/news/2019/01/25/nigeria-passes-disability-rights-law.

Eweje, Gabriel. "Environmental Costs and Responsibilities Resulting from Oil Exploitation in Developing Countries: The Case of the Niger Delta of Nigeria." *Journal of Business Ethics* 69, no. 1 (2006): 27–56.

Ewharieme, William, and Jude Cocodia. "Corruption and Environmental Degradation in Nigeria and Its Niger Delta." *Journal of Alternative Perspectives in the Social Sciences* 3, no. 3 (2011): 446–468.

Ezeah, Chukwunonye, and Clive L. Roberts. "Waste Governance Agenda in Nigerian Cities: A Comparative Analysis." *Habitat International* 41 (2014): 121–128.

Ezema, Ifeanyi, Christian Ezeah, and Benedict Ishiwu. "Social Networking Services: A New Platform for Participation in Government Programmes and Policies among Nigerian Youths." *Libres* 25, no. 1 (2015): 33–49.

Fadakinte, Mojibayo, and Babatunde Amolegbe. "Crisis of Citizenship and Nationhood in Africa: Reflections on Hegemony and the State." *Review of History and Political Science* 5, no. 1 (2017): 61–71.

Falola, Toyin. *Colonialism and Violence in Nigeria*. Bloomington: Indiana University Press, 2009.

Cultural Modernity in a Colonized World: The Writings of Chief Isaac Oluwole Delano. Austin: Pan-African University Press, 2020.

Economic Reforms and Modernization in Nigeria. Kent, OH: Kent State University Press, 2004.

The Humanities in Africa: Knowledge Production, Universities, and the Transformation of Society. Austin: Pan-African University Press, 2016.

Nigerian Political Modernity and Postcolonial Predicament. Austin: Pan-African University Press, 2016.

The Political Economy of a Precolonial African State: Ibadan. 1830–1900. Ile-Ife: University of Ife Press, 1984.

The Power of African Cultures. New York: University of Rochester Press, 2003.

"Technology, Culture and Society." Lecture, First Technical University, Ibadan, Nigeria, July 4, 2019.

The Toyin Falola Reader on African Culture, Nationalism, Development and Epistemology. Austin: Pan-African University Press, 2018.

Violence in Nigeria: The Crisis of Religious Politics and Secular Ideologies. Rochester: University of Rochester Press, 1998.

Falola, Toyin, and G. O. Oguntomisin. *Yoruba Warlords of the Nineteenth Century*. Trenton: Africa World Press, 2001.

Falola, Toyin, and Matthew M. Heaton. *A History of Nigeria*. Cambridge: Cambridge University Press, 2008.

Faye, Mamadou. "African Youth Integration in Politics." *Argumente Und Materialien Der Entwicklungszusammenarbeit* 21 (2017): 29–36.

Fayokun, Kayode Olatunbosun. "Legality of Child Marriage in Nigeria and Inhibitions Against Realization of Education Rights." *US-China Education Review* 5, no. 7 (2015). doi: 10.17265/2161-6248/2015.07.005.

Federal Government. *Nigeria's Vision 2020: Economic Transformation Blueprint*. Abuja: Nairametrics, 2009.

Folayan, Adekunle. *Agriculture and Economic Development in Nigeria: A Prescription for the Nigerian Green Revolution*. New York: Vantage Press, 1983.

Food and Agriculture Organization of the United Nations. "Nigeria: Women's Property and Use Rights in Personal Laws." *Food and Agriculture Organization of the United States*, n.d. www.fao.org/gender-landrights-database/country-pro files/countries-list/national-legal-framework/women's-property-and-use-right s-in-personal-laws/en/?country_iso3=NGA. Accessed June, 2019.

The State of Food Security and Nutrition in the World 2017. Rome: The United Nations, 2017. www.fao.org/state-of-food-security-nutrition/en/.

"Understanding the True Cost of Malnutrition." *Food and Agricultural Organization of the United Nations*, July 16, 2014. www.fao.org/zhc/detail-events/en/c/238389/.

Food Security Information Network. *Global Report on Food Crises 2018*. Rome: World Food Programme, 2018. https://docs.wfp.org/api/documents/WF P0000069227/download/?_ga=2.192785194.1048442300.1533835071–1305446390.1533835071.

Food Security Portal. "Country Resources: Nigeria." *Food Security Portal*, n.d. www.foodsecurityportal.org/nigeria/resources.

Forrest, Tom. *Politics and Economic Development in Nigeria.* Boulder: Westview Press, 1993.

Foster, John Bellamy. "Marx as a Food Theorist." *Monthly Review* 68, no. 7 (2016): 1.

"Marx's Theory of Metabolic Rift: Classical Foundations for Environmental Sociology." *American Journal of Sociology* 105, no. 2 (1999): 366–405.

Fukuyama, Francis. *The End of History and the Last Man.* Washington, DC: Free Press, 1992.

Gandhi, Dhruv. "Figure of the Week: Gaps in Nigeria's Public Infrastructure." *Brookings*, March 14, 2018. www.brookings.edu/blog/africa-in-focus/2018/03/14/figure-of-the-week-gaps-in-nigerias-public-infrastructure/.

Gardner, Levi David. "Down on the Farm: A Qualitative Study of Sustainable Agriculture and Food Systems Education at Liberal Arts Colleges and Universities." PhD dissertation, Michigan State University, 2012.

Gberevbie, Daniel, Adeola Oyeyemi, and Nchekwube Excellence-Oluye. "The Challenges of Good Governance, Accountability of Governmental Agencies and Development in Nigeria." *Acta Universitatis Danubius* 6, no. 2 (2014): 80–97.

Gellner, Ernest. *Nations and Nationalism.* Oxford: Basil Blackwell, 1983.

Gerard, Ronald. *Development Economics.* Boston: Pearson Publishers, 2014.

Gettlemen, Jeffrey. "Loss of Fertile Land Fuels 'Looming Crisis' Across Africa." *The New York Times*, July 29, 2017. www.nytimes.com/2017/07/29/world/africa/africa-climate-change-kenya-land-disputes.html.

Gichuki, Douglas. "Leadership in Africa and the Role of Youth in the Leadership Milieu." *Mandela Institute for Development Studies* (2014): 1–29.

Gikandi, Simon. "Chinua Achebe and the Post-Colonial Esthetic: Writing, Identity, and National Formation." *Studies in 20th Century Literature* 15, no. 1 (1991): 29–41.

Glasius, Marlies, and Geoffrey Pleyers. "The Global Movement of 2011: Democracy, Social Justice and Dignity." *Development and Change* 44, no. 3 (2013): 547–567.

Glazer, Nathan, and Daniel P. Moynihan. *Ethnicity: Theory and Experience.* Cambridge: Harvard University Press (1975).

Gleeson, J. "A Geography for Disabled People?" *Transactions of the Institute of British Geographers* (1996): 388–390.

Gordon, April A. *Nigeria's Diverse Peoples: A Reference Sourcebook* (Ethnic Diversity Within Nations Series). Santa Barbara: ABC-CLIO, 2003.

Gordon, Steven. "Fostering Social Movements with Social Media." *SSRN Electronic Journal* (2015): 1–30. http://ssrn.com/abstract=2708079.

Graham, Lucy Valerie, and Malibongwe Tuku. "A Captured Occupation? On Ngos, Accountability, and Grassroots Movements." *Bulletin of the National Library of South Africa* 72, no. 1 (2018): 93–104.

Grey, Sam, and Lenore Newman. "Beyond Culinary Colonialism: Indigenous Food Sovereignty, Liberal Multiculturalism, and the Control of Gastronomic Capital." *Agriculture and Human Values* (2018): 1–14.

Grinberg, Emmanuella. "What the 'Q' in LGBTQ Stands for, and Other Identity Terms Explained." *CNN*, June 14, 2019. https://edition.cnn.com/inter active/2019/06/health/lgbtq-explainer/.

Groninger, John W. "Building Watershed Management Capacity in Nigeria: Expanding the Role of Agriculture Colleges." *Journal of Contemporary Water Research & Education* 158, no. 1 (2016): 78–84.

Guidry, John A., Michael D Kennedy, and Mayer M Zald, eds. *Globalisations and Social Movements, Culture, Power and the Transnational Public Sphere*. Ann Arbor: University of Michigan Press, 2000.

Gumede, Vusi. "Exploring Thought Leadership, Thought Liberation and Critical Consciousness for Africa's Development." *Africa Development / Afrique et Développement* 40, no. 4 (2015): 91–111.

Gustafson, Ellen. "Obesity + Hunger = One Global Food Issue." TEDxEast video. 9: 23. May 2010. www.ted.com/talks/ellen_gustafson_obesity_hunger_1_glo bal_food_issue

Gwaza, Paul. "Romanticising Legal Pluralism through Religious Revival in Democratic Nigeria: Crusaders, Criminals, and Casualties." Paper presentation, the International Conference on Ethnicity, Religion and Peace Building, University of Jos, Jos, Nigeria, February 18–20, 2013. https://ssrn .com/abstract=2544836.

Gyimah-Boadi, Emmanuel. "Civil Society in Africa." In *Consolidating the Third Wave Democracies*, edited by LarryDiamond, Marc F. Plattner, Yun-han Chu and Hung-mao Tien, 278–294. Baltimore: Johns Hopkins University Press, 1997.

Habursky, Joshua, and Mike Fulton. "The Future of Politics is Grassroots." *The Hill*, March 12, 2017. https://thehill.com/blogs/pundits-blog/campaign/323 480-the-future-of-politics-is-grassroots.

Haider, Huma. "Helpdesk Research Report: Social Media and Reform Networks, Protests, Social Movements and Coalitions." *Governance and Social Development Resource Centre* (2011).

Hailey, Lord William Malcolm. *An African Survey: A Study of Problems Arising in Africa South of the Sahara*. Oxford: Oxford University Press, 1938.

Hall, Ruth. "Land Grabbing in Southern Africa: The Many Faces of the Investor Rush." *Review of African Political Economy* 38, no. 128 (2011): 193–214.

Hallett, Vicky. "What's the Difference Between Famine and Hunger? A Food FAQ." *NPR*, June 13, 2017. www.npr.org/sections/goatsandsoda/2017/06/1 3/532277316/what-s-the-difference-between-famine-and-hunger-a-food-faq.

Hamilton, Lawrence S., Helen F. Takeuchi, and East-West Center. *Ethics, Religion and Biodiversity: Relations between Conservation and Cultural Values*. Cambridge: White Horse, 1993.

Hardt, Michael, and Antonio Negri. *Multitude: War and Democracy in the Age of Empire*. New York: Penguin, 2004.

Harlow, Summer, and Guo, Lei. "Will the Revolution Be Tweeted or Facebooked? Using Digital Communication Tools in Immigrant Activism." *Journal of Computer-Mediated Communication* 19 (2014): 463–478.

Harsch, Ernest. "Civil Society Engages Africa Plan." *Africa Renewal*, October 2004. www.un.org/africarenewal/magazine/october-2004/civil-society-engages-african-plan.

Hassim, Shireen. "Democratization: A View from Africa." *Signs: Journal of Women in Culture and Society* 31, no. 4 (2006): 928–932.

Headey, Derek D., and T. S. Jayne. "Adaptation to Land Constraints: Is Africa Different?" *Food Policy* 48 (2014): 18–33.

Heidenheimer, Arnold J., and Michael Johnston. *Political Corruption: Concepts & Contexts.* 3rd ed. New Brunswick: Transaction Publishers, 2002.

Herald Scotland. "The Big Read: Can Federalism Ever Work in the UK?" *Herald Scotland*, April 22, 2018. www.heraldscotland.com/news/16175777.the-big-read-can-federalism-ever-work-in-the-uk/.

Hillocks, Roy J. "Farming for Balanced Nutrition: An Agricultural Approach to Addressing Micronutrient Deficiency Among the Vulnerable Poor in Africa." *African Journal of Food, Agriculture, Nutrition and Development* 11, no. 2 (2011).

The Historical Society of Nigeria. "The Place of History in Nigeria's School System and the Nation." Official memorandum. 1987.

Honey, Martha. *Ecotourism and Sustainable Development: Who Owns Paradise?* 2nd ed. Washington, DC: Island Press, 2008.

Honwana, Alcinda M., *The Time of Youth: Work, Social Change, and Politics in Africa*, 1–17. Boulder: Kumarian Press, 2012.

Hopwood, Bill, Mary Mellor, and Geoff O'Brien. "Sustainable Development: Mapping Different Approaches." *Sustainable Development* 13, no. 1 (2005): 38–52.

Hunger Notes. "Africa Hunger and Poverty Facts." *Hunger Notes*, August 2018. www.worldhunger.org/africa-hunger-poverty-facts/.

Hungtington, Samuel. *The Third Wave: Democratization the Late Twentieth Century.* Norman: University of Oklahoma Press, 1991.

Hussaini, Abdu, and Lydia Umar. "Ethnic and Religious Crisis in Kaduna." In *Hope Betrayed: A Report on Impunity and State-Sponsored Violence in Nigeria*, edited by I. Bawa and V. I. Nwogwu, 83–104. Lagos: World Organization against Torture and Center for Law Enforcement Education, 2002.

Ibelema, Minabere. "Explaining Sex-for-Marks." *Punch News*, October 28, 2018. https://punchng.com/explaining-sex-for-marks/.

Ibhawoh, Bonny. "Stronger than the Maxim Gun Law, Human Rights and British Colonial Hegemony in Nigeria." *Africa* 72, no. 1 (2002): 55–83.

"Nations and Nationalism: A Global Historical Overview." www .humanities.mcmaster.ca/~ibhawoh/documents/Nations%20&%20Nationalis m.pdf .

Ibori, Diana. "The Concept of Federalism and Its Features in Nigeria." *Nigeria News*, November 28, 2018. www.legit.ng/1136924-major-features-federalism-nigeria.html.

Ibrahim, M. 2017. "Child Marriage in Northern Nigeria." *Nigerian Reporter*, August 20, 2016. http://nigerianreporter.com/2016/08/20/child-marriage-in -northern-nigeria-nigerian-newspaper/.

Igodo, Cynthia. "The Power of Social Media: Nigeria's Changing Feminist Movement." *The Republic* 3, no. 1 (2019). www.republic.com.ng/vol3-no1 /the-power-of-social-media/.

Ihonvebere, Julius O. "The 1999 Presidential Elections in Nigeria: The Unresolved Issues." *Issue: A Journal of Opinion* 27, no. 1 (1999): 59–62.

Ikime, Obaro. *Can Anything Good Come out of History?* Ibadan: Bookcraft, 2018.

Ilorah, Richard. "Ethnic Bias, Favouritism and Development in Africa." *Development Southern Africa* 26, no. 5 (2009): 695–707.

Inamete. U. B. "Federalism in Nigeria: The Crucial Dynamics." *The Round Table: The Commonwealth Journal of International Affairs* 80, no. 318 (1991): 191–207.

Inegbedion, N. A., and E. Omoregie. "Federalism in Nigeria: A Re-appraisal." *Journal of Commonwealth Law and Legal Education* 4, no. 1 (2016): 69–83.

Inekwere, Bede E. "A History of Religious Violence in Nigeria: Grounds for a Mutual Co-Existence Between Christians and Muslims." Order No. 3711053. University of the West, 2015. http://ezproxy.lib.utexas.edu/login? url=https://search.proquest.com/docview/1703030998?accountid=7118.

Ingyoroko, M., E. T. Sugh, and Alkali Terfa. "The Nigerian Woman and the Reformation of the Political System: A Historical Perspective." *Journal of Socialomics* 6, no. 2 (2017): 2–8.

Ire, E. Uwem. "Multinationals and Corporate Social Responsibility in Developing Countries: A Case Study of Nigeria." *Corporate Social Responsibility and Environmental Management* 11, no. 1 (2004): 1–11.

Isaacs, D. "Nigeria's Emirs: Power Behind the Throne." *BBC*, September 29, 2010. www.bbc.com/news/world-africa-11418542.

Isoto, Rosemary E., Abdoul G. Sam, and David S. Kraybill. "Uninsured Health Shocks and Agricultural Productivity among Rural Households: The Mitigating Role of Micro-credit." *The Journal of Development Studies* 53, no. 12 (2017): 2050–2066.

Iweriebor, Ehiedu E. G. "State Systems in Pre-Colonial, Colonial and Post-Colonial Nigeria: An Overview." *Africa: Rivistatrimestrale di studi e documentazion-edell'Istitutoitaliano per l'Africa e l'Oriente* 37, no. 4 (1982): 507–513.

Iyorah, Festus. "True Federalism Beckons for Nigeria." *African Arguments*, September 12, 2017. https://africanarguments.org/2017/09/12/true-federalism-beckons-for-nigeria/.

Jachtenfuchs, Markus. "The Monopoly of Legitimate Force: Denationalization, or Business as Usual." *European Review* 13, no. S1 (2005): 37–52.

Jacobs, Sander, Nicolas Dendoncker, Berta Martín-López, et al. "A New Valuation School: Integrating Diverse Values of Nature in Resource and Land Use Decisions." *Ecosystem Services* 22 (2016): 213–220.

Jaffrelot, Christophe. "For a Theory of Nationalism." *Research in Question* 10 (2003): 2–51.

Jannah, Immanuel. "How RCCG Evangelist was Murdered while Preaching." *Vanguard*, July 10, 2016. www.vanguardngr.com/2016/07/abuja-evangelist-murdered-preaching/.

Jarmon, Charles. *Nigeria: Reorganization and Development since the Mid-Twentieth Century.* Leiden and New York: E. J. Brill, 1988.

Jasper, James. "A Strategic Approach to Collective Action: Looking for Agency in Social Movement Choices." *Mobilization: An International Journal* 9, no. 1 (2004): 1–16.

Jayne, Thomas S., David Mather, and Elliot Mghenyi. "Principal Challenges Confronting Smallholder Agriculture in Sub-Saharan Africa." *World Development* 38, no. 10 (2010): 1384–1398.

Jemison, Mae. "Teach Arts and Sciences Together." TED2002 video. 21: 10. February 2002. www.ted.com/talks/mae_jemison_on_teaching_arts_and_scien ces_together.

Jimoh, Ayodele. *The Nigerian Governance and Corruption Survey*. Ilorin: University of Ilorin, 2004.

Jinadu. A. L. "Federalism, the Consociational State, and Ethnic Conflict in Nigeria." *Plubius: Federalism and Consociationalism: A Symposium* 15, no. 2 (1985): 71–100.

"A Note on the Theory of Federalism." In *Readings on Federalism*, edited by A. B. Akinyemi, P. D. Cole, and Walter Ofonagoro. Lagos: Nigerian Institute of International Affairs, 1980, 26–35.

John of Salisbury. *The Statesman's Book*. Translated by John Dickinson. New York: Alfred A. Knopf, 1927.

John, Sokfa. "Genocide, Oppression, Ambivalence: Online Narratives of Identity and Religion in Postcolonial Nigeria." *Open Library of Humanities* 4, no. 2 (2018): 1–28.

Jonathan, Goodluck. "Consolidating Our Democratic System." *Strengthening Democratic Traditions and Institutions in Nigeria*, edited by Martin Uhomoibhi and Ehiedu Iweriebor. Abuja, Nigeria: Ministry of Foreign Affairs, 2014, x–xvii.

Joseph, M., and I. Benjamin. "Jonathan Gave CAN N7bn not N6bn, Pastor Dikwa Alleges." *Leadership*, 2015. http://leadership.ng/news/412848/jona than-gave-can-n7bn-not-n6bn-pastor-dikwa-alleges.

Kachaje, Rachel, Kudakwashe Dube, Malcolm MacLachlan, and Gubela Mji. "The Africa Network for Evidence-to-Action on Disability: A Role Player in the Realization of the UNCRPD in Africa." *African Journal of Disability* 3, no. 2 (2014), 86.

Kah, Henry Kam. "'Boko Haram Is Losing, but so Is Food Production': Conflict and Food Insecurity in Nigeria and Cameroon." *Africa Development* 42, no. 3 (2017): 177–196.

Kallen, M. H. *Cultural Pluralism and the American Idea*. Philadelphia: University of Philadelphia Press, 1956.

Kalu, Kenneth, Olajumoke Yacob-Haliso, and Toyin Falola, eds. *Africa's Big Men: Predatory State-Society Relations in Africa*. New York: Routledge, 2018.

Kamenka, Eugene, ed. *Nationalism: The Nature and Evolution of an Idea*. Canberra: Australian National University Press, 1973.

Kazeem, Yomi. "Nigeria's First Ever Corruption Survey Is as Bad as Most People Imagined." *Quartz Africa*, August 21, 2017. https://qz.com/africa/1058356/how-bad-is-corruption-in-nigeria/.

"Nigeria Has Become the Poverty Capital of the World." *Quartz Africa*, June 25, 2018. https://qz.com/africa/1313380/nigerias-has-the-highest-rate-of-extreme-poverty-globally/.

Kerr, Rachel Bezner, Emmanuel Chilanga, Hanson Nyantakyi-Frimpong, Isaac Luginaah, and Esther Lupafya. "Integrated Agriculture Programs to Address Malnutrition in Northern Malawi." *BMC Public Health* 16, no. 1 (2016), 1197.

Kettle, Martin. "Now Brexit Really Is Threatening to Tear the UK Apart." *The Guardian*, October 10, 2018. www.theguardian.com/commentisfree/2018/o ct/10/brexit-threat-theresa-may-uk-scotland-northern-ireland-union.

Kgosidintsi, Resego Natalie. "Student Activism and Youth Agency in Botswana." *BUWA!: A Journal on African Women's Experiences* 8 (2017): 39–40.

Khemani, Stuti. "Fiscal Federalism and Service Delivery in Nigeria: The Role of States and Local Governments." Paper, Nigerian PER Steering Committee, Abuja, Nigeria, 2001. www1.worldbank.org/publicsector/decentralization/march2003seminar/fiscalfedreport.pdf.

Kifordu, Henry. "Political Elite Composition and Democracy in Nigeria." *The Open Area Studies Journal* 4, no. 1 (2011): 16–31.

Kiikpoye, Aaron K., and George Dawari, eds. *Placebo as Medicine: The Poverty of Development Intervention and Conflict Resolution Strategies in the Niger Delta Region of Nigeria*. Port Harcourt: Kemuela Publications, 2010.

King, Jamilah. "How Black Lives Matter Has Changed US Politics." *New Internationalist*, March 9, 2018. https://newint.org/features/2018/03/01/black-lives-matter-changed-politics.

Klonick, Kate. "Peanut Paste Saves Starving African Children." *ABC News*, October 1, 2016. https://abcnews.go.com/Health/story?id=2497593&page=1.

Koné, Klohinlwélé. "Living and Narrating the Tensions of the Postcolonial Situation: Chinua Achebe Between Ambiguity and Ambivalence." *The International Journal of Social Sciences and Humanities Invention* 3, no. 11 (2016): 2943–2952.

Kooijman, Jaap. *Fabricating the Absolute Fake: America in Contemporary Pop Culture*. Revised ed. Amsterdam: Amsterdam University Press, 2013.

Kpessa, Michael, Daniel Béland, and André Lecours. "Nationalism, Development, and Social Policy: The Politics of Nation-Building in Sub-Saharan Africa." *Ethnic and Racial Studies* 34, no. 12 (2011).

Krause, Ruth. "Oil Spills Keep Devastating Niger Delta." *DW*, March 20, 2015. www.dw.com/en/oil-spills-keep-devastating-niger-delta/a-18327732.

Kweitsu, Richard. "Brain Drain: A Bane to Africa's Potential." *Mo Ibrahim Foundation*, August 9, 2018. mo.ibrahim.foundation/news/2018/brain-drain-bane-africas-potential/.

Kwemo, Angelle B. "Making Africa Great Again: Reducing Aid Dependency." *Brookings*, April 20, 2017. www.brookings.edu/blog/africa-in-focus/2017/04/20/making-africa-great-again-reducing-aid-dependency/.

Laffin, Martin, and Alys Thomas. "The United Kingdom: Federalism in Denial?" *Publius* 29, no. 3 (1999): 89–107.

Lam, Lucia L., Eldon Emberly, Hunter B. Fraser, et al. "Factors Underlying Variable DNA Methylation in a Human Community Cohort." *Proceedings of the National Academy of Sciences of the United States of America* 109, no. 2 (2012): 17253–17260.

Lamb, Russell L. "Food Crops, Exports, and the Short-Run Policy Response of Agriculture in Africa." *Agricultural Economics* 22, no. 3 (2000): 271–298.

Lambert, Michael, and University of KwaZulu-Natal. "On Rainbows and Butterflies: The Classics, the Humanities and Africa." *Acta Classica* 57 (2014): 1–15.

Lancaster University. "Traditional Beliefs Promote Sustainability in West Africa." *Science Daily*, March 4, 2015. www.sciencedaily.com/releases/201 5/03/150304110252. htm.

Lange, Matthew K. "British Colonial Legacies and Political Development." *World Development* 32, no. 6 (2004): 905–922.

Larsen, Svend, Susan Bassnett, Naomi Segal, et al. "No Future without Humanities: Literary Perspectives." *Humanities* 4, no. 1 (2015): 131–148.

Law, R. C. C. "The Heritage of Oduduwa: Traditional History and Political Propaganda Among the Yoruba." *Journal of African History* 14, no. 2 (1973): 207–222.

The Oyo Empire, c. 1600–1836: A West African Imperialism in the Era of the Atlantic Slave Trade. Oxford: Clarendon Press, 1977.

Lenin, Vladimir. *State and Revolution*. New York: International Publishers, 1932.

Levin, Michael. "The New Nigeria: Displacement and the Nation." *Journal of Asia and African Studies* 32, no. 1–2 (1997): 134–144.

Lewis, Peter M. *Oil, Politics, and Economic Change in Indonesia and Nigeria*. Ann Arbor: The University of Michigan Press, 2007.

Lisk, F. "'Land Grabbing' or Harnessing of Development Potential in Agriculture? East Asia's Land-Based Investments in Africa." *Pacific Review* 26, no. 5 (2013): 563–587.

Livingstone, S., N. Couldry, and T. Markham. "Youthful Steps Towards Civic Participation: Does the Internet Help?" In *Young Citizens in the Digital Age: Political Engagement, Young People & New Media*, edited by B. Loader, 21–34. London: Routledge, 2007.

Lovejoy, Paul E. "Interregional Monetary Flows in the Precolonial Trade of Nigeria." *The Journal of African History* 15, no. 4 (1974): 563–585.

Lu, Joanne. "'Unimaginable' Suffering in Southern Sudan. Is There Any Hope?" *NPR*, July 5, 2018. www.npr.org/sections/goatsandsoda/2018/07/05/62018 4859/unimaginable-suffering-in-south-sudan-is-there-any-hope.

Luckham, A. R. "Institutional Transfer and Breakdown in A New Nation: The Nigerian Military." *Administrative Science Quarterly* 16, no. 4 (1971): 387–406.

Lukpata, I. Victor. "Culture, Tourism, and Sustainable Development in Nigeria." *Journal of Good Governance and Sustainable Development in Africa* 2 (2014): 41–47.

Mabogunje, Akinlawon L., and John Omer-Cooper. *Owu in Yoruba History*. Ibadan: University of Ibadan Press, 1971.

Mackintosh, John P. "Federalism in Nigeria." *Political Studies* 10, no. 3 (1962): 223–247.

"Politics in Nigeria: The Action Group Crisis of 1962." *Political Studies* 11, no. 2 (1963): 126–155.

MacLachlan, Malcolm, Gubela Mji, Tsitsi Chataika, et al. "Facilitating Disability Inclusion in Poverty Reduction Processes: Group Consensus Perspectives from Disability Stakeholders in Uganda, Malawi, Ethiopia, and Sierra Leone." *Disability and the Global South* 1, no. 1 (2017).

Maddalena, C. "Introduction. Pluralism in Education and Implications for Analysis." *Italian Journal of Sociology of Education* 5, no. 2 (2013): 1–16.

Madu, Robert, and C. Shedrack Moguluwa. "Will the Social Media Lenses Be the Framework for Sustainable Development in Rural Nigeria?" *Journal of African Media Studies* 5, no. 2 (2013): 237–54.

Madueke, Onyedikachi, Celestine Nwosu, Chibuzo Ogbonnaya, Adaez Anumadu, and Vincent Okeke. "The Role of Social Media in Enhancing Political Participation in Nigeria." *IDOSR Journal of Arts and Management* 2, no. 3 (2017): 44–54.

Malthus, T. R. *An Essay on the Principle of Population; or, A View of Its Past and Present Effects on Human Happiness; with an Inquiry into Our Prospects Respecting the Future Removal or Mitigation of the Evils Which It Occasions.* England: 1898. Reprint, London: Pickering, 1986.

Mancur, Olson. *The Logic of Collective Action: Public Goods and the Theory of Groups.* Cambridge: Harvard University Press, 1971.

   The Rise and Decline of Nations: Economic Growth, Stagflation and Social Rigidities. New Haven: Yale University Press, 1984.

Mann, Alana. "Food Democracy: Why Eating Is Unavoidably Political." *The Conversation*, August 4, 2015, https://theconversation.com/food-democracy-why-eating-is-unavoidably-political-43474.

Manning, Carrie. "Assessing African Party Systems After the Third Wave." *Party Politics* 11, no. 6 (2005): 707–727.

Markovska, Anna, and Nya Adams. "Political Corruption and Money Laundering: Lessons from Nigeria." *Journal of Money Laundering Control* 18, no. 2 (2015): 169–181.

Marshall, Paul. *The Talibanisation of Nigeria: Sharia Law and Religious Freedom.* Washington, DC: Freedom House, 2002.

Marsonet, Michele. "Pragmatism and Political Pluralism: Consensus and Pluralism." *International Scientific Journal* 25, no. 12 (2015).

Martinez, Ibsen. "The Curse of the Petro-State: The Example of Venezuela." *Library of Economics and Liberty*, September 5, 2005. www.econlib.org/library/Columns/y2005/Martinezpetro.html.

Marx, Karl. *Grundrisse.* London: Penguin, 1973.

Marx, Karl, and Joseph J. O'Malley. *Critique of Hegel's "Philosophy of Right."* Cambridge: Cambridge University Press, 1970.

Maslow, Abraham, and Karen J. Lewis. "Maslow's Hierarchy of Needs." *Salenger Incorporated* 14 (1987).

Mazrui, Ali A. "A Fragment: Africa Between the Baobab Tree and the Owl of Minerva: A Post-Colonial Educational Narrative." Lecture, McGill University, Montreal, Canada, April 30–May 4, 2011.

   "On the Concept of 'We Are All Africans.'" *The American Political Science Review* 57, no. 1 (1963): 88–97.

Mbah, Peter, and Mwangu Chikodiri. "Sub-ethnic Identity and Conflict in Nigeria: The Policy Option for the Resolution of the Conflict Between Ezza and Ezillo in Ebonyi State." *Mediterranean Journal of Social Sciences* 5, no. 2 (2014): 681–688.

Mbatha, Nhlanhla C. "How to Understand, Evaluate and Influence Efficient Progress in South Africa's Land Reform Process: A Typology from Historical Lessons from Selected Sub-Saharan African Countries." *South*

African Journal of Economic and Management Sciences 20, no. 1 (2017): e1–e13.

Mbogoma, Gloria Ndisha. "Julius Nyerere's Education for Self-Reliance in Post-Colonial Tanzania: A Reconsideration." Thesis, University of Pretoria, 2018.

McIvor, David W., and James Hale. "Urban Agriculture and the Prospects for Deep Democracy." *Agriculture and Human Values* 32, no. 4 (2015): 727–741.

McMichael, Philip. "A Food Regime Analysis of the 'World Food Crisis.'" *Agriculture and Human Values* 26, no. 4 (2009): 281.

Meertens, Bert. "Agricultural Performance in Tanzania under Structural Adjustment Programs: Is It Really So Positive?" *Agriculture and Human Values* 17, no. 4 (2000): 333–346.

Mengistu, M. M. "The Quest for Youth Inclusion in the African Politics: Trends, Challenges, and Prospects." *Journal of Socialomics* 6, no. 1 (2017).

Meres, Ettobe David. "Nigeria: A Nation Divided by Hashtags, Two Protests with Half Momentum." *The Nerve Africa*, February 4, 2017. https://thener veafrica.com/9902/Nigeria-a-nation-divided-by-hastags-two-protests-with-half-momentum.

Mernissi, Fatema. *Islam and Democracy: Fear of the Modern World.* 2nd ed. Translated by Mary Jo Lakeland. New York: Basic Books, 2002.

Michels, Robert. *Political Parties: A Sociological Study of the Oligarchical Tendencies of Modern Democracy.* Kitchener: Batoche Books, 2001.

Migdal, Joel S. *Strong Societies and Weak States: State-Society Relations and State Capabilities in the Third World.* Princeton: Princeton University Press, 1988.

Miller, Gregory E., Edith Chen, and Karen J. Parker. Psychological Stress in Childhood and Susceptibility to the Chronic Diseases of Aging: Moving toward a Model of Behavioral and Biological Mechanisms." *Psychological Bulletin* 137, no. 6 (2011): 959–997.

Misselhorn, Alison, and Sheryl L. Hendriks. "A Systematic Review of Sub-national Food Insecurity Research in South Africa: Missed Opportunities for Policy Insights." *PLoS One* 12, no. 8 (2017).

Modibbo, Mohammed Ahmed. *European Trade, Imperialism and Under-Development of in Northern Nigeria 19th and 20th Centuries.* Zaria: Ahmadu Bello University Press Limited, 2016.

Momoh, Abubakar. "Does Pan-Africanism Have a Future in Africa? In Search of the Ideational Basis of Afro-Pessimism." *African Journal of Political Science* 8, no. 1 (2003).

"The Philosophy and Theory of the National Question." *The National Question in Nigeria: Comparative Perspectives,* edited by Abubakar Momoh, Said Adejumobi, Osarhieme Benson Osadalor, Mark Anikpo and Eskor Toyo, 1–20. Hampshire: Ashgate, 2002.

Morozov, Evgeny. *The Net Delusion.* London: Penguin Books, 2011.

Morreira, Shannon. "Steps towards Decolonial Higher Education in Southern Africa? Epistemic Disobedience in the Humanities." *Journal of Asian and African Studies* 52, no. 3 (2017): 287–301.

Morrison, Aaron. "The Fight to Increase Minimum Wage Will Be a Midterm Election Issue, the Poor People's Campaign Says." *Mic Network Inc*, August 28, 2018. https://mic.com/articles/190971/the-fight-to-increase-min imum-wage-will-be-a-midterm-election-issue-the-poor-peoples-campaign-says#.r3OyfoAQT.

Mosweunyane, Dama. "The African Educational Evolution: From Traditional Training to Formal Education." *Higher Education Studies* 3, no. 4 (2013): 50–53.

Muasher, Marwan. "The Second Arab Awakening." By Diane Rehm. National Public Radio, February 20, 2014.

Mueller, Dennis C. *Public Choice III*. Cambridge: Cambridge University Press, 2003.

Mugo, Tiffany Kagure. "African Queer Women Tackling Erasure and Ostracization: Love, Lust, and Lived Experience." In *The Palgrave Handbook of African Women's Studies*, edited by Olajumoke Yacob-Haliso and Toyin Falola. Cham: Palgrave Macmillan, forthcoming.

Mumba, Chisoni, Barbara Häsler, John B. Muma, et al. "Practices of Traditional Beef Farmers in Their Production and Marketing of Cattle in Zambia." *Tropical Animal Health and Production* 50, no. 1 (2018): 49–62.

Munasinghe, Mohan. "Environmental Economic and Sustainable Development." World Bank Environment Paper No. 3, Washington, DC, 1993.

Munyi, Chomba Wa. "Past and Present Perceptions Towards Disability: A Historical Perspective." *Disabilities Studies Quarterly*, 32, no. 2 (2012).

Murakami, Christopher D., Mary K. Hendrickson, and Marcelle A. Siegel, "Sociocultural Tensions and Wicked Problems in Sustainable Agriculture Education." *Agriculture and Human Values* 34, no. 3 (2017): 591–606.

Murray, Stephen O., and Will Roscoe, eds. *Boy-Wives and Female Husbands: Studies of African Homosexualities*. New York: Palgrave Macmillan, 1998.

Musarurwa, Hillary Jephat. "Closed Spaces or (In)competent Citizens? A Study of Youth Preparedness for Participation in Elections in Zimbabwe." *Commonwealth & Comparative Politics* (2018): 1–19.

Muse, Sulaimon. "Social Media and Public Participation in Nigeria: Challenges and Possibilities." *Advances in Social Sciences Research Journal* 1, no. 7 (2014): 43–48.

Mussoline, Benito. "The Doctrine of Fascism" in *Italian Encyclopedia*, 1932.

Mustapha, Abdul. "Ethnic Structure, Inequality and Governance of the Public Sector in Nigeria." UNRISD Programme on Democracy, Governance and Human Rights Paper Number 24, Geneva, Switzerland, 2006.

Ndichu, Esther. "Hunger Isn't a Food Issue. It's a Logistics Issue." TED@UPS video. 11:41. September 2015. www.ted.com/talks/esther_ndichu_hunger_isn_t_a_food_issue_it_s_a_logistics_issue#t-1564.

Negedu, Isaiah, and Augustine Atabor. "Nationalism in Nigeria: A Case for Patriotic Citizenship." *American International Journal of Contemporary Research* 5, no. 3 (2015): 74–79.

New Partnerships for Africa's Development. *Agriculture in Africa*. Johannesburg: African Union, 2013. www.nepad.org/resource/nepad-agency-2013-annual-report-0.

News 24. "Mugabe's Land Reform Cost Zimbabwe $17 Billion: Economists." *News 24*, May 12, 2018. www.news24.com/news24/africa/zimbabwe/muga bes-land-reform-costs-zimbabwe-17-billion-economists-20180512.

Nisbet, Robert Alexander. *Community and Power.* Oxford: Oxford University Press, 1965.

Nkandawire, Thandika, ed. *African Intellectuals: Rethinking Politics, Language, Gender and Development.* Dakar and London: CODESRIA and Zed Books, 2005.

Nnoli, Okwudiba. *Ethnic Politics in Nigeria.* Enugu: Fourth Dimension, 1978.

Nohlen, Dieter, Michael Krennerich, and Bernhard Thibaut, "Elections and Electoral Systems in Africa." In *Elections in Africa: A Data Handbook*, edited by Dieter Nohlen, Michael Krennerich, and Bernhard Thibaut. Oxford: Oxford University Press, 1999, 1–40.

Noll, Samantha. "Broiler Chickens and a Critique of the Epistemic Foundations of Animal Modification." *Journal of Agricultural and Environmental Ethics* 26, no. 1 (2013): 273–280.

"Northern People's Congress (NPC)." In *The Oxford Dictionary of Islam*, edited by John L. Esposito. Oxford: Oxford University Press, 2004. www .oxfordislamicstudies.com/article/opr/t125/e1773.

Nossiter, Adams. "Nigeria Tries to 'Sanitize' Itself of Gays." *The New York Times*, February 8, 2014. www.nytimes.com/2014/02/09/world/africa/nigeria-uses-law-and-whip-to-sanitize-gays.html.

Nowakowski, Kelsey. "Calories Count." *National Geographic Society* 224, no. 5 (2013): 24.

Ntamu, G. U., O. T. Abia, S. D. Edinyang, and Chris-Valentine Ogar Eneji. "Religion in Nigerian Political Space: Implication for Sustainable National Development." *International Journal of Academic Research in Business and Social Sciences* 4, no. 9 (2014). http://dx.doi.org/10.6007/IJARBSS/v4-i9/1159.

Nwabueze, B. O. *The Presidential Constitution of Nigeria.* Enugu: Nwamife Publishers, 1982.

Nwauche, Enyinna S. "Child Marriage in Nigeria: (Il)legal and (Un)constitutional?" *African Human Rights Law Journal* 15 (2015).

Nyirenda-Jere, Towela. "Strengthening Grass-Roots Participation in Agricultural and Rural Development Policy Processes." *NEPAD Planning and Coordinating Agency*, October 2013. www.nepad.org/resource/strengthen ing-grass-roots-participation-agricultural-and-rural-development-policy-pr ocess-0.

Obarisiagbon, Emmanuel, Osagie Agbontaen, and Mohammed Gujbawu. "A Sociological Investigation into the Influence of the New Media on Political Mobilization: A Study of Nigeria's 2015 Presidential Election." *New Media and Mass Communication* 58 (2017): 10–16.

Obi, Cyril I. *Nigeria: Democracy on Trial.* Uppsala: The Nordic Africa Institute, 2004. nai.uu.se/research/publications/electronic_publ/obi_nigeria.pdf.

Obi, S. N. and B. C. Ozumba. "Factors Associated with Domestic Violence in Southeast Nigeria." *Journal of Obstetrics and Gynecology* 27, no. 1 (2009).

O'Brien, Michael J. and Kevin N. Laland. "Genes, Culture, and Agriculture: An Example of Human Niche Construction." *Current Anthropology* 53, no. 4 (2012): 434–70.

Ochieng, Justus, Victor Afari-Sefa, Daniel Karanja, Radegunda Kessy, Srinivasulu Rajendran, and Silvest Samali. "How Promoting Consumption of Traditional African Vegetables Affects Household Nutrition Security in Tanzania." *Renewable Agriculture and Food Systems* 33, no. 2 (2018): 105–115.

Odiaka, Ngozi Oluchukwu. "The Concept of Gender Justice and Women's Rights in Nigeria: Addressing the Missing Link." *Journal of Sustainable Development, Law and Policy* 2, no. 1 (2013): 190–205.

Odimegwu, Ike. "Nigerian Nationalism and the Crisis of Patriotism: A Conceptual Dialogics in Philosophy and Africa." *World Philosophy* 1 (2006): 203–213.

Odisu, T. A. "Federalism in Nigeria: A Critique." *Journal of Political Sciences & Public Affairs* 3, no. 3 (2015).

Odoemelam, Uche, and Ebiuwa Aisien. "Political Socialization and Nation Building: The Case of Nigeria." *European Scientific Journal* 9, no. 11 (2013).

Odoh, Innocent. "FG, ASUU Move to Resolve IPPIS, Others as Talks Continue." Business Day, March 18, 2020. https://businessday.ng/educa tion/article/fg-asuu-move-to-resolve-ippis-others-as-talks-continue/.

Ofori-Parku, Sylvester, and Moscato, Derek. "Hashtag Activism as a Form of Political Action: A Qualitative Analysis of the #BringBackOurGirls Campaign in Nigerian, UK, and U.S. Press." *International Journal of Communication* 12 (2018): 2480–2502.

Ogbodo, Gozie, and Ngozi Stewart. "Climate Change and Nigeria's Sustainable Development of Vision 20–2020." *Annual Survey of International & Comparative Law* 20, no. 1 (2014): 16–34.

Ogbogbo, C. B. N., R. O. Olaniyi, and O. G. Muojama, eds. *The Dynamics of Intergroup Relations in Nigeria Since 1960: Essays in Honour of Obaro Ikime at 70.* Ibadan: University of Ibadan, 2012.

Ogbole, A. F., and A. O. Ogunrinade. "Nigerian Pluralistic Society and the Relevance of Religious Dialogue as an Instrument of Peace." *Journal of Educational and Social Research* 3, no. 3 (2013): 343–350.

Ogunbameru, Olakunle A. *Sociology: Origin, Development and Uses.* Ibadan: Penthouse Publications, 2008.

Ogunlesi, Tolu. "Nigeria's Internal Struggles." *The New York Times*, December 21, 2017. www.nytimes.com/2015/03/24/opinion/nigerias-internal-struggles.html.

Ogunremi, Deji. "Economic Development and Warfare in Nineteenth Century Yorubaland." In *War and Peace in Yorubaland 1793–1893*, edited by I. A. Akinjogbin, A. A. Adediran, and G. A. Adebayo. Papers, the Conference on the Centenary of the 1886 Kiriji/Ekitiparapo Peace Treaty, Obafemi Awolowo University, Ile-Ife, Nigeria, September 21–28, 1986.

Ojekunle, Aderemi. "Nigerians Are Signing a Petition against the High Cost of Internet Subscription." *Pulse*, November 22, 2018. www.pulse.ng/tech-niger ians-are-signing-a-petition–against-the-high-cost-of-internet-subscription/ h7sn64.

Ojigbo, Osai. "Hashtag Activism Makes the Invisible Visible." *The Mantle*, November 16, 2017. www.themantle.com/international-affairs/hashtag-activism-makes-inisible-visible/.

Ojo, John Sunday, and Godwin Chinedum Ihemeje. "Mushrooming Appointed Caretaker Committee: A Quagmire to Grassroot Democracy in Nigeria."

International Journal of Sociology and Anthropology 6, no. 7 (2014). doi:10.5897/ijsa2013.0523.

Ojo, Olatunji. "Heepa' (Hail) Òrìṣà: The Òrìṣà Factor in the Birth of Yoruba Identity. *Journal of Religion in Africa* 39, no. 1 (2009): 30–59.

"The Organization of the Atlantic Slave Trade in Yorubaland, ca. 1777 to ca. 1856." *The International Journal of African Historical Studies* 41, no.1 (2008): 77–100.

Ojoka, Donnas, and Tony Acolb. "Connecting the Dots: Youth Political Participation and Electoral Violence in Africa." *Journal of African Democracy and Development* 1, no. 2 (2017): 94–108.

Okafor, Chukwuemeka, E. O. Emma Chukwuemeka, and Jude O. Udenta. "Developmental Local Government as a Model for Grassroots Socio-Economic Development in Nigeria." *International Journal of Arts and Humanities* 4, no. 14 (2015).

Okechukwu, Uzoamaka Elizabeth, Gerald Nebo, and Jude Eze. "Women Empowerment: Panacea for Poverty Reduction and Economic Development in Nigeria." *Journal of Policy and Development Studies* 10, no. 2 (2016): 31–41.

Okere, Roseline. "Nigeria: Oil Production Dips to 1.3mbd Over Vandalism, Says NNPC." *The Guardian*, 2017. https://allafrica.com/stories/201709140086 .html.

Okey, Samuel. "Youth Involvement in Political Violence/Thuggery: A Counter Weight to Democratic Development in Africa." *Journal of Political Sciences & Public Affairs* 5, no. 3 (2017): 1–4.

Okeyezu, Chinwe R., P. Egbo Obiamaka, and J. U. J. Onwumere. "Shaping the Nigerian Economy: The Role of the Women." *Acta Universitatis Danubius, Economica* 8, no. 4 (2012): 15–24.

Okiro, Mike Mbama. "Law Enforcement, the Electoral Process and Democracy in Nigeria." In *Strengthening Democratic Traditions and Institutions in Nigeria*, edited by Martin Uhomoibhi and Ehiedu Iweriebor. Abuja: Ministry of Foreign Affairs, 2014, 91–102.

Okocha, Samuel. "Beyond the Hashtags: Nigerians Seek Lasting Solution to Boko Haram Insurgency." *Rewire News*, March 22, 2014. https://rewire.ne ws/article/201/05/22/beyond-the-hashtags-nigerians-seek-lasting-solution-t o-boko-haram-insurgency/

Okolie, Andrew C. "The Appropriation of Difference: State and the Construction of Ethnic Identities in Nigeria." *Identity* 3, no. 1 (2003): 67–92.

Okonjo-Iweala, Ngozi. *Reforming the Unreformable*. Cambridge: MIT Press, 2012.

Okonta, Ike. *When Citizens Revolt: Nigerian Elites, Big Oil and the Ogoni Struggle for Self Determination*. Trenton: Africa World Press, 2008.

Okpalike, Chika, J. B. Gabriel, and Kanayo Louis Nwadialor. "The Contributions of the Christian Missionaries in Building the Nigerian Nation, 1840–1960." *Academic Journal of Interdisciplinary Studies* 4, no. 2 (2015).

Okpanachi, Eyene. "Between Conflict and Compromise: Lessons on Sharia and Pluralism from Nigeria's Kaduna and Kebbi States." *Emory International Law Review* 25, no. 2 (2011): 897–919. http://law.emory.edu/eilr/content/v olume-25/issue-2/religious-nigeria/conflict-compromise-sharia-pluralism-k aduna-kebbi.html.

Okwu, Augustine S. O. "The Weak Foundations of Missionary Evangelization in Precolonial Africa: The Case of the Igbo of Southeastern Nigeria 1857–1900." *Practical Anthropology* 8, no. 1 (1980): 31–49.

Oladeinde O. "14 Nigerian States Insolvent have Ridiculously Low Internal Revenue-Report." *Premium Times*, May 30, 2017. www.premiumtimesng.co m/business/business-news/232507–14-nigerian-states-insolvent-%E2%808hav e-ridiculously-low-internal-revenue-report.html.

Olaiya, Taiwo. "Proto-Nationalisms as Sub-text for the Crisis of Governance in Nigeria." *SAGE Open* (2016): 1–13.

"Youth and Ethnic Movements and Their Impacts on Party Politics in ECOWAS Member States." *SAGE Open* (2014): 1–12.

Olakunle, Michael Folami, and Adejoke Olubimpe Folami. "Climate Change and Inter-Ethnic Conflict in Nigeria." *Peace Review* 25, no. 1 (2013): 104–110.

Olaniyi, Johnson O. "State Independent Electoral Commissions and Local Government Elections in Nigeria." *Africa's Public Service Delivery & Performance Review* 5, no. 1 (2017).

Olasupo, Olusola, Isaac Oladeji, and E. Ijeoma. "Nationalism and Nationalist Agitation in Africa: the Nigerian Trajectory." *The Review of Black Political Economy* 44 (2017): 261–283.

Olatunde, Diane. "Women's Participation and Representation in Nigeria's Politics in the Last Decade (1999–2009)." PhD thesis, University of the Witwatersrand, 2010.

Olatunji, Kehinde. "Thousands of Beggars Protest Against Undue Harassment, Arrest in Lagos." *The Guardian*, February 26, 2020. https://m.guarduan.ng/n ews/thousands-of beggars-protest-against-undue-harassment-arrest-in-lagos/.

Olawoyin, Oladeinde. "Perception of Corruption Worsens in Nigeria – Transparency International Report." *Premium Times*, February 22, 2018. www.premiumtimes.com/news/top-news/259494-perception-corruption-w orsens-nigeria-transparency-international-report.html.

Olawunmi, Bisi. "Ajimobi, the Constituted Kingmaker." *The Nation Newspaper*, 2017. https://thenationonlineng.net/ajimobi-constituted-kingmaker/.

Olukoshi, Adebayo O., and Liisa Laakso. *Challenges to the Nation-State in Africa.* Uppsala: Scandinavian Institute of African Studies, 1995.

Omenka, Nicodemus. "Appraising Nigeria's Implementation of the National Policy of 35% Affirmative Action for Women, 1999–2016." PhD thesis, Ebonyi State University, 2016. www.eajournals.org/wp-content/uploads/A ppraising-Nigeria%E2%80%99s-Implementation-of-the-National-Policy-o f-35-Affirmative-Action-for-Women-1999–2016.pdf.

Omofonmwan, Samson Imasogie, and Lucky Osaretin Odia. "Oil Exploitation and Conflict in the Niger-Delta Region of Nigeria." *Journal of Human Ecology* 26, no. 1 (2009): 25–30.

Omonobi, Kingsley. "46 Killed, 96 Wounded in Ile-Ife Yoruba-Hausa Clash – Police." *Vanguard*, 2017. www.vanguardngr.com/2017/03/46-killed-96-wounded-ile-ife-yoruba-hausa-clash-police/.

Onapajo, Hakeem. "Politics for God: Religion, Politics and Conflict in Democratic Nigeria." *The Journal of Pan African Studies* 4, no. 9 (2012): 42–66. www .researchgate.net/publication/273998985.

"Politics and the Pulpit: The Rise and Decline of Religion in Nigeria's 2015 Presidential Elections." *Journal of African Elections* (2016).

Oniang'o, Ruth. "Women Are Still the Key in Agriculture and Food Security in Africa." *South African Journal of Clinical Nutrition* 18, no. 2 (2005): 150–154.

Onwubu, C. "Ethnic Identity, Political Integration, and National Development: The Igbo Diaspora in Nigeria." *The Journal of Modern African Studies* 13, no. 3 (1975): 399–413.

Onwuzuruigbo, Ifeanyi. "Researching Ethnic Conflicts in Nigeria: The Missing Link." *Ethnic and Racial Studies* 33, no. 10 (2010): 1797–1813.

Opeyemi, Aluko. "Urban Violence Dimension in Nigeria: Farmers and Herders Onslaught." *Agathos: An International Review of the Humanities and Social Sciences* 8, no. 1 (2017): 187–206.

Organization of the Petroleum Exporting Countries. "Nigeria Facts and Figures." *Organization of the Petroleum Exporting Countries*, n.d. www .opec.org/opec_web/en/about_us/167. htm.

Oriaghan, Izehi. "A Quick Look at Women's Land and Inheritance Rights in Nigeria." *Landesa*, July 30, 2018. www.landesa.org-a-quick-look-at-wome n's-land-and-inheritance-rights-in-nigeria.

Orr, David. "Biological Diversity, Agriculture, and the Liberal Arts." *Conservation Biology* 5, no. 3 (1991): 268–270.

Osaghae, Eghosa. *Structural Adjustment and Ethnicity in Nigeria*. Uppsala: Nordic African Institute, 1995.

Otinche, Sunday Inyokwe. "Fiscal Policy and Local Government Administration in Nigeria." *African Research Review* 8, no. 33 (2018): 122–124.

Oviasuyi, P. O., W. Idada, and Lawrence Isiraojie. "Constraints of Local Government Administration in Nigeria." *Journal of Social Sciences* 24, no. 2 (2010): 81–86.

Oxfam Canada. "There is Enough Food to Feed the World." *Oxfam Canada*, September 5, 2017. www.oxfam.ca/there-enough-food-feed-world.

Oyedepo, O. Sunday. "On Energy for Sustainable Development in Nigeria." *Renewable and Sustainable Energy Reviews* 16, no. 5 (2012): 583–598.

Energy and Sustainable Development in Nigeria: The Way Forward. Nigeria: Springer, 2012.

Oyeniyi, Adeyemi B. "Dress and Identity in Yoruba Land, 1880–1980." PhD dissertation, Leiden University, 2012.

Oyesomi, K., and O. Oyero. "Newspaper Coverage of Women's Participation in the 2011 General Elections in Nigeria." *The Journal of the African council for Communication Education* 10, no. 1 (2012): 136–156.

Oyitso, Mabel, and C. O. Olomukoro. "Enhancing Women's Development Through Literacy Education in Nigeria." *Review of European Studies* 4, no. 4 (2012): 211–217.

Oyovbaire, E. *Federalism in Nigeria: A Study in the Development of Nigeria States*. New York: St. Martin's Press, 1984.

Panafrican Farmers' Organization. "Mission PAFO." *Panafrican Farmers' Organization*, September 14, 2017. http://pafo-africa.org/spip.php?article26.

Penney, Joel. "Social Media and Citizen Participation in 'Official' and 'Unofficial' Electoral Promotion: A Structural Analysis of the 2016 Bernie Sanders Digital Campaign." *Journal of Communication* 67, no. 3 (2017).

Pereira, Charmaine. "Domesticating Women? Gender, Religion and the State in Nigeria Under Colonial and Military Rule." *African identities* 3, no. 1 (2005): 69–94.

Pérouse de Montclos, Marc-Antoine, eds. *Boko Haram: Islamism, Politics, Security and The State in Nigeria*. Los Angeles: Tsehai Publishers, 2014.
  "Conversion to Islam and Modernity in Nigeria: A View from the Underworld." *Africa Today* 54, no. 4 (2008): 71–87.

Perullo, Alex. "Politics and Popular Song: Youth, Authority, and Popular Music in East Africa." *Journal of International Library of African Music* 9, no. 1 (2011): 87–115.

Pew Research Center. "The Global Divide on Homosexuality: Greater Acceptance in More Secular and Affluent Countries." *Pew Research Center*, June 4, 2013. www.pewresearch.org/global/2013/06/04/the-global-divide-on -homosexuality/.

Pittin, R. "Women, Work and Ideology in Nigeria." *Review of African Political Economy* 18, no. 52 (1991): 38–52, 46.

Pound, William T. "The State of Federalism Today." *National Conference of State Legislatures*, July 24, 2017. www.ncsl.org/bookstore/state-legislatures-magazine/the-state-of-federalism-today636359051.aspx.

Plamenatz, John. "Two Types of Nationalism." In *Nationalism: The Nature and Evolution of an Idea*, edited by Eugene Kamenka. Canberra: Australian National University Press, 1973, 22–36.

Premium Times. "Boko Haram Has Infiltrated My Government, Says Jonathan." *Premium Times*, January 8, 2012. www.premiumtimesng.com/news/3360-boko-haram-has-infiltrated-my-government-says-jonathan.html.

Provost, Claire. "World Social Forum: Grassroots Africa Takes Centre Stage." *The Guardian*, February 18, 2011. www.theguardian.com/global-development/po vertymatters/2011/feb/18/world-social-forum-reflections-back-ahead.

Punch News. "73 Parties Field Candidates for 2019 Presidential Election." *Punch News*, November 30, 2018. http://punchng.com/73-parties-field-candidates-for-2019-presidential-election-inec/.

Punjabi, Riyaz. "Autonomy in Jammu and Kashmir." *Strategic Analysis* 35, no. 2 (2011): 308–311.

Quijano, Anibal. "Coloniality and Modernity/Rationality." *Cultural Studies* 21, no. 2 (2010): 168–178.

Quirk, Joel. *The Anti-Slavery Project: From the Slave Trade to Human Trafficking*. Philadelphia: University of Pennsylvania Press, 2011.

Raja, Debolina. "9 Health Risks and Realities of Teenage Pregnancy." *Mom Junction*, n.d. www.momjunction.com/articles/health-risks-of-teenagpreg nancy_00377831/#Gref.

Luis Snyder, ed. *The Dynamics of Nationalism*, New York: Van Nostrand, 1964.

Ritzer, G. *Sociological Theory*. New York: McGraw-Hill, 2010.

Robert-Okah, I. "Insecurity in Nigeria: Implications for sustainable National Development in Nigeria." *International Journal of Academic Research* 6, no. 4 (2014): 242–50.

Roberts, Clive L., Glynne Watkin, Paul Philips, and Amos Odunfa. "Seasonal Variation and Municipal Solid Waste Composition: Issues for Development of New Waste Management Strategies in Abuja, Nigeria." *The Journal of Solid Waste Technology and Management* 36, no. 4 (2010): 210–219.

Roemer, J. E. "What Is Exploitation? Reply to Jeffrey Reiman." *Philosophy and Public Affairs* (1989): 90–97.

Rogers, P. Peter, F. Kazi Jalal, and A. John Boyd. *An Introduction to Sustainable Development*. New York: Earthscan, 2008.

Rosaldo, Renato. "The Cultural Impact of the Printed Word, A Review Article." *Comparative Studies in Society and History* 23 (1981): 508–513.

Rousseau, Jean Jacques. *The Social Contract and Discourses*. Translated by G. D. H. Cole. New York: E. P. Dutton & Co., Inc., 1950.

Rout, Sangram Keshari. "Indian Federalism – 15 Issues That Challenge the Federal Structure of India – Clear IAS." *ClearIAS*, May 12, 2017. www .clearias.com/indian-federalism-issues-challenges/

Rural Development and Land Reform. "Land Audit Report 2017." *Republic of South Africa*, 2017. www.ruraldevelopment.gov.za/publications/land-audit-report/file/6126.

Sachs, Jeffrey D. *The Age of Sustainable Development*. New York: Columbia University Press, 2015.

The End of Poverty: Economic Possibilities for Our Time. New York: Penguin, 2005.

Sachs, Jeffrey D., and Andrew M. Warner. "The Curse of Natural Resources." *European Economic* Review 45, no. 4–6 (2001): 827–838.

Sadighi, Darius. "How Hashtag Activism Helped Raise Awareness About Boko Haram: It Started with #BringBackOurGirls." *Teen Vogue*. May 12, 2017. www.teenvogue.com/story/how-hashtag-activism-helped-raise-awareness-about-boko-haram/.

Sahara Reporters. "At a Glance: The Final Positions of All 73 Parties That Contested Presidential Election. 2019." *Sahara Reporters*, February 27, 2019. http://saharareporters.com/2019/02/27/glance-final-positions-all-73-parties-contested-presidential-election.

Sahara Reporters. "How Governor Ganduje Plans to Oust Emir of Kano Sanusi." *Sahara Reporters*, May 7, 2019. http://saharareporters.com/2019/05/07/exclusive-how-governor-ganduje-plans-oust-emir-kano-sanusi.

Sahara Reporters. "NBS Data Reveals How Much Nigeria States Generated Internally in 2017."

Sahara Reporters. March 24, 2018. https://saharareporters.com/2018/03/24/nbs-data-reveals-how-much-nigerian-states-generated-internally-2017.

Salami, Adeleke. "Taxation, Revenue Allocation, and Fiscal Federalism in Nigeria: Issues, Challenges, and Policy Options." *Economic Options* 56, no. 189 (2011): 27–49.

Salanova, Regina. "Social Media and Political Change: The Case of the 2011 Revolutions in Tunisia and Egypt." Working paper 7, International Catalan Institute for Peace, Catalonia, 2012.

Salau, A. O. "Rivers State." In *Nigeria: Giant in the Tropics*, Vol. 2, edited by R. K. Udo and A. B. Mamman. Lagos: Gabumbo Publishing, 1993, 425–429.

Salau, A. O., Hamisu Kabir Matazu, Balarabe Alkassim, Chris Agabi, Francis Arinze Iloani, Umar Shehu Usman, and Saawua Terzungwe. "Nigeria: Revised Budget – Anger over Cuts in Health, Education Votes." *AllAfrica*, June 4, 2020. https://allafrica.com/stories/202006040446.html.

Sandler, Joe. "Clarke, Nigeria: Child Brides Facing Death Sentences a Decade After Child Prohibition Prohibited." *The Guardian*, Wednesday 11, 2015. https://theguardian.com/global-development-professionals-network/2015/mar/11/the-tragedy-of-nigerias-child-brides.

Sanusi, A. Yakeen. "Application of Human Development Index to Measurement of Deprivations Among Urban Households in Minna, Nigeria." *Habitat International* 32, no. 3 (2008): 384–398.

Sarsar, Saliba, and Julius O. Adekunle, eds. *Democracy in Africa: Political Changes and Challenges*. Durham: Carolina Academic Press, 2012.

Savelyev, Yuriy. "Essential Features of Modern Society in Sociological Discourse." *Journal of Humanities and Social Sciences* 6, no. 11 (2013): 1673–1691.

Schoofs, Mark, and Augustus Olakunle. "In Nigeria, a Bill to Punish Gays Divides a Family." *The Wall Street Journal*, January 12, 2007. www.wsj.com/articles/SB116855583554727450.

Schuck, P. H. "Federalism." *Case Western Reserve Journal of International Law* 38, no. 1 (2006): 5–12.

Secretary of State for the Colonies by Command of Her Majesty. *The Willink Commission Report: Report of the Commission Appointed to Enquire into the Fears of Minorities and the Means of Allaying Them*. Adaka Boro Centre, 1958. https://ijawnation.org/wp-content/uploads/2019/01/The-Willink-Commission-Report_conc_recom_lt.pdf.

Sengupta, Somini. "U.N.'s Famine Appeal Is Billions Shy of Goal." *The New York Times*, March 23, 2017. www.nytimes.com/2017/03/23/world/africa/un-famine-nigeria-somalia-south-sudan-yemen.html.

Shaka, Femi Okiremuete. "The Colonial Legacy: History and Its Impact on the Development of Modern Culture in Nigeria." *Third Text* 19, no. 3 (2005): 297–305.

Sheeran, Josette. "Ending Hunger Now." TEDGlobal video. 19: 03. July 2011. www.ted.com/talks/josette_sheeran_ending_hunger_now.

Shell-Duncan, Bettina and Ylva Hernlund. *Female "Circumcision" in Africa: Culture, Controversy, and Change*. Colorado: Lynne Rienner Publishers, 2000.

Shete, Maru, Marcel Rutten, George C. Schoneveld, and Eylachew Zewude. "Land-Use Changes by Large-Scale Plantations and Their Effects on Soil Organic Carbon, Micronutrients and Bulk Density: Empirical Evidence from Ethiopia. *Agriculture and Human* 33, no. 3 (2016): 689–704.

Shirazi, Farid. "Social Media and the Social Movements in the Middle East and North Africa." *Information Technology & People* 26, no. 1 (2013): 28–49.

Shirky, Clay. "The Political Power of Social Media." *Foreign Affairs* 90, no. 1 (2011): 28–41.

Sieff, Kevin. "Zimbabwe's White Farmers Find Their Services in Demand Again." *The Guardian*. September 25, 2015. www.theguardian.com/world/2015/sep/25/zimbabwe-land-reforms-mugabe-white-farmers.

Simon, L. Julian. *The Ultimate Resource*. Princeton: Princeton University Press, 1981.

Singer, Peter. *The Life You Can Save: How to Do Your Part to End World Poverty*. New York: Random House Incorporated, 2010.

Singhvi, A. "Federalism." *Indian Journal of Public Administration* 53, no. 4 (2007): 742–758.

Sinikangas, Maarit. "Yan Daudu: A Study of Transgendering Men in Hausaland West Africa." Master's thesis, Uppsala University, 2004.

Sklar, Richard. *Nigerian Political Parties*. Princeton: Princeton University Press, 1963.

Smith, Daniel Jordan. "AIDS, NGOs and Corruption in Nigeria." *Health & Place* 18 (2012): 475–480. doi: 10.1016/j.healthplace.2011.11.002.

Smith, Robert S. *The Lagos Consulate, 1851–1861*. Berkeley: University of California Press, 1979.

Sodiq Y. "Can Muslims and Christians Live Together Peacefully in Nigeria?" *The Muslim World* 99 (2009): 646–688.

Somerville, Keith. *Africa's Long Road Since Independence: The Many Histories of a Continent* London: Penguin Random House, 2017.

Sommers, Marc. "Creating Programs for Africa's Urban Youth: The Challenge of Marginalization." *Journal of International Cooperation in Education* 10, no. 1 (2007): 19–31.

Statista. "U.S. Food Waste – Statistics & Facts." Statista, May 19, 2018. www.statista.com/topics/1623/food-waste.

Stearns, Scott. "Nigerian Human Rights Group: At Least 500 Killed in Post-Election Violence." *VOA*, April 23, 2011. www.voanews.com/africa/nigerian-human-rights-group-least-500-killed-post-election-violence.

Steyn, Phia. "Oil Exploration in Colonial Nigeria, c. 1903–58." *The Journal of Imperial and Commonwealth History* 37, no. 2 (2009): 249–274.

Stock, Robert. "Environmental Sanitation in Nigeria: Colonial and Contemporary." *Review of African Political Economy* 15, no. 42 (1988): 19–31.

Suberu, Rotimi. "The Nigerian Federal System: Performance, Problems and Prospects." *Journal of Contemporary African Studies* 28, no. 4 (2010): 459–477.

Sullivan, Meg. "When Grassroots Activism Becomes a Commodity." *UCLA Newsroom*, May 29, 2014. http://newsroom.ucla.edu/releases/when-grassroots-activism-becomes-a-commodity.

Susser, E., J. B. Kirkbride, B. T. Heijmans, J. K. Kresovich, L. H. Lumey, and A. D. Stein. "Maternal Prenatal Nutrition and Health in Grandchildren and Subsequent Generations." *Annual Review of Anthropology* 41 (2012): 577–610.

Tade, Oludayo. "Why Nigerian Women in Oyo State Use Child Domestic Workers." *The Conversation*, October 27, 2019. http://theconversation.com/why-nigerian-women-in-oyo-state-use-child-domestic-workers-123890.

Taglialatela, Jared P., Jamie L. Russell, Jennifer A. Schaeffer, and William D. Hopkins. "Communicative Signaling Activates 'Broca's' Homolog in Chimpanzees." *Current Biology* 18, no. 5 (2008): 343–348.

Taiwo, Olufemi. "Colonialism and Its Aftermath: The Crisis of Knowledge Production." *Callaloo* 16, no. 4 (1993): 891–908.

"Reading the Colonizer's Mind: Lord Lugard and the Philosophical Foundations of British Colonialism." In *Racism and Philosophy*, edited by Susan E. Babbitt and Sue Campbell. Ithaca: Cornell University Press, 1999, 157–186.

Tajfel, Henri Tajfel. "Social Psychology of Intergroup Relations." *Annual Review Psychology* 33 (1982): 1–39.

Tangri, Roger. *The Politics of Patronage in Africa: Parastatals, Privatization and Private Enterprise*. Oxford: James Currey, 1999.

Taylor, Adam. "Meet the First Man to Come Out as Gay on Nigerian Television." *The Washington Post*, April 15, 2014. www.washingtonpost.com/news/world views/wp/2014/04/15/meet-the-first-man-to-come-out-as-gay-on-nigerian-tele vision/.

te Lintelo, Dolf J. H., Lawrence J. Haddad, Jennifer Leavy, and Rajith Lakshman. "Measuring the Commitment to Reduce Hunger: A Hunger Reduction Commitment Index." *Food Policy* 44 (2014): 115–128.

Tenuche, Marietu S. "Intra-Ethnic Conflict and Violence in Ebiraland." *Afrigov* 27, no. 2 (2002). http://works.bepress.com/marietu_tenuche/7/.

Thomas Aquinas. *Governance of Rulers*. Translated by G. B. Phelan. Toronto: Medieval Studies of Toronto, Inc., 1949.

Thomas Sankara : The Upright Man. Directed by Robin Sheffield. San Francisco: California Newsreel, 2006. search.alexanderstreet.com/view/wor k/bibliographic_entity%7Cvideo_work%7C3798038.

Tilly, Charles. "Political Identities in Changing Polities." *Social Research* 70, no. 2 (2003): 607–620.

Tilzey, Mark. "Reintegrating Economy, Society, and Environment for Cooperative Futures: Polanyi, Marx, and Food Sovereignty." *Journal of Rural Studies* 53 (2017): 317–334.

Toromade, Samson. "List of All 73 Candidates Contesting in February 16 Presidential Election." *The Pulse*, January 21, 2019. www.pulse.ng/news/pol itics/presidential-election-list-of-all-73-candidates-contesting-in-february-1 6-election/8y9l22j.

Treichel, Volker. *Putting Nigeria to Work a Strategy for Employment and Growth*. Washington, DC: World Bank, 2010.

Tschirley, David, Thomas Reardon, Michael Dolislager, and Jason Snyder. "The Rise of a Middle Class in East and Southern Africa: Implications for Food System Transformation." *Journal of International Development* 27, no. 5 (2015): 628–646.

Turner, David M. "Introduction: Approaching Anomalous Bodies." In *Social Histories of Disability and Deformity*, edited by David M. Turner and Kevin Stagg. New York: Routledge, 2006, 1–16.

Tusa, Felix. "How Social Media Can Shape a Protest Movement: The Cases of Egypt in 2011 and Iran in 2009." *Arab Media and Society*, no. 17 (2013): 1–19.

Tuthill, R. "Geographic Aspects of Cultural Pluralism in Nigeria." *High School Journal* 56, no. 1(1972): 26–44.

Ubaku, Kelechi, Chikezie Emeh and Chinenye Anyikwa. "Impact of Nationalist Movement on the Actualization of Nigerian Independence, 1914–1960." *International Journal of History and Philosophical Research* 2, no. 1 (2014): 54–67.

Uji, Brenda. "Social Media and the Mobilization of Youths for Socio-Political Participation." *New Media and Mass Communication* 42 (2015): 27–34.

Ukiwo, Ukoha. "On the Study of Ethnicity in Nigeria." Working paper, CRISE: Centre for Research on Inequality, Human Security and Ethnicity, Oxford University, Oxford, England, 2005.

Umozurike, U. O. "The African Charter on Human and Peoples' Rights. *American Journal of International Law* 77 (1983).

UNESCO. "Education for all: Global monitoring report." *Teaching and learning for all*. UNESCO Paris, n.d.

UNICEF. "Child Marriage." UNICEF, April 2020. http://data.unicef.org/topic/child-protection/child-marriage/

UNICEF. "Nutrition." UNICEF, n.d. www.unicef.org/nigeria/nutrition.html.

United Nations. "Africa." United Nations, n.d. www.un.org/en/sections/issues-depth/africa/index.html.

United Nations. *Corruption in Nigeria: Bribery: Public Experience and Response.* Vienna: United Nations Office on Drugs and Crime, 2017. https://drive.google.com/file/d/0B6jj-ulM0cLrOXFpMDh1Q1l1bm8/view.

United Nations. "Food." United Nations, n.d. www.un.org/en/sections/issues-depth/food/.

United Nations. *Innovation for Sustainable Development: Local Case Studies from Africa.* New York: United Nations, 2008.

United Nations. "Nigeria." United Nations, n.d. www.fao.org/emergencies/countries/detail/en/c/213439.

United Nations. "Population." United Nations, n.d. www.un.org/en/sections/issues-depth/population/.

United Nations. "Sustainable Development Knowledge Platform." United Nations, n.d. https://sustainabledevelopment.un.org/?menu=1300.

United Nations. *Universal Declaration of Human Rights*. 1948. www.un.org/en/universal-declaration-human-rights/.

United Nations. "World Population Projected to Reach 9.8 billion in 2050, and 11.2 billion in 2100." United Nations, June 21, 2017. www.un.org/development/desa/en/news/population/world-population-prospects-2017.html.

United Nations. "Zero Hunger Challenge." United Nations, n.d. www.un.org/en/zerohunger/challenge.shtml.

United Nations Development Programme. "Human Development Reports." United Nations Development Programme, January 1, 2014. http://hdr.undp.org/en/data.

Urry, J. *Sociology Beyond Societies: Mobilities for the Twenty-First Century.* London: Routledge, 2000.

U.S. Legal, Inc. "Federalism." *U.S. Legal System*, 2016. https://system.uslegal.com/federalism/.

Use Data Nigeria. "National Oil and Gas Map – Nigerian Oil and Gas Fields." Use Data Nigeria, 2014. www.usedatanigeria.com/dataset/national-oil-and-gas-map-ni/resource/51bad4aa-d3d8-46a1-86f6-137764b25540.

Ushe, Mike. "Christian Youths and Politics in Nigeria: Implications for Sustainable Development." *Journal of Sustainable Development in Africa* 16, no. 8 (2014): 15–29.

Usman, U. S. "Women and Poverty in Nigeria: Agenda for Poverty Eradication." *Developing Country Studies* 5, no. 3 (2015): 122–126.

Utz, Raphael. "Nations, Nation-Building, and Cultural Intervention: A Social Science Perspective." *Max Planck Yearbook of United Nations Law* 9 (2005): 615–647.

Uwadibie, O. Nwafejoku. *Decentralization and Economic Development in Nigeria: Agricultural Policies and Implementation.* Lanham: University Press of America, 2000.

Uwem, E. Ire. "Multinationals and Corporate Social Responsibility in Developing Countries: A Case Study of Nigeria." *Corporate Social Responsibility and Environmental Management* 11, no. 1 (2004): 1–11.

van Deth, Jan W. "Political Participation." In *The International Encyclopedia of Political Communication.* Hoboken: John Wiley & Sons, 2015.

van Gyampo, Ransford Edward, and Franklin Obeng-Odoom. "Youth Participation in Local and National Development in Ghana: 1620–2013." *The Journal of Pan African Studies* 5, no. 9 (2013): 129–150.

Vanguard. "Poverty: Foreign Aid Doing Nigeria More Harm Than Good." *Vanguard*, August 9, 2018. www.vanguardngr.com/2018/08/poverty-foreign-aid-doing-nigeria-more-harm-than-good-kalu-2/.

Vanlauwe, Bernard, A. Bationo, J. Chianu, K. E. Giller, et al. "Integrated Soil Fertility Management: Operational Definition and Consequences for Implementation and Dissemination." *Outlook on Agriculture* 39, no. 1 (2010): 17–24.

Vaughan, Olumide. *Religion and the Making of Nigeria.* Durham: Duke University Press, 2016. www.doabooks.org/doab?func=search&query=rid:20703.

von Bogdandy, Armin, Stefan Häußler, Felix Hanschmann, and Raphael Utz. "State-Building, Nation-Building, and Constitutional Politics in Post-Conflict Situations: Conceptual Clarifications and an Appraisal of Different Approaches." *Max Planck Yearbook of United Nations Law* 9 (2005): 579–613.

Walt, Vivienne. "The Breadbasket of South Korea: Madagascar." *Time*, November 23, 2008. http://content.time.com/time/world/article/0,8599,18 61145,00.html.

Wegner, Jarula M. I. "Reading Rap with Fanon and Fanon with Rap: The Potential of Transcultural Recognition." In *A Poetics of Neurosis: Narratives of Normalcy and Disorder in Cultural and Literary Texts*, edited by Elena Furlanetto and Dietmar Meinel. Bielefeld: Verlag, 2018, 75–94.

Weil, Connie. "Food and Agriculture in the Liberal Arts." *Professional Geographer* 36, no. 2 (1984): 243–44.

What Is Epigenetics. "DNA Methylation." *What Is Epigenetics*, n.d. www .whatisepigenetics.com/dna-methylation/.

Wheare, Kenneth C. *Federal Government.* London: Oxford University Press, 1946.

Wheeler, Stephen, and Timothy Beatley. *The Sustainable Urban Development Reader*. 3rd ed. New York: Routledge, 2014.

Whyte, Susan Reynolds. "In the Long Run: Ugandans Living with Disability." *Current Anthropology* 61, no. 21 (2019).

Whyte, Susan Reynolds, and Benedicte Ingstad, eds. *Disability and Culture*. London: University of California Press, 1995.

Widner, Jennifer. "Political Parties and Civil Societies in Sub-Saharan Africa." In *Democracyin Africa: The Hard Road Ahead*, edited by Marrina Ottaway. Boulder: Boulder: Lynne Rienner, 1997, 65–82.

The Willink Commission Report. *Report of the Commission Appointed to Enquire into the Fears of Minorities and the Means of Allying Them*. Adaka Boro Centre, 2014. eie.ng/wp-content/uploads/2014/03/TheWillinkCommissionReport_conc_recom_lt.pdf.

World Bank. *Helping Countries Combat Corruption: The Role of the World Bank*. Washington, DC: The World Bank, 1997.

World Bank. *World Development Report 1997*. New York: Oxford University Press, 1997.

World Commission on Environment and Development. *Our Common Future: Report of the World Commission on Environment and Development*. Oxford: Oxford University, 1987.

World Food Programme. "Hunger." World Food Programme, n.d. www.wfp.org/hunger.

"10 Facts About Hunger in Tanzania." World Food Programme, May 13, 2016. www.wfp.org/stories/10-facts-about-hunger-tanzania.

World Health Organization. "Increasing Breastfeeding Could Save 800,000 Children and US $300 Billion Every Year." World Health Organization, n.d. www.who.int/maternal_child_adolescent/news_events/news/2016/exclusive-breastfeeding/en/.

World Peace Foundation. "Nigeria: Civil War." Tufts Mass Atrocity Endings, August 7, 2015. sites.tufts.edu/atrocityendings/2015/08/07/nigeria-civil-war/.

World Population Review. "United States Population." World Population Review, June 18, 2018. http://worldpopulationreview.com/countries/united-states-population/.

Yaqub, Muneer. "SARS Has Turned Rogue. Nigeria Should End It Now." *African Liberty*, April 15, 2019. www.africanliberty.org/2019/04/15/sars-has-turned-rogue-nigeria-should-end-it-now/.

Yesufu, T. M. *The Human Factor in National Development: Nigeria*. Ibadan: Spectrum Books, 2000.

Zadrozny, J. *Dictionary of Social Science*. Washington, DC: Pacific Affairs Press, 1959.

Zappe, Florian. "'When Order Is Lost, Time Spits': The Abject Unpopular Art of Genesis (Breyer) P-Orridge." In *Unpopular Culture*, edited by Martin Lüthe and Sascha Pöhlmann, 129–145. Amsterdam: Amsterdam University Press. 2016.

Ziltener, Patrick, and Hans-Peter Mueller. "The Weight of the Past: Traditional Agriculture, Socio-Political Differentiation and Modern Development in

Africa and Asia: A Cross-National Analysis." *International Journal of Comparative Sociology* 48, no. 5 (2007): 371–415.

ZODML. "Herbert Macaulay." *ZODML,* September 19 2014. zodml.org/discover-nigeria/people/herbert-macaulay#.XDbEzc9KhQJ.

Zungura, M. E. Nyemba,F. Mutasa, and C. Muronza. "The Relationship Between Democracy and Women Participation in Politics." *Journal of Public Administration and Governance,* 3, no. 1 (2013): 168–176.

Index